D1521809

OLD TESTAMENT HISTORY

OLD TESTAMENT HISTORY

AN OVERVIEW OF SACRED HISTORY & TRUTH

WILBUR FIELDS

COLLEGE PRESS PUBLISHING COMPANY • JOPLIN, MISSOURI

Library of Congress Cataloging-in-Publication Data

Fields, Wilbur.
    Old Testament history: an overview of sacred history and
truth / Wilbur Fields.
        p.   cm.
    Rev. ed. of: Old Testament history / William Smith. 1983.
    Includes bibliographical references and index.
    ISBN 0-89900-646-9 (hardcover)
    1. Bible. O.T.–History of Biblical events.   2. Jews–
History–To 70 A.D.   I. Smith, William George, 1813–1893.
Old Testament history.   II. Title.
BS1197.F44 1996
221.9'5–dc20   96-36168
                                                          CIP

Table of Contents

Preface

This book of Old Testament History is a successor to two books: (1) *Sacred History and Geography*, by Don DeWelt, Joplin, MO: College Press, 1962; (2) *Old Testament History*, by William Smith, Revised by Wilbur Fields, Joplin, MO: College Press, 1992.

These two books have been used as textbooks for freshman students at Ozark Christian College (formerly Ozark Bible College) and similar colleges for over thirty years. Many of these students had never read the Old Testament completely. The books were prepared to acquaint students with the Bible text, and with the spiritual truths in the Scriptures. The books emphasized also the geography relating to the Bible.

I am indebted to many people for committing to me priceless truths from God's holy Scriptures. I recall the excitement and pleasure that came to my heart in my first year in Bible college when Dr. Claude Carson Taylor first revealed to me that the Old Testament told a continuous story and revealed the *eternal purpose* of God to bring Christ into the world as the Savior of all people. Dr. Taylor's little book *The Purpose of God* (Cincinnati: Standard, 1925) was a great light to me. I pray that this new book may bring to many future students the kind of inspiration that I found from his teaching and writings.

Our approach to the Old Testament is the approach of *faith*. We believe that all Scripture is God–breathed (2 Tim. 3:16). We believe that the men of God who spoke and wrote its words were carried along by the Holy Spirit (2 Pet. 1:21). We believe that all of the LORD's words in the sacred Scriptures are *true*, and all of God's righteous laws are *eternal*

(Ps. 119:160). We believe that the word of our God stands forever (Isa. 40:8; 1 Pet. 1:25). We believe that the Bible text as originally written has been preserved accurately and delivered to us in a trustworthy form. Jesus said, "It is easier for heaven and earth to disappear than for the least stroke of a pen to drop out of the Law" (Luke 16:17).

We should approach the Old Testament with the spirit expressed by Wilhelm Moeller as the motto for his *Introduction*: "Draw not nigh hither: put off thy shoes from off thy feet, for the place whereon thou standest is *holy ground*" (Ex. 3:5). (Quoted by Edward J. Young in *An Introduction to the Old Testament.*)

In this book we have continually tried to bring out the spiritual applications of the Bible. This book has an obvious "preachy" tone to it. Much information is given about how the Old Testament and the New Testament fit together. We do not apologize for this. The Bible is a preachy book, and anyone who presents it merely in a factual or academic way is not presenting the Bible in the way it presents itself.

We believe that the New Testament and the Old Testament are in complete harmony when they are properly understood. We believe that the Old Testament pointed ahead to Christ Jesus, and spoke much concerning Him. Jesus explained to all his disciples what was written in *all* the Scriptures concerning himself, in the Law of Moses, the Prophets and the Psalms (Luke 24:27, 44).

Our book contains questions over the Old Testament contents from Genesis through Esther. Most of these questions can be answered from the Bible text itself. Many students have expressed to us that they are grateful that we have insisted that they write out the answers to all these questions, even though much study wearies the body (Eccl. 12:12).

We have used the New International Version as our Bible text throughout this book. We have found it to be reliable and readable. We have occasionally quoted other versions, or given what we consider to be a literal translation when we felt it was helpful to do so. No one translation is completely perfect or always superior to other translations.

Reading this book must never replace reading the Bible itself. Read the Bible first, and then read the related sections from this book. Many events that are told in the Bible are not even mentioned in this book. The Bible's own words are more important than anything we could ever say about them.

It is our prayer and hope that those who are introduced to the study of the Bible through this book will find the *joy* that the Scriptures can bring.

They are more precious than gold,
        than much pure gold;
they are sweeter than honey,
        than honey from the comb (Ps. 19:10).

Introduction to Old Testament History

1. Why is the study of Old Testament History important?
2. The books of the Old Testament.
3. Bible history by periods.

1. *Why is the study of Old Testament history important?*

a. It is important because the holy Scriptures are able to make us wise unto salvation (2 Tim. 3:15). When the apostle Paul wrote of the "holy Scriptures," he was referring to the Old Testament Scriptures.

b. *The Old Testament is the background for the New Testament.* From the Old Testament *historical* books alone there are over 450 quotations or allusions in the New Testament. The New Testament cannot be understood without knowledge of its background, the Old Testament.

c. *All parts of the Old Testament contain prophecies and illustrations that predicted the coming of Christ or pointed toward it.*

Jesus said, "You diligently study the Scriptures because you think that by them you possess eternal life. These are the Scriptures that testify about me" (John 5:39; Luke 24:26). We should be able to begin at any point in the Old Testament and preach Jesus, for Christ is the theme of the whole Bible (Acts 8:35).

d. *The Old Testament history is completely true.*

Jesus our Lord said that the Old Testament Scriptures could not be broken, and were true in every detail (John 10:35; Matt. 22:29; Luke 16:17). Prophecy never had its origin in the will of man, but men spoke from God as they were carried along by the Holy Spirit (2 Pet. 1:21). All Scripture is God–breathed (inspired) and is useful for teaching (2 Tim. 3:16). The Old Testament is our only reliable source of knowledge about creation, the early history of humanity, and God's ancient dealings with mankind.

e. *The events in the Old Testament were written for our learning.* They are declared to be "examples" to us (1 Cor. 10:6; Rom. 15:4). In the Old Testament we have many examples of God's dealings with His people which should warn, instruct, and comfort us.

2. *The books of the Old Testament*

a. Every disciple of the Lord should learn the books of the Old Testament, and the divisions (or groupings) of the books. This is a **first** step in taking up the sword of the Spirit, which is the word of God (Eph. 6:17). Learn them in groups.

(1) *5 books of **Law:*** Genesis, Exodus, Leviticus, Numbers, Deuteronomy. These books are called the *Torah* (or *Law*) in Hebrew, or *Pentateuch* (meaning *five books*) in Greek.

(2) *12 books of **History***: Joshua, Judges, Ruth, 1 & 2 Samuel, 1 & 2 Kings, 1 & 2 Chronicles, Ezra, Nehemiah, Esther (3 single books, then 3 pairs of books, then 3 single books).

(3) *5 books of **Poetry*** (or devotion): Job, Psalms, Proverbs, Ecclesiastes, Song of Songs.

(4) *5 books called **Major Prophets:*** Isaiah, Jeremiah, Lamentations, Ezekiel, Daniel.

(5) *12 books called **Minor Prophets***: Hosea through Malachi. (The Hebrew Bible calls these *The Twelve*, and counts them as one book.)

b. The Hebrew Bible divides the books into three parts — the Law (or *Torah*), the Prophets (*Nevi'im*), and the Writings (*Kethubim*). These books all together are often called the *TaNaK*. The Hebrew Scriptures do not include the fourteen books often called the *Apocrypha*. The books in the Hebrew Bible are the same books as those in most Protestant Bibles, but the order of the books (after Kings) is different.

c. The **historical** portion of the Old Testament is contained in the books of Genesis through Esther. The poetic and prophetic books fit into the history at points that will be indicated later.

14

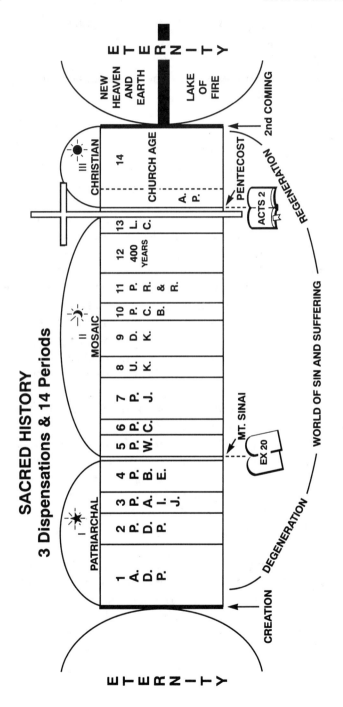

SACRED HISTORY
3 Dispensations & 14 Periods

3. *Bible history by periods.* All of the Bible's history (both the Old and New Testaments) can be summarized in fourteen periods. (See the chart.) Old Testament History can be outlined by the first eleven of the periods. This book follows the outline of Bible history as it is summarized by the periods.

Explanation of the chart

A. The three large arches across the top are the three great dispensations in God's program between creation and Christ's Second Coming. A *dispensation* is a period of time when God administered His kingdom in a particular way. In each dispensation God *dispensed* His laws in some particular manner.

B. The periods of Bible history within each dispensation are indicated by abbreviations. In the list that follows the portions of Scripture that tell of each period are given.

1. A.D.P. *Antediluvian* period, or period before the flood (Genesis 1–8). In this period mankind went rapidly into sin. Because of the wickedness of mankind God destroyed the world by the flood. This period lasted over 1600 years.

2. P.D.P. *Postdiluvian* period, or period after the flood (Genesis 9–11). People went back into sin after the flood and tried to build the tower of Babel.

3. P.A.I.J. Period of *Abraham, Isaac and Jacob* (Genesis 12–50; Book of Job). God called Abram and his family to separate themselves unto Him. Through these men all nations of the earth were to be blessed.

4. P.B.E. *Period of Bondage in Egypt* (Exodus 1–12). 430 years in Egypt. In Egypt the family of Abraham multiplied into a great nation.

5. P.W. *Period of Wandering* (Exodus 13–40, Leviticus, Numbers, Deuteronomy). Forty years in the desert with Moses. Israel became God's covenant nation at Mt. Sinai.

6. P.C. *Period of Conquest* (Joshua). About 7 years.

7. P.J. *Period of Judges* (Judges; Ruth; 1 Samuel 1–7). About 300 difficult years, when "everyone did as he saw fit."

8. U.K. *United Kingdom.* Reigns of Saul, David, and

Solomon. (1 Samuel 8–31; 2 Samuel; 1 Kings 1–11; 1 Chronicles 10–29; 2 Chronicles 1–9.

The poetic books of Psalms, Proverbs, Ecclesiastes and Song of Songs are from this period.)

9. D.K. *Divided Kingdom* (1 Kings 12–22; 2 Kings; 2 Chronicles 10–36). Two kingdoms: Judah and Israel.

10. P.C.B. *Period of Captivity in Babylon* (Books of Daniel and Ezekiel; Psalm 137). 70 years in Babylon.

11. P.R.& R. *Period of Return and Restoration* (Ezra, Nehemiah, Esther, Haggai, Zechariah, Malachi).

12. 400 years (or a few more) between the Old Testament and New Testament.

13. L.C. *Life of Christ* (Matthew, Mark, Luke, and John).

14. Church age. (Acts, epistles [Romans through Jude], part of Revelation). During this age men can receive Christ Jesus, and be saved from the world.

The first part of the church age (to about A.D. 100) was the A.P., the *Apostolic period.*

Questions
Introduction to Old Testament History
1. Give five reasons why the study of Old Testament history is important.
2. Learn the books of the Old Testament in order, and the divisions (groupings) of the books.
3. Which books of the Old Testament contain its historical portion?
4. Into how many periods can Bible history be outlined? How many of these periods are included in the Old Testament history?

"Tell of all
HIS WONDERFUL ACTS."

In Psalm 105:1–2, 5 we are told to . . .
> *Give thanks to the LORD, call on his name; make*
> *known among the nations what he has done.*
> *Sing to him, sing praise to him;*
> ***Tell of all his wonderful acts*** . . .
> *Remember the wonders he has done, his miracles,*
> *and the judgments he pronounced.*

After giving this exhortation to tell of God's wonderful acts, the psalm mentions God's covenant with Abraham and Jacob, the story of Joseph in Egypt, Moses leading Israel out of Egypt, Israel's wanderings in the wilderness, and Israel's conquest of the land of Canaan. The psalm identifies God's **"wonderful acts"** with the events in Old Testament history.

This book is a survey of Sacred History as told in the Old Testament, and the theological *truths* that are associated with that history. The book is designed to help us know what God's wonderful acts were, and to lead us to "Give thanks to the LORD, and call on his name."

Period I — Period before the Flood (Antediluvian Period)

From Creation to the flood (Genesis 1-9)

Section A
Introduction to Genesis

1. The name *Genesis* means origin, or source, or beginning. *Genesis* is the name given in the Greek Bible. In the Hebrew Bible Genesis is named *Bereshith*, which is the first word in the Hebrew Bible, and means "in the beginning." (The Old Testament was almost all written in Hebrew.)

2. *Moses was the author of Genesis*, as well as being the author of the four books which follow Genesis. Jesus said in John 7:19, "Has not *Moses* given you the law?" God's own words are recorded in Malachi 4:4: "Remember the law of my servant **Moses**, the decrees and laws I gave him." Moses was fully capable of doing this task. He was educated in all the great learning of the Egyptians (Acts 7:22). He had the time needed to write it while Israel journeyed in the desert. He had made the faith commitment to God that the author of such a book as Genesis would need (Heb. 11:24-25).

Certainly God is the ultimate author of Genesis and all the other books of the Bible. God inspired Moses for this task, and revealed truth to him. Moses could therefore write about things both known by him and things not known by him without error (2 Tim. 3:16; 2 Pet. 1:21).

Genesis nowhere states who its author was. Genesis, however, is clearly continued by the book of Exodus, and Exodus does state that Moses wrote certain sections of it (and probably wrote it all).

Most modern critics dismiss the idea that Moses wrote any of the law as "unscientific." They teach that an unidentified priestly writer (or writers) who lived about the time of the Babylonian captivity (550–450 B.C.) wrote Genesis chapter one, and the genealogical lists in Genesis 5, and parts of the flood story, and the genealogical lists in Genesis 10–11, and other passages of special interest to the priesthood. This unidentified priestly writer is often called "P."

Most critics assign narrative (story-telling) sections (like Genesis 2–4, and parts of the flood story, and Abraham's call in Genesis 12–13, and other passages) to another unknown author, who is called "J" (the *Jehovist,* or *Yahwist*). J is said to have lived about the time of king Solomon or Rehoboam (950 B.C.). He was a story teller and not a moralist or theologian. Some say J was a woman.

Those who hold this theory generally believe that there was a third writer who produced parts of the books of law. He is called "E" (for Elohist). "E" is supposed to have been a story-teller similar to J. The writings of E were later merged with the writings of J. Still later the writings of P were combined with the writings of J+E (a cut-and-paste production). With that done "out came" Genesis and finally the whole law.

This theory is widely held, but there are objections to it:

(1) No one has ever found a manuscript containing only the sections of Scripture assigned to J, or E, or P.

(2) Many of the writers of the Old Testament ascribed the entire law to Moses; and no Old Testament writer assigned it to anyone else. (See Joshua 8:31–32, Judges 3:4, and other references to Moses.)

(3) Jesus and His apostles often attributed to Moses passages which they quoted from the law. (See Matt. 8:4; Mark 7:10; 12:26; Acts 3:22; Rom. 10:5; and others). To us Jesus is the final authority.

(4) All of the ancient Jewish writers (The *Talmud,* Josephus, and others) attributed the books of law to Moses. (See Josephus, *Against Apion,* 1:8.)

(5) The source theory about the origin of Genesis leads to the "unedifying conclusion" that "nothing is authentic." (Cyrus Gordon)

3. *Genesis deals with events from the creation of heaven and earth to the death of Joseph* (son of Jacob). John J. Davis calls his

book on Genesis *Paradise to Prison* because Genesis tells of events from Paradise in the Garden of Eden to prison in Egypt.

4. *Genesis is scientifically and historically accurate.*

a. All the "waters" really are "gathered to *one* place" (Gen. 1:9). The oceans are connected, so that there is really just one large ocean. How could Moses, who never circled the globe, have known this if God had not revealed it to him?

b. Creatures reproduce "according to their various kinds" (1:11,21). Animals and plants reproduce their own kind, and there are limits on the amount of variability possible in their offspring.

c. Creatures reproduce *abundantly.* "Be fruitful and increase in number" (1:22). It has been estimated that one pair of robins would be capable of producing more than 19,500,000 offspring in ten years if there were no natural enemies to reduce this number (Alfred M. Rehwinkel, *The Wonders of Creation*, p. 157).

5. *Genesis divides itself into ten parts.* Each of these divisions begins with some words such as "This is the account of . . ." (or "These are the *generations* of . . ."). The Hebrew word for "account" [or "generations"] is *toledoth*, which means "generations" or "history" of a line from one stated ancestor. These *toledoth* statements appear to be introductions to the verses or chapters that follow them. (Note the uses of the term *toledoth* in Ruth 4:18; 1 Chronicles 1:29; Numbers 3:1. Also note its uses in Genesis 25:12; 36:1,9; 37:2.) The *toledoth* have been interpreted as endings (colophons, postscripts) to the paragraphs or chapters that immediately precede the statements. But that seems unlikely, in view of the way the term is used in these passages.

These are the sections labeled "accounts" ("generations") in Genesis:

(1) "The account of the heavens and the earth" (2:4–4:26)

(2) "The written account of Adam's generations" (5:1–6:8)

(3) "The account of Noah" (6:9–9:29)

(4) "The account of Shem, Ham and Japheth" (10:1,11:9)

(5) "The account of Shem" (11:10-26)

(6) "The account of Terah" (11:27–25:11). (This section deals mostly with Terah's son Abraham.)

(7) "The account of Abraham's son Ishmael" (25:12-18)

(8) "The account of Abraham's son Isaac" (25:19–35:39)

(9) "The account of Esau" (ch. 36. Note 36:1,9.)

(10) "The account of Jacob" (chs. 37-50). (This section deals mostly with Jacob's son Joseph.)

     6. **Outline of Genesis.** (Memorize this outline.)

       I. The earliest history (chs. 1–11)

        A. Creation (chs. 1-2)

        B. The fall (ch. 3)

        C. The two lines of humanity (chs. 4–5)

        D. The flood (chs. 6–9)

        E. Descendants of Noah (chs. 10–11)

       II. History of the patriarchs (chs. 12–50)

        A. Abraham (12:1–25:11)

        B. Isaac (25:12–28:9)

        C. Jacob (and Esau) (28:10–36:43)

        D. Joseph (and Jacob's other sons) (chs. 37–50)

   7. Genesis contains several significant *Messianic prophecies* (prophecies about the Messiah, or Christ):

    a. **Genesis 3:15** —The first promise of a Savior is given here. The passage foretold that the "seed of the woman" (who is Christ) would bruise the head of the serpent (Satan); and the serpent would bruise the heel of the woman's seed.

    b. **Genesis 12:3** and **22:18** — God promised to **BLESS** all peoples through Abraham and through his offspring ("seed"), who is Christ. See Acts 3:25–26 and Galatians 3:8, 16.

    c. **Genesis 49:10** — The tribe of Judah would be the ruling tribe in Israel until "he comes to whom it (the scepter) belongs," or "until *"Shiloh"* comes." The title *"Shiloh"* here refers to Christ.

Questions on Section A
Introduction to Genesis

1. What does the name *Genesis* mean?
2. In what language was the Old Testament written?
3. Who was the author (writer) of Genesis?
   Who was the ultimate author of Genesis?
4. What are the first and last events in Genesis?
5. Is Genesis a scientifically and historically accurate book?
6. How many divisions does Genesis divide itself into?
7. What expression is at the start of all of the divisions of Genesis?
8. Give the Scripture references for four Messianic prophecies in Genesis.
9. Write from memory the outline of Genesis, including the Scripture references.

Section B
The Creation (Genesis 1–2)

1. *The purpose of Scripture history.* The purpose of Scripture history is to set forth the steps by which God made for Himself a people, a *church.* God had an "eternal purpose" in mind when He made heaven and earth. Even before God laid the foundation of the earth, God planned to send Christ Jesus into the world to die for mankind and to *redeem* (rescue and purchase) mankind to Himself for His own people (Eph. 1:4; 3:11; 1 Pet. 1:4; Rev. 13:8).

The steps by which God worked out His program to bring mankind to Himself began with creation. God created man, and blessed him. Though man sinned, God gave forgiveness and promises of good things, which His people could yet inherit. God punished man when he sinned (by expelling him from the Garden of Eden, and by Noah's flood, for example). God especially directed and blessed certain people of faith (like Abraham), who could be examples to us all. Still later God gave good laws through Moses. But humankind failed in every generation.

Mankind's consistent failures to fear, love, and serve God

in the Old Testament age showed our fleshly weakness in sin, and also showed our need for the perfect system of grace that Jesus Christ would bring into the world. God planned something better for *us* so that only together with us would they [the saints of the Old Testament age] be made perfect (Heb. 11:40).

GOD is . . .

1. **Spirit** (John 4:24; Luke 24:39)
2. **Love** (1 John 4:8,16)
3. **Light** (1 John 1:5; 1 Tim. 6:16)
4. **Consuming fire** (Deut. 4:24; Heb. 12:29)
5. **HOLY** (Isa. 6:3; Lev. 11:44-45; 1 Pet. 1:16)
6. **Eternal** (Isa. 57:15; 40:28; Ps. 90:2)
7. **Merciful & gracious** (Ex. 34:6)
8. **Omnipresent** (Jer. 23:24; Isa. 66:1; Ps. 139:7-12)
9. **Omniscient** (Knows all) (Rom. 16:27; Heb. 4:13; 1 Tim. 1:17; Ps. 44:21)
10. **Omnipotent** (Almighty) (Jer. 32:17-18; Ps. 24:8; Gen. 17:1)

GOD'S descriptions of Himself
Exodus 34:5-7 — 13 attributes of God
Isaiah 57:15 — High, holy, eternal
Isaiah 40:25-29 — Creator, unwearied

---

2. *The universe was created by God only.* Without preface or argument for the existence of God, the writer of Genesis speaks of Him as the creator of the universe: "In the beginning God ('Elohim) created the heavens and the earth." (See chart on the Hebrew names for God.)

In this verse there is clear denial of many erroneous ideas about the origin of the universe. The world was created by God, not by *chance*, not by *self-generation*, not by impersonal *powers of nature*, nor by *many agents*, whether acting in har-

mony or in conflict (as in the Babylonian creation story). We
learn from John 1:1-3 that the *agent* in creation was the *Son*,
the *Word*. See also Hebrews 1:2; Colossians 1:16: "All things
were created *by* him and *for* him" (emphasis added).

3. *The work of creation was done at a definite time.* "In the
beginning God created the heavens and the earth." They did
not exist therefore from eternity. We should not think of
them as going back in time from age to age until we lose all
perception that they had a beginning. The Scripture links
together the creation of heaven and earth with God's making
of all the things on earth. See Exodus 20:11. We should
therefore believe that both the universe and the things on
earth are about the same age, only a few thousand years old,
according to Scripture. God alone knows when He made His
world, and we can know only what He has told us about this.

Attempts have been made to account for the existence of
the universe by a Big Bang blowup of all the matter in the
universe when it was compressed together.

This theory cannot account for the existence of matter,
nor for the orderly patterns in the elements and in the galaxies of stars. If *God* indeed made the universe, no other explanation will stand up under investigation. Scientific research
will probably reveal more and more of the marvels in God's
creation, but it can never explain the existence of the universe without acknowledging God.

HEBREW NAMES FOR GOD			
Hebrew names	**KJV, NKJV, NIV, NRSV, NASB**	American Standard vers.(1901)	Meaning of name
1.'Elohim אֱלֹהִים	God	God	*Mighty one.* This name refers to God as creator and preserver of man, or as God of all nations.

2. **Yahweh** יהוה	LORD (small capital letters)	Jehovah	The *EXISTING* (or being) one. The ETERNAL. This name comes from the verb of "I AM." *Yahweh* is the covenant name of God as God of Israel.
3. **'Adonai** אֲדֹנָי	Lord, or lord	Lord, or lord	Literally, "*My lord.*" *'Adonai* is a title of respect for men, as well as for God.

Other names for God include . . .

4. **'El** (Gen. 31:13) and **'Eloah** (Job 3:4), which are short singular forms of 'Elohim, meaning God or gods. **'Elohim** is plural in form, but usually singular in meaning.

5. **Shaddai** (often used in Job, as in 13:3) means The **Almighty**. Thus **'El Shaddai** (Gen. 17:1) means *God Almighty.*

6. **Yah**, or **Jah**, (Ex. 15:1; Ps. 116:1) is a short form of **Yahweh.**

4. *The Spirit of God was hovering over the waters* (Gen. 1:2). The reason for the Spirit's presence is not stated in Genesis, but Jesus said, "The Spirit gives life" (John 6:63; See also 2 Cor. 3:6). The Spirit of God was "hovering" over the newly-created earth like an eagle hovering over its young in the nest (Deut. 32:11).

The newly created earth was shrouded in thick, foggy vapor, so that sky and solid earth were not clearly separated. It was "formless and empty," or "unformed and unfilled" (Weston Fields).

5. *Light was God's first good gift upon earth* (Gen. 1:3-5). All living things depend on light for existence and operation. Light is marvelous and mysterious. It travels endlessly at great speed. Beams of light cross one another without appar-

ent collision. God is light (1 John 1:5). Jesus is the light (John 8:12). The light which God caused to shine on day one was light from His own glory. The sun and moon were made later (Gen. 1:16; Rev. 22:5).

GOD'S WORKS ON THE SEVEN DAYS OF CREATION

1. *First day* – Light and darkness
2. *Second day* – Expanse (firmament) of open sky
3. *Third day* – Dry ground and plants
4. *Fourth day* – Sun, moon, stars
5. *Fifth day* — Water creatures and birds
6. *Sixth day* — Living creatures and man
7. *Seventh day* – Rest

---

6. *At first, the earth was formless and empty* (Gen. 1:1-2). Many Bible interpreters have suggested that there was a long time gap (billions of years?) between Genesis 1:1 and 1:2. Some time long after the heavens and earth were first created the earth supposedly "*became* waste and void." After that, God remade the earth and the creatures now in it. According to this theory the first day of the seven days of creation is described in Genesis 1:3-5, but vv. 1-2 tell of time preceding the seven days of creation. This theory is called the "gap theory." The author once believed this theory. But there are objections to the theory:

a. Exodus 20:11 (spoken by God's own voice as part of the Ten Commandments) says that the LORD created heaven and earth and all things in them in *six* days. This indicates that all of the events in Genesis 1:1-5 are included on the first day of creation.

b. The grammar of the Hebrew language indicates that v. 2 refers to a condition (or event) existing at the same time as the events in v. 1. Verse 2 is simultaneous to v. 1, not subsequent to it. (See John J. Davis, *Paradise to Prison*, pp. 42-45. Also see Gesenius, Kautzsch, Cowley, *Hebrew Grammar*, pp. 453-454.)

c. The existence of fossils of hundreds of species of creatures which are identical (or nearly identical) to creatures now living indicates that there has been a general continuity of kinds of living things on earth since it was first created.

7. *The creation was completed within "days"* (Gen. 1:1–2:3). One theory (called the "day-age" theory) is that the "days" were not literal 24-hour solar days, but that they are to be understood figuratively as representing great geological periods of time. It is true that there are a few passages in the Bible where the Hebrew word for *day* (*yom*) is used to mean a period of indefinite length (such as Isaiah 2:12,20; 4:1; John 8:56.) But in most Bible passages "day" means an ordinary period of twenty-four hours.

There are several reasons to believe that the "days" of Genesis chapter one were brief periods, similar to our present "days":

a. Psalm 33:6,9 says, "By the word of the LORD were the heavens made . . . For he spoke, and it came to be; he commanded, and it stood firm." This sounds as if creation was instantaneous.

The existence in earth's oldest rocks of microscopic spheres of discoloration caused by radioactive decay of certain isotopes of elements that have a half-life of only minutes, and could leave the discolorations only in solid rock, suggests that the earth was created quickly in solid form. (See *Bible-Science Newsletter*, April 1986, p. 6.)

b. The analogies of other acts of creation suggest that God's original creation was done quickly. In an instant Jesus made enough bread and fishes to feed 5000 men (John 6:11). Jesus made the dead, rotting flesh of Lazarus into living flesh with one command. When Christ returns, the dead bodies of people that have decayed into dust will be made into living spiritual bodies "in the twinkling of an eye" (1 Cor. 15:52).

c. Adam was created on the sixth day. He lived in the garden of Eden through the sixth and seventh days. Some time after the seventh day he was expelled from the garden. He had two sons. They grew to maturity. Son Cain killed son Abel. Still later a third son, Seth, was born. Adam was 130 years old when Seth was born (Gen. 5:3). Plainly, the sixth and seventh days do not refer to periods of time thousands of years long. We assume the word *day* refers to the same period of time in *all* the references to "days" in Genesis 1.

d. Genesis 1:14 distinguishes between "days" and "years" and "seasons." This indicates that the first chapter of Genesis probably did not intend for the word *day* to mean *years*.

e. The "days" in Genesis 1 are divided into "evening" and "morning" (1:5). (The Hebrews regard a "day" as starting with the evening rather than the morning.) It is difficult to see how a long period of time could be said to have an evening and a morning. But "days" such as we now have would have had an evening and morning.

f. On the third "day" plants were made. The sun was not made until the fourth day. Many plants could not survive a "day" millions of years long without sunlight. Similarly, some plants depend upon certain insects and birds for their reproduction. But these flying creatures were not made until the fifth "day."

We conclude that in Genesis 1:1–2:3 the word *day* refers to ordinary days similar in length to those at the present.

8. *Creatures reproduce "according to their various kinds"* (or "according to their kind") (Gen. 1:12, 21, 24). Here is the great law of reproduction according to species. The possibility of some interbreeding between species is indicated in Bible passages such as Deuteronomy 22:9; but there appear to be limits on how much variation creatures can develop. Possibly the Hebrew word for "kind" (*min*) corresponds more closely to our word *genus* (referring to a *family* of creatures, like the dog family) than to *species*. Some creationist scholars have coined the word *baramin* to refer to the original created "kinds" (from the Hebrew *bara'*, to *create;* plus *min*, "kind").

9. *The two great lights were made on the fourth* day. These are the sun and the moon. God made the stars also. They did not form themselves by the coming together by gravitational attraction of hydrogen molecules or dust. The forces that drive matter apart in space are far greater than the gravitational attraction that might draw matter together (*Astronomy*, Dec. 1989, p. 14).

How galaxies of stars with their vast rotating structures might form by known laws of science is still a mystery, though researchers have diligently sought to explain the existence of the universe "without giving a nod to God" (*Astronomy*, Sept. 1995, pp. 37-38; Henry Morris, *Acts & Facts*, Jan. 1995).

How the light of stars thousands of light years from earth could have reached the earth in Adam's lifetime remains a mystery to us. The stars were set in the heavens to mark seasons and days and years from the very beginning. So they must have been visible. Nothing is too hard for God (Gen. 18:14). Possibly there are "laws" of relativity that permit light to pass through vast stretches of interstellar space quickly. (See *Bible Science News*, May 1995, pp. 14-17.)

10. *Fifth and sixth days* (Gen. 1:20-31). Having made the necessary preparations for life — light, land, and plants for food — God created a host of marvelous living creatures on the fifth and sixth days. Genesis tells that birds were made before the "creatures that move along the ground." We should not, therefore, believe that birds descended from dinosaurs.

On all of these days God saw that what He had made was *good* (1:10,12,18,21,25). The existence of disorder, death, and decay in our present world shows that the earth has suffered a great fall since the time when God first made it good.

THE WORD WAS WITH GOD AT CREATION

John 1:1-3 In the beginning was the *Word*, and the Word was with God, and the Word was God. He was with God in the beginning. Through him all things were made; without him nothing was made that has been made.

John 1:14 The *Word became flesh* and made his dwelling among us.   (Emphasis added.)

On the sixth day as His climax of creating, God said, "Let us make man in our image" (1:26). The use of the plural pronouns ("us" and "our") shows that God was in conversation

30

Man in God's Image

(or God's **likeness**. Genesis 1:26-27; 9:6;
1 Corinthians 11:7; James 3:9)

RESEMBLANCES	GOD	MAN
1. Spiritual nature	John 4:24	1 Thess. 5:23
2. Moral nature	Ex. 34:6-7	Eccl. 7:29
(conscience)		Gen. 1:27,31
3. Eternal existence	Ps. 90:1-2	Dan. 12:2
		Matt. 25:46
4. Ability to reason	Ps. 104:2-4	Prov. 14:22
	Rom. 16:27	Mark 2:6,8
5. Rule over the earth	Ps. 50:12	Gen. 1:26
	Ps. 24:1-2	Heb. 2:7-8
6. Freedom of choice	Ps. 115:3	Prov. 1:29
	Ps. 135:6	Ps. 119:30
7. Relationship capacity	Ex. 19:4-6	1 John 1:7
	Mal. 3:17	Ps. 133:1

Only in Jesus can we see what *man* would be like, if man were in full harmony with God. Jesus was perfect man, as well as perfect God.

with someone (or several) beings. From the New Testament we learn that there are three divine personalities that together make up what we call "God" or the "godhead" (that which is divine) — Father, Son, and Holy Spirit. Before the Son came into the world as Jesus Christ, He was known as the Word.

The existence of other divine personalities together with God is indicated even in the Old Testament. Isaiah 48:16 says "Come near me and listen to this: From the first announcement I have not spoken in secret; at the time it happens, I am there. And now the Sovereign LORD has sent *me*, with his *Spirit*" (emphasis added).

11. *The seventh day* (Gen. 2:1-3). By this day God had finished the work He had been doing, and rested, and blessed

the seventh day. God's rest, however, was not a complete ceasing from activity. He was done *creating*, but He continues to work to care for and bless His creatures. Christ said, "My Father is always at his work to this very day, and I, too, am working" (John 5:17). Thus God's seventh day of creation illustrated the true observance of the Sabbath day: "It is lawful *to do good* on the Sabbath" (Matt. 12:12).

The fact that God's work of creation was *finished* by the seventh day indicates that new creatures have not appeared on earth since then. Many kinds of creatures have become extinct, and many variations within species have appeared, but only within the limited boundaries of the "kinds" that God created.

Though God "rested" (or ceased to work) on the seventh day, there is no indication that He commanded man at that time to keep the seventh day as a weekly Sabbath. That command was given centuries later at Mt. Sinai when God gave the Ten Commandments to Moses and Israel: "You came down on Mount Sinai; you spoke to them from heaven . . . You *made known to them your holy Sabbath* and gave them commands . . . through your servant Moses" (Neh. 9:13-14, emphasis added).

12. *Man's place in God's world* (Gen. 2:4-7). After the magnificent summary of all of God's creative acts in Genesis 1, Genesis 2 narrows down the topic to tell of man's place in God's world. Genesis 2 is not a second creation story. Chapter 2 does not tell of the creation of such major items as sun, moon, stars, or earth. The chapter opens with the indication that earth already existed (2:4).

Genesis chapter 2 tells of . . .
GOD'S GIFTS TO MAN
1. Life (2:5,7)
2. A dwelling place (2:8)
3. Beauty to see (2:9)
4. Food (2:9,16; Acts 14:17)
5. Work (2:15)
6. Rules (2:17)
7. Companionship (2:18-25)

---

13. *Critical view of Genesis chapter 2.* Many Bible critics
have said that Genesis 2 was written by a different author
than the author of Genesis 1. Genesis 1 has been attributed
to a ritualistic priestly writer living about 450 B.C. Genesis
2-4 is assigned to a story-telling author (called "J") who lived
about 850 B.C. "J" is said to picture God in an anthropomorphic way, as if God had human hands that planted a garden,
and shaped man out of the dust, and took out one of the
man's ribs, while P described God as transcendent spirit. But
this objection is superficial. An anthropomorphic conception
of God also appears in chapter one. Indeed it is impossible
for the finite mind to speak of God without using anthropomorphic language. Chapter 1 asserts that God "called,"
"saw," "blessed," "deliberated" (v. 26, "let us make"), and
"rested" (Edward J. Young, *Intro. to O.T.* [1963], p. 53).

Genesis 2:4 is the place where for the first time we find
the name LORD God (Heb. *Yahweh 'Elohim*), and therefore it
has been regarded as the place in the text where the "J" section begins. But the name *Yahweh* (or Jehovah) is the name
customarily used in sections of Scripture where God is
making *covenant* relationships with His people. (See Genesis
12:1; 15:17; 17:1.) Genesis 2 gives God's original covenant
with Adam, and therefore the name LORD is appropriate in
it.

14. *The earth was made for man* (Gen. 2:4-7). When the
plants were made on the third day, no "plant of the field"
(cultivated herbs) had yet sprung up. God delayed their
appearance until he had formed man. The beautiful earth
was made for man, and not for its own sake. Chemically man
is made of dust, but God breathed into man's body the
"breath of life" so that man became a "living being," or
"living *soul*" (Hebrew *nephesh*, soul or life).

15. *Provisions for man* (Gen. 2:8-17). Adam ("man" in a
generic sense) was placed in a garden (Greek, *paradise*). The
garden was located "east" from where Moses wrote Genesis,
"in Eden." (*Eden* means loveliness, delight.) The garden lay in
Mesopotamia, possibly in the far north (toward Mt. Ararat),
or in the far south (toward the Persian Gulf). Beauty and

food were present. There was work assigned to man, work which would provide his needs, and give him the joys of achievement (2:15).

A moral test for man was created. In the middle of the garden was "the tree of the knowledge of good and evil" (2:9,17). God stated a rule plainly: If "you eat of it you will surely die." If humankind was to have opportunity to choose to love the LORD, it was necessary that some other choice be available to man. When God provided this choice for man, God took a risk that mankind would choose to do that which He could not approve.

In some way we do not understand, the tree could impart forbidden knowledge to man. It was not useful knowledge, but knowledge of matters that would harm and destroy man and break his relationship with his creator. It is better not to know some things.

The fact that Adam named the animals proves that he was endowed with the power of *language* from the beginning. The story of his fall bears indirect but certain testimony to his close fellowship with God. Adam had all the talents that his most gifted descendants have shown. We see man's marvelous potential most perfectly demonstrated in Christ, "the second Adam" (1 Cor. 15:47).

16. *Adam was a pattern of Christ.* Romans 5:14 tells that "Adam was a *pattern* (a symbol, or *type*) of the one to come" (Christ). A *type* is some person or event in the Old Testament that God designed to resemble some person or thing in the New Testament. The *antitype* is the person or thing in the New Testament that was foreshadowed by the Old Testament type. There are many such *types* in the Old Testament. We include information about several of them in this book.

17. *Companionship provided for man* (Gen. 2:18-25). God made the woman from the side of the man. This is a surprising manner of creating the woman. God did it that way to illustrate the future close relationship of Christ to His church (Eph. 5:29-32). The woman was to be a helper to the man, though not his slave (1 Cor. 11:9). She was called *woman* (Hebrew, *Ishah*, the feminine of *Ish*, Man). God's creation of

Adam, a pattern (type) of Christ

ADAM	CHRIST JESUS
1. Son of God (Luke 3:38)	1. Son of God (Luke 1:35)
2. A living soul (Gen. 2:7)	2. A life-giving spirit (1 Cor. 15:22)
3. Dominion over all things (Ps. 8:4-8)	3. Dominion over all (Matt. 28:18; Heb. 2:5-9)
4. One flesh with his bride (Gen. 2:24)	4. One flesh with His church (Eph. 5:30-31)
5 Disobedient (Rom. 5:19)	5. Obedient (Heb. 5:8)
6. Brought death to all (1 Cor. 15:22)	6. Brought life to all (1 Cor. 15:22)
7. Affected all those after him	7. Affected all those after Him

The Garden of Eden — A Type of Heaven

1. A dwelling place for man (Gen. 2:8)	1. A dwelling place for man (John 14:2)
2. Tree of life (Gen. 2:9; 3:25)	2.Tree of life (Rev. 2:7; 22:2)
3. River (Gen. 2:10)	3. River of life (Rev. 22:1)
4. Presence of God (Gen. 1:15-22)	4. Presence of God (Rev. 21:3)
5. Work to do (Gen. 2:15)	5. Work to do (Rev. 21:26; 22:3)
6. Beautiful (Gen. 2:9). A "Paradise" (Gen. 2:8; 3:24, Greek)	6. Beautiful (Rev. 21:2, 11). A "Paradise" (Rev. 2:7)
7. Cursed (Gen. 3:14-19; 5:29)	7. No more curse (Rev. 22:3)

EVE, A type of the Church (the people of God)

EVE	The CHURCH
1. Taken from the side of Adam (Gen. 2:21-22)	1. Taken from the side of Christ (John 19:34; Acts 20:28)
2. One flesh with Adam (Gen. 2:24)	2. One flesh with Christ (Eph. 5:30-32)
3. Tempted and deceived (1 Tim. 2:14)	3. Tempted and deceived (2 Cor. 11:3)
4. Saved by the "seed of the woman" (Gen. 3:15)	4. Saved by the "seed of the woman" (Gal. 4:4-5; 1 Tim. 2:15)
5. ONE wife for one husband (Mal. 2:15)	5. ONE church for one Lord (John 10:16; Eph. 4:4-5)
6. Loved (Gen. 2:23; 3:20)	6. Loved by Christ (Eph. 5:29)
7. To bear children (Gen. 1:28)	7. To bear "fruit" (John 15:2-5)

---

humankind as male and female was Christ's basis for teaching the permanence of marriage: "What God has joined together, let man not separate" (Matt. 19:5).

Principles of marriage shown by the creation of man and woman:

(a) The *unity* of man and wife, shown by her creation from man, and from the command to become "one flesh" (referring to sexual union) (Gen. 2:24; 1 Cor. 6:16).

(b) The lifelong *permanence* of marriage, which is not to be broken except for the most serious causes (Matt. 19:9).

(c) *Monogamy* — one wife for one man — as God's pattern for marriage (Mal. 2:15-16; Rom. 7:1-3; 1 Cor. 7:39; 1 Tim. 3:2; Titus 1:6; Lev. 21:13).

(d) The *subordination* of wife to husband as a result of her being made after the man was made (1 Cor. 11:8-9; 1 Tim. 2:13).

(e) Man's responsibility to *toil* for his wife (his own flesh) and to love and cherish her (Gen. 2:15; Eph. 5:28-29).

The last word in the description of man and woman shows a perfect innocence by the absence of a sense of shame. "The man and his wife were both naked, and they felt no shame" (Gen. 2:25). The sense of shame became very real after Adam's sin.

Questions on Section B
The Creation (Gen. 1–2)

1. What was the condition of the earth after its creation? (1:2)
2. What was hovering over the waters? (1:2)
3. Make a concise list of the things done or made on the seven days of creation.
4. List three reasons for arguing that the "days" of creation were successive days about the same length as days now.
5. Why are the days of creation said to have evenings first, then mornings?
6. What does the word *firmament* mean? To what does it refer? (1:6,14,20)
7. What did the expanse (firmament) separate? (1:6)
8. What did God call the expanse (firmament)? (1:8)
9. Where were the waters under the sky gathered? (1:9)
10. What did God call the dry land? (1:10)
11. What did God cause the earth to produce and bear? (1:11)
12. According to what rule do plants bear fruit and seed? (1:12)
13. What were the lights in the expanse of heaven to serve as? (1:14-15)
14. With what command did God bless the birds and the sea creatures? (1:22)
15. In what likeness and image did God make man? (1:26)
16. Over what was man given rule (dominion)? (1:26)
17. Was man told to reproduce before his first sin? (1:28)
18. What was originally given to man for food? What was given to the beasts? (1:29-30)
19. What word describes everything God made? (1:31)
20. Is Genesis chapter 2 a second creation story?
21. What is the relationship of Genesis chapter 2 to chapter 1?

22. How completely was God's work of creation finished? (2:1,3)
23. What did God say about the seventh day? What quality did God declare it would have? (2:3)
24. From what did God form man? (2:7)
25. What did God breathe into man?
26. In what two ways are the trees in Eden described? (2:9)
27. What two special trees in the garden are named? (2:9)
28. How did the river from Eden divide? (2:10)
29. Name the four rivers out of Eden. (2:11-14)
30. What work was given to man? (2:15)
31. What was man prohibited from eating, and what was the penalty if he ate? (2:17)
32. What did God determine to make for man? (2:18)
33. How did the animals get their names? (2:20)
34. From what was the woman made? (2:22-23)
35. Why was the woman called *Woman*? (2:23)
36. Whom is the man to leave when he marries? (2:24)
37. What are man and wife to become? (2:24; 1 Cor. 6:16)

Section C
The Fall of Man (Genesis 3)

1. *The serpent tempted the first man and woman* (Gen. 3:1-13). In the Garden of Eden the serpent tempted the woman (Eve) to eat the fruit of the tree of knowledge of good and evil, which God had specifically forbidden them to do (2:17). The serpent may at that time have been a creature that walked upright (3:14).

In later chapters of the Bible we learn that this "serpent" was actually the evil spirit-being called *Satan*, who is now at work in those who are disobedient to God (Eph. 2:2).

Scripture Information about Satan

The Bible says little about the origin of Satan. He seems to have been one of the angels who sinned soon after heaven and earth were created and did not stay in their assigned positions of authority (Jude 6; 2 Pet. 2:4). The Bible passages of Ezekiel 28:12-19 and Isaiah 14:12-15 perhaps refer to Satan by making the kings of Tyre and Babylon symbolic of Satan. If so, then Satan was once a beautiful angel who rebelled against God and said, "I will make myself like the Most High" (Isa. 14:14). His heart became proud because he had been in Eden, the garden of God, and was anointed as a guardian cherub (Ezek. 28:13-14). God drove him in disgrace from the mount of God. (This seems possible, but is not certain.)

Long ago Satan was allowed to come into God's presence (as in Job 1:6). There he accused the people of God of doing evil (Rev. 12:10). Later Satan was cast out of heaven. He goes about now on the earth with great wrath (Rev. 12:9, 12), looking for someone to devour (1 Pet. 5:8).

At the end of the age we now live in, Satan and his angels will be cast into the lake of burning sulphur, and they will be tormented day and night for ever and ever (Rev. 20:10; Matt. 25:41).

By means not known to us, Satan took possession of the serpent and spoke with the serpent's voice. The serpent craftily suggested that God was not good because He would not allow the man and woman to eat of any tree in the garden they desired. He accused God of trying to keep people from enjoying the knowledge that He alone had access to. The serpent denied that they would die, though God had clearly said they would die if they ate the fruit of the tree.

The woman was deceived by the serpent and ate of the fruit. She also gave some to her husband, who was *with her*, and he ate it (3:6). The apostle Paul said, "Adam was not the one deceived; it was the woman who was deceived" (1 Tim. 2:14).

God's first question to man: "WHERE ARE YOU?" (Gen. 3:9). God asked this question for conviction, not for information. Where are WE now in relation to God?

The results of their sin were immediate and catastrophic.
They were at once aware they were naked and ashamed of it.
They felt fear of God and hid themselves. They tried to shift
blame for their actions upon others. The man blamed the
woman, and indirectly blamed God. The woman blamed the
serpent (3:12-13). The man and woman had entered into a
state of spiritual death (separation from God, Eph. 2:1; Col.
2:13). Physical death would occur later. God's warning had
come true: "In the day you eat of it you shall surely die"
(Gen. 2:17, NKJV).

This story was accepted as a true event by the apostles of
Jesus Christ, and therefore by Christ himself (John 16:12-14).
We also should accept the story as truth, and as the explanation for the existence of evil in our world. Paul wrote, "Sin
entered the world through one man [Adam], and death
through sin" (Rom 5:12). He wrote also, "I am afraid that just
as Eve was deceived by the serpent's cunning, your minds
may somehow be led astray" (2 Cor. 11:3). The apostle John
wrote of "the great dragon . . . that ancient serpent called the
devil, or Satan, who leads the whole world astray" (Rev. 12:9).

2. *Penalties for the disobedience of man* (Gen. 3:14-19).
    a. Penalties upon the serpent (3:14-15)
       (1) Crawl upon his belly and eat dust
       (2) The offspring of the woman would crush his
          head.
    b. Penalties upon the woman (3:16)
       (1) Increased pains and childbirth
       (2) Husband would rule over her
    c. Penalties upon Adam (3:17-19)
       (1) The ground is cursed with thorns and thistles.
          The whole creation has been subjected to futility
          and decay (Rom. 8:20-21).
       (2) Physical death ("return to the ground"). "As in
          Adam all die, so in Christ all will be made alive"
          (1 Cor. 15:22).

The effects of Adam's "fall" upon the nature of the whole
human race are not as clearly stated in Scripture as the writers of creeds have tried to state them. When Adam sinned,

Genesis 3:15 — The first prophecy of the Messiah

a. There will be *enmity* between the serpent and the woman.
b. There will be *enmity* between the offspring of the woman and the offspring ("seed") of the serpent.
c. The offspring of the woman will *crush the head* of the serpent.
d. The serpent will *crush the heel* of the woman's offspring.

The offspring of the woman is a single individual ("he") who will destroy the serpent and the effects of all the serpent's deeds. The woman's "seed" will destroy guilt and fear and pain and death and decay. Christ does all these things!

The ***serpent*** in the prophecy was Satan, the devil. Satan inflicted great pain upon Christ, such as crushing his heel. But Satan could not bruise Christ with a fatal blow.

The ***woman's offspring*** (or *seed*) is Christ Jesus (Gal. 4:4; Matt. 1:18). He crushed the serpent's head when he died on the cross for mankind, and then rose again.

The ***offspring of the serpent*** seems to be a title for all sinners collectively (John 8:44). They have enmity toward Christ. They even crucified Him.

The ***woman*** in the prophecy perhaps represents the human race, born from the woman. Satan has a great hatred for the human race that God created, and tries to destroy all of us by tempting us to sin.

This prophecy was man's only promise of hope for nearly two thousand years. In the symbolism of this verse all the wonderful things that Christ has accomplished for us were summarized, though in a veiled form.

his descendants did not lose their free will or ability to *choose* to serve God (Deut. 30:19; Josh. 24:19). People can still believe and repent (Mark 1:15).

The fall of Adam did not bring about a condition wherein God had to choose some to be saved and be with Him, and some to perish. God does not want anyone to perish, but wants everyone to come to repentance (2 Pet. 3:9; 1 Tim. 2:4).

Mankind has inherited many consequences from Adam's sin. It does not appear, however, that we are born condemned to eternal punishment for Adam's sin. "The son will not share the guilt of the father, nor will the father share the guilt of the son" (Ezek. 18:20). We all soon acquire guilt of our own! Probably we should avoid using the nonbiblical expression "original sin."

Adam's sin certainly did affect man's nature to a large degree. God made man good and upright. Jesus said that we are now "evil" (Matt. 7:11). "There is no one who does good, not even one" (Ps. 14:3). "Even from birth the wicked go astray; from the womb they are wayward and speak lies" (Ps. 58:3). All of us should cry out, "What a wretched man I am!" (Rom. 7:24). We need a new birth and need to become new creatures.

"As through the disobedience of the one man [Adam] the many were made sinners, so through the obedience of the one man [Jesus] the many will be made righteous" (Rom. 5:19).

The story of man's fall has been preserved in part in the legends of many nations. The Greek legend of Pandora traces the entrance of evil to a woman. The Babylonian myth of Adapa tells how man forfeited an opportunity for eternal life. Delitzsch well says, "The story of the Fall, like that of the Creation, has wandered over the world."

Adam named his wife *Eve* because she would become the mother of all living people (Gen. 3:20). The name *Eve* is the feminine form of the Hebrew word for life, or living. We should not have racial or national prejudice, because we are all descended from one original mother, and are therefore all related to one another.

It is clear that God now disapproves of nudity and immodesty (1 Tim. 2:9; Rev. 3:18). God clothed Adam and his wife with garments of skins (Gen. 3:21).

God did not want man to live forever in the earth suffering decay and pain. He banished man from the Garden of Eden, lest man should eat from the tree of life and live forever in the present earth (Gen. 3:22-23). The tree of life will

The Origin of Sacrifice (Gen. 3:21).

Almost certainly, animals had to be killed to provide skins to cover Adam and his wife. Fig leaves could not cover (3:7). From the time of man's first sin, God made it plain that the wages of sin is death, but that He accepts the offering of *blood* and life as a sacrifice and substitute for the life of the one who has sinned. God Himself provides the sacrifice.

In the holy eyes of God, only the sacrifice of blood can take away the sin of man. "Without the shedding of blood there is no forgiveness" (Heb. 9:22). This seems to have been known to all godly people — Abel, Noah, Abraham, and others — because all offered sacrifices. The law of Moses required many sacrifices.

God planned even before the creation (foundation) of the world to send Christ Jesus as the perfect and final sacrifice for man. Jesus was the "Lamb that was slain from the creation of the world" (Rev. 13:8). The previous sacrifices were imperfect, but they pointed toward Christ's all-sufficient sacrifice of Himself upon the cross.

be provided for mankind in the new heaven and earth yet to appear (Rev. 22:2).

Cherubim (plural of *cherub*) were placed at the garden of Eden, to keep man out (Gen. 3:24). Cherubim are supernatural (angelic?) created beings which were seen when God's presence was being shown in glory (Ezek. 10:20; Ex. 25:18-20; Rev. 4:6).

Questions on Section C
The Fall of Man (Gen. 3)

1. How did the serpent differ from other wild animals? (Gen. 3:1)
2. What question did the serpent ask the woman? (3:1)
3. Who actually spoke through the serpent? (Rev. 12:9; 2 Cor. 11:3)
4. Had God forbidden them to *touch* the fruit of the tree in the midst of the garden as the woman stated? (3:2; 2:16-17)
5. What statement of God did the serpent plainly deny? (3:4)

6. Why did the serpent say that God did not want them to eat the fruit? (3:5)
7. What three things about the tree tempted the woman? (3:6) How do these three temptations compare to the worldly temptations listed in 1 John 2:16?
8. Where was the man when Eve ate the fruit? (3:6)
9. What was the first thing they became aware of after eating? (3:7)
10. What was used to make coverings? (3:7)
11. What was God's question when he called for the man? (3:9)
12. Whom did the man blame for his eating the forbidden fruit? (3:12)
13. Whom did the woman blame for her eating it? (3:13)
14. What punishment was pronounced on the serpent? (3:14)
15. What was the serpent's seed to do to the woman's offspring, and the woman's offspring to the serpent? (3:15)
16. What were the punishments pronounced on the woman? (3:16)
17. What were the punishments pronounced on the man? (3:17-19)
18. What effect did Adam's sin have on the whole subsequent human race? (Rom. 5:12; 1 Cor. 15:21-22) What effect on the whole material creation? (Rom. 8:20-22)
19. Does God approve of nudity now? (3:21;1 Tim. 2:9)
20. Why did God drive man from Eden? (3:22)
21. What blocked man's way back into Eden? (3:24)

Section D
The Old Testament World

The events we read about in the Bible occurred at real places on earth and at real times in history. The Bible is a book based on history and geography. It is necessary to know some of the principal lands, rivers, seas, mountains, etc. to understand the history in the Bible.

Thirty-two places are located on the map that follows. The names and locations of all of these should be memorized. It is easy to memorize them one group at a time.

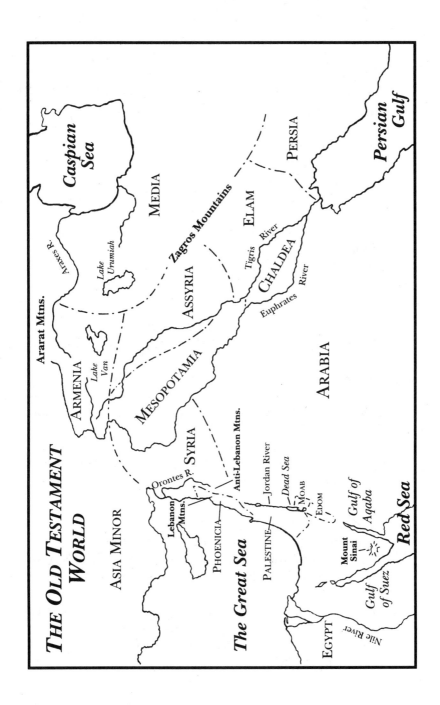

THE OLD TESTAMENT WORLD

ASIA MINOR

The Great Sea

ARMENIA

Caspian Sea

Ararat Mtns.

Araxes R.

Lake Urumiah

MEDIA

Zagros Mountains

Lake Van

ASSYRIA

MESOPOTAMIA

Tigris River

ELAM

CHALDEA

Euphrates River

PERSIA

Persian Gulf

ARABIA

SYRIA

Orontes R.

Anti-Lebanon Mtns.

Lebanon Mtns.

PHOENICIA

PALESTINE

Jordan River

Dead Sea

MOAB

EDOM

Gulf of Aqaba

Red Sea

Mount Sinai

Gulf of Suez

EGYPT

Nile River

1. *Rivers*
    a. *Araxes* — North boundary of Media and the eastern Bible lands. It flows eastward from Mt. Ararat into the Caspian Sea.
    b. *Orontes* — King Solomon fought a battle at Hamath by the Orontes river. North of Israel and Lebanon.
    c. *Tigris* — Called *Hiddekel* in Hebrew. The wicked city of Nineveh lay by this river. It merges with the Euphrates. 1150 miles long.
    d. *Euphrates* — Abram and Ezekiel looked upon its waters. It starts near Mt. Ararat, and flows into the Persian Gulf. 1650 miles long.
    e. *Nile* — The stream of life for Egypt. Once it became blood.
    f. *Jordan* — Israel crossed the Jordan into the Promised Land.

2. *Bodies of Water*
    a. *Caspian Sea* — Northern limit of eastern Bible lands
    b. *Persian Gulf* — The Tigris and Euphrates rivers flow into this gulf.
    c. *Red Sea* — Israel crossed this sea when they left Egypt. It has two arms: the Gulf of Suez and the Gulf of Aqaba.
    d. *Dead Sea* (or *Salt Sea*) — The lowest place on earth's surface
    e. The *Great Sea* — The Mediterranean
    f-g. *Lake Van* and *Lake Urumiah* – These are not mentioned in the Bible, but they are near Mt. Ararat, where the ark came to rest.

3. *Mountains*
    a. *Ararat* mountains — Where the ark came to rest
    b. *Zagros* mountains — East of Mesopotamia. The key to the ancient Babylonian language was discovered on the Behistun mountain in the Zagros range.
    c. *Lebanon* mountains — These lie along the east coast of the Mediterranean. The Lebanons are parallel to the *Anti-Lebanon* mountains on their east, with the Great Rift Valley between them.

d. *Mt. Sinai* — Moses received the law at Mt. Sinai.

4. *Lands.* (Memorize in groups of 2-3, 2-3, 2-3, in the order listed.)

a. *Armenia* — Noah's residence after the flood. All humans now living descended from forefathers in this land.

b. *Media* — South of the Caspian Sea. The Medes were conquered by Cyrus the Persian, and joined Cyrus in capturing Babylon.

c. *Assyria* — The cruel empire that captured the kingdom of Israel.

d. *Elam* — People from this land captured Lot, Abram's nephew.

e. *Persia* — Esther, a Jewish maiden, became queen of Persia.

f. *Mesopotamia* — The name means "between the rivers." In the Bible the name refers to the northern area between the Euphrates and the Tigris, or between the Euphrates and the Habor river.

g. *Chaldea* (called *Sumer* in ancient times) Abram lived at the city of Ur of the Chaldeans. It was called *Babylonia* in later times.

h. *Asia Minor* — This was the center of the Hittite empire.

i. *Syria* (or, more correctly, *Aram*) — Jacob worked for Rachel there.

j. *Arabia* — This land is mostly desert, inhabited by nomads.

k. *Phoenicia* — Now called *Lebanon*. This land was dominated by the cities of Tyre and Sidon. Queen Jezebel came from this land.

l. *Palestine* — Also called Canaan and Israel.

m. *Moab* — East of the Dead Sea. Homeland of Ruth.

n. *Edom* — Southeast of the Dead Sea. Homeland of Esau's descendants.

o. *Egypt* — The Israelites lived in Egypt 430 years.

Section E
The Two Classes of Humanity (Genesis 4–5)

1. *Cain and Abel* (Gen. 4:1-16). The earliest history of the human race demonstrated that "knowing good and evil" was not a happy experience, as the serpent had suggested to Eve it would be. People should not attempt to "know" evil by experimenting with it. It is better to follow the instructions of our holy God concerning what we should do or not do. For Eve, "knowing evil" brought her to suffer the anguish of the violent death of her son.

Eve displayed a godly faith when *Cain* was born, saying (literally), "I have acquired a man, the LORD." Cain's name comes from the verb *acquire* and therefore meant "Acquired." Possibly she thought that she had acquired the son who would be the woman's "offspring" who would bruise the serpent (Gen. 3:15). If so, she found she was wrong.

Eve's second son was named *Abel*, meaning "vapor, breath, vanity" (BDB lexicon). By the time of his birth the pains and weariness and futility in life upon earth had affected her zest for life.

Cain and Abel occupied themselves in careers of growing plants and livestock. From the beginning of the human race mankind has had the knowledge and practice of these occupations. We believe the record of Cain and Abel is a true history of real events. Jesus spoke of the "blood of Abel" as being real (Luke 11:51). See also Hebrews 11:4 and 1 John 3:12.

Cain and Abel brought offerings to the LORD, each bringing the products of his labor. Abel brought the "fat portions" of the firstborn of his flock. The animals obviously were slain. We have no record of what instructions about the offerings God may have given to man. Abel's sacrifice of animals is the oldest blood sacrifice given by a human that is known to us. God has always required the sacrifice of blood to cover human sins against him, and Abel's sacrifice seems to be a part of the continual offering of blood that mankind needs to offer to God.

"By *faith* Abel offered a better sacrifice than Cain did" (Heb. 11:4). "Faith comes from *hearing* the message (Rom. 10:17). We think that Cain and Abel had received instructions about the offering that the LORD desired. Abel did what he was told and Cain did not.

When Cain presented his offering, God did not look upon "Cain and his offering" with favor. God looked upon Cain's nature and life, and not just upon his offering. "The sacrifice of the wicked is detestable" (Prov. 21:27).

Cain would not accept God's warning to him (4:6-7). Cain was angry, and felt condemned by the righteous example of his brother, and killed him. "The wicked detest the upright" (Prov. 29:27). Jesus said that the devil was a "murderer from the beginning" (John 8:44). "Do not be like Cain, who belonged to the evil one and murdered his brother. And why did he murder him? Because his own actions were evil and his brother's were righteous" (1 John 3:12).

A GOOD QUESTION & A BAD ANSWER

"Where is your brother?"

"I don't know . . . Am I my brother's keeper?" (Gen. 4:9)
(We all should consider ourselves keepers of our brothers.)

God punished Cain by driving him away from productive land and from people. "You will be a restless wanderer in the earth." Cain had stained the earth with his brother's blood, and now found himself unable to settle down upon the earth. God asserted His power and His control over the productivity of the earth.

Cain had been bold in killing his brother, but at once became a crybaby when sentenced to punishment. God in his mercy "put a mark on Cain so that no one who found him would kill him" (4:15). We do not know what this mark was, but it was obviously visible. The fact that God placed a protective mark upon Cain indicates that God's treatment of evildoers is often kinder than human treatment of them.

49

The Two Classes of Mankind (Genesis chapters 4 & 5)

1. *The godless class* (descendants of Cain) (Gen. 4)
   a. Had *material prosperity* — Jabal (4:20)
   b. Had *musical skill* — Jubal
   c. Had *mechanical technology* — Tubal-Cain
   d. Had *moral viciousness* — Lamech (4:23-24)
2. *The godly class* (descendants of Seth) (Gen. 5)
   a. *Simple* (Not flashy. No details about their long lives are told.)
   b. *Spiritual*
      (1) Men called upon the LORD (4:26).
      (2) Enoch walked with God (5:22).
      (3) Noah was a preacher of righteousness.
   c. *Saved.* Enoch was taken from this life. Noah was saved in the ark.

Cain went out from the LORD's presence, and lived in the land of Nod, east of Eden." *Nod* means *wandering*, and therefore does not refer to a particular land with boundaries, but to a general area east of Eden where Cain wandered. (Eden still existed then.)

2. *The family of Cain* (Gen. 4:17-24). "Cain lay with (literally *knew*) his wife, and she became pregnant and gave birth to Enoch. Cain was then building a city" (Gen. 4:17). (The "city" was probably only a few houses with protective posts around them.)

Cain must have married a sister or niece of his. After the birth of Adam's third son, Seth, Adam and Eve had other "sons and daughters" — plural of both (Gen. 5:4). There is nothing inherently evil in marrying a close relative. Jacob married his cousin Rachel; Abram married his half-sister; Adam married his own flesh.

The descendants of Cain advanced in the skills and arts of human civilization, but quickly began to practice evil. The seventh man in the line from Adam through Cain was named *Lamech* (4:18-19). Lamech married two women — Adah and Zillah. This is the first known example of one man marrying

50

more than one woman. God made one wife for one man, because God was seeking a godly offspring from mankind (Mal. 2:15).

Lamech's three sons were pioneers in various skills and arts of civilization. (a) *Jabal* — the father of those who live in tents and raise livestock; (b) *Jubal* — the father of all who play the harp and flute (stringed and wind instruments); (c) *Tubal-Cain* — who forged all kinds of tools out of bronze and iron. Tubal-Cain's sister was *Naamah* (meaning *delightful, pleasant*).

The benefits of these ancient skills were much jeopardized by the character of Lamech. He demanded that his two wives listen to his speech (4:23). He recited a poem, the oldest known poetic composition. In it he boasts that he has killed a man who had wounded him. In our imagination we picture Lamech brandishing a shining bronze sword forged by his son Tubal-Cain as he boldly boasts before his wives, "If Cain is avenged seven times, then Lamech seventy-seven times" (4:24). Lamech is scornful of divine protection, such as God promised to Cain (4:15). Lamech is sure he can protect himself, and will inflict far worse vengeance upon his enemies than God would.

The Two Classes of Humanity (Genesis 4–5)
The godless line   **The godly line**

1. Adam

The godless line	The godly line
2. Cain	2. Seth
3. Enoch	3. Enosh
4. Irad	4. Kenan
5. Mehujael	5. Mahalalel
6. Methushael	6. Jared
7. Lamech	7. Enoch
8. Jabal, Jubal, Tubal-Cain	8. Methuselah
	9. Lamech
	10. Noah

INTERMARRIAGE

DESTRUCTION

3. *The godly line of Seth* (Gen. 4:25–5:32). After the death of Abel, God granted Adam and Eve another son, whom Eve named *Seth*, from the verb meaning *put* or *set*. "God has granted (or set) me another child in place of Abel." In Seth's time men began to call on the name of the LORD. This seems to refer to public group worship (H.C. Leupold, *Exposition of Genesis*, Vol. 1, p. 228).

Genesis 5:1 begins the second of the sections in Genesis that are introduced as "accounts" of something or someone. Literally it says, "This is the book (or scroll) of the generations (offspring) of Adam." It appears possible that this chapter was once a separate document before Moses incorporated it into Genesis. Observe that the word of God was *written* down from the beginning, and not just passed on orally.

Genesis chapter five gives the names of the men descended from Adam to Noah. The same names are given in the genealogy of Jesus in Luke 3:36-38. This is the list that led to the Messiah. Genesis 5 tells how long each man lived, and in every case (except Enoch) says, "then he died." The repetition of these words has been called the "tolling of the funeral bell" of the patriarchs (Bonar). Satan had said to Eve, "You will not surely die." But over and over we read in Genesis 5, "Then he died . . . then he died."

When God created man in the likeness of God, he created them male and female, and blessed them. When man and woman were created, God called them *"man"* (5:2). Literally, "He called their name *Adam* (or *man*)." Adam had called the woman *Eve* (living, or life), but God called her *Man* (Mrs. *Adam*).

The thing that immediately impresses us about Genesis 5 is how long the patriarchs lived. All but one of them lived over seven hundred years and several lived more than nine hundred. Many critics have assumed that this list is only legendary. We accept it as true. God created Adam with potential vigor to live forever, and even after the fall of Adam man retained enough force to live for long periods.

A clay tablet from ancient Babylonia (Sumer) tells that there were eight kings who ruled in that land for 241,000 years before the Flood swept over the earth. Each of these kings is said to have reigned over 20,000 years. This is clearly legendary, but it does indicate that long ago people knew that men lived long lives before the Flood, and that there had been a real flood. (See "The Sumerian King List" in *Ancient Near Eastern Texts*, edited by James B. Pritchard. Princeton Univ. Press, 1955, pp. 265-266.)

H.C. Leupold in his *Exposition of Genesis* (Vol. 1, p. 237) wrote of the effects that the long lives of the patriarchs had:

> Enoch's translation (987) occurred about midway between creation and Flood (1656). Again, Adam was still living when Lamech, Noah's father, was born (874). Any tradition that Adam desired to hand down was only in the second generation at the time the Flood came: Adam to Lamech. Methuselah died in the year of the Flood (1656), yet he need not have perished in the Flood. . . Apparently the Flood did not sweep a single one of the Sethites, the true "seed of the woman" away. Besides, it may be remarked that Noah barely missed knowing Adam and Seth . . . What a power for godliness that should have been to see so many staunch believers living simultaneously and encouraging one another.

After the flood of Noah there was a dramatic decrease in the length of people's lives, compared to their longevity before the flood. Compare Genesis 5 and Genesis 11. The life span of people has leveled off at about seventy years (Ps. 90:10).

Some have objected that there probably are "gaps" in the genealogical list in Genesis 5, so that the names of many people in the generations are not given (C.C. Crawford, *Genesis*, Vol. II, pp. 464-467). The possibility of missing names makes it somewhat easier to reconcile the millions of years that scientists say man has been on earth with the young age for the human race given in the Bible. The example of the genealogy of Christ in Matthew 1:1-17 is used as an illustration that genealogical lists sometimes omitted names not considered necessary to the purpose of the list. It is true that Matthew 1 does omit six or seven names that are known from other Scripture passages. Also the genealogical list in Genesis 11 (tracing the line from Noah to Abram) omits the name of *Cainan*, which is given in Luke 3:36 and also in the Greek Septuagint Bible in Genesis 11:13.

It is plain that there are a few gaps in some genealogical lists in the Bible. But to extrapolate from the existence of a few known gaps totalling a few hundred years to the conclusion that the gaps may cover several million years of hypothetical human history far exceeds the firm evidence in Scripture. We believe that the human race has only been on earth a few thousand years, surely not more than ten thousand.

The Greek Septuagint Bible gives longer age spans for the patriarchs in Genesis 5 than the Hebrew Bible does. Generally the Greek text makes their ages about a hundred years older at the time of the births of their sons.

Name of Patriarch	Age at birth of son (acc. Hebrew)	Age at birth of son (acc. Greek)
1. Adam	130 yrs.	230 yrs.
2. Seth	105	205
3. Enosh	90	190
4. Kenan	70	170
5. Mahalalel	65	165
6. Jared	162	162
7. Enoch	65	165
8. Methuselah	187	167
9. Lamech	182	188
10. Noah	500 (Gen. 5:32)	500
11. Shem (before flood)	100 (5:32; 7:13) (Total yrs. to flood: 1656)	100 (6:1; 7:11) (Total yrs. to flood: 2242)

The statistics in the Hebrew Bible would date the flood about 2,458 B.C., and creation about 4,114 B.C. The figures in the Greek date the flood about 3,238 B.C., and creation about 5,480 B.C. We are more comfortable with the Greek dating than the Hebrew, but either set of dates is preferable to the millions of years the human race is usually said to have existed.

The high point in the list of Seth's descendants (Genesis 5) is the story of Enoch (5:18-23). Enoch was the seventh from Adam (Jude 14). Enoch had sons and daughters, and still "Enoch walked with God." (This shows that raising a family does not necessarily destroy godliness.)

Seven generations in the godless line of people produced the murderous LAMECH. Seven generations in the godly line produced an ENOCH, who walked with God and was taken home with God.

**Enoch *walked* with God (Gen. 5:24).
Let us *walk* (live) as children of light (Eph. 5:8).**

During his life of three hundred and sixty-five years, Enoch prophesied against the godless men of his time. He proclaimed, "See, the Lord is coming with thousands upon thousands of his holy ones [angels] to judge everyone, and to convict all the ungodly of all the ungodly acts they have done." (Enoch's words are quoted from the *Book of Enoch*, 1:9. Though this book was not accepted by the Jews as Scripture, and is classed as one of the Pseudepigrapha [writings under false authorship], Jude's quotation of the verse gives that one verse the authority of Scripture.)

"By faith Enoch was taken from this life, so that he did not experience death; he could not be found, because God had taken him away (translated, or transferred, him). For before he was taken, he was commended as one who pleased God" (Heb. 11:5).

**Only Enoch and Elijah were taken from this world
without dying (Gen. 5:24; 2 Kgs. 2:11).**

55

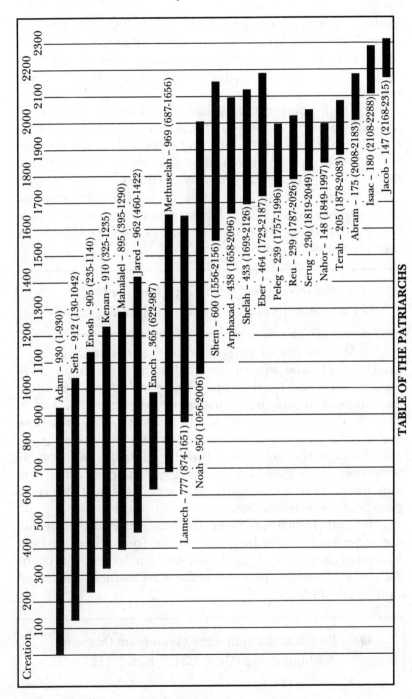

TABLE OF THE PATRIARCHS

Adam – 930 (1-930)
Seth – 912 (130-1042)
Enosh – 905 (235-1140)
Kenan – 910 (325-1235)
Mahalalel – 895 (395-1290)
Jared – 962 (460-1422)
Enoch – 365 (622-987)
Methuselah – 969 (687-1656)
Lamech – 777 (874-1651)
Noah – 950 (1056-2006)
Shem – 600 (1556-2156)
Arphaxad – 438 (1658-2096)
Shelah – 433 (1693-2126)
Eber – 464 (1723-2187)
Peleg – 239 (1757-1996)
Reu – 239 (1787-2026)
Serug – 230 (1819-2049)
Nahor – 148 (1849-1997)
Terah – 205 (1878-2083)
Abram – 175 (2008-2183)
Isaac – 180 (2108-2288)
Jacob – 147 (2168-2315)

Creation 100 200 300 400 500 600 700 800 900 1000 1100 1200 1300 1400 1500 1600 1700 1800 1900 2000 2100 2200 2300

Noah was in the tenth generation of humanity. When he was born, his father named him *Noah*, meaning *rest*. People had come to feel the painful toil of their hands caused by the ground the LORD had cursed (Gen. 5:29; 3:17). Besides that, there was an almost overwhelming pressure to join the wicked people all around them in their ungodliness (Gen. 7:11; 2 Pet. 2:5,9). Noah's parents hoped he would grow up and become one who would bring *rest* to them. They would have been amazed if they had known that Noah (six hundred years later!) would deliver the earth from the evil people in it by the flood.

Noah's three sons — Shem, Ham, and Japheth — were born after Noah was five hundred years old. God exercises much control over when children are born (Ps. 127:3). Perhaps God delayed their births, so that they would live longer after the flood to give a witness of it to many generations.

Questions on Section E
The Two Classes of Humanity (Gen. 4–5)

1. Who was Adam's first son? His second? (4:1)
2. What were the sons' occupations? (4:2)
3. What did the sons bring as offerings to the Lord? How did the Lord regard the offerings? (4:3-5)
4. What was Cain's reaction to God's rejection of his offering? (4:5-6)
5. What warning did God give Cain? (4:7)
6. What did Cain do to Abel? Where? (4:8)
7. What question did God ask Cain after his crime? What was Cain's answer? (4:9)
8. What was Cain's punishment? (4:11-12)
9. What was Cain's reaction to his punishment? (4:13)
10. How did God protect Cain from being killed? (4:15)
11. Into what land did Cain go after his crime? (4:16)
12. Who built the first city? (4:17)
13. Who first married two women? What were his wives' names? (4:19)
14. What was the occupation of Jabal? Jubal? Tubal-Cain? (4:20-22)

15. What did Lamech brag about doing? To what degree did Lamech threaten vengeance on anyone who harmed him? (4:23-24)
16. Who was Adam and Eve's third son? (4:25)
17. What did men begin to do in Seth's time? (4:26)
18. What name did God call the first couple? (5:2)
19. How long did Adam live? (5:5)
20. Name the people in the generations from Adam to Noah. (5:5-29)
21. How did Enoch's life on earth end? (Compare Heb. 11:5)
22. How long did Methuselah live? (5:27)
23. What does the name *Noah* mean? (5:29)
24. Who were Noah's three sons? (5:32)

Section F
Noah and the Flood (Genesis 6:1–9:17)

> **Genesis chapters 6–9 tell the story of Noah's flood.**

1. *Noah before the flood* (Gen. 6). A population explosion occurred in the earth before the flood. Dr. Henry Morris in his book *The Genesis Flood* (pp. 25-26) calculates that in the pre-flood world, there could have been as many as a billion people, if each generation had only six children (three sons and three daughters), and each generation was born ninety years after the previous one.

Noah found himself in a world where there was an explosion of evil. Every inclination of the thoughts in the hearts of people was only evil all the time (6:5; 8:21). (God cares about what we think.) All the people had corrupted their ways (Gen. 6:12). The "sons of God" (probably the godly descendants of Seth) intermarried with the "daughters of men" (probably the godless descendants of Cain). This produced many great heroes, possibly even *giants,* according to the Greek Bible (6:4), but no righteous people. God found only Noah to be righteous (7:1).

The *Nephilim* (6:4) were probably "the *fallen* ones," or "those who *fall* upon others." The word comes from the verb

58

meaning to *fall*. It probably refers to thugs and bandits. The world was full of violence in Noah's time (6:11).

The "sons of God" (6:4) certainly were not angelic beings from outer space who came to earth and took earth women. Jesus said that angels do not marry (Matt. 22:30). It would be strange if angelic beings sinned, and then the people on earth were destroyed by the flood for the sins of angels. In a few Bible passages the expression "sons of God" does refer to angels (Job 1:6; 2:1; 38:7). But in the Bible it is applied also to God's people (as in Hosea 1:10; Deut. 14:1; 2 Cor. 6:18), and probably means that in Genesis 6:4.

The third "account" ("generations" or "history") in Genesis begins at Genesis 6:9: "the account of Noah." (This statement does not force us to believe that Noah was the author of the preceding paragraphs, or of what follows the statement. Noah did keep a log on the ark (Gen. 7:11, 17), and his records may have furnished information for the Genesis story.

God told Noah that He was going to destroy life on the earth (6:13,17). Noah was to build an *ark* to save his family (6:14).

The ark was basically a huge floating wood box. The ark had a capacity of about a million and a half cubic feet, the capacity of over five hundred standard railroad box cars (Henry M. Morris, *The Genesis Flood*, p. 67). The ark was made of *gopher* wood (6:14). (The NIV translation "cypress wood" is perhaps correct, but no one really yet knows what kind of wood is referred to by the Hebrew term *gopher*.)

2. *The flood* (Gen. 7:1-24). The flood occurred one hundred and twenty years after God first warned Noah (6:3; 7:6).

Noah was instructed to bring the animals into the ark (7:8-9). The animals were to "come" to Noah, so that he did not have to go out and capture them (6:20). At this point we read for the first time in the Bible about "clean" and "unclean" animals (7:2). Seven of each clean animal would enter the ark, and two of each unclean animal (6:20; 7:2). Clean animals were those that God accepted for sacrifices, and after the flood could be eaten (9:3). God gave instructions about these animals to the patriarchs like Noah, although no record of His instructions is given in the Bible. In later years in the law of Moses rather detailed information is given about clean and unclean animals (Leviticus 11).

We assume that the continents were then still linked, or that species of animals now existing only in separate continents were then more widely found over the earth, so that a few of all kinds could come to Noah. (See Henry M. Morris, *The Genesis Flood*, pp. 79-86.)

The flood was a miracle. It was a miracle the animals came to Noah. It was a miracle they boarded the ark. It was a miracle Noah could care for the animals, estimated to number about 35,000 (Morris, *op.cit.*, p. 69). It was a miracle their breeding instincts were limited. (Perhaps the animals spent considerable time in semi-hibernation.) Those who cannot accept the possibility of miracles will find the flood story unbelievable.

Why do we believe the flood story is true?

1. Jesus said it really happened (Luke 17:27). So also did the apostle Peter (1 Pet. 3:20; 2 Pet. 3:5-6).
2. There are legends about the flood among nearly all "primitive" tribes and races. (See Alfred M. Rehwinkel, *The Flood*, chapter IX.)
3. Billions of creatures are fossilized all over the world. Fossilization requires quick burial, something rarely occurring today. Coal beds were mats of dense vegetation buried quickly, as shown by unwilted leaf fossils in the coal. (Rehwinkel, *op. cit.*, chs. XII, XIII)
4. Vast erosion of earth's ancient surface and rocks.

Genesis 7:11-12. The flood waters had two sources: (a) the springs of the great deep (seas) burst forth (literally, "were broken up"); (b) the floodgates (or windows) of heaven were opened, releasing rain.

The breaking up of the earth's crust at the sea bottom

probably produced tidal waves, earthquakes, avalanches, and also volcanoes. The flood was a cataclysm, not a tranquil rise of water. Such a flood would cause great erosion of the earth's crust. The disturbed material would be redeposited as sediments and rock layers. The flood caused catastrophes on earth's surface.

Many interpreters believe that before the flood a dense canopy of water vapor was in the sky over our atmosphere. This canopy may have been the reason that the earth once had a warmer climate over all of it, even in the polar regions, where forests once grew. If such a canopy was precipitated as rain, it would have furnished much of the water necessary to cover the whole earth. The breakup of the water canopy may have caused the quick freeze in Siberia and Alaska, where millions of elephants froze quite suddenly (Rehwinkel, *op. cit.*, ch. XV). We think the canopy theory is probably true, and that the collapse of the canopy was associated with the flood of Noah.

Genesis 7:17-23. "The waters rose . . . and all the high mountains under the entire heavens were covered." This verse indicates that the flood covered the entire earth, and was not a local flood in part of Mesopotamia. Evidences of such local floods have been found at Ur and Nineveh and other places in Mesopotamia. These local floods were not the same event as the worldwide flood of Noah. (See G. Frederick Owen, *Archaeology and the Bible*. Westwood, NJ: Revell, 1961, pp. 152-155.)

If the flood were not universal, no ark would have been needed, and the animals would not have needed to come to Noah.

Jesus said, "The flood came and took them *all* away" (Matt. 24:39, emph. added).

The statements that "the waters *rose*" (7:18) and "the waters *flooded*"(7:24) both use the same verb in Hebrew (translated "prevailed" in NKJV and NASB). It means *to be strong, or mighty* (BDB). The fact that the waters "prevailed" during both the forty days of rainfall and the one hundred and fifty days (7:24 and 8:3) indicates that the forty days of

The FLOOD —
A Type (Symbol) of Christ's Second Coming
"As it was in the days of Noah, so it will be at the coming of the Son of Man" (Matt. 24:37).

Similarities	The Flood	Second Coming
1. Advance warning given	Gen. 6:17; 2 Pet. 2:5	Matt. 24:42; Rev. 1:7
2. Unexpected by the world	Matt. 24:38-39	1 Thess. 5:2-3; Matt. 24:44
3. Expected by believers	Heb. 11:7	1 Thess. 5:4
4. Sudden	Gen. 7:11-13	1 Thess 5:3
5. Total and final	Gen. 7:21-23	2 Peter 3:10
6. Destruction	By water — 2 Pet. 3:5-6	By fire — 2 Pet. 3:7, 12
7. A new world afterward	Gen. 8:15-17	2 Pet. 3:13

rainfall are probably to be included within the one hundred and fifty days. The flood reached its greatest depth after the first forty days, instead of rising throughout the one hundred and fifty days.

3. *End of flood* (Gen. 8:1-19). "God *remembered* Noah" and all the animals. In the Bible to *remember* sometimes meant to take action to fulfill a promise (Gen. 30:22; Ex. 6:5).

Two hundred and twenty four days after the rain began the ark came to rest on the mountains (plural) of *Ararat* (8:3). The traditional mountain named *Ararat* is in the extreme east end of Turkey, about twenty miles from where Turkey, Russia (Armenia), and Iran meet. The mountain is named in Turkish *Agri Dagh* (The Painful Mountain), or Greater Ararat in English. It is a volcanic mountain, 16,946 feet high. It is perpetually snow-capped and stormy. Seven miles away is Lesser Ararat, 12,782 feet high. If Noah built the ark in Mesopotamia, the rising flood waters had created a water movement that carried the ark northward to the higher elevations by Ararat. That land nearby was later named Urartu (from Ararat), and is now called Armenia.

Noah sent birds from the ark to see if they found dry land. A *raven* and a *dove* were sent (8:6-12). There is a Babylonian story called *The Gilgamesh Epic* written on clay tablets. The story includes, as an incidental part of it, a story of the great flood (tablet XI). The Babylonian story has several similarities with the biblical story, though also some striking differences. Among the similarities between the biblical flood story and the Gilgamesh Epic is the sending out of birds. The Epic tells of sending out a *dove*, a swallow, and a *raven*. The stories obviously have a connection. Some scholars have suggested that the two stories have a common original story; others that the Bible writer borrowed from the Babylonian story; others that the Babylonian epic was a corrupted version of the story preserved in the Bible. (See *The Ancient Near East*, Vol. 1, James B. Pritchard, ed. Princeton Univ. Press, 1973, pp. 40-75. Also M. F. Unger, *Archaeology and the Old Testament*. Grand Rapids: Zondervan, 1964, pp. 55-71.)

The Chronology of Events During the Flood

7 days shut up in the ark after it was loaded (Gen. 7:10)

40 days of rain, starting on 2nd month, 17th day (7:11,12,17)

110 more days the waters "prevailed." Total = 150 days (7:24)

74 days until the ark rested on Ararat on 10th month,1st day (8:5)

40 day interval until the raven was sent out (8:6)

7 days until the dove was sent (8:8,10. "Seven other days." NASB)

7 day interval. Dove sent again (8:10)

7 day interval. Dove sent, but did not return (8:12)

29 days until ground was dry (8:13. Next year, 1st month, 1st day)

_57_days until departure from ark (8:14-16. 2nd month, 27th day)

378 days on the ark (371 since rain began). (1 year, 13 days).

(Adapted from J.C. Whitcomb & Henry M. Morris, *The Genesis Flood*, p. 3)

The FLOOD –
A Type (Symbol) of Baptism
"This water symbolizes baptism that now saves you also"
(1 Pet. 3:21).

Similarities	The Flood	Baptism
1. Preceded by preaching	2 Pet. 2:5	Rom. 10:14
2. Faith required	Heb. 11:7	Col. 2:12; Gal. 3:26-27
3. Obedience required	Heb. 11:7	2 Thess. 1:8
4. Destruction of old life	2 Pet. 3:6	Rom. 6:2-3, 6
5. "Saved through water"	1 Pet. 3:20	Mark 16:16
6. A new life follows	Gen. 9:8-15	Col. 1:13

---

4. *God's covenant with Noah* (Gen. 8:20–9:17). Noah's first act after leaving the ark was to offer to the LORD a sacrifice from the clean animals. Noah's sacrifices show the importance of worship in the lives of God's holy people, and they indicate the necessity for sacrifices of *blood*. The LORD was pleased with Noah's sacrifice (8:21). (The LORD is now pleased when we accept the sacrifice of Christ as OUR sacrifice.)

God then established with Noah and his descendants a new *covenant* (an agreement or arrangement) containing several promises and regulations.

a. God would never again curse the ground (8:21). The promise here refers to "cursing" the ground by destroying all living creatures on it. God repeated twice more that the waters would never again become a flood to destroy all life (9:11, 15).

b. Seasons of seedtime and harvest, and cold and heat, will continue as long as the earth remains (9:22). This seems to indicate that before the flood there was a more uniform climate over all the earth all year long than we now experience.

c. Animals will fear people (9:2).

d. Meat may be eaten (9:2-3). Previously God had given to man only seed-bearing plants and fruit (Gen. 1:29).

e. Blood must not be eaten (9:4-5). This rule was later repeated in the law of Moses (Lev. 17:10-14), and by the apostles of Christ (Acts 15:20, 29). "The life of a creature is in the blood, and I have given it to you to make atonement for yourselves."

f. Murderers will be put to death (9:6). Sometimes God spared murderers as He spared Cain. God does not enjoy seeing the wicked put to death (Ezek. 33:11), but the use of capital punishment as a penalty still has God's authorization. See Exodus 21:12; Acts 25:11; Romans 13:4.

God placed His rainbow in the clouds to be the sign of His covenant between himself and the earth. (Does the rainbow that encircles God's throne in heaven give the same message? [Rev. 4:3])

God's covenant with Noah and his descendants has never been revoked.

Questions on Section F
Noah and the Flood (Gen. 6:1-9:17)

1. Who are the "sons of God" and who are the "daughters of men" in Genesis 6:1?
2. What did the sons of God observe about the daughters of men? (6:2)
3. Whom did the sons of God take as wives? Was monogamy practiced?
4. What had been contending with men? (6:3)
5. How many years of probation did God grant the world before the flood? (6:3)
6. What sort of people were the offspring of the sons of God and the daughters of men? (6:4)
7. What did men have on their minds before the flood? (6:5)
8. What did God determine to do with mankind and other living things? (6:7)
9. Who found grace in the eyes of the Lord? (6:8)
10. How is Noah's character described? (6:9)
11. Of what wood was the ark made? (6:14)
12. What was the ark coated with to make it watertight? (6:14)

13. What was the length, breadth and height of the ark? (6:15)
14. How many stories were there in the ark? (6:16)
15. What was Noah doing during the years before the flood? (2 Pet. 2:5)
16. What did God promise to establish with Noah? (6:18-19)
17. How were the animals brought to the ark? (6:20)
18. How fully did Noah obey God's commands? (6:22)
19. How many of each type of clean beast were taken on the ark? How many unclean? (6:19; 7:2)
20. How many days elapsed between the command to board the ark and the start of the rainfall? (7:10)
21. How old was Noah when the flood began? (7:11)
22. How many people were saved in the ark? (7:13, 1 Pet. 3:20)
23. What were the two sources of the waters of the flood? (7:11)
24. How long did it rain? (7:12)
25. How high upward above the mountains did the waters prevail? (7:20)
26. What died in the flood? (7:21)
27. How long did the waters prevail upon the earth? (7:24)
28. What did God cause to pass over the earth that made the waters recede? (8:1)
29. Where did the ark come to rest? (8:4)
30. How many times were birds sent forth from the ark before it was opened? What birds were sent each time? What were the results each time? (8:6-12)
31. How long was Noah in the ark altogether? (Compare Gen. 7:11 and 8:14)
32. What did God tell Noah and the animals to do when they left the ark? (8:17; 9:1)
33. What did Noah build right after leaving the ark? (8:20)
34. What did Noah offer upon his altar? (8:20)
35. What did God say he would never do again? (8:21)
36. What seasons are not to cease as long as the earth remains? (8:22)
37. What feeling toward people did the beasts have after the flood? (9:2)
38. What was given to man for food after the flood? (9:3)
39. What part of living creatures is not to be eaten by mankind? (9:4)
40. What law was given about men or beasts that killed people?
41. What provision did God's covenant contain about future floods? (9:11)
42. What was the token of God's covenant with Noah? (9:13-16)

Period II — Period after the Flood (Postdiluvian Period)

(Genesis 9:18–11:32)

Section A
The Table of Nations (Genesis 9:18–10:32)

1. *The sons of Noah* (Gen. 9:18-19). In the Bible story the names of the sons of Noah are listed first of all following the completion of God's covenant with Noah (9:18-19). Noah's sons were the ancestors of all people now living. All the people in the human race are related because all are descended from one ancestor (Noah) through his three sons. We should treat one another like loving family members.

NOAH'S THREE SONS (Gen. 9:18)

1. **SHEM** — Ancestor of **Semites**, who lived in the Fertile Crescent and Arabia. They include Jews, Arabs, Syrians, Assyrians, and others.

2. **HAM** — Ancestor of **Hamites**, who lived in north Africa, and Canaan, and lower Mesopotamia (Sumer). They included the Egyptians, Ethiopians (and probably other Africans), and Canaanites. Hamites include the black races, but also others.

3. **JAPHETH** — Ancestor of **Japhethites**, often called Indo-Europeans. They lived in southern Russia, Asia Minor, Greece, and Iran (Media). Japheth is the ancestor of Europeans and Asians, probably including Oriental peoples.

---

2. *Noah drunken. The curse upon Canaan* (Gen. 9:20-28). Noah soon demonstrated that the curse that Adam brought on the earth and mankind continued on after the flood. He

fell victim to drunkenness. Intoxication was surely practiced by the evil generation before the flood, who were "eating and drinking" (Matt. 24:36). Noah was "a man of the soil" and planted a vineyard. The land of Armenia (the area around Mt. Ararat) is very favorable for growing grape vines. Noah drank of the wine, and became drunk and lay naked in his tent. In that condition he was seen by his son Ham.

At that time the differences in the character of people showed clearly. Ham appears to have considered his father's nakedness almost amusing and a topic for conversation. Shem and Japheth very modestly covered their father. A mind focused on God does not delight in jokes about fleshly things.

When Noah awoke from intoxication, he found out (or knew by some means) what his youngest ("little") son had done. Noah then spoke prophetically of the future character and experiences of his sons. Noah's prophecy appears to possess a divine inspiration.

Though Ham was the offender when Noah was drunken, no curse was pronounced by Noah upon him. Rather a curse was pronounced three times upon Ham's son *Canaan* (9:24, 26, 27). The exact reason for the curse upon Canaan is not told at this point. The prophecy looked ahead to the time when the Canaanites would be expelled from their land, primarily because of their involvement in sexual excesses and in cruelty. The Canaanites became involved in the worship of Baal and Anath. The legends about these false gods are full of ungoverned sex stories. Probably the character shown by Ham was concentrated most greatly in his descendants through Canaan.

The curse upon Canaan does not imply that there was a curse pronounced upon all of Ham's other descendants, in particular upon the black races. No other Hamites were cursed except Canaan, and the Canaanites who were cursed were not a black race, but similar in appearance to Jews or Arabs.

Noah said of Shem, "Blessed be the LORD (Yahweh), the God of Shem." The Semites (in particular the Jews) preserved the knowledge of the true God in a godless world. Semites like Job and Abraham have been lights for mankind. Canaan became the slave of Shem when the Jews (Semites) led by Joshua and King David conquered the land of Canaan.

Noah said of Japheth, "May God extend (or enlarge) the territory of Japheth; may Japheth live in the tents of Shem, and may Canaan be his slave." Japheth was to have territory more extended than his brothers. This has come to pass. Japheth was the ancestor of Europeans and Asians, and they occupy by far the largest portion of land on earth. Japheth's descendants came to live "in the tents of Shem" when many of them accepted the God of the Jews and the Christians. Canaan became a slave to Japheth when the Greeks (like Alexander the Great) and the Romans conquered the lands where Canaanites lived.

Noah lived 350 years after the flood, and died at the age of 950. He outlived the fifth and eighth of his descendants, *Peleg* and *Nahor*. He was for 128 years contemporary with *Terah*, the father of Abraham, and died only two years before the birth of Abraham himself (2008 B.C.). The information about man's most ancient history did not have to pass through many generations before Moses began his huge work of writing the Biblical history. This adds trustworthiness to the Bible as a historical record.

3. *Descendants of Noah's sons* (Gen. 10). Genesis chapter ten is often called "The Table of Nations." It is an amazing chapter. It traces the family descent of peoples all the way from Greece (Javan) in the West to Media (Madai) in the East, over 1,500 miles. It traces the ancestry of peoples living from southern Russia (Gomer and Magog) in the north, to Ethiopia in Africa (Cush) in the south, nearly 2,000 miles apart. About sixty-seven names are given. Whoever compiled this table of nations possibly had to travel great distances, and get information from people speaking different languages. Such research is difficult. For example, the ancestry and relationship of American Indian tribes has been very hard to discover. In spite of these difficulties, the Table of Nations has been found to be a record of real people who, in

most cases, have been identified in records outside the Bible. (See Ira M. Price, O.R. Sellers, E. L. Carlson, *The Monuments and the Old Testament,* Judson Press, 1958, ch. 8. Also see chs. 6–8 in Merrill F. Unger, *Archaeology and the Old Testament,* Zondervan, 1954.)

It is difficult to determine whether some of the names in the Table of Nations are names of individuals, or countries, or cities, or of ethnic groups. Some are clearly individuals — like Gomer, or Cush, or Nimrod. Some are names of ethnic groups — like Kittim (Cyprus?), and Jebusites, and Hittites. Some seem to be cities or lands — like Sidon (10:15) or Ophir. But this does not destroy the value of the list for understanding the relationship of peoples.

God placed the nations and peoples where He wanted them to live when the earth was being repopulated after the flood. God "determined the times set for them and the exact places where they should live" (Acts 17:26; Deut. 32:8). People have frequently tried by war to take over lands from the peoples God placed in them.

Genesis 10:25 mentions *Peleg* and says in his time "the earth was divided." We do not know what that means. Did the continents pull apart at that time? We lean toward that view, but it is uncertain. Perhaps it means that the tower of Babel was built in his time, and people were divided by that event into language groups.

The children of *Japheth* (Aryans):

a. **Gomer** — The *Cimmerians*, a people that lived in the far north (Ezek. 38:6) near Armenia and Media.

b. **Magog** — Probably the name of northern barbarians near the Black Sea. Josephus (*Ant.* I, vi, 1) said that Magog was a name for the *Scythians* (in southern Russia).

c. **Madai** — Medes

d. **Javan** — The Greeks

e. **Tubal** — Probably these are the people called *Tabal* in Assyrian inscriptions. They lived in the mountains south of the Black Sea.

f. **Meshech** — A people called *Mushki*, near the Black Sea.

g. **Tiras** — Uncertain. Perhaps the Thracians NE of Greece.

The children of *Shem* (Semites):

a. **Elam** — The Elamites east of Mesopotamia.

b. **Asshur** — The Assyrians around the upper Tigris River.

c. **Arphaxad** — Uncertain. Ancestor of Hebrews. Perhaps lived east of Assyria, near Nuzi. (G.F.Owen, *Archaeology and the Bible*, p. 112).

d. **Lud** — Perhaps Lydia, in western Asia Minor.

e. **Aram** — The Syrians

The children of *Ham* (Hamites):

a. **Cush** — Ethiopia, south of Egypt (Nubia, or the Sudan)

b. **Mizraim** — Egypt (One of the first areas settled after the flood)

c. **Put** — The Kingdom of **Punt**, on both sides of Red Sea.

d. **Canaan** — Canaanites

Nimrod is named as a famous warrior, hunter, and builder of cities (10:8-12). He is considered to have been a tyrant, and probably a "hunter" of people as well as animals. He founded several famous cities in both southern and northern Mesopotamia, including *Babylon* (Babel), *Erech* (Uruk), *Akkad, Nineveh*, and others. Some of the cities he built became centers of cruel, idol-worshipping empires. He was a great-grandson of Noah. Josephus tells that Nimrod was the leader of the revolt against God, and esteemed it a piece of cowardice to submit to God. He changed the government into tyranny, and stirred up the people to build the tower of Babel (Josephus, *Antiquities*, I, iv, 1-2). We do not know if this information from Josephus is true or not.

Questions on Section A
The Table of Nations (Gen. 9:18-28; ch. 10)

1. Who was the father of Canaan? (Gen. 9:18)
2. From what three people was the whole earth repopulated? (9:19; 10:32)
3. What did Noah plant after the flood? (9:20)
4. What degrading thing happened to Noah? (9:21)

5. What did Ham do that suggests he had a leering nature? (9:22)
6. Who covered Noah as he lay in his tent? (9:24)
7. What did Noah say would happen to Canaan? (9:25)
8. What do we call the descendants of Shem?
9. Who that was associated with Shem was blessed? (9:26)
10. What future did Noah prophesy for Japheth (two things)? (9:27)
11. How many sons did Japheth have? (10:2) Name them.
12. In what general area did the descendants of Japheth settle?
13. How many sons did Ham have? (10:6) Name them.
14. In what general area did most of the Hamites settle?
15. Who became a mighty warrior and hunter? (10:8-9)
16. Name three cities associated with Nimrod? (10:10)
17. What cities in Assyria did Nimrod build? (10:11)
18. Name five locations or people descended from Canaan. (10:15-19)
19. How many sons did Shem have? (10:22) Name them.
20. Who was *Eber*? (10:21,25; 11:14-16) What people get their name from *Eber*?
21. Which of the sons of Shem was ancestor of the Israelites and Arabs? (10:24; 11:10)
22. What happened on earth in the time of Peleg? (10:25)

Section B
The Tower of Babel; The Descendants of Shem (Genesis 11)

1. *The tower of Babel* (Gen. 11:1-9). God had directed Noah and his family to be fruitful and increase in number. "Multiply (literally, *swarm*) on the earth and increase upon it" (Gen. 9:7). As Noah's descendants migrated south and east from the Mt. Ararat area, they came to a pleasant plain in *Shinar*. They did not want to be scattered from this comfortable location.

Shinar may be equivalent to *Sumer*, the name for the world's oldest civilization, which developed in southern Mesopotamia, near where the Euphrates and Tigris rivers merge. The Sumerians invented writing. They built cities, and had schools. They organized governments. They made musical instruments and had a musical scale. They discovered medicines for many ills. They also had over two thousand gods. As the apostle Paul said, they exchanged the glory of the immortal God for images made to look like mortal man (Rom. 1:23).

To prevent their getting scattered and to make a name for themselves, they proposed to build a city with a tower to the heavens. Mesopotamia lacks building stones and timber. Therefore, they planned to use well-baked mud bricks with tar (asphalt) for mortar. Remains of numerous such structures have been found in Mesopotamia. Walls made of these materials were very strong.

The typical shape of temple towers in Mesopotamia was pyramidical, with large flat steps (or stages) on their sides. These towers were called *ziggurats*. That name meant "hill of heaven" or "mountain of God." The three most famous towers in Mesopotamia were (1) the Ziggurat of Ur (70 feet high); (2) *Birs Nimrud* (the Tower of Nimrod) 150 feet tall, at Borsippa; (3) A tower at Babylon named E-temen-an-ki, is said to have stood 660 feet high. Its ruins still rise in places to a height of 200 feet. The fire-burnt bricks of which it is built are still so well cemented together it is almost impossible to separate them or extract one whole (G.F. Owen, *Archaeology and the Bible*, pp. 129-130). This is perhaps the ruins of the Tower of Babel.

The LORD defeated the people's project of building the tower by confusing their language, so that they could not understand one another. The LORD said, "Let *us* go down and confuse their language" (11:7 emphasis added; compare Gen. 1:26). By this confusion of language "the LORD scattered them over the face of the whole earth" (11:9). The LORD's will shall be done, in spite of man's lack of cooperation.

The Bible does not say that the confusion of languages at Babel produced all of our presently used languages, but it seems to have been the start of the process of language division.

George Smith, a pioneer translator of many of the Babylonian clay tablets, found one tablet from the library of

King Asshurbanipal at Nineveh which read: "Babylon brought to subjection, [small] and great he *confounded their speech* . . . their strong place (tower) all the day they founded; to their strong place in the night entirely he made an end" (G. Smith, *The Chaldean Account of Genesis*. New York: Scribners, 1876, pp. 158-163).

The separation of people into groups speaking the same language would lead to inbreeding within the language groups, and then to the development of races. According to Dr. Gary E. Parker, it would take only *one generation* of controlled inbreeding to get all the variations of skin color we see among the races today (H.M. Morris and G.E. Parker, *What is Creation Science?* El Cajon, CA: Master Books, 1987, p. 113).

The name *Babel* means *gate of god*. *Babel* is similar in sound to the verb *balal*, which means to *confuse*. The name *Babel* (or *Babylon*) therefore came to stand for *confusion* (Gen. 11:9).

2. *From Shem to Abraham* (Gen. 11:10-26). The chosen line of descendants that was begun in Genesis 5 resumes at Genesis 11:10. That verse is also the start of the fifth "account" (or "generations") in Genesis — the "account of Shem." (See 2:4; 5:1.) This "account" does not give the total age of each patriarch, as Genesis 5 does, but the full age of each can be calculated easily.

The list of descendants in Genesis 11:10-32 gives the same names as those in the genealogy of Jesus in Luke 4:34-37, except that Luke includes the name of *Cainan*. Cainan's name is given in the Greek LXX Bible, but is not in the Hebrew. We think the name Cainan should be included, primarily because the New Testament has it. The Genesis 11 list tells that the life spans of people were hundreds of years shorter after the flood than before. Also the ages at the births of the first sons were much lower.

Genesis 11:16 names *Eber*. From his name the name *Hebrew* is derived. An ancient king at the Syrian city of Ebla about 2350 B.C. was named *Ebrum*. His name is perhaps the same as *Eber*. During his time the name *Ya* (=Yahweh?) began to be used more than before. This suggests a new religious development occurred. (G. Pettinato, "The Royal Archives of Tell-Mardikh-Ebla," in *Biblical Archaeologist*, May 1976, p. 48.)

Genesis 11:16-19 mentions Peleg. See Genesis 10:25 notes.

Generations from the Flood to Abraham (Gen. 11:10-32)				
Name	Life span in Hebrew	Life span in Greek	Age son born (Heb)	Age son born (Gr.)
Shem	602	602	100	100
Arphaxad	438	435	35	135
Cainan	not listed	460	not listed	130
Shelah	433	460	30	130
Eber	464	404	34	134
Peleg	239	339	30	130
Reu	239	339	32	132
Serug	230	330	30	130
Nahor	148	304	29	179
Terah	205	275	70	70

From the flood to Abram's birth in Hebrew = 292 yrs. (Abram born 2166)
From the flood to Abram's birth in the Greek Bible = 1,042 yrs.

In Genesis 11:10-26 the only information about human history for nearly a thousand years is the list of names. This period is approximately 3000 to 2000 B.C. It is the period called the Early Bronze age by archaeologists. Numerous great civilizations rose and fell during this period. In Egypt it was the time of building the pyramids during Egypt's Old Kingdom. In Mesopotamia it was the time of the Sumerian city-states, such as the Ur I dynasty. In Palestine it was a time of building strongly fortified cities, which indicates that wars occurred. (See Carl G. Rasmussen, *Zondervan NIV Atlas of the Bible*, Zondervan, 1989, pp. 73-75.) God looks upon individuals of faith in any time period as more important in human history than the battles and national power struggles that historians usually write up as the most important events of a period.

3. *The "account" of Terah* (11:27-32). After giving the genealogical list in 11:10-26, the Scripture writer narrowed down his area of discussion to one family, the family of Terah. Even the information about Terah's family is mostly limited to the story of Terah's son *Abram*. Genesis frequently presents its history in this manner — narrowing down information about a whole family to a focus on an individual in that family.

The "account" ("generations") of Terah is the sixth such introduction to a new section in Genesis. See Genesis 2:4 and others.

Abram, Nahor and Haran were brothers, sons of Terah, but not triplets. Haran appears to have been much older than Abram, and died while his father was yet living (12:28). Haran's son Lot was old enough to have a family of his own before Abram had a son.

Terah, Abram's father, "worshipped other gods" beyond the River Euphrates (Josh. 24:2). We are not told how he was converted from this.

Terah and his family moved six hundred miles up the Euphrates River from the city of Ur of the Chaldeans, to the city of Haran, which was on the Balikh River, a branch of the Euphrates.

Genesis does not reveal the fact that Abram had been called by God at Ur of the Chaldeans, to leave his country and his people and go to the land which God would show him. This is revealed in the speech of Stephen in Acts 7:2-3.

Abram and his wife, Sarai, left Ur and settled in Haran. Abram did not know when he left Ur where his destination was to be (Heb. 11:8). By faith he went forth, and Sarai loyally stayed with him (1 Pet. 3:6). Their faith seems to have inspired faith in other members of Abram's family, because several of them went with Abram and settled in Haran. Terah and Lot moved with Abraham to Haran. In later years we read that other family members of Nahor's family were then living in the Haran area. Jacob went to Haran, and met his cousin Rachel.

When Abram left the city of Ur of the Chaldeans (about

2100 B.C.), it was at a time of great prosperity and power for Ur. Ur was a commercial center. It had great temples and the Ziggurat of Ur. We urge students to do research on the archaeology and history of Ur. Abraham forsook Ur because of his faith, not because Ur was a miserable place to live.

Questions on Section B
The Tower of Babel; The Descendants of Shem (Gen. 11)

1. How did human speech immediately after the flood differ from speech at present? (11:1)
2. Name the plain where Noah's descendants at first settled. (11:2) Where was it?
3. What materials were used for building? (11:3)
4. What were the two purposes for building a tower? (11:4)
5. How was the tower project stopped? (11:7)
6. Name the city where the tower was built. (11:8)
7. What did the name of the city mean? (11:9)
8. Make a list of the names of the generations from Shem to Abram. (11:10-26)
9. Name Terah's three sons. (11:26)

Period III — Period of Abraham, Isaac and Jacob
From the Call of Abram to the Death of Joseph (Genesis 12–50; Book of Job)

God's Eternal Purpose was carried out through Abraham.

During the period of Abraham, Isaac, and Jacob God began to carry out His *"eternal purpose"* (or plan) for mankind through one family and nation, the family of **Abraham** and the nation of **Israel**. Other nations were mostly allowed to walk in their own ways (Acts 14:16), until the Christ would come and be born from the descendants of Abraham. (The ways that other nations lived were mostly violent, immoral, and self-destructive.) God concentrated His attentions on the Hebrew people (descended from Abraham), and blessed and guided them with special attention. After that period all nations would be blessed by Christ turning them from their wicked ways (Acts 3:25-26). All nations could then share in the blessing given to Abraham (Gal. 3:8,14; Eph. 3:11).

What was God's Eternal Purpose for Mankind?

1. To **RESCUE** (redeem) mankind
   (Titus 2:14; Isa. 63:16; 59:20)
2. To **BLESS** mankind (Gen. 12:3; 22:18;
   Gal. 3:8; Eph. 1:3)
3. To **BE WITH** mankind forever (Rev. 21:3;
   Mal. 3:17; Ex. 19:5–6; 2 Cor. 6:16)

This period of Abraham, Isaac, and Jacob is often called the Patriarchal Period. Abraham, Isaac, and Jacob were the greatest of the patriarchs, so we have chosen to call the period by their names.

A *patriarch* is a father-ruler, or head of a tribe or large family. In lands where there was no central federal government, the patriarch of each family (ordinarily the father) was provider, lawgiver, ruler, and judge.

During the periods before and after the flood, God demonstrated that mankind would not become righteous just because He gave them good things (as in the Garden of Eden), or because He gave them rules, or gave warnings of punishment, or actual punishments (like the flood). God knew that only by the death of His Son and the power of His Spirit within man would we become righteous. **Abraham** was the key man in bringing into reality God's eternal purpose (Gal. 3:8,14; Eph. 3:11).

GOD'S PROMISES TO ABRAHAM

"All peoples on earth will be *BLESSED* through you" (Gen. 12:3).

"Through your offspring (seed) all nations on earth will be *BLESSED*" (Gen. 22:18).

(If we desire God's blessings we will need to seek them through Abraham and through his offspring [Christ], because God promised His blessing to come through Abraham.)

What Blessings are in the BLESSING of ABRAHAM ?

1. The promise of the Holy Spirit (Gal. 3:14, 5-6)
2. The promise of justification by faith (Gal. 3:8-9)
3. Christ turning us from our wicked ways (Acts 3:25-26)

Section A
The Land of Promise

During the life of Abraham the land of Canaan became the main center of events in Bible history, and it continued to be such afterwards. We should therefore learn certain facts about that land.

1. *Facts about the land of promise.*
   a. Palestine is about 5200 miles from America, and is located on the east end of the Mediterranean Sea.
   Palestine is part of the "Fertile Crescent," a land area stretching in an arch around the desert, from Egypt, through Palestine and Syria, and downward through Mesopotamia.
   b. Palestine is the natural bridge between Egypt, Arabia and Africa on the south and Syria, Mesopotamia and Asia Minor to the north.
   c. Palestine is a small land. It is only about 150 miles from Dan to Beersheba (1 Sam. 3:20). Dan and Beersheba were cities in the northern and southern ends of the land.

2. *Names of the land.* At various times the land of promise has been divided up differently and called by different names.
   a. *Canaan.* This name applies to the area west of the Jordan River, about 6000 square miles, an area slightly smaller than Massachusetts. It was named after Ham's son Canaan.
   b. *Palestine.* A larger area, including Canaan and the land east of the Jordan, about 12,000 square miles. The name *Palestine* is derived from the *Philistines*, who inhabited its lower coastal area.
   c. *Israel.* Same territory as Palestine. Named for Jacob (Israel).
   d. *Judah* (or Judea). This name applies only to the southern part of Canaan. Judah was for a time separated from the rest of Israel.
   e. The *Holy Land.* This name is given to it because many holy events occurred there.
   f. The *promised land.* God promised this land to Abraham and his descendants forever (Gen. 13:15; 17:8).
   The boundaries of the Promised Land were as follows:
   North — Euphrates River, and Lebo Hamath (on the Orontes River)
   South — Kadesh Barnea and the River of Egypt (Wadi el-Arish)

West — The Great Sea

East — Deserts of Syria and Arabia. (See Numbers 35:1-12.)

These boundaries enclosed an area of about 60,000 square miles. This entire area was under Israelite control only during the reigns of David and Solomon.

3. *Divisions of the land*

Five Geopolitical divisions. (As indicated on the map)

Ⓐ Upper Galilee — Northwest of Sea of Galilee.

Ⓑ Lower Galilee — Plain of Esdraelon and hills just north.

Ⓒ Samaria — Central area with hills and valleys.

Ⓓ Judah — Dominant political area.

Ⓔ Negev —Desert area, extending from Judah south to the Gulf of Aqaba. The word *Negev* means South.

Four natural divisions

① Coastal plains

② Mountain region

③ Jordan valley

④ Eastern tableland

Four Plains

a — Akko (also called Acre or Asher)

b — Esdraelon (often called Jezreel)

c — Sharon   d — Philistia

Thirteen Mountains

A — Lebanon	F — Ebal	K — Hermon
B — Carmel	G — Gerizim	L — Gilead
C — Tabor	H — Olives	M — Nebo
D — Hill Moreh	I — Zion	
E — Gilboa	J — Hebron (Jebel Jalis)	

Three Bodies of Water

x — Lake Huleh (sometimes called the Waters of Merom)

y — Sea of Galilee (or Lake Kinnereth)

z — Salt Sea (Dead Sea) (Elevation = 1300 ft. below sea level)

Ten Brooks or Rivers

(1) Kishon	(6) Jordan
(2) Besor	(7) Yarmuk
(3) River of Egypt (=Wadi el-Arish)	(8) Jabbok
(4) Wadi Qelt (not the Cherith)	(9) Arnon
(5) Kidron	(10) Zered

50 FACTS ABOUT THE LAND OF PROMISE

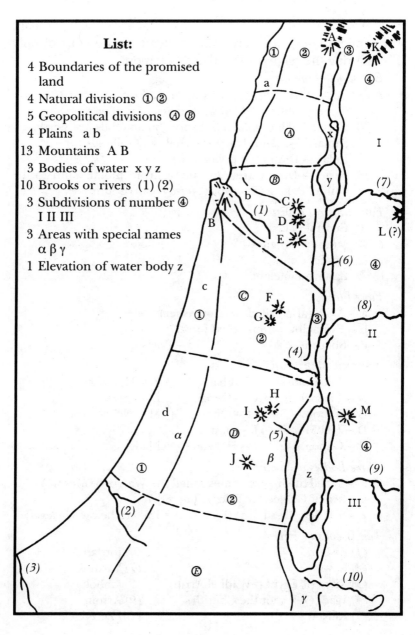

List:

4 Boundaries of the promised land

4 Natural divisions ① ②

5 Geopolitical divisions Ⓐ Ⓑ

4 Plains a b

13 Mountains A B

3 Bodies of water x y z

10 Brooks or rivers (1) (2)

3 Subdivisions of number ④ I II III

3 Areas with special names α β γ

1 Elevation of water body z

Three Divisions of Eastern Tablelands
 I. Bashan   II. Gilead   III. Moab

Three Areas with Special Names
 α – The Shephelah (foothills east of Philistine plain)
 β – The desert of Judah (The Jeshimon)
 γ – The Arabah (Valley between Dead Sea and Red Sea)

Section B
Life of Abraham until Birth of Isaac (Genesis 11:27–20:18)

WHY ABRAHAM IS SO IMPORTANT TO US . . .

1. He is a great example of faith (Heb.11:8-12).
2. He is "father" of Jews and Arabs.
3. He is "father" of Christians, those who have faith like his (Gal. 3:29; Rom. 4:11-12,16).
4. God's BLESSING upon mankind was to come through Abraham and his offspring (Gen. 12:3).

The Life and Journeys of Abraham
 1. *Ur of the Chaldeans* (Gen. 11:27-31).
   a. Original call to Abram; Acts 7:2-3
   b. Terah's migration; Gen. 11:27-31
 2. *Haran* (Gen. 11:32-12:3).
   a. Death of Terah; 11:32
   b. Second call to Abram; 12:1-3
 3. *Shechem* (Gen. 12:4-7).
   a. First promise of land
 4. Between *Bethel* and *Ai* (Gen. 12:8-9).
   a. Altar built
 5. *Egypt* (Gen. 12:10-20).
   a. Lie about Sarai
 6. Back at *Bethel* (Gen. 13:1-17).
   a. Separation from Lot
 7. *Hebron* (Gen. 13:18–14:12).
   a. Invasion from the East

8. *Dan* (Gen. 14:13-16).
   a. Rescue of Lot
9. Returning to *Hebron* and at Hebron (Gen. 14:17–19:38).
   a. Meeting with King of Sodom and Melchizedek; 14:17-24
   b. God's covenant with Abram; ch. 15
   c. Hagar and Ishmael; ch. 16
   d. Covenant of circumcision; 17:1-14
   e. Promise of Isaac; 17:15-21
   f. Circumcision of household; 17:22-27
   g. Destruction of Sodom and Gomorrah; chs. 18–19
10. *Gerar* (Gen. 20:1–21:20).
   a. Lie about Sarah to Abimelech; ch. 20
   b. Birth of Isaac; 21:1-7
   c. Removal of Hagar and Ishmael; 21:8-21
11. *Beersheba* (Gen. 21:22-34).
   a. Covenant of Abraham and Abimelech
12. Land of *Moriah* (Gen. 22:1-18).
   a. Offering of Isaac
13. *Beersheba* (Gen. 22:19-24).
   a. Abraham learns of Nahor's family
14. *Hebron* (Gen. 23).
   a. Death and burial of Sarah
15. *Beersheba* (Gen. 24:1-25:8).
   a. Wife for Isaac; ch. 24
   b. Marriage to Keturah; 25:1-4
   c. Last days of Abraham; 25:5-8
16. *Hebron* (Gen. 25:9-10).
   a. Burial of Abraham

---

1. *God's Call to Abram* (Gen. 12:1-3). The call to Abram in Genesis 12 was actually the second call to Abram. He was called the first time at Ur of the Chaldeans (Acts 7:2-3). Abram and his family moved up to Haran, where Abram's father, Terah, died. After Terah's death the LORD called Abram again. The first and second call were much alike: "Leave your country, your people, and your father's household and go to the land I will show you."

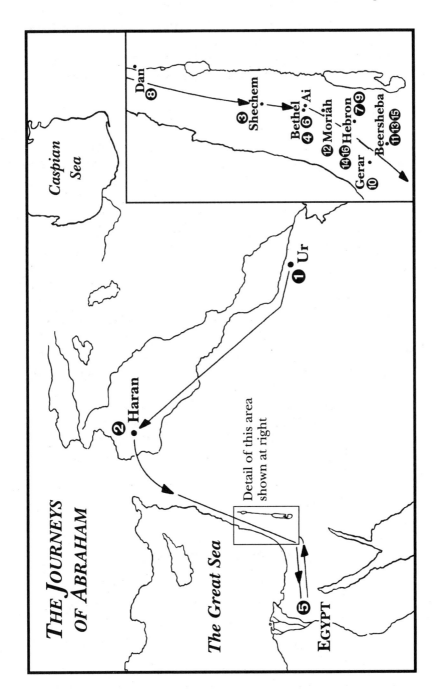

THE JOURNEYS OF ABRAHAM

Caspian Sea

Dan ⓫

③ Shechem

Bethel ④ ⑥ •Ai

⑫ Moriah
⑭⑯ Hebron ⑦⑨
Gerar •
⑩ Beersheba ⑪⑬⑮

① Ur

② • Haran

Detail of this area shown at right

The Great Sea

⑤

EGYPT

The name *Abram* meant *Exalted Father*. Later his name was changed to *Abraham*, which means *father of a multitude* (Gen. 17:5). He is our *"father,"* if we are God's children. Abram lived 2166–1991 B.C. He was living in 2000 B.C., four thousand years ago.

God's call to Abram involved the principle of *separation*. Abram was to separate from his family. Often God's children must separate from their earthly families if they wish to serve God (Luke 14:26). The character of some of Abram's relatives — like Laban and Lot — was such that it was necessary to get away from them. "Bad company corrupts good character" (1 Cor. 15:33).

Abram did not want his son to intermarry with the daughters of the Canaanites (Gen. 24:3). Neither did Isaac and Rebekah want Jacob to marry someone from the "women of this land" (27:46). These are examples of the principle of *separation*.

The principle of *separation* was not intended to prevent Abram or any other godly person from associating with other people. God clearly said to Abram, "I will make your name great, and *you will be a blessing*." By separating ourselves from evildoers and devoting ourselves to God's service, we can gain the strength of faith to go back among people and be a blessing to them. We are not to be Pharisees or monks.

God promised to make Abram **GREAT**. That promise has been fulfilled wonderfully. Abram is honored by Jews, Arabs, and Christians alike.

Genesis 12:3 (and 22:18) is the verse that links the Old and New Testament together.

"All peoples on earth will be *blessed* through you."

"The Scripture foresaw that God would justify the Gentiles by faith, and announced the gospel in advance to Abraham: 'All nations will be *blessed* through you'" (Galatians 3:8).

2. *Abram arrives in Canaan* (Gen. 12:4-9). The journey from Haran to Canaan was about four hundred miles. Abram was then seventy-five years old. His wife (Sarai), and his nephew Lot, and many people they had acquired in Haran accompanied them.

Abram had a private "army" of 318 "trained men born in his household" (Gen. 14:14).

Abram's first encampment in the land was at *Shechem* (12:6). This place is near the center of the land, on the road through the central mountains toward Bethel, Jerusalem and Hebron. Shechem became very important in the later history of the patriarchs. Jacob bought his first land there and dug his well there. Joseph (Jacob's son) was buried there.

Genesis 12:6 says "the Canaanites were in the land" when Abram arrived. The Canaanites were descendants of Ham (Gen. 10:15-19). They entered the land, probably immigrating from Phoenicia (north of Israel), and gave their name (*Canaan*) to the land. Archaeologists call the period when the Canaanites dominated the land the Middle Bronze II period, approximately 1950–1450 B.C. The Canaanites were people of culture. They rebuilt cities destroyed before their arrival. They made artistic pottery. They also had bad morals.

When Abram arrived in Canaan, there was a famine in the land. What a welcome after travelling a thousand miles! Abram continued to migrate southward, probably seeking pasture (Gen. 13:2,6). From Shechem he travelled south about thirty miles to the "hills" (literally "mountain") east of Bethel, with Bethel on the west and 'Ai on the east.

At every stop where Abram camped he worshipped the LORD and built an altar (Gen. 12:7,8). Abram left a trail of altars behind him. What are we leaving behind us as we go through life?

The author has worked ten seasons at the archaeological excavations at Khirbet Nisya ten miles north of Jerusalem. This place is on the east slope of a large mountain. We believe it is the location of the town of 'Ai, where Abram camped. The modern Arab town of Bireh is west of the mountain, probably on the location of ancient Bethel. The pottery fragments we have found at Khirbet Nisya are types made in all the periods when the Bible says 'Ai was occupied.

3. *Abram in Egypt* (Gen. 12:10-20). Because of the famine in Canaan, Abram travelled on southward to Egypt. This would be a journey of two hundred miles across barren desert. Egypt usually had food because of the annual flooding of the Nile each summer. Egypt suffered a continual flow of destitute people who entered into their land. (See Werner Keller, *The Bible as History in Pictures*, New York: Morrow, 1964, p. 42.)

In Egypt Abram gave in to fear, and said that Sarai, his wife, was his sister. He hoped this would protect him from death at the hands of the Egyptians, who might want to take Sarai into a harem. Abram's statement left Sarai defenseless, and she was taken into Pharaoh's palace. The LORD protected Abram and Sarai (in spite of his failing). The Egyptians expelled Abram from their land — with Sarai.

The Bible exposes the sins of its heroes !

Abraham (Gen. 12:13).   Moses (Num. 20:11-12).
King David (2 Sam. 11:2-5)

---

4. *Abram and Lot separate* (Gen. 13). When Abram and his household returned from Egypt to the place between Bethel and 'Ai (12:8), it was necessary for them to separate their families and flocks to different places because the land could not support them both. Lot moved to the green Jordan valley, and then on to the city of Sodom. The LORD sent Abram on a tour of the Promised Land, and Abraham settled near Hebron. (Hebron is west of the Dead Sea, in a green area in the central mountains.)

Abram was very wealthy (13:2). Wealth is not always evidence that the owner is selfish and heartless.

Abram was a peacemaker, and was very generous to Lot, allowing him to choose which area he desired to live in (13:7-9). "A generous man will prosper" (Prov. 11:25).

The area around the Jordan River and Dead Sea was once

productive and supported large populations (Gen.13:10). This is confirmed by the presence of the huge cemeteries just east of the Dead Sea. The cemetery at Bab edh-Dhra is composed of more than 20,000 tombs in which over 500,000 people were buried together with over three million pottery vessels! (*Biblical Archaeology Review*, Sept./Oct. 1980, p. 28). That area is now so barren that it is nearly uninhabitable.

Genesis 13:13: "The men of Sodom were wicked and were sinning greatly against the LORD."

Sins of Sodom:

Ezekiel 16:49 (NKJV): "Look, this was the *iniquity* of your sister **Sodom**:
1. She and her daughter had *pride*,
2. fullness of food, and abundance of idleness [**luxury**];
3. neither did she strengthen the hand of the poor and needy [**selfishness**]."
4. Genesis 19:5: "Where are the men who came to you tonight? Bring them out to us so that we can have sex with them" (Hebrew: "*know*" them).

God was emphatic about giving the land of Canaan to Abram's descendants forever (13:15; 17:8; Ps. 105:9-11). Sometimes God removed the Israelites from the land when they sinned (Deut. 28:36), but a remnant always later came back.

5. *Lot rescued* (Gen. 14:1-17). Four powerful kings from the East invaded the land of Canaan. *Shinar* is probably the land of Sumer. *Ellasar* (14:1) was probably the Sumerian city of Larsa. *Goiim* means "the nations" (probably a confederation). None of these four kings is yet identified from sources outside the Bible. *Amraphel* is not Hammurabi, the king of Babylon who ruled about 1700 B.C., at least three hundred years after the time of Abram.

Dr. Nelson Glueck wrote that in his extensive explorations east of the Jordan valley he discovered a long line of sites in Transjordan and in the Negev that had been occupied in the

Middle Bronze I period (2100–1850 B.C.). They had all been destroyed no later than about the middle of the nineteenth century B.C. and for the most part were never rebuilt. (See *The Other Side of the Jordan*, Cambridge, MA: 1970, p. 139). He considered these destructions the work of the invaders mentioned in Genesis 14.

These four powerful kings met and defeated five puny kings of the cities of Sodom, Gomorrah, and nearby towns. None of these five kings are known, except perhaps *Birsha*, king of Gomorrah (13:2). Dr. Giovanni Pettinato, former epigrapher of the excavations at Tell Mardikh (Ebla) in Syria, says that he saw a clay tablet there which contained the name of Birsha, king of Gomorrah. (See *Biblical Archaeologist*, Dec. 1978, p. 154.) His claim has been disputed, but may yet be proved to be correct.

The invaders swept down from northern Mesopotamia, through Ashteroth Karnaim in the region east of the Sea of Galilee, on southward almost two hundred miles to El Paran on the north tip of the Red Sea gulf of Aqaba. From there they went to Kadesh Barnea (14:7), and northeast toward the Dead Sea. They struck Hazazon Tamar, which is En Gedi, on the west side of the Dead Sea (2 Chr. 20:2). There the four powerful invading kings met the five puny kings of Sodom, Gomorrah and the neighboring towns. (See *Bible and Spade*, Summer 1974, p. 78.)

The battle occurred in the Valley of Siddim, which is identified as the "Salt Sea" (14:3), apparently the shallow south part of the sea, which was then not covered with water.

The invaders were triumphant and carried off all the loot from Sodom and Gomorrah. They also kidnapped Abram's nephew Lot, who was living in Sodom. (Lot's selfishness hurt him.)

The capture of Lot was reported to Abram at Hebron, at least thirty miles from Sodom. From Hebron Abram and his private army of 318 men pursued the invaders as far as Hobah north of Damascus, a distance of over 150 miles.

6. *Melchizedek meets Abram* (Gen. 14:18-24). When Abram returned triumphant, he was met by a great priest named

Melchizedek. He appears suddenly on the scene, and we have no subsequent information about him. He is one of the greatest of all the types of Christ, being both priest and king.

Abram would accept no reward from the king of Sodom for rescuing his subjects when he rescued Lot (Gen. 14:22-24).

Melchizedek — A type (symbol) of Christ Jesus (Psalm 110:4; Hebrews 5:6; 6:1)		
Similarities	*Melchizedek*	*Jesus*
1. *Priest* of God Most High	Gen. 14:18; Heb. 7:3	Heb. 7:3
2. *King* of *Salem* (=King of Jeru*salem*, and of peace)	Gen. 14:18	Heb. 7:2
3. *King* of *righteousness*	*Melchizedek* means "my righteous king"	Heb. 7:2
4. Brought Abram bread and wine	Gen. 14:18	Luke 22:19-20
5. Blessed Abram	Gen. 14:19	Rev. 1:3
6. Received *tithes* from Abram and his family	Gen. 14:20	Matt. 23:23
7. Had no beginning of days or end of life	Heb. 7:3	Heb. 7:15
8. Very *great* (greater than Abram and Levi)	Heb. 7:4-10	Heb. 8:6

7. *God's Covenant with Abram* (Gen. 15). In a vision God said to Abram, "Do not be afraid, Abram. I am your shield, your very great reward" (wages, payment). This is a precious promise that every child of God can receive as if spoken to him. But Abram felt that since he had no child, he had no earthly reward that would outlive him. Abram spoke of his servant Eliezer from Damascus: "Behold a son of my house is inheriting me!" (literal Hebrew).

The LORD promised Abram that his offspring would come from his own body, and be as innumerable as the stars of heaven (15:5).

> **"Abram believed the LORD, and he credited** [his belief] **to**
> **him** [Abram] **as righteousness"** (Gen. 15:6).
> Abram was NOT a completely righteous man. No person is.
>
> Our unrighteousness + God's + our = RIGHTEOUSNESS
>   grace   faith   for us
>
> OUR faith is also imputed to us as righteousness (Rom. 4:9-12).

In the Scriptures "faith" is more than belief that certain events happened. Faith is giving ourselves in total confidence to the LORD, ready to do whatever He says. Faith is not divorced from doing good works (Jas. 2:14-26). Baptism is described as an expression of faith (Gal. 3:27, 29). We all fall short in the works we should do for Christ. Our faith and God's grace bridge the gap from us to God. (Concerning Abram's faith and works, see Hebrews 11:8-19; Romans 4:16-22; James 2:17-18.)

God's covenant with Abram was stamped with divine verification by a vision of a solemn covenant-making ceremony. The custom of cutting an animal into two halves and having the two parties making a covenant to walk between the two halves is alluded to in Jeremiah 34:17. It was as if the parties were saying to one another, "If either of us do not do what we promised in this covenant, we will be as dead as these animal carcasses."

The smoking pot of fire that floated between the two pieces of meat (Gen. 15:17) symbolized the presence of God.

God foretold to Abram that his descendants would live as aliens in a country not their own [Egypt] for four hundred years and endure enslavement before they returned to settle as residents in the land of Canaan. The only land Abraham ever owned in the land of Canaan was the burial cave for Sarah at Hebron (Heb. 11:9-10; Acts 7:5).

God's reason for delaying His promise to give the land to Abram and his seed was that "the sin of the Amorites has not yet reached its full measure" (15:16). (The Amorites were the largest of the seven Canaanite "nations.") These people had many sins in Abram's time. But by the time of Moses six hundred years later the iniquity of the Canaanite nations was a full, overflowing cup that was contaminating everyone who touched it. (See Deut. 9:4-6.)

Lists of the Canaanite nations can be found in Genesis 10:15-18; 15:19-21; Joshua 3:10; 24:11; and Nehemiah 9:8.

8. *Hagar and Ishmael* (Gen. 16). Abram and Sarai ran ahead of God's timetable for blessing them by causing the birth of Ishmael. The son, Ishmael, was one whose "hand will be against everyone . . . and he will live in hostility toward all his brothers" (16:12). Ishmael's descendants include many of the Arab peoples of the Middle East.

Abram had waited about eleven years since God promised him a son (16:15). It is sometimes difficult to wait for years upon the LORD (Ps. 27:14; 33:20).

Hagar, Sarai's servant from Egypt (Gen.12:16?), became conceited and overbearing when she conceived the child and felt this gave her an advantage over Sarai. Sarai treated her harshly and Hagar fled.

Out in the desert on the east of Egypt the "angel of the LORD" told Hagar to return to her mistress and "SUBMIT to her." Servants even yet should obey earthly masters in everything (Col. 3:22-25).

The ANGEL (messenger) of the LORD is the same divine being who later came to earth visibly as Jesus Christ. This "angel" spoke with all the foreknowledge and power of God. See the special study at Judges 6:11, p. 364.

The well where God revived Hagar was named *Beer Lahai Roi* (16:14). It is three Hebrew words meaning . . .

```
Beer . . . . . . . . .Lahai . . . . . . . . . . .Roi
Well of . . . . .the living one . . . .(who) sees me.
```

Hagar's son was named *Ishmael*, which means *"God hears."* (16:11, 15).

9. *The covenant of circumcision* (Gen. 17). When Abram was ninety-nine years old The LORD (Yahweh) appeared to him

and said, "I am God Almighty" (Heb., *'el Shaddai*). *Shaddai* (Almighty) is a name often used for God in the book of Job. God at this time gave Abram the new name *Abraham*, meaning "father of a multitude" (17:5). Also Sarai's name was changed to *Sarah*, meaning *princess* (17:15).

God commanded Abraham to circumcise every male in his family. This was to be the "sign" of God's covenant with Abram (17:11). Any male not circumcised was regarded as cut off from his people.

Circumcision was a custom practiced in Egypt at least by 2300 B.C., before Abram's time. (See Werner Keller, *The Bible as History in Pictures*, New York: Morrow, 1964, p. 124.) This does not prove that Abram borrowed the custom from Egypt.

Circumcision is no longer commanded by God as a religious law. (See Gal. 5:6; 2:3; 1 Cor. 7:19.) Circumcision was never the MEANS of becoming righteous before God, because Abram had been declared righteous because of his faith years before he was circumcised (Rom. 4:9-11).

Circumcision – A symbol of Baptism		
Similarities	**Circumcision**	**Baptism**
1. Initiates into special religious privileges and immunities	Gen. 17:9-13; Ex. 12:48	Col. 2:11-13
2. Represents a righteousness which is obtained by faith	Rom. 4:1	Mark 16:16; Acts 2:38
3. More than just outward. Symbolic of inward change	Jer. 4:4; Rom. 2:29	1 Pet. 3:21; Rom. 6:1-7
4. Neither means anything apart from faith.	Rom. 2:25; Acts 7:51	1 Pet. 3:21

(Adapted from Gary Zustiak notes: "Circumcision and Baptism")

Baptism now replaces circumcision as the mark of the true people of God (Col. 2:11-13). In Christ Jesus we were circumcised not with a circumcision done by the hands of men but with the circumcision done by Christ, having been buried with him in *baptism* and raised with him through your *faith* in the power (or supernatural *working*) of God (Col. 2:11-12).

Baptism differs from circumcision in that baptism is for both males and females. Also baptism requires *faith* in those being baptized, and is therefore only for those old enough to believe. There are, nonetheless, several similarities between them.

After God's instructions concerning circumcision God told Abraham that his wife Sarah would bear a son, and "you will call his name *Isaac*" (meaning *laughter*) (17:19). Abraham fell face down and laughed. We might think he laughed in incredulity. But Romans 4:18-21 tells us that Abraham did **NOT** waver through unbelief regarding the promise of God, and was fully persuaded that God was able to do what He had promised. Therefore, Abraham's laughter must have been a laugh of delight rather than a laugh of doubt.

10. *Three visitors to Abraham* (Gen. 18:1-15). The LORD appeared to Abraham near the great trees (lit., *oaks*) at Mamre, which are two miles northwest of Hebron (18:1; 13:18).

It is amazing that the LORD *appeared* to Abraham, because the LORD said to Moses, "No one may see me and live" (Ex. 33:20; John 1:18). It is true that no man has seen God the Father. But God's "Messenger" (angel), who is "one" with the Father, was in the world, and was seen by people (like Isaiah), even before he took the form of flesh and made His dwelling among us as the man Jesus (John 10:30; 17:22; 1:10, 14; 12:41). See Judges 6:11 (p. 364) for the special study "The Angel of the LORD."

The other two visitors to Abraham were angels (19:1). Abraham and Sarah fed their visitors (18:3-8).

> *"Do not forget to entertain strangers, for by so doing some people have entertained angels without knowing it"* (Heb. 13:2).

The LORD told Abraham that his wife Sarah would have a child "about this time next year" (lit., "at the time of life," or "in due season" [NRSV]). Sarah, then aged eighty-nine, over-heard the LORD's promise, and "laughed." Her laughter revealed that she *almost* doubted the promise. The LORD said to Abraham, "Is anything too hard for the LORD?" Sarah was embarrassed that she had laughed.

Sarah did have faith, even if her faith was not perfect. By *faith* Sarah herself also received strength to conceive seed, and she bore a child when she was past the age, because she judged Him faithful who had promised (Heb. 11:11, NKJV).

11. *Abraham pleads for Sodom* (Gen. 18:16-33). Abraham's prayers to the LORD caused God to promise to save Sodom if there were only ten righteous people in it (18:32). "The prayer of a righteous man is powerful and effective" (James 5:16).

12. *Sodom and Gomorrah destroyed* (Gen. 19:1-29). The two angels with the LORD came to Sodom in the evening of the day the LORD had promised to Abraham the birth of his son. By the next morning Sodom and Gomorrah and the neigh-boring towns had been destroyed by burning sulfur raining down upon them from the LORD out of the heavens.

Regarding the sins of Sodom, see Genesis 13:13 notes. Their principal sins were (1) homosexuality (19:15), and (2) pride, and (3) neglect of the poor (Ezek. 16:49-50).

We sometimes describe Abraham's nephew Lot as an evil man. But Lot was distressed by the ungodliness in Sodom. 2 Peter 2:7-8: The LORD "rescued Lot, a righteous man, who was distressed by the filthy lives of lawless men (for that right-eous man, living among them day after day, was tormented in his righteous soul by the lawless deeds he saw and heard)."

Lot's daughters were virgins (19:8), but they were pledged to be married, so that their husbands-to-be are referred to as Lot's sons-in-law (19:14). These men would not listen to Lot.

Lot's willingness to sacrifice his daughters to the lust of evil men to save his guests (19:6-8) is hard for us to under-stand. Lot did not seem to recognize the divine power within his guests.

The determined persistence of the evildoers, even after they were struck blind, amazes us (19:11). Literally: "And they were *weary* (trying) to find the door" (of Lot's house) (19:11).

"Don't even look back!" the angels told Lot, his wife, and their two daughters as they practically pushed them out of Sodom the next morning. "Flee to the mountains!"

Lot begged to go to the little neighboring town of *Zoar* (19:19-20). His wife "looked back," and became a pillar of salt (19:26). (The verb "looked back" means to look back with consideration, to gaze. Her interests were still in Sodom.)

The entire area of Sodom and the plain nearby were overthrown by the fire from heaven. The area had once been well-watered everywhere (13:10). The LORD destroyed the cities and the vegetation in the land (13:25).

Thirty miles away at Hebron Abraham saw the smoke rising from the deep valley where Sodom had been (19:28). There had not been ten righteous people in the city!

The Cities of the Plain (south and east of the Dead Sea)

1. **SODOM**	3. Zoar	4. **Admah**
2. **GOMORRAH**		5. **Zeboiim**

Where were Sodom and Gomorrah located? They were near the Dead Sea, but probably not at the north end of it. No significant burned locations have been found north of the Dead Sea. The valley which the shallow waters of the south end of the Dead Sea cover (the Valley of Siddim) has often been thought to be their location. *Biblical Archaeology Review* (Sept.–Oct. 1980, pp. 27-29) says that this theory about their location has now been disproved. Since the water level in the Dead Sea has dropped much in recent years, archaeologists have been able to examine much of the sea floor. They found no ancient remains there.

Research just east of the Dead Sea Lisan (the tongue of land on the sea's east side) has revealed the remains of five (and five only) destroyed ancient sites there. The sites are named Bab edh-dhra, Numeira, Safi, Feifa, and Khanazir. These sites each lie by a wadi (brook). Each was destroyed near the end of the Early Bronze age (2350 B.C.?). A huge cemetery appears to lie by each place, with possibly half a million people buried in some of them. The sites that have been examined appear to have perished in a fiery destruction. The excavators report that at the site named Numeira there was spongy charcoal all over the ground, so that it could be scooped up by hand. See *Newsletter of the American Schools of Oriental Research,* April 1974, and Oct.–Nov. 1975. Also *Biblical Archaeology Review*, Sept.–Oct. 1980, pp. 26-36; and *Bible and Spade,* Summer 1974 (pp. 65-89) and Winter 1977 (pp. 24-30).

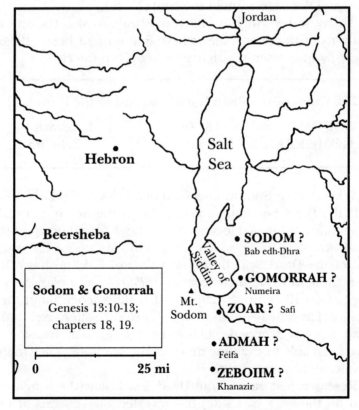

Map of Possible Locations of Sodom and Gomorrah

We think that these five locations were those of Sodom and its neighboring cities, though definite proof is still lacking. The destruction of the places at the end of the Early Bronze age seems to be a century or two before the time of Abraham, according to the date presently assigned to the Early Bronze age; but this might be modified in the future.

13. *Lot and his daughters* (Gen. 19:30-38). Lot had begged to go to the village of Zoar when he fled Sodom (19:20). But when Sodom was burned he and his daughters fled to a cave in the mountains. The great population that had been in Sodom was wiped out, so that the older daughter said, "There is no man around here." The two daughters deceived their father with wine and conceived children of their father. Their children (sons) were named *Moab* and *Ben-Ammi* (meaning "son of my people"). These sons became ancestors of the Moabites and Ammonites. These races had centuries of hostilities with the Israelites, though they were closely related.

God later forbade the Israelites to accept Moabites and Ammonites into Israel (Deut. 23:3-4). This exclusion was the result of the hostility of these nations toward the Israelites, not because of the immoral events of their origin.

14. *Abraham and Abimelech* (Gen. 20). Abraham moved from his residence near Hebron to the Negev desert area west and southwest of Beersheba. For a while he stayed at *Gerar*. His son Isaac was born at Gerar. Gerar is probably Tell Abu Hureira, on the Valley (wadi) of Gerar, which is a branch of the Wadi Besor. (See *Israel Exploration Journal,* 6,1 (1956), pp. 26-32.)

The story of Abram in Egypt saying that Sarai was his sister (12:9-20) has similarities to the story of Abraham and Abimelech at Gerar. The stories are introduced with very similar words (12:9 and 20:1). The two stories seem to show the relationships of Abraham with different types of people (12:3). When Pharaoh in Egypt took Sarai, the LORD inflicted serious diseases on Pharaoh. Pharaoh expelled Abram, but could not harm him. Pharaoh was the prototype of all ungodly cruel nations. Such nations found God's special man

(Abram) to be protected by his God, but they did not respect him nor his God. The fact that they could not harm Abram should have warned them not to defy his God. Moses' experiences with a later Pharaoh showed that the Egyptians did NOT learn this clearly-revealed lesson.

On the other hand, Abimelech is described as a righteous Gentile or a righteous sojourner in the land. He had been deceived by Abraham's words about Sarah, and took her "with a clean conscience and clean hands" (20:5). When Abimelech learned of Abraham's special status with God, he accepted it, and offered gifts to "cover the offense against you," (literally, "a covering of the eyes" so those with Sarah could not see the wrong Abimelech had done) (20:16). Abraham prayed for Abimelech, and his family again produced offspring. With such people as Abimelech, Abraham could live in the same land in harmony.

It is easy for us to condemn Abraham for his half-lie about Sarah, and that certainly was outside the will of God. We are not accustomed to giving God's prophets the respect that their ministries should have. All the prophets were men subject to weakness (Heb. 5:2), but they were *God's* agents. When God told Abimelech, "Abraham is a *prophet*, and he will pray for you, and you will live," Abimelech did the right thing and submitted. In much the same way we submit gladly to Christ's twelve apostles.

Questions on Section B
Life of Abram until Birth of Isaac (Gen. 11:27–20:18)

1. Why did God choose one family through which to work out his program? (Gal. 3:6-9)
2. Whose family was chosen? (Gen. 11:31;12:1)
3. Who were Terah's three children? (11:27)
4. Who was Lot's father? (11:27)
5. Where did Terah first live? To what place did he go? (11:31)
6. What do the names *Abram* and *Abraham* mean?

7. Where did Abram receive his first call? (Acts 7:2)
8. Where did Abram receive his second call? (Gen. 11:32)
9. Where did Terah die? (11:32)
10. Tell four things God promised to Abram when He called him the second time. (12:2-3)
11. How old was Abram when he left Haran? (12:4)
12. Into what land did Abram come? What was his first stopping place there? (12:5-6)
13. Why did Abram go into Egypt? (12:10)
14. What deceitful thing did Abram do in Egypt? (12:11,13)
15. Why did Abram and Lot separate? Where did the separation take place? (13:2, 6-7)
16. Where did Lot go to live? (13:12)
17. What blessing was announced to Abram after his separation from Lot? (13:14-16)
18. Where did Abram live? (13:18)
19. Who invaded the city where Lot lived? (14:1-2,12)
20. Who told Abram of Lot's capture? (14:13)
21. How many men did Abram have? (14:14)
22. Where did Abram rescue Lot? (14:14)
23. What would Abram not accept from the king of Sodom? (14:17, 21-23)
24. Who was Melchizedek? (14:18) What did he give Abram?
25. What did Abram give Melchizedek? (14:20)
26. Who did Abram assume would be his heir and possessor of his house? (15:2)
27. How many offspring (descendants) did God promise Abram? (15:5)
28. What did God credit (or account) as righteousness unto Abram? (15:6)
29. How long did God foretell that Abram's descendants would sojourn in a country not their own? (15:13)
30. What were the limits of the land God promised to Abram? (15:18)
31. Who was Sarai's maidservant? (16:1)
32. What was the attitude of the maidservant when she conceived? (16:4)
33. Who called a well *Beer Lahai Roi*, and why? (16:7, 13-14)
34. What was Hagar's son's name? What was Abram's age at his birth? (16:16)
35. How old was Abram when his name was changed? (17:1,5)
36. What did the change of names indicate about the change of Abraham's status? (17:5-6)
37. What was the sign of God's covenant with Abraham? (17:11)

38. To what was Sarai's name changed? What does the new name mean? (17:15)
39. What caused Abraham to laugh? (17:17)
40. How many rulers were to come from Ishmael? (17:20)
41. Who were the three visitors who came to Abraham at Mamre? (18:1; 19:1)
42. What did Abraham feed his guests? (18:8)
43. What promise was given concerning Abraham's son by his visitors? (18:10)
44. Why did Sarah laugh? (18:12)
45. What plans did Jehovah reveal to Abraham about Sodom? (18:20,23)
46. How many righteous people could have saved Sodom? (18:32)
47. Where did the angels stay in Sodom? (19:2-3)
48. How was an assault on Lot's house stopped? (19:11)
49. What members of Lot's family got out of Sodom? (19:15)
50. To what small city did God permit Lot to flee? (19:23)
51. What was the fate of Sodom and Gomorrah? (19:24)
52. What was the fate of Lot's wife? (19:26)
53. Give the names of the sons of Lot's two daughters, and the people descended from each. (19:37-38)
54. Who was Abimelech? Where did he live? (Gen. 20:2)
55. What lie did Abraham tell Abimelech? (20:2)
56. How did Abimelech discover the deception? (20:6)
57. What was the main difference between Pharaoh's taking Sarah and Abimelech taking her? (Gen. 12:14-20; 20:3-6)

Section C
Life of Abraham: Birth of Isaac
until Death of Abraham (Genesis 21:1–25:18)

1. *The Birth of Isaac* (Gen. 21:1-7). The LORD *visited* Sarah, as He had said (Gen. 21:1; 1 Sam. 2:21; Ex. 3:16), and she bore a son. What ineffable joy! The name *Isaac* means *laughter.*

It was through Isaac that Abraham's offspring was to be reckoned (21:12). God gave to Isaac and to his son Jacob the same promise that He gave to Abraham, that in their offspring all the nations on earth would be blessed (Gen. 26:4; 28:14).

**Abraham was 100 years old,
and Sarah was 90 when Isaac was born.**

---

2. *Hagar and Ishmael sent away* (Gen. 21:8-21). A child was usually about three years old when weaned, old enough to be taken from the care of its mother (1 Sam. 1:22).

At the great feast at the weaning of Isaac, his half-brother Ishmael was "mocking" (literally, "laughing," from the same verb as Isaac's name). Sarah demanded that the slave woman and her son be sent away at once and permanently. Abraham was reluctant, but God directed him to do it. (The law code of Hammurabi, about 1700 B.C., directed that the free woman could not sell her slave woman who had borne children to her husband. [Hammurabi, Law 146, in *Ancient Near East*, Vol 1, Princeton, 1973, p. 154]).

The LORD cared for Hagar and the boy, and brought her to a well of water. Ishmael grew up in the desert of Paran (in the southeast part of the Sinai peninsula). His mother got a wife for him from Egypt. (She herself was an Egyptian.) Future conflicts between the descendants of Isaac and Ishmael were inevitable.

3. *The treaty at Beersheba* (Gen. 21:22-34). Though Abimelech, king at Gerar, was not openly hostile to Abraham, he was suspicious and envious of him. He supposed Abraham had the same attitude toward him. (Most humans feel that other people's attitudes toward them are about the same as their attitudes toward the people.) Abraham swore to show kindness to Abimelech and his territory.

Abraham confronted Abimelech over the seizure by his servants of a well of water, a necessity in the desert. The two men swore an oath of peace, and Abraham gave Abimelech seven ewe lambs. The place where this was done was called *Beersheba*. That name means both *Well of the oath* and *Well of the seven* (lambs).

The tamarisk tree (21:33) is a small tree that grows in valleys in semi-arid places. Modern visitors to Tell Beer-Sheba can see tamarisk trees growing.

103

Abraham stayed (literally, "sojourned" as an alien) in the land of the *Philistines* for a long time, perhaps twenty years. The reference to *Philistines* in the story of Abraham is considered to be an anachronism by many Bible critics, because most of the Philistines did not immigrate into Canaan until after 1200 B.C. That is true, but it does not prove that **NO** Philistines lived in Canaan in the time of Abraham. (See G.E. Wright, "Fresh Evidence for the Philistine Story," in *Biblical Archaeologist*, Sept. 1966, pp. 70-74.)

4. *Abraham tested* (Gen. 22). The LORD *tests* His people (Gen. 22:1; Jer. 11:30; 1 Thess. 2:4). God's test of Abraham revealed, as nothing else could have, the depth of the faith of Abraham. (Our tests reveal our depth!)

Abraham was sent to the "region (lit., *land*) of *Moriah*" to offer Isaac as a burnt offering on one of the mountains there. King Solomon built the temple of the Lord on Mt. *Moriah*, where David had purchased the threshing floor of Ornan the Jebusite (2 Chr. 3:1). It is commonly believed that the mount of Moriah where Abraham almost sacrificed Isaac is the same place where Solomon built his temple (and the Dome of the Rock now is). This may be true, but it is not a certainty. Abraham saw the place "in the distance" (22:4). This description of the distance is quite vague, but one cannot see Mt. Moriah from more than about a half mile away because it is surrounded by higher hills.

Abraham believed that he would return with Isaac — alive. God had promised that Abraham's offspring would be reckoned through Isaac. Isaac as yet had no children. God's promises never fail; but dead men do not beget sons. Therefore if he killed Isaac, God would of necessity bring him back to life (Heb. 11:19). Abraham had faith that great at a time when no human had ever yet come back from the dead (as far as we know).

Abraham and Isaac went to Moriah TOGETHER (22:6). They came back TOGETHER (22:19).

According to Josephus Isaac was then twenty-five years old. Isaac yielded himself to be sacrificed when his father told him it was God's command (*Antiquities*, I, xiii, 1-4). We do not know whether these statements are true or not.

On the way to the sacrifice Isaac asked, "Where is the lamb for a burnt offering?" Abraham answered, "God will *provide for Himself* the lamb" (NKJV). This translation is supported by the Greek and Latin versions. The Revised English Bible reads, "God will provide himself with a sheep." This wording directs our minds to Christ Jesus, whom God provided to the world and to Himself as an offering and sacrifice on our behalf.

The Angel of the LORD stopped Abraham as he sent forth his hand and took the knife to kill his son, his only son, whom he loved. The Angel of the LORD is almost certainly the same divine being who later came to earth as the man Jesus. See special study "The Angel of the LORD" (p. 364).

When the Angel said, "Now I know that you fear God, because you have not withheld from me your son," the Angel was not indicating that He did not know all secrets, even the future. Rather, he then *knew* Abraham's faith by the demonstration of it, by experience with it. Compare Judges 2:22.

Abraham called the name of the place where the ram was provided as a substitute for Isaac *The LORD will provide*, or *The LORD will SEE* (22:14). The Hebrew name is *Yahweh-yireh* (or *Jehovah-jireh*).

Genesis 22:18 (& 12:3) – The Greatest Prophecy in the Old Testament.

(The gospel of Christ is the fulfillment of God's promise to Abraham in Genesis 22:18. See notes on Gen. 12:1-3.)

God promised Abraham that his descendants would take possession of the cities (literally, the *gate*) of their enemies (22:17). When conquerors captured the gates of the cities of their enemies, the cities were doomed. God's people have always been at war with the forces of evil. Through God's heroes — like Abraham, Isaac, and Rebekah (24:60), and Jesus (the *offspring* of Abraham) — God's righteous kingdom shall rule over all.

Jesus is the offspring (seed) of Abraham through whom all nations on earth will be blessed.

"The Scripture does not say 'and to seeds,' meaning many people, but 'and to your *seed*,' meaning one person, who is Christ" (Gal. 3:16, quoting Gen. 22:18; emphasis added).

Abraham appears to have been in the land of the Philistines (Gerar?) when the call came to him to go and sacrifice Isaac. After that event Abraham dwelt at *Beersheba* for the rest of his life (22:19), except for the burial of Sarah at Hebron (Gen. 23). He lived at Beersheba about fifty years. Genesis 26:33 indicates there was a "city" at Beersheba in the time of Isaac. No traces of a *city* at Beersheba before about 1000 B.C. have yet been found, but some remains may yet be discovered.

At Beersheba Abraham learned of the family of his brother Nahor, who lived up in the Haran area of north Mesopotamia. Nahor's wife Milcah had borne him eight sons! The names of Nahor's son Bethuel and Bethuel's daughter *Rebekah* soon became prominent in the story of God's chosen family (Gen. 22:20-24; 24:24).

5. *The death and burial of Sarah* (Gen. 23). Sarah was absent from their residence at Beersheba when she died at Hebron. Abraham "went to mourn" for her, and to bury her. He purchased a cave and field for a burial place. He paid four hundred shekels, the first asking price, for the place. (Jacob later bought a farm for a hundred pieces of silver. Gen. 33:19). This cave became the burial place for three couples — Abraham and Sarah, Isaac and Rebekah, and Jacob and Leah.

This cave — called the cave of Machpelah — and the enclosure and mosque above it are still major landmarks at Hebron, and sacred to Jews and Arabs alike. (An interesting article about the cave is in *Biblical Archaeology Review*, May–June 1985, pp. 26-43.)

The large amount of information about *Sarah* in Genesis shows she was a person of great importance.

a. Sarah was willing to leave a nice house in Ur to spend

the rest of her life living in tents (Heb. 11:9).

b. Sarah was loyal to Abraham in spite of his half-lies about her being his sister.

c. Sarah sometimes expressed very strong feelings (Gen. 16:5; 21:9-10).

d. Sarah wanted a son for Abraham so much that she offered Hagar to bear the son (16:1-2). By doing this she ran ahead of God, and caused herself a lot of trouble.

e. Sarah was a good cook, and able to care for unexpected guests (Gen. 18:6; Prov. 31:10, 15).

f. Sarah really believed she would bear a son, and she did (Heb. 11:11).

6. *Rebekah, wife for Isaac* (Gen. 24). Abraham desired strongly that his son Isaac marry one of his own relatives and NOT marry from the daughters of the Canaanites. (We also should marry "in the Lord" [1 Cor. 7:39].) This was a carrying out of the principle of *separation*. See notes on Genesis 12:1-3.

Abraham's servant set out with ten camels for *Aram Naharaim* – Syria of the Two Rivers — to the town of Nahor (Haran?). At the well he prayed for the LORD to direct him to the right maiden. His prayer was answered "before he had finished praying" (24:15). The beautiful virgin Rebekah appeared, and offered to draw water for his ten camels. (That was perhaps fifty gallons of water.)

When the servant identified himself, Rebekah *ran* and told her family about these things (24:28). Rebekah's brother *Laban* is introduced at this time (24:29).

The servant of Abraham was faithful in his assignment, and quickly revealed his mission (24:33-49). The family agreed to the marriage proposal (24:51).

Throughout her life Rebekah showed great energy and efficiency — a whiz-bang person. She quickly made the decision to pack up and depart the next day with Abraham's servant (24:58). She was an excellent cook (27:9), and seamstress (27:16). She was overly ambitious for her son Jacob.

When Rebekah left home the family blessed her and said, "Our sister, may you increase to thousands upon thousands; may your offspring *possess the gates of their enemies*" (24:60).

These words are like those the Angel of the LORD spoke to Abraham at Mt. Moriah (22:17). Through people like Rebekah, God's battle will be won upon earth.

Rebekah's maids and her nurse, Deborah, accompanied her on her trip to meet Isaac (Gen. 24:61; 34:8). She was a blessing to people for many years.

Rebekah was presented to Isaac with dignity (24:62-66). Isaac brought her into the tent of his mother Sarah (who had been dead three years [17:17; 23:1; 25:20]). "So she became his wife, and he loved her; and Isaac was comforted after his mother's death" (24:67).

The marriage of Rebekah to Isaac has similarities to the presentation of the church to Christ as His bride. She is sought for. She comes willingly, even eagerly. She comes as a pure virgin. She comes to stand with the all-conquering groom (2 Cor. 11:2; Rev. 19:7-8; Eph. 5:25-27).

7. *The death of Abraham* (Gen. 25:1-11). Sarah died when Abraham was 137 years old, and he died at age 175. After Sarah's death he took another wife named *Keturah*. She bore him six children, the most famous being *Midian* (25:2). The Midianites in later years had conflicts with Israel, especially in the time of Gideon (Judg. 6:1-6).

Genesis 25:6 mentions "concubines" of Abraham. Abraham gave "gifts" to their sons, and sent them away to the East, the deserts of Arabia and nearby, away from his son Isaac. Abraham left everything he owned to Isaac.

Abraham died at a good old age, "an old man and *full.*" (The phrase "of years" is not in the Hebrew.) What is needed for a life to be *full?* Such things as faith in God, fellowship with God, fellowship with family, experiences of hardships and success, and hope in this life and for eternity — all these are necessary.

Abraham in his lifetime often confessed to his Philistine neighbors or others that he was only an alien and a sojourner on earth (Heb. 11:13-16). He looked for a better country — a heavenly one, where Abel and Enoch and Noah and Sarah had gone.

We can join Abraham in the life to come, and be at

"Abraham's side" (bosom) (Luke 16:22). "Many will come from the east and the west, and will take their places at the feast with Abraham, Isaac and Jacob in the kingdom of heaven" (Matt. 8:11).

8. *The account of Ishmael* (Gen. 25:12-18). Ishmael had twelve sons. They lived from Havilah to Shur, near the border of Egypt. Havilah was probably a place in southern Arabia. (See Gen. 10:29; 1 Sam. 15:7).

Ishmael's descendants "lived in hostility toward all their brothers" (25:18). This translation has been influenced by the prophecy in Genesis 16:12. Literally 25:18b reads, "before (or upon) the face (presence) of all his brothers he fell." (Did Ishmael die a violent death?)

Questions on Section C
Life of Abraham: Birth of Isaac until Death of Abraham
(Gen. 21:1–25:18)

1. What was the name of Abraham's son, and the meaning of his name? (21:3,6; 17:19)
2. What was the age of Abraham at the birth of his son? (21:5)
3. What was done to Hagar and Ishmael when Isaac was weaned? Why? (21:9-10)
4. How did God save Hagar and Ishmael? (21:19)
5. Where did Ishmael's wife come from? (21:21)
6. In (or through) what person was Abraham's seed to be reckoned (or called)? (21:12)
7. Why did Abimelech seek to make a covenant with Abraham? (21:22-23)
8. Concerning what did Abraham complain to Abimelech? (21:25)
9. Why was a well called *Beersheba*? (21:31)
10. How did God test Abraham? (22:1-2)
11. Where did the test take place? (22:2)
12. What question of Isaac surely pained Abraham deeply? (22:7-8)
13. Was Abraham willing to do everything God commanded? (22:10)
14. What animal was provided as a substitute offering? (22:13)
15. What did Abraham call the place? (22:14)

16. What blessings were promised to Abraham because he was willing to offer Isaac? (22:17-18)
17. Who was to be blessed in Abraham's offspring? (22:18)
18. How many children did Milcah bear to Nahor? (22:23)
19. Where did Sarah die? (23:2)
20. From whom did Abraham purchase a burial ground? (23:8-10)
21. What sort of property did he buy? (23:17)
22. Who was sent to find a wife for Isaac? (24:2-3)
23. Where was he sent? (24:4,10)
24. What sign did the servant ask God to show him to identify the right woman? (24:14)
25. What woman was found as a wife for Isaac? (24:15)
26. Who was her father, and who was her brother? (24:15,29)
27. How was Isaac related to his wife? (24:24;11:27-29)
28. How long did the servant stay at the girl's house? (24:54-56)
29. Where was Isaac when he met his bride? (24:62)
30. Why did Isaac take the woman to Sarah's tent? (24:67)
31. Who became Abraham's wife in his old age? (25:1)
32. How many children did Abraham have by this wife? (25:2)
33. How were this woman's children treated differently from Isaac? (25:5-6)
34. How long did Abraham live? (25:7)
35. Where was Abraham buried? By whom? (25:9)

Section D
Isaac (Genesis 25:19–28:9)

The "account" of Ishmael's descendants (25:12–18) is followed at once by the "account" of Isaac (25:19). This is typical of the way the book of Genesis presents its material. Genesis repeatedly presents information about a whole family or topic by giving a brief summary or genealogical list. Then it NARROWS DOWN the subject to one person in the chosen line, and gives the story of that one person and his family.

Genesis 1 tells of the whole earth, and then Genesis 2 narrows down the subject to MAN only. Genesis 4 deals with ALL the descendants of Adam, but chapter 5 narrows down the topic to the descendants of Seth only. Genesis 10 listed all of the family of Noah; but Genesis 11 narrows the subject to the descendants of Shem. Genesis 36 tells of Esau's family, but the following chapters tell only of Jacob's family. (This arrangement of material probably indicates that Genesis was put together by one author.)

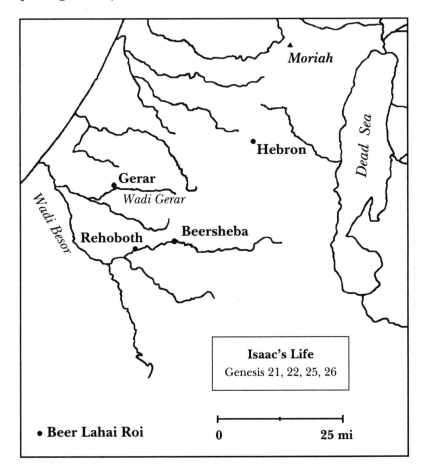

Life of Isaac
1. *Gerar*
   a. Birth; Gen. 20:1-21:7
   b. Rejection of Ishmael; 21:8-21

2. *Beersheba*
   a. Boyhood home; 21:32-34
3. *Moriah*
   a. Sacrifice of Isaac; 22:1-19
4. *Beersheba*
   a. Death of mother; ch. 23
5. *Beer Lahai Roi*
   a. Marriage to Rebekah; ch. 24
6. Trip to *Hebron* and back
   a. Death and burial of Abraham; 25:7-10
7. *Beer Lahai Roi*
   a. Birth of twin sons; 25:11,19-26
   b. Birthright sold; 25:27-34
8. *Gerar*
   a. Lie about Rebekah; 26:1-11
   b. Great crops and herds; 26:12-17
   c. Disputed wells; 26:18-21
9. *Rehoboth*
   a. Undisputed well; 26:22
10. *Beersheba*
    a. Covenant with Abimelech; 26:26-33
    b. Esau's wives; 26:34-35
    c. Blessing given to Jacob; ch. 27
    d. Jacob sent away; 28:1-5
11. *Hebron*
    a. Reunion with Jacob; 35:27
    b. Death and burial of Isaac; 35:28-29

1. *The account of Isaac and his sons* (Gen. 25:19-34). Isaac's wife Rebekah bore twin sons after twenty years of childless marriage, and after Isaac made supplication to the LORD.

Before the sons were born God said, "The older will serve the younger" (25:23). The apostle Paul used this event as an illustration of God's royal right to choose whom he wishes and place them in positions of His own choice (Rom. 9:10-13; Mal. 1:2-3). We must not say that God is unjust or partial in these choices, even if we do not know His reasons for the choices.

Isaac — A type (symbol) of Christians *(Gal. 4:21-31; Gen. 21–27)*		
Similarities	**Isaac**	**Christians**
1. A child born through promise	Gen. 18:9-14; Rom. 4:16-21	Gal. 4:28
2. A son of Abraham	Gen. 21:2-3	Gal. 3:29; Rom. 4:12,16
3. His birth brought joy. (*Isaac* means *laughter.*)	Gen. 21:6	Acts 8:8,39; Luke 15:7
4. Born free!	Gen. 21:10	Gal. 4:31
5. Saved by a substitute sacrifice	Gen. 22:13	Heb. 9:23-26
6. Peaceable	Gen. 26:18-22	Rom. 12:18
7. Persecuted	Gen. 21:9	Gal. 4:29
8. Received inheritance	Gen. 25:5-6	Gal. 4:30; 1 Pet. 1:3-4

The older twin son was born red and hairy. His name *Esau* means hairy, rough. The younger son was born with his hand grasping his brother's heel. His name *Jacob* comes from the Hebrew word for *heel* and could be translated "heel-grabber" or "supplanter" (one who takes over the place of another). On several occasions Jacob took over privileges or honors that Esau might customarily have had because he was the firstborn.

When they grew up Jacob and Esau were quite different in the ways they lived. Esau was a hunter, and Jacob was a home-boy, a mother's boy (25:27-28).

One day Esau came home from hunting quite hungry. Jacob was cooking red lentil stew. Esau asked for stew, and Jacob said, "First sell me your *birthright*" (25:31). Esau talked as if he were starving, though he could not actually have been at death's door if he was still up walking about. Esau despised (scorned) his birthright, and sold it for a single meal (Heb. 12:16-17).

The *birthright* bestowed certain benefits and honors upon its owner. He became head of the family when the father died. He received twice as much inheritance as his brothers (Gen. 48:22). In the family of Abraham and Isaac the birthright carried the rich spiritual promise that "in your offspring all the nations of the earth will be blessed." Esau cared for none of these things. He was a "godless" or "profane" man, interested only in his stomach and the excitement of a hunt. Jacob may have been overly ambitious and possibly even a bit unscrupulous. But Jacob was interested in the spiritual realities, while Esau disdained them. The Scripture criticizes Esau and not Jacob.

2. *Isaac and Abimelech* (Gen. 26). Isaac found himself in conflict with his Philistine neighbors, as had his father Abraham.

Isaac sojourned in the land of the Philistines around Gerar (where he was born) because of famine around Beer Lahai Roi. The king named Abimelech that Isaac met was not the same Abimelech that Abraham had been with eighty years before.

The LORD gave to Isaac the same promise that He gave to Abraham — that all nations would be blessed by his offspring (26:4).

Isaac told the same lie about Rebekah that Abraham had told about Sarah — that she was his sister (26:7). Sons have often have imitated the sins of their fathers. God protected Isaac from the consequences of his words, as He had protected Abraham.

Isaac became very wealthy because the LORD blessed his harvests (26:12). (All wealth is ultimately derived from the earth, which God has created.) The Philistines, in envy and fear, stopped up all the wells that Abraham had dug (26:15). Isaac reopened the wells (a hard, disagreeable task), and dug some new ones.

Isaac would not fight or risk his life for a well. He dug two wells the Philistines claimed, but a third one was uncontested.

The WELLS of ISAAC

1. **ESEK** (Gen. 26:20) — Its name meant *CONTENTION*.
2. **SITNAH** (Gen. 26:21) — Its name meant *HOSTILITY*, or *ENMITY*. (This name is related to the name *Satan*.)
3. **REHOBOTH** (Gen. 26:22) — Its name meant *ROOMS* (broad open spaces).
4. **SHIBAH** (Gen. 26:33) — The name means *SEVEN* (21:30), and comes also from the verb *to SWEAR* (21:31). *Shibah* is part of the name of Beersheba.

Esau married two Hittite women, who were a grief of mind to Isaac and Rebekah (26:34-35; 27:46). These marriages showed that Esau was not devoted to the family faith as his grandfather Abraham had been, and was therefore not entitled to the blessing.

3. *Jacob gets the blessing* (Gen. 27:1-40). It was common in Bible times for fathers to bestow their goods to their sons by a spoken (oral) will (testament). Jacob did this with his sons and Joseph's sons (48:9). King David spoke his final wishes to his son Solomon. Isaac sought to give such an oral blessing to his son Esau. Once spoken it was considered unchangeable.

Isaac had become nearly blind, but he was not near death (27:2). He was still alive more than twenty years later when Jacob returned from Paddan Aram (35:27).

By deception Rebekah and Jacob obtained for Jacob the blessing Isaac intended for Esau. Isaac was suspicious, but was deceived. Isaac's words have become a proverb to describe suspicious actions:

**"The voice is the voice of Jacob,
but the hands are the hands of Esau" (Gen. 27:22).**

Isaac blessed Jacob with the riches of the land (27:28). When Esau came in to Isaac with tasty food, Isaac suffered shock and trembled greatly (27:33). When Esau cried out for a blessing, his father did bestow a blessing upon him:

115

"Lo! of the fat parts of the earth shall be thy dwelling" (Gen. 27:39. Rotherham's *Emphasized Bible,* 1897).

Esau's blessing was much less than Jacob's; and Jacob was still to be Esau's lord (27:37). Nonetheless, Esau did get a blessing, and the blessing was not meaningless. Both the blessing to Jacob and the blessing to Esau have the same Hebrew words in the phrases "of earth's riches" (27:28) and "from the earth's riches" (27:39). The land where Esau and his descendants settled was in the Mt. Seir region southeast of the Dead Sea. The area is mountainous, but the high mountains cause condensation of moisture so that rain falls and sometimes snow. This waters the valleys between the mountains, so that the area is productive.

JACOB DID NOT NEED TO RESORT TO TRICKERY TO GET ISAAC'S BLESSING.

1. God had protected his grandfather, Abraham (Gen. 20:2-3).
2. God prevented Isaac from going to Egypt, and protected him in the land of the Philistines (26:2-3). Somehow God would have prevented Isaac from giving Esau the blessing.
3. God protected Jacob from Laban (Gen. 31:24).
4. Jacob himself declared later that God was with him, even when he did not know it (Gen. 28:15-16).

What were the consequences of Jacob's trickery?

1. Fear of detection by his father (Gen. 27:11-12)
2. Enmity from Esau (27:41)
3. Need to flee from home (27:43-45)
4. Never saw his mother again after he left home.
5. Involvement with dishonest Laban (31:38-41)
6. In danger of losing his life (32:6,11)

Though Jacob did wrong acts (as we all do), he was fundamentally a man of faith. Though Esau appears to have gotten a raw deal, he was basically a man of earthly and selfish interests only.

4. *Jacob flees to Laban* (Gen. 27:41–28:9). Rebekah planned at once to send Jacob from home to her brother Laban at Haran (27:43). Rebekah spoke to Isaac of her fear that Jacob would do as Esau had done and marry one of the women of the land of Canaan. Isaac sent Jacob away to the land of *Paddan Aram*, to Laban, the son of Bethuel and brother of Rebekah. *Paddan Aram* means the Field (or land) of Aram (= Syria).

Rebekah did foretell correctly that Esau's fury against Jacob would subside (27:44). Many years later the brothers were reunited with a great display of affection (33:4).

After Jacob left the family home, Esau went and married two more women, this time from the family of Ishmael. It is not plain whether Esau did this to show spite toward his mother and father or to placate them by marrying some women more closely related to their family. (Perhaps both motives were involved.)

Questions on Section D
Isaac (Gen. 25:19–28:9)

True or False? Correct all false statements.
1. Isaac was forty years old when he married Rebekah (Gen. 25:20).
2. Rebekah was barren thirty years after marriage (25:20,26).
3. Rebekah had twin boys (25:24).
4. God said the younger son would serve the older (25:23).
5. Esau was a quiet man, staying at home in tents (25:27).
6. The name *Edom* means *red*, and was given to Esau (25:30).
7. Jacob sold his birthright for some red stew (25:30,33).
8. Jacob despised his birthright (25:34).
9. Abimelech was king of Philistines at Gerar (26:1).
10. Isaac went into Egypt because of famine (26:7).
11. Isaac told a lie similar to one told by Abraham (26:1).
12. Isaac suffered famine around Gerar (26:1,12).
13. The Philistines and Isaac got along well (26:15-16,27).
14. Esek and Sitnah were Isaac's sons (26:20-21).
15. *Rehoboth* means *room* (26:22).

16. God appeared to Isaac in Beersheba (26:23-24).
17. Abimelech made a treaty with Isaac (26:28,31).
18. Esau married two Amalekite women (26:34).
19. Esau sent Isaac to take wild game (27:1-3).
20. Rebekah desired that Jacob get the blessing (27:5-10).
21. Rebekah put Esau's clothing on Jacob (27:15).
22. Isaac heard the voice of Esau, but felt the hands of Jacob (27:22).
23. Isaac made Jacob lord over his brothers (27:29).
24. Esau came in soon after Jacob left (27:30).
25. Isaac took back the blessing pronounced on Jacob (27:33,37).
26. Esau soon forgave Jacob (27:41).
27. Rebekah planned to send Jacob to her brother Laban (27:43).
28. Isaac agreed with Rebekah's plan to send Jacob away (28:1-2).
29. Esau married the daughter of Israel (28:9).

Section E
The Family of Jacob (Genesis 28:10–36:43; ch. 38)

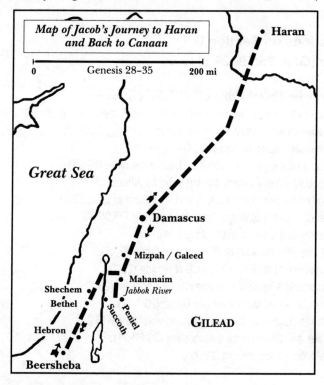

118

Life and Journeys of Jacob

1. *Beer Lahai Roi* (Gen. 25:19-34)
   a. Birth of Jacob and Esau
   b. Birthright sold
2. *Gerar* (26:1-21)
   a. Accompanies parents
3. *Rehoboth* (26:22)
   a. Accompanies parents
4. *Beersheba* (26:23–28:9)
   a. The LORD's appearance, and the covenant with Abimelech
   b. Esau's two wives
   c. Jacob gets blessing (ch. 27)
   d. Jacob sent away (28:1-9)
5. *Bethel* (28:10-22)
   a. Jacob's dream
6. *Haran* (29:1–31:21)
   a. Jacob's dealings with Laban
   b. Jacob's wives and children
7. *Mizpah* (31:22-25)
   a. Final meeting with Laban
8. *Mahanaim* (32:1-21)
   a. Meeting with angels
   b. Preparations to meet Esau
9. *Peniel* (32:22–33:16)
   a. Wrestling with angel (32:22-32)
   b. Meeting with Esau (33:1-16)
10. *Succoth* (33:17)
    a. House and shelters built
11. *Shechem* (33:18–35:5)
    a. Purchase of ground (33:18-20)
    b. Sin of Shechem (ch. 34)
    c. Sent to Bethel (35:1-5)
12. *Bethel* (35:6-15)
    a. Altar built
    b. Deborah dies
    c. The blessing of God
13. *Bethlehem* (35:16-20)
    a. Benjamin born; Rachel dies
14. *Hebron* (35:21–45:28)
    a. Sin of Reuben (35:21-22)
    b. Death of Isaac
    c. Descendants of Esau (ch. 36)
    d. The story of Joseph (37:1–45:28)
15. *Beersheba* (46:1-7)
    a. God appears to Jacob
16. *Egypt* (46:8–50:6)
    a. Jacob's family in Egypt
17. *Hebron* (50:7-13)
    a. Burial of Jacob

1. *Jacob's dream at Bethel* (Gen. 28:10-22). Jacob's flight from Beersheba to Bethel was at least sixty-five miles. Bethel (Luz) was ten or twelve miles north of Jerusalem. Jacob travelled to Bethel apparently without a stop. He was exhausted and felt alone. Jacob later said, "I had only my staff" in the early part of his journey (Gen. 32:10). Perhaps he had left home "out the back door," so Esau would not see him depart.

At Bethel Jacob lay down with a stone under his head. He dreamed of a stairway (or ladder) with angels ascending and descending on it, and above it stood the LORD. In that lonely place the LORD appeared to Jacob and gave to him the same glorious promise that He had given to Abraham and Isaac.

> **"All peoples on earth will be blessed through you and your offspring"** (Gen. 28:14).

Because of God's promise to Jacob, the descendants of Abraham are also called the "children of *Israel*." (Jacob was later named *Israel* [32:28].) The New Testament refers to Christians as "Israel" (Gal. 6:16; Phil. 3:3; James 1:1).

Jacob had thought that he was in a God-forsaken place. But he discovered that he was in the very House of God. Jacob named the place Beth-el, which means **HOUSE OF GOD**.

Jacob promised that the LORD would be his God, and that he would give a tenth of all that God gave to him. All of us need to make a similar commitment.

Jacob's Ladder – A Type (symbol) of Christ Jesus		
Similarities	**Jacob's ladder**	**Jesus Christ**
1. Heaven opened to view	Gen. 28:12	John 1:51; Matt. 3:16
2. Ladder reached to earth	Gen. 28:12	John 12:46
3. Ladder reached to God	Gen. 28:12	1 Pet. 3:18
4. Angels of God ascending and descending	Gen. 28:12	John 1:51; Heb. 1:6; Luke 2:9,13
5. A place of blessing	Gen. 28:14-15	Eph. 1:3
6. Gate of heaven	Gen. 28:17	John 10:9; Rom. 5:2
7. Tithing commitment	Gen. 28:22	Acts 2:44-45; 4:32

2. *Jacob's arrival at Haran* (Gen. 29:1-14). Upon his arrival at Haran, Jacob was informed that Laban's daughter *Rachel* was coming to the well with the sheep. Jacob tried to arrange a private meeting with Rachel, but the local shepherds made a flimsy excuse about why they could not leave. Jacob kissed his

cousin (Rachel) and then introduced himself. Rachel's father (Laban) embraced Jacob and brought him to his home.

3. *Jacob marries Leah and Rachel* (Gen. 29:14-30). Jacob stayed with Laban a month, and had said nothing about going back home. Laban perceived that Jacob was not a temporary visitor and requested that Jacob might work for him. Jacob agreed to work for him for seven years in return for his younger daughter, Rachel.

The seven years of service passed in dream-like hope. The marriage day came. Laban performed a huge deceit upon Jacob and gave him Rachel's older sister, Leah. (She must have been veiled and about the same size as Rachel.) Leah was a worthy woman, but no man had sought her, perhaps because of her weak eyes.

One week later Laban gave Rachel to Jacob, but then asked Jacob to work seven more years for her. Jacob had gained a reputation for trickery by deceiving Esau and his father. But Jacob met his match for trickery in Laban.

Jacob was not a young man when he met Rachel. He was about seventy-seven years old then, and their son Joseph was born when Jacob was ninety-one. (See Gen. 37:3.) Joseph was thirty-nine when Jacob's family moved to Egypt. Jacob was then one hundred and thirty years old (Gen. 47:9; 41:46,53; 45:6).

4. *Jacob's children* (Gen. 29:31–30:24). In the seven years following Jacob's marriages twelve children were born, eleven sons and a daughter. There was much jealousy between Leah and Rachel, and rivalry for Jacob's attention. Both Leah and Rachel had a maidservant, and the maidservants bore four of Jacob's children. The evils of polygamy were clearly experienced.

Jacob's sons became the ancestors of large families (tribes) called the Twelve Tribes of Israel. Many Bible critics do not accept as fact that the Israelite people nearly all came from a common ancestor, but that is the Biblical account of their origin.

Rachel suffered the humiliation of bearing no child until all the other children were born (except Benjamin). Then she bore *Joseph*, who became Jacob's favorite son and saved his family during a famine.

JACOB'S WIVES AND CHILDREN What their names meant			
LEAH's children	**Bilhah's**	**Zilpah's**	**RACHEL's**
1 *Reuben* — "Behold! a son!"	5 *Dan* — "Vindicated"	7 *Gad* — "Good Fortune!"	11 *Joseph* — "Add"
2 *Simeon* — "Heard"	6 *Naphtali* — "Struggle"	8 *Asher* — "Happy"	12 *Benjamin* — "Son of right hand"
3 *Levi* — "Attached"			
4 *Judah* — "Praise"			
9 *Issachar* — "Hired"			
10 *Zebulun* — "Habitation"			
Dinah — (daughter)			

5. *Jacob's flocks increase* (Gen. 30:25-43). After completing the required years of service for his wives, Jacob worked for Laban six more years. As his pay he agreed to take only the speckled and spotted sheep that would be born. This would be five to ten percent of an average herd. Laban continually tried to take advantage of Jacob. He took away the spotted breeding animals from Jacob. He changed their agreement "ten times" (an indefinite large number) (31:7). Jacob retaliated by causing the animals to breed in front of tree branches cut and peeled to show speckles. Jacob acquired great herds and flocks (30:42-43). We believe this happened by the blessing of God, not by breeding tricks based on superstition that Jacob practiced. God blessed Jacob in spite of his deeds and not because of them.

6. *Jacob flees from Laban* (Gen. 31). Laban grew more and more selfish, malicious and disagreeable. Even his daughters said to Jacob, "Not only has he sold us, but he has used up what was used to pay for us" (31:15). Leah and Rachel were quite willing to leave their homeland and flee away with Jacob when Laban was away. Laban lost the love of his family. The Hebrew wording is very expressive: "And Jacob stole the heart of Laban the Aramean by not telling him he was fleeing" (31:20). Laban surely felt pain over what he brought upon himself.

Prov. 11:29 — He who brings trouble on his family will inherit only wind.

When Laban discovered that Jacob and his family had fled, he pursued after them seven days. "Then God came to Laban the Aramean in a dream at night and said to him, 'Be careful not to say anything to Jacob, either good or bad'" (31:24). This event shows that God will protect His children. He may let them suffer or even die, but nothing separates them from His love (Rom. 8:38-39).

Rachel had stolen her father's household gods (*teraphim*) when they left (31:19). These were crude statuettes of gods, six to eight inches long. At a place named *Nuzi* in the land east of the Tigris river several such *teraphim* were found. Possession of these images ensured that the owner would be head of the family and heir to the estate! (See Werner Keller, *The Bible As History in Pictures,* New York: Morrow, 1964, p. 55.) The Nuzu discoveries are dated about three centuries after Jacob's time, but the custom was probably similar in Jacob's time.

Laban accused Jacob of stealing his gods (31:30). Jacob knew nothing about Rachel's theft. Laban did not find his gods in Jacob's goods. Jacob told Laban what he thought of him (31:38-42). An offended brother can hardly be won back (Prov. 18:19).

Laban parted from Jacob after they made an unfriendly

covenant. "May the LORD keep watch between you and me when we are away from each other" (31:49). Laban returned home, and never saw his grandchildren again.

7. *Jacob prepares to meet Esau* (Gen. 32:1-21). On his way back to Canaan, Jacob saw the angels of God! Jacob called the place *Mahanaim*, meaning *two camps* (or two groups) — Jacob's camp and the angels' camp. Jacob was a very important person to God.

Jacob sent messengers ahead of him to his brother Esau in the country (*field*) of Edom. Jacob's act of taking Esau's blessing had consequences, even years later. Jacob was told that Esau was coming to meet him with four hundred men. Such an army indicated that WAR was imminent.

In great fear and distress, Jacob divided his family and flocks into groups (32:7-8). He prayed (32:9). He sent groups of goats, sheep, camels, cows, and donkeys ahead of him with their drovers, hoping that these gifts for Esau would pacify him.

8. *Jacob wrestles with God* (Gen. 32:22-31). Beside the brook Jabbok that night Jacob was alone, apart from his family. (The Jabbok "jabs" into the Jordan River valley from the east, about halfway between the Sea of Galilee and the Dead Sea.) There a "man" wrestled with him until daybreak (32:24).

Hosea 12:2-4 says of Jacob, "In the womb he grasped his brother's heel; as a man he *struggled* with God. He *struggled* with the angel and overcame him; he wept and begged for his favor." (The verb *struggled* is the root word of the name *Israel*, which means "he who struggles with God," or *persists*, and *strives* with God.)

Jacob faced a potentially life-destroying situation. After twenty years of frustrating service with Laban, now he must meet Esau! If God did not save Jacob that night, Jacob was doomed — or felt that he was. So Jacob prayed all night, and his prayer was combined with actual physical wrestling with God's "man." (Angels are frequently called *men* in Scripture.) Jacob hung on, and Jacob achieved deliverance. Jacob became an overcomer!

> Jacob received a new name — *ISRAEL* (Gen. 32:28).
> Jacob, the heel-grabber, the supplanter, became **ISRAEL**, "he who strives with God" and "prevails."

Jacob called the place where he wrestled *Peniel*, a name meaning the *face of God*, saying, "It is because I saw *God* face to face, and yet my life is spared" (32:30). (We believe Jacob saw the divine being who later came to earth as Jesus Christ.)

Jacob came back to his camp limping (32:25, 31). But his soul was leaping.

9. *Jacob meets Esau* (Gen. 33). Before he met Esau, Jacob arranged his people so that Rachel and Joseph were in the rear of their column. If Esau massacred those he first met, perhaps he would spare others farther back. Jacob was brave enough to go ahead of his family and face Esau first.

The meeting with Esau was friendly and gracious, amazingly so. Esau offered to leave some of his men to escort Jacob's family. Jacob probably still felt some unease, and declined the offer.

After Esau's departure, Jacob journeyed on to *Succoth* near the Jordan River. The name *Succoth* means *booths* or *shelters*. There Jacob built a place (lit., *house*) for himself and made shelters (*sukkoth*) for his livestock. The location of Succoth is a mound now named Tell Deir 'allah, east of Jordan, seven miles from where the Jabbok now enters the Jordan. (See the *International Standard Bible Encyclopedia* [Rev. Ed., 1988], article "Succoth.")

Jacob must have stayed at Succoth about five years or more. When he left Laban's home, Dinah was only about seven years old. When Jacob arrived at Shechem, Dinah was old enough that the men there wanted her in marriage (34:1-4).

From Succoth Jacob moved his family across the Jordan into the land of Canaan, and came to *Shechem*, where his grandfather Abraham had camped first. There at Shechem Jacob purchased the first land he owned (33:19). There he dug a deep well through bedrock (John 4:11-12). There he set up an altar, and called it *El Elohe Israel*, meaning God, the

God of Israel. In later years Jacob sent his son Joseph to Shechem to see about his brothers (37:12-13).

Shechem lay between Mt. Ebal and Mt. Gerizim. Jacob arrived at Shechem about 1900 B.C. There was not a great fortified city there when Jacob came (34:10), but it developed into a strong city during the century that followed.

While Jacob was absent from his land, it appears that squatters settled upon it, so that Jacob had to take it back by fighting with his sword and bow (Gen. 48:22).

10. *Dinah and the Shechemites* (Gen. 34). At Shechem Jacob's daughter, Dinah, suffered the humiliation of being raped by *Shechem*, the young prince of the country. Literally, he *humbled* her. (Compare Deut. 22:28-29.)

We are surprised to read that after violating the young woman, he was attracted to her and wanted to get her as a wife (34:12). Shechem showed no sense of guilt.

When Dinah's brothers heard of this, they were filled with grief and fury. This was "a thing that should not be done" (34:7). That appears to be a parenthetical remark by the author of Genesis. We have no record of what rules or laws God had given to the patriarchs about sexual conduct. They clearly had some limits that were generally accepted (34:31). The law of Moses set strict rules about sexual conduct. See Leviticus 18 & 20; 19:29; Deuteronomy 22.

Shechem's father's name was *Hamor* (meaning a male donkey). He earnestly sought to obtain Dinah as wife for his son. "Make the price for the bride and the gift I am to bring as great as you like, and I'll pay whatever you ask me" (34:12). Meanwhile the girl was still detained at his house (34:26).

The eagerness of the Canaanites to take Dinah shows the constant temptations the Israelites were under to merge with the Canaanites in a permissive society. The separation principle that Abraham lived by was incomprehensible to the Canaanites.

Jacob's sons Simeon and Levi slaughtered the men of Shechem while they were in pain after being circumcised. Jacob did not approve of their violence (34:30).

Jacob had the last word about Simeon and Levi in his final prophecy about his sons. "Cursed be their anger, so fierce, and their fury, so cruel! I will scatter them in Jacob and disperse them in Israel" (49:5-7). The Simeonites were the only tribe that did not receive a blessing in the blessing of Moses (Deut. 33).

11. *Jacob returns to Bethel* (Gen. 35:1-15). God sent Jacob back to Bethel, where He had appeared to him in the dream (28:11-13).

Preparations to go to Bethel:
1. Get rid of the foreign gods with you (Gen. 35:2,4).
2. Purify yourselves.
3. Change your clothes.
(Could these guidelines help us prepare for worship?)

As Jacob set out for Bethel, the terror of God fell upon all the towns around them (35:5). God was a shield to Jacob. We must honor Jacob as God honored him.

At Bethel Jacob built an altar, and set up a stone pillar and poured out a drink offering on it (35:14; Lev. 23:13). God confirmed to Jacob the change of his name to *Israel,* and promised to him the land (35:12).

Deborah, the old nurse of Rebekah, died at Bethel (35:8; 24:61). She was probably the beloved "Nanny" in the family for several generations. She must have been 160 years old.

12. *The deaths of Rachel and Isaac* (Gen. 35:16-29). Though God had protected Jacob for many years, his beloved wife Rachel died in childbirth as the family journeyed toward Bethlehem. (Bethlehem is six miles south of Jerusalem.) Her death occurred some distance (ten miles?) north of Bethlehem, probably near Ramah (Jer. 31:15; Gen. 48:7). She named the son *Ben-Oni,* meaning *Son of my trouble.* But Jacob called his name *Benjamin,* meaning *Son of my right hand.* (The right hand was considered to bestow a greater blessing than the left hand [Gen. 48:14].)

The tomb of Rachel stands today as a small domed building beside the road at the north edge of Bethlehem.

Jacob's son Reuben lay with his father's concubine Bilhah while they were beyond Migdol Eder (meaning *Tower of the Flock*). Because of this sin Reuben lost his rank as the first-born of the family to Joseph and to Judah (35:21-22; 49:3-4). Joseph received the double portion of land that the firstborn received (1 Chr. 5:1). Judah received the right of ruling over the Israelites.

Jacob was reunited with his elderly father (Isaac) at Hebron (35:17-19). It had been about twenty-five years since he had seen his father. His mother (Rebekah) had died in that time. Isaac died, and his sons Esau and Jacob buried him in the cave of Machpelah (23:19). The family was united at Isaac's death.

13. *The account of Esau* (Gen. 36). Esau, who was also called *Edom* (meaning *red*), moved to a land some distance from his brother Jacob (36:6). His descendants settled in the Mt. Seir region, south and east of the Dead Sea. Esau seems to have accepted the fact that Jacob had received the blessing, so that he could not continue to live where Jacob was. Some things cannot be changed, and must be accepted with grace.

A people called the *Horites* lived in the Mt. Seir region before the Edomites took it over (38:20-21). These were probably the same people known as *Hurrians* in northern Mesopotamia.

Genesis 36 lists many descendants of Esau and the Horites. This indicates that God cares about people from *all* nations. It indicates that God keeps a record of everyone's name. The mention of the discovery of hot springs in the desert (36:24) suggests to our minds that God knows every event in our lives and remembers all of them.

14. *Judah and Tamar* (Gen. 38). Genesis 38 is a distasteful story. It shows the need of God's people for a new nature. The chapter shows God's grace to sinners. We deal with the chapter here because it interrupts the story of Joseph, which began in chapter 37.

Jacob's son Judah begat twin sons by his own daughter-in-law, Tamar. The chosen line of Abraham's descendants continued on through Isaac, Jacob, Judah, and Judah's son *Perez*. Perez and his twin brother (Zerah) were born through deceit and harlotry (Gen. 38:25-26; Matt. 1:3). But Perez became a fleshly ancestor of Jesus our Lord. Jesus does not care whom He is related to, or what His ancestors may have done. He is very willing to call us His "brothers" (Heb. 2:11-12). (See Ruth 4:17-22.)

Why did Judah separate himself from his brothers? (38:1). We do not know for certain. Perhaps he felt uncomfortable around them after they had sold Joseph into slavery (37:26-27). Perhaps they were angry at him.

Genesis 38 shows how great was the danger of contamination that Israel faced from the Canaanites. Judah could "buddy up" with Hirah, a Canaanite. It was easy for Judah to marry the daughter of a Canaanite named Shua. The presence of Canaanite prostitutes in the land (38:15) seems to have been a common sight.

In Genesis 38 we are introduced to the custom of LEVIRATE (pronounced LEVER-ate) marriage. *Levir* is a Latin word meaning brother-in-law. This was "marriage" to the childless widow of a man's brother (or other relative), so that she might bear a child that would be counted as heir to the deceased man. See Deuteronomy 25:5-10. The story of Ruth is based on the Levirate marriage custom, as is also the question of the Sadducees to Jesus in Matthew 22:23-28.

Questions on Section E
The Family of Jacob (Gen. 28:10–36:43; ch. 38)

1. Learn the names of the places on the map of the journeys of Jacob, and at least one event at each place.
2. What was Jacob's dream at Bethel? (Gen. 28:12)
3. What does the name *Bethel* mean? (28:19) What was the place previously called?
4. What were three promises God made to Jacob in the dream? (28:13-15)
5. What did Jacob promise God? (28:22)
6. Where did Jacob meet Rachel? (29:2,6)
7. How was Jacob related to Rachel? (29:10)

8. Who was Rachel's father? Her sister? (29:16)
9. How did Jacob obtain Rachel? (29:20,30)
10. What deception did Laban practice on Jacob? (29:23)
11. Write the names of Jacob's thirteen children, and the mothers of each. (29:32-30:24)
12. How did Jacob acquire great flocks? (30:31-43)
13. How did Jacob and Laban get along together? (31:7)
14. What was Laban doing when Jacob left? (31:19-20)
15. What did Rachel steal? (31:19)
16. What did God tell Laban as he pursued Jacob? (31:24)
17. What made Jacob angry with Laban? (31:36-37)
18. What two names were given to the heap of stones set up between Jacob's and Laban's territories? (31:48-49)
19. What does the name *Mahanaim* mean, and why did Jacob call it that? (32:1-2)
20. How did Jacob prepare to placate Esau before they met? (32:1-21)
21. At what brook did Jacob wrestle? (32:22-24)
22. What were two results of Jacob's wrestling? (32:25-28)
23. What does the name *Israel* mean? (32:28)
24. Did Esau harm Jacob? (33:4,15-16)
25. What does the name *Succoth* mean? (33:17)
26. Where did Jacob first buy property in Canaan? (33:18-19)
27. Who took Dinah? (34:1-2)
28. Who massacred the Shechemites? (34:25-26)
29. How did Jacob react to the massacre? (34:30)
30. Who called Jacob to Bethel? (35:1)
31. Who died at Bethel? (35:8)
32. What was said of Jacob's name at Bethel? (35:10)
33. Where was Benjamin born? (35:16,19)
34. What did Rachel call Benjamin? Why? What does the name mean? (35:18)
35. How did Reuben lose his right as firstborn son? (35:22;49:3-4)
36. Where did Isaac die? (35:27-29)
37. Who was Shuah? (38:2)
38. Who were Judah's first three sons? (38:3-5)
39. Who was Tamar? (38:6)
40. Name Tamar's twin sons. (38:29-30)
41. Who was Judah's son who carried on the chosen line? (Matt. 1:3)

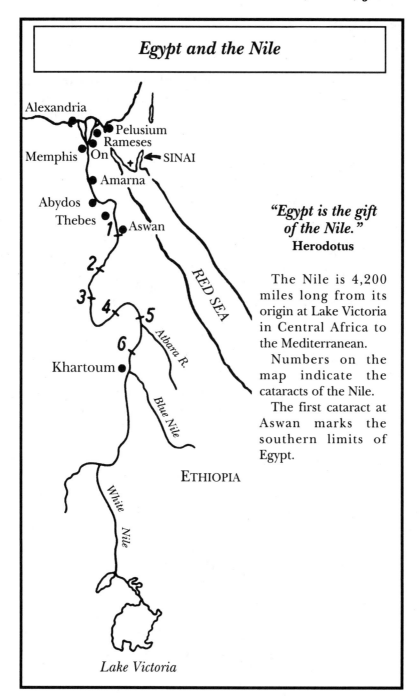

Egypt and the Nile

Alexandria

Pelusium

Rameses

Memphis On

SINAI

Amarna

Abydos

Thebes

Aswan

RED SEA

Albara R.

Khartoum

Blue Nile

ETHIOPIA

White Nile

Lake Victoria

"Egypt is the gift of the Nile."
Herodotus

The Nile is 4,200 miles long from its origin at Lake Victoria in Central Africa to the Mediterranean.

Numbers on the map indicate the cataracts of the Nile.

The first cataract at Aswan marks the southern limits of Egypt.

Section F
Land of Egypt

Beginning with the story of Joseph, the history of God's people Israel becomes inseparably linked with the land of Egypt. It is therefore necessary to present some information about Egypt.

I. NAMES OF EGYPT
  A. *Kem* (or Kemet)
    1. Most ancient name.
    2. Means black land.
    3. Evidently it was the name given to the land by the people themselves.
  B. The *Land of Ham*
    1. See Psalms 78:51; 105:23; 106:22.
    2. Called "the land of Ham" because Mizraim, the son of Ham, moved here.
  C. *Mizraim*
    1. Used over eighty times. Name of Ham's son (Gen. 10:6; 12:10,11,13; 13:1).
    2. Plural (or dual) in form, perhaps because of Egypt's division into Upper and Lower Egypt, or the Nile Valley and the Delta.
  D. *Rahab*
    1. A poetic name for the land.
    2. See Psalms 87:4, 89:10; Isa. 51:9.
  E. *Egypt*
    1. Greek name for the land.
    2. This name was never used by the inhabitants themselves during ancient times.
II. DIVISIONS OF THE LAND OF EGYPT (See Charles Pfeiffer, *Egypt and Exodus*, pp. 11-19.)
  A. According to location (direction)
    1. Southern Egypt from the first cataract (at Aswan) to the Delta is called *Upper Egypt*.
      a. Tableland from one to twenty-four miles in width, hugging the shores of the Nile.

    b. From this fertile valley the Egyptian could look to the east or the west and see barren desert cliffs as high as 1800 feet rimming the valley.

  2. Northern Egypt (the Delta area) is called *Lower Egypt.*

    a. As the Nile waters entered the Delta they divided into a number of branches, only two of which have persisted into modern times, the others having largely dried up.

    b. At its widest extent the Delta extends up to 125 miles. The Delta has the shape of a large triangle with the point at the bottom.

    c. In the Delta grew papyrus plants, which provided the writing material of ancient Egypt.

B. According to the character of the land

  1. Desert

    a. Egypt is 96% desert.

    b. Without the Nile, all would be barren desert.

    c. Rainfall is almost nil, except for the Mediterranean coast area.

  2. Nile Valley

    a. This extends from Aswan to Mediterranean Sea.

    b. It is only two to twelve miles wide, with steep cliffs on both sides.

    c. In Lower Egypt, land of Goshen portion of Delta and was suitable for raising flocks.

    d. A branch of the Nile goes west through a break in the cliffs near Amarna, and drains into a low productive area called the *Faiyum.*

III. THE NILE RIVER

A. Three sources of the Nile

  1. *White Nile*

    a. Flows from Lake Victoria in Central Africa (a tropical area).

    b. Provides a steady source of water throughout the year.

    c. The White Nile flows through grassy land and rocks, and thus it is relatively clean and clear.

      d. The rise in the White Nile from April to November is six feet annually.

  2. *Blue Nile*

      a. Flows from Lake Tana in the Abyssinian plateau (Ethiopian plateau). Joins White Nile at Khartoum.

      b. Very tempestuous, muddy stream.

      c. Rises 26 feet from April to August; causes the Nile to flood.

  3. *Atbara River* (200 miles downstream from Blue Nile)

      a. Only other significant tributary of Nile.

      b. Brings additional flood waters from highlands of Ethiopia.

B. Annual overflow of the Nile

  1. Begins at Aswan at the end of May or the beginning of June.

  2. Continues to rise until early in September.

  3. Remains stationary twelve days at a height of about 36 feet above its ordinary level at Thebes, 25 feet at Cairo, and four feet at its mouth.

  4. Keeps the land fertile as it brings with it new soil.

C. Two principal mouths of the Nile at the Delta

  1. The west mouth: *Rosetta* (Canopic).

  2. The east mouth: *Damietta* (Pelusiac).

D. Cataracts of the Nile

  1. Six cataracts. (These are not falls, but rocky rapids which prevent navigation.)

  2. First cataract at Aswan.

  3. Sixth cataract at Khartoum, where the Blue Nile runs into the White Nile.

E. Miscellaneous information regarding Nile and Nile Valley

  1. Second longest river valley on earth.

  2. Nile is approximately 4200 miles long.

  3. The Nile valley provides Egypt with about 13,300 square miles of cultivable land (about area of Massachusetts and Connecticut). (Total area of Egypt is about 350,000 square miles.)

IV. IMPORTANT CITIES OF EGYPT
  A. In Lower Egypt
    1. *Memphis* (Noph — See Isa. 19:13): one of the ancient capitals in lower Egypt.
    2. *Heliopolis* (city of Sun) — called *On* in Bible (Gen. 41:45). It was a priestly city.
    3. *Rameses* in land of Goshen.
      a. Starting point of Exodus.
    4. *Pelusium*
      a. Also called Sin (Ezek. 30:15,16).
      b. Very obscure as far as history goes.
      c. Alexander the Great fought a battle there.
    5. *Alexandria*
      a. Founded by Alexander the Great around 331 B.C.
      b. Most prominent city in later history.
  B. In Upper Egypt
    1. *Thebes*
      a. Most important city in upper Egypt.
      b. In Bible is called *No* or *No-Amon* (Jer. 46:25).
      c. Long the capital of Egypt.
    2. *Amarna*
      a. Capital of Egypt during the brief time of Akhenaton (1376-1362 B.C.).
V. HISTORY OF EGYPT
  A. Predynastic period (about 3200-2800 B.C. The flood probably was about 3500 B.C.)
    1. Local lords ruled small areas.
    2. Hieroglyphic writing developed.
      a. Picture writing.
      b. Used throughout the history of Egypt.
    3. Earliest settlers domesticated cattle and finally became cultivators of the soil.
  B. Early dynasties, I and II (2800-2600 B.C.)
    1. Local lords in Upper and Lower Egypt were united into one kingdom under King Menes (or Narmer).
    2. Capital at Abydos.
  C. Old Kingdom (Dynasties III-VI, 2600-2150 B.C.)
    1. Capital at Memphis (Noph).

2. Great material progress:
   a. Step Pyramid Sakkara.
   b. Great Pyramid at Giza (481 feet high, on a thir-
      teen-acre base).
   c. Gigantic Sphinx representing King Khephren of
      the Fourth Dynasty.
   d. Approximately seventy pyramids built during
      this period.
3. Breakup of the kingdom near end of 6th century.
   (Intermediate period of breakup and decline.
   Dynasties VII-X, with minor kings at Memphis and
   Thebes.)

D. Middle Kingdom (Dynasties XI-XII, 2050-1720 B.C.)
   1. Reappearance of a powerful centralized govern-
      ment.
   2. Although native to Thebes, the Twelfth Dynasty
      established its capital near Memphis.
   3. Conquests into Palestine.
   4. Literature dealing with religious matters devel-
      oped.
   5. Burials in Valley of the Kings (tombs in cliffs).
   6. Abraham visited Egypt 2090 B.C.
   7. Joseph became ruler about 1883 B.C.

E. Hyksos Period (Second Intermediate period; Dynasties
   XIII-XVII, 1750-1570 B.C.)
   1. Following the Middle Kingdom, there were two
      centuries of disintegration, decline and invasion.
      (History is very obscure.)
   2. The feeble Thirteenth and Fourteenth Dynasties
      were terminated by an invasion of Hyksos warriors.
      The intruders, who possibly came from Asia Minor,
      overpowered the Egyptians by means of horse-
      drawn chariotry and the composite bow, both of
      which were unknown to the Egyptian troops. The
      Hyksos established Avaris in the Delta as their capi-
      tal. However, the Egyptians maintained a sem-
      blance of authority at Thebes. Shortly after 1600
      B.C. the Theban rulers became powerful enough to

expel this foreign power and to establish the
Eighteenth Dynasty, introducing the New
Kingdom. (Adapted from S.J. Schultz, *The O.T.
Speaks* (New York: Harper & Row, 1960, p. 16).

F. New Kingdom (Dynasties XVIII-XXI, 1580-935 B.C.)
   1. Capital at Thebes.
   2. The 18th and 19th dynasties constitute the period of Egypt's greatest glory.
   3. A woman, *Hatshepsut*, was ruler of Egypt 1501–1479 B.C. She may have taken the baby Moses.
   4. Thutmose III (1490-1447) made seventeen campaigns into Palestine and Syria. Perhaps he was the Pharaoh of oppression.
   5. Amenhotep II (1447-1421). Perhaps Pharaoh of the exodus.
   6. Exodus of Israelites — 1446 B.C. (Memorize this date.)
   7. Thutmose IV — non-firstborn ruler, successor of Amenhotep II.
   8. Akhenaton (1376-1362); monotheistic reformer; capital at Amarna.
   9. Tutankhamen (1360-1350); King "Tut."
   10. Seti I (1320-1300); 19th dynasty conqueror.
   11. Rameses II (1300-1234); conqueror and builder; thought by some to be the Pharaoh of the oppression.
       a. Under Rameses IV-XII, the power of the Egyptian kings declined considerably (1167-1085).
       b. At the time of decline, the rule was wrested from the political leaders and placed in the hands of the priestly class.

G. Foreign dynasties (Dynasties XXII-XXV, 935-663)
   1. Shishak (a Libyan) (947-925); 1 Kings 14:25-26.
       a. In Shishak's time (contemporary with King Rehoboam) Egypt again became powerful enough to invade Palestine (926 B.C.).

2. Tirkahah (a Nubian, or Ethiopian) (689-663);
2 Kings 19:9.

H. Native Egyptian dynasties (XXVI-XXVIII, 662-525)
1. Pharaoh Necho (609-593)
   a. King Josiah was slain by Necho as he was going
   to help Assyria against Babylon, 608 B.C. (2 Kgs.
   23:29-30).
   b. Necho made Jehoiakim king of Judah (2 Chr.
   36:4).
2. Pharaoh Hophra (588-567) tried to aid Zedekiah
(Jer. 37:5-7).

I. Persian rule (525-406, 343-332; interrupted by three
Egyptian dynasties). Alexander the Great conquered
Egypt in 331 B.C. (Hellenistic)

J. Period of Ptolemies (323-31 B.C.). The Ptolemies were
Greek rulers descended from one of Alexander's generals.

VI. RELIGION OF EGYPT
A. Egypt was a land of many gods.
1. There was never one religion in Egypt.
2. "With local deities as the basis of religion, Egyptian
gods became numerous" (Schultz, p. 46).
3. The religion was a conglomeration of many ideas
about life, death, nature and the gods.

B. Some of the earliest gods were animal gods.
1. Baboon, cat, cow, hippo, ichneumon fly, cobra, and
others.
2. In later times many of the gods "took" the forms of
these animals, or these animals became sacred to
them.

C. The Egyptians did believe in the immortality of the
soul (called the Ba).
1. Some thought the dead wandered in the cemeteries
seeking food.
2. Some thought the dead went to Osiris for judgment and eternal life.
3. Some thought the dead joined the gods who
floated in the heavenly ocean on boats of the sun.

4. Some thought the dead were carried off by a Hathor cow or bull to wait for the bodily resurrection.

D. The Egyptians had at least three types of gods, but these were often confused in the people's thinking, and the names of gods in one place were taken by residents of other areas.

1. Gods of places
   a. At Memphis: Ptah (creator god, who was incarnate in the sacred Apis bull).
   b. At Thebes: Amon (often confused or combined with the sun god, Re).
   c. At Abydos: Osiris, (god of the underworld); Isis, his wife; their son, Horus.

2. Cosmic gods
   a. Sun god, Re (national deity of Egypt).
   b. Sky goddess, Nut.
   c. Earth god, Geb.

3. Gods responsible for functions of life
   a. Sekhmet, lion-headed goddess of war and disease.
   b. Hathor, cow-goddess of love.
   c. Thoth, Ibis-headed god of wisdom; recorder of gods.

E. A popular religious legend: Osiris was slain by his brother, Seth. Isis found his body, and embalmed and buried it. Osiris revived and became *king of the underworld*. Isis bore Horus to Osiris. Egyptians associated the rising and the falling of the Nile with Osiris' legend. Egyptians desired to be buried at Abydos where Osiris was buried.

For detailed bibliographies on Egypt: See pages 54-55 of *The Old Testament Speaks* by Samuel J. Schultz (New York: Harper and Row Publishers, 1960); *Egypt and the Exodus* by Charles F. Pfeiffer (Grand Rapids: Baker Book House, 1964), pp. 89-91.

Questions on Section F
Land of Egypt

1. List five names for Egypt.
2. Which part of Egypt is called *Lower* Egypt? *Upper* Egypt?
3. What is the Delta of the Nile?
4. What percentage of the land of Egypt is desert?
5. How wide is the Nile valley?
6. What are the three sources of the Nile River?
7. During what months does the Nile overflow each year?
8. What are the *cataracts* of the Nile? How many of them are there?
9. What was the ancient capital in Lower Egypt?
10. What was the most important city in Upper Egypt?
11. Who were the Hyksos? Did they rule while the Israelites were living in Egypt?
12. What woman ruled over Egypt during part of the New Kingdom?
13. Name the Egyptian king who possibly was the pharaoh during the oppression of Israel.
14. Name the Egyptian king who possibly was ruling at the time of the exodus.
15. What date is suggested for the exodus?
16. What did the Egyptians consider necessary for them to do to have immortality?
17. Who was the Egyptian god over the underworld?

Section G
Joseph and Jacob in Egypt (Genesis 37, 39–50)

1. *Joseph's dreams* (Gen. 37:1-11). Jacob and his family lived at Hebron (35:27; 37:1, 14).

Observe that a new section begins at 37:2: "the account (*generations*) of *Jacob*." It extends to the end of Genesis. The section deals mostly with the career of Joseph. The career of Joseph is very significant, but in the larger context Joseph's deeds were the working out of the promises that God gave to Jacob, and to Isaac and to Abraham. So it is proper to call the section "the account of *Jacob*."

Joseph at age seventeen brought to his father an evil

report about his brothers (37:2). They probably deserved correction, but Joseph showed questionable wisdom in giving the report. The brothers of Joseph were also envious of their father's partiality to Joseph.

Joseph had been born to Jacob when he was about ninety-one years old. Jacob gave to Joseph a "richly ornamented robe" (37:3). (Older translations read "coat of many colors." The meaning of the Hebrew phrase is uncertain.) A tomb painting at Beni-Hasan in Middle Egypt shows a group of Asiatics entering Egypt about 1890 B.C. Their leader is wearing a colorful robe with embroidered stripes, perhaps similar to Joseph's robe.

Joseph's dreams were the last straw to his brothers. The meaning of the two dreams was obvious. As the brothers' sheaves of grain bowed down to the sheaf of Joseph, and as the sun, moon, and stars bowed down to Joseph, so Joseph's family would bown down to him. Even Jacob rebuked Joseph for the second dream (37:10). But the dreams were a revelation from God to Joseph. He could not ignore them. The dreams were fulfilled completely (42:6,9).

2. *Joseph sold by his brothers* (Gen. 37:12-36). Joseph was sent by Jacob from Hebron to Shechem (about sixty miles) to see if all was well with his brothers. Joseph did not find the brothers at the Shechem farm of Jacob, and went on to Dothan, twenty miles further, northwest from Shechem. He found the brothers, but they were ready to kill him. They placed him in a cistern (or pit) at Reuben's suggestion (37:21,24; 42:22). They stripped off Joseph's beautiful robe, and sat down to eat.

Dothan was by the road through the valley between Mt. Carmel and Mt. Gilboa. The road came from Gilead east of Jordan. A caravan of Ishmaelites came by, loaded with spices they were taking down to Egypt to sell. Judah urged them to sell Joseph to these Ishmaelites (37:26-27).

There were Midianites travelling with the Ishmaelites (37:28, 36). (The Midianites were descendants of Keturah, Abraham's second wife [Gen. 25:1-2].) The Midianites were closely associated with the Ishmaelites. (See Judges 8:12, 24.)

They travelled together, and fought together, and probably were intermarried.

The Midianite merchants came by where Joseph was in the pit, and (literally) "*they* pulled Joseph up out of the cistern and sold him for twenty shekels of silver to the Ishmaelites." Whether the brothers pulled Joseph up out of the pit or the Midianites did it is unclear. Probably the brothers did not lay their hands on him (37:27).

Joseph pleaded for his life, but his brothers would not listen (42:21).

Joseph's brothers dipped his robe in the blood of a goat. They took the robe back to their father saying, "We found this. Examine it to see whether it is *your son's* robe" (37:32).

Jacob could only assume that Joseph had been torn to pieces by some animal. "In mourning will I go down to the grave (*Sheol*) to my son" (37:35).

> **SHEOL** (= Greek **HADES**, the unseen world) is the place of the dead, both the body and the soul (Ps. 16:10; 49:15).

Joseph was sold in Egypt to Potiphar, one of Pharaoh's officials, the captain of the *guard*. (BDB Lexicon defines *guard* as *bodyguard* [originally, royal *slaughterers*].)

Joseph – An Illustration (type?) of Christ		
Similarities	**Joseph**	**Christ**
1. Both reproved evil	Gen. 37:2	John 7:7
2. Hated by their brothers	Gen. 37:4,11	John 7:5
3. Hated without a cause	Gen. 37:4	John 15:25
4. Sold for the price of a slave	Gen. 37:28	Matt. 26:15; Ex. 21:32
5. Tempted, but triumphant	Gen. 39:7-13	Luke 4:1-12
6. Suffered	Ps. 105:17-18; Gen. 42:21	Heb. 5:8
7. Exalted to second place	Gen. 41:40,43	Phil. 2:9-11; 1 Cor. 15:27

8. Sent to save life	Gen. 45:7	Luke 19:10
9. Forgiving	Gen. 45:14-15	Luke 23:34
10. Searched the hearts of sinners	Gen. 42:9-17,25	Rev. 2:23

3. *Joseph tested in Egypt* (Gen. 39:1-18). "The word of the LORD *tested* (or *proved*) him" (Ps. 105:19).

In Egypt Joseph was *tested* by (1) service as Potiphar's slave (3:2-4); (2) temptations by Potiphar's wife (39:7-10); (3) false accusations by Potiphar's wife (39:14-15); (4) imprisonment (39:20; Ps. 105:17-18); (5) loneliness for his family (43:27-30).

Throughout all his tests Joseph never quit trying to be the best he could possibly be. He was successful wherever he was, for "the LORD was with Joseph." Four times this statement is made (39:2, 3, 21, 23). Others could see that the LORD was with him (39:3).

Joseph would not commit adultery with his master's wife. He said, "How could I do such a wicked thing and sin against *GOD*?" (39:9). Joseph knew that sin hurts GOD even more than it hurts people. Compare Psalm 51:4.

Joseph *fled* from the temptations by Potiphar's wife (39:12).

"*Flee* from sexual immorality" (1 Cor. 6:18).

There is an Egyptian story about two brothers named *Anubis* and *Bata*, which slightly resembles the story of Joseph and Potiphar's wife. Anubis' wife tempted Bata, as Potiphar's wife tempted Joseph. Bata refused her. The Egyptian story is dated about 1225 B.C., six hundred years after the time of Joseph. (See *The Ancient Near East*, Vol 1, J.B. Pritchard, ed., Princeton Univ. Press, 1973, pp. 12-16.)

4. *Joseph, a prisoner in Egypt* (Gen. 39:19–40:23). Potiphar placed Joseph in the prison where the king's prisoners were confined (39:20). In prison at first "they bruised his feet with shackles; his neck was put in irons" (Ps. 105:18). But the LORD was with Joseph, so that he was soon made a trusty, and the warden put Joseph in charge of all those held in the prison.

If Joseph had not been purchased by Potiphar, he would not have been placed in the prison with the king's prisoners. If he had not been in that prison, he would not have met Pharaoh's cupbearer and baker, and would not have been brought before Pharaoh, and would not have had the opportunity to save his people during the famine. Truly "in all things God works for the good of those who love him" (Rom. 8:28).

In the prison Joseph interpreted the dreams of the king's cupbearer (or butler) and baker. The Egyptians regarded dreams as important prophecies of the future. Between the forelegs of the great Sphinx at Giza is a large stone tablet recording a dream of King Thutmose IV (1401–1391 B.C.), telling that the Sphinx spoke to him in a dream, saying that he would become king.

Joseph openly gave testimony to God: "Do not interpretations (of dreams) belong to God?" (40:8; 41:16). Joseph's interpretations of the dreams came to pass.

Joseph described his being brought to Egypt as being "forcibly carried off" (lit., "stolen"), and also as being "sold" (40:15; 45:5). Kidnapping includes both stealing and selling people.

5. *Pharaoh's dreams* (Gen. 41:1-36). Joseph spent two years in prison after interpreting the dreams. The LORD sometimes makes his people wait for long periods, though God does not view time as humans do. "*Wait* for the LORD" (Ps. 37:34).

It was a marvelous miracle that the LORD caused Pharaoh to dream the dreams of the seven cows and seven heads of grain (41:1-6). Without these dreams as warnings that seven years of abundant harvests would be followed by seven years of famine many people would have perished, including Joseph's family.

Egypt suffers famine when the Nile River does not overflow in the summer months. There is an old Egyptian inscription telling of seven years when the Nile did not overflow. This occurred in the time of King Zoser of the third dynasty, eight hundred years before Joseph's time. Such periods of famine were remembered and feared. (See *The Ancient Near*

East, Vol. 1, Princeton Univ. Press, 1973, pp. 24-27.)

When Joseph was called in to interpret the dreams, he *shaved* himself (41:14). Egyptian paintings show that the Egyptians were clean-shaven, but Asiatics wore beards then.

Joseph's interpretation of Pharaoh's dreams was so completely in harmony with the dreams that it was accepted at once, and Joseph's recommendations about making preparations for the famine were also accepted. Joseph got the job!

6. *Joseph, ruler in Egypt* (Gen. 41:37-57). As the second ranking ruler in Egypt (41:43), Joseph was (1) an honored man (41:37-45); (2) an efficient man (41:46-49); (3) a family man (41:50-52); (4) a benefactor (41:53-57).

Pharaoh called Joseph *Zaphenath-Paneah*, an Egyptian name perhaps meaning "The god speaks and he [Joseph] lives." Pharaoh gave to Joseph Asenath, daughter of Potiphera, priest at the city of On (later called Heliopolis). Potiphera was priest of the sun god Re.

Joseph had two sons: (1) *Manasseh*, whose name means *forgetting*; and (2) *Ephraim*, meaning *fruitful* (or perhaps "doubly fruitful," because the name has a dual ending).

Joseph stored up so much grain in the seven good years that he stopped keeping records of it (41:49). Egyptian relief carvings show pictures of rows of state granaries. (Werner Keller, *The Bible as History in Pictures*, p. 72.)

The famine that came upon Egypt affected the countries around Egypt (41:54). This was a necessity so that Joseph's family would be compelled to move into Egypt. In Egypt they would be in much less danger of losing their religious distinctiveness by assimilation into the native population than they were in Canaan. (Does the "world" want to absorb us also?)

7. *Joseph's brothers go to Egypt* (Gen. 42). When Jacob said that the brothers should go to Egypt for food, the brothers kept "looking at each other." Their last association with Egypt was the view of Joseph being taken toward that land.

In Egypt Joseph spoke roughly to his brothers, though they did not recognize him (42:7). This was not done to punish them but to test them and see if they still had their old jealousies and cruel tendencies.

Joseph remembered his dreams (42:9). Reuben remembered Joseph's pleas (42:21).

Joseph kept Simeon in Egypt (42:24) to make sure that the others would return with their youngest brother, whom they had left home.

The discovery of their money in their grain sacks was a great shock (42:35). It gave them much to think about.

Jacob said, "You have deprived me of my children. Joseph is no more, and Simeon is no more" (42:36). Jacob spoke truer than he knew, but the brothers felt it.

8. *The second journey to Egypt* (Gen. 43). Jacob was very reluctant to let Benjamin be taken to Egypt. He was the only son of Rachel left to Jacob.

Judah offered himself as a guarantee of the safety of Benjamin (43:8-9). Judah was as good as his word (44:16-34).

Jacob sent some of the "best products of the land" as a gift to "*the man*" (43:11). Their best was not much, but "A gift opens the way for the giver and ushers him into the presence of the great" (Prov. 18:16).

Jacob's feeling of total helplessness and dependence on "God Almighty" echoes the ultimate experience of all people (43:13; 35:11).

Events in the brothers' second visit to Egypt:
   (a) Attempt to return the money (43:15-18)
   (b) Emotional meeting with Benjamin (43:29-30)
   (c) Banquet with the brothers (43:31-34)

Seating the brothers in the order of their ages without having asked them their ages was a large clue as to who "the man" was (43:33).

Joseph's giving Benjamin five times as much food as the other brothers received was a severe test of the jealousy the brothers once had taken out upon Joseph (43:34).

9. *Joseph's silver cup in the sack* (Gen. 44:1-34). Joseph's statement that the cup found in Benjamin's grain sack was the cup used by his lord (Pharaoh) for "divination" would strike terror into many people (44:5,15).

When the cup was found in Benjamin's sack, the brothers could only conclude that Benjamin had stolen the cup. "Then they tore their clothes" (44:13).

Judah's plea to Joseph for Benjamin is very heart-touching
(44:16-34).

10. *Joseph makes himself known* (Gen. 45). Joseph had NOT
enjoyed the experiences of concealing his identity from his
brothers, and testing them, and causing them anguish. He
could control himself no longer! He cried out, "Have everyone leave my presence." He desired a private meeting with
his brothers.

Joseph's true motives toward his brothers were quickly
revealed. "Do not be distressed and do not be angry with
yourselves for selling me here, because it was to save lives
that God sent me ahead of you" (45:5; 50:19-20).

Israel was to come down to Egypt, and live in the region
(lit., *land*) of *Goshen* (45:10). This was the green valley
between the east side of the Nile delta and Lake Timsah (in
the Suez Canal). The area is now called the Wadi Tumilat.

Joseph gave his brothers one more test. He gave them all
new clothing, but gave Benjamin five sets of clothes and
three hundred shekels of silver (45:22). This would show if
the brothers could still be free of jealousy when the pressure
was off of them. By that time they were very satisfied to have
escaped with their lives!

"Don't quarrel" on your way home! It would be very easy
for them to blame one another for past events (45:24). It was
not going to be easy when they returned to Jacob and told
him Joseph was alive. Jacob would have a LOT of questions
to ask.

When Jacob heard the news, he was "stunned" (45:26).
(Literally, "His heart became cold" [numb, feeble].) But when
he saw the carts (wagons) Joseph had sent to move them to
Egypt, he replied, "This is GREAT! . . . I will go and see him
before I die."

11. *Jacob goes to Egypt* (Gen. 46:1-30). God had often
spoken to or appeared to Jacob. God spoke again to him at
Beersheba as he journeyed to Egypt: "Do not be afraid to go
down to Egypt, for I will make you into a great nation there"
(46:3). God surely did increase Jacob's family in Egypt, from
70 men to 603,550 men (Num. 1:32).

Neither the death of Rachel nor the long separation from Joseph had separated Jacob from God's love (Rom. 8:38-39).

A list of Jacob's sons and grandsons is in 46:8-27. These total seventy men. The Greek Septuagint Bible gives a total of seventy-five, by adding names of five grandsons of Joseph (46:20,27; LXX).

Joseph went out in his chariot to meet Jacob in the land of Goshen, and threw his arms around his father and wept for a long time. The capital of Egypt at that time (about 1876 B.C.) was in the vicinity of Memphis, west of the Nile near the south end of the Delta. From the capital to the land of Goshen was about a hundred miles — a rather long ride.

12. *Jacob and his family visit Pharaoh* (Gen. 46:31-47:12). Joseph selected five of his brothers to visit Pharaoh. He cautioned them not to say they were *shepherds*, for all shepherds were detestable to the Egyptians. Egypt was subjected to a constant inflow of "sandcrossers," who sought to enter the green area of Egypt with only a few sheep or goats to maintain their livelihood. Joseph told his brothers to say that they were "men of cattle" (or livestock).

Pharaoh asked the brothers, "What is your occupation?" "Your servants are *shepherds*," they replied to Pharaoh. In spite of their unwise statement Pharaoh welcomed them to Egypt, to the best part of his land. He invited Joseph to appoint any of their "men of valor" to be over his "livestock" (cattle) (47:6).

The meeting of Jacob with Pharaoh was an epochal event. Jacob "blessed Pharaoh" (47:7, 10). That is amazing. The thought that a starved-out sheepherder could bless one of the greatest kings in Egyptian history jolts our set of worldly values. "Without doubt, the lesser person is blessed by the greater" (Heb. 7:7). Jacob was indeed greater than Pharaoh. God had said to Jacob, "All peoples on earth will blessed through you and your offspring" (28:14).

The Pharaoh at that time was probably Senwosret III (Sesostris III). He was king 1878-1841(?) B.C., during the Middle Kingdom. He made the most lasting reputation of any of the Middle Kingdom rulers. He conquered the land of

Nubia south of Egypt. He removed the power from the provincial governors. (We wonder if part of his success was not caused by Joseph's service.) The fact that Jacob could bless such a strong ruler shows the greatness of Jacob. (See John Baines and Jaromir Malek, *Atlas of Ancient Egypt*, New York: Facts on File, 1980, pp. 36-40.)

Jacob was one hundred and thirty years old when he visited Pharaoh (47:9). He said, "The years of my pilgrimage . . . have been few and difficult" (lit., *evil*).

Jacob's family settled in the "district of *Rameses*," the same area also called Goshen. Rameses II was not king until 1290–1224 B.C., six hundred years after the time of Joseph, and about one hundred fifty years after Moses. It appears that the name *Rameses* was used as a name for part of the country many years before kings bearing that name came to power.

13. *Joseph and the famine* (Gen. 47:13-26). During the seven years of famine Joseph acquired for Pharaoh all the people's money (47:14), their livestock (47:17), and their land (47:20). Joseph moved the people into the cities. (This is the Hebrew reading of 47:21. The NIV follows the reading in the Samaritan and Greek Bibles.) Joseph gave those who cultivated the land the seed to plant, and asked that they pay to Pharaoh a fifth of the produce of the land. (Many countries charge more than 20% tax!)

14. *Jacob in Egypt* (Gen. 47:27-31). Jacob lived in Egypt seventeen years, and saw his family increase greatly in number.

Before his death Jacob made Joseph swear to bury him where his fathers were buried, at the cave of Machpelah in Hebron (47:30; 35:28-29).

Jacob then worshipped as he leaned on the top of his staff (47:31). The Hebrew word for *staff* has the same consonants as the word for *bed*. The vowels that were supplied by scribes called Masoretes (A.D. 500–900) make the word read *bed*. But the Greek Bible translates it as *staff*, and the quotation in Hebrews 11:21 confirms this reading. This has been strangely perverted. The Latin Bible (Vulgate) translates the passage, *worshipped the top of his staff*, and this text is cited as an authority for image worship!

149

15. *Manasseh and Ephraim* (Gen. 48). Genesis chapter 48 tells of the blessing that Jacob bestowed upon Joseph's sons, Manasseh and Ephraim. Jacob blessed the younger son, Ephraim, to become greater than his older brother, Manasseh. Jacob also claimed the sons of Joseph as if they were his own first generation sons (48:16), so that their names would be included as part of the "twelve tribes."

Jacob suffered the blindness and forgetfulness that often comes in advanced age (48:8,10). When he saw Joseph's sons, He asked, "Who are these?"

When he blessed Manasseh and Ephraim, Jacob placed his right hand upon Ephraim, indicating that Ephraim would get the greater blessing.

When the land of Canaan was divided up among the twelve tribes, no area was designated as the "tribe of Joseph." Rather, two areas were selected and named after Joseph's sons. See Joshua, chapters 16 and 17.

**"By faith Jacob, when he was dying,
blessed each of Joseph's sons"** (Heb. 11:21).

---

16. *Jacob blesses his sons* (Gen. 49:1-28). Genesis 49 is a chapter of great poetic beauty, and great prophetic significance. Jacob called for his sons and prophesied concerning what they would be like and do. It is very helpful to compare the blessings of Jacob with the blessing of Moses upon the twelve tribes (Deut. 33).

Jacob spoke of the tribes mostly in the order of their births. Many of the tribes are symbolized by an animal or some object. These symbols of the Twelve Tribes have been used on banners and other artistic media.

We shall see the names of the twelve tribes of Israel upon the gates of pearl in the New Jerusalem (Rev. 21:10-12).

    a. *Reuben* — See Gen. 35:22.

    b. *Simeon* and *Levi* — Gen. 49:5-7; 34:25. These two tribes were to be the "scattered" tribes. Simeon was scattered

---

SYMBOLS OF THE TWELVE TRIBES :

1. **REUBEN** — Mandrake (Gen. 30:14)
2. **SIMEON** — Sword over Shechem (Gen. 34:25)
3. **JUDAH** — Lion (Gen. 49:9)
4. **ZEBULUN** — Ships (Gen. 49:13)
5. **ISSACHAR** — Strong donkey (Gen. 49:14)
6. **DAN** — Serpent (Gen. 49:17)
7. **GAD** — Horseman (Gen. 49:19)
8. **ASHER** — An olive tree (Deut. 33:24)
9. **NAPHTALI** — Doe (Gen. 49:21)
10. **JOSEPH** — A fruitful vine (Gen. 49:22)
      10A. **EPHRAIM** — Ox (Deut. 33:17)
      10B. **MANASSEH** — Vine (Gen. 49:22)
11. **BENJAMIN** — A ravenous wolf (Gen. 49:27)

---

by being assigned to live in scattered towns within the tribe of Judah (Josh. 19:1-9). Levi was scattered by being designated as the priestly tribe, so that the Levites would live in the territories of all the other tribes (Josh. 21:1-2, 41).

c. *Judah* was given the honor of being the tribe from which the kings of Israel would come (49:8-12).

A great Messianic prophecy —
"The **scepter** will not depart from *JUDAH*,
Nor the ruler's staff from between his feet,
Until he comes to whom it belongs *(SHILOH)*
and the obedience of the nations is his" (Gen. 49:10).

A *scepter* is the jeweled staff in a king's hand, which is the symbol of his authority. Judah was to retain the scepter of Israel, until *Shiloh* comes !

The name *Shiloh* can mean . . .
  (1) *Restgiver* (Matt. 11:28-29). (H.C. Leupold, *Exposition of Genesis*, p. 1179)
  (2) *Peaceful, peaceable* (from *Shalom*). (Isa. 9:6)
  (3) *"He whose it* [the scepter] *is"* (Luke 1:32)
  (4) *Messiah*. (Leupold, *op.cit.*, p. 1180)
We believe that *Shiloh* is a title for Jesus. The throne of His father David belongs to Him.

Eusebius, "The Father of Church History," (A.D. 265–334, in Palestine), wrote a very interesting paragraph on how the prophecy in Genesis 49:10 was fulfilled.

> At the time that Herod [the great] was king, who was the first foreigner that reigned over the Jewish people, the prophecy by Moses received its fulfillment, viz. "That a prince should not fail from Judah, nor a ruler from his loins, until he should come for whom it is reserved" . . . The prediction was evidently not accomplished, as long as they were at liberty to have their own native rulers, who continued from the time of Moses down to the reign of Augustus. Under him, Herod was the first foreigner that obtained the government of the Jews. Since, as Josephus has written, he was an **Idumean** [Edomite] by his father's side, and an Arabian by his mother's . . . (See Josephus, *Antiquities of the Jews*, IV, vii, 3.). (From Eusebius, *Ecclesiastical History*, Book I, Ch. VI)

It is amazing to learn that in the time of the first king over the Jews who was not an Israelite (king Herod the Great) that Jesus was born. Thus when the scepter departed from Judah to a man from another nation, *Shiloh* ("he to whom the scepter belongs," who is Jesus) was born.

  d. *Dan* – (Gen. 49:16-17). A fighting tribe which took the northern city of Laish by the sword (Judg. 18:27-30). Samson was a judge from the tribe of Dan (Judg. 13:2).

  e. *Joseph* – (Gen. 49:22-26). The Joseph tribes of Ephraim and Manasseh received the best land (Samaria) and the most land.

f. Benjamin — (Gen. 49:27). Benjamin was a predatory tribe. It fought the other tribes at Gibeah (Judg. 20:14).

17. *Death and burial of Jacob* (Gen. 49:29–50:14). Jacob died immediately after he gave his final blessings to his twelve sons (49:28, 33).

Jacob's death produced great mourning (50:1,3). His body was embalmed like the kings were embalmed (50:2). A very large company of Jacob's descendants and Egyptians of high rank joined in a long procession to bear Jacob's body to its resting place (50:7-9).

It appears that the procession crossed northern Sinai, and then went up on the east side of the Dead Sea and crossed the Jordan back into Canaan, and came to Hebron, where Jacob was buried. This was a very long trip, nearly four hundred miles, and may have taken a month.

When the procession came to the threshing floor of Atad "near the Jordan" (literally, "beyond the Jordan," east of the Jordan), there was a loud and bitter seven-day period of mourning for Jacob (50:10).

It was very befitting that the death of the great man Jacob be brought to the attention of as many people as possible. In his life Jacob had demonstrated the power of faith in God, and had shown an intensity of faith in the midst of many difficulties and personal failings that should inspire others to imitate his example.

Jacob's testimony to every generation could be, "If God could work through *me*, He can work through anyone."

18. *Joseph reassures his brothers* (Gen. 50:15-21). After the burial of Jacob Joseph's brothers were afraid that Joseph would pay them back for all the wrong they had done to him. They were not fully able to trust Joseph or his good will. (Are WE willing to trust the grace of the Lord Jesus completely?) The brothers came to Joseph and said (literally), "Behold, we are slaves for you" (50:18).

Joseph reassured them and spoke kindly to them, literally, "He spoke to their heart" (50:19-21).

19. *The death of Joseph* (Gen. 50:22-26). Joseph lived about fifty-five years after his father died, until age 110. He lived to

see the third generation of Ephraim's children. Joseph's body was embalmed and kept in Egypt. His bones were carried out of Egypt about three hundred and fifty years after his death, when the Israelites left Egypt led by Moses (Ex. 13:19).

> Heb. 11:22 — By *faith* Joseph, when his end was near, spoke about the exodus of the Israelites from Egypt and gave instructions about his bones.

20. *Chronology of the patriarchs*:
a. *Abraham* – 2166–1991 B.C.
  (1) Age 75 when he entered Canaan (Gen. 12:4)
  (2) 100 when Isaac was born (21:5)
  (3) 175 at death (25:7)
b. *Isaac* – 2066–1886 B.C.
  (1) 40 at marriage (25:20)
  (2) 60 at birth of Jacob and Esau (25:26)
  (3) 180 at death (35:28)
c. *Jacob* — 2006–1859 B.C.
  (1) 91 at the birth of Joseph (41:46; 45:6; 47:9)
  (2) 130 when before Pharaoh (47:9)
  (3) 147 at death (47:28)
d. *Joseph* — 1915–1805 B.C.
  (1) 30 when brought before Pharaoh (41:46)
  (2) 110 at death (50:26).

> Heb. 11:13 — All these people were still living by faith when they died. They did not receive the things promised; they only saw them and welcomed them from a distance. And they admitted that they were aliens and strangers on earth.

Questions on Section G
Joseph and Jacob in Egypt (Gen. 37, 39–50)

1. How old was Joseph when he brought a bad report about his brothers? (Gen. 37:2)
2. What special gift did Jacob give to Joseph? (37:3)
3. What were the two dreams of Joseph, and what did they mean? (37:5-10)
4. Where did Jacob send Joseph to find his brothers? (37:13)
5. Where had the brothers gone? (37:17)
6. Which brother kept the others from killing Joseph? (37:21)
7. Who suggested that Joseph be sold? (37:26-27)
8. To what people was Joseph sold? (37:28)
9. What was the price for Joseph? (37:28)
10. What was done with Joseph's coat? (37:31-32)
11. What did Jacob say when he saw the coat? (37:33,35)
12. To whom was Joseph sold in Egypt? (37:36)
13. What office did Joseph's Egyptian owner hold? (39:1)
14. How did Joseph get along in his master's house? (39:2)
15. How greatly did Joseph's master trust him? (39:6)
16. Who tempted Joseph? (39:7)
17. Joseph declared that his sin would be against whom? (39:9)
18. How did Joseph escape the woman? (39:12)
19. What lie did the woman tell? (39:14)
20. What did the master do with Joseph? (39:20)
21. What prisoners were kept in the place where Joseph was confined? (39:20)
22. How did Joseph get along in prison? (39:21-23; Ps. 105:17-18)
23. What two officials of the king were placed in prison? (40:1)
24. What made these prisoners sad? (40:8)
25. What was the cupbearer's dream? (40:10-11)
26. What interpretation did Joseph give of this dream? (40:12-14)
27. What request did Joseph make of the cupbearer? (40:14)
28. What was the baker's dream? (40:16-17)
29. What interpretation did Joseph give of his dream? (40:18-19)
30. Who forgot Joseph? (40:23) For how long? (41:1)
31. What were Pharaoh's two dreams? (41:1-6)
32. Who among the Egyptians could interpret the dreams? (41:8,24)
33. Who told Pharaoh of Joseph? (41:9,12)
34. What preparations did Joseph make before coming before Pharaoh? (41:14)

35. Whom did Joseph give credit to for interpreting dreams? (41:16)
36. What did Joseph say the dreams of Pharaoh meant? (41:26-27)
37. Why was Pharaoh's dream given in two forms? (41:32)
38. What advice did Joseph give Pharaoh? (41:33-36)
39. Why did Pharaoh select Joseph as food collector? (41:38-40)
40. How high did Joseph rank in Egypt? (41:40)
41. Who was given to Joseph as a wife? (41:45)
42. Who was Joseph's father-in-law? (41:45)
43. What was Joseph's age when he stood before Pharaoh? (41:46)
44. How much food did Joseph collect? (41:49)
45. What were the names of Joseph's two sons? Which was the older? (41:51-52)
46. What area did the famine cover? (41:54,56)
47. Why should Jacob's sons have gone into Egypt? (42:1-2)
48. Why did they look at one another instead of going to Egypt? (42:1)
49. Which son of Jacob did not go into Egypt? Why not? (42:4)
50. Whom did the brothers face in Egypt? (42:6)
51. How did their visit fulfill a dream? (42:6; 37:9)
52. What did Joseph accuse the brothers of? (42:9)
53. How long were the brothers kept in custody (jail)? (42:17)
54. Whom were the brothers ordered to bring back to Egypt? (42:20)
55. Why did the brothers think they suffered this penalty? (42:21)
56. How had Joseph spoken when his brothers sold him? (42:21)
57. What made Joseph weep? (42:22-24)
58. Which brother was detained in Egypt? (42:24)
59. What did Joseph have placed in the brothers' sacks? (42:25)
60. How did the brothers react when they discovered the contents of their sacks? (42:28,35)
61. What did Jacob accuse the brothers of? (42:36)
62. What security did Reuben offer Jacob as proof he would care for Benjamin? (42:37)
63. Why did the brothers return to Egypt a second time? (43:2)
64. Who told Jacob that they had to take Benjamin to Egypt? (43:3)
65. Who promised to guarantee Benjamin's safety? (43:8-9)
66. What did Jacob tell the brothers to take into Egypt? (43:11-12)
67. What hospitality did Joseph show to the brothers when they returned to Egypt? (43:16)
68. What did Joseph say when the brothers tried to return their money? (43:23)
69. What did the brothers offer to Joseph? (43:25-26)
70. Whom did Joseph ask the brothers about? (43:27)

71. How did Joseph react when he saw Benjamin? (43:29-30)
72. Why didn't Joseph sit at the table with his brothers? (43:32)
73. How were the brothers arranged at the table? (43:33)
74. Who got the most food? How much more? (43:34)
75. What was placed in the brother's sacks and in Benjamin's sack? (44:1-2)
76. What did Joseph have the steward accuse the returning brothers of taking? (44:4-5)
77. What was the cup of Joseph (supposedly) used for? (44:5)
78. What did the brothers say could be done to them if they were guilty? (44:9)
79. How did the brothers react when the cup was found? (44:12-13)
80. How did Joseph say that Benjamin would be punished? (44:17)
81. Who interceded for Benjamin? (44:18)
82. What did the interceding brother offer to do to get Benjamin released? (44:33)
83. Why did he make this offer? (44:31,34)
84. Why did Joseph send everyone except his brothers out of the room? (45:1)
85. Whom did Joseph ask about first after revealing his identity? (45:3)
86. How did the brothers react when Joseph identified himself? (45:3)
87. Who did Joseph say had sent him into Egypt? (45:5,8)
88. How many years of the famine had passed by then? (45:6)
89. What instructions did Joseph send to his father? (45:9)
90. In what land was Jacob to dwell in Egypt? (45:10)
91. How were Joseph's feelings toward Benjamin shown? (45:14)
92. How did Pharaoh react to the coming of Joseph's brothers? (45:16)
93. What arrangements for transporting Jacob's family did Pharaoh make? (45:17-19)
94. What clothing was given to the brothers? What clothing and what else was given to Benjamin? (45:22)
95. How did Jacob react to the news about Joseph? (45:26)
96. Did Jacob agree to go into Egypt? (45:28)
97. At what city did God speak to Jacob in a vision as he went to Egypt? (46:1-2)
98. What did God promise Jacob that he would do for him in Egypt? (46:4)
99. What does "Joseph will close your eyes" mean? (46:4)
100. How many souls (people) of the family of Jacob came into Egypt? (46:26-27)
101. Who was sent ahead of Jacob to direct the way into Goshen? (46:28)
102. Describe the meeting of Joseph and Jacob. Where did this meeting occur? (46:29)
103. What were the Israelites to tell Pharaoh was their occupation? (46:32,34)

104. How did the Egyptians feel about shepherds? (46:34)
105. How many brothers of Joseph went in with him to see Pharaoh? (47:2)
106. In what land in Egypt did Pharaoh let them dwell? (47:6)
107. What job offer did Pharaoh make to the brothers? (47:6)
108. With what sort of speech did Jacob speak to Pharaoh? (47:7,10)
109. How old was Jacob then? (47:9)
110. What was another name for the area where Jacob's family lived? (47:11)
111. What three things did Joseph get from the people for Pharaoh? (47:14,16,20,23)
112. Who relocated the people of Egypt? (47:21)
113. What class of people retained their land? (47:22)
114. What part of the production of the land was collected for Pharaoh? (47:24)
115. How did the Israelites get along in Egypt? (47:27)
116. How long did Jacob live in Egypt? (47:28)
117. What promise did Jacob require Joseph to make to him? (47:29-30)
118. Who was brought to Jacob when he was sick? (48:1)
119. What event did Jacob recall before Joseph and his sons? (48:3-4)
120. What relationship did Jacob claim toward Joseph's sons? (48:5)
121. Under what names would Joseph's sons' inheritance be reckoned? (48:6)
122. What is another name for Bethlehem? What happened to Jacob there? (48:7)
123. How did Jacob show affection for Joseph's sons? (48:10)
124. How did Jacob arrange his hands on Joseph's sons? (48:14)
125. How did Joseph react to Jacob's hand position on his sons? Why? (48:17-18)
126. Which of Joseph's sons was to become greater? (48:19-20)
127. How had Jacob acquired land from the Amorites? (48:22)
128. What did Jacob call his sons together to tell them? (49:1-2)
129. What honor and symbol did Jacob foretell for the tribe of Judah? (49:10)
130. Explain the term *Shiloh* in Gen. 49:10 (NASB & NKJV). What Messianic application is in it?
131. Where did Jacob command his sons to bury him? (49:29-30)
132. What five other persons besides Jacob were buried there? (49:31)
133. What class of professionals embalmed Jacob? (50:2)
134. How long did the embalming take? (50:3)
135. What request did Joseph make of Pharaoh after Jacob died? (50:5)
136. Who all went up into Canaan to bury Jacob? (50:7-9)
137. What did the Canaanites notice about the mourning for Jacob? What did they call it? (50:10-11)
138. What did the brothers of Joseph fear after Jacob was buried? (50:15)

139. How did Joseph react to their fears and message? (50:17,21)
140. How long did Joseph live? (50:22)
141. How many generations of his descendants did Joseph live to see? (50:23)
142. What did Joseph make the children of Israel swear to do when they left Egypt? (50:24-25; Ex. 13:19)
143. Where was Joseph's body kept? (50:26)

Period IV — Period of Bondage in Egypt

From Israel's Settlement in Egypt until their departure under Moses. 1876–1446 B.C. (Exodus 1–12)

Section A
Introduction to Exodus

1. The name *Exodus* means "a going out" or "departure." The name is taken from the Greek Old Testament (the Septuagint). The Greek form of the name (*exodos*) occurs in Exodus 19:1. The name applies more precisely to the early chapters (1–19) of the book than to the entire book.

The Hebrew name of the book is *Shemoth*, meaning "names." It is taken from the opening line of the book.

2. Exodus continues the history from the point where Genesis left off. It *starts* by telling of Israel's bondage in Egypt and *ends* with the construction of the tabernacle.

3. *Moses* was the human author of Exodus, as he was of Genesis. See Mark 12:26, where Jesus said, "Have you not read in the book of *Moses*, in the account of the bush [Ex. 3], how God said to him, . . .?" Moses was the author of the first five books of the Old Testament, which are called the *Torah* (or Law) and the *Pentateuch* (meaning *five books*).

4. There are two important dividing points in the story in Exodus:

a. Ex. 12:36/12:37. Before this dividing point the Israelites are in Egypt. From 12:37 on they are in the desert.

b. Ex. 19/20. This dividing point marks the division between the patriarchal dispensation and the Mosaic dispensation. The giving of the law at Mt. Sinai was the start of a new dispensation (administration) in God's eternal program.

During the patriarchal dispensation [from Adam to Moses] God dealt with individuals and families of all nations.

During the Mosaic dispensation God dealt primarily with the nation of Israel, to prepare for the future coming of the Messiah.

    5. *Outline of Exodus.* (Memorize this. At the least memorize the three main parts and their Scripture limitations.)

      I. The Hebrews in Egypt (1:1–12:36)
        A. Bondage in Egypt (ch. 1)
        B. The preparation of Moses (chs. 2–4)
        C. The plagues (chs. 5–11)
        D. The passover (12:1-36)

      II. The Hebrews from Egypt to Mt. Sinai (12:37–18:27)
        A. The exodus (12:37–15:21)
        B. The journey to Mt. Sinai (15:22–17:16)
        C. The visit by Jethro (ch. 18)

      III. The Hebrews at Mt. Sinai (chs. 19–40)
        A. The law given (chs. 19–24)
        B. Instructions about the tabernacle (chs. 25–31)
        C. The golden calf (idolatry) (chs. 32–34)
        D. Construction of the tabernacle (chs. 35–40)

    6. *Why study Exodus?*
    a. From Exodus we learn more about the LAW of God than from any other book. (For example, the Ten Commandments are in Exodus chapter 20.)
    b. In Exodus we find many events that were illustrations (or *types*) for Christians now. 1 Corinthians 10:11: "These things happened to them as examples and were written down as warnings for us." As an example, Israel's deliverance across the Red Sea illustrates our baptism into Christ (1 Cor. 10:2; Gal. 3:27).
    c. In Exodus we learn much about the character and work of the LORD God. Exodus 34:6,7: "The LORD, the LORD, the compassionate and gracious God, slow to anger, . . ." (See W. Fields, *Exploring Exodus*, College Press, 1976, pp. 49-53.)
    All people should learn that God is the LORD, Yahweh (Jehovah). This is a frequent teaching in Exodus. (See Ex. 6:7; 7:5; 7:17; 24:4; 16:12). God is the Eternal One, who causes things to exist and to happen.

161

7. *What is the theme (or themes) of the book of Exodus?*

a. *Redemption* and *leading*. "In your unfailing love you will *lead* the people you have *redeemed*" (Ex. 15:13). This appears to be a key verse in the book. Compare Exodus 3:8; 6:6-7. (To *redeem* people is to *rescue* or *ransom* them from a dangerous situation.)

b. *The making of a holy nation*. "You will be for me a kingdom of priests and a *holy nation*" (Ex. 19:6). Israel became God's *holy nation* when He provided for them a . . .

    (1) leader (chs. 1-6)
    (2) liberation (chs. 7-12)
    (3) leading (chs. 13-18)
    (4) laws (chs. 19-24)
    (5) divine worship (chs. 25-40).

c. *From a family to a nation*. "I will make you into a great nation" (Gen. 12:2). This transition came about through these stages that are told in Exodus:

    (1) Population (Ex. 1)
    (2) Liberation (Ex. 2-12)
    (3) Legislation (Ex. 19-24)
    (4) Organization (Ex. 25-40) (rules for worship and for government)

d. *The journey into God's presence*. "I brought you to *myself*" (Ex. 19:4). Israel came to the glorious time when they saw God! (Ex. 24:9-11).

Their journey had a distant beginning, many obstacles and detours on the journey, much help in their journey, and many demands upon the travellers. The spiritual journey of Israel to God was a longer trip than the journey from Egypt to the promised land.

8. *Date of Israel's exodus* from Egypt: **1446** B.C. (See 1 Kings 6:1). Please remember this date.

Questions on Section A
Introduction to Exodus

1. What does the name *Exodus* mean?

2. With what events does the history in Exodus begin and end?
3. Who was the author of Exodus?
4. What are the two important dividing points in the story in Exodus? What goes before and what comes after these dividing points?
5. Write the three main parts of the outline of Exodus, and the Scripture sections that tell of each.
6. What are two themes that have been proposed as the themes of the book of Exodus?
7. What is the date of the exodus from Egypt?

Section B
The Hebrews in Egypt (Exodus 1:1–12:36)

1. *The Israelites oppressed* (Ex. 1).

Exodus 1 — **TRANSITION** !
   a. From few to many (Ex. 1:1-7)
   b. From remembrance to rejection (Ex. 1:8)
   c. From harmony to hostility (Ex. 1:9-10)
   d. From freedom to slavery (Ex. 1:11-14)
   e. From bad to worse (Ex. 1:22)

The "new king(s) who did not know about Joseph" were probably the Hyksos kings who ruled over the delta region in Egypt after the Middle Kingdom, during dynasties XIII to XVII, 1750–1570 B.C. They were non-Egyptian rulers (actually Canaanites!) who had settled into Egypt in large numbers. They gained control in the land, but were outnumbered by the Israelites in Egypt, and feared them. (See Ex.1:9-10. Gleason L. Archer, Jr., *A Survey of Old Testament Introduction*, Chicago: Moody, 1994, pp. 228-233.)

After the Hyksos rulers were driven out of Egypt (about 1550 B.C.), the native Egyptian kings of the XVIII dynasty ruled the land. They continued and increased the persecutions of the Israelites.

The city of *Rameses* (1:11) appears to have no connection

EXODUS- CHAPTER TOPICS

GOD'S MAN	PLAGUES	PATHWAY	COVENANT
1 Need for God's Man (Transition)	7 The Conflict Begins ! ———— (Plague 1)	13 Demands and Direction to the Redeemed	19 Preparations to Receive Covenant
2 Preparation of God's Man	8 Plagues 2, 3, 4	14 Baptized unto Moses	20
3 Call of God's Man	9 Plagues 5, 6, 7	15 From Song to Bitterness	21
4 Hesitancy of God's Man	10 Plagues 8, 9	16 Bread from Heaven	22
5 Resistance to God's Man	11 The Last Warning !	17 Two Tests: Water and War	23
6 Strengthening of God's Man	12 Plague 10 ———— Over and Out !	18 Jethro and Judges	24 Covenant Ratified

God's Covenant Ordinances

TABERNACLE INSTRUCTIONS	GOLDEN CALF	TABERNACLE CONSTRUCTION
25 Tabernacle Instructions (Ark, table, lampstand)	**32** Rupture of Covenant	**35** Offerings and Workmen
26 Enclosings (Curtains, boards, bars, veil, screen)	**33** God and Israel in Tension	**36** Enclosings
27 Altar and Court	**34** Renewal of Covenant	**37** Inside Furniture
28 Priests — Garments **29** Priests — Consecration		**38** Outside Furniture ——— Total Cost
30 Incense, etc.		**39** Priests' Garments; Finished Work Presented
31 Craftsmen; Sabbath		**40** All Set Up! Glory of LORD

with King Rameses II, who ruled 1301–1234 B.C. The place was probably at Tell el-Dab'a near Qantir in the eastern edge of the Nile Delta.

If the Israelites had not experienced the persecutions in Egypt, they probably would never have been willing to leave Egypt, for it was a comfortable homeland in many ways.

Exodus 1 — THE **NEED** for God's Man (Moses)

a. Death of the previous generation and leadership (Ex. 1:1-6)
b. Multiplication of God's people (Ex. 1:7)
c. Afflictions of God's people (Ex. 1:15-22)

---

2. *Birth of Moses* (Ex. 2:1-10). The baby Moses was born of parents from the priestly tribe of Levi. His father was *Amram* and his mother was *Jochebed* (Ex. 6:20). His older sister was *Miriam* (Num. 26:59) and his brother was *Aaron*, three years older than Moses (Ex. 7:6). The baby Moses was "beautiful (like) unto God" (Acts 7:20). His godly parents hid him three months from the Egyptians. He doubtless heard words about God, and the Messiah to come, and God's promise to Abraham, and God's care while he was very young in his mother's care (2:8). This influence led Moses in later life to choose to stand with the people of God rather than to enjoy the comforts of Egypt and the pleasures of sin for a short time (Heb. 11:24-25).

Exodus 2 — The **PREPARATION** of God's man (Moses)
(Things needed to prepare God's man)
  a. God-fearing parents (Ex. 2:1-2; 2 Tim. 1:5)
  b. Divine direction and providence (Ex. 2:3-9)
  c. Training (Acts 7:22)
  d. Personal decision (Ex. 2:11; Heb. 11:24)
  e. Courage to act (Ex. 12:11-13)
  f. God's chastening (Ex. 2:14-15, 21-22)
  g. Patient endurance (Heb. 11:27; Ex. 18:4)

The name *Moses (Moshe)* is from the Hebrew verb *mashah* (to *draw* out), or from the Egyptian word for *bear* (a son). (Ex. 2:10)

Acts 7:22 — Moses was educated in all the wisdom of the Egyptians and was powerful in speech and action. This excellent education helped prepare Moses to be a great leader and writer.

Hebrews 11:24-25 — By faith Moses, when he had grown up, refused to be known as the son of Pharaoh's daughter. He chose to be mistreated along with the people of God. Moses was forty years old when he made this decision (Acts 7:23).

The day when Moses walked out of the palace and went to HIS PEOPLE (Ex. 2:11) was a decisive moment for all the world. God would use Moses to give His divine laws to mankind!

3. *Moses flees to Midian* (Ex. 2:11-25). Moses failed in his first attempt to save the Israelites from oppression, and from their evil relationships among themselves (Ex. 2:11-15; Acts 7:23-28).

Moses fled to the land of *Midian,* located mostly east of the Red Sea gulf of Aqaba, but partly west of the gulf. (Moses probably went to that side.) It was a three hundred mile flight across deserts from Egypt to Midian. (Moses must have been extremely frightened.)

In Midian Moses showed that he had not lost his "spunk" and his courage to defend the oppressed. He helped young women at a well (Ex. 2:16-17). Moses did not give up after one failure in Egypt. In Midian Moses married *Zipporah* ("bird"), daughter of *Jethro,* the priest of Midian. (Jethro was also called *Reuel* [Ex. 2:18].) Moses had two sons: *Gershom* (meaning *alien,* or foreigner) and *Eliezer* ("God is my help").

Three Periods in Moses' Life

a. 40 years in Egypt, as a **PRINCE**
b. 40 years in Midian, as a **SHEPHERD**
c. 40 years in the desert, as **LEADER** of the Israelites.

---

4. *Moses and the burning bush* (Ex. 3). After forty years as a shepherd in Midian, God called Moses from a burning bush to go back to Egypt and lead the Israelites out. (See Deuteronomy 33:16 on the burning bush.) Forty years before Moses felt he could deliver Israel by himself. Now he has lost his excessive self-confidence, and he offers many excuses.

Moses' five excuses why he could not go and lead Israel out:

    a. Who am I? (3:11)

    b. What shall I tell them is your NAME? (3:13)

    c. What if they do not believe me? (4:1)

    d. I am not eloquent, but slow of speech. (4:10)

    e. Send someone else to do it. (4:13)

The burning bush was seen on the "far side" of the desert, literally, the "back side." To the Hebrews the *west* side was the *back* side. Moses was at Mt. *Horeb*, which is another name for Mt. Sinai. The name *Horeb* means *dry*. It is dry around *Jebel Musa* (the mount of Moses), the traditional location of Mt. Sinai in the south part of the Sinai peninsula, but not as dry as most of the peninsula. There was a little pasture there.

At the burning bush Moses *saw* the Angel of the LORD (3:2). The angel said, "I am the God of your father, the God of Abraham" (3:6). (See notes on Judges 6:11.)

Exodus 3 — The **CALL** of God's man (Moses)

    a. Comes in unexpected ways (3:2)

    b. Must be heard with reverence (3:5)

    c. Is in harmony with God's former revelations (3:6)

    d. Given to help people (3:7-8)

    e. Sends us to BIG jobs (3:8)

    f. Comes to people who feel inadequate and fearful (3:11)

    g. Comes with God's directions (3:16)

    h. Comes with reassurance (3:17)

    i. Sends us against human opposition (3:19)

    j. Comes with divine help (3:20)

God told Moses that His name was **"I AM WHO I AM"** (3:14). His name was the LORD, *Yahweh*, the Everlasting One. The name Yahweh is derived from the Hebrew verb meaning to "be" or to "become." God's name is His memorial; He wants to be remembered by it. (Jesus is as much entitled to be called *Yahweh* as is His Father. See Isaiah 40:3,5; Matthew 3:3; Jeremiah 23:5-6.) If the name LORD (*Yahweh*) is not significant to you, meditate on it a while.

God forewarned Moses that the king of Egypt would not let Israel go unless a mighty hand (GOD's hand) compelled him (3:19).

5. *God empowers Moses for his mission* (Ex. 4:1-17). God answered all of Moses' objections. God enabled him to work miracles that would convince the people (4:3-9). God supplied him with a spokesman — his brother Aaron — when Moses said he was not capable of speaking. (Actually, Moses proved to be a powerful speaker. He gave all the stirring sermons in Deuteronomy.) God told him to take "this *staff* in your hand so you can perform miraculous signs with it" (4:17,20; 7:19; 17:5-6).

Exodus 4 — The **HESITANCY** of God's man

   a. Fear that people would not believe (4:1)

   b. Fear of his slow speech (4:10; 6:30)

   c. In need of having his commission repeated (4:19)

   d. Personal failure to obey God's covenant (4:24-26)

   e. Victory when hesitancy is overcome (4:27-31)

---

6. *Moses returns to Egypt* (Ex. 4:18-31). Jethro was willing to allow Moses to return to Egypt. Moses did not tell Jethro what his true mission to Egypt was (4:18).

After Moses had committed himself to go back to Egypt, God told Moses that "the men who wanted to kill you are dead" (4:19). Up until this time Moses did not know this, and could only have supposed that he would be confronting the same king who had tried to kill him forty years before. This shows Moses' courage.

The king of Egypt who had tried to kill Moses was probably the great Thutmose III, who ruled Egypt 1502–1448 B.C. He was son-in-law of Hatshepsut, the woman ruler of Egypt who may have been "the daughter of Pharaoh" who took the baby Moses. Thutmose III died shortly before Moses came back to Egypt. Thutmose was succeeded by his son Amenhotep II (1448–1422 B.C.) Amenhotep was probably the Pharaoh at the time of the exodus, the one who tried to prevent the Israelites from leaving. According to his inscriptions he was physically very strong, and also insufferably boastful. (See *Ancient Near Eastern Texts*, James B. Pritchard, ed., Princeton Univ. Press, 1955, pp. 243-244.)

As Moses returned toward Egypt, his wife and two sons went with him, riding on "a donkey," just *one* (4:20).

Exodus 4:24-26 tells of a deathly illness Moses experienced at a lodging place on the way. It is not a pleasant story. Zipporah had to circumcise her son to save Moses' life. Moses could not become the leader of God's covenant people if he himself had not obeyed God's command about circumcision, which was the sign of God's covenant with Abraham (Gen. 17:14). Before men can be successful leaders, they must be obedient followers of those over them. (Zipporah returned to her father after this incident [Ex. 18:2].)

The LORD directed Aaron to meet Moses (Ex. 4:27). They met with the Israelites, who believed that God was now concerned about (lit., had visited) the children of Israel (4:31).

7. *Resistance to Moses* (Ex. 5:1-21).

Exodus 5 — **RESISTANCE** to God's man (Moses)

   a. Resistance from sinners (Pharaoh). (5:1-14)
   b. Resistance from God's people. (5:15-21)
(The Israelites bypassed Moses and criticized him. It is more painful to get opposition from those we are trying to help than from known enemies.)

Pharaoh refused the request to let Israel leave Egypt to hold a festival to the LORD in the desert. He increased their

Moses as a Type of Christ

People living on the Old Testament side of the wall of time could see in Moses and such leaders a FORE-SHADOWING, or TYPE, of Christ, the greater one who was to come.

171

slave burdens to a level they could not possibly fulfill. The Israelites turned against Moses after this initial failure by Moses to deliver them.

Pharaoh said to Moses, "Who is the LORD, that I should obey him?" (5:2). Pharaoh was soon to become well-acquainted with the LORD! One of the main purposes for telling the story in Exodus is that people will know that God is the *LORD* (7:17; 8:22; 6:7, 28).

8. *The strengthening of God's man* (Ex. 5:22–6:30).

Exodus 6 — The **STRENGTHENING** of God's man

Moses needed strengthening after the resistance described in chapter five. How was God's man strengthened?

a. By God's name (6:2-3, 6, 29)
b. By God's promises (6:1, 6-8)
c. By God's covenant (6:4-5)
d. By God's command (6:10-13, 28-29)
e. By association with the people of God (6:14-27)

God's *name* (Yahweh) was to be a strength to Moses (6:2). Because God is truly what His name means — the Eternal living one — His name is a strength to us. (See Psalms 124:8; 118:10; 148:5.) The *name* of the LORD is equivalent to the LORD Himself (Isa. 24:15).

God said to Moses, "I appeared to Abraham . . . as God Almighty (*'El Shaddai*), but by my name the LORD I did not make myself known to them" (6:3). It is certainly obvious that Abraham knew the name *LORD* (Yahweh). See Genesis 15:8; 22:14. How, then could Abraham have NOT known God's name? Bible critics have often said that the Jehovist (Yahwist) author of parts of Genesis knew that Abraham used the name *Yahweh*, but that "P" (the Priestly author of other parts) used only the name *'Elohim* (God) up until this verse (Ex. 6:2-3). (See N. Gottwald, *The Hebrew Bible*, p. 211.) This explanation (?) makes the Bible self-contradictory.

A better explanation is found in the Bible itself. Centuries after the time of Moses the prophet Jeremiah (about 600 B.C.) wrote, "I will teach them . . . then they will know that my name is the LORD" (Jer. 16:21). Also Ezekiel the prophet (590 B.C.) wrote, "I will make known my holy *name* among my people Israel" (Ezek. 39:7). These passages show that "knowing God's *name*" meant more than knowing the word *Yahweh*. It meant knowing God by experience, by personal association with Him, and by seeing His works for us. Abraham did not live to see all the wondrous works of Yahweh that Moses saw, and therefore he did not fully know the *name* of the LORD.

The LORD strengthened Moses by commanding him bluntly, "Bring the Israelites out of Egypt!" (6:13). "Quit griping and get going!"

The genealogical list in Exodus 6:14-25 appears there as a surprise when we first read it. But what could strengthen Moses any more than to write a list of his forefathers, and think about what they had believed and done? They were part of a "cloud of witnesses" to him and to all (Heb. 12:1).

9. *Confrontation with Pharaoh* (Ex. 6:28–7:13).

Exodus 7 — **THE CONFLICT BEGINS!** (The first plague)

    a. The command (7:1-7)
    b. The confrontation (7:8-13)
    c. The calamity (7:14-21)

Moses was shuddering with fear at the thought of going in to Pharaoh. "I speak with faltering (lit., *uncircumcised*) lips. Why would Pharaoh listen to ME?" (6:30)

God allowed Aaron to be Moses' "prophet" (7:1). A "prophet" is a person who speaks for God or someone else.

Pharaoh thought that Moses' miracle of the staff turning into a serpent was merely human magic that his magicians could outdo. The magicians did do something similar by their "secret arts" (sorcery). The apostle Paul mentions the names of two of the magicians who opposed Moses — Jannes and Jambres (2 Tim. 3:8).

> **LIST of the TEN PLAGUES** (Exodus 7–12)
>
> (1) River to blood   (6) Boils
> (2) Frogs   (7) Hail
> (3) Gnats (lice)   (8) Locusts
> (4) Flies   (9) Darkness
> (5) Death of livestock   (10) Death of firstborn

10. *The first plague* (Ex. 7:14-24). Turning the waters of the Nile into blood got the attention of all Egypt at once. Without the Nile Egypt is all desert.

The Egyptians worshiped the Nile as a god, named *Hapi*. They pictured him as a man, but with drooping female breasts, carrying a tray of flowers and food. They sang hymns to the Nile and offered sacrifices to it. (See Ezekiel 29:3.) Their Nile was changed into blood, and the fish died, and the river smelled bad. The "blood" was not exactly the same as the blood of any particular creature, but it resembled blood more than anything else.

All of the ten plagues were attacks on certain *gods* in Egypt. "I will bring judgment on all the *gods* of Egypt" (Ex. 12:12). "The LORD had brought judgment on their *gods*" (Num. 33:4). (See Harry Rimmer, *Dead Men Tell Tales,* ninth ed.(1952) pp. 85-122. Wilbur Fields, *Exploring Exodus,* College Press, 1976, pp. 167-177. E.A. Wallis Budge, *The Mummy,* New York: Collier, 1974, pp. 266-301.)

What is a *plague?* It is not just a disease or epidemic, but any event that afflicts, smites, or troubles. The plagues are often called *signs* or *wonders.* (See Ex. 7:3; 8:23; 10:1; Deut. 4:34.) A *sign* is a miracle with a message. The plagues were to teach something, as well as to punish. The plagues were to show God's *power* (Ex. 9:16). The plagues were *judgments,* that is, punishments (Ex. 12:12). The English word *plague* is the translation of three different Hebrew words, meaning a slaughter, a blow or stroke, and a smiting or stumbling.

The Egyptian magicians also made blood from water (7:22). The Egyptians needed less blood, not more blood.

The magicians later made frogs, which the Egyptians did not need more of (8:7).

Pharaoh did not "take even this (the first plague) to heart" (7:23). This is the first reference to Pharaoh's responses to the plagues. He hardened his own heart at the beginning. Later during the plagues God took Pharaoh's reactions out of his own control and God Himself hardened Pharaoh's heart to punish him for the cruel hardness he had chosen to follow.

The plagues covered a time span of perhaps six months, from about October to March.

11. *Plagues of frogs, gnats, and flies* (Ex. 8).

Exodus 8 — **Plagues 2, 3, & 4.** Little Creatures — Big Plagues!

(The supremely great smitten by the supremely contemptible)

FROGS (8:1-15). GNATS (Lice) (8:16-19). FLIES (8:20-32)

The plague of frogs was an attack upon the frog goddess *Heqt*, wife of the great ram-horned creator god *Khnum*. Heqt is pictured on a porch of the mortuary temple of Hatshepsut (Deir el Bahri) west of Thebes. She is pictured with a woman's body and a frog head. She supposedly gave life to the unborn children.

The Egyptians were very fastidious about cleanliness, and shaved their bodies so lice would not cling to them. That did not deter the lice (or gnats) of the third plague.

When the Egyptian magicians could not duplicate the lice, they said, "This is *finger* of God" (8:19). This is an authentic Egyptian expression. (See George L. Robinson, *The Bearing of Archaeology on the Old Testament*, New York, 1944, pp. 42-43.)

The plague of "flies" may refer to several kinds of insects. The Hebrew word means "swarms." The scarab beetle was particularly important to the Egyptians as a symbol of immortality.

After the plague of flies Pharaoh offered Moses a compromise: "Go, sacrifice to your God in the land" (8:25). This was the first of four compromise offers that Pharaoh made during the plagues. They were compromises that would have continued the captivity.

Pharaoh's Compromise Offers to Moses:

(1) "Go, sacrifice in the land" (8:25).
  (The compromise of remaining in the "world")
(2) "Go . . . but not very far" (8:28).
  (The compromise of lukewarmness)
(3) "Only the men go" (10:11).
  (The compromise of undedicated families)
(4) "Go . . . but leave your flocks and herds" (10:28).
  (The compromise of undedicated livelihoods)

---

12. *The death of livestock; the boils; and hail* (Ex. 9).

Exodus 9 — Wealth and Health Destroyed by Disobedience
  (1) Plague of death of livestock (9:1-7)
  (2) Plague of boils (9:8-12)
  (3) Plague of hail (9:13-35)

The death of the livestock was especially significant in Egypt. Every animal in Egypt was sacred to some god. They had the cow goddess of love, Hathor. Amon-Re, the great god at Thebes, was depicted as a ram. When the sacred animals died, the gods of Egypt were silent.

The Israelites were not affected by the plagues that struck the Egyptians all around them (8:22; 9:6,26). This protection over the Israelites showed that the plagues were *miracles*, and not just natural calamities affecting everyone, as some have said they were.

After the sixth plague, the plague of boils, "the LORD hardened Pharaoh's heart" (9:12). Pharaoh had been allowed to make his own decisions after the first five plagues. He chose the cruel and God-defying path. As punishment God hardened Pharaoh's heart. Perhaps Pharaoh sensed that he was being compelled to say and do things by a power outside of himself.

Very little rain falls in Egypt except along the Mediterranean coast. Hail is almost unknown. "Hail fell and lightning flashed back and forth" (9:24). The Egyptians worshiped a sky goddess (*Nut*), but she could not stop the storm. The hail beat down the flax (9:31). The Egyptians depended on flax to make linen for the wrapping of mummies.

After the plague of the hail Pharaoh summoned Moses and confessed, "This time I have sinned" (9:27). But when the hail stopped, Pharaoh sinned again and hardened his heart (9:34). The LORD had given Pharaoh that chance to choose the humane way, and he refused, even after God had hardened his heart once before. From that time onward, the choices were taken from Pharaoh (11:10).

13. *The plagues of locusts and darkness* (Ex. 10).

Exodus 10 — Two Terror Plagues
    (1) Locusts (10:1-20)   (2) Darkness (10:21-23)

The story of the plagues of locusts and darkness were to be told to children and grandchildren (10:2).

Locust plagues are terrible disasters. (See *National Geographic*, April 1953, pp. 545-562.) The locusts in this plague were even worse than ordinary locusts (10:14).

The darkness was an especially significant plague, because the chief god at the capital city of Thebes was Amon (Amon-Re), a sun god! The darkness was so dense it could be *felt* (10:21). The darkness was worse than that in any sand storm or dust storm.

Pharaoh said to Moses, "Get out of my sight! . . . The day you see my face you will die" (10:28). Pharaoh was forcing a finale.

14. *The final warning to Pharaoh* (Ex. 11).

Exodus 11 — The Last Warning
    "There will be one more plague! . . . Every firstborn son in Egypt will die" (Ex. 11:1, 5).

When we leave Egypt "ask for articles of silver and gold" (11:2). These materials would be used in the tabernacle (25:3).

Moses was highly regarded in Egypt by Pharaoh's officials and by the people (11:3).

The LORD would "pass over" Egypt (11:4; 12:12). No "death angel" is mentioned. A "destroyer" is mentioned in Exodus 12:23. Compare Psalm 78:49.

15. *The Passover* (Ex. 12:1-36). The month of the Passover feast would be the first month of Israel's religious year (12:2). The month is called *Abib* or *Nisan*, and comes in March–April of our calendar.

Exodus 12 — **Over and Out !**

   a. God passed *over* Egypt (12:1-36).
   b. Israel went *out* of Egypt (12:37-51).

A lamb was to be selected for each family (12:5). It was to be eaten "at twilight," literally "between the two evenings" (12:6).

The Passover in Egypt – A Type of Christ, our Passover		
Similarities	**Passover**	**Christ**
1. An unblemished lamb	Ex. 12:5	John 1:29; Heb. 4:14-15
2. Lamb selected in advance	Ex. 12:3	Christ foreknown 1 Pet. 1:19-20
3. Lamb slain	Ex. 12:6, 21	Rev. 5:6; 13:8
4. Not a bone broken	Ex. 12:46; Num. 9:12	John 19:33, 36
5. Blood applied to doors	Ex. 12:7, 22	Blood on hearts. Heb. 10:22
6. Leaven removed	Ex. 12:15, 19-20	Sin removed. 1 Cor. 5:8
7. Followed by Feast of Unleavened Bread	Ex. 12:17-20; 13:6	Christian life. 1 Cor. 5:8

Israel was delivered from Egypt when the blood of the Passover lamb was placed on their doors. They did not escape from Egypt by their own power or resolutions. We do not escape from sin by our own works but by the blood of Christ.

The Passover feast was to be observed each year. In the seven days that followed the Passover no food containing leaven was to be in the Israelites' homes. This period was called the Feast of Unleavened Bread (12:17). In the New Testament the Feast of Unleavened Bread is used as a symbol of the Christian life. As the Israelites had no leaven in their homes, "let us keep the Festival, not with the old yeast (leaven) of malice and wickedness, but with bread without yeast, the bread of sincerity and truth" (1 Cor. 5:8).

The meaning of the Passover feast was to be explained to the Israelites' children each year at the feast (Ex. 12:24).

Pharaoh had threatened to kill Moses if he ever saw his face again. After the Passover he came seeking Moses, begging them to depart.

> "He brought out Israel, laden with silver and gold, . . . Egypt was glad when they left" (Ps. 105:36-38).

Hebrew Weights and Measures

Weights (often used as monetary units)
a. **Talent** (Ex. 38:25) . . . . .60 minas, about 75 pounds
   (A talent of gold would be worth about $300,000, and a talent of silver about $2,000.)
b. **Mina** (Ezek. 45:12; 1 Kgs. 10:17) . . . . .50 shekels. 20 oz.
c. **Shekel** . . . . .4 oz.
d. **Beka** (Ex. 38:26) . . . . .½ shekel
e. **Gerah** (Lev. 27:25; Num. 3:47; 18:16) . . . . .¹⁄₂₀ shekel

Liquid Measure
a. **Log** (Lev. 14:10) . . . . .Approx. 1 pint
b. **Cab** (kab, qab) (4 logs; 2 Kgs. 6:25) . . . . .2 quarts
c. **Hin** (12 logs; Ex. 20:24). . . . . .1 gallon
d. **Ephah**, or bath (Ezek. 45:10) . . . . 6 gallons
e. **Homer**, or cor (Ezek. 45:14) . . . . 60 gallons
   (A cor consists of ten baths or one homer.)

Dry Measure

a. *Cab* (kab, qab) (2 Kgs. 6:25) . . . . Approx. quart, or liter
b. *Omer* (Ex. 16:16) . . . . .Approx. ½ gallon (2 liters)
c. *Seah* (1 Kgs. 18:32) . . . . About 2 gallons
d. *Ephah* (Ten omers in an ephah. Ex. 16:36) . . . Approx. 5 gallons

Length

A *cubit* is approximately 1½ feet (18 inches).

The Hebrew Calendar

MONTH	OUR MONTH	FESTIVALS	SEASON
1. **Abib**, or **Nisan** Ex. 23:15; Neh. 2:1	Mar./Apr.	14. Passover 15-21. Feast of Unleavened Bread	Latter rains. Jordan in flood. Barley ripe in lowlands.
2. **Ziv**, or **Iyar**	Apr./May	14. Passover for those who could not keep regular one. Num. 9:10-11	Early figs. Barley harvest in hill country.
3. **Sivan** Esth. 8:9	May/June	6. Feast of Weeks (Harvest)	Wheat harvest.
4. **Tammuz**	June/July		Dry season from late April to early Oct. First grapes.
5. **Ab**	July/Aug.		Olives in lowlands.
6 **Elul** Neh. 6:15	Aug./Sept.		Grape gathering. Summer figs.
7. **Ethanim**, or **Tishri** 1 Kgs. 8:2	Sept./Oct.	1. Feast of Trumpets 10. Day of Atonement 15-21. Tabernacles	Pomegranates ripe. Former (early) rains begin.
8. **Bul**, or **Marchesvan** 1 Kgs. 6:38	Oct./Nov.		Olives gathered in northern Galilee. Planting time for barley and wheat.
9. **Kislev** Zech. 7:1	Nov./Dec.	25. Feast of Dedication (Hanukkah)	
10. **Tebeth** Esth. 2:16	Dec./Jan.		
11. **Shebat** Zech. 1:7	Jan./Feb.	14-15. Feast of Purim	
12. **Adar** Esth. 3:7	Feb./Mar.		Oranges and lemons ripe in lowlands. Almond trees blossom.

Each new month (new moon) began with the blowing of trumpets and offering of sacrifices (Num. 28:11; 10:10; Ps. 81:3).

Questions on Section B
The Hebrews in Egypt (Ex. 1:1–12:36)

1. Make a list of the 12 sons of Jacob. (Ex. 1:2-6)
2. How many descendants of Jacob came into Egypt? (1:5)
3. How greatly did the children of Israel multiply? (1:7)
4. Why did the new king in Egypt oppress Israel? (1:8-10)
5. Name the two store-cities the Israelites built. (1:11)
6. What types of slave work did Israel do? (1:14)
7. Name the two Hebrew midwives. (1:15)
8. Why did the midwives not kill the Israelite babies? (1:17)
9. What commandment did the king make about the Hebrew babies? (1:22)
10. Of what tribe was Moses? (2:1)
11. How long was the baby Moses hidden? (2:2)
12. Who raised Moses? (2:8-9)
13. Who adopted Moses? (2:10)
14. How much education did Moses receive? (Acts 7:22)
15. Which did Moses choose when he became a man — Egypt or Israel? (Heb. 11:26)
16. Why did Moses flee from Egypt? (Ex. 2:11-15)
17. To what land did Moses flee? (2:15)
18. How many daughters did Reuel have? (2:16)
19. Who became Moses' wife? (2:21)
20. Name Moses' two sons. (2:22; 18:3-4)
21. How long did Moses live in Midian? (Acts 7:30)
22. Near what mountain did Moses see a burning bush? (Ex. 3:1)
23. Who spoke to Moses from the bush? (3:2,6)
24. What was Moses sent to do? (3:10)
25. What five excuses did Moses give to God? (3:11,13; 4:1,10,13)
26. What did God say his name was? (3:14; Compare John 8:58)
27. To whom was Moses to go first? (3:16-17)
28. What did God foretell about Pharaoh's reaction to Israel's proposed departure? (3:19)

29. Explain: "You will not go empty-handed." (Ex. 3:21; 12:35; Ps. 105:37)
30. What three miracles was Moses empowered to perform? (4:3,6,9)
31. What made God angry with Moses? (4:10-14)
32. Who was to be the spokesman for Moses? (4:14)
33. What threat was to be made about Pharaoh's firstborn? (4:22-23)
34. Why did God try to slay Moses (perhaps by a deadly plague)? (4:24-26)
35. Where was Zipporah sent as Moses went into Egypt? (4:26; 18:2)
36. Did the Israelites accept Moses and Aaron? (4:29-31)
37. With what question did Pharaoh respond to Moses' request that he let Israel go? (5:2)
38. What did Moses ask permission for the Hebrews to do? (5:3)
39. Why did Pharaoh increase the workloads of the Israelites? (5:5-9)
40. Why did the Israelites become displeased with Moses? (5:19-21)
41. By what name had God been known to Abraham? By what name was God not made known to him? (6:3)
42. Name the generations from Levi to Moses. (6:16-20)
43. Name Moses' mother. (6:20)
44. What relation was Korah to Moses? (6:16-21)
45. Who were Aaron's four sons? (6:23)
46. Why did God harden Pharaoh's heart? (7:3-5)
47. Give the ages of Moses and Aaron when they led Israel out of Egypt. (7:7)
48. What miracle of Moses did Pharaoh's magicians (apparently) duplicate? (7:10-11; Compare 2 Tim. 3:8)
49. List the ten plagues in order.
50. How many of the plagues did Pharaoh's magicians duplicate?
51. What four compromise offers did Pharaoh make to Moses during the plagues? (8:25,28; 10:11,24)
52. Why had God made Pharaoh to be king? (9:14-16; Rom. 9:17)
53. What did Pharaoh's servants urge him to do? (10:7)
54. What did Pharaoh threaten Moses with after the ninth plague? (10:28)
55. How safe were the Israelites to be during the last plague? (11:7)
56. What feast marked the beginning of months, the start of the new year? (Ex. 12:2,11)
57. When was the Passover lamb selected? When was it slain and eaten? (12:3,6)
58. What was to be done with the blood of the lamb? (12:7)
59. What were the Israelites to be ready to do on the night of the Passover? (12:11)

60. On what condition would Jehovah pass over any house? (12:13)
61. What period (or feast) followed the Passover for a week? (12:15-20)
62. How often was the Passover to be observed? (12:24-27)
63. What happened at midnight in Egypt? (12:29)
64. What did the Israelites ask the Egyptians for when they departed? (12:35-36)
65. Make a list of the months in the Hebrew calendar.
66. How much is a talent? What was its value in gold and in silver? (Ex. 25:39)

Period V — Period of Wandering

From the Exodus from Egypt to Israel's Entry into Canaan.
(Exodus 12:37–40:38; Leviticus; Numbers; Deuteronomy)

Section A
From Egypt to Mt. Sinai (Exodus 12:37–18:27)

1. *The Sinaitic peninsula*
   a. The Sinaitic peninsula is a large, triangular desert area bordered on the north by the Mediterranean Sea, on the west by the Gulf of Suez, and on the east by the Gulf of Aqaba and the Arabah valley. The Sinai peninsula is of importance in sacred history because the children of Israel wandered there for forty years after they left Egypt under the leadership of Moses.
   b. Dimensions of the Sinaitic peninsula — 150 miles wide across the north part; 260 miles from north to south.
   c. Inhabitants – The *Amalekites*, Israel's enemies, wandered as nomads between Mt. Sinai and Canaan.
   d. Deserts (wildernesses) of the Sinaitic Peninsula —
      (1) *Wilderness of Shur* – A sandy desert in the northwest.
      (2) *Wilderness of Etham* – A southward extension of the wilderness of *Shur* along the Red Sea side (Num. 33:8; Ex. 15:22).
      (3) *Wilderness of Paran* – A large stony desert in the southeastern part of the peninsula. It is a sterile table of limestone, 2000 to 3000 feet above sea level. Has many hills and a few springs of impure water.
      (4) *Wilderness of Sin* — Probably the small (6 x 13 mi.) plain known as el Murkah, which lies along the side of the Gulf of Suez northwest of Mt. Sinai. The modern oil-producing center of Abu Rudeis is in this plain. It is very barren and hemmed in by hills. The manna was first given in this desert (Ex. 16:1).

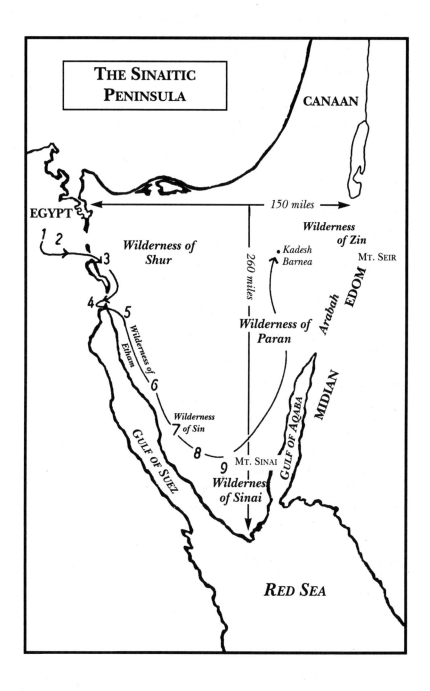

THE SINAITIC
PENINSULA

CANAAN

EGYPT

150 miles →

Wilderness of Zin

Wilderness of Shur

• *Kadesh Barnea*

Mt. Seir

260 miles

Wilderness of Paran

Arabah

EDOM

Wilderness of Etham

Wilderness of Sin

6

7

8

GULF OF AQABA

MIDIAN

GULF OF SUEZ

Mt. Sinai

9

Wilderness of Sinai

RED SEA

(5) *Wilderness of Sinai* — A rugged wasteland of granite mountains in the southern part of the peninsula. Mountains up to 8000 feet high.

(6) *Wilderness of Zin* (or *Tsin*) – A rugged depression (valley) in northeastern Sinai. It is a branch of the Arabah valley, on its west side. It included the area as far west as Kadesh Barnea (Num. 34:3; 20:1; 33:36; Deut. 32:51; Josh. 15:1).

e. Locations in and around the Sinaitic peninsula

(1) Land of *Midian* – The Midianites mostly lived east of the Gulf of Aqaba, but Jethro and Moses probably lived on the west side.

(2) The *Arabah* — A southward continuation of the deep depression (the Great Rift Valley) in which the Dead Sea lies. The Arabah extends south to the Red Sea Gulf of Aqaba. Extremely dry and hot. (The Jordan valley north of the Dead Sea is also sometimes called the *Arabah*.)

(3) *Edom* – The mountainous area (*Mt. Seir*) along the east side of the Arabah. It was inhabited by the descendants of Esau.

(4) *Kadesh Barnea* – The center of the Israelites' wanderings in the wilderness for many years. Probably at the springs named 'Ein Qadis or the nearby springs of 'Ein el Qudeirat. These are about fifty miles southwest of Beersheba.

Questions on the Sinaitic Peninsula

1. What is the general shape of the Sinaitic peninsula?
2. What borders the Sinaitic peninsula on its north, west and east sides?
3. What are the dimensions of the Sinaitic peninsula east to west and north to south?
4. What people inhabited the Sinaitic peninsula?
5. On a map locate the wildernesses (deserts) of Shur, Etham, Sin, Paran, and Sinai.
6. On a map locate Midian, the Arabah, Edom, and Kadesh Barnea.

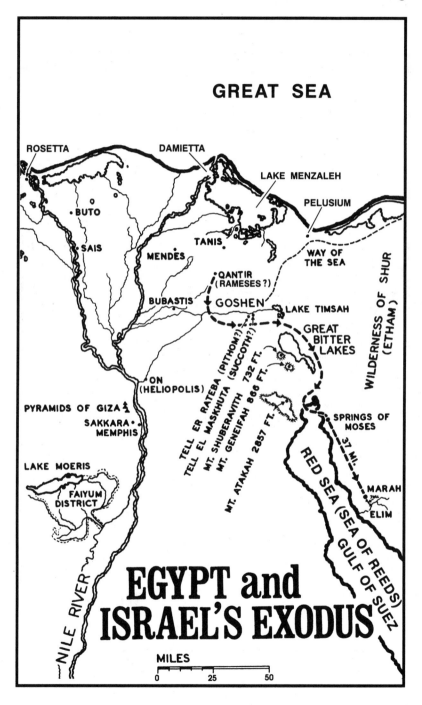

GREAT SEA

ROSETTA

DAMIETTA

LAKE MENZALEH

PELUSIUM

• BUTO

• SAIS

TANIS

MENDES

WAY OF
THE SEA

QANTIR
(RAMESES ?)

BUBASTIS

GOSHEN

LAKE TIMSAH

GREAT
BITTER
LAKES

WILDERNESS OF SHUR
(ETHAM)

ON
(HELIOPOLIS)

TELL ER RATEBA (PITHOM?)

TELL EL MASKHUTA (SUCCOTH?)

MT. SHUBERAVITH 732 FT.

MT. GENEIFAH 866 FT.

MT. ATAKAH 2857 FT.

PYRAMIDS OF GIZA

SAKKARA •
MEMPHIS

LAKE MOERIS

FAIYUM
DISTRICT

SPRINGS OF
MOSES

37 MI.

MARAH

ELIM

RED SEA (SEA OF REEDS)

GULF OF SUEZ

NILE RIVER

**EGYPT and
ISRAEL'S EXODUS**

MILES

0   25   50

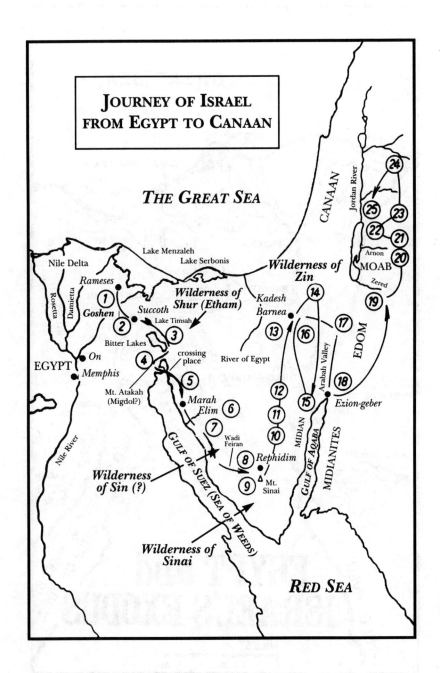

JOURNEY OF ISRAEL
FROM EGYPT TO CANAAN

THE GREAT SEA

CANAAN

Jordan River

24
25 23
22 21
20

Wilderness of
Zin

Lake Menzaleh
Lake Serbonis

Nile Delta

Arnon
MOAB

Zered

Rameses

Wilderness of
Shur (Etham)

Kadesh
Barnea

14

Goshen

Succoth
Lake Timsah

1

2

3

19

13

16

17

EDOM

Bitter Lakes

crossing
place

River of Egypt

Rosetta
Damietta

On

EGYPT
Memphis

4

5

Mt. Atakah
(Migdol?)

Marah
Elim

6

12

15

18

Arabah Valley

Ezion-geber

11

7

Wadi
Feiran

MIDIAN

10

GULF OF SUEZ (SEA OF WEEDS)

8 Rephidim

Wilderness
of Sin (?)

9

Mt.
Sinai

GULF OF AQABA

MIDIANITES

Nile River

Wilderness of
Sinai

RED SEA

2. *Three parts* (or periods) *of Israel's wilderness wanderings:*
   a. *From Egypt to Mt. Sinai.* This journey lasted fifty days.
   b. *From Mt. Sinai to Kadesh Barnea.* Israel stayed at Mt. Sinai for about eleven months. They received God's law at Mt. Sinai and built the tabernacle there. The journey from Sinai to Kadesh is mostly northward. It required about three months. This part of Israel's journeys is related in the book of Numbers.
   c. *From Kadesh Barnea to the Plains of Moab.* Israel failed to enter Canaan from the south (from Kadesh Barnea). They wandered in the Sinai deserts for thirty-eight years, until the older generation all died. In the fortieth year of their wanderings they journeyed eastward, around the mountains of Edom, and northward along the east side of the Dead Sea and Jordan valley. By the end of the forty years, Israel was camped in the Plains of Moab, just east of the Jordan River across from Jericho, and north of the Dead Sea.

There Moses died, and Joshua soon led Israel across the Jordan into the promised land.

Places and Events in Israel's Journey
From Egypt to Canaan
   1. *Rameses*
      a. Starting point (Ex. 12:37)
   2. *Succoth*
   3. *Etham*
      a. Pillar of cloud and fire (Ex. 13:20-22)
   4. *Camp near Pi Hahiroth*
      a. Pursuit by Egyptians
      b. Crossing Red Sea (Ex. 14)
   5. *Marah*
      a. Bitter water made sweet (Ex. 15:22-26)
   6. *Elim*
      a. Twelve springs and seventy palm trees (Ex. 15:27)
   7. *Wilderness of Sin*
      a. Quails and manna provided (Ex. 16)

8. *Rephidim*
   a. Water from the rock (Ex. 17:1-7)
   b. Attack by Amalek (Ex. 17:8-16)
   c. Jethro meets Moses (Ex. 18:1-12)
   d. Judges appointed (Ex. 18:13-27)
9. *Mt. Sinai*
   a. The law given (Ex. 20). (By this means Israel became a nation, a theocracy.)
   b. Golden calf made by the people (Ex. 32–34)
   c. Tabernacle constructed (Ex. 25-40)
   d. Consecration of the priests (Lev. 8-9)
   e. Deaths of Nadab and Abihu (Lev. 10:1-7)
   f. A blasphemer stoned (Lev. 24:10-23)
   g. The first census taken (Num. 1)
   h. The Passover kept (Num. 9)
10. *Taberah*
    a. Murmurers burned (Num. 11:1-3)
11. *Kibroth Hattaavah*
    a. Craving for meat and food. Quails given (Num.11:4-34)
    b. Seventy elders appointed (Num. 11:24-25)
    c. Eldad and Medad prophesy (Num. 11:26-27)
12. *Hazeroth*
    a. Miriam gets leprosy for complaining (Num. 11:35–12:15)
13. *Kadesh Barnea* ("You stayed in Kadesh many days" Deut. 1:46.)
    a. Expedition of the twelve spies (Num. 13:1–14:38)
    b. Futile invasion of Canaan (Num. 14:39-45)
    c. Korah's rebellion (Num. 16)
    d. Budding of Aaron's rod (Num. 17)
14. *Seventeen stopovers* (Num. 33:18-34). (No events at these places are told. Most are unknown, except Moseroth [Num. 33:30], which is the same as Moserah in Deut. 10:6. This was near Mt. Hor, where Aaron later died.)
15. *Ezion Geber* (Num. 33:35)
16. *Kadesh Barnea* (Num. 33:36; 20:1-21). (This was the second stopover around Kadesh, and was in the thirty-ninth or fortieth year of wandering. See Num. 33:37-38.)

17. *Mt. Hor* (Moserah)
   a. Death of Aaron (Num. 20:22-29; Deut. 10:6)
   b. Attack by king of Arad (Num. 21:1-3)
18. *Elath* and *Ezion-Geber* (Deut. 2:8)
   a. Snakes sent among the people (Num. 21:4-9)
19. *Zered Valley*
   a. Camps set up (Num. 21:10-12)
20. *Arnon River* (Num. 21:13-15. Note that Israel went around the land of Moab. Judg. 11:18)
21. *Beer*
   a. Well dug (Num. 21:16-19)
22. *Pisgah*
   a. View of wasteland (Jeshimon) (Num. 21:20)
23. *Jahaz*
   a. Defeat of Sihon, king of Amorites (Num. 21:21-32)
24. *Edrei*
   a. Defeat of Og, king of Bashan (Num. 21:33-35)
25. *Plains of Moab*
   a. Balaam's prophecies (Num. 22–24)
   b. Sin at Peor (Num. 25)
   c. The second census (Num. 26)
   d. Midianites defeated (Num. 31)
   e. Messages in Deuteronomy
   f. Death of Moses (Deut. 34)

(The more complete list of Israel's stopping places is given in Numbers chapter 33.)

3. *Route of Israel's departure from Egypt* (Ex. 12:37-39; 13:17-22). "When Pharaoh let the people go, God did not lead them on the road through the Philistine country, though that was shorter" (Ex. 13:17). The short road from Egypt to Canaan ran along the Mediterranean coast of the Sinai peninsula. This road would have been a route to Canaan of less than two hundred miles, a journey of perhaps two weeks. God intended that Israel go to the "mountain of God" in their journey (Ex. 3:12). Furthermore, the Israelites were quite unprepared to meet the armies and forts of the Philistines which had already been placed along the coastal road. "So God led the people around by the desert road toward the *Red Sea*" (13:18).

It appears that the Israelites left Egypt travelling east toward the desert, and not toward the north. They would have crossed the line now marked by the Suez Canal near Lake Timsah, where they would have entered the Desert of Shur, also called *Etham* (Ex. 13:20). From there they began to journey south, toward the mountain of God, where they would receive the law of God.

The Egyptians never did rule southern Sinai. This would have influenced the Israelites to travel through southern Sinai on their journey, rather than to go across northern Sinai. Furthermore, northern Sinai has almost no water sources, while southern Sinai has more adequate water supplies. Southern Sinai has a relatively comfortable climate, compared to the sandy wastelands of northern Sinai. (See Itzhaq Beit Arieh "The Route Through Sinai," in *Biblical Archaeology Review*, May–June 1988, pp. 28-37.)

Israel's journey was a spiritual journey. Israel's journey must not be viewed as only a travel over *land*. Israel's true journey was a spiritual journey, from unbelief to faith in the LORD, from idolatry to the worship of the LORD, from the love of the food of Egypt (Num.11:5) to loving the LORD with all their hearts (Deut. 6:4-5). During their long stay in Egypt most Israelites had lost the devotion to God that Abraham and Jacob and Joseph had. They did not know God's name (Ex. 3:13). They worshiped the gods of Egypt! (Josh. 24:15). "In their hearts they turned back to Egypt" (Acts 7:39). The generation that left Egypt with Moses never seemed to develop trust in the LORD, though He did great miracles before them.

God said of the Israelites, "I brought you to *myself*" (Ex. 19:4). The journey from Egypt to GOD was a much longer journey than the journey from Egypt to Canaan.

4. *Red Sea, or Sea of Reeds?* The sea now called the *Red Sea* was called the *Sea of Weeds* or *Sea of Reeds* (Hebrew, *Yam Suph*). Nonetheless, the names *Red Sea* and *Sea of Reeds* refer to the same body of water, namely the Red Sea. The Greek Septuagint Bible consistently translated *Yam Suph* as *"Red Sea."* The New Testament refers to the sea the Israelites crossed as the Red Sea (Acts 7:36; Heb. 11:29). (The author-

ity of the New Testament should settle the question.) Furthermore in such passages as 1 Kings 9:26 and Numbers 21:4 and 33:10-11, the term *Yam Suph* clearly refers to the body of water we call the Red Sea. Therefore, *Yam Suph* almost certainly refers to the Red Sea in such passages as Exodus 15:4, 22. "The best of Pharaoh's officers are drowned in the *Red Sea*."

Some writers have said that Israel crossed a swampy place when they crossed the "Sea of Reeds." This is not the way the Bible describes the place they crossed. There was a "wall of water on their right and on their left" (Ex. 14:22). When Pharaoh's chariots pursued the Israelites, "the deep waters have covered them; they sank to the depths like a stone" (Ex. 15:5). "The sea covered them. They sank like lead in the mighty waters" (Ex. 15:10).

The "weeds" in the Sea of Weeds probably are the seaweeds, as in Jonah 2:5, where the word *suph* refers to seaweeds in the Mediterranean Sea.

The waters at the north tip of the Gulf of Suez (near the modern town of Suez) are about seventeen feet deep and four miles across. We are strongly convinced that this was the place where Israel crossed the sea.

5. *A long sojourn ends* (Ex. 12:40-42). The Israelites had lived in Egypt 430 years, "to the very day." This extended from Jacob's coming to Egypt in 1876 B.C. to their departure in 1446 B.C.

The Greek Bible adds a phrase to 12:40: "the sojourning of the children of Israel, while they sojourned in the land of Egypt *and the land of Canaan*, was four hundred and thirty years." The insertion of this phrase causes the "430 years" to include the time from Abraham's entry into Canaan until Jacob went into Egypt (215 years), as well as the years actually spent in Egypt. If this chronology of the Greek Bible is followed, we shall have to believe that Jacob entered Egypt in 1661 B.C.

It is very improbable that the population of Israel could have multiplied from 70 men to 603,550 men in 215 years. That time span is only four or five generations. We prefer the Hebrew Bible over the Greek Bible in most cases where they differ, though the Septuagint is NOT always wrong. (The Greek Bible is a translation from the Hebrew, and they agree far more often than they disagree.)

6. *Demands and directions to the redeemed* (Ex. 13).

A. God's demands (Ex. 13:1-16)
    1. Consecrate the firstborn (13:1-2, 11-16)
    2. Keep the feast (13:3-10)
B. God's directions (Ex. 13:17-22)
    1. Safe direction (13:17)
    2. Rigorous direction (13:18)
    3. Clear and constant direction (13:21-22)

---

7. *Crossing the sea* (Ex. 14). When the Israelites were in the desert of Etham, almost out of Egypt, The LORD gave Moses some surprising directions: "Turn back and encamp near Pi Hahairoth, between Migdol (a Tower) and the sea." This resulted in a turn back toward Egypt. More than that, the turn led them into a very narrow corridor (.3 mi.) between the Red Sea Gulf of Suez and steep-sided Mt. Atakah just west of the gulf. (See map on p. 187.)

Pharaoh had trackers and runners following the Israelites. When he heard of their unexpected turn back toward Egypt, he supposed they were wandering around the land in confusion. The Israelites were the bait that God used to bring the Egyptian army to the sea. There Pharaoh met his doom. When his army tried to follow the Israelites over the dry strip across the sea, the waters closed upon them.

The Israelites were very fearful when Pharaoh's army came.

Directions in dilemma (Ex. 14:13-16)

1. "Do not be afraid" (14:13)
2. "Stand firm" (14:13)
3. "See the deliverance (lit., *salvation*) of the LORD."
4. "Move on! Go forward!" (14:15)

Israel crossed the Red Sea after midnight (Ex. 14:24), probably between midnight and 3:00 a.m. If they marched across on a mile-wide front, with people five feet apart and ranks five feet behind each other, all two to three million of the Israelites could have crossed the sea in about three hours. Their column would have been two to three miles long. The shining light from the cloud made their way clear. Psalm 77:16-18 indicates that a storm of rain and lightning occurred there the night Israel crossed the sea.

Exodus 14 — *"Baptized into Moses"*

"They were all *baptized into Moses* in the cloud and in the sea" (1 Cor. 10:2). Before crossing the sea they were all in Egypt's kingdom. After crossing the sea, they were under the authority of Moses. Crossing the sea was the time of transition, and a time of triumph.

"All of you who were *baptized into Christ* have clothed yourselves with Christ" (Gal. 3:27).

ISRAEL — A Type of the Church (1 Cor. 10:1–11)

ISRAEL		RED SEA		JORDAN	CANAAN
I S R A E L	1. Bondage in Egypt 2. Deliverer (Moses) 3. Moses believed 4. Egypt forsaken 5. Passover	→ R E D S E A	6. Freedom from Egypt 7. Heavenly food provided 8. Law of Moses 9. Tabernacle worship 10. Unfaithful perish 11. Faithful enter → → →	J O R D A N →	C A N A A N
C H U R C H	1. Bondage in sin 2. Deliverer (Christ) 3. Christ believed 4. Sin forsaken 5. Death of Christ	→ B A P T I S M	6. Freedom from sin 7. Heavenly food provided 8. Law of Christ 9. Church worship 10. Unfaithful to perish 11. Faithful enter → → →	D E A T H →	H E A V E N

8. *The Song of Moses and Miriam* (Ex. 15:1-21). The Song declared the greatness of the LORD. It is an exciting song.

Exodus 15 — **FROM TRIUMPH TO TESTING**
(1) Songs of triumph (15:1-21)
(2) Situations of testing (15:22-26)
God's children often experience severe testing soon after times of spiritual triumph. Even Jesus went from his baptism directly into his temptations in the desert (Matt. 3:13–4:1).

The Song of Moses (Ex. 15:1-18)

1. What the LORD *IS* (15:1-3) — My strength, my song, my salvation, my God (Ps. 118:14; Isa. 12:2).

2. What the LORD *DID* (15:4-16)

3. What the LORD *WILL DO* (15:13-18)
"You will bring them in and plant them" (15:17)
"The LORD will reign for ever and ever" (15:18)

Israel came across the Red Sea into the Desert of Shur. This is nearly all a barren sandy wasteland. They went three days and found no water. When they did find a spring in the sand, the water was bitter. They called it *Marah*, which means bitter. The LORD used it as a test to see if they would obey His *commands*. *Marah* is probably the bitter spring named 'Ain Hawwara, thirty-seven miles from the north tip of the Gulf of Suez.

Another seven miles of travel south, along the gulf side, brought Israel to *Elim*, probably the Wadi Gharandel, where Israel found twelve springs of good water and seventy palm trees in the wadi channel (15:27).

Exodus 16 — **BREAD FROM HEAVEN**

---

9. *Quail and manna* (Ex. 16). Numbers 33:10-11 says, "They left Elim and camped by the Red Sea. They left the

Red Sea and camped in the Desert of Sin." The modern road along the east side of the Gulf of Suez follows the ancient road, and at one point comes to the seaside. Concerning the Desert of Sin, see Period V, Section A, 1, p. 184.

Israel arrived at the Desert of Sin exactly one month after their departure from Egypt. If any Israelites had thought they were setting out on a three days' journey (Ex. 5:3), they had by then used up all food supplies that they had brought with them from Egypt.

Quail migrate back into the Middle East from Africa in the springtime. The LORD directed their arrival time and their landing place to supply the Israelites' needs (16:13).

The Israelites called the bread *manna* (or *man*). This word means "What is it?" It was not a food that they had known before (Deut. 8:3). It was a miraculous product. There was no possibility that the mostly barren Sinai desert could supply food for two to three million Israelites without God's intervention.

A memorial jar of manna was to be kept by the ark (16:33).

GOD'S PURPOSES IN GIVING MANNA

a. To fill them with food (Ex. 16:12, 16; Matt. 6:31-33)
b. To see if they would walk in His laws (Ex. 16:4; Deut 8:16)
c. To show that the LORD had led them out of Egypt (Ex. 16:6)
d. To show that He was the LORD their God (Ex. 16:6)
e. To show God's glory (Ex. 16:7)
f. To silence their murmurings (Ex. 16:7, 8, 12)
g. To introduce the Sabbath law (Ex. 16:23, 25, 29)
h. To humble them (Deut. 8:16, 3)
i. To teach that man does not live by bread alone, but by every word of God (Deut. 8:3)
j. To point toward Jesus, the living bread from heaven (John 6:41, 48-51)

---

10. *Water from the Rock* (Ex. 17:1-7). The major wadi (brook) draining the southern part of the Sinai peninsula into the Gulf of Suez comes to shore near the Wilderness of

Sin. The wadi is called the Wadi *Feiran*. It has a branch upstream, called the Wadi *Sheikh*, that goes inland almost to Mt. Sinai (Jebel Musa). The Wadi Feiran is the main route from the sea up to Mt. Sinai, and the modern road goes through it. Almost certainly the Israelites would have gone through this valley up to Mt. Sinai. In places it is up to half a mile in width. Pink granite mountains lie all around it. A few thorny, tough acacia trees grow in the valley. (The tabernacle was made from the acacia wood.)

In the Valley of Feiran at a place called *Rephidim* God supplied Israel water from a large rock (Deut. 8:15). But the boulder of stone did not give them the water. "They drank from the spiritual rock that accompanied them, and that rock was Christ" (1 Cor. 10:3).

Moses called the place where they received the water *Massah* and *Meribah*. *Massah* means *testing*, or *tempting*. *Meribah* means *quarreling*, or strife or contention. The Israelites *tested* the LORD by saying, "Is the LORD among us or not?" We should not test the LORD by questioning His presence or His goodness (Deut. 6:16).

Exodus 17 — TWO TESTS: WATER and WAR
  a. Water from the rock (Ex. 17:1-7)
  b. War with the Amalekites (Ex. 17:8-15)

In every crisis they faced, the Israelites did not show faith, but grumbled. God does not like our complaining against Him (Num. 14:27).

The Water-producing ROCK — A Type of Christ

1. Struck by God's order (Ex. 17:6; Zech 13:7; Isa. 53:4)
2. Produced abundant water (Ps. 78:15; John 7:37-39; 4:10)
3. To be struck only once (Num. 20:8-12; Heb. 9:28)

---

11. *The Amalekites defeated* (Ex. 17:8-15). The Amalekites were descendants of Esau (Gen. 36:12). They lived as preda-

tory nomads. The Israelites were strung out in a long column in the wadis of Sinai. The Amalekites attacked the stragglers in the rear ranks (Deut. 29:17-19). For this offense they were as a race sentenced to extermination (Ex. 17:16; Num. 24:20, 24). King Saul was sent to wipe them out (1 Sam. 15:2-5; 18:18).

In this story we are introduced for the first time to *Joshua*, who became the successor to Moses. He was a warrior, and defeated the Amalekites.

We read also of *Hur*. He and Aaron held up Moses' hands as Joshua fought the Amalekites. "Lifting up the hands" is usually associated with prayer (Ps. 141:2; 1 Tim. 2:8). God must have desired to show vividly that the victory over the Amalekites was His victory, and not a victory by human power. Exodus 24:14 indicates that Hur was an official appointed to judge disputes. Josephus (*Antiquities* III, ii, 4 [III, 54]) says that Hur was the husband of Miriam, Moses' sister. We do not know if that is true or not.

12. *Jethro's visit and judges appointed* (Ex. 18). Jethro came to meet Moses with the Israelites, as he came near to Mt. Sinai. Jethro brought Moses' wife and two sons, who had returned to Midian after the illness of Moses at the lodging place (Ex. 4:24-26). Jethro was delighted with the report of what the LORD had done through Moses (18:10). God had said to Abraham, "I will bless those who bless you." Jethro received a blessing by blessing Moses, who was from the offspring of Abraham.

Though Jethro was the priest of Midian, Jethro learned about the LORD Yahweh from Moses, and not Moses from Jethro (18:11). There is a theory called the Kenite theory, that the Israelites got their conception of Yahweh from the Midianites or Kenites.

Jethro found Moses spending all his hours judging the disputes of the people. Jethro knew the folly of one-man rule, and urged Moses to appoint subordinate judges. One out of every ten men would be a judge. The judges were to be capable men who feared God and hated dishonest gain and bribes (18:21).

Questions on Section A
From Egypt to Mt. Sinai (Ex. 12:37–18:27)

1. Make a list of the first nine places on the map of Israel's journey from Egypt to Canaan, and give at least one event at each place.
2. Who left Egypt with Israel? (Ex. 12:38; Num. 11:4)
3. How long had Israel lived in Egypt? (12:40)
4. What regulation was given about the bones of the passover lamb? (Ex. 12:46; Compare John 19:36)
5. What people and animals were claimed by the Lord? (13:2)
6. What was the feast of unleavened bread to remind the people of? (13:7-10)
7. What was to be done with firstborn animals? (13:11-13,16; Num. 18:15-17)
8. Why did God not lead Israel into Canaan by the short seacoast way through the land of the Philistines? (13:17)
9. Whose bones were carried out of Egypt by Moses? (13:19)
10. Where did the pillar of cloud begin to lead Israel? (13:20-21)
11. Near what place did the Israelites camp by the Red Sea? (14:2)
12. Why did Pharaoh think Israel was trapped? (14:3)
13. Why did Pharaoh desire to keep Israel in Egypt? (14:5)
14. How many Egyptian chariots set out after Israel? (14:7)
15. How did Israel react when they saw the Egyptians coming? (14:10)
16. What was Israel told to do to see the salvation (deliverance) of the Lord? (14:13)
17. What separated Israel from Egypt at night? (14:19-20)
18. What cleared a path across the sea? (14:21)
19. What hindered the Egyptians as they tried to follow Israel? (14:25)
20. What was the fate of the Egyptians? (14:28)
21. How did the Israelites feel toward God and toward Moses after they crossed the Sea? (14:31)
22. Who sang a song after the deliverance? (15:1)
23. Who sang and danced and played music? (15:20)
24. Into what wilderness did Israel enter after crossing the sea? (Ex. 15:22; Num. 33:8)
25. Name the place where Israel found bitter water. (15:23)
26. How was the water sweetened? (15:25)
27. What would guarantee the health of the Israelites? (15:26)
28. What was found at Elim? (15:27)
29. What did Israel lack in the Wilderness of Sin? (16:1-3)

30. On how many days each week was food provided for Israel? (16:4-5)
31. When was twice as much food to be gathered? (16:5)
32. What meat was given to Israel? (16:13)
33. What does the name *manna* mean? (16:15)
34. How much manna was gathered each day for each person? What happened to those who gathered more or less? (16:16-18)
35. On what day was no manna found? (16:23-27)
36. Where was a pot of manna to be kept as a memorial? (16:32-34; Heb. 9:4)
37. Where did Israel come and find no water? (17:1)
38. How was the water provided for Israel? (17:6)
39. What do the names *Massah* and *Meribah* mean? To what were they applied? (17:7)
40. What tribe attacked Israel? Where? (17:8)
41. Who held up Moses' arms? Why? (17:10-12)
42. Who led Israel's army in battle? (17:10)
43. What was written in a book about the attacking tribe? (17:14)
44. What was the altar made at Rephidim called? (17:15)
45. Whom did Jethro bring to Moses? (18:1-5)
46. What did Jethro conclude after hearing the report of Moses' deeds? (18:11)
47. How long was Moses occupied in judging the people? (18:13)
48. What did Jethro counsel Moses to do? (18:17-22)
49. In what month after the departure from Egypt did Israel arrive at Sinai? (19:1)

Section B
Giving of the Law (Exodus 19–24, 32–34)

Exodus 19 — **Preparations for God's covenant**

(1) The journey completed (19:1-2)

(2) The offer from God (19:3-6)

(3) The people's acceptance (19:7-8)

(4) Acts of consecration (19:9-16)

(5) The descent of God (19:16-25)

---

1. *The journey completed* (Ex. 19:1-2). Israel had left Egypt on the fifteenth day of the first month. They arrived at Sinai

in the third month, "on the very day," probably referring to the first day of the month. Their journey had taken *fifty* days, or nearly that long. Their journey had provided them many examples of God's power and care. It should have imparted to them strong faith in the LORD. They encamped in front of the mountain, probably in the plain of er-Rahah, beside the northern summit of Mt. Sinai named Ras Safsafeh (6500 feet high).

2. *The offer from God* (Ex. 19:3-6). God's offer to Israel was nearly too marvelous for humans to grasp. "If you *obey* me fully and keep my *covenant*, then out of all nations **YOU** will be my treasured possession . . . *you* will be for me a kingdom of priests and a holy nation" (19:5-6, emphasis added). The apostle Peter quoted this verse in 1 Peter 2:9, and applied it to Christians in our dispensation. What will YOU do with God's offer to you?

A covenant is a pledged agreement between people or groups. When God makes an offer, He makes it plain and certain.

3. *The people's acceptance of God's offer* (Ex. 19:7-8). "The people all responded together, 'We will do everything the LORD has said'" (19:8; 24:3). God knew their promise was shallow. But He loved them, and wanted them deeply. "When Israel was a child, I loved him, and out of Egypt I called my *son*" (Hosea 11:1). God does not force Himself upon us, but calls for our own individual and collective acceptance of His covenant.

4. *Acts of consecration* (Ex. 19:9-15). These acts included washing their clothes, putting a fence about the mountain, abstaining from sexual relations, and gathering at the mountain. They needed to be totally focused on the great event coming. The *fence* around the mountain was an indication that there is a gap between sinful humankind and our holy God. We cannot see His face and live. We cannot inherit His kingdom in our present flesh.

5. *The descent of God upon the mountain* (Ex. 19:16-25). On the third day God descended upon Mt. Sinai in a thick cloud, with a loud trumpet blast, and an earthquake. It was so terri-

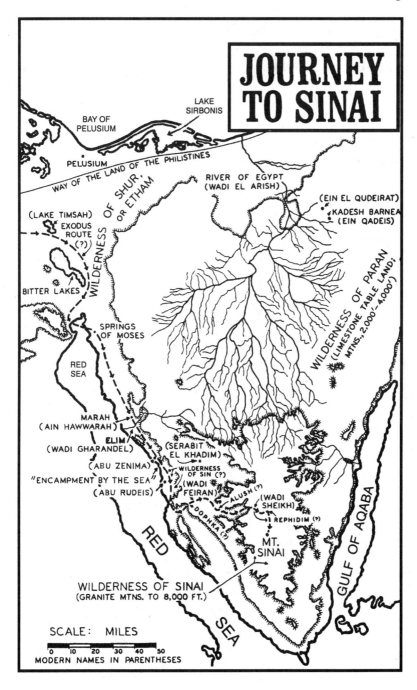

JOURNEY TO SINAI

LAKE SIRBONIS

BAY OF PELUSIUM

PELUSIUM

WAY OF THE LAND OF THE PHILISTINES

RIVER OF EGYPT (WADI EL ARISH)

WILDERNESS OF SHUR, OR ETHAM

(EIN EL QUDEIRAT) KADESH BARNEA (EIN QADEIS)

(LAKE TIMSAH)

EXODUS ROUTE (?)

WILDERNESS

BITTER LAKES

WILDERNESS OF PARAN (LIMESTONE TABLE LAND; MTNS. 2,000'-4,000')

SPRINGS OF MOSES

RED SEA

MARAH (AIN HAWWARAH)

ELIM (WADI GHARANDEL)

(SERABIT EL KHADIM)

(ABU ZENIMA)

WILDERNESS OF SIN (?)

"ENCAMPMENT BY THE SEA" (ABU RUDEIS)

(WADI FEIRAN)

ALUSH (?)

(WADI SHEIKH)

DOPHKA (?)

REPHIDIM (?)

RED

MT. SINAI

GULF OF AQABA

WILDERNESS OF SINAI (GRANITE MTNS. TO 8,000 FT.)

SEA

SCALE: MILES

0   10   20   30   40   50

MODERN NAMES IN PARENTHESES

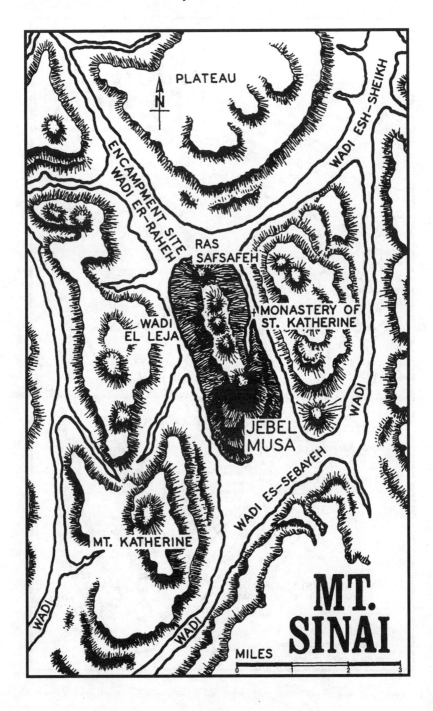

PLATEAU

WADI ESH-SHEIKH

ENCAMPMENT SITE
WADI ER-RAHEH

RAS
SAFSAFEH

WADI
EL LEJA

MONASTERY OF
ST. KATHERINE

JEBEL
MUSA

WADI

MT. KATHERINE

WADI ES-SEBAYEH

WADI

WADI

MT.
SINAI

MILES
0   1   2   3

fying that even Moses said, "I am trembling with fear" (Heb. 12:18-21). This spectacular display of God's presence is contrasted with the more gentle and heavenly way the good news of Jesus is presented to us (Heb. 12:22-24).

In our mind's eyes we stand with Moses, ready to hear God's law. The giving of the law of Moses (starting with the Ten Commandments in Exodus chapter 20) was the beginning of a new dispensation in God's government, the period of the Law of Moses. While the law would prove to be an impossible burden to keep, it would be our tutor, our guardian, and our preparation for an even better covenant, to be revealed later by Christ Jesus.

6. *The ten words* (Ex. 20:1-21). In the Hebrew Bible the Ten Commandments are called the "ten words" (or sayings) and the "Testimony" (Ex. 31:18; 34:28; Deut. 4:13; Ex. 25:16, 21). The term *Decalogue* also means "ten words."

The Ten Commandments are in
Exodus 20 and Deuteronomy 5

The Ten Commandments — A Protection

1. Protection from false gods (20:2-3)
2. Protection from false worship (20:4-6)
3. Protection from misusing God's name (20:7)
4. Protection of rest, and the remembrance of creation (20:8-11)
5. Protection of parents (20:12)
6. Protection of human life (20:13)
7. Protection of marriage and personal purity (20:14)
8. Protection of property (20:15)
9. Protection of truth (20:16)
10. Protection of the heart (20:17)

(Adapted from John J. Davis, *Moses and the Gods of Egypt*, 2nd ed., Grand Rapids: Baker, 1986, pp. 210-220).

The first four commandments are duties to God. The last six are duties to man.

The Ten Commandments are unique in their comprehensiveness and their conciseness. Almost every duty and sin known to man is summed up in them. They are unique in making duties to mankind on a par with duties to God. They are unique in their teaching that it is impossible to separate morality from religion. There is really no parallel to them in the world. Without them our social system probably could not survive.

Ex. 20:3 — "You shall have no other gods *before* me." "Before me" means "in my presence," or "against me," or "in addition to me" (Gen. 31:50). The verse teaches a strict monotheism.

Ex. 20:5 — "Punishing the children for the sin of the fathers." This may seem unjust. But God did this only to those who hated him. Those who loved him and kept his commandments were recipients of God's love, regardless of what their forefathers had done.

Ex. 20:7 — "You shall not *misuse* the name of the LORD." This commandment forbids falsehoods and blasphemy. But it also forbids *vain* (useless, meaningless) use of God's name. The same Hebrew word used with the meaning of *vain* can be found in Psalm 60:11; 108:12; Malachi 3:14.

Ex. 20:8 — The Sabbath day is the seventh day of the week, our Saturday. The Sabbath was first revealed to man in the Desert of Sin when the manna was given, and was first commanded as a law in the Ten Commandments. The apostles of Christ regarded the Sabbath as a shadow of the things that were to come (Col. 2:17), and met for group worship on the first day of the week, Sunday (Acts 20:7). The purposes of the Sabbath law were (1) for rest (Ex. 23:12), (2) to remember creation, (3) to remember their deliverance from Egypt (Deut. 5:15).

The Sabbath law was quite strict in forbidding work. See Exodus 31:12-17; 35:1-3; Numbers 15:32-36; Nehemiah 13:15-22.

Ex. 20:13 — The older translation, "You shall not KILL" is better than "You shall not murder," because the Hebrew word for *kill* is also applied to manslaughter and accidental killing, as well as to murder (Deut. 4:42; Num. 35:6,11; Josh. 20:3).

Nine of the Ten Commandments are repeated in the New Testament, mostly in an intensified form. (See Matthew 5:21-30.) Only the Sabbath command is lacking. The law of God is to be written on our hearts, rather than on stone tablets (Heb. 8:10; 2 Cor. 3:7). We are no longer under the law of Moses as a covenant (Rom. 6:15). But through love we fulfill the law (Rom. 13:10), and serve one another (Gal. 5:13).

7. *Idols and altars* (Ex. 20:22-26). Altars were to be made for the serious and solemn purpose of sacrifice, not to exhibit human skill in sculpture.

8. *First serving of God's just laws* (Ex. 21-23). The word translated "laws" in Exodus 21:1 means "judgments" or righteous decisions by a judge. God's laws are all righteous and good.

The Ten Commandments that all Israel heard are simple, comprehensive principles. But human life is complicated and crooked. Is all killing murder? Do all sexual wrongs deserve the same punishment? The Israelites needed a LOT of instruction besides the Ten Commandments. They had almost NO knowledge of what was God's will for their lives. It was impossible to teach all of God's laws in one day (or one year!). The covenant ordinances in Exodus 21-23 were a first "sampler" of the many teachings that Israel would receive. They dealt briefly with a mixture of topics. There were laws about slaves (21:2-6), personal injuries (21:12), criminal laws (21:16), property laws (21:35), sex laws (22:16), laws about relationships between people (22:21-22), laws about the Sabbath (23:12) and feast days (23:14-19).

> ". . . teaching them to obey everything I have commanded you" (Matt. 28:20).

Many of the laws are extremely attractive, and have applications in many situations. Read Exodus 23:1-9 for examples.

All of these laws derive their force from a personal relationship with God (Ex. 23:25).

Both the *Old Testament and the New Testament*
teach us to ***LOVE OUR NEIGHBOR AS OURSELVES.***
(Lev. 19:18; Matt. 5:43-44)
"If you see the donkey of someone who hates you fallen down under its load, do not leave it there; be sure you help him with it" (Ex. 23:5).

This first serving of God's laws is called "The Book of the Covenant" (24:7). Moses read it to the people when he came down from the mountain. The people promised to obey these laws (24:3).

9. Exodus 24 — *The High Point in Exodus*

Exodus 24 — ISRAEL ENTERS COVENANT RELATIONSHIP WITH THE LORD.

Israel entered into covenant relationship with God by . . .
(1) God's offer to accept Israel as His people (Ex. 19:5-6).
(2) Hearing God's word (His book) (Ex. 24:4, 7).
(3) Promising to obey God's law (Ex. 24:3, 7).
(4) Sprinkling the blood (Ex. 24:8; Heb. 9:18-20).
People in every age have entered into covenant relationship with God by these same means.

Before the covenant was made, the Israelites did not dare even to touch the mountain where God was appearing (Ex. 19:12-13, 21-24). *After* the covenant was made, the Israelites could *see* God and *eat* and drink with Him in perfect safety (Ex. 24:9-11). (God's people now share a similar experience [2 Cor. 3:18].)

Sadly, Israel's happy relationship with God that is described in Exodus 24 was soon broken when Israel made the golden calf (Ex. 32). They broke the covenant, and Israel was again estranged from God (Ex. 32:10).

10. *Israel Sins at Sinai* (Ex. 32).

(Exodus chapters 25–31, 35–40 will be discussed after chapters 32–34 are considered.)

> Exodus 32 — *The Golden Calf. The Covenant Broken*

"The people are out of Egypt, but Egypt is not out of the people!" In Egypt they had worshiped Hathor, the cow-goddess of love, and the sacred bulls at Memphis. Now they dance in ecstasy around the golden calf.

The echoes of God's command, "You shall not make for yourself an idol in the form of anything," had hardly ceased to bounce from the mountainsides when the people said to Aaron, "Make us gods, who will go before us" (32:1). "They forgot the God who saved them" (Ps. 106:21).

Moses had been up on Mt. Sinai for forty days (24:18). Aaron showed weakness of character by yielding to the people's request (32:4). Aaron's story to Moses about how the golden calf was made was truly a "tall tale" (32:24). God was angry with Aaron for doing this. Only Moses' prayer saved him (Deut. 9:20).

The calf was probably made of wood covered with thin sheets of gold, with features engraved upon it. It could be burned.

Aaron tried to put a good face on the idolatry by building an altar before the golden calf, and proclaiming a festival to the LORD (32:5). But God refused to honor a festival to Him when "other gods" were "before him." God looked upon the calf not as a representation of Him; but as an idol (Ezek. 20:8; Acts 7:39-41). God was ready to destroy Israel (32:9).

The prayers of Moses saved Israel (32:11-14, 31-32). He did not seek honors for himself, but glory for God (32:10-12). Moses was a spiritual statesman, who was more concerned with his people than with himself, even when the people were abusive toward him. But not even the prayers of Moses could save the Israelites from all of the consequences of their sin (32:34-35).

> Moses prayed, "Please forgive their sin — but if not, then **blot me out of the book** you have written" (32:32).
>
> (This prayer of Moses is almost as great as the prayer of Christ in the Garden of Gethsemane (Matt. 26:39).

Moses himself became angry when he saw the golden calf (32:19). He broke it into pieces, burned it, threw the ashes in water, and made the people drink it. He set an example to the people: "The images of their gods you are to burn in the fire" (Deut. 7:25).

The success of Moses in rallying many people against the idolatry, particularly the Levites, shows that Aaron could have resisted the request to make the idol, if he had tried (32:25-28).

The Levites redeemed their reputation that day. Instead of appearing only as cruel ruffians (Gen. 49:5-7), they showed that they were committed to God so fully that they would go against their own family members, if need be (32:26-29). They became the tribe from which the priests came. In Moses' final blessing he gave the Levites great honor (Deut. 33:8-11).

> Exodus **32** — The covenant with God broken
>
> Exodus **33** — Israel and God in tension
>
> Exodus **34** — The covenant restored

11. *God and Israel in tension* (Ex. 33). The period between Moses' prayer for Israel (32:31-34) and God's re-acceptance of Israel was a tense time (33:14, 17).

> Exodus 33 — God's presence withdrawn (33:1-3)
>
> The people in mourning (33:4-6)
> The tent of meeting removed from the camp (33:7-11)
> The mediator in prayer (33:12-23)

Exodus 33:7-10 tells of a "tent of meeting." This term was

later applied to the first room in the tabernacle, the Holy Place (Ex. 27:21). Here it refers to another tent — probably Moses' own tent — where Moses talked to God before the tabernacle was built.

Moses loved God so much that he wanted to see His glory (33:18). God said, "You cannot see my face" (33:20). But God did grant to Moses part of what he requested. "I will hide you in a cleft (a crevasse) in the rock, and cover you with my hand until I have passed over. Then I will remove my hand and you will see my back" (my afterglow). In heaven Moses now beholds God face to face, and we also may behold Him (1 John 3:2).

Exodus 34 — **The covenant renewed**

1. The tablets were restored (34:1-4).
2. God proclaimed His Name (34:5-9).
3. God pledged His covenant (34:10).
4. God commanded His ordinances (34:11-26).
5. God's words were written (34:27-28).
6. God's commands were reported (34:31-32).
7. Moses' face shone (34:29-30, 33-35)

In Exodus 34:5-7 there is one of the most complete and wonderful descriptions of God in the Bible. It is God's own Sermon on His name. God is what His name says He is.

(1) The LORD (Yahweh), the LORD (a doubly-declared name)
(2) God (the mighty one)

(3) Compassionate	(8) Forgiving wickedness
(4) Gracious	(9) Forgiving rebellion and sin
(5) Maintaining love to thousands	(10) Not leaving the guilty unpunished
(6) Abounding in love	(11) Punishing children for the
(7) Abounding in faithfulness	sins of the fathers

Moses veiled his face, which had acquired a glow from his association with God on the mountain (34:29-33). He veiled it so that the people would not see the glory fade away (2 Cor. 3:13-18). The apostle Paul used the fading glory of Moses' face as a symbol of the fading glory of the old covenant (the law of Moses). Like Moses, "We, who with unveiled faces all reflect the Lord's glory, are being transformed into his likeness with ever-increasing glory" (2 Cor. 3:18).

Questions on Section B
Giving of the Law (Ex. 19–24, 32–34)

1. From what place did God call Moses in the wilderness of Sinai? (Ex. 19:1-3)
2. What was God's condition for Israel to become His own possession from among all peoples? (19:5-6)
3. What did Israel promise Moses and God that they would do? (19:8)
4. When God came to Israel, what did He come in? (19:9)
5. How many days' notice of His coming did God give Israel? (19:1)
6. What was the penalty for touching the mount? (19:12-13; compare Heb. 12:18-22.)
7. Describe the scene as God descended on Mt. Sinai. (19:16-18)
8. About how many times did Moses go up on Mt. Sinai?
9. Who all heard the words of the Ten Commandments? (Ex. 20:9, 18; Deut. 5:22-23)
10. Learn from memory Exodus 20:2-17.
11. How did Israel react when they heard God's voice? (20:19-20)
12. What material was Israel to use in making God an altar? (20:24-25)
13. How long could a Hebrew servant be held in slavery? (21:2)
14. What responsibility did a man with a mean bull have? (21:28-29)
15. What people were especially under God's protection and concern? (22:22)
16. How long could a man's garment be held as security for a loan? (22:26-27)
17. What law was given about following a mob? (23:2)
18. How often did the land lie unused for a year? (23:10-11)
19. How many compulsory feasts were to be kept each year? Name them. (23:14-16; 34:22-23; Deut. 16:16)
20. Who was sent before Israel to keep them? (23:20-21)
21. What did the people promise concerning the words of the covenant which God spoke? (24:3-5)
22. By what means did Moses ratify the covenant between God and Israel? (Ex. 24:8. Compare Heb. 9:18-26.)
23. What group of people went up on Mt. Sinai with Moses on one trip? (24:1, 9)
24. Describe the appearance of God to Moses and to the others. (24:10)

25. Who went up with Moses when he received the tables of the Ten Commandments? (24:12-13)
26. How long did Moses stay up on the mount on that trip? (24:18)
27. What did the people say when Moses delayed coming down? (32:1)
28. What was used to make an idol? Who built it? (32:2-4)
29. What did the people do before the idol? (Ex. 32:6; 1 Cor. 10:7)
30. What did God threaten to do to Israel, and do with Moses? (32:20; Deut. 9:14,20)
31. What saved Israel from God's wrath? (32:11-14)
32. What did Moses do with the tablets of the Ten Commandments? (32:19-20).
33. What tall tale did Aaron tell Moses? (32:24)
34. What tribe stood with Moses against the idolatry? (32:26)
35. How many died because of the idolatry? (32:28; compare Acts 2:41.)
36. With what words did Moses pray to God to forgive Israel? (32:32)
37. Why did God not go with Israel, but rather sent an angel? (33:1-3)
38. What was the tent called where Moses sought the LORD? (33:7)
39. In what manner did God speak to Moses? (33:11)
40. What did Moses ask God to show him? (33:13, 18)
41. Why could Moses not see God's face? (33:20)
42. Where did God hide Moses as His glory passed by? (33:21-23)
43. What was Moses to bring up on the mountain during his final ascent? (34:1-2)
44. What did God promise and covenant to do before Israel and all the people? (34:10-11)
45. What was Israel to do to the Canaanites? (34:11-16)
46. What words are called "the words of the covenant"? (34:11-16)
47. What was very noticeable about Moses' appearance when he came down from the mount? (34:29; compare 2 Cor. 3:13.)

You be the Judge (Exodus 21–23)

Case A — A Hebrew by the name of Dan bought a slave from one of his brothers. The slave served the allotted six years, but during that time he married the niece of his master with the help and encouragement of his master. They had three children. Now he wishes to leave, but the master says that the wife and children belong to him, and that he must leave by himself. What is to be done? (Ex. 21:4-6)

Case B – While securing lumber for the building of the tabernacle, a workman felled a tree which fell on another workman and killed him. The man who was killed had a brother working in the crew, and he swears that he has the right to avenge the blood of his brother. Has he? If so, what is to be done? (Ex. 21:12-14; Num. 21:15)

Case C – Here appear four brothers who all state they caught their sister cursing and attacking their mother. What is to be done? (Ex. 21:15)

Case D – A man was startled out of his sleep one night, and saw someone in his tent. He reached under his pillow and took hold of his sword. Almost before he knew it, he had run the intruder through, and he lay dead on the tent floor. What is to be done? (Ex. 22:2)

Case E — A man comes to say that he has borrowed his neighbor's ox, and it had fallen sick while with him, and finally died. What shall be done? (Ex. 22:10, 12-14)

Section C
Tabernacle and Priesthood (Exodus 25:1–31:11; 35:4–40:38; Leviticus 8–10)

1. *Introduction to the Tabernacle.*

a. *What was the tabernacle?* The tabernacle was the movable house of worship which the Israelites made at Mt. Sinai and carried with them through their forty years of wilderness wanderings. It could quickly be dismantled and reassembled. After the Israelites settled in the Promised Land, the tabernacle was set up at a permanent location (Shiloh). It continued to be the center of their worship activities for over four hundred years, until the time of the prophet Samuel. In the days of King Solomon (970–931 B.C.) a temple was built, which replaced the tabernacle, but some of the furniture of the original tabernacle was used in the temple.

b. *What was the purpose of the tabernacle?* It was to be a *sanctuary* (a holy place) where God would dwell among His worshiping people (Ex. 25:8; 29:45). God lives among His people, not in a building or a box. The tabernacle was the place where God chose to make His name (meaning Himself) to dwell (Jer. 7:12; Deut. 12:11). There all the Israelites were to bring their sacrifices and rejoice before the LORD.

The tabernacle was set up in the very center of the encampments of the tribes of Israel (Num. 1:52-53). God desired to be in the center of everything in the Israelites' lives.

c. *Where is the biblical information about the tabernacle found?* The instructions about how to build it are in Exodus 25-31. The record of its construction is in Exodus 35-40. There is much information in Leviticus about the worship to be conducted at the tabernacle. The books of Numbers and Deuteronomy, as well as Hebrews in the New Testament, say much about the tabernacle. A large amount of space is devoted to the tabernacle in the Scripture.

d. *Why is the study of the tabernacle important?* The tabernacle was a copy and shadow of what is in heaven (Heb. 8:4; 9:23). The tabernacle was a small model on earth of what is in heaven above. The tabernacle had an *ark* (box) of the covenant; heaven has an ark (Rev. 11:19). The tabernacle had an *altar* for sacrifice; heaven has an altar (Rev. 6:9; 14:18; 16:7). The tabernacle had a shining *cloud of glory* in its innermost room; heaven shines with the glory of God's presence (Rev. 21:23). In the tabernacle there was a *"throne"* for God above the ark of the covenant and the atonement cover upon it (Ps. 99:1); in heaven the throne of God is central (Rev. 22:3). In the tabernacle *incense* was burned each morning and evening; in heaven incense (people's prayers) is offered before God (Rev. 8:3). In the tabernacle figures of worshiping *cherubim* (angels) were on its veil and on the ark (Ex. 25:18-20); in heaven the living cherubim worship before God's throne (Ezek. 10:1-3; Rev. 4:6-8).

The tabernacle was also important because it was a *type* (a symbol, or illustration, or foreshadowing) of our Christian religion of the present time. "This is an illustration for the present time" (Heb. 9:8-9). Every room (or area) in the tabernacle, and every piece of furniture resembled something in our present religion of Christ. For examples, the altar of incense was a type of prayer; and the Holy of Holies (the innermost room) was a picture (type) of heaven.

It is very impressive to learn that God designed the tabernacle in such a marvelous way that it resembled both His dwelling in the heavens, and foreshadowed the features of our present Christian faith.

    e. *Where were the materials for the tabernacle obtained?* They were obtained from free will offerings from each man whose heart prompted him to give (Ex. 25:2). The people contributed very willingly, until the builders had to say, "The people are bringing more than enough for doing the work" (Ex. 36:5). (There is a lesson for us in this.)

The materials used in making the tabernacle are listed in Exodus 38:21-31. Their value would have been nine million dollars or more. The tabernacle was an impressive structure, even though it was movable.

    f. *Who built the tabernacle?* The two principal builders were *Bezalel* of the tribe of Judah and *Oholiab* of the tribe of Dan. The LORD filled Bezalel with the Spirit of God and with skill. God gave all the craftsmen special skill (Ex. 31:1-6; 36:1,8; 37;1; 38:22-23). In a similar way Christ gave to His twelve apostles special help by sending the Holy Spirit upon them to help them remember all that He had taught them, and to reveal new things to them, and give them power (John 14:26; 16:12-13; Acts 1:8).

(We shall present the information about the parts of the tabernacle in the order that the Scripture presents it.)

    2. *The ark of the covenant* (Ex. 25:10-22; 37:1-9). The ark appears to have pictured God's throne in heaven (Ps. 99:1; Lev. 16:2). The information about the tabernacle begins with the ark. God's perspective is first, not man's. The ark was a wooden chest, made of acacia wood, covered with gold inside and out. It was 2½ cubits long (almost four feet) × 1½ × 1½ cubits. The ark contained the stone tablets of the original Ten Commandments (Ex. 25:16; 40:20; 1 Kgs. 8:9). A jar of manna was kept "before the LORD" near the ark (Ex. 16:33). Also the staff (rod) of Aaron that blossomed in the desert was kept "in front of the Testimony" (the Ten Commandments) (Num. 17:8, 10).

General view of the tabernacle and court.

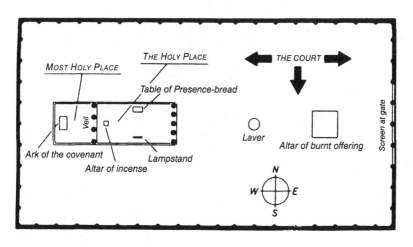

Floor plan of the tabernacle and court.

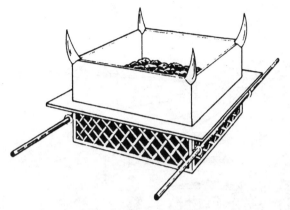

Altar of burnt offering or brazen altar.

The laver
and its
base.

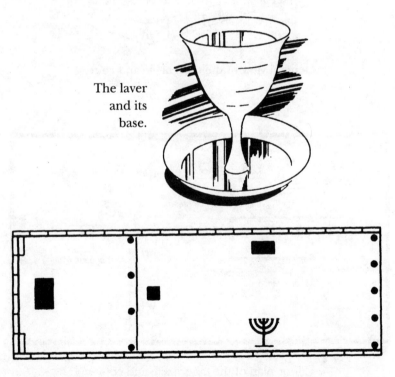

Floor plan of the tabernacle building, showing its boards.

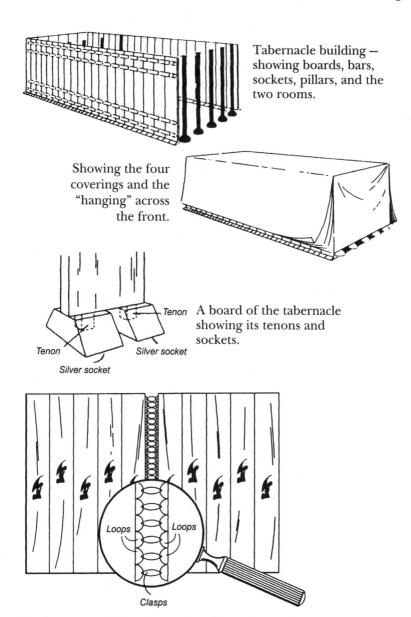

Tabernacle building —
showing boards, bars,
sockets, pillars, and the
two rooms.

Showing the four
coverings and the
"hanging" across
the front.

A board of the tabernacle
showing its tenons and
sockets.

Tenon

Tenon

Silver socket

Silver socket

Loops

Loops

Clasps

The innermost (linen) curtain of the tabernacle.
Note that it was formed of two groups of five
curtains decorated with cherubim, and joined by
loops and clasps.

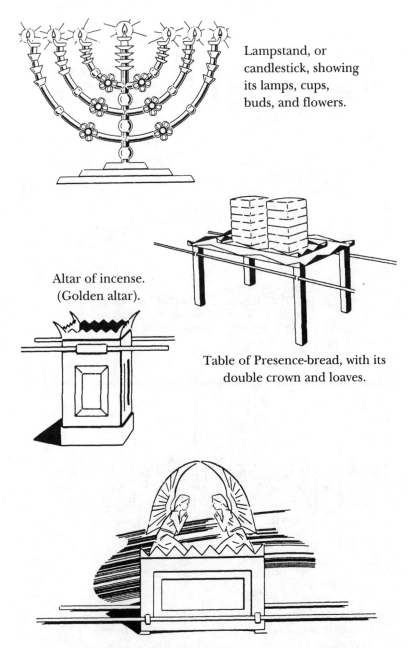

Lampstand, or candlestick, showing its lamps, cups, buds, and flowers.

Altar of incense. (Golden altar).

Table of Presence-bread, with its double crown and loaves.

The ark of the covenant and the mercy seat with cherubim.

The ark was covered by a lid of solid gold, called the "atonement cover" (or mercy seat) (Ex. 25:17-22). The high priest sprinkled blood on the atonement cover on the Day of Atonement each year (Lev. 16:11-16; Heb. 9:7). Gold figures of cherubim were upon the atonement cover, made of one piece with it. They faced one another, with their wings spread above the atonement cover.

God communicated with Israel from His "throne" above the ark (25:22; Num. 7:89).

The Ark of the Covenant — A symbol of God's throne	
1. Ten commandments inside	1. Righteousness and justice, the foundation of God's throne (Ps. 89:14)
2. Jar of manna there	2. Lovingkindness (Ps. 89:14)
3. Aaron's staff there	3. Christ alone is priest
4. Atonement cover (mercy seat) covered ark	4. Christ, our place of mercy and atonement
5. Cherubim	5. Worshiping angels

3. *The table of Presence-bread* (Ex. 25:23-30; 37:10-16; Lev. 24:5-9). This was a small table, two cubits (three feet) long. It was used to hold the twelve loaves of the bread of the Presence, set out each Sabbath day. Its exact meaning is not stated in Scripture. The bread is called the bread of the Presence. Twelve loaves suggests the twelve tribes. We therefore suppose that the Table of Presence-bread pictured *God's people in God's presence.*

The Table of Presence-bread —	*God's People in God's Presence*
1. Twelve loaves / tribes	1. All Christians
2. Continually before God	2. Continual fellowship with God
3. Frankincense applied	3. Prayer (Acts 2:42)
4. Eaten weekly	4. Weekly assembly (Heb.10:25)

The loaves were very large, each made of two-tenths of an ephah of flour (about a gallon!). Frankincense was placed upon the loaves. Incense is a symbol of prayer in the Scriptures.

4. *The lampstand* (Ex. 25:31-40; 27:20-21; 37:17-24; Num. 8:1-4. The ritual is told in Lev. 24:1-4). The lampstand is called the **menorah** in Hebrew. It was made of a talent of pure gold. It had a central upright shaft, and six branches, three from each side. The shaft and branches were decorated with carvings in the shapes of almond flowers and buds (or knops) and cups (perhaps the calyxes of the flowers). On the shaft and on each branch a golden lamp was placed. Each morning and evening pure olive oil was placed in the lamps, and they were lighted to burn continually.

In Scripture the number *seven* seems to indicate completeness and perfection. The *olive oil* is sometimes symbolic of the Holy Spirit (Heb. 1:9; Acts 10:38).

The LAMPSTAND (Menorah) — The Light of God & Christ	
1. Seven lamps	1. A perfect, complete light
2. Olive oil burned	2. Holy Spirit "fuel"
3. Seen by priests only	3. Seen by saints only (2 Cor. 4:4)
God is light (1 John 1:5). Jesus is the light (John 8:12). You are the light of the world (Matt. 5:14).	God's word is a light (Ps. 119:105; 2 Pet. 1:19).

5. *The tabernacle building and its coverings* (Ex. 26:1-37; 36:8-38).The tabernacle building was formed of "frames" (or boards) of wood ten cubits (fifteen feet) long, stood up on their ends on silver bases (sockets), and held together by crossbars through them and through rings on their exterior. The frames were covered with gold. These frames could be set up quickly.

The tabernacle building was covered by four large fabric coverings draped over it. These were made of (1) linen cloth

decorated by figures of cherubim worked into them; (2) goats'
hair (probably dark colored); (3) rams' skins dyed red;
(4) hides of sea cows (or manatees) (26:14). (These are listed
from inner covering to outer coverings.)

The tabernacle building had two rooms — the *Holy Place*,
the first room inside the entrance, and the *Most Holy Place*
(Holy of Holies), the innermost room. The Holy Place was
10 × 10 × 20 cubits in size; the Most Holy Place was 10 × 10 ×
10. The priests went each day into the Holy Place to burn
incense and light the lamps, and on the Sabbath days to
replace the Presence bread. Only the high priest went into
the Most Holy Place, and he went only on one day each year,
the Day of Atonement.

A beautiful curtain (veil) separated the Holy Place from
the Most Holy Place (26:31-34; 36:35-36). The veil was made
of blue, purple and scarlet yarn, with cherubim figures
worked into it. A similar veil was in the temples in later years.
The veil was torn apart by God's power the hour that Jesus
died on the cross (Matt. 27:51).

The entrance to the Holy Place from the outside had a
beautiful curtain similar to the veil, but lacked the cherubim
figures. See Exodus 26:36-37; 36:37-38.

Three items of furniture were in the Holy Place: (1) The
table of Presence bread; (2) the lampstand (menorah), (3) the
altar of incense. In the Holy of Holies there was only one
item, the ark of the covenant, which contained the tablets
with the Ten Commandments written on them.

The tabernacle was placed inside an enclosed courtyard
50 × 100 cubits. The courtyard had within it (in front of the
tabernacle building) a bronze *altar* for burnt offerings and a
basin (or *laver*) where the priests washed (Ex. 30:17-22).

The apostle Paul said that he could not discuss the items
in the tabernacle in detail just then (Heb. 9:5). We do not
feel we are wiser than Paul, or know anything about the
tabernacle except that which the Scripture states. The following charts show some of the similarities (types) between the
tabernacle parts and the church revealed in the New
Testament:

The HOLY of HOLIES – A Type of Heaven
(The Holy of Holies was God's Throne Room! Psalm 99:1)

1. A perfect cube	1. Foursquare (Rev. 21:16)
2. Golden (Ex. 26:29)	2. Golden (Rev. 21:18, 21)
3. Ark of covenant there	3. God's throne and ark there (Rev. 22:3; 11:19)
4. Glory cloud (shekinah) (Lev.16:2)	4. Light of God's glory (Rev. 22:5)
5. Approached through the veil	5. Approached through Christ's broken body (Heb. 10:20)
6. Priests entered it bearing blood (Heb. 9:7).	6. Christ entered heaven with His own blood (Heb. 9:12).

The Holy Place – A Type of the Church
(The Scripture does not state what the Holy Place represented, but its position and functions suggest it was a type of the church. The true church consists of all people who are saved by Christ. Heb. 12:23-24)

1. Only priests could enter it. (Aaron and his sons were the only priests [Num. 3:10].)	1. Only "priests" enter it. (All Christians are priests [1 Pet. 2:5,9; Rev. 1:6]).
2. The lampstand gave light in it.	2. The light of Christ is upon His people (John 12:46; Acts 26:23).
3. Incense offered in it daily.	3. Prayers offered (Acts 2:42; Rev. 5:8; 8:3).
4. Bread of Presence always there.	4. Christ said, "I am with you always" (Matt. 28:20).
5. Passage to the Holy of Holies was through the Holy Place.	5. Christ will come to take his *church* (Eph. 5:27; Rev. 19:7,8).

6. *The altar of burnt offering* (Ex. 27:1-7; 38:1-7; Ps. 118:27). In the courtyard of the tabernacle was an altar for burning the bodies of animals offered as sacrifices. It was made of wood covered with bronze. (It is called the bronze, or brazen, altar, to distinguish it from the altar of incense, which was

---

The Veil – A Type (symbol) of the body of Christ

Hebrews 10:19-20 – "We . . . enter the Most Holy Place by the blood of Jesus, by a new and living way opened for us through the curtain (the veil), that is, his body."

1. Once the veil blocked the entrance into the Most Holy Place (Heb. 10:8).

2. The veil was torn apart when Christ died (Matt. 27:50-51).

3. Heaven is now opened (Acts 7:59; 2 Cor. 5:8; Phil. 1:23).

4. The cherubim figures on the veil remind us of the angels that were so often with Christ (Luke 2:13, 15; Matt. 4:6; John 1:51; 20:12).

---

called the "golden altar.") The altar was square in shape, 5 × 5 cubits in size and three cubits high. It had a horn projecting from each upper corner. It had a "ledge" projecting out from its sides (presumably to lay equipment or sacrifices upon), and a grating under the ledge, which would allow air circulation up through the altar.

"Horns" in the Bible are often a symbol of strength and power (1 Sam. 2:1, 10; 2 Sam. 22:3; Ps. 75:4; 89:24; 132:17). This shows that the altar was a place of strength.

Upon this altar a lamb was sacrificed every morning and evening (Ex. 29:38-41). Many other offerings were made on the Sabbath days and on feast days.

The Altar of Burnt-Offering – A Type of the Death of Christ

(The altar of burnt-offering also pictures the doom of sinners.)

1. Offerings of blood	1. Blood of Christ shed
2. Had horns (power)	2. Has power (Matt. 28:18; Rev. 12:11)
3. Continuous burning	3. Continuous atonement
4. Special offerings made	4. Every need met
5. Only priests ministered at the altar	5. Only Christ is the high priest

7. *The courtyard* (Ex. 27:9-15). The tabernacle building was enclosed by a courtyard, framed in by posts set upon bronze bases, and holding up linen curtains five cubits (7½ feet) high. The courtyard was 50 × 100 cubits, not large enough to hold a large crowd. Most of the people stood outside the court on major feast days. The entrance to the court was closed by a beautiful curtain 20 cubits across (27:16).

Inside the courtyard was the altar of burnt offerings, and also a laver where the priests washed, and the tabernacle building.

Revelation 11:2 mentions an "outer court" associated with the temple of God, and says it was "given to the Gentiles." It is difficult to say what time period this court was to exist in, but it does show that the "court" was in the world. We therefore view the courtyard *God's Outreach into the World*.

The Courtyard – God's Outreach into the World	
1. Open to all (1 Kgs. 8:41-42)	1. Whoever desires may come (Rev. 21:17)
2. Altar of burnt-offering there	2. Death of Christ for everyone
3. Laver there	3. Cleansing through water and the word (Eph. 5:26)

8. *The garments of the priest* (Ex. 28; Lev. 8:5-9).

Moses' brother Aaron and his sons were the only priests in Israel that God appointed. "Appoint Aaron and his sons to serve as priests; anyone else who approaches the sanctuary must be put to death" (Num. 3:10). The high priesthood passed from Aaron to his son Eleazar and on to later generations.

The high priest had six special garments. They were (1) the ephod, (2) the breastpiece (or breastplate), (3) a robe under the ephod, (4) a turban bearing a gold plate engraved with the words HOLY TO THE LORD, (5) an inner tunic, and (6) a sash, or girdle.

The *ephod* (Ex. 28:6-14; 39:2-7) was a like an apron, with front and back sections united at the shoulders, where two onyx stones were placed. The ephod was made in beautiful colors, and had gold threads in it.

The *breastpiece* (or breastplate) (Ex. 28:15-28; 39:8-21) was attached to the ephod over the priest's breast. It was made of colorful fabric, and had upon it twelve gemstones, upon which were engraved the names of the twelve tribes of Israel. Golden rings and cords held it upon the breastplate. When Aaron wore this he bore "the names of the sons of Israel over his heart" (28:29).

Inside the breastplate two objects called *Urim* and *Thummim* were placed (28:30; Deut. 33:8). The form or material of these items is not revealed. Perhaps they were gemstones. It is certain that they were used to obtain information from God about matters that humans could not know (Num. 27:21; 1 Sam. 28:6; Ezra 2:63).

The *robe of the ephod* (28:31-35; 39:22-26) was like a sleeveless dress of blue, worn under the ephod. Around its lower hem dangled small bells of gold and pomegranate-shaped pendants made of fabric.

The *tunic* (or coat) (Ex. 28:39; 39:27) was a linen undergarment worn under the robe of the ephod.

A *turban* was made for Aaron's head (Ex. 28:36-38; 39:30-31). It bore upon it a plate of gold, with the inscription HOLY TO THE LORD.

A *sash* (or girdle) held the ephod and the robe of the ephod securely on the body (28:39; 39:29).

The garments of Aaron were for "glory and for beauty" (Ex. 28:2). ("Glory and beauty" is a better translation than "dignity and honor.") The clothes did not "make the man" but they surely pointed him out and called attention to him.

The New Testament says that Christ Jesus is now our high priest (Heb. 6:20; 7:24). He is our priest upon his throne, like Melchizedek and Joshua (Zech. 6:13). In some ways Jesus resembled Aaron, and in several respects He differs from Aaron.

While Jesus was on earth He lived among us as a poor carpenter and teacher. Now Jesus has garments of glory, even greater than Aaron's. While He waits in heaven until His return, He has garments of glory resembling the priest's garments. See Revelation 1:12-13.

Aaron, the high priest – Like Christ, our High Priest	
1. High priest	1. High priest (Heb. 3:1)
2. Called by God	2. Called by God (Heb. 5:4-5)
3. Anointed with oil (Ex. 29:7)	3. Anointed with the Holy Spirit (Acts 10:38; Heb. 1:9)
4. Offered gifts and sacrifices (Heb. 5:1)	4. Offers gifts and sacrifices
5. Names of tribes on breastplate	5. Our names on His heart

Aaron UNLIKE Christ	
1. Tribe of Levi (Heb. 7:11-14)	1. Tribe of Judah (Rev. 5:5)
2. Sinful (Heb. 7:27-28)	2. Sinless (Heb. 4:15)
3. Ministered in earthly tabernacle	3. Ministers in heaven (Heb. 8:1-2; 9:11-12, 24)
4. Repeated sacrifices	4. Once-for-all sacrifice (Heb. 10:1-4, 11-12)
5. Dying (Heb. 7:23-25)	5. Continues forever

9. *The consecration of the priests* (Ex. 29:1-45; 30:22-23; Lev. 8–9). "Consecrate" (in 29:1) means "to make holy" or "sanctify." The consecration ritual is more fully described in Leviticus 8 and 9. See notes on that passage.

10. *The altar of incense* (Ex. 30:1-10; 37:25-28). This altar was called the "golden altar" (Num. 4:11). It was a small altar (1½ × 1½ × 2 cubits). It was placed in the Holy Place, on its west side up against the veil. At this altar the priest was as near to being inside the Holy of Holies as he could come, except on the Day of Atonement. The incense would penetrate into the Holy of Holies, so that in Hebrews 9:3-4 the golden altar of incense was spoken of as if it were part of the furniture of the Most Holy Place. A special formula for the incense to be burned is described in Exodus 30:34-38.

Incense was burned morning and evening. When a sin-offering was offered, some of the blood was placed on the horns of the altar of incense (Lev. 4:7).

In the Bible incense is a symbol of prayer. "May my *prayer* be set before you like *incense*" (Ps. 141:2; compare Rev. 5:8; 8:3).

The Altar of Incense – A Type of Prayer	
1. Close to the Most Holy Place	1. Close to Heaven
2. Powerful (horns)	2. Powerful
3. Golden	3. Precious
4. Fire from the altar of burnt-offering (Lev. 16:12)	4. Power from Christ's death
5. Twice-daily incense	5. Regular prayers. "Pray without ceasing" (1 Thess. 5:17)

11. *Laver (basin) for washing the priests* (Ex. 30:17-20). A bronze basin (laver) for washing the priests was placed between the altar of burnt-offering and the tabernacle building. It was made of the bronze from the mirrors of the women who served at the tabernacle. (38:8. That was a big sacrifice.) It had some kind of base under it (Ex. 39:39). The priests washed at the laver when they were consecrated (Lev. 8:6). After that they were to wash at the laver each time they went into the Holy Place to minister (Ex. 30:20-21).

It is probable that the apostle Paul alludes to the laver in Titus 3:5: "He saved us through the *washing* of rebirth and renewal by the Holy Spirit." This is usually understood to refer to our baptism into Christ. Also in Ephesians 5:25-26: "Christ loved the church and gave himself up for her to make her holy, cleansing her by the *washing* with water through the word."

The Laver (basin) – Symbol of CLEANSING for Christians	
1. Priests were washed during their consecration (Ex. 40:12).	1. Baptism (?)
2. Priests washed whenever they ministered.	2. Continual cleansings (1 John 1:7,9)

12. *Moses inspects the tabernacle* (Ex. 39:32-42). God had been very insistent that the tabernacle be built according to the pattern He had given (Ex. 25:9,40; 26:30). When the tabernacle was completed, "Moses inspected the work and saw that they had done it just as the LORD had commanded. So Moses blessed them" (39:43). The LORD's insistence about following His pattern for the tabernacle should cause us to take care to follow the Bible exactly in those things it tells us to do.

13. *Setting up the tabernacle* (Ex. 40:1-33). The LORD instructed Moses himself to set up the tabernacle the first time. "So the tabernacle was set up on the first day of the first month in the second year" (40:17). This was only ten months after they had arrived at Mt. Sinai. They left Mt. Sinai on the twentieth day of the second month of the second year (Num. 10:11). The Israelites had a busy first year "on the road."

14. *The cloud and the glory* (Ex. 40:34-37; Num. 9:15-23). The cloud that guided the Israelites covered the Tent of Meeting and the glory of the LORD filled the tabernacle. In a similar way the glory of the LORD filled the temple of Solomon during its dedication (2 Chr. 7:1).

The continual presence of the cloud above the tabernacle and the camp of Israel should have been a constant reminder to Israel that God was in their midst, both for protection and for judgment. God has never left us without witness of His presence.

Questions on Section C
Tabernacle and Priesthood (Ex. 25–31; 35–40; Lev. 8–10)

1. Where was Moses when the Lord gave him instructions about the tabernacle? (Ex. 24:15-16)
2. What was the tabernacle? (Ex. 26:30)
3. Why is the tabernacle important to us? (Heb. 9:8-9,24)
4. Where did God dwell in the time of the tabernacle? (Ex. 25:8)

5. Where within the tabernacle did God particularly reveal His presence? (Ex. 25:21-22)
6. Who were camped about the tabernacle? (Num. 2:2)
7. What were some of the names for the tabernacle? (Ex. 25:8; 29:10)
8. From whom were the materials obtained for the tabernacle? (Ex. 36:3)
9. What men actually constructed the tabernacle? (Ex. 36:1)
10. What special guidance did the builders of the tabernacle have? (Ex. 36:2)
11. How many tabernacles did all the parts of the tabernacle combine to form? (Ex. 26:6)
12. What kind of money was collected for the service of the tabernacle? (Ex. 30:16)
13. By what means was the tabernacle sanctified for holy use? Of what is anointing oil a symbol? (Ex. 40:9)
14. What covered over (or hovered over) the tabernacle? (Ex. 40:34)
15. What is the estimated value of the materials in the tabernacle?
16. Draw a sketch of the tabernacle floor plan and the court, the Holy Place and the Holy of Holies, and the locations of all items of furniture.
17. Give the dimensions of the court, including its entrance. (Ex. 27:9-16)
18. What were the dimensions of the Holy Place? The Holy of Holies?
19. What items or materials were used in making the court? (Ex. 27:9-18)
20. What were the dimensions of the altar of burnt offering? (Ex. 27:1)
21. When was fire kept burning on the altar of burnt offering? (Lev. 6:12-13)
22. Of what material was the laver made? (Ex. 30:17-21)
23. Where was this material for the laver obtained? (Ex. 38:8)
24. When did the priests wash in the laver? (Ex. 29:4; 30:20-21)
25. What were the walls of the tabernacle made of? (Ex. 26:15-25)
26. What held the boards together? (Ex. 26:26-29)
27. What materials were used in the four coverings of the tabernacle? (Ex. 26:1-14)
28. What separated the Holy Place from the Most Holy Place? (Ex. 26:31-35)
29. What does the name "bread of the presence" (or showbread) indicate was the symbolism of the bread? (Ex. 25:30)
30. How many loaves were placed on the table of presence-bread? How often were new loaves put out? (Lev. 24:5-9)
31. How often was the lampstand tended to? (Lev. 24:1-4)
32. How often was incense burned on the altar of incense? (Ex. 30:7-8)
33. Name the three items kept in or beside the ark of the covenant. (Ex. 16:33; Num. 17:10; 1 Kgs. 8:9)

34. What was the lid or covering of the ark called? Describe this lid or covering. (Ex. 25:17-22)
35. Describe the ark of the covenant. Give its dimensions. (Ex. 25:10-16)
36. Who only went into the Holy of Holies? How often? At what time? (Heb. 9:7; Lev. 16:2; 23:27-28)
37. Of what was the altar of burnt offering a type? (Heb. 13:10-12)
38. Of what was the laver a type? (Titus 3:5; Heb. 10:22)
39. Of what was the altar of incense a type? (Ps. 141:2; Rev. 5:8)
40. Of what was the veil a type? What would the tearing of the veil when Christ died represent? (Matt. 27:51; Heb. 10:19-20; 9:7-8)
41. Of what was the Holy of Holies a type? (Heb. 9:11-12, 24)

The Priesthood

1. Who was Israel's first high priest? (Lev. 8:12)
2. List the six distinctive garments of the high priest and describe them briefly. (Lev. 8:7-9; Ex. 28:4)
3. What was *Urim* and *Thummim*? (Ex. 28:30)
4. What was the high priest's distinctive function on the Day of Atonement? (Lev. 16)
5. What was the high priest's distinctive function in the cities of refuge? (Num. 35:25)
6. List three duties of the priests. (Lev. 6:12; 10:11; Ex. 27:20-21; 29:38-44)
7. How were the Levites supported? (Num. 18:21)
8. How were the priests supported? (Num. 18:26-28)
9. Who were the assistants of the priests? (Num. 3:6-9)
10. Name the three families of the Levites. (Num. 3:17-20)
11. How many cities were given to the Levites? (Num. 35:6-7)

Section D
Leviticus

1. *Introduction to Leviticus.*

a. What Bible verse is on the United States Liberty bell?

Answer: Leviticus 25:10 — "Proclaim **liberty** throughout all the land unto all the inhabitants thereof" (KJV).

What Bible verse has the SECOND GREATEST COMMAND in it? Answer: Leviticus 19:18 — "Love your neighbor as yourself."

b. Leviticus is a book of **Regulations for divine worship**. (See Hebrews 9:1.) Leviticus 18:5 — "Keep my decrees and laws, for the man who obeys them will *live* by them." The book tells the laws about sacrifices, the priesthood, the dietary laws, the laws about feast days, and similar things.

c. Leviticus is meaningful to us because Christ is the fulfillment of all the sacrifices, the priesthood, and the rituals in Leviticus. An acquaintance with Leviticus will help us to comprehend the unsearchable riches of Christ, who is our sacrifice, our Passover, our altar, our priest.

I never felt the impact of Christ's being our "offering and sacrifice" (Eph. 5:1) until I learned of the burnt offering described in Leviticus chapter one. The burnt offering was killed, and skinned, and cut to pieces, and totally burned. Christ's death was likewise a total sacrifice of Himself for us.

d. *Authorship of Leviticus.* **Moses** was the human author of Leviticus. Compare Leviticus 14:1-4 with Matthew 8:4.

No other book of the Bible so often affirms that GOD spoke its words. In no less than thirty-nine verses the book says that **God** spoke to Moses. See Leviticus 1:1; 4:1; 6:1,8,24; 8:1; and other verses at the beginnings of chapters.

Leviticus 26:46: "These are the decrees, the laws and the regulations that the LORD established on Mount Sinai between himself and the Israelites through *Moses*."

Many Bible critics have said that Leviticus is part of a "Priestly Code," a group of writings supposedly produced during and after the Babylonian captivity, about 500 B.C., a thousand years after the time of Moses. Norman Gottwald wrote that most of the latter half of Exodus and the whole of Leviticus come from the P [priestly] writer (*The Hebrew Bible*, Philadelphia, 1987, p. 140).

Not one of the ancient writings that speak of the origin of the Bible (Josephus, the Talmud, etc.) tells of any priestly production of Leviticus. Also the theory goes against the emphatic statements in the text of Leviticus about its own authorship.

At the ancient city of Ugarit the Canaanites around 1400 B.C. observed several sacrifices with names very similar to those in Leviticus 1-5. These included trespass-offerings, peace-offerings, and others. This supports the belief that the laws of Moses in Leviticus and other books were written near 1400 B.C., and not down in the fifth century B.C., the date given to the imaginary P source. (See Chas. Pfeiffer, *Ras Shamra and the Bible*, Baker, 1962, pp. 37-38.)

  e. ***Brief outline of Leviticus.*** (Memorize)
   (1) The five sacrificial offerings (chs. 1–7)
   (2) Consecration of the priests (chs. 8–10)
    (Deaths of Nadab and Abihu; ch. 10)
   (3) Clean and unclean things (chs. 11–15)
   (4) The Day of Atonement (ch. 16)
   (5) Prohibitions for the people (chs. 17–20), and prohibitions for priests (chs. 21–22)
   (6) Feasts (chs. 23–25)
   (7) Blessings and curses (ch. 26); Vows and tithes (ch. 27)

  f. Leviticus is a very practical, down-to-earth book. It tells us to bring our tithes (27:30). It condemns homosexuality and all forms of sexual abuse (chapter 18). The idea of TRUST in God's care is prominent in Leviticus (19:23-24; 23:39-43; 25:18-22; 26:2-5). Our obligation to care for the poor is stated (19:10; 23:22).

  Christians should "fulfill the law through love" (Gal. 5:13-14). We are free from ordinances in Christ (Col. 2:20; Heb. 9:10). But we are not to use this freedom to indulge our sinful flesh, but to serve one another in love (Gal. 5:13).

  g. A key word in Leviticus is *holy* or *holiness*. The word occurs over seventy times in the book. The word *holy* means "being set apart" or "consecrated to God." Lev. 19:2: "Be *holy*, because I, the LORD your God, am *holy*."

  2. *The five sacrificial offerings* (Lev. chapters 1–7).

---

(1) **BURNT OFFERING** (Lev. 1; 6:8-13). This offering was completely burned. It pictured the future death of Christ and the doom of sinners in the lake of fire.

---

(2) **GRAIN OFFERING** (Lev. 2; 6:14-23). This offering was partly burned and partly eaten by priests. It consisted of grain placed upon the burnt offering (Num. 15:4). Its symbolism is not stated.

---

(3) **FELLOWSHIP OFFERING** (peace offering) (Lev. 3; 7:11-21). This offering was partly burned, partly eaten by priests, and partly by the offerer. It was given to express thanks or joy, or as a gift.

(4) **SIN OFFERING** (Lev. 4; 6:24-30). This offering was partly burned and partly eaten by priests. It was offered for sins done without the person being aware of sinning.

(5) **GUILT OFFERING** (trespass offering) (Lev. 5:14–6:8; 7:1-10). This offering was partly burned and partly eaten by priests. It was mostly offered for sins of dishonesty and for ceremonial violations. This offering required *restitution*, as well as the offering itself (5:16; Num. 5:5-10). We can sin by failure to do the religious activities God commands. (See James 4:17.)

3. *Consecration of the priests* (Lev. chapters 8–10; Ex. 29).

To *"consecrate"* (Lev. 8:12) means (in Hebrew) "to fill the hands." Consecrated people are doers, not just learners.

Aaron (the brother of Moses) was Israel's first high priest. Only Aaron and his sons (descendants) had the authority to perform priestly ceremonies (Num. 3:10). Only the high priest entered the Holy of Holies in the tabernacle. Aaron was a type (symbol) of Christ Jesus, who is our high priest. (Heb. 4:14; 5:4).

Aaron's sons were priests of lesser rank. As such, they may have been symbols of Christians, who are *all* priests unto God (Rev. 1:6; 5:9; 1 Peter 2:5,9). The New Testament does not establish a group of individuals in the church to be priests for all the rest of the people.

Aaron and his sons were *anointed*. This was done by pouring oil upon their heads (8:12). The ceremony of anointing installed a person into some office, like the priesthood or kingship.

Jesus was anointed with the Holy Spirit (Acts 10:38) when he was baptized. Thus Jesus is the *Anointed One*. The terms *Messiah* (in Hebrew) and *Christ* (in Greek) mean the *Anointed One*.

During his consecration ceremony, blood was placed upon Aaron's right ear, right thumb, and right big toe (8:24). His ears, hands, and feet were set apart for God's exclusive use.

Tragedy struck during the consecration ritual, when Aaron's two sons Nadab and Abihu were burnt with fire from God because they used unauthorized fire (not that from the altar of burnt offering) in offering the incense (10:1). Probably Nadab and Abihu were drunk at the time they died (10:9). We must do exactly what God says or we may suffer a fate like that of Nadab and Abihu, or of Ananias and Sapphira (Acts 5).

4. *Laws of clean and unclean meats* (Lev. 11). "Clean" meats had to come from animals that both chew the cud and have a split hoof. Clean fish had both scales and fins. These laws kept the Israelites apart from other nations, who ate animals forbidden to Israelites. The laws also had some basis as wholesome dietary rules.

Jesus abolished the diet restrictions of the Old Testament. See Mark 7:19; Romans 14:14, 17; 1 Timothy 4:3; 1 Corinthians 8:8. Even so, we are not to judge people on the basis of what they eat or do not eat.

5. *Circumcision*, and *Purification of women after childbirth* (Lev. 12). A son was circumcised when eight days old. Circumcision is no longer a commanded religious rite (Gal. 6:16).

A sacrifice of purification was to be made by a mother forty days after the birth of a son and eighty after birth of a daughter (12:3-5). If parents were poor, as Joseph and Mary were (Luke 2:24), they could offer a dove instead of a lamb.

The purification ritual indicates that God was pained enough with the unpleasant features of childbirth (which Adam and Eve brought upon humanity) that He required sacrifices to *cover* (atone for) it. The sacrifice of Christ covers all the things that we humans have brought upon ourselves.

6. *Leprosy* (Lev. 13–14; Num. 5:1-4). The "leprosy" of these chapters is not the same disease that is now called leprosy (Hansen's disease). The word seems to refer to several types of skin diseases, and also to mildew, dry rot, and decay that could affect clothing and buildings. All of these corruptions are the result of the fall of man.

Jesus commanded ten lepers that He cleansed to go and

do the ritual prescribed in Leviticus (Luke 17:14). This ritual lasted eight days (Lev. 14:8,10), and is called a *cleansing* rather than a healing.

7. *The day of atonement* (Lev. 16; 23:26-32). This "feast" was held on the tenth day of the seventh month (early in our month October). It was a solemn occasion with fasting. On that day each year the high priest went into the Holy of Holies with blood and sprinkled it upon the atonement cover (mercy seat) upon the ark of the covenant.

The fact that sacrifices had to be offered each year on the day of atonement for the sins committed during the past year, shows that the sacrifices offered every day did not really take away sins so that they would be remembered no more. Christ takes away sins so that they are remembered no more (Heb. 10:1-4; 8:12-13). Christ is now the atonement, the priest, the sacrifice, and the altar. He ministers at the true tabernacle in heaven for us (Heb. 8:5; 7:27).

8. *Various good laws* (Lev. 19).

    a. Do not reap the corners of your fields. Leave grain for the poor (19:9-10).

    b. Pay wages promptly (19:13).

    c. Don't curse the deaf (19:14).

    d. Don't try to talk to the dead (19:31; 20: 6).

    e. Use honest weights and measures (19:36).

9. *The sabbath year* and the *Year of Jubilee* (Lev. 25).

    a. The sabbatical year was every seventh year (25:1-7). The land was not farmed in those years. This restored fertility into the land, and provided food for people and animals. God strongly insisted that the land "keep its sabbaths" (Lev. 26:43; 2 Chr. 36:21).

    b. The Year of Jubilee came every fiftieth year (25:8-10).

      (1) The word *Jubilee* (Hebrew, *yovel*) means a "ram's horn" trumpet. The trumpet was blown to signal liberation from all debts and servitude (25:10).

      (2) In that year all lands that had been mortgaged or sold were returned debt-free to the original family owners (25:13, 23). This prevented greedy wealthy men from obtaining all the poor people's lands. This preserved family feelings

and loyalty. This encouraged the keeping of genealogical records.

      (3) Slaves were released (Lev. 25:40).

      (4) The produce of the land was not harvested in the Year of Jubilee, as it was not harvested in the Sabbatical years (25:11). Much faith was required to keep the Sabbatical year and the Year of Jubilee.

The Year of Jubilee seems to have been a type of the Christian life we now enjoy, and our blessings in heaven hereafter. See Isaiah 61:1-2 and Luke 4:19.

      10. *Blessings for obedience, and punishments for disobedience* (Lev. 26; Deut. 27–28)

      a. Blessings listed (Lev. 26:1-13)

      b. Punishments listed (Lev. 26:34-35)

      c. God's will shall be done, whether man cooperates or not (Lev. 26:34-35).

      d. Disobeying God could bring the people to cannibalism! (Lev. 26:29; compare Deut. 28:53-57; 2 Kgs. 6:28)

Our study of Leviticus should make us say, "Oh, how I love your law!" (Ps. 119:97). Also it should lead us to say, "The law is GOOD" (1 Tim. 1:8). But it also should make us glad that we are NOT under the law but under grace (1 Cor. 9:20; Rom. 6:14; Acts 15:10).

Questions on Section D
Leviticus

Leviticus 1 (also 6:8-13) — "The burnt offering"
1. What animals could be offered as burnt offerings (4 answers)? (1:3,10,14)
2. Who killed the burnt offering? (1:5)
3. What was done with the blood of the burnt offering? (1:5)
4. What was done to the body of the burnt offering? (1:9)
5. When were burnt offerings regularly made? (Ex. 29:38-42)
6. What regulation was made about the fire on the altar of burnt offering? (6:12-13)

Leviticus 2 (also 6:14-23 and 7:9-10) — "The grain offering"
1. In what three forms could a grain offering be brought? (2:1,4,14)
2. What three things were always added to the grain offering? (2:2,6,13)

3. What was done with the grain offering? (2:9-10)
4. What was excluded from the grain offering? (2:11)

Leviticus 3 (also 6:12 and 7:11-38) — "The fellowship (or peace) offering"
1. What part of the fellowship offering was burned? (3:3-4)
2. Where was it burned? (3:5)
3. What two parts of an animal were not to be eaten? (7:22)
4. Name three purposes for which fellowship offerings might be made.
5. Who ate the flesh of fellowship offerings? (7:15,31-32)

Leviticus 4:1-5:13 (also 6:24-30) — "The sin offering"
1. What type of sins were sin offerings offered for? (4:2)
2. From the Scriptures give two types of sins requiring sin offerings? (5:1-4)
3. What was done with the blood of the sin offering? (4:5-7)
4. What classes of people are mentioned as possibly offering sin offerings and what was each required to bring? (4:3,13,22,27)
5. What provision was made for poor people who had to bring sin offerings? (5:7; Luke 2:22-24)
6. What was done with the body of the sin offering? (4:10-11; 6:29)

Leviticus 5:14-6:7 (also 7:1-8) — "The guilt (or trespass) offering"
1. What types of sins were guilt offerings offered for? (6:14)
2. What was required in addition to the sacrifice when trespass offerings were made (2 things)? (5:16)

Summary from Leviticus 1-7 (See 7:37-38)
1. List the 5 types of offerings described in Leviticus 1-7.
2. Which offering was wholly burned? (1:9)
3. Which offerings were partly eaten by priests? (2:10; 6:29-30; 7:6)
4. Which offering was shared by priest and offerer? (7:13-14)

Leviticus 8
1. What is the topic of chapter 8? (8:33)
2. Who were set apart to be the priests? (8:1)
3. Where was the blood placed upon the priests? (8:24)
4. How many days did the consecration ritual last? (8:33)

Leviticus 9
1. When Aaron entered into his office what four offerings did he offer? (9:2,7,17,18)
2. How was Aaron's burnt offering on the altar consumed? (9:24)

Leviticus 10
1. What is the topic of chapter 10? (10:1)

2. Which of Aaron's sons died and why? (10:1)
3. Why was Aaron not to mourn over the death of his sons? (10:6-7)
4. What were the priests not to do when they entered the tent of meeting? (10:8)

Leviticus 11

1. What is the topic of chapter 11? (11:41,47)
2. What were the two qualifications of animals that could be eaten? (11:3-39)
3. What word describes the type of life the people were to live? (11:44)

Leviticus 12

1. What is the topic of chapter 12? (12:1)
2. When was a baby circumcised? (12:3)
3. How long after the birth of a male child was it until sacrifice was offered? A female child? (12:3-4; 12:5)
4. Why did Joseph and Mary offer turtle doves? (12:8; 5:7; Luke 2:22-24)

Leviticus 13

1. What is the topic of Leviticus 13? (13:1)
2. What did a leper in public have to cry out? (13:45)
3. What did contamination affect besides people? (13:47; 14:34)

Leviticus 14

1. What creatures were employed in the ceremony for cleansing lepers? (14:4,10)
2. What could contamination affect besides people and garments? (14:34)

Leviticus 15

1. What is the general topic of chapter 15? (15:2,19)

Leviticus 16

1. What is the topic of chapter 16? (16:17)
2. On what month and day was the ritual described in chapter 16? (24:26)
3. How often did Aaron enter the (Most) Holy Place? (16:2,34)
4. What was done with the two goats? (16:15,21)

Leviticus 17

1. Where were the people required to offer sacrifices? (17:5)
2. What item was not to be eaten? Why? (17:11)
3. Where is the life of the flesh? (17:11)

Leviticus 18

1. Israel was not to do according to the doings of what two countries? (18:3)
2. What was the penalty for moral violations? (18:29)

Leviticus 19
1. What character were the children of Israel to have? (19:2)
2. What was to be left at harvest time? Why? (19:9)
3. How much time was to elapse before fruit from trees could be eaten? (19:23-24)
4. What restriction was placed on animal breeding? (19:19)
5. How were the old people to be treated? (19:32)

Leviticus 20
1. What were people not to give to Moloch? (20:2-3)
2. What was the penalty for one who turns to mediums? (20:6)

Leviticus 21
1. Could the priest weep for the dead? Could the high priest? (21:1-2,10)
2. What disqualified a man for the priesthood? (21:7-20)

Leviticus 22
1. Were the priests always as holy as the things in the tabernacle? (22:2)
2. What made animals not acceptable for sacrifice? (22:18-20)
3. How old did an animal have to be before it could be sacrificed? (22:26)

Leviticus 23
1. What was the date of the Passover and the feast of unleavened bread? (23:5)
2. What was done with the first sheaf of the harvest? (23:10-11)
3. How many days from the bringing of the first sheaf to the next feast (the feast of weeks or Pentecost)? (23:16)
4. What three feasts were in the seventh month? (23:24,26,33)
5. Where were the people to live during the feast of tabernacles? (23:42)

Leviticus 24
1. What was burned in the lampstand? (24:1)
2. When was bread placed on the table of presence-bread? (24:8-9)
3. What was done to the man who cursed God's name? (24:23)

Leviticus 25
1. How would the land keep a Sabbath? (25:2-4)
2. What was released on the Year of Jubilee? How often did this year occur? (25:10-11,28)
3. What was the law about taking interest? (25:36)

Leviticus 26
1. List three of the blessings for obedience. (26:4,6,7, etc.)
2. List three of the punishments for disobedience. (26:16,17,22, etc.)

Leviticus 27
1. What was to be given when a vow was accomplished (or fulfilled)? (27:2-3; Acts 21:23-24)
2. What had to be done with all things given or devoted to the Lord? (27:28)
3. What part of all produce was the Lord's? (27:30)

Section E
Numbers

1. *Introduction to Numbers*
   a. The book of *Numbers* gets its name from the censuses of the Israelites recorded in chapters 1,3, and 26. The Greek name is *Arithmoi*, also meaning *numbers*. The Hebrew name is *Bemidbar,* meaning *In the Desert* (or *In the Wilderness*). This title describes the book's contents better than the name *Numbers*, which describes only a few chapters of it.

   I have sometimes called the book of Numbers the story of *A Tragic Journey*. Only two of the people who were over twenty years of age when Israel left Egypt lived through the wanderings in the desert and entered the promised land.

   Numbers could also be called *Journey to God's Rest-Land*. The Promised Land is frequently referred to as a place of "Rest" (Deut. 3:20; 12:10; 25:19; Josh. 1:13-15; 21:24; 23:1; Heb. 4:3). The theme of *REST* is common in the Scriptures. The wicked, like Cain, cannot rest (Isa. 57:20). Jesus said, "Come to me . . . and I will give you *rest*" (Matt. 11:28). "Blessed are the dead who die in the Lord . . . they will *rest* from their labor" (Rev. 14:13).

   b. Numbers tells of Israel's wanderings in the desert, from the time they were at Mt. Sinai until they arrived at the edge of the promised land, on the east side of the Jordan River (Deut. 1:3).

   c. Moses was the human *author* of the book of Numbers. See Numbers 1:1; 33:2. The entire Law (referring to the first five books of the Bible) was attributed to Moses by Jesus and by writers of other books of the Bible (John 1:17; Josh. 23:6; 2 Chr. 33:8).

d. *Date* of the book of Numbers: The book was completed shortly before Moses' death in 1406 B.C., in the fortieth year of Israel's wanderings (Num. 33:38). The book covers a span of thirty-nine years. Numbers begins with the census of the Israelites that was taken at Mt. Sinai a month after the tabernacle was completed (Num. 1:1-2; Ex. 40:17).

e. Numbers records seven murmurings of the Israelites against God and against Moses. (See Num. 11:1; 11:4; 14:2; 16:1; 16:41; 17:12; 20:2-3; 21:5.) These murmurings brought much trouble upon the Israelites.

f. "The spiritual lesson enforced throughout the book (of Numbers) is that God's people can move forward only so far as they trust His promises and lean upon His strength." (Gleason L. Archer, Jr., *A Survey of Old Testament Introduction*, Chicago: Moody, 1994, p. 265.)

g. *Outline of the book of Numbers*:
(1) Events at Mt. Sinai in preparation for departure (Num. 1:1–10:10)
(2) Events from Mt. Sinai to Kadesh Barnea (10:11–14:45)
(3) Wanderings from Kadesh Barnea to the Plains of Moab (chs. 15–21)
(4) Events in the Plains of Moab (chs. 22–36)

2. *The first census of Israel* (at Mt. Sinai) (Num. 1). Only the men over twenty were counted. Twelve men helped Moses take the census. One of them was *Nahshon*, son of Amminadab of the tribe of Judah (1:7; 7:17; 10:14). He was an ancestor of Christ (Matt. 1:4).

The tribes were counted individually. The tribe having the largest population was Judah; the smallest was Manasseh. The Levites were not counted in this census (but see chapter 3). The population total was 603,550 (1:46; 2:32). Truly, Abraham's offspring had become "a great nation" (Gen. 12:2).

3. *The arrangement of the tribal camps, and the order of march for the tribes* (Num. 2). The twelve tribes were grouped into four groups of three tribes each. These groups were camped around the tabernacle on four sides. The Levites and priests

were camped close to the tabernacle, with the other tribes around them (3:38). When Israel set out on their marches, the Levites and the tabernacle were in the center of their column (2:17).

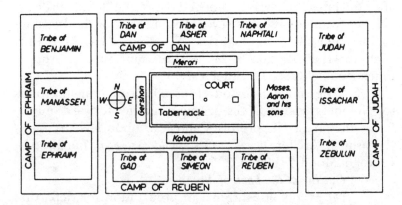

4. *Census of the Levites* (Num. 3). The Levites were taken by God for His service instead of the firstborn from each family (Num. 3). (See Ex. 13:1). There were 22,000 Levites counted (3:39). The firstborn sons in all the other tribes totalled 22,273. The 273 firstborn in excess of the number of Levites were "redeemed" by their families for payment of five shekels of silver for each.

**Sons of Aaron, the High Priest –
Nadab, Abihu, Eleazar, Ithamar** (Num. 3:2).

---

5. *Work of the Levites* (Num. 4). The Levites were to pack up the tabernacle in preparation for moving to other places. They had a clever method of packing the ark of the covenant without ever looking upon it (4:4-5, 20). The Levites transported the tabernacle, parts of it by poles on their shoulders, and part in wagons.

The Levites also assisted the priests in the work around the tabernacle (3:8-9; 8:22).

Levi had three sons — Kohath, Gershon, and Merari. The *Kohathites* (from whom the priests descended) carried the furniture of the tabernacle. The *Gershonites* transported the fabric items of the tabernacle. *Ithamar,* son of Aaron, supervised the work of the Gershonites. Ithamar was the ancestor of Eli, the priest in the time of Samuel (1 Sam. 4:28; 1 Chr. 24:2). The *Merarites* transported the heavy wood parts of the tabernacle and everything related to their use (4:29, 31; 7:6-7).

6. *The purity of the camp* (Num. 5:1-4). The Israelites were to send out of their camp anyone with "leprosy," that is, with an infectious skin disease. Regarding "leprosy," see Leviticus, chapters 13 and 14.

7. *Restitution for wrongs* (Num. 5:5-10). When people did wrongs, they were to *confess* their wrongdoing, and then make full *restitution* for what they had taken, and also make a penalty payment of one fifth of its value. (See Leviticus 5:16). This same principle should still be practiced, even though we are no longer under the law of Moses.

8. *The test of an unfaithful wife* (Num. 5:11-31). If a man suspected his wife of adultery with another man, he could bring her to the tabernacle for a test. She was to drink water containing dust from the tabernacle floor (5:16-24). If she was innocent, no ill effects followed. If she was guilty her abdomen swelled (5:27).

This test may sound like superstition, or at least seem very primitive and unpleasant. But adultery is a serious matter before God and in the lives of people, in spite of Hollywood's and TV's delight in it. If the woman was innocent, she was cleared of guilt. If a man had committed adultery, he was executed (Lev. 20:10).

People in the ancient Near East frequently employed a trial by ordeal to determine if someone was guilty of something. Hammurabi's law (# 132) dictated that a suspected woman was to throw herself in the river. If she survived, she was innocent! The procedure in Numbers 5 is quite different. The procedure itself was not life-threatening, as the trial by ordeal was. The effectiveness of the test was totally dependent upon the infinite knowledge of God and His actions to reveal the truth.

According to the Jewish Talmud the procedure began with the husband being suspicious and giving his wife a warning before two witnesses to avoid any kind of contact with a certain man. If she ignored his warning and was seen with this man, then the process was begun. (*Mishnayot*, Vol. III, *Nashim* ["Women"] Tractate *Sotah* ["Errant Wife'], New York: Judaica Press, 1983)

9. *The Nazirites* (Num. 6:1-21). Nazirites were a special class of men set apart for some unusual service. Most of the information about them is in Numbers 6. The three most famous Nazirites were (a) Samson, (b) Samuel the prophet, (c) John the baptizer. (See Judges 13:5; 1 Samuel 1:12; Luke 1:15.)

Three things Nazirites were *NOT* to do:

(1) Drink wine or fermented drink, or eat grapes (Num. 5:3-4)
(2) Shave or cut their hair (6:5-7)
(3) Touch a dead body (6:6)

There were two types of Nazirites, the temporary and the perpetual. The first class was far more common. Insofar as we know, only the three most famous Nazirites were perpetual Nazirites. There seem to have been many temporary Nazirites. Amos 2:11 and Lamentations 4:7 refer to temporary (?) Nazirites.

The Israelites were condemned for tempting their Nazirites to sin (Amos 2:12). Do not tempt God's leaders to sin.

The New Testament never refers to Nazirites. No one should now claim to be one.

10. *Offerings by the leaders* (Num. 7). When the tabernacle was completed and consecrated, the leaders of Israel made special gifts for its operation. Six carts (wagons) and twelve oxen were given to help transport it (7:3; 4:29, 31). The leader of each tribe gave a silver plate, a silver bowl, a gold dish, a bull, rams, lambs, two oxen, and goats. Nahshon,

leader of Judah, was one of the donors (7:17; 1:7).

The list of gifts is repeated for all twelve of the tribes. This seems repetitious, but it reminds us that God observes all of our gifts individually.

11. *The purification of the Levites* (Num. 8:5-26). The presentation and purification of the Levites for their service in the tabernacle was an event to be witnessed by everyone and to be participated in by the community (8:9, 10, 13, 15, 21).

Those who minister to the LORD must be purified (Num. 8:6-7; Mal. 3:3; Heb. 9:14).

The Levites were an "offering" to the Lord (8:15). The Levites were to do service for the priests (8:19, 22). Are we willing to give our family members and children as an offering to the LORD?

12. *The second Passover observed* (Num. 9:1-14). Israel observed its second Passover feast at Mt. Sinai, one year after the original Passover in Egypt. The first Passover was held at a time of anxiety and tension. The second Passover was held in freedom and triumph. Probably fifty thousand lambs were required for Israel's Passover.

Some people could not observe the Passover on its scheduled day because they were unclean. God sympathizes with our unavoidable problems and makes allowance for them (9:9-11). But God does not accept our lack of obedience, self-discipline, or carelessness in observing His laws (9:13).

13. *The guiding cloud* (Num. 9:15-23; Ex. 40:36-37). God makes His directions in our life plain (9:17-23).

14. *Two trumpets* (Num. 10:1-10). Two silver trumpets were made and used to give signals to the Israelites to march forward, or assemble, or prepare for a battle. The two silver trumpets were pictured on the Arch of Titus in Rome, as part of the booty from the temple in Jerusalem. (See Jack Finegan, *Light From the Ancient Past*, Princeton Univ. Press, 1969, pp. 283 (fig. 120), 329.)

Numbers 10:10 is the last verse in the story of Israel's stay at Mt. Sinai. They had been here eleven months and twenty days. The story of their journey from Sinai to Kadesh Barnea begins at 10:11.

15. *The Israelites leave Sinai* (Num. 10:11-36). Israel set out from Mt. Sinai, and journeyed to the Desert of Paran (in the eastern side of the Sinai Peninsula). The journey from Mt. Sinai to Kadesh Barnea should have taken about eleven days (Deut. 1:2). They left early in the month of May. Because of Israel's grumbling their journey was not completed until the time of the grape harvest, probably in August (13:23). Their trip to Kadesh Barnea took about three months. The terrain in eastern Sinai is very rugged, and Israel would need to follow the wadies in the valleys.

Moses asked Hobab, the son of Reuel (Jethro), to go with Israel as they left Sinai (10:29-32). Hobab was not willing at first, but did go with them when Moses told him how much he was needed.

At every start and stop in Israel's journeys Moses would pray that the LORD's will would be done (10:36).

16. *Fire from the LORD* (Num. 11:1-3). This chapter records the first of many times of complaining and rebellion by Israel against Moses and God after they left Mt. Sinai.

17. *The plague at Kibroth Hattaavah* (Num. 11:4-35). Many non-Israelites left Egypt with the Israelites. This "rabble," or "mixed multitude," did not share Israel's history of fellowship with God, and caused problems for the Israelites. They complained about the manna (11:4-6). They remembered all the food items they had eaten in Egypt. All of the items they mentioned are grown in Israel in abundance.

Moses was distressed over these people. The LORD instructed Moses to appoint seventy elders in Israel to help him govern the uncooperative people. The Spirit that was upon Moses would come upon them (11:17, 25; compare Ex. 18:21.).

Two of the seventy men, named *Eldad* and *Medad*, continued to prophesy in the camp after most of the rest had ceased (11:26-29). Joshua protested their actions, as if they were trying to rival Moses. But Moses felt no jealousy.

The LORD sent great flocks of quail into the Israelites' camp. No one gathered less than ten homers of them — a wagon load! But many Israelites died there (11:33-34). The place was named *Kibroth-Hattaavah*, meaning *graves of craving*, or *graves of lust* (11:34).

18. *Miriam gets leprosy* (Num. 12). Moses had married Zipporah forty years previous to this time. She is never mentioned in the stories of Israel's journeys, and probably had died. Moses had married a Cushite, an Ethiopian (Nubian). (Josephus mentions Moses marrying an Ethiopian while he still lived in Egypt.) Miriam *and Aaron* spoke against Moses because of his Cushite wife. But God knew that Miriam's basic motive for complaining was jealousy over the authority that Moses had. (She may not have even recognized that in herself.) She was a "prophetess" (Ex. 15:20), but still jealous of Moses' authority.

Moses is said to have been "more humble than anyone else on the face of the earth" (12:3). Could Moses himself have written that about himself in his own book? Probably he could have. Jesus spoke of Himself as "meek and lowly in heart" (Matt. 11:29).

Numbers 12:6 could possibly be translated very literally, "If the LORD (himself) was your prophet, I the LORD would make myself known to him in a dream (which) I would speak to (or *in*) him." But God communicated to Moses "face to face"! (Deut. 34:10). Moses had a unique association with God. Miriam was very much in the wrong for speaking against Moses.

Miriam was punished with leprosy for her talk, and her illness delayed the march of the Israelites for seven days (12:15).

19. *Expedition of the twelve spies* (Num. 13).The spies were sent out by *God's* command, but also by the people's request (Deut. 1:22). The sending out of the spies was a *test* of the people's faith. How would they respond to the spies' report?

The names of the ten faithless spies are practically forgotten and unknown. But everyone remembers *Joshua* and *Caleb*, the two believing spies (13:6, 16).

The name *Joshua* (13:16) is *Hoshea + Yah*. It means *Yah* (Jehovah) *is salvation*, and is the same name as *Jesus*.

The journey of the twelve spies was a long one. From Kadesh Barnea to Beersheba is fifty miles, and from there on to the far north toward Lebo Hamath would be nearly two hundred miles.

Grapes begin to ripen in August, but most are picked in September (13:20)

Beware of grasshopper faith (13:3). There is no harm done if others view us as grasshoppers, but when we begin to feel like grasshoppers in our own eyes, we flee away like grasshoppers from anything that looks threatening.

20. *Rebellion and rejection at Kadesh Barnea* (Num. 14). The Israelites accepted the report of the ten spies who did not believe they could conquer the land of Canaan. Israel actually chose a new leader (Korah?) to lead them back to Egypt (Neh. 9:17).

Moses' prayers again saved Israel, as they had at Mt. Sinai (14:13-19; Ex. 32:11-14). Moses had no self-seeking ambitions to become the founder of the nation (14:12).

God's sentence of punishment was taken from the Israelites' own words. They had said, "Our wives and children will die" (14:3, paraphrase). God said, "*YOU* will die, but your children will enter the promised land" (14:31, paraphrase).

The next day the Israelites changed their minds about not trying to enter the land of Canaan from its south side (14:39-40). Against Moses' advice they attempted to invade Canaan. The Amalekites and Canaanites chased the Israelites back, "like a swarm of bees" (Deut. 1:44).

21. *Laws about offerings* (Num. 15). The fact that God would give to the Israelites laws about sacrifices for forgiveness would reassure them that they might yet live, even though they had sinned by unbelief at Kadesh Barnea.

The Israelites had not actually intended to sin. But sins done even unintentionally by the whole congregation or by a leader required sacrifices of sin-offerings (15:22-24; Lev. 4:13).

A man who gathered sticks on a sabbath day was stoned to death (15:32-36; compare Ex. 20:8).

Tassels (or fringes) were to be placed on the corners of

the Israelites' robes. These were to remind them of God's commandments. In later centuries the Jews developed this simple decoration into an elaborate system of threads and knots that were designed to set forth symbolically the 613 precepts which they believed the law to consist of. Jesus denounced those who made these fringes extra wide to show off (Matt. 23:5).

22. *The rebellion of Korah* (Num. 16). The most serious threat ever to Moses' leadership occurred at Kadesh Barnea soon after Israel was forbidden to enter Canaan until forty years passed. This rebellion was led by Korah, a cousin of Moses (Ex. 6:18-21). Korah became a prime example of an ungodly rebel (Jude 11).

Korah (from the priestly family of the Kohathites) conspired with the Reubenites named *Dathan* and *Abiram.* (The Reubenites and Kohathites were camped close to one another, so that it was convenient for making conspiracies.) Korah acquired 250 followers, and most of the Israelites sided with him (16:19). He was a powerful politician.

Moses proposed a test to show who was God's chosen priest — Aaron's family or Korah's? Let each attempt to offer incense before the LORD. Only the true priest would survive such a test (16:16-17).

Korah and his chief henchmen were swallowed up into the earth (16:31-33). Fire from the LORD burned his 250 followers. "It is a dreadful (fearful) thing to fall into the hands of the living God" (Heb. 10:31). The sons of Korah were not burned, and later became famous musicians in the temple (26:10-11; Titles of psalms 42, 45-50). The incense burners (censers) of Korah and his men were hammered into plates to cover over the altar of burnt offering (16:37-38).

When Korah was destroyed, the Israelites said to Moses, "You have killed the LORD's people" (16:41). If Moses could actually have killed people as Korah was killed, he was no person for anyone to be speaking against!

When the plague broke out among the people for supporting Korah, Aaron, the true priest, went out among them with his incense burner and stood between the living and the

dead (16:48). Observe the power of God's true priests —
Aaron and Christ.

23. *The budding of Aaron's staff* (Num. 17). The Levites, led
by Korah, had recently rebelled. It was necessary to establish
the true priesthood of Aaron once for all. God did that
(17:3-5).

A *GREAT* miracle occurred! Buds formed, and blossoms
bloomed, and almonds were produced in one night on a
detached branch (17:8).

The staff (rod) of Aaron was to be kept "before the LORD
in the Tent of the Testimony," near the ark of the covenant.

24. *Priests and Levites: their work and support* (Num. 18).
Only the priests could minister in the tabernacle. The Levites
were merely their helpers. Many Bible critics say that the distinction in rank between priests and Levites was not made
until the time of the Babylonian captivity, and was not
enforced until the Priestly (P) writer wrote his document.
This notion is not biblical and it is not supported by any hard
evidence outside the Bible.

The Levites were supported by tithes from the people
(one-tenth of the people's incomes). The Levites themselves
were to give to the priests a tenth of the tithes they received
(18:26, 28).

25. *The water of cleansing* (Num. 19). A red heifer was to be
sacrificed. Then its ashes were to be placed in water (19:1-9).
This water was used to sprinkle those who had touched a
dead body (19:11-13). God views the death that we humans
have brought upon ourselves with great anguish, and plans to
destroy death. The ashes of the red heifer were a temporary
relief.

If "the blood of goats and bulls and the *ashes of a heifer*
sprinkled on those who are ceremonially unclean sanctify
them so that they are outwardly clean, How much more,
then, will the blood of Christ . . . cleanse our consciences
from acts that lead to death, so that we may serve the living
God" (Heb. 9:13-14).

26. *The fateful fortieth year* (Num. 20). The forty years of
Israel's wanderings are almost a blank page in Israel's history.

A list of names of some of the places Israel camped at during those years is given in Numbers 33. From this list we learn that during those years they made one trip down to the north tip of the Gulf of Aqaba to Ezion Geber (Num. 33:36), and from there returned to Kadesh Barnea shortly before Aaron died (33:37-39).

Events in the fortieth year of Israel's wanderings:

(1) Miriam died (20:1);

(2) Moses struck the rock, instead of just speaking to it (20:2-13; Ex. 17:1-7);

(3) The Edomites refused to let the Israelites pass through their land (20:14-21);

(4) Aaron died on Mt. Hor (20:22-29).

The Desert of Zin (Tsin) is a desolate, rugged depression, a branch off the west side of the Arabah valley south of the Dead Sea. Kadesh Barnea was considered to be in the Desert of Zin (27:14; 33:36).

Moses was to *SPEAK* to the rock to get water this time. (Compare Ex. 17:56 and Num. 27:12-14). This might seem like a small command, but God does not consider any of His commands to be small (Matt. 5:19). Besides that, there was an important reason from the typology of the Rock. The Rock that gave the Israelites water was Christ (1 Cor. 10:4). Christ was only smitten (struck) on one occasion. We may now speak to Him, but sinners cannot crucify Him again. The Rock is smitten but once!

The Israelites were now aware that they would never successfully invade Canaan from the south. So they travelled east, planning to go around the south end of the Dead Sea and up along its east side, and then enter Canaan from the east. To do this they had to go across the mountainous land of Edom, which lay along the east side of the Arabah valley south of the Dead Sea. The Israelites asked the Edomites for permission to pass through their land. Many of the roads through Edom are narrow passages with cliffs on both sides, like the road through Petra, which in places is not fifty feet wide. These would be easy to block. Edom refused passage to the Israelites.

Aaron, Israel's first high priest, died in the fifth month of the fortieth year (33:37-39), on Mt. Hor. Aaron's son *Eleazar* became Israel's second high priest. The traditional place of Aaron's death and burial is at *Jebel Harun* (mount of Aaron) west of Petra about three miles, on the east edge of the Arabah valley. This seems to me to be the correct location, but many scholars favor *Jebel Madurah* twenty-four miles northwest of Kadesh Barnea.

27. *Arad destroyed* (Num. 21:1-3). Arad was a Canaanite city between Beersheba and the Dead Sea. The king of Arad attacked Israel. In return his city was destroyed, and the place was named *Hormah*, meaning "devoted," that is, set apart to be destroyed. Some other places were also called *Hormah*.

28. *The Bronze Snake* (Num. 21:9). Because the Edomites would not let Israel pass through their land, the Israelites had to make a long detour around Edom. They went toward the south so they could go around Edom instead of going through it. The way from Mt. Hor south goes through the Arabah valley. I travelled through the Arabah valley in 1974, and in many places the temperature was 120 degrees or higher. The Israelites complained, and the Lord sent venomous (lit., the *burning*, or *seraphim*) snakes. When they cried out, the LORD told them to make a snake of bronze and put it up on a pole. Those who looked with faith upon the bronze snake were healed.

The Bronze Serpent — A Type of Jesus on the Cross (Num. 21:4-9; John 3:14-15; 2 Kgs. 18:4)	
The Bronze (brazen) serpent	**Jesus on the cross**
1. Death without it (Num. 21:6)	1. Death without Him (John 8:21,24)
2. Lifted up on a pole (Num. 21:8)	2. Lifted up on the cross (John 3:14; 12:32-33)
3. Available to all (Num. 21:8)	3. Available to all (John 3:16)
4. The ONLY cure	4. The ONLY savior (Acts 4:12)
5. A SURE cure (Num. 21:8-9)	5. A SURE cure

6. Required faith	6. Requires faith (John 3:15)
7. Look and live! (Num. 21:8)	7. Look and live! (Isa. 45:22)
8. Must not become an idol (2 Kgs. 18:4)	8. Must not become an idol (a charm or crucifix; 1 John 5:21)

29. *The journey to Moab* (Num. 21:10-20). Israel went on southward to the north tip of the Gulf of Aqaba at Ezion Geber (Deut. 2:8). There they turned northward and went along the desert road of Moab, and came up to the Zered River. The Zered comes from the east and flows into the Rift Valley (or Jordan Valley) just south of the Dead Sea.

By the time Israel reached the Zered valley not a man was living among them who had been numbered at the census at Mt. Sinai, except Moses, Caleb and Joshua (Deut. 2:13-14).

North of the brook Zered lay the land of Moab. The Lord sent the Israelites east along the Zered so they would detour around the land of Moab and not harass the Moabites (Deut. 2:9; Judg. 11:15-22).

Israel crossed the Zered, and came to the well called Be'er (21:16-18). It was dug out by the nobles and princes of Israel. The refreshment from this well, and the singing that accompanied its cleaning reminds us of the streams of living water that Jesus promised to us (John 7:37-39).

Much of the land east of the Dead Sea is high, and from those heights (*Bamot)* Israel had a view overlooking the "wasteland" (or *Jeshimon*) west of the Dead Sea in the Wilderness of Judah (21:20).

30. *Defeat of Sihon and Og* (Num. 21:21-35; Deut. 2:24–3:11).

Israel defeated *Sihon,* king of the Amorites east of the Jordan River at a place named *Jahaz* (21:23). Jahaz was probably located north of the Arnon River, near the city of Dibon. The territory of Sihon included the lands between the Arnon river (east of the Dead Sea) and the Jabbok River (on the east side of the Jordan, about halfway between the Dead Sea and Galilee). Israel took all these lands in one or two battles. Archaeologists have found that this area was sparsely populated at the time of Moses.

From Jahaz Israel journeyed north about eighty miles to the city of *Edrei* on the Yarmuk river. There Israel defeated the forces of a giant king named *Og*, and took all his lands, which included the lands of *Gilead* (east of the Jordan) and *Bashan* (the Golan Heights east of the Sea of Galilee). Og had an iron bedstead thirteen feet (9 cubits) long and six feet (four cubits) wide (Deut. 3:11).

From their victory at Edrei Israel journeyed back to the south, to the area called the Plains of Moab, just north of the Dead Sea and east of the Jordan, across the river from the town of Jericho. In the Plains of Moab all of the remainder of the events told in Numbers and in Deuteronomy occurred.

31. *Deliverance from Balaam* (Num. chs. 22–24; 31:8, 15–16; Josh. 24:9-10; Mic. 5:8). Balak, the king of Moab, had nothing to fear from the Israelites (Deut. 2:9). But he thought he did and called for a prophet named Balaam to come from a great distance and pronounce curses upon the Israelites, which would destroy them. Balaam was very willing to come, but the LORD prevented him from pronouncing curses on Israel. Instead blessings came out of his mouth.

> **An undeserved *curse* does not come to rest** (Prov. 26:2).

Balaam lived far off at Pethor, up by the Euphrates River (Num. 22:5).

God told Balaam NOT to go with the Moabites and curse Israel (22:12). But Balaam LOVED the money he would get for unrighteous prophesying (2 Pet. 2:15). The LORD allowed Balaam to go on, but on the way to pronounce his curses, Balaam's donkey veered twice and a third time squatted down on the ground beneath him.

Balaam's donkey (a she-donkey, Hebrew, *'athon*) spoke to him, "Am I not your own donkey, which you have always ridden?" (22:30). Balaam "was rebuked for his wrongdoing by a donkey — a beast without speech — who spoke with a man's voice and restrained the prophet's madness" (2 Pet. 2:15-16; Jude 11).

At that point Balaam saw what the donkey had seen before — an angel on the road with a sword drawn (22:31).

Balaam thought he could get God to change His mind and let him pronounce the curses if he would offer sacrifices, or move around to different spots (23:1, 27), or use sorcery (24:1). None of these schemes worked.

Balaam uttered four prophecies, which God placed in his mouth:

1. I cannot curse the people that God has blessed (Num. 23:7-10).
2. God will not change His mind (23:18-24).
3. How good Israel is (24:3-9).
4. Israel's enemies will perish (24:15-24).

Balak was perturbed. "I summoned you to curse my enemies, but you have blessed them these three times. Now leave at once and go home" (24:10-11).

Balaam's most famous prophecy is Numbers 24:17:

"I see him, but not now;
   I behold him, but not near.
A star will rise out of Jacob; ✡ ☆
   A scepter will rise out of Israel."

In this prophecy Balaam looks into the future four hundred years, to the time of King David (1010–970 B.C.). King David defeated the Moabites (even though his great grandmother Ruth was a Moabitess). See 2 Samuel 8:2.

Balaam also probably foretold in this prophecy the time when Magi (wise men) from the East would come to Jerusalem, and say, "Where is the one who has been born king of the Jews? We saw his *star* in the East and have come to worship him" (Matt. 2:2).

It appears that Balaam did not go directly back home to Mesopotamia, but stayed around Moab. There he counselled the Moabites and Midianites somewhat in this manner: "We will never be able to pronounce a curse on these Israelites as long as they are in the favor of Yahweh their God. What we need to do is get their God angry at them, and then he will destroy them himself. Why not invite the Israelite men down to your yearly Ba'al festival, where you have all the holy prostitutes? That is almost certain to make their God angry with them." (See Numbers 31:16.)

Revelation 2:14 — Jesus said, "You have people there who hold to the teaching of Balaam, who taught Balak to entice the Israelites to sin by eating food sacrificed to idols and by committing sexual immorality."

The name of *Balaam* has been found written in a wall inscription at Tell Deir 'Alla, near the Jordan, on its east side. The inscription is dated about 900 B.C. Except for the name, it has no direct biblical connections.

32. *The sin at Baal of Peor* (Num. 25). Israel was encamped at *Shittim*, about ten miles east of the Jordan River. The men went and joined the Moabites in their immoral religious festival to Baal at a place called Peor. Moses was instructed to put to death those involved in this (25:4).

An Israelite man came into their camp with a Moabite woman by his side. They disappeared into his tent. Aaron's grandson *Phinehas* ran into his tent with his spear and ran it through both of them at once. The Israelite man was from the tribe of Simeon. Phinehas was praised for his zeal. He became Israel's third high priest.

24,000 Israelites died of a plague after this mass immorality (25:9). First Corinthians 10:8 gives the figure of 23,000, but that figure may include only those who died of the plague, but not a thousand who were executed.

33. *The second census* (Num. 26). The second census was taken in the Plains of Moab; the first had been taken at Mt. Sinai. The second census was taken about thirty-nine years after the first. The second census showed a decline of about 1,820 people since the first census. There would have been an increase if 24,000 people had not perished just a few months before the census was taken (Num. 25:9). The second

census may have been taken in preparation for the war coming up against the Midianites (Num. 26:2; 25:17; 31:1-3).

In the second census Judah remained the largest tribe, as it had been in the first census. Manasseh had made the largest growth in population. Simeon had made the largest drop. This tribe appears to have been deeply involved in the sin at Baal of Peor, which caused many to die (25:14).

All of the older generation had perished before the second census was taken (26:64-65).

34. *Zelophehad's daughters* (Num. 27:1-11). The daughters of Zelophehad of the tribe of Manasseh desired to inherit their father's property because there were no brothers in their family to inherit it (27:4). Their request was granted, but a restriction was later placed on such cases. Women who inherited land had to marry within their own tribe (36:6-9). The patriarch Job left land to his daughters (Job 42:15).

35. *Joshua to succeed Moses* (Num. 27:12-23). When Moses was warned of his imminent death, he did not begin to whine and plead, as King Hezekiah did (2 Kgs. 20:2). Moses' first concern was that God appoint a leader for Israel. Joshua was the choice of both God and men (27:18; Ex. 18:10; 24;13; 32:17).

36. *Offerings* (Num. 28). There was a continual burnt-offering, a lamb offered each morning and another in the evenings (28:3). A double offering was made on the Sabbath days (28:9), and additional offerings on various feast days (28:11, 16-19, 26-27). Sin is expensive.

37. *Offerings on feasts in the seventh month* (Num. 29; compare Leviticus 23.)

a. *Feast of Trumpets* (29:1-6). This was held on the first day of the seventh month, about mid-September by our calendar. The Feast of Trumpets was a day of solemn rest (Lev. 23:24-25).

b. *Day of Atonement* (29:7-11). This was a day to "deny yourselves" ("afflict your souls"), that is, to fast. See Acts 27:9.

c. *Feast of Tabernacles* (29:12-40). It was also called Booths (Heb., *Sukkoth*), and Ingathering. It lasted eight days. A complicated system of decreasing numbers of bulls were sacrificed each day (29:13, 17, 20, 23, 26, 29, 32, 36). During this feast people were to live outdoors in temporary brush arbors (Lev. 23:39-42). Also during this feast, every seven years, the entire law was to be read (Deut. 31:10-11).

38. *Vows made by women* (Num. 30). A vow or a spoken word is serious in God's eyes, and is not to be broken (30:2; Eccl. 5:4-5; Deut. 23:21). Under the law of Moses, a woman's vows were binding for life, unless her father or husband forbade the vow at the time she spoke it (30:4-5, 6-8).

39. *Slaughter of the Midianites, and dividing of the spoils* (Num. 31). Israel fought against Midian because the Midianites seduced Israel into the immorality at Baal of Peor (25:16-18; 31:2). Phinehas led the war against Midian (31:6; 25:7-8, 10-13). Phinehas had taken a firm stand against evil. We need men who are firm against evil, and yet compassionate.

Balaam was killed in this war (31:8). What we sow, we shall reap (Gal. 6:7-8).

Of the women prisoners captured in the war, one out of every fifty were given to the LORD's work in the tabernacle by the whole congregation of Israelites. One out of five hundred of those owned by the men of war was given to the LORD's work. These people worked as slaves around the tabernacle, and apparently their children did after them.

40. *The tribes east of Jordan* (Num. 32). The tribes of Reuben, Gad and one-half of Manasseh received their land allotment in the land east of the Jordan (32:1, 4-5, 33).

These tribes had to help the other tribes conquer their land west of the Jordan. All must bear a share of the load and battle. If they did not help the other tribes, "Be sure that your sin will find you out" (32:23).

The tribes that asked for special lands were later the first to go into captivity. Being on the border and frontier caused them to be the first to be invaded (2 Kgs. 15:29).

41. *Stages in Israel's journeys* (Num. 33). God told Moses to keep a record (a log) of the places they journeyed through (33:2).

The plagues in Egypt had been judgments upon the gods (idols) of Egypt (33:4; Ex. 12:12).

Aaron died at age 123. He was three or four years older than Moses (33:39).

DRIVE OUT the Canaanites! (33:52; Deut. 7:1-5). If you do not drive them out, they will be barbs in your eyes and thorns in your sides (33:55). The Canaanites that were left in the land would corrupt Israel (Deut. 7:4).

The promised land was to be divided among the twelve tribes (1) by lot, and (2) by population size (33:54).

42. *The borders of Israel* (west of Jordan) (Num. 34).

a. *South border:* From the south end of the Salt Sea, eastward along the Zered River, southward to the Scorpion Pass (the Ascent of Akkrabim), to Kadesh Barnea, to the Wadi of Egypt (the Wadi el-Arish), and north to the Great (Mediterranean) Sea. (The Scorpion Pass is a twisty trail up out of the Wilderness of Zin into the Negev.)

b. *North border:* From the Great Sea, to Lebo Hamath on the Orontes River. The Mt. Hor mentioned in 34:8 is not the same Mt. Hor referred to in 33:38.

c. *East border:* From Riblah on the Orontes River, to the Sea of Kinnereth (Galilee) and the Jordan River to the Salt Sea.

43. *Levitical Cities and Cities of Refuge* (Num. 35). Concerning the cities of refuge, see Numbers 35:9-34; Deuteronomy 4:41-43; 19:1-13; Joshua 20:7-8. Three cities of refuge were set on each side of the Jordan, so that one would be accessible from any area. Manslayers had to remain in a city of refuge until the high priest then living died (35:25). He could not buy his way out of the city of refuge.

Forty-eight cities were to be given to the Levites throughout the land. These forty-eight included the six cities of refuge. Besides the cities themselves, the land immediately surrounding the cities belonged to the Levites for pasture land.

Two or more witnesses were required for conviction of a murderer (35:30). The penalty for murder was death (35:31).

44. *Marriages of women who inherited property* (Num. 36). Women who inherited property because they had no brothers had to marry within their own tribe (36:8). God wants people to have their own land and keep it.

261

Questions on Section E
Numbers

Numbers 1
1. What is the topic of chapter one? (1:2)
2. What people were counted in the numbering? (1:3)
3. Make a list of the tribes, their populations and the total number. (1:46)
4. Which tribe was not numbered and why not? (1:47)

Numbers 2
1. What is the topic of chapter two? (2:1)
2. List the order (or positions) of the various camps as Israel moved about. (2:3,9; etc.)
3. As the tribes marched, where was the tabernacle carried in relation to the camps? (2:17)

Numbers 3
1. What is the topic of chapter three? (3:1,6)
2. Whom did God take instead of the firstborn of Israel? (3:13)
3. Name the three families of the Levites. (3:17)
4. What was the total number of the Levites? (3:39)
5. Were there more Levites or firstborn Israelites? How many more? (3:39,42)
6. What was done to adjust the difference between the number of Levites and the number of the firstborn? (3:46)

Numbers 4
1. Give the chapter topic for chapter four. (4:2,21,29)
2. How was the ark of the covenant packed up for moving? (4:4-6)

Numbers 5
1. What was used to determine if a wife had committed adultery? (5:16-22)

Numbers 6
1. What is the topic of most of chapter six? (6:2)
2. What things was a Nazirite not to do? (6:3-6; Compare Judges 13:4-5,7,24)

Numbers 7
1. What was given to help in transporting the tabernacle? (7:3)
2. Did the leaders of the various tribes offer different gifts for the tabernacle? (7:11-17)

Numbers 8
1. What is the topic of 8:5-26?

Numbers 9

1. What feast was kept early in the second year after Israel left Egypt? (9:1-2)
2. What rule was given about those who could not keep the Passover because they were unclean? (9:11)
3. What guided the Israelites and determined their moving about? (9:15)

Numbers 10

1. What was used for calling the congregation of Israel together? (10:1)
2. How long after leaving Egypt was it when Israel left Sinai? (10:11; 33:3)
3. How long were the Israelites at Mt. Sinai altogether? (Compare Ex. 19:1 and Num. 10:11)
4. Into what desert did Israel come after leaving Sinai? (10:12)
5. Whom did Moses ask to accompany Israel from Mt. Sinai? (10:29)
6. Did he desire to accompany Moses and Israel? (10:30)

Numbers 11

1. What happened when the people complained? (11:1)
2. What was the place called where they murmured? (11:3)
3. What did the rabble with Israel crave after? (11:4)
4. How did God react to their lustful weeping? (11:10)
5. How did Moses react to it? (11:10-11)
6. Whom did God appoint to help Moses bear the burden of the people? (11:16)
7. How long did God promise that Israel would eat flesh? (11:19)
8. What did the men who were appointed to help Moses do when the Spirit rested on them? (11:25)
9. What two men prophesied in the camp? (11:26)
10. How did Joshua react to their prophesying? (11:28)
11. What type of meat was given to the people? (11:31)
12. With what did Jehovah strike the people? (11:33)
13. What was the place called where God gave them meat, and what did its name mean? (11:34)

Numbers 12

1. What did Miriam and Aaron speak against Moses about? (12:1)
2. How is Moses described in this chapter? (12:3)
3. How did Jehovah feel about their speaking against Moses? (12:7-8)
4. How was Miriam punished? (12:10)
5. How long did Miriam's sin delay Israel's progress? (12:15)

Numbers 13

1. What did Jehovah command Moses to do? (13:2)

2. Who were the spies from the tribes of Judah and Ephraim? (13:6,8)
3. How much of the land did the men look over? (13:21-22)
4. What was obtained at Eschol? (13:23)
5. How long did the men take on their trip? (13:25)
6. How did the spies describe the land and its inhabitants? (13:27-28)
7. Which spy said that Israel could possess the land? (13:30)
8. How did the men say they looked to the inhabitants of the land? (13:33)

Numbers 14
1. How did the people react to the words of the ten unbelieving spies? (14:1)
2. Whom did the Israelites say would be a prey and perish? (14:3)
3. Did the Israelites appoint a captain to lead them back to Egypt? (14:4; Compare Neh. 9:17)
4. What did God threaten to do to Israel? (14:12)
5. What prevented God from killing Israel? (14:19-20)
6. What judgment and punishment did God pronounce upon Israel? (14:30-34)
7. What happened to the ten spies? (14:37)
8. What was the result of Israel's attempted invasion of Canaan? (14:44-45)

Numbers 15
1. What two offerings were to be made along with burnt or peace offerings? (15:5-7)
2. If a person sinned unknowingly, what types of offerings did he have to bring? (15:22-25)
3. What was to be done to those who sinned defiantly, "with the high hand"? (15:30)
4. What was the punishment upon the man who gathered sticks on the Sabbath? (15:32,36)
5. What were the Israelites to place on the borders of their garments? (15:38)

Numbers 16
1. What is the chapter topic of Numbers 16? (16:1,3)
2. Who rebelled against Moses (3 names)? How many men joined the rebels? (16:2)
3. What did Moses tell the rebels to do to determine whom the Lord had chosen to be priests? (16:6-7)
4. Was the congregation of Israel favorable to Moses or to the rebels? (16:9)
5. What was the fate of the rebel leaders? Of their followers? (16:31-32,35)
6. What was done with the censers of the rebels? (16:38)
7. How did the congregation react to the deaths of the rebels? (16:41)
8. How many in the congregation died as a result of this? (16:49)

Period V: Wandering

Numbers 17
1. What did God use to demonstrate which man was His chosen priest? (17:2)
2. Where was the rod (staff) to be kept? Why? (17:4,10)
3. What was Israel's reaction to the budding of Aaron's rod? (17:12-13)

Numbers 18
1. What was the penalty upon unauthorized people who did the work of priests? (18:3)
2. What was to be given to Aaron and his sons to provide for their needs? (18:8-9)
3. What was to be done with firstborn animals? (18:14,15,17)
4. What was the redemption price of firstborn sons? (18:15-16)
5. Why did the priests receive no inheritance of land? (18:20)
6. What was to be given to the Levites as their inheritance? (18:21)
7. What were the Levites to take out of their tithes? To whom was this given? (18:26,28)

Numbers 19
1. What were the ashes of a red heifer to be used for? (19:9; compare Heb. 9:13)
2. How long was a man unclean after touching a dead body? (19:11)

Numbers 20
1. Where did Miriam die? (20:1)
2. What did God tell Moses to do to the rock? What did Moses do? (20:8,11)
3. What was Moses' punishment? (20:12)
4. What unkind thing did Edom do to Israel? (20:21)
5. Where did Aaron die? (20:23-24)
6. Who became Aaron's successor as high priest? (20:26)

Numbers 21
1. What Canaanite king attacked Israel? (21:1)
2. What was the result of this attack? (21:3)
3. How did the Israelites feel as they went around the land of Edom? (21:4-5)
4. What was the bronze serpent used for? What did Jesus compare this incident to? (21:8-9; John 3:4-15)
5. What was the border between Moab and the Amorites? (21:13)
6. What did Moses and Israel do at Beer? (21:16-18)
7. Who was Sihon? (21:21)
8. What was the extent of Sihon's kingdom? (21:24; compare Joshua 12:2-3)
9. What did Israel request of Sihon? (21:22)
10. Where did Sihon fight against Israel? (21:23)

11. Between what two rivers did Israel occupy the land of Sihon? (21:24)
12. What was the capital city of Sihon's kingdom? (21:26)
13. What land had Sihon previously captured? (21:26)
14. Who was Chemosh? (21:29; Compare 1 Kings 11:33)
15. To what city did Moses send spies? (21:32)
16. Who was Og? (21:33)
17. What was the extent of Og's kingdom? (21:33; Deut. 3:3-5; Josh. 12:4-5)
18. How big was Og's bedstead? (Deut. 3:11)
19. Where did Israel fight Og? (21:33)
20. What encouragement did Israel receive for the battle against Og? (21:34)
21. What was the outcome of the battle of Og? (21:35)

Numbers 22

1. Who was Balak? (22:4)
2. What was worrying Balak? (22:2-3)
3. Who was Balaam? (22:4-5)
4. What did Balak want Balaam to do? (22:6)
5. What did God tell Balaam not to do? (22:12)
6. How did Balak try to persuade Balaam? (22:17)
7. What blocked Balaam's path as he rode to Balak? (22:22)
8. What unusual thing did Balaam's ass do? (22:28; 2 Peter 2:15-16; Jude 11)
9. Did Balaam really want to please God or to please Balak? (22:38)

Numbers 23

1. What did Balaam do in the hope that God might change his mind? (23:1)
2. In Balaam's first prophecy did he curse or bless Israel? (23:11)
3. What was done in preparation for the second attempt to curse Israel? (23:13-14)
4. Did God change his mind about Israel, according to Balaam's second prophecy? (23:19)
5. What did Balak say after Balaam's second prophecy? (23:25)
6. Did Balak think that God was the same everywhere? Give a reason for your answer. (23:27)

Numbers 24

1. What had Balaam used sorcery for? (24:1)
2. What is the main point in Balaam's third prophecy? (24:5,9)
3. What (apparently) good statement did Balaam give to Balak after the third prophecy? (24:13)
4. In Balaam's fourth prophecy what did he say would rise out of Jacob and Israel? (24:17)
5. Relate this prophecy (24:17) to Matthew 2:2.

6. In his fourth prophecy what nations did Balaam predict God would destroy? (24:20-22)

Numbers 25

1. What sin did Israel fall into? (25:1-2)
2. Whose counsel had brought about this sin by Israel? (Num. 31:16)
3. What priest slew a couple? How? Why? (25:6-8)
4. How many Israelites died as a result of this sin? (25:9; 1 Cor. 10:8)
5. What did God tell the Israelites to do to Midian? (25:16)

Numbers 26

1. What is the topic of chapter 26? (26:2)
2. Prepare parallel lists of the populations of the tribes in the two censuses (Num. 1, 26).
3. How many men survived the 40 years' wilderness wanderings? (26:64-65)

Numbers 27

1. What did the daughters of Zelophehad want? (27:4)
2. Was their request granted? (27:6)
3. What dramatic demand did God make to Moses? (27:12-13)
4. What did Moses ask God to do before he (Moses) died? (27:15-16)
5. Who was appointed as leader to succeed Moses? (27:18)

Numbers 28

1. On what occasions were the Israelites to offer additional sacrifices besides the daily continual burnt offerings? (28:9,11,16,26)

Numbers 29

1. What three feasts were to be observed in the seventh month? (29:1,7,12; Lev. 23:23-36)
2. On what days of the month were these feasts to be observed?

Numbers 30

1. How seriously were vows to be taken? (30:2; Eccl. 5:4-6)
2. Who had power to break a vow made by a woman? A wife? A widow? (30:5,8,9)

Numbers 31

1. With whom did Israel go to war? (31:2)
2. What prophet was slain in the war? (31:8)
3. How did the war come out? (31:7,10)
4. How were the prisoners of war divided? (31:27-30)
5. What part of the prisoners were given to Jehovah from the men of war? From the congregation of Israel? (31:28-30)

Numbers 32

1. What land did the children of Reuben and Gad request? (32:1,5)
2. How did Moses react to their request? (32:6,14)
3. What did the tribes of Reuben and Gad promise to do if they could have the requested land? (32:17-18)
4. What other tribe received land in the same area as Gad and Reuben? (32:33)
5. Who dispossessed the Amorites in Gilead? (32:39)

Numbers 33

1. What is the general topic of chapter thirty-three? (33:1)
2. What caused Moses to write a record of the journeys of Israel? (33:2)
3. What were the Egyptians doing while the Israelites left Egypt? (33:4)
4. In what year of Israel's wanderings did Aaron die? (33:38)
5. What did God command Israel to do to the inhabitants of Canaan? (33:52)
6. What would the Canaanites be to the Israelites if the Israelites failed to drive them out? (33:55)

Numbers 34

1. What was the south border of the promised land? (34:3; Gen. 15:18)
2. What was the north border of the promised land? (34:7-8)
3. What part of the land was allotted to Gad, Reuben and half of Manasseh? (34:15)

Numbers 35

1. How many cities were to be given to the Levites altogether? (35:7)
2. What six special cities were included in this number? (35:6,13)
3. How much territory surrounding these cities was to be given to the Levites? (35:4)
4. What were the cities of refuge used for? (35:11)
5. Where were the cities of refuge to be located? (35:14)
6. What was the penalty for murderers? (35:16)
7. Who decided if a man had a right to safety in a city of refuge? (35:24)
8. How long did a manslayer have to stay in a city of refuge? (35:25)
9. How could a manslayer lose his security in a city of refuge? (35:26-27)
10. How many witnesses were required to convict a killer? (35:30)

Numbers 36

1. What problem worried the descendants of Manasseh? (35:2-3)
2. What restriction about marriage was placed on women who inherited property? (35:6)

Section F
Deuteronomy

1. Introduction to Deuteronomy

The name **DEUTERONOMY** *means the SECOND LAW
(or the LAW REPEATED).*

a. The law was given at first at Mt. Sinai (Ex., Lev., Num.).

b. The law was repeated (and enlarged) forty years later in the Plains of Moab, and recorded in the book of Deuteronomy.

---

a. In Moses' last month of life he spoke to the Israelites. He reviewed their journeys and the laws God had given them at Mt. Sinai and in the desert. He strongly urged them to keep God's laws and covenant. This second giving of the law is recorded in the book of Deuteronomy.

In Deuteronomy many of the laws given previously are repeated or expanded. The Ten Commandments are given in Exodus 20, and again in Deuteronomy 5.

This repetition of the law was needed because a new generation had grown up in the desert who had not heard the law at Mt. Sinai. The Israelites who had once heard the law showed by their behavior that they needed to hear it again.

b. Author, date, and place of writing of Deuteronomy.

(1) *Author: Moses* was the author of all the book except the last chapter, which tells of his death. The last chapter was possibly written by Joshua after Moses' death. (See Joshua 8:32 and 24:26.)

Deuteronomy 1:1 — "These are the words *Moses* spoke to all Israel."

Deuteronomy 4:44 — "This is the law *Moses* set before the Israelites."

Deuteronomy 31:9 — "*Moses* wrote down this law and gave it to the priests."

Deuteronomy 31:24-26 — "After *Moses* finished writing in a book the words of this law from beginning to end, he gave this command to the Levites who carried the ark . . . 'Take this Book of the Law and place it beside the ark of the covenant of the LORD.'"

Deuteronomy 32:45 — "*Moses* finished reciting all these words."

1 Corinthians 9:9 — "It is written in the law of *Moses*: 'Do not muzzle an ox while it is treading out the grain.'" (This is a quotation of Deuteronomy 25:4. Compare also Romans 10:19 and Deuteronomy 32:21.)

(2) *Date* of Deuteronomy: 1407 B.C. Deuteronomy was spoken and written in the fortieth year, the eleventh month after Israel's exodus from Egypt (Deut. 1:1). It took approximately one month to do it. Deuteronomy was a thirty-day riverside revival. It was completed just before Moses' death.

Joshua 4:19 tells that Israel crossed into Canaan in the forty-first year, the first month, tenth day. That was seventy days after Moses began to deliver Deuteronomy. Several events occurred after Moses' death until the crossing into Canaan: (1) a thirty-day period of weeping for Moses (Deut. 34:8); (2) the sending of spies into Jericho, an event that occupied several days; (3) three days of preparation (Josh. 3:2). These events occupied about forty days, leaving about thirty days for the delivering of the messages in Deuteronomy.

(3) *Place* of delivering Deuteronomy. It was delivered in the Plains of Moab by the Jordan River across [east] from Jericho. The place was named Shittim (or Acacia Grove) (Josh. 2:1). This was about ten miles east of the Jordan River and seven miles north of the Dead Sea.

c. Contents and style of Deuteronomy.

(1) The book contains three long addresses by Moses (chs. 1–30), followed by a few closing words and events (chs. 32–34).

Deuteronomy contains (mainly in chs. 12–26) many laws of social, civil and political nature such as Israel would need when they entered the promised land, but which would have been superfluous in the desert. (See Deuteronomy 12:8-11 as an example.)

(2) The book has mostly the *style* of a sermon or fatherly exhortation. The book is emphatic and emotional. Deuteronomy 32:46-47: "Obey carefully all the words of this law. They are not just idle words for you — they are your life. By them you will live long in the land you are crossing the Jordan to possess."

d. *Outline of Deuteronomy*. (Memorize the main parts.)
I. Three addresses by Moses (chs. 1-30)
   A. (Chs. 1-4) Review of God's leading Israel from Mt. Sinai to the Plains of Moab (1:1-4:40). Cities of refuge east of Jordan (4:41-43)
   B. (Chs. 5-26) Laws and exhortations. (4:44-49 is introduction.)
      1. Old laws (chs. 5-11). (An extended exposition of the Ten Commandments)
      2. New laws (chs. 12-26) (to be observed in Canaan)
   C. (Chs. 27-30) Blessings for obedience and curses for disobedience
II. Closing words and events (chs. 31-34)
   A. Final commands (ch. 31)
   B. The song of Moses (ch. 32)
   C. The blessing of Moses (ch. 33)
   D. The death of Moses (ch. 34)
e. New Testament uses of Deuteronomy

(1) Jesus quoted Deuteronomy three times during His temptations (Matt. 4:4-10; Deut. 6:13,16; 8:3).

(2) Paul quoted Deuteronomy to prove the teachings of the gospel. See Romans 10:8.

(3) Peter quoted Deuteronomy 18:15 in his sermon on Solomon's porch (Acts 3:22-23; 7:37).

f. *Memorize* from Deuteronomy. Jesus obviously memorized passages from Deuteronomy. We should also. The following passages seem especially significant: Deuteronomy 4:2, 35, 39; 6:4-5,7; 8:3; 10:12; 18:15; 29:29; 30:11-15; 31:6; 33:27.

g. *Critical views of the authorship of Deuteronomy*. Most biblical critics hold that the book of Deuteronomy was first brought forth to the people in 622 B.C., in the time of King

Josiah, when the book of the law (supposedly only Deuteronomy) was "found" in the temple rubble (2 Kgs. 22:3-8). This was almost eight hundred years after the time of Moses. Supposedly the book had been written not long before, and planted in the rubble so it would certainly be found, and could be represented as an actual writing by Moses. Robert Pfeiffer says that the Deuteronomist [the author of Deuteronomy] "timed" the appearance of his book, and placed the book in the Temple's collection box (*Old Testament Introduction*, p. 57).

Norman Gottwald says that the Deuteronomic tradition "surfaced" in the major reform of the kingdom of Judah launched by King Josiah (*The Hebrew Bible*, pp. 138-139).

The beliefs and teachings in Deuteronomy are said to be the productions of religious men in the northern kingdom who were influenced by the prophets like Amos and Hosea, and believed that obedience to the covenant with Yahweh was significant. Moses taught that idea long before! They advocated that there should be only ONE central sanctuary where the worship of Yahweh was practiced. They wrote these beliefs in a highly sermonic and hortatory (exhorting) form. Deuteronomy is said (by some critics) to be the first book actually accepted as "canon" by the Israelites (Pfeiffer, *op. cit.*, p. 52). The Deuteronomic writers supposedly inserted into other books (Joshua through 2 Kings) many moralizing introductions and comments that presented their theological viewpoints.

If we accept this critical theory about the authorship of Deuteronomy, we must reject everything the book says about its own authorship, and everything that Jesus said about it. The theory does not have any support from ancient writings or from documents that have been found. The theory is built on the presupposition that we can simply disregard any statements about God *speaking* to people (R. Pfeiffer, p. 50).

For futher information, see Gleason L. Archer, *A Survey of Old Testament Introduction* (Chicago: Moody Press, 1994), pp. 271-283. Also see G.T. Manley, *The Book of the Law* (Grand Rapids: Eerdmans, 1957).

Questions on the Introduction to Deuteronomy

1. What does the name *Deuteronomy* mean? Why is it called that?
2. Who was the author of Deuteronomy? What was its date of production? Where was it written?
3. In what two passages (books, chapters) are the Ten Commandments given?
4. In what style is most of Deuteronomy presented?
5. When did Jesus make a conspicuous use of passages from Deuteronomy?
6. What are the two main parts in the outline of Deuteronomy? What chapters in the book are included in each part?
7. When do many Bible critics say that Deuteronomy was first brought forth to the Israelites?

2. *First address by Moses* (Deut. 1–4). Moses spoke the words in Deuteronomy "east of the Jordan," literally, "beyond the Jordan," a title applied to the lands east of Jordan, regardless of where the speaker was (Deut. 1:1; 4:31).

Moses told the people of many experiences they had shared during the forty years of wandering in the desert, from Mount Horeb (Sinai) to the Plains of Moab. They had passed through a vast and dreadful desert (1:19). They had rebelled against God's commandment to go in and conquer the land of Canaan (1:26). But through all of their agony "The LORD your God has blessed you . . . He has watched over your journey through this vast desert" (2:7). They spent many days — thirty-eight years in fact (2:14) — wandering from Kadesh Barnea to the border of the promised land. During that time an entire generation of men had died (2:14). Nonetheless, they had conquered the lands east of Jordan, the territories of Kings Sihon and Og (2:32; 3:3). The Israelites had the LORD's promise that Joshua would lead them across the Jordan (3:28).

Moses reviewed this history (much of which is told also in the book of Numbers, chapters 10–21) so that the Israelites would follow the laws of God after he died (4:1).

Deuteronomy 4:8: "What other nation is so great as to have such righteous decrees and laws as this body of laws I am setting before you today?" None! No other people have ever received their laws by hearing the voice of God speaking out of fire, as Israel did at Mt. Sinai (4:33).

Therefore, "Acknowledge and take to heart this day that the LORD is God in heaven above and on the earth below. There is no other" (4:39).

Deuteronomy 4:41-43 tells of cities of refuge east of the Jordan River (literally, "beyond the Jordan"). Regarding the cities of refuge, see Numbers 35:6-32, Deuteronomy 19:1-13, and Joshua 20:1-9.

3. *Moses second address – Laws (partly old laws)* (Deut. 5–11).

The Ten Commandments as given in Deuteronomy 5:6-21 are slightly paraphrased from the wording in Exodus 20. (We assume that the Exodus 20 wording is a copy of the original words as written by God Himself.) Deuteronomy 5:15, for example, tells the Israelites to "Observe" the Sabbath day (rather than "Remember" it, as in Exodus 20:8), because the LORD brought you out of Egypt. In Exodus, the reason given for remembering the seventh day was to remember that God created the world in six days. Both the Exodus and Deuteronomy versions of the Ten Commandments are God's truth.

If the Sabbath day was given to remember Israel's exodus from Egypt, that suggests that the Sabbath day was not designed to be an everlasting observance for people of all nations.

Deuteronomy 6:2. The commandment to teach the children the law of God is often given (6:7; 4:10; 11:19).

The greatest law in the Old Testament is Deuteronomy 6:4-5. Jesus called it the *greatest* commandment (Matt. 22:38). Christians as well as Jews believe that the LORD is **ONE** (1 Cor. 8:6). We do believe that this oneness is displayed as three personalities — Father, Son, and Holy Spirit. The Old Testament itself suggests this. See Isaiah 48:16.

The LORD's people are to *love* Him with all their hearts (Deut. 6:5; Ps. 116:1; 18:1).

Deuteronomy 6:4-5 is often called the **SHEMA**, from the Hebrew word for "Hear" at the beginning.

Deuteronomy 6:4-5 — The SHEMA — שְׁמַע

"Hear, O Israel: The LORD our God, the LORD is ONE.
Love the LORD your God with all your heart
    and with all your soul
    and with all your strength."

Deuteronomy 6:8; 11:18. "Bind them (the law) on your foreheads." Jews have followed this law literally, and often wear little leather boxes called phylacteries strapped to the forehead and forearm. These boxes contain small scrolls of Scriptures. See Matthew 23:5.

Deuteronomy 7:1-5. Destroy the nations of Canaan! The seven Canaanite nations are named here. These were Canaanite races more than nations. Canaan was not a united nation before the Israelite conquest, not even united states, but rather a group of independent city-states fighting among themselves. Each large city had its own "king," such as the king of Jericho or king of 'Ai.

Deuteronomy 8:2. God led the Israelites through the desert to humble them and test them. It is easy to feel that God hates us when we are suffering hardships, but that is not true.

Deuteronomy 8:3,16. The manna was a miraculous food. It was something that no one had known or seen before, not some kind of known plant or insect. The miraculous way it appeared and disappeared each day should have taught them that "man lives on every word that comes from the mouth of the LORD." Jesus quoted this verse at His temptation (Matt. 4:4).

Deuteronomy 9:4-5. It was not because of Israel's righteousness that God was letting them take possession of the land of Canaan, but because of the extreme wickedness of the Canaanites. They offered their children as sacrifices to their gods (Deut. 12:31). They were cruel to one another (Judg. 1:7). They were not sexually regulated as the Israelites were (Num. 25:1).

The Israelites were not much better than the Canaanites (2 Kgs. 17:14-17). God's grace and God's promise to their faithful forefather Abraham carried them through (Num. 25:1).

Deuteronomy 10:12: "What does the LORD your God ask of you, but to *fear* the LORD your God, to *walk* in all his ways, to *love* him, to *serve* the LORD your God with all your heart?"

Deuteronomy 11:10-11, 14. In Egypt the land was watered by water wheels and irrigation ditches. But in Canaan the land was dependent upon the rain that the LORD sent. It was a land where the inhabitants had to depend on God. If the people obeyed, then God would send rain on the land in its season, both the autumn and spring rains (the former and latter rains).

Deuteronomy 11:29-30. When Israel crossed into Canaan, they were to read the blessings promised in the law and the curses that the law warned of (Lev. 26 and Deut. 27, 28). The blessings were to be read on Mt. Gerizim and the curses on Mt. Ebal. These mountains were in the center of the land, with the city of Shechem in the valley between them. Mt. Gerizim is green and tree-covered, a symbol of blessings. Mt. Ebal is bald, being mostly bare rock, a symbol of curses (Deut. 27:4; Josh. 8:30-33).

4. *Moses' second address – More laws (partly new)* (Deut. 12–26).

Deuteronomy 12:1. This is the start of a new part of Moses' second address. "These are the decrees and laws you must be careful to follow in the land that the Lord . . . has given you."

Deuteronomy 12:13-14. The Israelites were to offer their sacrifices only at the place the Lord would choose. Compare Deut. 16:2,16,22. This place was first at the tabernacle, and later at Shiloh, and still later at Jerusalem.

The people of God need to worship together so that each group will not be worshiping in its own way.

Deuteronomy 13. This chapter contains warnings about being misled. They were not to be led to follow other gods than Yahweh. The Israelites could be misled by someone who claimed to be a *prophet* (13:1), or by their *relatives* (13:6), or by *towns* in the land (13:12-13). They were not listen to them. Rather, they were to put them to death or destroy them.

Prophets were not to be believed just because they could perform some miraculous sign or wonder (13:1; 18:20; Matt. 7:22; 24:24; 2 Thess. 2:9-10; Rev. 13:13).

Deuteronomy 14. The chapter directs us to live as children of God. (Compare Ephesians 5:1; 1 John 3:1-3.) Being children of God will regulate our (1) physical appearance (14:1); (2) diet (14:3); (3) use of wealth (14:22).

Deuteronomy 15:1-11. "At the end of every seven years you must cancel debts." There is a contrast between God's ideal for man — "There should be no poor among you" — and man's performance — "There will always be poor people." Money was to be lent freely to the poor (15:7-10), and no interest was to be collected.

Deuteronomy 16 tells of the three annual compulsory feasts. (Compare Exodus 23:14-17.) The three feasts were:

(1) The PASSOVER, on the first month, fourteenth day. The Passover was eaten in the evening at sundown. Jesus ate His last Passover with His disciples at that time (Matt. 26:20).

(2) The Feast of WEEKS (or harvest), fifty days after the first harvest).

(3) The Feast of TABERNACLES (or BOOTHS), in the seventh month, starting on the fifteenth day, and lasting seven days.

Deuteronomy 17:5-6. Execution was to be done by stoning the evildoer. Two or three witnesses were required before a man or woman could be condemned to death.

Executions were to be done at the city gate (that is, outside the gate). Jesus and Stephen were slain outside of Jerusalem (Heb. 13:12; Acts 7:58).

Deuteronomy 17:16-17. Kings of Israel were not to multiply wives, or horses, or silver and gold. King Solomon greatly violated all three of these restrictions (1 Kgs. 10:26–11:3).

Deuteronomy 18:11; 26:14. The law of Moses and the

prophets strictly forbade attempts to talk to the dead (Lev. 19:31; 20:27; Isa. 8:19). We learn from the Scripture that it is probably impossible to speak to the dead. The doomed dead are kept "in prison" and "under punishment" until the day of judgment (1 Pet. 3:19; 2 Pet. 2:9). The dead are not brought out of Hades until the last judgment (Rev. 20:13). The dead are not allowed to return to the land of the living (Luke 16:27-31). If we attempt to talk to the spirits of the dead, we might make contact with some Satanic spirit who pretends to be the spirit of the dead we seek.

Deuteronomy 18:15, 18-19. The LORD promised to raise up a prophet *like Moses* from among the Israelites. God demanded that the people listen to this prophet, or He would call them to account. According to the New Testament this prophet was JESUS (Acts 3:22; 7:37). There are many similarities between Moses and Jesus.

MOSES, a Type of Christ (Deut.18:15)		
SIMILARITIES	MOSES	JESUS
1. Both saved in infancy from cruel kings	Ex. 2:5-9	Matt. 2:19
2. Peacemakers	Ex. 2:13	Matt. 5:9; Luke 19:42
3. Sent by God	Ex. 3:10	John 5:30
4. Worked miracles	Ex. 4:4-9	John 20:30
5. Proclaimed deliverance	Ex. 3:17	Luke 4:18
6. Prophet	Deut. 34:10	Matt. 13:57
7. Lawgiver	John 1:17	John 14:15
8. Rejected by many	Acts 7:23-29	John 12:37
9. Placed his people before himself	Ex. 32:32	Matt. 20:28

Deuteronomy 19–21 teach the sacredness of human life.

Deuteronomy 19:1-13. Concerning cities of refuge, see Deuteronomy 4:41-43.

Deuteronomy 19:14. The right of private property is a divinely-given and divinely-protected right. Not even a king, such as King Ahab, dared to take a citizen's property (1 Kgs. 21:17-19).

Deuteronomy 21:1-9. An unidentified slain man had to be atoned for by the people of the village nearest to where he was found slain. Life is sacred. Not even a sparrow falls without the Father knowing of it (Matt. 10:29).

Deuteronomy 21:21. A stubborn and rebellious son could be stoned to death. But the judgment was administered only through the courts. This regulation adds force to the command to "Honor your father and your mother."

Deuteronomy 21:22-23. Bodies of executed people left hanging upon a tree were regarded as accursed. Christ Jesus became a *curse* for us when he was hanged upon the cross (Gal. 3:13).

Deuteronomy 22:1-3. Love should lead us to do what the law commanded when it told the Israelites to return a neighbor's lost ox. In Israel people were not to practice Finders-Keepers.

Deuteronomy 22:22. Both an adulterer and the adulteress were to be put to death. Compare John 8:3-5.

Deuteronomy 23:12-13. The sanitation laws of Israel would have prevented many diseases.

Deuteronomy 23:24-25. Grapes or grain from a man's field could be eaten by those passing by, but they could not be gathered to be carried away. Jesus' disciples were criticized for doing a very legal act (Matt. 12:1-2).

Deuteronomy 24:1. A woman could not be kicked out of her house by her husband unless he gave her a divorce document, which would allow her freedom to seek another (and kinder?) man. Moses did not *command* men to divorce their wives, but he tolerated it to protect the woman from becoming destitute (Matt. 19:7-8). God *hates* divorce (Mal. 2:16).

Deuteronomy 25:5-10. A brother-in-law of the childless widow of his brother was to marry her and raise a child to continue the deceased man's line. This practice is called "Levirate" marriage, meaning "brother-in-law marriage." On the basis of this custom Ruth was married to Boaz (Ruth 4:7-8). The argument of the Sadducees against the resurrection of the dead was based on this custom (Matt. 22:24).

Deuteronomy 25:13-16. Just, equal, and honest weight (used in balances, for buying or selling) were required. Our God is a just God (Prov. 11:1; Lev. 19:35-36; Amos 8:5).

Deuteronomy 26:1-14. Firstfruits of the products of the land were to be brought to the Lord, with an open declaration of obedience to God. The "wandering Aramean" ("Syrian about to perish") was Jacob, who fled to Egypt because of famine in Canaan.

5. *Moses' third address – Curses and blessings* (Deut. 27-30).

a. *The altar on Mt. Ebal* (Deut. 27:1-8). The law of God was to be written upon large stones that were to be set up on Mt. Ebal and covered with plaster. God wants His word to be WRITTEN as well as spoken. (See Isaiah 8:1; Jeremiah 36:1-2; Habakkuk 2:2; John 20:31.). This command to write the law was carried out by Joshua (Josh. 8:30-33).

See Deuteronomy 11:29 for notes on the location of Mt. Ebal. The acoustics are excellent in the valley between Mt. Ebal and Mt. Gerizim, so that words spoken on the mountains can be heard by people in the valley between. (See *Biblical Archaeologist*, Dec. 1976, pp. 138-139.)

A large stone installation has been excavated on Mt. Ebal, and some scholars think it may be the remains of Joshua's altar. (See Adam Zertal, "Has Joshua's Altar Been Found on Mt. Ebal?" *Biblical Archaeology Review*, Jan.–Feb. 1985, pp. 26-43. Also *Biblical Archaeology Review*, Jan.–Feb. 1986, pp. 42-53.)

b. *Curses read from Mt. Ebal* (Deut. 27:9-26). Moses had told the people the laws they were to keep. With the acceptance of his words the people would again become the people of the LORD (27:9). They were renewing the *covenant* they had made with God at Mt. Sinai (Deut. 29:1,12). The curses that would come upon them if they did not obey God's covenant were a powerful incentive to obey. The Levites were to recite the curses to all the people in a *LOUD* voice. The curses were very plain and unambiguous.

All the people were to respond with "Amen" after each curse was read (Deut. 28:15). *Amen* means "surely," or "truly," or "Let it be established," or "So be it." Christians should speak the "Amen" to words they approve (1 Cor. 14:16; Rev. 22:20).

    c. *Blessings for obedience* (Deut. 28:1-14; 30:1-10; 29:9). The blessings that were promised were all material blessings, but such blessings are desired and needed by everyone.

The teaching of this chapter that material blessings will come when people obey God is sometimes scorned as being "Deuteronomic" theology. It has been said that the book of Job was written to correct this false view of life, and "stultify the Deuteronomist." Norman Gottwald wrote that Job undermined the dogma of retribution by affirming amoral suffering (*The Hebrew Bible*, p. 582). This is a very incomplete view of the teachings in Deuteronomy, and of Job also.

The book of Deuteronomy certainly does not present the idea that God's people will never endure sufferings (32:23-24). Deuteronomy foretells that curses and punishments will come upon the people, as well as blessings. The truth that God blesses those who serve Him is taught throughout the Bible (Heb. 11:6). Many people do not like the idea that all things that happen to us — good and evil alike — are in the hands of God, and we are accountable to Him (Eccl. 9:1).

One of the blessings for obeying the LORD is that His people will "be the head and not the tail" (28:13, 44).

    d. *More curses for disobedience* (Deut. 28:15-68). The long list of punishments in this chapter is terrifying, mainly because history reveals that Israel — and all mankind — has suffered all of the punishments.

Mental diseases would come upon the disobedient, as well as physical diseases (28:28). (The chapter does not say that mental diseases would never afflict the righteous.) The mental depression of King Saul is a vivid example of this (1 Sam. 16:14).

All of us should thank God for whatever degree of "sound mind" He has granted to us (2 Tim. 1:7).

Another punishment that would come was deportation

and captivity in foreign lands (Deut. 28:36-37, 64). The Israelites in later centuries suffered such captivity in Assyria and Babylon (2 Kgs. 17:6).

"Because of the suffering . . . you will eat the fruit of the womb, the flesh of the sons and daughters the LORD your God has given you" (Deut. 28:53). This actually occurred (2 Kgs. 6:28-29).

The LORD would send them back to Egypt if they disobeyed Him (28:68). This came to pass in later centuries (Josephus, *Wars of the Jews*, VI, ix, 2).

e. *Renewal of the covenant* (Deut. 29). A *covenant* is an agreed-upon arrangement between parties. The LORD commanded Moses to make a covenant between the Israelites and Him in the Plains of Moab, in addition to the covenant He had made with them at Horeb (Mt. Sinai) (29:1-2). It was a reaffirmation of the same covenant that was made at Mt. Sinai.

Israel's shoes did not wear out in the desert for forty years (29:5). God bestowed this favor upon them even in their unbelief. Much more would He bless them, if they were obedient.

f. *Call to choose blessings or curses* (Deut. 30). Moses' three addresses in Deuteronomy 1–30 close with a stirring call to the Israelites: "This day I call heaven and earth as witnesses against you that I have set before you life and death, blessings and curses. Now **CHOOSE LIFE,** so that you and your children may live and that you may love the LORD your God, listen to his voice, and hold fast to him. For the LORD is your life" (30:19-20).

Even if Israel was unfaithful for a time, God would regather them when they returned to Him (30:1-3). God is gracious.

God's covenant was very close to them — in their mouth and in their heart (30:11-14; Rom. 10:6-8). It was not far off and unreachable.

6. *Final commands and events* (Deut. 31–34).
    a. *Final commands* (Deut. 31):
        (1) Conquer the land (31:1-6)

(2) To Joshua — "Be strong!" (31:7-8, 23)
(3) Read the law publicly (31:9-13)
(4) Write the words of this song (31:14-22)
(5) Keep the law beside the ark (31:24-29)

Moses was one hundred and twenty years old at the time of his death (31:2; 34:7).

The command to "Be strong and courageous" (31:7) is quoted to Christians in Hebrews 13:5.

The entire law was to be read publicly to the people every seven years (31:10-13). The word of God read well is powerful. See Nehemiah 8:1-8.

Moses was to write the words of a song that the LORD would put in his mind (31:19). The song was a warning that the Israelites were going to forsake the LORD in the future. The song was given to delay or prevent some of the Israelites from forsaking the LORD, though God knew that most of them would do that. The song is given in chapter 32.

b. *The Song of Moses* (Deut. 32). The Song of Moses tells of (1) praise to God (32:3) and (2) the perverseness of the people (32:5). The overall idea of the song is stated in 32:4-6.

Outline of the *Song of Moses* (32:1-43):
(1) Call to praise (32:1-3)
(2) God's faithfulness and Israel's faithlessness (32:4-18)
(3) Chastisement upon Israel, and its necessity (32:19-23)
(4) God's compassion on His humbled people (32:34-42)
(5) Conclusion — Call to praise (32:43).

Five times in the song God is called "The Rock" (32:4, 15, 18, 30, 31). Compare Habakkuk 1:12. The Hebrew word for *rock* here means a rock, or cliff, or rocky wall (BDB Lexicon, p. 849).

God called Israel by the title *Jeshurun*, meaning "the righteous one" (32:15; 33:5,26). It is a poetic and idealized name.

The song closes with the joyful invitation "Rejoice, O nations (Gentiles), with his people; for he will avenge the blood of his servants" (32:43). This profound passage foreshadowed the joy of the Gentiles, who would come to share God's blessings with Israel. See Romans 11:25-26; Isaiah 42:1; 49:6.

After he recited the song, Moses addressed the people: "Take to heart all the words I have solemnly declared to you this day" (32:46).

Deuteronomy 32:48-52. *Moses sent up to Mt. Nebo.* On that same day when Moses completed teaching the song God sent him up into the Abarim range of mountains, to Mt. Nebo in Moab, where he would die after seeing a view of the promised land (32:48-52).

Abarim means "those beyond, or on the other side." The name refers to the range of mountains east of the Dead Sea and north of Moab. *Nebo* is the particular headland at the extremity of the Abarim range. Mt. Nebo is about ten miles east of the point where the Jordan enters the Dead Sea. *Pisgah* is probably the peak joined by a saddle to Mt. Nebo on its northwest. From Pisgah Moses saw a view of the promised land (Num. 21:20; 23:14; Deut. 3:27; 34:1).

c. *The Blessing of Moses* (Deut. 33). The Blessing of Moses is addressed to the twelve tribes, although there is no blessing to the tribe of Simeon. (See Joshua 19:1-9). The Blessing is an idealized prophecy of what the tribes of Israel MIGHT have become, if they had fully achieved God's blessings and God's desires for them. It contains no words of warning or reproof. It is full of tenderness and beautiful expressions. The Blessing is in striking contrast with the Song in chapter 32. It is helpful to compare the words of Jacob in Genesis 49 concerning the future of his sons with the statements in Deuteronomy 33 about the twelve tribes.

The tribe of Levi is highly praised (33:8-11). Levi disregarded his father and mother so as to serve God (Ex. 32:26, 28). The Levites were the tribe from which the priests came. "He (Levi) teaches your precepts to Jacob and your law to Israel."

On *Jeshurun* as a title for Israel, see notes on 32:15. "There is no one like the God of *Jeshurun* .... The eternal God is your refuge, and underneath are the everlasting arms" (33:26,27).

d. *The death of Moses* (Deut. 34). See notes on Deuteronomy 32:49 concerning *Abarim, Nebo,* and *Pisgah.* These three names were all applied to the same mountain.

From Mt. Nebo God gave Moses a miraculous view of the promised land. He saw the land from Naphtali in the far north beyond Galilee (over a hundred miles from Mt. Nebo), to the western sea (the Mediterranean), and to Zoar southeast of the Dead Sea (Gen. 19:22).

Moses died and was buried by God in the valley in front of Beth Peor. God must have revealed this to the final writer of Deuteronomy, because no one knows the place of Moses' burial. Beth Peor (34:6) had been the place where the Israelites joined in the idolatry with the Moabites (Num. 25:1-3).

Moses was the greatest of all the prophets. Although he began as an unwilling spokesman for God, he became one who wanted God's will to be done, and one who loved his people more than his own life. It is significant that the law is called the Law of *Moses,* and not just the law of God. Moses had a passion for God and His law. All the great prophets who came later built upon the law that Moses had established.

In heaven we shall sing the song of *Moses,* the servant of God, and the song of the Lamb (Rev. 15:3): "Great and marvelous are your deeds, Lord God Almighty."

Questions on Section F
Deuteronomy

Deuteronomy 1
1. In what year and month did Moses speak the words of Deuteronomy? (1:3)
2. Why had Moses appointed wise men from the tribes to be heads over the people? (1:9-13)
3. What sort of a place was the wilderness which Israel passed through after leaving Horeb? (1:19)
4. How did the Lord feel toward Moses when the Israelites did not have faith to conquer the promised land? (1:34)

5. How did the invasion of Canaan work out when Israel decided they would try to enter? (1:43-44)
6. How long did Israel abide at Kadesh? (1:46)

Deuteronomy 2
1. With what three peoples was Israel not to contend? (2:4-5,9,19)
2. How many years did it take Israel to get from Kadesh Barnea to the Brook Zered? (2:7,14)
3. Who was Sihon? (2:24)
4. How did Sihon respond to Israel's messengers of peace? (2:30)

Deuteronomy 3
1. Who was Og? What did Israel do to him? (3:1)
2. How big was Og's bed? (3:11)
3. What tribe received the land of Bashan? (3:13)
4. What command was given to the men of the Israelite tribes who inherited land east of the Jordan? (3:18)
5. What request of Moses did God deny? (3:25-26)

Deuteronomy 4
1. What was Israel neither to add to nor diminish from? (4:2)
2. What words were God's covenant which he commanded to Israel? (4:13)
3. What lesson was Israel to learn from the fact that they saw no form of God on the day God spoke the law to them in Horeb? (4:15)
4. What would be Israel's punishment if they made graven images in the land? (4:26)
5. Name the three cities of refuge east of (or beyond) the Jordan. (4:43)

Deuteronomy 5
1. What did God make with the Israelites at Horeb? (5:2)
2. What notable words are repeated in Deuteronomy 5? (5:6-21)
3. What was the Sabbath day to cause Israel to remember besides the seventh day of creation? (5:15)
4. How did the Israelites react when they heard the voice of the Lord at Sinai? (5:23-25)

Deuteronomy 6
1. What wonderful truth about God is given in this chapter? (6:4) (This verse is called the *Shema*, from the opening word in Hebrew, meaning "Hear.")
2. How important is the command in 6:5? (See Matthew 22:37-38)
3. Where was the law to be placed? (6:8-9) (For further study, look up "Phylactery" in a Bible dictionary. Matt. 23:5)
4. How can men *tempt* the Lord? (6:16; Ex. 17:2,7)

Deuteronomy 7

1. How many nations of Canaanites were in the promised land? (7:1)
2. What was Israel to do (and *not* do) with these nations? (7:2-5)
3. Did God promise to cast out these nations suddenly? (7:27)

Deuteronomy 8

1. Why did God give them manna other than to keep them alive? (8:3)
2. What agricultural products and minerals were in the promised land? (8:8-9)
3. What was Israel likely to forget when they enjoyed abundance? (8:11-14)

Deuteronomy 9

1. What was the reason for which God determined to drive out the Canaanites? (9:5)
2. How long had Israel been rebellious against the Lord? (9:24)
3. What had made God angry with Israel? (9:8,16)
4. How did God feel toward Aaron when he made the golden calf? (9:20)

Deuteronomy 10

1. Who wrote on the second set of tables of Ten Commandments? (10:4)
2. What did God require of Israel? (10:12)
3. Why were the Israelites to love aliens? (10:19)

Deuteronomy 11

1. What did Moses declare that the Israelites had seen? (11:7)
2. How was the land of Egypt and the land of Canaan watered? (11:10)
3. What two things did Moses set before Israel? (11:26)
4. Where were the blessings to be proclaimed and where were the curses to be proclaimed? (11:29)

Deuteronomy 12

1. What was to be done to Canaanite places of worship? (12:2-3)
2. Where were the Israelites to offer their burnt offerings? (12:11)
3. What was not to be eaten? (12:16)

Deuteronomy 13

1. Were the people to believe prophets because they worked miracles? (13:1-3)
2. What was to be done to relatives who tried to get the people to worship other gods? (13:6-9)
3. What was to be done to towns that served other gods? (13:12-15)

Deuteronomy 14

1. Of whom were the Israelites called children? (14:1)
2. What was taken out of the yearly increase of crops and livestock? (14:22)
3. What was the tithe of the third year to be used for? (14:28-29)

Old Testament History

Deuteronomy 15
1. What was to be canceled every seven years? (15:1)
2. How were Israelites to treat the poor of their people? (15:7-8)
3. What could Israelites do to other nations that they could not do to their own people? (15:6)
4. What was to be given to a Hebrew bondservant when he was released? (15:13)

Deuteronomy 16
1. All three of the compulsory feasts were to be observed in a certain place. Where was it? (16:6,11,15)
2. At what hour of the day was the Passover to be eaten? (16:6)
3. How was the date of the feast of weeks determined? (16:9-10)
4. What does the command "They shall not appear before the Lord empty" mean? (16:16)
5. What is the effect of a bribe upon a wise man? (16:19)

Deuteronomy 17
1. What rendered an animal unfit for sacrifice? (17:1)
2. How was a person who transgressed God's covenant to be slain? (17:5)
3. Who gave the judgment concerning hard cases of disagreement? (17:9)
4. Who was to select the king over the Israelites? (17:15)
5. What three things was a king not to multiply to himself? (17:16-17)
6. What was the king to read every day? (17:18-19)

Deuteronomy 18
1. How did the Levites get their living? (18:1)
2. What is a divination? (18:10)
3. What individual did God promise to raise up? (18:15)
4. How would the people know when God had not spoken to a prophet? (18:22)

Deuteronomy 19
1. How many cities west of Jordan were to be set apart as cities of refuge? (19:2)
2. What was the purpose of the cities of refuge? (19:4)
3. How many additional cities might have been designated as cities of refuge? (19:9)
4. What law was given about boundary stones? (19:14)
5. What punishment was to be given to false witnesses? (19:16-19)

Deuteronomy 20
1. How could Israel confidently face greater armies than they had? (20:3-4)
2. What four classes of men were excused from military duty? (20:5-7)

3. What offer was to be made to every city the Israelites attacked? (20:10)
4. How were the Israelites to treat differently the Canaanite cities from distant cities under siege? (20:14-16)
5. What restriction was imposed about cutting down trees during a siege? (20:19)

Deuteronomy 21

1. Who was held responsible for an unknown man who was slain? (21:3)
2. What could be done to a stubborn and rebellious son? (21:18-21)
3. How long were those who were hanged to remain on a tree? (21:22-23)

Deuteronomy 22

1. What was a man to do when he found his neighbor's lost ox? (22:1)
2. What restriction was imposed about types of clothing that could be worn? (22:5)

Deuteronomy 23

1. What peoples could not enter the assembly of Jehovah for several generations? (23:3)
2. What interest could be charged on money lent to an Israelite? (23:19)
3. What was the law about eating grapes from a man's vineyard? (23:24)

Deuteronomy 24

1. What was to be given to a woman by her husband if he hated her? (24:1; compare Matt. 19:7-9)
2. What freedom did a new bridegroom have? (24:5)
3. What was the law about taking a garment as security for a loan? (24:12-13)

Deuteronomy 25

1. How many stripes could be given to a criminal? (25:3)
2. What privilege did an ox treading grain have? (25:4)
3. What was to be done for a childless widow by her husband's brother? (This is called "levirate" marriage.) (25:5)
4. What was to be done to the tribe of Amalek? Why? (25:19)

Deuteronomy 26

1. What was to be done with part of all the firstfruits of the ground? (26:1-2)

Deuteronomy 27

1. Where was the law to be written after Israel crossed Jordan? (27:2-4)
2. Upon what mountain were curses to be pronounced? Blessings? (27:12-13)

Deuteronomy 28

1. What was to happen to Israel if they hearkened and obeyed the Lord's commandments? (27:1-2)

2. What was to happen if Israel did not hearken and obey God's commandments? (28:15)
3. What would other nations do to Israel if Israel was disobedient to God? (28:49-52; 2 Kgs. 17:7-18)
4. What would cause cannibalism? (28:53; compare 2 Kgs. 6:28-29)
5. To what nation would God bring Israel back if they were disobedient? (28:68; compare Josephus, *Wars* VI, ix, 2)

Deuteronomy 29
1. What does Moses in this chapter remind the Israelites that they had seen? (29:2)
2. How did Israel have shoes during the forty years' wanderings? (29:5)
3. What did Moses want Israel to enter into that day, as they were all camped on the plains of Moab? (29:12)

Deuteronomy 30
1. What would happen when Israel returned unto God while in captivity? (30:1-4)
2. Where did God say that his word and commandments were? (30:11-14; compare Rom. 10:6-8)
3. What two things did Moses set before the people? (30:19)

Deuteronomy 31
1. How old was Moses when he spoke the words in Deuteronomy? (31:2)
2. How often was the law to be read orally? At what time of the year? (31:10)
3. What did God foretell that the Israelites would do? (31:16)
4. Why was Moses to teach Israel a song? (31:19)
5. What charge was given to Joshua? (31:23)
6. Where were the Levites to keep the copy of the law? (31:24-26)

Deuteronomy 32
1. Is the song of Moses mainly a song of warning or of joy or of praise? (32:5-6)
2. What does the name *Jeshurun* mean? (32:15)
3. Where was Moses told to go to die? (32:48)

Deuteronomy 33
1. To whom did Moses address the various parts of his blessing? (33:6,7) (For further study, make a comparison of this chapter with Genesis 49.)
2. What was the refuge of Israel and what was underneath Israel? (33:27)

Deuteronomy 34
1. Where did Moses die? (34:1)
2. What did God show Moses before he died? (34:1-3)

3. How old was Moses when he died? (34:7)
4. How long did Israel lament for Moses? (34:8)
5. How did Moses compare to other prophets? (34:10)

Period VI — Period of Conquest
(Book of Joshua)

Section A
Introduction to Joshua

1. *Name of the book.* The book gets its name from its principal character, Joshua. Joshua became the leader of the Israelites after Moses' death.

Joshua and **Jesus** are the same name. The name *Joshua* is from the Hebrew *Yehoshua'*, and Jesus is from the Greek *Iesous*. The name comes from the verb meaning to *save*. Both Joshua and Jesus were saviors (Matt. 1:21).

---

2. *Beginning and ending points.* The book of Joshua *begins* with God's call to Joshua very soon after the death of Moses (Josh. 1:1). The book tells of the *invasion* and *conquest* of the land of Canaan, the dividing of the land among the twelve tribes, and *ends* with the death of Joshua.

3. *Authorship of the book.* The Jewish Talmud says that *Joshua* himself was the author (*Baba Bathra*, 14b). This is an attractive view. Certainly Joshua did do some writing (8:32; 24:26).

Rahab the harlot, whose story is told in Joshua chapter 2 and in 6:25, was still living when the book was written. This dates the book within Joshua's lifetime.

Joshua 5:1 and 5:6 use first-person pronouns ("we" and "us") to tell of Israel's crossing the Jordan. This seems to indicate that the author was one of those who, like Joshua, crossed the Jordan into Canaan. But the reading in the Hebrew Bible margin of 5:1 says "until *they* crossed over"; and the Greek Bible supports this wording.

The closing verses in the book of Joshua tell of the death of Joshua, and of the priest Eleazar (24:29,33). The last person named in the book is *Phinehas*, the grandson of Aaron (Num. 25:7,10). Phinehas was a zealous man for the LORD, and may well have been the author of the book, or the editor of documents written by Joshua and others. We favor this view. Whoever the human author was, the Holy Spirit was the ultimate editor of the book.

Critics who seek to account for the Bible by human means alone say that the book developed from an original core of stories and poems, but was expanded and embellished over decades and centuries until it reached a final form about 600 B.C. (N. Gottwald, *The Hebrew Bible*, p. 146).

4. The book of Joshua deals with the *period of conquest* of the land of Canaan. This period lasted about seven years (1406–1400 B.C.). Note that Caleb was forty years old when he served as one of the spies into Canaan. After that Israel wandered in the desert about thirty-eight years. Caleb was eighty-five years old when the conquest was completed (Josh. 14:7,10). 85 years − (40 + 38 years) = 7 years.

The conquest was important in God's plan. God planned to send His Son to *earth*. It would be of great benefit when God's eternal kingdom was established to start it in a land where God's law was known and honored. The prophet Malachi foretold that the Lord would suddenly "come to his temple" (3:1). A temple requires a land for it. God had promised to Abraham and his descendants that He would give them the land of Canaan as an eternal possession (Gen. 13:15,17; 17:8; Deut. 34:4).

> Psalm 105:44-45 — **He gave them the lands of the nations . . . that they might keep his precepts and observe his laws.**

The *law* of God was more important to Israel's identity than the *land*. They would lose the land if they were unfaithful to the law (Josh. 23:16). It was, nonetheless, God's intention for Israel to possess the land.

293

5. "The *theme of the book* concerns the irresistible power of God's people in overcoming the world and taking permanent possession of their promised inheritance, provided only they maintain a perfect trust in God's strength and permit no sin of disobedience to break their covenant relationship with Him" (Gleason L. Archer, *Survey of Old Testament Introduction* [1994], p. 285).

6. *Outline of the book.*

OUTLINE OF THE BOOK OF JOSHUA

a. **Invasion and Conquest of Canaan (chs. 1–12)**
b. **The land divided among the twelve tribes (chs. 13–22)**
c. **Joshua's farewell addresses and his death (chs. 23–24)**
(Memorize this outline.)

---

7. *Verses to memorize:* Joshua 1:8; 23:14; 24:15.

Questions on Section A
Introduction to Joshua

1. Where does the book of Joshua get its name?
2. What other famous person has the same name as Joshua?
3. With what event does the book begin? End?
4. Who does the Jewish Talmud say was author of the book?
5. Who is the last person named in the book?
6. What period of Bible history does the book tell of?
7. How long did this period last? What was its date?
8. Why was the conquest of the LAND of Canaan important?
9. What is the *theme* of the book? (Be brief.)

Section B
Invasion and Conquest of Canaan (Joshua 1–12)

1. *Joshua, the new leader of Israel* (Josh. 1:1-9). MOSES, the lawgiver, was succeeded by JOSHUA, the warrior. God raises up leaders with gifts and abilities needed in their own times.

The death of Moses was a time when Israel might have

perished. They had no homeland, and had shown little commitment to be a nation under God. Their new leader would determine their national character and destiny.

Joshua's name at first was Hoshea, meaning *salvation* (Num. 13:16). Moses prefixed the God's name *Yah* to his name so that his name meant *Yahweh is salvation.* This name was descriptive of his work, and was a type of the greater work of Jesus, who would "save his people from their sins" (Matt. 1:21). (The name *Jesus* in Greek is the same as *Joshua* in Hebrew.)

Joshua was well-prepared for his new responsibility. He had been Moses' aide for forty years. He had led in battle against the Amalekites (Ex. 17:10). He was with Moses on Mt. Sinai (Ex. 32:17). He served as one of the twelve spies into Canaan (Num. 13:16), so that he knew the land well. Only Joshua spoke out with Caleb expressing confidence that they could take the land. Joshua was God's own choice to be leader (Num. 27:18; Deut. 31:3). Moses had laid his hands upon Joshua, as an act of ordination (Deut. 34:9). Joshua is one of the very few Old Testament heroes of whom no personal failures are recorded.

God spoke a long and emphatic commission to Joshua. With words like those in Deuteronomy 11:24-25, God sent Joshua to conquer ALL the land. God described the land to be taken — from the southern desert to the Lebanon mountains in the north, to the great river Euphrates — all the Hittite country — to the Great Sea (the Mediterranean) on the west. The Hittites were a powerful people whose empire had been centered in Asia Minor, but who also had controlled part of Canaan. Against such enemies the conquest appeared impossible; but God declared that no one would be able to stand up against Joshua, for "I will never leave you nor forsake you."

The Conquest of Canaan was *GOD's* battle,
not man's (Ex. 34:11; Deut. 31:3; Josh. 1:3; 13:6; 23:5).

(Though it was God's battle, the people of Israel
still had to get up and "Go get 'em.")

In all of his service Joshua was to obey the LAW of Moses, and to meditate on it day and night (1:7-8). "Meditation" in the Bible involves making sounds — singing, praising, speaking. Joshua later read the entire law to the people (8:34) and charged them to obey all that was written (23:6). Joshua had available to him all five of the books of Moses (Gen. to Deut.), and not just parts of Deuteronomy, or fragments of Genesis, Exodus, etc. (which some critics have alleged). Joshua knew of Abraham, Isaac, and Jacob, and the exodus (Josh. 24:2-7).

Joshua, a Type of Jesus Christ.	
1. Same name — **Yehoshua** — meaning Yahweh is salvation	1. Same name — Jesus — See Matthew 1:21.
2. Replaced Moses as leader	2. Replaced Moses as covenant giver
3. Brought the people into the promised land	3. Brings us into heaven with Him
4. Great warrior	4. Great warrior (Isa. 63:1-6; Rev. 19:11-16)

2. *Joshua prepares to cross into Canaan* (Josh. 1:10-18). Joshua began to carry out God's instructions at once. He instructed the officers to get the people ready. He set a time when he planned to cross the Jordan — "three days from now" — though it actually took a few days longer (2:22; 3:5). He reminded the two and one-half tribes that were to live east of the Jordan River (Gad, Reuben, and half of Manasseh) of their responsibility to go with the other tribes across the Jordan River to help them fight for the territory west of the Jordan. (See Numbers 32; Deuteronomy 3:18-20).

3. *Joshua sends spies to Jericho* (Josh. 2). The Israelites were encamped at *Shittim* (short for *'Abel-Shittim*, meaning *Meadow of Acacia Trees* [Num. 33:49; 25:1; Mic. 6:5]; NKJV translates it *Acacia Grove*). Shittim was about five miles north of the Dead Sea and ten miles east of the Jordan.

The first military obstacle Israel faced was the city of Jericho. Joshua secretly (literally, *silently*) sent two spies into Canaan, that is, to Jericho.

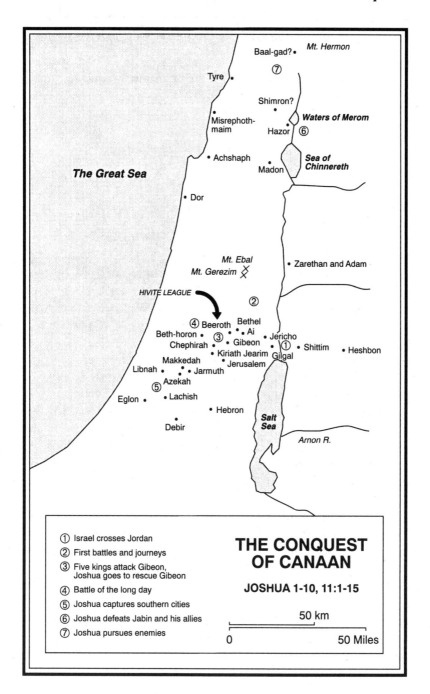

Baal-gad?•   *Mt. Hermon*

⑦

Tyre •

Shimron?
•
Misrephoth-   *Waters of Merom*
maim   Hazor • ⑥

• Achshaph   *Sea of*
         Madon *Chinnereth*

The Great Sea

• Dor

Mt. Ebal   • Zarethan and Adam
Mt. Gerezim ⚔

HIVITE LEAGUE ●

②

④ Beeroth Bethel
Beth-horon • •• Ai
Chephirah • ③ • Gibeon • Jericho
         • Kiriath Jearim ① • Shittim • Heshbon
Makkedah   • Jerusalem Gilgal
Libnah • • • Jarmuth
  ⑤ • Azekah
Eglon • • Lachish
         • Hebron **Salt**
•   **Sea**
Debir   *Arnon R.*

① Israel crosses Jordan
② First battles and journeys   **THE CONQUEST**
③ Five kings attack Gibeon,   **OF CANAAN**
  Joshua goes to rescue Gibeon
④ Battle of the long day   **JOSHUA 1-10, 11:1-15**
⑤ Joshua captures southern cities
⑥ Joshua defeats Jabin and his allies   50 km
⑦ Joshua pursues enemies
                          0   50 Miles

297

Facts about the Old Testament city of Jericho :

1. Located 5 mi. W. of Jordan, & 7 mi. N. of Dead Sea.
2. A small city (7–10 acres) on a mound (now named Tell es-Sultan).
3. Fortified by 2 walls of mud bricks. The outer wall was built upon a stone retaining wall over 4 meters high.
4. A large spring was beside the city (2 Kgs. 2:21).
5. Called the "City of Palm trees" (Deut. 34:3).
6. The "lowest city in the world," 800' below sea level. It has a very warm climate.
7. A mountain "wall" stands 1½ miles west of Jericho. (It is called the "Mount of Temptation." [Matt. 4:8])

Some have said that Jericho had been destroyed before 1400 B.C. (the end of the Late Bronze 1 period), and therefore there was no city there then for Joshua to have conquered. But recent researches by Dr. Bryant G. Wood have brought to light pottery fragments from Jericho made at that time period. (See *Biblical Archaeological Review*, March–April 1990, pp. 44-57.) The spies entered the house of Rahab, a prostitute. (Hebrews 11:31 indicates Rahab was definitely that.) Her house was part of the city wall, and the window in her house could be an exit from the city. She hid the spies when the king's "men" came seeking them, and directed the men to pursue the spies, as if they had left. (Because of her faith, God did not punish Rahab for her lies, though God hates lies.)

Much of the content of Joshua chapter 2 is Rahab's dialogue with the spies. She showed an amazing knowledge of Israel's crossing the Red Sea, and their victory over the kings east of the Jordan. (Modern critics say the stories of Israel's exodus and wilderness wanderings never happened; but Rahab, who lived then, knew they did. Rahab made a wonderful confession to the spies: "The LORD [Yahweh!] your God is God in heaven above and on the earth below" (2:11).

Rahab obtained the promise that the Israelites would spare her family when the LORD gave Israel the land. Three conditions were imposed upon Rahab: (1) Keep all your family inside your house; (2) Tell no one what we are doing; (3) Hang the scarlet cord from your window (2:17, 21). (This would identify her dwelling.)

At Rahab's direction, the spies fled westward to the "hills" (literally "mountain") west of Jericho. A towering scarp of rock cliffs forms a jagged wall about a mile west of Jericho. One of these mountains is now called the Mt. of Temptation, from the belief that there the devil tempted Jesus (Matt. 4:8).

The spies returned to Joshua with exciting news: "The LORD has surely given the whole land into our hands!" God had sent the "hornet" before Israel to break down their enemies' courage to fight (Deut. 7:20).

4. *Israel crossed the Jordan River* (Josh. 3). Joshua and all the Israelites seemed eager. They set out "early in the morning" (the next day after the spies returned?). It was about ten miles from their camp at Shittim to the Jordan (a long day's walk). There they camped before crossing.

The people were instructed to follow the priests, who would be carrying the ark of the covenant. They had not travelled across the Jordan before, and therefore needed a divinely-directed guide. Moreover, the way was dangerous, for the Jordan was at spring flood stage (3:15).

The Israelites were to stay back away from the ark about a thousand yards (*Heb. two thousand cubits*). Though the ark was covered when it was being transported (Num. 4:5), God's presence was still concentrated at the ark. Sinful humankind cannot look upon God and live (Ex. 33:20). Israel had to keep a distance away from the ark and follow the priests.

The LORD promised to exalt Joshua in the eyes of all Israel (3:7; 4:14). Honor for leaders is necessary (Heb. 13:17).

Joshua risked all the credibility he had gained when he foretold to the people that when the priests set foot in the Jordan, its waters would be cut off. But Joshua had no doubts.

God did not fail. As the priests touched the water's edge, the waters stopped flowing. Below (south of) the crossing place the waters flowed on down into the Salt Sea. The waters were blocked off near a town named Adam about 20 miles upstream (north) from where the Israelites crossed. This location is known for occasional landslides that block the Jordan during earthquakes. But that is NOT necessarily the explanation for the complete cutting off of the Jordan waters. It is marvelous that the waters stopped coming at the moment the priests stepped into the water. And it is marvelous that the people crossed "on *dry* ground" (3:17). This is the same expression used to refer to the Red Sea crossing place (Ex. 14:21). It suggests a supernatural and quick drying out.

The crossing of the Jordan has furnished inspiration for many songs ("I Won't have to Cross Jordan Alone" and others). The Scripture does not present a list of similarities between the Jordan crossing and other events. But some come to mind:

a. Crossing the Jordan resembles our baptism and resembles death.

b. The promised land resembles the Christian life and also heaven.

5. *Memorial stones from the river bed* (Josh. 4). When the whole nation had finished crossing the Jordan, the LORD said to Joshua, "Choose twelve men from among the people, one from each tribe . . . to take up twelve stones from the middle of the Jordan" (4:2-3). Before the people crossed the Jordan, Joshua had told them to select twelve men (3:12). The people had delayed in doing this, so Joshua himself appointed twelve men and sent them back into the river channel to gather twelve stones from the middle of the Jordan. The men carried the stones over to their new camp (Gilgal) and put them down.

Everyone should be involved in the LORD's work.
Joshua selected one man from each tribe. Every person in every tribe could feel that *his* tribe had been involved in the memorial.

Then Joshua himself went to the middle of the Jordan, to the spot where the priests who carried the ark of the covenant into the Jordan had stood. There Joshua set up twelve other stones in the channel as a memorial to the crossing. There were *two* memorial stone markers, one in the middle of Jordan and one in the new camp west of the riverside. Probably the stones in the river bed soon toppled down. The author of the book of Joshua says, "They are there to this day" (3:9). Even after the stones tumbled, the memory of the stones would bring to mind the story of how the Israelites crossed.

The NIV translation of 3:9 gives the meaning that there was only *one* memorial of twelve stones. But the NIV margin, and the KJV, NKJV and NASB all follow the Hebrew, which says that Joshua set up "twelve stones [not *the* twelve stones] in the middle of the Jordan." The Greek LXX is even plainer: "Joshua set also *other* twelve stones in the Jordan itself."

Joshua himself later set up at Gilgal the twelve stones that had been taken out of the Jordan (4:20). This memorial probably stood for centuries.

The famous Madaba mosaic map of the Holy Land (about A.D. 600) pictures a building beside Jordan with twelve stones imbedded in its wall and the caption "GALGALA [Gilgal], also the TWELVE STONES" [ΔΩΔΕΚΑΛΙΘΟΝ].

MAKE MEMORIALS of great events. We forget so soon! Samuel made *Eben Ezer* (1 Sam. 7:12). Jesus gave the Lord's Supper. Mordecai created the feast of Purim (Esth. 9:28).

When the Israelites crossed the Jordan, the men of the tribes of Gad, Reuben and half Manasseh crossed the Jordan "in front of (or "in the presence of") the Israelites," leaving their wives and children behind. That surely encouraged the other Israelites.

The priests remained in the river, probably for hours, until all had crossed over. When they left, the Jordan River waters returned to their place and ran at flood stage as before (4:18).

The Israelites' camp west of the Jordan was named *Gilgal* which means *circle.* The name comes from the Hebrew verb meaning to *roll*. (See 4:19; 5:9.) Gilgal lay only two or three miles east of Jericho. At Gilgal the stone monument was set up "so that all the peoples of the earth might *know* that the hand of the LORD is powerful and so that you might always *fear* the LORD your God." Psalm 114 celebrates the crossing of Jordan in vivid poetry.

6. *Events at Gilgal* (Josh. 5). The Canaanite "kings" over cities west of the Jordan soon heard the news: "ISRAEL HAS CROSSED THE JORDAN!" Their hearts (courage) then "melted" even more than before (2:9,11).

a. Circumcision was the sign of God's covenant with Abraham and his descendants (Gen. 17:10). It was a matter of life or death for the Israelites with Joshua to observe this ordinance. To Christians now fleshly circumcision is of no significance (1 Cor. 7:19). When we put away the sinful nature (and practices), and are baptized with faith in God's working, God regards us as having a circumcision not done by the hands of men (Col. 2:11-12).

"Make flint knives" (5:2). These are made by chipping off convex blades from nodules of flint. They are extremely sharp. The place of circumcising near Gilgal was named *Gibeath Haaraloth*, a vivid name meaning "hill of foreskins."

b. The Passover feast was THE memorial to Israel's deliverance from Egypt. It was to be observed yearly. Now in the promised land Israel observed the Passover in the forty-first year since the first passover in Egypt.

At the feast they ate fresh produce of the land, made into unleavened bread. (In the warm climate around Jericho the wheat matures by Passover time in April, earlier than in the cooler hill country of Canaan.) On the day after Passover, the manna that God had supplied six days each week for forty years ceased. But God's true bread for His people never ceased (John 6:32-33).

c. The commander of the army of the LORD appeared to Joshua as Joshua was near Jericho (5:13-15). He appeared as a "man" with his sword drawn. He called Himself the "Commander" (Hebrew *sar*, often translated "prince" or "captain"). Perhaps He was the angel Michael (Rev. 12:7;

THE FALL OF JERICHO

Gene Fackler.

"Jericho's wall will collapse!" (Josh. 6:5). Literally, "The wall of the city will fall beneath itself." The outer wall of mud bricks sat upon a stone retaining wall. When the wall fell down beside the retaining wall, it made an instant ramp for the Israelites to ascend into Jericho and attack. The window in the wall locates Rahab's house.

(Drawing courtesy of Associates for Biblical Research)

Dan. 10:13,21, where Michael is called "your prince"); or He was the Angel of the LORD, who is not distinguishable from the LORD Himself (Ex. 3:2; Judg. 6:11-16), and sometimes bore a sword (2 Chr. 21:15-16).

The mission of the Commander to Joshua is not stated. Certainly it was strong encouragement to Joshua and Israel to know that the LORD's commander was with them. Perhaps the Commander told Joshua the strategy for conquering Jericho. The military tactics used by Joshua were hardly what any man would plan.

"Take off your sandals, for the place where you are standing is holy." These words by the Commander to Joshua are almost identical to the words spoken by God to Moses (Ex. 3:5). It elevated Joshua's prestige to be spoken to by God with the same words He spoke to Moses.

7. *The LORD delivers Jericho to Joshua* (Josh. 6).

"By faith the walls of Jericho fell, after the people had marched around them for seven days" (Heb. 11:30).

Joshua 6 tells of the fall of Jericho.

(See notes on 2:1-22 for information about the city of Jericho.)

WAS GOD JUSTIFIED IN DESTROYING THE CANAANITES?

Joshua 6:21: "They *devoted* the city to the LORD and *destroyed* with the sword every living thing in it — men and women, young and old, cattle, sheep and donkeys." (See Joshua 9:24.)

1. The LORD had been very longsuffering with the Canaanites. In the days of Abraham (2000 B.C.) God said that his descendants would not at once possess the land of Canaan, but would sojourn in a foreign country [Egypt] 400 years. Only then would they come back to Canaan, "for the sin of the Amorites has not yet reached its full measure" (Gen. 15:16).

Six hundred years after the time of Abraham, the iniquity of the Amorites (Canaanites) was fully developed. God then said, "It is on account of the *wickedness* of these nations the LORD is going to drive them out before you" (Deut. 9:4). This was God's decision, not man's.

---

2. The Canaanites had become very cruel to one another. Judges 1:7 tells of the Canaanite king Adoni-Bezek, who had cut off the thumbs and big toes of seventy other "kings" he had captured, and then forced them to pick up scraps under his table for their food.

The clay tablets found at Tell el-Amarna in Egypt tell of continual hostilities among the cities of Canaan.

3. The Canaanite society was pervaded by an *obsession with sex*. Statuettes of the goddess Asherah nude are among the commonest classes of religious objects found in the archaeological digs in Late Bronze levels. (W.F. Albright, *Archaeology of Palestine*, p. 104.) The legends of the Canaanite gods Ba'al and Anath are full of sexual references. When the Israelites went to the worship of Ba'al at Peor, they soon became involved in immorality (Num. 25:1-3), because religious prostitution was part of the ritual.

4. The Canaanites practiced offering their children as sacrifices to their gods (Deut. 12:31; 18:9-10).

We must at all times accept that God's judgments show us what is right and wrong (Ps. 51:4; Rom. 3:4).

When the Israelites began their siege of Jericho, Jericho was "tightly shut up," meaning perhaps "shut up inside and out" (Josh. 6:1, NRSV).

God spoke of the city as if its defeat had already happened:

"I have delivered Jericho into your hands" (6:2).

Jericho's walls probably appeared too strong to capture. The great walls of Canaanite cities had dismayed the ten spies in Canaan (Num. 13:28). The Israelites were not experienced in the tactics of siege warfare.

The central position of the ark and the priests in the marches around Jericho (6:4,8) put stress upon the fact that this was a war directed by *God*, not just an ordinary military campaign.

The statement "the wall of the city will collapse" could more literally be translated "the wall will fall *beneath* itself" (6:5,20; 7:21). The archaeological remains at Jericho show that a mud brick wall was built upon a lower stone retaining wall. When the wall fell, it tumbled down before the lower retaining wall and formed a slope of debris that permitted the Israelites to walk up into the city from any point around it. (See *Biblical Archaeology Review*, Mar.–Apr. 1990, p. 47.)

Jericho was a small city (about 200 × 300 meters, 7–10 acres), and therefore walking around it seven times in a day was very feasible (6:15). All of Jericho would have fit in three city blocks.

"Devoted" (6:17-18) is a term meaning something that is totally and irrevocably given to God. (The Hebrew term is *ḥerem*; Greek *anathema*.) *Devoted* things were often killed or utterly destroyed (Lev. 27:29; Josh. 7:12).

God's instructions about giving all the metals found in Jericho to the LORD's treasury (6:19) was the occasion for the sin of Achan (7:1).

Perhaps the LORD employed an earthquake to bring down the walls of Jericho. The area is subject to quakes (*BAR*, ibid., 54). But the quake (if such it was) struck precisely at the time Israel shouted. And it struck with such precise focus that Rahab's house did not fall when the rest of the city did (6:22).

Rahab was temporarily segregated from Israel (6:23), but was later married to an Israelite named Salmon, and became the great-great-grandmother of King David and an ancestor of the Lord Jesus (1 Chr. 2:11-15; Matt. 1:5-6).

Joshua pronounced a curse upon the one who would rebuild Jericho (6:26). Jericho was reoccupied soon after its destruction (18:21); and a structure was built there in the period of judges (Judg. 3:13,20). Perhaps this was the "Middle Building" found by archaeologist John Garstang, and dated in the Late Bronze 2 period (J. Garstang, *The Story of Jericho* [1948], p. 123). The rebuilding of the walls was not attempted until the time of King Ahab (874–853), almost 600 years after Joshua. The rebuilder, named Hiel, suffered the loss of his oldest and youngest sons, as Joshua foretold (1 Kgs. 16:34).

8. *The sin of Achan* (Josh. 7). After Israel's great victory at Jericho, they suffered a serious, though temporary, setback at their second battle site, named 'Ai. This happened because an Israelite named *Achan* secretly took some of the spoils of

Jericho for himself. (Achan's name is spelled *Achar* in the Greek Bible and in 1 Chronicles 2:7. *Achar* means *trouble*. See 7:26.) The LORD viewed Achan's act seriously, as if the whole nation of Israel had "acted unfaithfully." "He was not the only one who died for his sin" (Josh. 22:20). The Scripture frequently tells of entire nations suffering punishment for the sin of one person in the group. (Note 2 Samuel 21:1; 24:15-17.) No one sins without hurting others.

'Ai was a small Canaanite city near Bethel, up in the hills west from Jericho about 15 miles (but about 25 on foot through the twisting brook valleys). *'Ai* means "ruins" or "heap" or rubble. 'Ai has generally been located at a large (27-acre) mound now named Et-tell, about 12 miles north of Jerusalem, though no remains have been found there that can be dated to the time of Joshua. (Remains are from Early Bronze Age layers, 3100–2350 B.C.; and Iron Age 1 layers, 1220–1050 B.C. See *Biblical Archaeologist*, March 1976, p. 19.)

A suggested alternate location for 'Ai is *Khirbet Nisya*, a small (3–4 acre) mound ten miles north of Jerusalem, and a mile east of the Arab cities of Ramallah and Bireh. Remains have been found there from every period when 'Ai was occupied according to the Bible and the early Christian historians like Eusebius. (See *Bible and Spade*, Summer 1993, pp. 69-75.) The author of this book has been involved in the excavations at Khirbet Nisya. But the exact location of 'Ai remains uncertain. Likewise, the identification of *Beth Aven* (7:2) is uncertain, though some interpret the name as a derogatory title (meaning "House of Wickedness") applied to *Bethel* ("House of God"). (See Hosea 10:5; 1 Kings 12:28-29.)

Joshua sent spies up to 'Ai. They reported it was a place with a small population and could be taken by a few thousand troops. "Do not *weary* all the people." The climb up from Jericho 800 feet below sea level to the 'Ai area 2500 feet above is exhausting.

In the first attack upon 'Ai Israel was defeated, and 36 were killed. This distressed Joshua. He prayed face down to the ground. Though his own leadership was threatened by the defeat, Joshua was mostly concerned with God's honor:

"What will you do for your own great name?" Israel faced no greater disaster than that God would not be with them anymore (7:12).

God directed Joshua to discover the one who had stolen the "devoted things" and destroy him with fire (7:15). By use of drawn lots, Achan was exposed. (The use of lots to discover secret information from God was frequent in the Old Testament age. See Proverbs 16:17. But the practice seems to have ceased after the selection of Matthias [Acts 1:26].)

Achan was told, "Confess to the LORD" (7:19 NIV marg.; NRSV). He admitted taking a "wedge" (literally a *tongue*) of gold, and silver, and a beautiful robe. These things were found hidden in his tent.

Then Achan and all that he had were taken to a remote valley and stoned to death and burned. These included his sons and daughters and livestock. (The children must have known what Achan had done. We suppose his wife was dead because she is not mentioned.) The valley was called *Achor*, meaning trouble or disturbance. It is a desolate place in the cliffs west of Jordan, fourteen kilometers north of Jericho. Achan, the troubler of Israel, suffered trouble in a valley named Trouble. These events taught many lessons about God.

9. *'Ai destroyed* (Josh. 8:1-29). Though God had punished Israel after Achan's sin, God was still definitely with Israel, and God encouraged Joshua to press the attack upon 'Ai. The spoils from 'Ai were to be taken by the Israelites, unlike those from Jericho (8:2, 22).

Joshua slipped 5000 men into hiding west of 'Ai as an ambush. The rest of the army was to make a feigned attack from the north, and draw the Canaanites from the city, so the ambush could enter it and set it ablaze. That night Joshua stayed in the valley north of 'Ai. (Both of the proposed locations for 'Ai — Et-tell and Khirbet Nisya — have deep valleys on their north sides.) The next morning Joshua and the "leaders" (literally, "elders") of the people went up toward 'Ai in the presence of the people of the city. The Canaanites were decoyed and all came out against Israel. Very quickly they found themselves caught between their city burning behind them and the Israelite army in front of them. The people of 'Ai were completely destroyed, and their king was captured and hanged. Joshua burned 'Ai and made it a *tell* forever (8:28). (A *tell* is a mound of ruins. There are thousands of such *tells* in the Middle East.)

'Ai had a gate (8:29); but its gate and walls were destroyed. Their king was buried under a large pile of rocks "at the *entrance* (literally "opening") of the gate."

It appears that *Bethel* was defeated near the same time that 'Ai was (8:17; 12:16). Bethel was near (1-2 miles?) to 'Ai, with a mountain between them (Gen. 12:8).

10. *The law read on Mt. Ebal* (Josh. 8:30-35). After the victory over 'Ai Joshua and all the Israelites travelled to Mt. Ebal to build an altar and to read the law of Moses. Ebal is about 30 miles north from 'Ai. Mt. Ebal and its neighbor Mt. Gerizim are in the center of the country, with the narrow (½ mile wide) Valley of Shechem between them. The town of Shechem is in the valley, with Ebal on its north and Gerizim on the south.

On Ebal Joshua built an altar according to the instructions in Exodus 20:26 and Deuteronomy 27:1-8. Archaeological remains of this altar have perhaps been found (*BAR*, Jan.–Feb.1985, p. 26 ff). At Mt. Ebal Joshua copied on stones the law that Moses had written (perhaps only its principal sections). There the blessings for obedience and curses for disobedience written in the law were read to all the people, to citizens and aliens within Israel alike (8:33; Lev. 26 and Deut. 27:9-28:66). Then Joshua read the entire law (8:34). These events stress again the importance of God's written law as man's divine guidebook.

Acoustical tests have been made at Shechem. These show that words spoken up on the mountainside can be heard clearly in the valley below (*Biblical Archaeologist*, Dec. 1976, pp. 138-139).

How was Israel able to hold a large mass meeting at Mt. Ebal in unconquered territory, with Canaanites living all around? A possible answer to this may be in the letters found at Tell el-Amarna in Egypt (dated about 1375 B.C.). These state (in epistle #289) that 'Abdu-Heba (king of Jerusalem) protested to the king of Egypt that Lab'ayu (king of Shechem) had given the land to the 'Apiru (*The Ancient Near East*, Vol 1., Princeton Univ., 1973, p. 274). The 'Apiru were roving groups of marauding peoples in Canaan who were outside the established groups in society. The 'Apiru probably included the Hebrews, but also included other socially unsettled and unaccepted groups.

Some doubtful interpretations have been made of Israel's assembly at Mt. Ebal. N. Gottwald (*The Hebrew Bible*, pp. 270, 274) proposes that at this Shechem assembly oppressed segments of Canaanite populace became initially incorporated together with people who were worshipers of Yahweh, and that this event was the actual origin of "Israel" as a people. Evidence for this idea is very limited.

After the mass meeting at Mt. Ebal, Joshua and Israel returned to their camp at *Gilgal*, near Jericho (9:6). They returned to this place frequently, even though the journey to it was long and difficult (Josh. 10:43; 14:6; Judg. 2:1).

11. *The Gibeonites deceive Israel* (Josh. 9). The Canaanite cities existed as independent kingdoms, even hostile kingdoms. But when Joshua defeated Jericho and 'Ai, they realized they had to unite to resist Joshua. They assembled themselves together to fight Joshua "with one mouth" (literal wording).

The people of Gibeon, a Canaanite city, realized that Joshua would soon destroy them as he had destroyed Jericho and 'Ai. They came to Gilgal and deceived the Israelites, so that they made a treaty (literally, a *covenant*) of peace with them. This caused friction in Israel; but the covenant was accepted by both the people and by God as a promise that Israel had to comply with. (See 2 Samuel 21:1.)

The Gibeonites had heard of the "fame" (literally, *name*) of the LORD (9:9). One's *name* in the Bible stands for his character and doings. See Joshua 7:9. Like Rahab, they knew God's name.

Gibeon is a village on a knoll about eight miles northwest

of Jerusalem (modern name, *el-Jib*). It was scarcely seven miles from 'Ai. (2 Samuel 2:13 mentions a "pool" at Gibeon, and Jeremiah 41:12 refers to a "great pool" there.) The hill of Gibeon was partially excavated by Dr. James Pritchard of the University of Pennsylvania in 1956–63. He found a huge water pool and well. The pool was 37′ in diameter and 35′ deep in bedrock, with a well shaft on down 45′ below the pool to the water. Also he found a tunnel with steps leading down from inside the city to a water-drawing room. (See Pritchard, *Gibeon Where the Sun Stood Still.* Princeton, 1962). Whether these large water works were all there in Joshua's time is uncertain. Joshua sentenced the Gibeonites to be water carriers for the community (Josh. 9:26). This hints that even then the Gibeonites had some type of water supply facilities.

The Gibeonites deceived Israel by claiming they were ambassadors from a distant country. They wore old clothes and had old supplies. (Their words should have aroused suspicion. Food spoils long before clothes get old. And if they really had come from a distant land, they did not need to make a treaty.)

Israel made a mistake by not asking the LORD for guidance in this matter (9:14). The LORD had promised to guide their decisions through the priests using Urim and Thummim (Num. 27:18-21).

ASK THE LORD FOR GUIDANCE,
in everything you do.

Joshua sentenced the Gibeonites to be become a perpetual race of slaves as woodcutters and water carriers for the "house of God" (the tabernacle) and the community (congregation) (9:22, 26). The Gibeonites seemed relieved to have insured themselves against annihilation.

CENTRAL CONQUEST OF CANAAN – Three Unusual Battles:
1. *Jericho* – The walls fell down (Josh. 6).
2. *'Ai* – Initial defeat (Josh. 7–8). City taken by an ambush.
3. *Beth Horon* – Sun & moon stood still (Josh. 10).

12. *Battle of Gibeon and Beth Horon* (Josh. 10:1-15). The other Canaanite cites near Gibeon were greatly alarmed (fearful) when they heard that Gibeon had made a treaty of peace with Israel. Five of the "kings" of cities joined together to attack Gibeon, to force it to rejoin them in resisting Israel. This attack was led by *Adoni-Zedek*, king of Jerusalem. (His name means "lord of righteousness," as *Melchizedek* [Gen.14:18] means "king of righteousness.")

The Gibeonites sent word to Joshua to come quickly and save them. Joshua and his men made a hard, 25-mile, all-night march up from Gilgal to Gibeon. They had moonlight; the moon was still visible in the western sky the next morning (10:12).

At Gibeon Joshua defeated the Canaanites in a great victory, and chased them westward toward Beth Horon. The terrain is rugged and rocky in the four miles from Gibeon to Upper Beth Horon. Layers of smooth rock alternate with upturned edges of limestone strata and loose rectangular stones. Beth Horon is actually two towns — Upper Beth Horon and Lower Beth Horon — about two miles apart, with a descent of over 800 feet between them. In the descent the LORD hurled large hailstones down on the fleeing Canaanites, and many died (Josh. 10:9-11).

At that time Joshua spoke to the LORD, praying, "O sun, stand still over Gibeon, O moon, over the valley of Aijalon."

From Joshua's location at Beth Horon, the morning sun appeared to be standing in the east over Gibeon, and the moon in the southwest above the Valley of Aijalon. In those positions the sun and moon stood still about a full day longer, until Israel had avenged itself upon its enemies. The verb "stand still" may also be translated "be silent." We believe this occurred exactly as described, even though scientific explanations cannot account for it. (No "lost day" has been found in astronomical time calculations.)

Joshua 10:15 says that Israel returned to camp at Gilgal. It is surprising that they would have made the hard trip back to Gilgal in the midst of a battle. This verse is lacking in the Greek LXX.

13. *Five Amorite kings killed* (Josh. 10:16-28). Joshua pursued the Amorite kings seventeen miles south to Azekah and nearby Makkedah. Azekah was on a high hill about 25 miles west of Bethlehem. The location of Makkedah is uncertain. At Makkedah the five Amorite kings were trapped in a cave, and afterwards killed and hanged in disgrace. These kings had gone up to attack (lit., *smite*) Gibeon (10:4). But they themselves were destroyed. They reaped what they had sown (Gal. 6:7).

14. *Southern cities defeated* (Josh.10:29-43). After the great victory over the five Amorite kings Joshua and his army made a sweep through the western foothills (the Shephelah) and then into the southern hill country around Hebron.

Southern Sweep by Joshua's Army –

From **MAKKEDAH** to **LIBNAH** to **LACHISH**
to **EGLON** to **HEBRON** to **DEBIR**.

The location of Libnah (10:29) is uncertain. Perhaps it was at Tell Bornat, five miles south of Gath.

In each of these battles we are told that Joshua left no survivors. But none of the cities were burned, and none of them were occupied at that time by Israelite settlers. Canaanites reoccupied them after Joshua's sweep, so that we read in Judges chapter 1 that Hebron and Debir had to be defeated again after Joshua's death before being occupied by Israelites.

Lachish was a large (31 acre) city in the Shephelah foothills west-northwest of Hebron. The mound is now called Tell ed-Duweir. It was one of the most important Canaanite cities in the country. It was unfortified in the time of Joshua (Late Bronze 1 & 2 periods). The king of the important city-state of Gezer came over twenty miles to help the king of Lachish defend his city, but both were defeated.

The location of ancient Eglon also is uncertain. Possibly it was at Tell el-Hesi southwest of Lachish. It took Joshua two days to defeat Lachish, but only one to defeat Eglon.

Joshua turned eastward into the highlands, and defeated Hebron (20 miles south of Jerusalem). (Hebron was the place where Abraham, Isaac, and Jacob had been buried.) The villages around Hebron — like Ziph, Carmel, Maon, and Juttah (Josh. 15:55) — were taken in the same campaign.

Debir (10:38) was probably at Khirbet *(ruins of)* Rabud, five miles southwest of Hebron. It was recaptured early in the period of judges, by Caleb's nephew Othniel (Judg. 1:11-15). Joshua at a later time did some "mopping up" of unconquered spots in the hill country around Hebron (Josh. 11:21).

"So Joshua subdued the whole region" (10:40). The areas conquered are listed. It is clear that Joshua captured many more locations than are named in Joshua chapter 10. *Kadesh Barnea* (where the twelve spies were sent from) was taken, though it is fifty miles southwest of Beersheba. *Goshen* (10:41) was probably the area around the town of Goshen (15:51) twelve miles southwest of Hebron. This is not the Land of Goshen in Egypt (Gen. 46:34).

It was a time of great triumph when the Israelites returned to their families at Gilgal near Jericho (10:43). God leads His people in triumph (2 Cor. 2:14).

15. *The northern conquest of Canaan* (Josh. 11). The Canaanite kings in the northern part of the land had not learned to fear the God of Israel by the defeat of the southern kings. Joshua 11:20 says, The LORD "hardened their hearts to wage war against Israel, so that he might destroy them totally." Led by Jabin, king of the city-state of Hazor (pronounced Hot-SORE), they came together by agreement "to fight against Israel."

(This Jabin was not the same Jabin we read of in Judges 4:21, 23, who was defeated by Deborah and Barak about 150 years later. Perhaps he was his ancestor.)

The northern kings included those around the Sea of Galilee (called Kinnereth in O.T.), and westward toward the Mediterranean, and north toward Mt. Hermon.

These kings gathered at the Waters of Merom to prepare their battle. They had many horses and chariots, and an army "as numerous as the sand on the seashore" (11:4).

The Israelites scorned chariots and horses in warfare. Psalm 20:7: "Some trust in chariots and some in horses, but we trust in the name of the LORD our God." (See Deuteronomy 17:16; 2 Samuel 8:4.)

The *Waters of Merom* were formerly thought to be Lake Huleh, north of the Sea of Galilee. Most scholars now favor a location in the mountainous area near Mt. Meron, about 10 miles northwest of the Sea of Galilee. The exact location is uncertain.

The LORD sent Joshua against the northern Canaanites.

Perhaps Joshua was fearful. The LORD said to him, "Do not be afraid. . . by this time *tomorrow* I will hand all of them over to Israel." Obviously Joshua was within a day's journey of the Waters of Merom when the LORD sent him (11:6). There were several cities near northern Canaan which Joshua defeated — Megiddo, Taanach, and Jokneam (11:21-22). He may have been fighting one of these when he was sent to the Waters of Merom.

In a sudden attack Joshua defeated them and pursued them all the way to Greater Sidon (at least 60 miles) and other distant places. "He hamstrung their horses and burned their chariots" (11:9). (To *hamstring* is to cripple by cutting the hamstring tendon above the hock of the rear leg.)

Joshua came back from pursuing the northern kings and captured Hazor, which was the dominant city among the northern Canaanite kingdoms. Joshua burned Hazor (11:13), the only city in the area actually burned.

Hazor lay four miles southwest of Lake Huleh, on the west side of the Jordan valley. Extensive excavations (ongoing) at Hazor have revealed it was the largest city in Canaan, with a lower city of 170 acres enclosed by a great rectangular earthen bank. It had an upper mound of 30 acres. Layer XV is dated in the Late Bronze 1 period (15th cent. B.C.). This layer was destroyed and burned (B. Waltke, *Bul. Near East Arch. Soc.*, #2 [1972], p. 13). Layer XV at Hazor is probably the remains of the destruction by Joshua about 1400 B.C.

With the destruction of Hazor, Joshua's conquests were practically completed. Only a few mopping-up operations followed (11:25). It had been a long war (11:18), about seven years. Joshua "left nothing undone of all that the LORD commanded Moses" (11:15). "Joshua took the entire land" (11:23).

These statements must be understood as slightly hyperbolic because in Joshua 13:1-5 there is a list of areas that remained unconquered in Joshua's old age. Also in 23:5 we read Joshua's exhortation to the Israelites to complete the conquest of the land. In the Bible "all" or "entire" sometimes means "almost all" or "the greater part." Note Joshua 21:43: "The LORD gave Israel *all* the land he had sworn to give their forefathers, and they took possession of it and settled there." This passage is near the exhortations of Joshua to Israel to drive out the Canaanites that remain (23:5). But nothing can diminish the glory and greatness of Joshua's conquest. It was GOD's victory.

16. *Summary of the conquests* (Josh. 12). All the conquered cities are listed in a grand summary. The conquests led by Moses against kings Sihon and Og are recalled (Josh. 12:1-6; Num. 21:21-35; Deut. 2:26–3:11). The north and south limits of the conquered areas are named (12:1,7).

A list of the thirty-one cities west of the Jordan that were defeated closes the victory record. The word *one* is inserted after the name of each city. This compels us to think of each one as a struggle and a triumph. It is not a list of which only the total is important.

The defeated cities are listed with the first two to be captured named first (12:9). Then cities in the southern conquest are itemized (12:10-16). These are followed by cities in the northern sections (12:17-24). Very few cities in the central part of the country are listed, perhaps only Tappuach in Ephraim (Josh. 16:8; 17:8), and Tirzah in Manasseh (12:24).

In reality Joshua's conquests were quite limited. Only three cities were actually burned — Jericho, 'Ai, and Hazor. Archaeological surveys have discovered nearly 15,000 sites of ancient ruins in Israel. Some have argued that since there are remains of numerous destructions in Israel between 1300 and 1200 B.C. that the conquest should be dated in that period (G.E. Wright, *Biblical Archaeology* [1966], p. 70). But the very scarcity of destruction deposits datable around 1400 B.C. fits better with the biblical description of a limited conquest by Joshua, than would the later period when many cities were being destroyed.

Questions on Section B
Invasion and Conquest of Canaan (Josh. 1–12)

1. When did God speak to Joshua? (Josh. 1:1)
2. What does the name *Joshua* mean?
3. How much of Canaan was to be given to Israel? (1:3)
4. What was Joshua to do with the book of the law? (1:8)
5. What command of Moses to the tribes of Gad, Reuben, and half of Manasseh did Joshua remind them of? (1:13-15)
6. From what place did Joshua send spies? How many spies? To what city? (2:1)
7. How far is Jericho from the Jordan river? From the Dead Sea?
8. Into whose house did the spies come? (2:1)
9. Where were the spies hidden in Jericho? (2:6)
10. Which way did the men pursue after the spies? (2:7)
11. What feeling did the people in Canaan have about the invading Hebrews? (2:9-11)
12. What promise did the woman ask of the spies? (2:12-13)
13. How did the spies escape from Jericho? (2:15)
14. What signal was the woman to hang in her window? (2:18)
15. Whom was Rahab to gather in her home? (2:18)
16. Who led the procession across Jordan? (3:3,14)
17. How much space was to be between the ark and the people? (3:4)
18. Where did the priests stand during the crossing? (3:8, 17)
19. What was the crossing of Jordan to reassure the people about? (3:10-11)
20. What was the condition of Jordan when Israel crossed it? (3:15)
21. Where did the Jordan waters stop and pile up? (3:16)
22. What were twelve men appointed to do after the Jordan was crossed? (4:1-3)
23. Where were the stones to be set? (4:3,20)
24. What purpose were the stones from Jordan to serve? (4:6-7)
25. Where was a second group of stones set up? By whom? (4:9)

26. How did the crossing of Jordan cause the Israelites to feel toward Joshua? (4:14)

27. What was the name of the first encampment after crossing the Jordan? (4:19)

28. How did the crossing of Jordan affect the Canaanites? (5:1)

29. At what location were the people circumcised? (5:9)

30. Why was the mass circumcision necessary? (5:5)

31. What does the name *Gilgal* mean? Why was that name given to the place? (5:9)

32. What feast was kept in Gilgal? (5:10)

33. When did the manna cease? (5:12)

34. Who appeared to Joshua when he was near Jericho? (5:13-14)

35. What did the LORD's commander tell Joshua to do? (5:15)

36. How many times did Israel march around Jericho? (6:4-5)

37. List the order of the various groups as they marched around Jericho. (6:4, 6-7, 9,13)

38. What sound was heard during the marching? (6:9, 13)

39. When did the people shout? (6:16)

40. What does *devoted* mean? (6:17)

41. What was to be done with the goods of Jericho? (6:17-19)

42. What was to be done to Jericho itself? (6:21,24)

43. Who brought out Rahab and her family? (6:22,23)

44. Where did Rahab live after that? (6:25)

45. What did Joshua pronounce upon the one who would rebuild Jericho? (6:26)

46. Who acted unfaithfully at Jericho? What was his unfaithful act? (7:1)

47. What did Joshua's spies report about 'Ai? (7:2-3)

48. How many Israelites died in the first assault on 'Ai? (7:4-5)

49. How did the defeat at 'Ai affect Israel's courage? (7:5)

50. What did Joshua do after this defeat? (7:6-7)

51. Why did God say that Israel had been defeated? (7:11-12)

52. How was the sinner pointed out? (7:14)

53. What did Joshua tell Achan to say? (7:19)

54. What things had Achan stolen? (7:21)

55. Who were killed along with Achan? (7:24)

56. What name was given to the place Achan was killed? (7:26) What does the name mean?

57. Who were to go up and attack 'Ai? (8:1)

58. How was the spoil of 'Ai to be handled differently from that of Jericho? (8:2)
59. How was Joshua directed to capture 'Ai? (8:3-7)
60. What lay between 'Ai and Israel? (8:11)
61. What city had joined with 'Ai in fighting Israel? (8:17)
62. How did Joshua signal his men to enter 'Ai? (8:18)
63. How many people of 'Ai fell to Joshua? (8:25)
64. What was done to the city? (8:28)
65. What was done to the king of 'Ai? (8:29)
66. What did Joshua build on Mt. Ebal? (8:30)
67. What was read to the whole assembly of Israel? (8:34)
68. What did the kings in Canaan come together to do? (9:1-2)
69. What city made a treaty of peace with Joshua? (9:3-6)
70. How did they deceive and convince Israel? (9:4-5, 11-13)
71. What did Israel neglect to do before making the treaty of peace? (9:14)
72. When was the deception discovered? (9:16)
73. Name the four cities in the group that deceived Israel. (9:17)
74. How did the assembly (congregation) respond when the deception became known? (9:18)
75. Why was the treaty of peace not broken? (9:20)
76. What were the Gibeonites made to be? For how long? (9:23)
77. Who was the king of Jerusalem? (10:1)
78. How important a city was Gibeon? (10:2)
79. How many kings joined together to attack Gibeon? (10:5)
80. What did the Gibeonites do when they were attacked? (10:6)
81. Where did Joshua defeat the kings? (10:9)
82. To what places did Israel pursue the enemy kings? (10:10)
83. How did the LORD help in the battle? (10:11)
84. In what book was a record of this victory written? (10:13)
85. Over what places did the sun and the moon stand still? (10:12)
86. Where did the five kings hide? (10:16)
87. What significance was there in putting feet on the kings' necks? (10:24)
88. How were the bodies of the kings disgraced? (10:26)
89. What five cities were taken after Makkedah fell? (10:29-39)
90. How much of the Negev (South) did Joshua take? (10:40)
91. What were boundaries of this part of the conquest? (10:41)
92. Who was Jabin? (11:1).
93. How many people made camp together to fight Israel? (11:2-4)
94. Where did they gather? (11:5)

95. What was Joshua to do with their horses and chariots? (11:6)
96. How far did Joshua pursue these northern enemies? (11:8)
97. What city in the north was taken and burned? (11:18)
98. Was Joshua's conquest brief or long? (11:18)
99. Why did the Canaanites not make peace with Joshua? (11:19-20)
100. Where did the Anakites live? (11:21-22)
101. How fully did Joshua conquer the land? (11:23)
102. What two kings east of the Jordan did Israel defeat? (12:1-2,4)
103. What word follows the name of each city that was conquered? (12:9-24)
104. How many kings did Joshua and the Israelites conquer on the west side of the Jordan? (12:24)

Section C
The Land Divided among the Twelve Tribes
(Joshua 13–22)

> There is *no retirement* from the LORD's service! (Josh. 13:1)

When Joshua was old and well advanced in years (lit., *in days*), the LORD said to him, "You are very old, and there are still very large areas of land to be taken over." We do not know exactly how old Joshua had become, probably over eighty. He died at 110 years (23:2; 24:29).

1. *Considerable land unconquered* (Josh. 13:1-7). Even in Joshua's old age the LORD continued to speak to him and direct him. The LORD reminded him of large unconquered areas.

Three Principal Unconquered Areas:

1. **Philistia** (the southern coastal zone).
   This included the five *Philistines* rulers (lit., *lords, tyrants*) of the cities of Ashdod, Ashkelon, Gath, Gaza, and Ekron.
2. The northern coastal zone, called *Phoenicia* in later times. This area was dominated by cities like Sidon and Gebal (40 miles north of Sidon).
3. The *Lebanon* **mountains**, east of Phoenicia, and north from Mt. Hermon to Lebo Hamath (the "entrance of Hamath").

The work of dividing the land among the twelve tribes had been part of the original commission of Joshua (1:6; Deut. 31:7). But it was *God* who would drive out the inhabitants (13:6).

The unconquered areas were large. From Mt. Hermon north to Lebo Hamath on the Orontes River was eighty miles (13:5). At no time in history has Israel ruled the Phoenician coast as far north as Sidon and Gebal (later called Byblos).

The land of Canaan was to be Israel's *inheritance* (13:7,8).

To the Israelites (and to others) an *inheritance* was very important for the survival and prosperity of every family.

2. *Inheritance of the tribes east of the Jordan* (Josh. 13:8-32).

> The tribes east of the Jordan:
> *Reuben, Gad,* & half of *Manasseh.*

Great emphasis is given to the territories to be allocated to the tribes who would live east of the Jordan River. Their territories are described first and at length. A list of cities in each tribe is given. This land was excellent for production of livestock (Num. 32:4).

Probably the reason for the emphasis was the natural tendency for the tribes east of the Jordan to feel detached from the tribes west of the Jordan (Num. 32:31-32; Josh. 22:24-27).

> The LORD wants all His people to be associated together.
> *How good and pleasant it is when brothers*
> *live together in unity* (Ps. 133:1).

a. *Reuben* (13:15-23). The south border of Reuben's land was the rim of the Arnon gorge. This gorge is 2000 feet deep and flows into the center of the Dead Sea east side. Reuben's land was mostly a productive plateau. It contained many places (such as Dibon and Beth Peor) where great historical events had occurred. Balaam had tried to curse Israel at Dibon (Num. 22:41). Israel had sinned at Beth Peor (Num.

23:28; 25:1-2), and Moses was buried near there (Deut. 34:6). Great events should be remembered.

b. *Gad* (13:24-28). The land of Gad was productive. The territory of Gad is frequently called *Gilead*. It lay east of the Jordan.

c. *Half-tribe of Manasseh* (13:29-31). This tribe was in the area north of the Yarmuk River, mostly east of Galilee. The area was called *Bashan*, and is now called the Golan Heights. It is an extremely productive and desirable area.

One of the famous descendants of Manasseh was *Makir* (Num. 26:29). He was a warrior, and conquered Gilead and Bashan (Num. 32:39; Deut. 3:15; Josh. 17:1).

3. *Inheritance of Levites* (Josh. 13:14, 33). The tribe of Levi received no land in a single area, because the priestly service was their inheritance (Josh. 18:7; 14:3-4; Num. 3:5-7). They were to be "scattered" in Israel (Gen. 49:7). They did receive forty-eight cities (Josh. 21:41; 14:3). But the LORD, the God of Israel, was their inheritance; and they received tithes from the people for their living (Num. 18:24).

4. *Inheritance of areas west of the Jordan* (Josh. 14:1-5). The LORD had directed Joshua and Eleazar the priest to divide up the land among the tribes (Num. 34:16-29). The heads of the tribal clans of Israel helped them (Josh. 14:1,5).

The LORD had commanded that the land be divided among the nine and one-half tribes by lot and by population size (Num. 26:52-56; Josh. 14:2).

The LORD had told Moses to give the Levites towns and pasturelands around their towns (Num. 35:2-5; Josh. 14:3-4).

> The **LORD** made all the plans, and provided power.
> But the people had to carry out the plans.

5. *Hebron given to Caleb as inheritance* (Josh. 14:6-15). Caleb, the faithful old spy, came to Joshua, requesting as his inheritance the hill country around Hebron. The area around Hebron is higher in elevation than any part of Canaan (over 3000′ in places), except northern Galilee. The

LORD had promised this area to Caleb (Num. 14:24; Deut. 1:36). Caleb was 85 years old, but still full of faith and eager to fight for his inheritance. He wanted a legal grant of his allotment, and the endorsement of the leaders.

Judges 15:13-17 tells of Caleb's capture of Hebron and the three Anakite giants there. Judges 1:9-13 tells of the same battle, led by the "men of Judah." (The two accounts harmonize well.)

From Joshua 14 we could get the impression that Caleb captured Hebron while Joshua was still living, although the text does not actually state that. From Judges we learn that Hebron was taken after Joshua's death (Judg. 1:1,10).

6. *Allotment for the tribe of Judah* (Josh. 15). Judah was the most important and powerful of all the twelve tribes (1 Chr. 5:2). It had the largest population. The Bible in telling the territories of the tribes west of the Jordan describes the territory of Judah FIRST, and devotes more space to it than to any other tribe's land.

Judah was the fourth son of Jacob and Leah (Gen. 29:35). When the oldest son, Reuben, sinned and lost his rank as firstborn (Gen. 35:22; 49:3-4), that honor passed to son Joseph (1 Chr. 5:1-2); but Judah became the most powerful tribe, and most of the kings and rulers came from Judah (Gen. 49:10).

JESUS — Lion of the tribe of JUDAH ! (Rev. 5:5)

The territory of Judah was in the SOUTH part of the land. It included the southern Negev desert. Judah's south border was the south border of Israel (Josh. 15:2-4; Num. 34:3-5).

Judah's south border ran from the south end of the Salt (Dead) Sea, westward into the Negev, to the Scorpion Pass, through the desert of Zin to Kadesh Barnea, and on west to the Wadi (brook, valley) of Egypt (Wadi el-Arish), and up to the Great Sea.

The Desert of Zin is a low-level valley about 25 miles southwest of the Dead Sea; it branches off westward from the Arabah

Valley (south of the Dead Sea). The Scorpion Pass (Ascent of Akkrabim) is now identified as the pass Es-Sufah, a twisty trail up out of the Desert of Zin, northward into the Negev desert.

The north border of Judah extended from the north end of the Dead Sea mostly westward, and passed along the south edge of Jerusalem. Judah's border went by En Rogel, a well at the southeast corner of Jerusalem, made famous by events associated with David and Absalom (2 Sam. 17:17-20), and Solomon (1 Kgs. 1:9-10).

> *Jerusalem was in the land of Benjamin. But the tribe of JUDAH was "next door" south of Jerusalem.*

Judah's north border went through the Valley of Ben (sons of) Hinnom, which goes around the south side of Jerusalem.

The Judeans attempted at some time to dislodge the Jebusites living in Jerusalem (15:63), but could not do so. King David later (1003 B.C.) did capture Jerusalem (2 Sam. 5:6-7).

Caleb, the faithful spy, was from Judah. He took Hebron and Debir. (See 15:13-19; 14:6-15.)

Lists of the towns in different sections of Judah fill much of Joshua 15. 115 towns are named. Many of them are said to have had "villages." These were unwalled settlements near the larger cities, where the people who worked on the land lived except in wartime. (The locations of many of these towns are shown on Map 32 in Barry J. Beitzel, *The Moody Atlas of Bible Lands*, Chacago: Moody, 1985, p.100.)

Ziklag (15:31) was a town 12 miles northwest from Beersheba, actually assigned to the tribe of Simeon (Josh. 19:5), and later given to David by the Philistine king Achish (1 Sam. 27:6).

Several of the towns of Judah — Ekron, Ashdod, Gaza — remained under the control of Philistines. David later captured these.

7. *Allotment for Ephraim and Manasseh* (Josh. 16 & 17).

> **Joseph** (son of Jacob) received TWO portions of land, named after his sons — **EPHRAIM & MANASSEH** (Gen. 48:22).

The tribes of Ephraim and Manasseh, which were descended from Jacob's son Joseph, received large areas of some of the best land, in the central part of the country. The territory of Ephraim and Manasseh included the productive Plain of Sharon, and the lovely hill country of Samaria, with its round-topped hills and productive valleys in between. Manasseh was in the north part of their lands, and Ephraim in the south.

> *Ephraim* and *Manasseh*, the tribes that received the most land and the best land, were the tribes that **complained** about their allotment! (Josh. 17:14-18)

The east border of Ephraim "reached to Jericho and came out at the Jordan" (Judg. 16:7). The eastern boundaries of Ephraim and Manasseh are not clearly related. Most Bible atlases (e.g., *Moody Atlas, NIV Atlas, McMillan*) show Manasseh's territory extending in a narrow strip southward along the west side of the Jordan to Jericho and the border of Benjamin. This layout would cut Ephraim off from the Jordan. Perhaps Ephraim and Manasseh jointly occupied the territory alongside their eastern boundary at the Jordan.

The south border of Ephraim went from Bethel (ten miles north of Jerusalem) southwest to Gezer (16:3). Gezer (GEZZ-er) was on a large prominent mound, the northernmost hill of the Shephelah foothills, on the south edge of the Valley of Aijalon. The Canaanites were not driven from Gezer until the time of King Solomon (1 Kgs. 9:15-17).

The north border of Ephraim went westward through the Kanah Ravine (lit., Wadi Kanah) (16:8). This enters the Mediterranean Sea just north of Joppa (modern Tel Aviv). Ephraim's territory lay south of the Kanah, and Manasseh's north of it (17:9-10).

Ephraim was the younger son of Joseph. But Ephraim became a stronger tribe than Manasseh (Gen. 48:19-20). Ephraim became so dominant in the north that the entire northern kingdom called "Israel" was sometimes called "Ephraim" (Hosea 11:8; Isa. 7:2).

Joshua 17 tells of the allotment of the tribe of Manasseh. Half of Manasseh was east of the Jordan and the Sea of Galilee, in what is now called the Golan Heights.

Makir, a son of Manasseh, was a warrior who conquered the territory of Bashan and Gilead (east of Jordan), and received this large area as his inheritance (Josh. 17:1; Num. 26:28-29; 32:39-40; 1 Chr. 5:23). It was suitable for their great flocks and herds (Num. 32:1-5).

Six other clans (extended families) of the Manassites received territory west of the Jordan. The most well-known of these clans was *Abiezer* (17:2; or *Iezer* in Num. 26:20), because Gideon was of that clan (Judg. 6:11; 8:2). The clan of Hepher received five tracts of land in the names of the five daughters of Zelophehad (17:3-6; Num. 27:1-11; 36:2-12).

The eastern border of Manasseh (by the Jordan) is not clearly defined. Perhaps Ephraim and Manasseh jointly occupied the area by the Jordan (16:5-7).

Several towns in Manasseh's territory were occupied by Ephraimites. Also some towns north of Manasseh in the tribes of Issachar and Asher were occupied by Manassites (17:9-11).

Manasseh failed to capture several large Canaanite towns in its territory: Megiddo, Dor, Taanach, Beth Shan (17:11-12).

The tribes of Manasseh and Ephraim complained to Joshua about the lands allotted to them. Only these tribes complained. Their complaint stressed the fact that heavily armed Canaanites lived in their territory (17:16). Much of their land also was covered with forests (17:15, 18).

Though Joshua was from the tribe of Ephraim, he did not grant the request of his fellow-tribesmen, but challenged them to go forth and drive out the Canaanites, and clear the forest land.

Manasseh and Ephraim were troublesome tribes (Isa. 9:21).
But God still loved them. Psalm 60:7:
"Manasseh is mine; Ephraim is my helmet."

---

8. *Survey of the rest of the land* (Josh. 18:1-10). Israel experienced a happy and climactic day! The whole body of Israelites gathered at Shiloh, and set up the Tent of Meeting (the tabernacle of Moses) there. No more would they need to carry their tabernacle about in their wanderings.

The location of the town of Shiloh is plainly stated in Scripture (Judg. 21:19). It lies north of Bethel about ten miles, and three miles east of the highway from Bethel to Shechem. It was certainly "off the beaten track" and "out of the way." The choice of Shiloh as the tabernacle site was God's choice. God said of Shiloh, "[There] I first made a dwelling for my Name" (Jer. 7:12; Deut. 12:11).

Probably the very location where the tabernacle was set up at Shiloh has been found. A large (77' × 400') levelled area of bedrock lies on the north side of Tell Shiloh. This place is the only level space near Shiloh large enough to contain the tabernacle and its court. (See *Biblical Archaeology Review*, Nov.–Dec. 1988, pp. 46-52.)

Considerable time seems to have gone by before all the tribes were assigned certain areas to live in. They had become complacent, and lost their zeal to conquer new places. Joshua urged the seven tribes to "take possession of the land" that the LORD had given them. They needed to make a survey of the land not yet assigned to tribes, divide it into seven parts (18:5), write up a description of it (18:6,9), and list the towns in each part. Then Joshua and Eleazar the priest would cast lots (18:8; 19:51) to determine the areas which would be assigned to each tribe.

9. *Territory allotted to Benjamin* (Josh. 18:11-28). The territory of Benjamin lay between the tribe of Judah on its south and Ephraim on its north. It was a small area, approximately twelve miles north to south, and 25 east to west. The city of Bethel lay on the north edge of Benjamin, and Jerusalem on its south edge. Many important towns — like Gibeah, Ramah, Beeroth, and Gibeon — were clustered in the land just north of Jerusalem. (See Joshua 15:7-8 concerning the Valley of Hinnom and En Rogel.)

Twenty six towns in Benjamin are named. They are listed

in two groups: cities in east Benjamin (18:21-24), and then in west Benjamin (18:25-28).

Several of the towns assigned to the Levites were located in Benjamin (Josh. 21:4,17). This seems providential, because the temple was later built at Jerusalem in Benjamin, and the Levites worked in the temple.

About **Benjamin** he said, "Let the beloved of the LORD rest secure in him, for he shields him all day long" (Deut. 33:12).

Most of eastern Benjamin is in the dry Judean wilderness. Its western part is a hard limestone plateau. But its thin reddish soil is fertile, and it receives sufficient (25″) annual rainfall. Deep valleys cut down from its high central watershed toward the west and east.

10. *Allotments for six tribes* (Josh. 19:1-48). Joshua 19 continues the description of the territories assigned to the seven tribes that were slow in possessing their inheritance. The selection of areas was made by Joshua and by Eleazar the priest at Shiloh in the presence of the LORD (19:51).

a. *Simeon* (19:1-9). Simeon had the smallest population in the census in Numbers 26. The Simeonites had been conspicuously involved in the immorality at Ba'al of Peor (Num. 25:14). Simeon received only seventeen towns (with nearby villages), which were *scattered* within the territory of Judah. Beersheba was their major city. Several of the towns of Simeon were also assigned to Judah (Josh. 15:21-31). Perhaps some parts of the towns were inhabited by Simeonites, and some by Judeans.

The Simeonite towns were in the southern Negev desert.

The scattering of Simeon was a fulfillment of the prophecy by Jacob in Genesis 49:5,7: "Simeon and Levi are brothers . . . I will *scatter* them in Jacob, and disperse them in Israel." The Simeonites were eventually absorbed by Judah, so that Beersheba was called "Beersheba in Judah" (1 Kgs. 19:3).

The Simeonites had a harsh cruel character (Gen. 49:5-7; 34:25-31).

b. *Zebulun* (19:10-16). Zebulun was a small but desirable land. Zebulun's territory was in the hills north of the Plain (valley) of Esdraelon (Jezreel) These hills are called Lower Galilee. The area consists of four rows of hills (up to 2000') running east to west, with productive valleys in between. On its western extremity Zebulun did extend south to the south side of the valley of Esdraelon at Jokneam. Jokneam is at an exit from the valley, southward through the Mt. Carmel ridge.

Zebulun was a landlocked tribe, but had openings for exit through valleys in all directions. Perhaps Moses referred to this in Deuteronomy 33:18: "Rejoice, Zebulun, in your going out."

Judge Elon was a Zebulunite (Judg. 12:11). The town of Gath Hepher was in Zebulun. It was the hometown of Jonah the prophet (2 Kgs. 14:25), and lay about three miles northwest of modern Nazareth.

c. *Issachar* (19:17-23). Issachar's inheritance corresponded to the great valley of Jezreel (Esdraelon), except for its west end, which was in Zebulun. On the east end of Zebulun was a five-mile wide valley that extended eastward to the Jordan, and lay along the north side of Mt. Gilboa. This was a natural passageway to the Jordan, along the Brook Harod (Jezreel, or Jalud).

Issachar was a very desirable area, but hilly in the east part. (Note Mt. "Tabor" in 19:22.) Some towns in Issachar were occupied by Manassites (17:11).

d. *Asher* (19:24-31). The territory of Asher occupied the northern coastal plain north of Mt. Carmel. The plain (called the Plain of Akko) is only 5–10 miles wide. East of the plain Asher had land in the volcanic heights of Upper Galilee.

Asher was assigned territory northward as far as the cities of Tyre and Sidon in Phoenicia, but it never conquered that area.

Asher was a small tribe, but productive (Gen. 49:20).

> "Most blessed of sons is **ASHER** . . . and your strength will equal your days" (Deut. 33:24-25).

e. *Naphtali* (19:32-39). Naphtali was in the extreme north of Israel. It lay west of the Jordan River and the Sea of Galilee. Naphtali's eastern portion was in the Jordan valley, with Hazor as its dominating city (Josh. 11:10). The west part of Naphtali was in the heights of Upper Galilee.

Sixteen fortified cities in Naphtali are named. Naphtali was on Israel's northern frontier, and therefore would be the first tribe to be attacked by invasions from Syria or by more distant invaders (like Assyria and Babylon).

Jesus' ministry in Galilee was mostly in the territory of Zebulun and Naphtali (Matt. 4:13-15; Isa. 9:1).

f. *Dan* (19:40-48). Dan was a tribe with a large population, but a small narrow territory. It lay west of Benjamin, and extended westward, sloping down into the coastal plain near Joppa and south.

Dan's territory overlapped land occupied by the Philistines on its south side (as at Ekron and Gath). Though Dan was warlike and contentious (like a coiled serpent — Gen. 49:17), it could not take possession of all its territory. Some Danites therefore sought a more peaceful area to dwell in. They found and captured a town in the far north (in Naphtali) named *Leshem* (also spelled *Laish*). The cruel conquest of this city is related in Judges 18.

Samson was from the tribe of Dan. The towns of Zorah, Eshtaol, and Timnah (Josh. 19:41-42) are mentioned prominently in the story of Samson (Judg. 13:25; 14:1).

Me Jarkon (19:46) could be translated "the waters of the Yarkon." That is a name for the Brook Kanah, just north of Joppa (modern Tel Aviv). Philistines occupied some of that area, as at Tell Qasile by the Yarkon River.

11. *Joshua's inheritance* (Josh. 19:49-51). After all the tribes had been assigned their territories, the Israelites gave to Joshua a town of his own — a richly deserved reward. The LORD had commanded that they do this (Num. 14:24,30), and Joshua had asked for a particular site. Joshua built up the town and settled there. The place was named *Timnath Serah* in the hill country of Ephraim. (Joshua was from Ephraim.) *Timnath* means "allotted portion of"; and *Serah* means *remain-*

ing or *leftover* (possibly *overhanging*). Joshua's town is spelled *Timnath Heres* (by reversing the letters of *Serah*) in Judges 2:9, a name meaning *Portion of the Sun.* Perhaps by changing the name Israel was commemorating the day when Joshua prayed the sun would stand still (10:13). (That event occurred about eight miles south of Timnath Serah.)

12. *Cities of Refuge* (Josh. 20:1-9). Cities of refuge were designated as places of protection for those who accidentally and unintentionally killed a person.

The LORD had commanded Moses to designate six cities as cities for refuge (Num. 35:6, 9-32; Deut. 19:1-13). The law of that time was that a relative of someone who had been killed ("the avenger of blood") was to seek and slay the killer. God made an emphatic distinction between planned murder and accidental manslaughter, though manslaughter brought restrictions on freedom. The manslayer could flee to a city of refuge and remain there safe, as long as he remained inside the city.

Upon the death of the high priest who was serving at the time, the manslayer could return to his former home protected by law from vengeance by relatives of the dead.

The six cities of refuge were dispersed all over the land, so that a manslayer could quickly flee to one nearby. Three were designated east of the Jordan River and three west; and then on each side of Jordan the cities were placed in the north, center and south parts.

CITIES OF REFUGE		
	West of Jordan	**East of Jordan**
North	*Kadesh* (in Naphtali)	*Golan* (in Manasseh)
Center	*Shechem* (in Ephraim)	*Ramoth-Gilead* (in Gad)
South	*Hebron* (in Judah)	*Bezer* (in Reuben)

Jesus is our "city" of refuge (Heb. 6:18). His death has given us freedom from the guilt of *all* our sins — both intentional and unintentional.

13. *Towns for the Levites* (Josh. 21:1-42). The head men of the families of the Levites came to the town of Shiloh to Eleazar the priest, and to Joshua, and to the heads of the other tribes. They requested that towns be given to the Levites, as the LORD had commanded Moses (Num. 35:2-4; Lev. 25:32-34; Josh. 14:3-4).

This request was granted, and 48 cities were assigned to the Levites (21:41). These included the six cities of refuge (Josh. 20). The names of the 48 cities are listed, and also the names of the Levite families that were to live in each city. Pasturelands for the flocks of the Levites were allotted around their cities.

The Levites were the tribe the *priests* came from.

Even those Levites who were not priests were privileged to be servants of the priests (Num. 3:5-9).

Levi was a son of Jacob (Gen. 46:8,11). He had three sons: Kohath, Gershon, and Merari (Ex. 6:16). The priests came from the family of Aaron, which came from the family of Kohath. During the wanderings in the wilderness, the Kohathites had cared for the furniture of the tabernacle (Num. 4:4-12). The Gershonites had cared for the cloth items of the tabernacle (Num. 4:24-26). The Merarites transported the heavy boards, pegs, and posts.

It seems providential that the Kohathite Levites (from which the priests came) received towns in the tribes of Judah, Simeon and Benjamin (21:4, 9-19; 1 Chr. 6:54-61). These tribes' territories were located nearest to Jerusalem, where the temple would be built.

One of the priests' towns in Benjamin was *Anathoth*, a village two miles north of Jerusalem, and home of the prophet Jeremiah (Josh. 21:13-18; Jer. 1:1).

The tribe of *Levi* was to be *scattered* in Israel, as was the tribe of Simeon (Gen. 49:7). Simeon was scattered as a punishment for his cruelty. But Levi redeemed himself by standing with Moses in opposition to the golden calf at Mt. Sinai

(Ex. 32:26-29). They were *scattered* to teach the word of God throughout all the land (2 Chr. 17:8-9; 35:3).

14. *The LORD's triumph completed!* (Josh. 21:43-45). With the completion of the conquest and the allotment of the land to the tribes, it was appropriate to break forth in a paean of praise to the LORD.

The **LORD'S TRIUMPH COMPLETED!** (Josh. 21:43-45)

1. The LORD gave all the land He promised (21:43).
2. The LORD gave them **rest** on every side (21:44; 23:1).
3. The LORD handed over all their enemies.
4. The LORD fulfilled ALL his good promises (21:45).
   "Give thanks to the LORD" (Ps. 105:1).

Though the LORD gave Israel a "rest" in the promised land (21:44; 22:4), the LORD said later in Psalm 95:11, "They shall never enter my *rest*." Their *rest* therefore involved more than a land to live upon. The true rest consisted of fellowship with God. The apostle Paul said, "There remains, then, a Sabbath-rest for the people of God" (Heb. 4:9-11). Jesus spoke of the *rest* He would give us (Matt. 11:28). Revelation 14:13 speaks of a future *rest* for the dead who die in the Lord.

15. *The eastern tribes return home* (Josh. 22). When the promised land had been conquered, and the land had been assigned to the tribes, Joshua summoned to Shiloh the men of the tribes of Reuben, Gad, and the half-tribe of Manasseh. Nearly seven years previously these men had left their wives and children east of the Jordan, and had come across the river with the other tribes to help them conquer the lands west of the Jordan (Josh. 1:12-18; Num. 32:1-27).

Joshua praised the men of the eastern tribes for their obedience and sacrificial service (22:3). He also warned them to be very careful to obey the law that Moses gave. Keeping the law was their most important duty (23:6). Joshua dismissed them to return to their homes with great wealth and booty (22:8). Their return would be a happy, emotional one; but it would be hard to readjust to family members they had been separated from for several years.

> Sometimes we must forsake father and mother, wives and children for the service of the Lord (Mark 10:29-30).

As the eastern tribes were returning, they built an "imposing altar" (lit., "an altar great in appearance") by the Jordan River. ("Geliloth" in 22:10 may mean *territories* or *districts*, and not be a proper name.) When the other tribes heard about the altar, they assumed that the tribes east of the Jordan were setting up a worship center of their own, and would not be joining the other tribes at the tabernacle in Shiloh. The Israelites west of the Jordan gathered at Shiloh to go to war against them.

The Israelites sent an investigating team — Phinehas the priest and ten representatives from the western tribes — to question the eastern tribes about the altar. Phinehas was a man who spoke and acted decisively. (See Numbers 25:7-8; Psalm 106:30). His interrogation of the eastern tribes was very sharp (22:16-20). At least the Israelites did not "shoot first and ask questions later." Open confrontation is sometimes a necessity.

Phinehas compared their building the altar to Israel's sin at Baal of Peor (22:17; Num. 25:1-3). He said, "Up to this very day we have not cleansed ourselves from that sin." Israel had a lingering longing for lawlessness that needed to be kept tightly in control.

Phinehas stated a real danger: "If you [eastern tribes] rebel against the LORD today, tomorrow he will be angry with the whole community of Israel" (22:18). When Achan sinned, all the Israelites suffered (22:20; Josh. 7:4-5,11).

The eastern tribes responded graciously, but emphatically. Twice they called upon God as their witness, using three names for God (22:22). They assured the Israelites that their altar was *not* being made for offering sacrifices, but was only a memorial to teach future generations that the Israelites were all ONE people, to offer sacrifices together at God's one sanctuary. The tribes west of the Jordan needed to remember that, as well as those east (22:27-28).

This reply pleased Phinehas and the leaders. When they returned to Canaan (west of the Jordan), their report made the Israelites glad (22:33). Talk of war ceased.

The eastern tribes called their altar *'Ed*, a Hebrew word meaning "Witness" or "Testimony." It was "a witness between us that the LORD is God" (22:34).

Because the eastern tribes were on Israel's frontier with foreign nations, they were exposed in later centuries to invasions, both by armies, and by temptations to worship the gods of their neighbors. The Ammonites to the east worshiped Molech, and the Israelites practiced the same worship (2 Kgs. 23:10).

Questions on Section C
The Land Divided among the Twelve Tribes (Josh. 13–22)

1. What were the three principal areas that were not conquered by Joshua? (13:2-5)
2. How many tribes received inheritance in the land west of the Jordan? (13:7)
3. Which three tribes received land east of the Jordan? (13:8,32)
4. Which tribe received no inheritance of land? (13:14,33) What was the inheritance of this tribe? (13:33)
5. From the rim of what gorge and northward was the tribe of Reuben located? (13:15-16)
6. Which tribe's territory lay east of the Jordan, and north up to the end of the Sea of Kinnereth (Galilee)? (13:24-27)
7. What is another name for the territory of the half-tribe of Manasseh (east of Galilee)? (13:29-31)
8. How were the areas to be assigned to each tribe determined? (14:2; 18:8-10)
9. What had Moses promised to Caleb? (14:9)
10. How old was Caleb when the land was divided? (14:10)
11. What city was given to Caleb? What was its former name? (14:13-15)
12. Whom did Caleb drive out of this city? (15:14)
13. Who took the city of Debir? What was his reward for taking it? (15:15-17)

14. What did Caleb's daughter ask for? (15:19)
15. The north border of Judah ran along the south edge of what city? (15:8)
16. What people occupied Jerusalem? Were they driven out?(15:63)
17. Whose names were given to the two allotments for Joseph's inheritance? (16:1, 4)
18. Which tribe had territory touching Jericho on its south side, and had the Kanah ravine as part of its north border? (16:5-8)
19. From what city did the Ephraimites not dislodge the Canaanites? (16:10)
20. Which son of Manasseh received Gilead and Bashan east of the Jordan? Why? (17:1)
21. What man of the tribe of Manasseh had daughters that inherited his land? (17:3-4)
22. Which tribe had territory near Shechem and south to the Kanah Ravine? (17:7-9)
23. What cities did Manasseh have within the tribes of Issachar and Asher? (17:11)
24. What people lived in those towns? (17:12-13)
25. Which tribes complained about the size of the lands allotted to them? (17:14-17)
26. What did Joshua tell the complaining tribes to do?(17:15,17-18)
27. At what place was the tabernacle set up? (18:1)
28. How many tribes were slow to possess their land? (18:2)
29. Between what two tribes did the territory of Benjamin lie?(18:17)
30. What was the major city in Benjamin? (18:28)
31. Where was the inheritance of the tribe of Simeon? (19:1,9)
32. Which tribe received land around the Valley of Esdraelon, and the town of Gath Hepher? (19:10-13)
33. Which tribe's territory touched Mt. Tabor and went east to the Jordan? (19:17-22)
34. Which tribe had territory in the west part of the land touching Mt. Carmel? (19:24-26)
35. Name two great Phoenician cities that were assigned to the territory of Asher. (19:28-29)
36. Which tribe in the far north had the Jordan river along its east border? (19:32-34)
37. Which tribe had territory around the towns of Zorah and Eshtaol and Joppa? (19:40-46. See Judges 13:24-25.)
38. What town in the far north was occupied by the tribe of Dan? (19:47)

39. What town was given to Joshua? In which tribe's territory was it? (19:49-50)
40. At what place was the land divided? (19:51)
41. What were the cities of refuge used for? (20:1-6)
42. Give the names of the six cities of refuge. Tell what tribe each city was located in. (20:7-8)
43. What was given to the Levites?(21:1-2)
44. How many cities altogether did the Levites get? (21:41)
45. How fully had the promises of God been fulfilled? (21:45)
46. Which tribes had kept a promise? (22:1-3)
47. What were these tribes to be careful to keep when they returned home? (22:5)
48. What did these tribes take back home with them? (22:8)
49. What did these tribes build? Where? (22:10-11)
50. What was the response of the other tribes to this construction? (22:12,16)
51. Who was sent to question the returning tribes? (22:13-14)
52. Why had the returning tribes built the altar? (22:24-28).
53. What was the altar named? (22:34)

Section D
Joshua's Farewell Meetings (Joshua 23–24)

Joshua 23 — Exhortations to Israel's leaders (at Shiloh?)
Joshua 24 — Joshua's covenant for the people (at Shechem)

1. *Exhortations to Israel's leaders* (Joshua 23):
   a. Remember what you have received (23:4).
   b. Obey the law of Moses (23:6).
   c. Finish the conquest of the land (23:5, 9-10).
   d. Don't ally yourselves with the nations or intermarry with them (23:12-13). Don't serve their gods (23:16).
   e. Remember that God's promises never failed (23:14-15).
2. *Assembly with Israel's leaders* (Josh. 23:1-3). "After a long time" seems to refer to the period, perhaps twenty years, after the LORD gave Israel "rest" from the conquests. ("Rest" is a frequent word in the book of Joshua. See Joshua 1:13, 15; 11:23; 14:15; 21:44; 22:4; 23:1.)

The location of the gathering in ch. 23 is not stated. We assume it was at Shiloh, as in 22:9; 21:1; and 19:51. The statement in 24:1 that the later meeting was "at Shechem" suggests that the previous meeting was elsewhere.

"All Israel" was called to this meeting, but it was primarily for their elders, heads, judges, and officers. Exactly the same groups of people gathered for the later meeting (Josh. 24:1).

3. *Obey the law of Moses* (Josh. 23:6-8). Joshua's command to the people to obey the law of Moses was similar to God's command to him at the start of his conquests (1:7). The people had responsibilities to carry out, just as the leaders did.

This command clearly indicates that the Book of the law of Moses existed in Joshua's time. Compare Deuteronomy 31:9-13. Critical Bible scholars often say that the law of Moses was not even written until the time of King Josiah (621 B.C.) or the Babylonian captivity.

4. *Do not associate with the Canaanites* (Josh. 23:7,12-13). Joshua was emphatic that the Israelites should NOT intermarry with the Canaanites or associate with them. Most of all, they must not serve their gods. The religion of the Canaanites was the root of their violent and immoral conduct. Intermarriage with the other nations would become a major cause of apostasy from God. See Judges 3:5-6.

If Israel was unfaithful to God, the LORD would no longer drive out the nations before them (Josh. 23:16). This came to pass (Judg. 2:1-3). The Israelites would perish from the land God gave them. This also came to pass (2 Kgs. 17:15-18).

5. *Final covenant assembly at Shechem* (Josh. 24:1-28). The same groups of people gathered at the assembly at Shechem as those at the earlier meeting (Josh. 23:2; 24:1). But the statement that "Joshua sent the *people* away, each to his own inheritance" (24:28) suggests that a larger assembly of Israelites was present than the leaders only. The people "presented themselves before GOD" (24:1). It was a serious occasion, as well as a happy one.

Shechem was a very historic place. Shechem lay in the center of the land, in a narrow valley between Mt. Ebal and

---

Outline of Joshua's Farewell with Israel (Josh. 24:2-28)

1. Review of Israel's history (24:2-13)
   a. Terah, Abraham, Isaac, Jacob (24:2-4)
   b. Moses and the exodus (24:5-7)
   c. Conquest of the land east of the Jordan (24:8-10)
   d. Conquest of Canaan (24:11-13)
2. Joshua's call for decision (24:14-15)
3. The people's commitment to the LORD (24:16-18)
4. Foreign gods thrown away (24:19-24)
5. Stone of witness set up (24:25-28)

Mt. Gerizim (Josh. 8:33). At Shechem Abraham made his first encampment in the promised land (Gen. 12:6-7). At Shechem Jacob purchased his first land in Canaan (Gen. 33:18-19). The law had been read at Shechem (Josh. 8:30,34); and the place had become "the holy place of the LORD" (Josh. 24:26). Having the gathering at Shechem added much impressiveness to Joshua's assembly with the people.

Joshua 24:2 says that Terah (Abraham's father) and Nahor (his brother) "worshiped other gods" beyond the River (Euphrates). This important information is not told in Genesis. We do not know what influences later caused Abraham's family to turn and serve Yahweh.

Joshua 24:4 mentions God's giving land to *Esau* (Jacob's brother). If God gave Esau land, he would surely give a land to Jacob's descendants. God loves even godless men like Esau.

Some of the Israelites who heard Joshua were old enough to remember being in Egypt and the exodus (probably then sixty years in the past). "You saw with your own eyes" (24:5-7).

The curses that Balaam had sought to lay upon Israel when Balak hired him were a deadly threat to Israel (24:9-10; Num. 22:2-6). The reality of evil powers and demons is taught in Scripture. But the LORD had delivered Israel from Balaam.

The LORD gave Israel a land already developed for human occupation (24:13). This fulfilled God's promise in Deuteronomy 6:10-11.

Joshua reminded Israel, "The citizens (literally, *lords*, or *Ba'als*) of Jericho fought against you, as did also the Amorites . . ." (24:11). This information about Jericho is not reported in Joshua 6.

The LORD had sent the "hornet" ahead of Israel (24:12; Deut. 7:20). The "hornet" refers to all the influences which had weakened the Canaanites before Israel entered their land (Josh. 2:11,24). John Garstang suggested that the "hornet" might refer to Egyptian kings who had repeatedly invaded Canaan in the previous generation (*Joshua-Judges*. London: Constable, 1931, pp. 258-260). King Thutmose III (c. 1480–1448 B.C.) made seventeen invasions into Canaan.

Joshua said, "Now *fear* the LORD" (24:14). It is very necessary to fear the LORD (Eccl. 12:13; Matt. 10:28; 1 Peter 1:17). But those who do fear God should not have fear (1 John 4:18).

It is a painful shock to learn that the Israelites had idols hidden among their possessions (Josh. 24:14,23). Joshua told them to throw these away. Joshua called for an open decision by the people:

> **"Choose for yourselves this day** whom you will serve. . . . But as for me and my household, we will serve the LORD" (Josh. 24:15).

When the people declared they would serve the LORD, Joshua made a *covenant* for the people. Joshua recorded their words in the Book of the Law of God, and set up a large stone as a Witness (testimony). This covenant by Joshua is similar to the covenant Moses made at Mt. Sinai (Ex. 24:3-8). On both occasions the people made an open commitment, and a record was written, and memorials were set up.

6. *Three historic burials* (Josh. 24:29-33):

> a. **JOSHUA** (Josh. 24:28-31)
>
> b. **JOSEPH** (son of Jacob) (Josh. 24:32)
>
> c. **ELEAZAR** (son of Aaron) (Josh. 24:33)

See notes on Joshua 19:50 concerning Timnath Serah, the burial place of Joshua.

Joshua had a powerful influence on the character of the Israelites. They served the LORD all the lifetime of Joshua, and of those elders who had been with Joshua and outlived him (24:31).

Joseph's bones, which the Israelites had brought up from Egypt (Gen. 50:25; Ex. 13:19; Heb. 1:22) were buried at Shechem. Many of his family had been buried at Hebron, but Joseph was buried at Shechem in the tract of land that Jacob had purchased there, probably because that portion of the country was allotted to Joseph's descendants, the children of Ephraim and Manasseh.

Eleazar, Aaron's son, had helped Joshua divide up the land (Num. 34:17; Josh. 19:1). He was buried at Gibeah in the hill country of Ephraim (24:33). *Gibeah* means *hill.* The name often refers to the *Gibeah* of King Saul three miles north of Jerusalem in the territory of Benjamin (1 Sam. 15:34). The location of the Gibeah where Eleazar was buried is not yet known with certainty. The Greek Bible (LXX) adds a verse at the end of 24:33, stating that Phinehas (son of Eleazar) later was also buried at Gibeah (Gr. *Gabaar*).

Questions on Section D
Joshua's Farewell Meetings (Josh. 23–24)

1. What was Joshua's physical condition? (23:1,2)
2. What groups were present at Joshua's assembly? (23:2)
3. What did Joshua ask Israel to remember? (23:4-5)
4. What did Joshua charge Israel to obey? (23:6)
5. What was Israel NOT to do with the Canaanites? (23:7,12)
6. What would the remaining Canaanites be to the Israelites if they did not drive them all out? (23:13)
7. What had NOT failed? (23:14-15)
8. What would happen if Israel violated the covenant of God?(23:16)
9. Where was Joshua's final assembly with Israel? (24:1)
10. What groups were present at this assembly? (24:1)

11. What evil thing had Terah and Nahor done? (24:2)
12. What had the LORD done to the Egyptians? (24:7)
13. Who had attempted to curse Israel, but blessed them? (24:9-10)
14. What had God sent ahead of Israel? (24:12)
15. What choice did Joshua call on the people to make? (24:15)
16. What promise did the people make to Joshua? (24:18)
17. Why did Joshua say the people could not serve the LORD? (24:19-20)
18. What did Joshua command the people to throw away? (24:23)
19. What did Joshua write? Where? (24:25-26)
20. Why did Joshua set up a large stone? (24:26-27)
21. How long did Joshua live? (24:29)
22. Where was Joshua buried? (24:30)
23. How long did Israel serve the LORD? (24:31)
24. Where were Joseph's bones buried? (24:32)
25. What priest died after Joshua's lifetime? (24:33)

Period VII – Period of Judges

From the death of Joshua until the start of King Saul's reign
(Judges, Ruth, 1 Samuel 1-7)

Section A
Introduction to Judges and Ruth

1. The books of Judges and Ruth, along with 1 Samuel 1-7, tell of that period of Bible history we call the *Period of Judges.*

2. The book of Judges begins with the history after the death of Joshua and ends (chronologically) near the death of Samson. This history covers slightly more than 300 years, about 1350-1050 B.C. The period of the judges includes the priesthood of Eli and the administration of Samuel the prophet.

3. The "judges" whose history we read in the book of Judges were not courtroom judges. Rather, they were military deliverers (or guerrilla leaders) who saved their people from invading enemies. After saving the Israelites, these "judges" functioned as the rulers, police, lawgivers, and civil judges, because there were then no civil rulers or kings in Israel.

4. The book of Judges appears to have been written by a *prophet,* because it condemns the evil deeds of leaders in the true spirit of a prophet. It was written before King David captured Jerusalem (1003 B.C.), but apparently after Israel had a king (after 1050 B.C.). (See Judges 1:21; 21:25.) *Samuel,* the prophet of that time, was probably the author of Judges. The Jewish *Talmud* attributes the book to Samuel (*Baba Bathra,* 14b).

5. The book of Judges tells of repeated cycles of history in Israel. The diagram below illustrates these cycles.

6. The history in the book of Judges tells of evil, depressing and repetitive events. The verse that most sharply character-

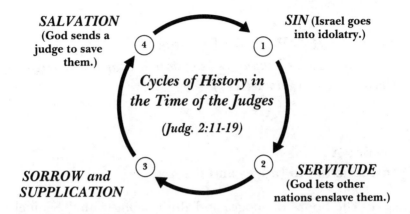

SALVATION
(God sends a
judge to save
them.)

SIN (Israel goes
into idolatry.)

Cycles of History in
the Time of the Judges

(Judg. 2:11-19)

SORROW and
SUPPLICATION

SERVITUDE
(God lets other
nations enslave them.)

izes the entire book of Judges is 21:25: "In those days Israel had no king; everyone did as he saw fit." (Please memorize this verse.)

7. The events described in the last five chapters of Judges occurred *early* in the period of judges, even though they are told last. The fact that these events occurred early during the period is shown by the fact that Judges 18:30 mentions Moses' grandson Jonathan as living when the events occurred. Moses' son was born nearly forty years before the exodus, perhaps about 1470 B.C. (Ex. 2:22). It is improbable that Moses' grandson was living after 1300 B.C. Judges 20:28 also mentions Aaron's grandson *Phinehas* as being alive at the time of the events in Judges 19–21. Another evidence that Judges 17–21 tells of events *early* in the period of judges is that Hosea 10:9 refers to the sin at Gibeah (described in Judges 19) as the *beginning* of Israel's sins in the land. Also, in Judges 20:47 we learn that the tribe of Benjamin was reduced to 600 men by warfare during the period of judges. But by the time of Kings Saul and David enough years had passed that Benjamin had increased back to many thousands (1 Chr. 12:29).

8. The book of Ruth gives a lovely story of one family that lived in the time of the judges. The love and goodness described in Ruth make a welcome contrast to the ugliness of much of Judges. The book gives a marvelous picture of

family affection and devotion. (Memorize Ruth 1:16-17.)

The book of Ruth shows God's wonderful grace in accepting Gentiles into His chosen nation of Israel. Ruth, the Moabite foreigner, became the great-grandmother of King David. The book also has value because it tells the names of the chosen line of Abraham's descendants from Judah's son Perez through David, who became king. The author of Ruth is unknown, but he probably wrote during King David's reign.

9. *Outline of Judges*. (Please memorize this outline.)

I. Events and conquests after Joshua died (1:1–2:5)

II. History of the judges (2:6–16:31)

  A. Cycles of history during the period of judges (2:6–3:6)

  B. The 7 oppressions and 13 judges (3:7–16:31)

1. Oppression by Mesopotamia	(1) Othniel (3:8-11)
2. Oppression by Moab	(2) Ehud (3:12-20)
3. Attack by Philistines	(3) Shamgar (3:31)
4. Oppression by Canaan	(4) Deborah (chs. 4–5)
5. Oppression by Midian	(5) Gideon (chs. 6–8)
	(6) Abimelech (ch. 9)
	(7) Tola (10:2)
	(8) Jair (10:1-5)
6. Oppression by Ammon	(9) Jephthah (10:6–12:7)
	(10) Ibzan (12:8-10)
	(11) Elon (12:11-12)
	(12) Abdon (12:13-15)
7. Oppression by Philistia	(13) Samson (chs. 13-16)

III. Events showing conditions in the time of the judges (chs. 17–21, and the book of Ruth)

  A. The idolatry of Micah (ch. 17)

  B. Migration of the tribe of Dan (ch. 18)

  C. Crime and civil war in Benjamin (chs. 19–21)

  D. The story of Ruth (Ruth 1–4)

10. The *chronology of the judges*. The chronology of this period is difficult. Several facts must be fitted together:

a. In Judges 11:26 there is the statement by judge Jephthah that Israel had occupied the towns of Heshbon, Aroer and others nearby for three hundred years before the Ammonites took over the area. Jephthah made this statement near the start of his judgeship. Israel had come into the Heshbon area in the fortieth year of their wanderings with Moses (1406 B.C.; Num. 21:25). Therefore Jephthah must have become judge *after* 1106 B.C.

b. 480 years elapsed between the exodus from Egypt (1446 B.C.) and the fourth year of King Solomon (966 B.C.) (1 Kgs. 6:1). The judges fit into this period of 480 years. The apostle Paul mentions this period as being about 450 years (Acts 13:19-21).

c. Besides the history told in Judges, several additional events must be fitted into this 480-year period. These include four years of Solomon's reign, the forty years of David's reign (1 Kgs. 2:11), forty years of Saul's reign (Acts 13:21), approximately 20 years of Samuel's judgeship (1 Sam. 7:1; 14:18), the lifetimes of Joshua and the faithful elders after Canaan was conquered (Josh. 24:31), the seven years of the conquest, and the 40 years of wandering in the wilderness. These events occupied more than 150 years.

d. The book of Judges contains many statements telling how many years each conqueror of Israel oppressed them, and how many years of peace Israel had after each judge delivered them. (See 3:8,11, 14,30; 4:3; 5:31; 6:1; 8:23; 9:23; 10:2,3,8; 12:7,9,11,14; 13:1; 15:20; 16:31.) When added together, these total 410 years.

It is obvious that if 410 years is added to the 150 years filled by other known events that we have far more years to account for than the 480 years allowed by 1 Kings 6:1. We accept the Bible as true. How can we solve this difficulty?

e. Some interpreters have tried to explain the problem by saying that the numbers of years assigned for each period are rounded off or imprecise, because many numbers end in zeroes, like 20 or 40 (Judg. 3:11; 4:3; 5:31; 8:28; 13:1; 15:20; 16:30). But not all the numbers end in zeroes (3:14; 9:22; 10:2,3; 12:9); and those numbers which do could be the exact numbers.

f. The explanation of the chronological difficulties in Judges seems to be that some of the judges judged at the same time, though in different tribal areas; or at least they had overlapping judgeships. Judges 10:7 hints that the Ammonite oppression (associated with Jephthah) was near the same time as the Philistine oppression that Samson fought against in another area. Also the phrase "after him" (12:8,11,13) does not necessarily mean "after one judge had died," but may mean "after his judgeship was underway." The early judges (Othniel through Abimelech) are said to have served as judges one after another; but the judges Tola through Samson probably overlapped one another by several years. A list of suggested dates for the judges is given below (Sec. h).

g. There appears to be a correlation between the history in Judges and the history of Egypt and the other nations that lived around Israel. The periods when Israel had peace were the periods when the Egyptians or Hittites had strong rulers and kept the small nations around them in submission. (See M.F. Unger, *Archaeology & O.T.*, ch. 16.) These small nations (like Moab and Midian) oppressed Israel whenever they could get away with it. When the big nations did not control the small predatory peoples, these oppressed Israel. Probably the big nations thought they were doing this by their own power, not knowing that God was using them either to punish Israel, or to protect Israel from small predatory countries around them.

h. Dates of the judges and related events:

(1) Wilderness wanderings of Israel — 1446–1406 B.C.

(2) Conquest of Canaan (7 yrs.) — 1406–1399.

(3) Peace following Joshua's death — 1399–1389 (?)

(4) Oppression by Aram-Naharaim (Mesopotamia) — 1389–1381 (8 yrs., Judg. 3:8)

(5) Peace under Othniel — 1381–1341 (40 yrs., Judg. 3:11)

(6) Moabite oppression by Eglon — 1341–1323 (18 yrs., Judg. 3:14)

347

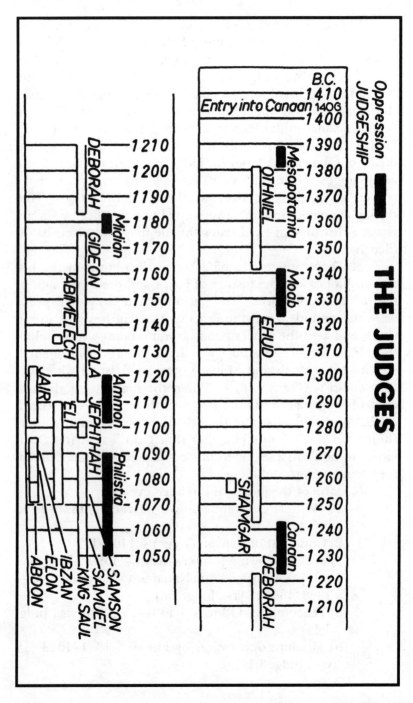

(7) Peace under Ehud — 1323-1243 (80 yrs., Judg. 3:30)

(8) Oppression by Canaanites — 1243-1223 (20 yrs., Judg. 4:3)

(9) Peace under Deborah — 1223-1183 (40 yrs., Judg. 5:31)

(10) Oppression by Midianites — 1183-1176 (7 yrs., Judg. 6:1)

(11) Peace under Gideon —1176-1136 (40 yrs., Judg. 8:28)

(12) Abimelech — 1136-1133 (3 yrs., Judg. 9:22)

(13) Tola and Jair — 1133-1110 (Tola 23 yrs. and Jair 22, Judg. 10:1-5. Jair is said to have come *after* Tola (10:3). But probably both of them served during part of the Ammonite oppression from which Jephthah delivered Israel.)

(14) Oppression by Ammonites — 1120-1102 (18 yrs., Judg. 10:8)

(15) Jephthah — 1102-1096 (6 yrs., Judg. 12:7)

(16) Ibzan, Elon, Abdon — 1096-1071 (25 yrs., Judg. 12:8-15). These three judges probably served during part of the Philistine oppression with which Samson was involved.

(17) Samson — 1090-1070 (20 yrs., Judg. 16:31). Samson is said to have judged Israel 20 years *in the days of the Philistines* (Judg. 15:30). The Philistine oppression lasted 40 years (Judg. 13:1). It appears that the first twenty years of the Philistine oppression were the same years as the twenty years of Samson's judgeship, and also the time when Eli was judge. The Philistine oppression of Israel did not truly cease until Samuel's victory at Ebenezer (1 Sam. 7), shortly before Saul became king. Samuel's judgeship lasted about 20 years. (Compare 1 Sam. 7:2; 13:1; 14:18.) This period probably constituted the remaining twenty years of the Philistine oppression.

(18) Eli — 1110-1070. Probably contemporary with Samson.

(19) Samuel — 1070-1050 B.C.

Questions on Section A
Introduction to Judges and Ruth

1. What period of Bible history do the books of Judges and Ruth tell of?
2. With what events does Judges begin and end?
3. How many years of history are covered in Judges?
4. What was the nature of the service the judges did for Israel?
5. Who was the probable author of the book of Judges?
6. What are the four (or five) words that describe the cycles of history during the period of judges?
7. What type of ruler did Israel not have during the period of judges? (21:25)
8. Did the events told in the last five chapters of Judges happen late in the period of judges or early?
9. How does the book of Ruth contrast with the history in Judges?
10. What genealogical information is given in the book of Ruth?
11. How many years elapsed from the exodus until King Solomon's fourth year? (1 Kgs. 6:1)
12. What is the difficulty we have with the chronology in Judges?
13. What is the possible explanation of this difficulty?
14. How does the history in Judges seem to relate to the history of Egypt and other nations around Israel?
15. What other judge led Israel during the time when Samson was judge?

Section B
The Earlier Judges — Othniel to Deborah (Judges 1–5)

1. The *period of judges* extended from the death of Joshua to the choice of Saul as king. It was a time of great anarchy and distress. Our principal source of information about it is the book of *Judges*, to which *Ruth* is a supplement. The last five chapters (17–21) of Judges tell two or three ugly examples of idolatry and anarchy during the period of judges.

2. *General summary of the period.* The history of the whole period of judges is summed up in Judges 2:6–3:5. After Joshua died, the people remained faithful to the LORD only as long as that generation lasted which had seen all the great things the LORD had done for Israel (2:7). The next generation did not know the LORD nor what he had done for Israel

---

WHY STUDY THE JUDGES ?

1. They are very *interesting* people.
2. They are named in the New Testament as *examples of faith.* (Heb. 11:32). Some were bad examples we should avoid imitating (1 Cor. 10:6).
3. The book of Judges *continues the story* of God's eternal program of redeeming (rescuing) Israel and mankind.
4. The judges *illustrate God's astounding longsuffering;* and also they illustrate God's punishments upon evildoers.
5. The judges are useful *illustrations* of human character and behavior. (They are a good study in psychology.)
6. *Archaeological remains* from the time of the judges require knowledge of the history in Judges to be interpreted correctly.
7. The period of judges *shows man's need for a righteous king* (Judg. 21:25). Happily for us, we have a righteous king, JESUS (Isa. 32:1).
8. The story of the judges is part of God's Scripture, and *all scripture is profitable* (2 Tim. 3:16).

(2:10). They forsook the LORD, and turned and served the Ba'als and the Ashtoreths (2:13).

Ba'al was the Phoenician and Canaanite god of rain, storm, and fertility. The name *Ba'al* means *lord* or *master.* It was applied to the gods of many local worship centers, for example, Ba'al-Gad, Ba'al-Peor, Ba'al-Zebub, etc. *Ashtoreth* was one of the Canaanite goddesses of love, sex, and war. Other similar deities were named Anath, Astarte, and Asherah. These were associated with Baal as wife, sister, or lover. Their worship included acts of prostitution.

The LORD punished Israel's idolatry by causing them to be defeated in battle and raided by the nations around Israel (2:15). But though they were punished, they were not forsaken by God. God raised up *judges,* who saved them out of the hands of these raiders. When the judges died, the people went back to serving other gods again.

351

The LORD was very angry because of this (2:20), and said that He would NOT drive out all the Canaanite "nations" that still lived in the land (2:21). God's foreknowledge that Israel would go into idolatry had caused God not to drive out all the Canaanites during the conquests of Joshua (Judg. 3:1-2). The Canaanites were to remain in the land as *tests* of Israel's faith. The presence of these idolaters would force the Israelites to take an open stand as to what god they would serve.

Three principal areas in Canaan remained unconquered as the period of judges began. They were (1) the southern coastal plains ruled by five lords of major *Philistine* cities; (2) the northern coastal area of Phoenicia around Sidon; and (3) the Lebanon mountains east of Phoenicia (Judg. 3:1-3).

3. *Conquests after Joshua's death* (Judg. 1:1-2:4). After Joshua's death the individual tribes of Israel continued the conquest of the land, with individual tribes attempting to conquer territory near their assigned areas. This was different from Joshua's conquests, which were campaigns by all the tribes together to conquer large areas. Generally the attempts to conquer more areas after Joshua's death were ineffective. The tribe of *Judah*, assisted by the Simeonites, struck down ten thousand men at a place named Bezek (Judg. 1:4). (The location of Bezek is uncertain. Probably it was north of Judah, near Mt. Gilboa.) Adoni-bezek (meaning the *lord of Bezek*) was captured. The Israelites cut off his thumbs and big toes, because he had done the same cruelty to seventy other petty "kings" of Canaanite towns. Then he had amused himself by watching these mutilated "kings" attempt to pick up scraps of food under his table (1:7). He confessed that God had paid him back for what he had done to them.

This event shows that Canaan was NOT a united nation, but a land of warring, independent city-states. Also it shows the cruelty of some Canaanites. Adoni-bezek died at Jerusalem, which the men of Judah captured at least partially, though only temporarily (1:21). (Josephus says the Israelites captured only the the lower part of Jerusalem, not its upper part. *Ant.* V,2,2.)

The men of Judah, led by the faithful old spy Caleb, also captured the city of Hebron (Kiriath Arba) (Judg.1:10,20).

CALEB — *His faith led him to victory!*
(Num. 13:30; Josh. 15:13-14; Judg. 1:10-11)

Following the capture of Hebron, Caleb's nephew Othniel captured the town of Debir (Kiriath Sepher). (Debir was probably located five miles south of Hebron, at ruins now named Khirbet Rabud.)

For this brave act Othniel received as his reward Acsah, the daughter of Caleb, as his wife (Judg. 1:13). Judah defeated the cities of Gaza, Ashkelon, and Ekron, but could not hold them. (Later these cities would become Philistine centers.) Judah could not capture the "plains" because the inhabitants had iron war chariots (1:19). The "plain" referred to is probably the coastal plains west of Judah (1:34).

Judges 1:16 reports that the descendants of Moses' father-in-law (Jethro), moved away from Jericho to the desert of Judah near Arad (which is east of Beersheba). Jethro is called the *Kenite* (probably meaning "smith"). Some from his family had come into Canaan with the Israelites. They were involved in important events later (Judg. 4:11,17; 5:24).

Other conquests and other failures to conquer are described in Judges 1:21-36. The Benjamites could not dislodge the Jebusites from Jerusalem (1:21). The "house of Joseph" (the tribe of Ephraim, perhaps with Manasseh) captured the city of Bethel (Luz), which was located about ten miles north of Jerusalem. A man from Bethel who showed the Israelites how to get into the city was afraid to go back there, and went to the far-off land of the Hittittes (in Asia Minor!) to build a town.

Five of the tribes — Manasseh, Ephraim, Zebulun, Asher, Naphtali — failed to dislodge the Canaanites from major cities in their assigned territories. The Amorites, a Canaanite group, continued to control several large areas. These included the coastal plains, and the southern area around the

Scorpion Pass (called *Akkrabim* in Hebrew, and located about 30 miles southeast from Beersheba) to Sela (the cliff, or Petra, south of the Dead Sea), and beyond.

The LORD's reproof of Israel (2:1-5). Israel's lack of sufficient faith to conquer the land caused the "angel of the LORD" to come to their camp and announce that he would not drive out all the Canaanites from before them (2:3,21). This caused the people to weep, and they called the place *Bokim*, meaning "weepers." Its location is uncertain, perhaps near Gilgal. (The "Angel of the LORD" [Judg. 2:1] seems to have been the LORD Himself. We believe He was the preincarnate Word, who later came as Jesus.)

4. *Summary of the period of judges* (Judg. 2:6–3:6). (See section 2 above.) The period is an illustration of man's failure to take hold of God's promised power. The Israelites failed to conquer the cruel, immoral Canaanites in the land, and even intermarried with them (Judg. 3:6). The period illustrates people's need for a righteous king; but even a righteous king can rule only if the people are in submission to the rule of God.

5. *The first three judges* (Judg. 3:7-31). The missions of most of the judges were preceded by a period of oppression under a foreign conqueror.

– The Book of Judges–
The Book of the ACTS of the Holy Spirit

1. The Spirit of the LORD came upon Othniel (Judg. 3:10).
2. The Spirit of the LORD came upon Gideon (6:34).
3. The Spirit of the LORD came upon Jephthah (12:29).
4. The Spirit of the LORD came upon Samson (14:19).

---

a. *Othniel, the first judge* (Judg. 3:7-11; 1:13). The first foreign invader of Israel was Cushan-Rishathaim, king of Aram-Naharaim (*Aram of the two rivers,* i.e., Mesopotamia). Aram-Naharaim was the area around Haran that had been the home of Abraham's family (Gen. 24:10). Cushan-Rishathaim is not yet known from historical sources besides the Bible and Josephus (who calls him "king of the Assyrians"). Possibly he was a Hittite commander, because the Hittites controlled northern Mesopotamia until about 1200 B.C. When the Spirit of the LORD came upon Othniel (Caleb's nephew), Othniel delivered Israel and the land had peace forty years (Judg. 1:13).

b. *Ehud, the second judge* (Judg. 3:12-30). Ehud was son of Gera, a Benjamite (Judg. 3:15; 1 Chr. 8:1-6), and was left-handed. Many left-handed warriors came from the tribe of Benjamin (Judg. 20:15-16). Ehud saved Israel from an alliance of Moabites, Ammonites, and Amalekites (3:13. See Exodus 17:8-15 for information about the Amalekites). Eglon, king of the Moabites, established his control center at Jericho, called the "City of Palms." (Many date palm trees are still cultivated there.) After eighteen years of subjection, Israel was delivered by *Ehud*, who thrust a long dagger (about a foot and a half, or cubit, long) and its handle into the belly of King Eglon, who was a very fat man. Then the Israelites struck down about ten thousand Moabites, and the land had peace for eighty years.

Throughout the story Ehud is not called a judge, but only a deliverer (3:15). Even so, he led the Israelites in the battle, and almost certainly functioned as judge after his victory.

Ehud's deceit and assassination of Eglon may make some Christian believers uneasy. Second Corinthians 10:4: "The weapons we fight with are not the weapons of the world." We must remember that God has no pleasure in the death of the wicked (Ezek. 18:23). But wicked people like Eglon who will not cease their wickedness will all perish, often in violent ways.

c. *Shamgar, the third judge* (Judg. 3:31). Shamgar displayed great strength and speed by smiting down six hundred Philistines with only an oxgoad as his weapon. There is no reason to call him a judge, except that he is mentioned third in the record of judges who saved Israel. His heroic act (or acts) was a personal act of prowess; and he is not called a judge. Probably his deeds occurred during the eighty years of peace of Ehud. The next oppression is said to have begun

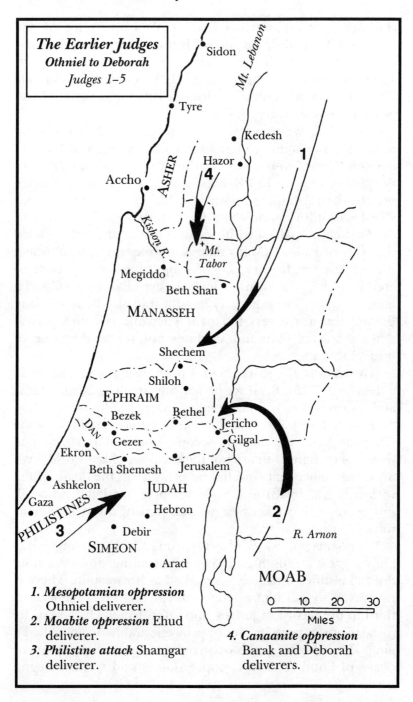

The Earlier Judges
Othniel to Deborah
Judges 1–5

Sidon

Mt. Lebanon

Tyre

Kedesh

1

ASHER

Hazor

4

Accho

Kishon R.

+Mt. Tabor

Megiddo

Beth Shan

MANASSEH

Shechem

Shiloh

EPHRAIM

Bezek

Bethel

Jericho

DAN

Gezer

Gilgal

Ekron

Beth Shemesh

Jerusalem

Ashkelon

JUDAH

Gaza

Hebron

PHILISTINES

2

3

Debir

R. Arnon

SIMEON

Arad

MOAB

1. *Mesopotamian oppression*
   Othniel deliverer.
2. *Moabite oppression* Ehud
   deliverer.
3. *Philistine attack* Shamgar
   deliverer.

0   10   20   30
Miles

4. *Canaanite oppression*
   Barak and Deborah
   deliverers.

"after Ehud died" (4:1). The fact that Shamgar's father was named *Anath*, the name of an immoral Canaanite goddess, suggests that idolatry had infected his grandparents.

The Philistines, whom Shamgar fought, were becoming a severe "thorn in the side" of the Israelites on their southwest frontier. They immigrated into Israel from the Mediterranean islands around Crete in huge numbers after about 1200 B.C. They became Israel's most fearsome enemy by the time of Samson and Samuel. But some Philistines had already come into the land by the time of Ehud (1323–1243 B.C.) and Shamgar. (A few lived in the land back in the time of Abraham and Isaac.)

d. *Deborah* and *Barak* (Judg. 4, 5). The first three oppressions during the period of judges were from foreign oppressors. But after Ehud died, the Canaanites whom the Israelites had not driven out of their land became powerful, and cruelly oppressed the Israelites for twenty years, until they cried to the LORD for help. The Canaanites were led by *Jabin*, king of the city of Hazor. About 150 years previously Joshua had defeated another Jabin, king of Hazor, and probably an ancestor of this Jabin (Josh. 11:1-14). Jabin's military commander was *Sisera* from Harosheth Haggoyim (meaning Harosheth of the Gentiles). This place was near the Kishon River, probably in the vicinity of Megiddo, and thus only about ten miles from his battle place with Barak. Deborah was the only woman judge, and also a prophetess. She spoke messages revealed directly to her by God (Judg. 4:6). Deborah's place for holding court was under a palm tree about ten miles north of Jerusalem, between Ramah and Bethel.

Prophetesses in the Bible include: 1. Miriam (Ex. 15:20); 2. Deborah; 3. Huldah (2 Kgs. 22:14); 4. Nodiah (Neh. 6:14); 5. Wife of Isaiah (Isa. 8:3); 6. Anna (Luke 2:36); 7. Philip's daughters (Acts 21:9); 8. "Jezebel" (Rev. 2:20).

DEBORAH — Her name means "honey-bee." She was busy as a bee — being prophetess, wife, judge, and battle leader.

Conditions in Israel in Deborah's time were dangerous! In her song following her victory Deborah sang that "In the days of Shamgar . . . the roads were abandoned; travelers took to the winding paths. Village life in Israel ceased . . . they chose new gods, [and] war came to the city gates" (5:6-8). Deborah called for Barak to come lead a battle against the Canaanites. Barak lived in Kadesh near the Sea of Galilee, in the tribe of Naphtali, over a hundred miles from Deborah's base. He must have been a well-known warrior. The New Testament lists Barak as one of the heroes of faith (Heb. 11:32).

Barak was unwilling to lead the battle unless Deborah accompanied him (Judg. 4:9). This reveals much about the honored place of some women in the Old Testament.

TWO WOMEN — **Deborah** & **Jael** —
won the battle honors instead of the man Barak.

Barak assembled ten thousand men on the slopes of Mt. Tabor. Tabor is 1,843 feet high, and stands out prominently at the northeast corner of the plain of Esdraelon (often called Jezreel), southwest of the Sea of Galilee. Tabor's sides are steep, rocky, and brush-covered — very safe from the Canaanites' iron chariots of war (4:13). At the foot of Tabor on its west side the broad plain (about ten miles across) lies in clear view. It is called the plain of Megiddo (2 Chr. 35:22) — or Armageddon. The little brook Kishon runs along the south edge of the plain. The gentle slope of this brook causes slow runoff of water, so that the plain becomes quite muddy in the winter (Carl Rasmussen, *Zondervan NIV Atlas*, p. 36).

A sudden storm seems to have struck as Barak's men came down the mountain to attack Sisera's troops in the plain. The little brook became a torrent. "From the heavens the stars fought . . . against Sisera. The river Kishon swept them away, the age-old river, the river Kishon" (Judg. 5:20-21). The chariots were bogged down in mud. "Then thundered the horses' hoofs — galloping, galloping go his mighty steeds" (5:22). Barak pursued the chariots and army westward clear back to Sisera's home village. Not a man of Sisera's troops was left. Years later this slaughter was remembered in Psalm 83:9-10: "Do . . . as you did to Sisera and Jabin at the river Kishon, who perished at Endor and became like refuse (lit., *dung*) on the ground."

Sisera found his chariot stuck in mud. He dismounted and fled on foot. In panic he ran about twenty-five miles to Kedesh, a village near the southwest corner of the Sea of Galilee. There in an exhausted condition, he sought a hiding place at the tent of Heber the Kenite. (See Judges 1:16.) Jael, the wife of Heber, gave Sisera milk to drink and then drove a tent peg through his temple as he slept. Barak in pursuit of Sisera came by. Jael went out to meet Barak and to show him the dead body of Sisera. Faith — even imperfect faith — had triumphed.

The victory *Song of Deborah* occupies Judges chapter five. The song is vivid, and "pulls no punches."

Outline of Song of Deborah (Judg. 5)

1. Praise to the LORD for victory (5:2-5)
2. Dangerous conditions before the battle (5:6-11)
3. Praise for brave fighters and scorn for the slackers (5:12-18, 23)
4. The battle (5:19-22)
5. Praise of Jael (5:23-27)
6. Sarcastic mocking poem about Sisera's fate (5:28-31)

In a sarcastic poem at the close of Deborah's song, Deborah describes Sisera's mother (probably old) as looking out her window, worrying why her son (probably a big, burly fighter) was taking so long to get home. The mother's "wise" women reassure her: "You know how men are. After the battle they are collecting the spoil; and each man has found a girl or two!" But Sisera's decaying body and peg-shattered head were not coming home! Deborah concludes: "So may all your enemies perish, O LORD!"

Should we condemn the deceit of Ehud and the violence of Jael? Probably not. Neither of them actually lied about their intentions, even if they did not tell everything. Jael herself was requested by Sisera to lie to save his life. We must remember that the Bible does not always approve the morality of all the acts that it records, not even of acts done by great servants of God. Nor should we forget the years of stealing and killing done by evil men like Eglon and Sisera. They reaped what they had sown.

Questions on Section B
The Earlier Judges — Othniel to Deborah (Judg. 1–5)

1. How long did the people remain faithful to the LORD after Joshua died? (Judg. 2:7)
2. Who was *Ba'al*? *Ashtoreth*? (2:13). What does the name *Ba'al* mean?
3. What punishment did the LORD send upon Israel for their idolatry? (2:14)
4. Who saved Israel from those who raided them? (2:16)
5. For what purpose did the LORD allow the Canaanites to remain unconquered in the land? (2:22)
6. Where were the three principal unconquered areas at the time when the period of judges began? (3:3)
7. How did the battles to conquer Canaan after Joshua died differ from the campaigns during the life of Joshua?
8. Which tribe was sent up first to fight the Canaanites after Joshua died? (1:1-2)
9. What was done to Adoni-bezek? Why? (1:6-7)
10. Did Judah take Jerusalem? (1:8). Did the Israelites keep control of it? (1:21)
11. What warrior took Hebron? (Josh. 15:13; Judg. 1:11)
12. Who was Acsah? (1:12)
13. Who took the town of Debir? What was his reward?(1:12-13)
14. Who were the Kenites? (1:16)
15. Where did the Kenites go from, and go to? (1:16)
16. Why could Judah not drive out the inhabitants of the plains? (1:19)
17. What people controlled Jerusalem? (1:21)
18. Who captured the town of Bethel? (1:22)
19. Who built a new city he called *Luz*? Where did he build it? (1:26)
20. What six tribes did not drive out the inhabitants from their territories? (1:21-34)
21. What message did the angel of the LORD give Israel? (2:1-3)

22. What does the name *Bokim* mean? What happened there? (2:4-5)
23. What forbidden marriages occurred? (3:6; Deut. 7:1-4)
24. Of what land was Cushan-Rishathaim king? (3:8)
25. Who delivered Israel from Cushan-Rishathaim? (3:9)
26. Name the king of Moab (3:12). What was his physical appearance? (3:17)
27. What city did the Moabites and others take over? (3:13)
28. Who was left-handed? (3:15)
29. Who slew Eglon? Where? (3:20-21)
30. Where did Israel cut off the Moabites from escaping?(3:28)
31. What people did Shamgar fight? With what weapon? How many did he slay? (3:31)
32. Near what date did the Philistines immigrate into Canaan in large numbers?
33. Who was king of the Canaanites? (4:2)
34. Who was captain of the army of the Canaanites?(4:2)
35. How many iron chariots did the Canaanites have?(4:3)
36. What was Deborah's occupation? Where did she live?(4:4-5)
37. Whom did Deborah call to deliver Israel? (4:6)
38. To what mountain was he sent? (4:6)
39. Why did a woman get the honor a man might have won? (4:8-9)
40. Where had Heber the Kenite moved to? (4:11)
41. Near what river did Israel fight the Canaanites? (4:13)
42. To what place did Sisera flee? (4:17, 11)
43. Who met Sisera? (4:18)
44. How did Sisera die? (4:21)
45. What actions by travellers showed that conditions in Israel were dangerous in the time of the judges? (5:6)
46. Which tribes did Deborah praise for helping in the battle? (4:14-15, 18)
47. Which tribes were scorned for not helping in battle? (4:16-17)
48. What had helped Israel defeat Sisera? (5:20-21)
49. In her song what did Deborah picture the mother of Sisera as worrying about? (5:28)

Section C
The Later Judges — Gideon to Samson (Judges 6–16)

1. *Oppression by the Midianites* (Judg. 6:1-10). After the peace won for Israel by the victory of Deborah and Barak, Israel again did evil in eyes of the LORD. The worship of Ba'al

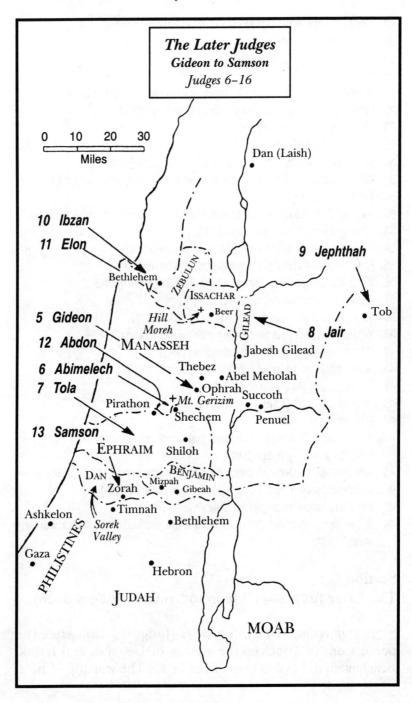

The Later Judges
Gideon to Samson
Judges 6–16

0   10   20   30
Miles

Dan (Laish)

10 Ibzan
11 Elon

9 Jephthah

Bethlehem

ZEBULUN

ISSACHAR

Beer

Tob

5 Gideon

Hill
Moreh

GILEAD

12 Abdon

MANASSEH

8 Jair

Jabesh Gilead

6 Abimelech

Thebez

Abel Meholah

7 Tola

Ophrah

Succoth

Pirathon

Mt. Gerizim

Shechem

Penuel

13 Samson

EPHRAIM

Shiloh

BENJAMIN

DAN

Mizpah

Gibeah

Zorah

Timnah

Bethlehem

Ashkelon

PHILISTINES

Sorek
Valley

Gaza

Hebron

JUDAH

MOAB

was publicly practiced, and the people were eager to declare zeal for the false god (Judg. 6:30). Therefore the LORD delivered them into the hands of their old nomadic enemies from the desert, the Midianites and Amalekites (6:3. Num. 25:17-18; Ex. 17:8). (The Midianites were descendants of Abraham and his wife Keturah [Gen. 25:1]; and the Amalekites were descendants of Esau [Gen. 36:15-16].) For seven years these raiders swept into Israel on camels from across the Jordan "like swarms of locusts" devouring the crops, until the Israelites were utterly impoverished (Judg. 6:5-6).

Israel cried to the LORD, but the LORD rebuked them: "You have not listened to me" (6:10).

Lessons: We, like the Israelites, are all *easily entangled* by sin (Heb. 12:1). If we disown the LORD, He will disown us; and the *consequences are severe* (2 Tim. 2:12).

---

2. *Call of Gideon, the fifth judge* (Judg. 6:11-24). The angel of the LORD (the LORD Himself) appeared to a "mighty warrior" named Gideon, and called him to go and save Israel. Gideon protested that God had apparently neglected or forsaken Israel. But the angel promised to be with Gideon, and said he would strike down all the Midianites. Gideon wanted to bring an offering to the "angel" to prove that he was indeed the angel of the LORD. The angel burned the young goat and the bread Gideon brought. "So Gideon built an altar to the LORD there and called it The LORD is Peace" (Yahweh Shalom; 6:24). This altar still stood at the time the book of Judges was written.

Gideon was from the tribe of Manasseh, and the clan (the extended family) of Abiezer (Josh. 17:2). He humbly said, "My clan is the weakest in Manasseh, and I am the least in my family" (Judg. 6:15). Gideon lived in Ophrah, a village about five miles west of the Hill Moreh (near modern Afula). He was a grown man with at least one son at the time he was called (8:20).

3. *Gideon destroys the altar of Baal* (Judg. 6:25-32). Gideon's mission of delivering Israel had to begin at home! At the house of Gideon's father stood an idol of Baal and a sacred wooden Asherah pole (the emblem of this goddess). God spoke to Gideon (in some manner not described): "Tear down your father's altar." Gideon was a bit fearful, but he and ten men did it that night. The citizens were outraged and ready to kill Gideon. But Gideon's father, Joash, inspired by the faith of his son, asked them: "Are you going to plead Baal's cause? . . . If Baal really is a god, he can defend himself" (6:31). After this Gideon was sometimes called *Jerub-Baal*, meaning "Let Baal fight" for himself. (Some Israelites would not say the name *Baal*, and would substitute for it the word *bosheth*, which means *shame*. Thus Gideon was sometimes called *Jerubbesheth*, meaning "Let the *shameful* one [Baal] fight" for himself [2 Sam. 11:21].)

Special Study
THE ANGEL OF THE LORD

There are several references in the Old Testament to the "Angel of the LORD" that suggest that this angel of the LORD was the LORD (Yahweh) Himself. (Emphasis added on Scriptures.)

a. Genesis 16:10 — The *angel* told Hagar, "*I* will so increase your descendants." Hagar said to him, "You are the *God* who sees me" (16:13).

b. Genesis 22:11-18 — The "*angel* of the LORD" called out to Abraham. The angel spoke again, "Now I know that you fear *God*, because you have not withheld from *me* your son"(22:12).

c. Genesis 31:11-13 — The *angel* of God spoke to Jacob, saying, "I am the *God* of Bethel."

d. Genesis 32:24-30 — Jacob wrestled with a *man* (really an *angel*) who was also *called "God"* (Hosea 12:2-4). Jacob said, "I saw *God* face to face" (Gen. 32:30).

e. Genesis 48:15-16 — Jacob spoke of the *angel* who redeemed him as being identical with *God.*

f. Exodus 3:2 — "The *angel* of the Lord" appeared to Moses at the burning bush; but the words spoken to Moses are attributed to *God* (3:5-6).

g. Exodus 13:21 — The *Lord* went ahead of Israel when they left Egypt. But Exodus 14:19 and Numbers 20:16 indicate that it was an *angel* who went before them.

h. Exodus 23:20-21 — The *angel* that was sent before Israel had power to forgive rebellion and sins, and God's Name was in him! Only *God* has such authority. (See Mark 2:7.)

i. Judges 2:1-5 — The *angel* of the Lord spoke to Joshua and Israel. The *angel* said, "*I* will never break my covenant with you." "*I* will not drive them out before you." Only God could speak in this manner.

j. Judges 6:11-16 — The "angel of the Lord" is specifically called "the Lord" (Yahweh).

The Scripture also records numerous *appearances* of God during the Old Testament age when no angel is mentioned. (1) To Abraham (Gen. 12:7). (2) To Jacob (Gen. 28:13; 32:34). (3) To the elders of Israel (Ex. 24:10). (4) To Isaiah (Isa. 6:1; John 12:37-41). (5) To Ezekiel (Ezek. 1:1).

These appearances are significant, because the Scriptures declare that no man has seen or can see God (Ex. 33:20; John 1:18; 6:46; Col. 1:15; 1 Tim. 6:16; 1 John 4:12). How can these passages be harmonized? We believe that the appearances of the Lord or the angel of the Lord were appearances of that divine One called the Word (John 1:1), who was in the beginning "with God" and later came into the world in the person of Jesus of Nazareth. Note the following passages:

(1) Isaiah 48:16 quotes someone who had spoken openly "from the beginning," and was sent by the Sovereign Lord.

(2) Micah 5:2 prophesied that the ruler to be born in Bethlehem is he "whose origins are from of old." (This could hardly refer to anyone other than Jesus.)

(3) The Lord whom Isaiah saw (Isa. 6:1-5) is specifically identified in John 12:37-41 as Jesus.

(4) God has always revealed Himself through Christ the

Word, "who is at the Father's side" (John 1:18). Even before He was born of Mary, Christ was "in the world," and the world was "made through him," though the world did not recognize Him (John 1:10). The Word Himself had the nature of God, and was "with God" (John 1:1). Jesus said, "Anyone who has seen me has seen the Father" (John 14:9).

(5) If it was Jesus the Word who appeared as the *angel of God* or as *God* during the Old Testament age, then both statements are true, that no man has ever seen God (the Father), but that men truly did see the LORD when they saw the preincarnate Word.

---

4. *Sign of the fleece* (Judg. 6:33-40). Near the very time when Gideon was called, the Midianites and their fellow-raiders descended upon Israel again (6:33). The Midianites seem to have resided mostly in the Sinaitic peninsula and east of the Gulf of Aqaba (at least in the time of Moses; Ex. 2:15-21). But they were nomadic and migrated wherever they could find pasturage.

Gideon's confidence faltered a little, and he asked the LORD to make wet with dew a fleece of wool while the ground around it remained dry. Then he asked that the fleece remain dry while the ground was wet. Heavy dews are common in Israel.

The LORD granted Gideon's requests, but Gideon probably should not have put God to this test. God had already made it quite plain that *He* had spoken. Gideon himself recognized that God might be angered by his request (6:39).

5. *Gideon's victory over Midian* (Judg. 7:1-25).

a. *Gideon chose 300 men* (7:1-8). A great army assembled in response to Gideon's call (6:34-35). Thirty-two thousand gathered by the spring of Harod. (*Harod* means "trembling.") This spring flows from the north foot of Mt. Gilboa, and supplies water for pools nearby and a brook. In plain view to the north six miles away is the ridge called the Hill of Moreh ("Hill of the Teacher"), where 135,000 Midianites were encamped (8:10). God told Gideon to let those who were fearful return home, and 22,000 were honest enough to confess fear, and departed. But the 10,000 who remained were still so many that Israel might boast that its own strength won the battle. Gideon reduced his forces to three hundred men, those who lapped water from their hands at their mouths, rather than going to their knees to drink.

Reducing Gideon's army to three hundred took all day (7:1,9). An all-night battle yet awaited them. Only the most valiant could endure it.

God often wins His battles with just a few brave, faithful people.

---

b. *Final reassurance to Gideon* (7:9-14). God gave Gideon a final reassurance before the battle. With his servant Purah, Gideon slipped into the Midianite camp and overheard a Midianite telling of a dream. The Midianite dreamed of a round loaf of barley bread rolling into their camp and smiting *the* tent (perhaps the chief's tent). He interpreted this as a portent that Gideon would smite Midian (Judg. 7:9-14). Barley was used to make bread only in times of distress or famine because of its somewhat bitter taste.

GIDEON – WITH ONLY 300 MEN *plus God* defeated 135,000 Midianites! (Judg. 8:10)

---

c. *Slaughter of the Midianites* (7:15-25). In the middle of the night Gideon divided his men into three groups, "armed" with ram's horn trumpets (*shophars*) and torches in earthen jars. Breaking their jars and blowing the trumpets, they panicked the Midianite host, which ran in disarray "crying out as they fled." They fled eastward, downwards toward the Jordan. Thousands perished, as the Midianites in the darkness turned their swords on one another. Men of the tribe of Ephraim were summoned to intercept the fleeing Midianites at the fords of the Jordan River, all the way south to Beth Barah (near the Dead Sea) (7:24). The Ephraimites captured and beheaded two Midianite leaders (princes), Oreb (the "Raven") and Zeeb (the "Wolf"). These names may have been emblems on their banners (7:25).

Psalm 55:23 — But you, O God, will bring down the wicked into the pit of corruption; bloodthirsty and deceitful men will not live out half their days. But as for me, I trust in you.

---

6. *Jealousy of Ephraim* (Judg. 8:1-3). The tribe of *Ephraim* complained to Gideon that they had not been allowed to share in the honors of winning the victory over Midian. (Were they pleased that *God* received the honor?) Gideon answered them very politely: "You did more than I did. You captured the Midianite *princes.*" (Proverbs 15:1: "A gentle answer turns away wrath.") We shall hear more of Ephraim's complaints (Judg. 12:1-6).

7. *Pursuit of Midianites beyond the Jordan* (Judg. 8:4-21). Gideon and his 300, now exhausted and lacking supplies, continued their pursuit of the Midianites who had escaped the initial slaughter, and crossed the Jordan. They found the Israelite towns in that area — Succoth and Peniel — were unwilling to give Gideon aid because they had long been under Midianite domination and feared that the Midianites would come back and wipe them out.

Gideon continued his pursuit of the fleeing Midianites, and overtook them on the "routes of the nomads" (the "back roads") far east of the Jordan (8:11). Nobah and Jogbehah were places in the area of ancient Rabbah, modern Amman, Jordan (Judg. 8:11). Gideon captured the two Midianite kings.

As Gideon returned victorious, he passed through the towns of Succoth and Peniel, which had refused to aid his weary men (8:5-6,15). Gideon punished them by scourging them with thorns, tore down their tower, and killed some men. Gideon probably should have graciously forgiven them.

A young man of Succoth wrote down for Gideon the names of officials in Succoth (8:14). This act shows that literacy was more common in that age than some critics have

MAP OF PLACES IN THE LIFE OF GIDEON:
1. **Ophrah** (Judg. 6:11) – Home village of Gideon. Here the Angel of the LORD called him.
2. **Spring of Harod** (means *trembling*) (Judg. 7:1) – Where Gideon reduced his army to 300.
3. **Hill Moreh** – Gideon fought the Midianites here (Judg. 7:1)
4. **Beth Shittah** (NKJV: Beth Acacia) (Judg. 7:22) – The Midianites fled through this area as they tried to escape from Gideon back east across the Jordan.
5. **Abel Meholah** and **Tabbath** (Judg. 7:22) – Places near the Jordan River where the Midianites fled to escape from Gideon.
6. **Succoth** and **Peniel** (Judg. 8:5,8,15,17) – Israelite towns that would not supply Gideon's men food as they pursued the Midianites east from the Jordan.
7. **Nobah** and **Jogbehah** (Judg. 8:11) – Rural tent-villages where Gideon overtook and destroyed the remnants of the fleeing Midianites.
8. **Mt. Tabor** (Judg. 8:18) – Round-topped mountain where the Midianite kings had killed some of Gideon's brothers.

369

claimed. (For example, see N. Gottwald, *The Hebrew Bible* [1987], p. 95.)

Back in Israel Gideon held a "trial" for the Midianite kings, Zeba and Zalmunna (8:18-21). They confessed to killing some princely men at Mt. Tabor. Gideon replied, "Those were my brothers." Gideon personally executed them, because his firstborn son, Jether, was too young and timid to do it.

Genesis 9:6 — "Whoever sheds the blood of man, by man shall his blood be shed."
Proverbs 6:16-17 — "Six things the LORD hates . . . hands that shed innocent blood."

---

8. *Gideon refuses the crown, but makes an ephod* (Judg. 8:23-32). The Israelites in gratitude offered to Gideon the position of HEREDITARY KING: "Rule over us — you, your son and your grandson." Gideon refused with words too noble for most of the Israelites: "The LORD will rule over you." (Cf. Deut. 33:5.) Gideon would probably have been a good king. Gideon's refusal of the kingship made him like the olive tree in the fable, who would not rule over the trees of the forest, but by not taking the position it left the throne to a thorn-bush (Judg. 9:8).

Gideon did ask the Israelites for gold from the spoil of the Midianites (8:24), and with this gold he made an *ephod*, which he placed in Ophrah, his town. An ephod was a *priest's* garment (Ex. 28:4,6). Gideon was from the tribe of Manasseh. The Levites had exclusive rights as priests (Num. 3:9-10). The ephod of Gideon became a "snare to Gideon and his family," because "all Israel prostituted themselves by worshiping it."

The land had forty years of peace (8:28-32). Gideon lived to a good old age. He had many wives and seventy sons. (See Deut. 18:17.) Gideon's concubine at Shechem bore him a son whom he named *Abimelech* ("My father is king"). The name is a surprise and seems inappropriate.

9. *Abimelech's failure as "king"* (Judg. 8:33–9:56). After

Gideon's death the Israelites forgot the LORD and went back to Baal worship, calling him *Baal-Berith* ("Baal-of-the-covenant"). They forgot their covenant with the LORD (Deut. 29:1).

a. Abimelech, the son of Gideon's concubine at Shechem, conferred with his relatives there and succeeded in having himself made "king" at Shechem (Judg. 9:1-3). His first "royal" act was to take his hired enforcers to Gideon's home village of Ophrah and kill all of his seventy brothers (9:5). Only the youngest, named Jotham, escaped. Abimelech had grown up vicious, probably because he never had a father at home to counsel him and to model a godly life.

b. Abimelech was crowned king beside the great tree at the *pillar* in Shechem. Shechem was rebuilt in the Late Bronze II age (after 1400 B.C.). The remains of the great temple there at that time have been found. The building has been identified by archaeologists as none other than the structure mentioned in Judges 9 as the temple of El (or Baal) Berith. (See James Ross and Lawrence Toombs, "Six Campaigns at Biblical Shechem," in *Archaeological Discoveries in the Holy Land*, 1967, pp. 124-125.) Clearly it had been destroyed violently. (See Judges 9:46-49.) In the forecourt of the temple was found an altar platform that once had a huge flat limestone slab, six feet high, set in a stone socket. Both the socket and slab were raised to their original positions. This may be the very "pillar" of Judges 9:6.

c. *Jotham's fable* (9:7-21). (A fable differs from a parable by its use of physical impossibilities, such as trees and animals talking.) The first rebuke of Abimelech's cruel reign was well-described by his only surviving half-brother, Jotham. Jotham spoke a fable from the slopes of Mt. Gerizim. The Valley of Shechem is about a half mile wide, with Mt. Gerizim on its south side and Mt. Ebal on its north. The acoustics in this valley are amazingly good, with sounds and speaking clearly audible between the mountains and the valley. (See *Biblical Archaeologist*, Dec. 1976, pp. 138-139.)

ABIMELECH, the "THORNBUSH KING"
(or Bramble Bush King). (Judg. 9:14)

Jotham's fable told of the trees of the forest seeking one tree to become king over all the trees. The worthwhile trees declined the honor(?); but a thornbush finally accepted the kingship. The thornbush spoke in a very demanding and threatening manner. This story illustrated Gideon and Abimelech. Useful people like Gideon are too busy doing good to desire kingly positions; but worthless people like Abimelech seek royalty and demand submission from the people. Then they destroy those who trust them.

Jotham closed his fable with the wish and warning that Abimelech and the Shechemites who made him king might destroy one another (9:19-20).

d. *Destruction of Abimelech* (9:22-57). Jotham's curse was soon fulfilled (9:57). Within three years the inhabitants of Shechem rose up in rebellion. While waiting in hiding to attack Abimelech, they robbed others passing by (9:25). Gaal, a leader of the opposition to Abimelech, spoke at a wine festival like a drunken man, challenging Abimelech to bring out his army and fight.

In the fights that followed the rebellion Abimelech captured Shechem, killed its people, and scattered salt upon it to make it unfruitful (9:45). Salt was sometimes placed on land as a curse (Jer. 17:6; Zeph. 2:9). (Concerning the uses of salt, see F. Chas. Fensham, "Salt as Curse," in *Biblical Archaeologist*, May 1962, pp. 48-50.)

The citizens remaining in the tower of Shechem sought safety in the stronghold of the temple of El-Berith. But Abimelech and his men gathered fuel and set the stronghold on fire above them. About a thousand people died. (We should not be able to read this story without sorrow and without resolution to raise our children in godliness.)

The town of *Thebez* (modern Tubas, eight miles northeast of Shechem) had joined in the rebellion again Abimelech. While attempting to burn Thebez as he had burned Shechem, Abimelech was struck on his head when "a woman dropped (Hebrew, *threw*) an upper millstone" and cracked his skull. He died more concerned that people might say "A woman killed him," than in sorrow for his crimes.

Abimelech is usually counted as the sixth judge, but neither his character nor his deeds make him worthy of this title. The Scripture does *not* state that "he led (judged) Israel."

10. *Tola* and *Jair* (Judg. 10:1-5). Little is told of the two judges that followed Abimelech. *Tola*, a man of Issachar, lived in Shamir, a town in Ephraim (about 40 miles from Issachar). The location of Shamir is unknown. Perhaps he lived in Ephraim because it was more central in Israel than Issachar. He judged Israel 23 years.

TOLA and **JAIR** — Judges we know little about.
But God knows us all!

Judge *Jair* led Israel for 22 years after Tola. He was probably from the tribe of Manasseh, and judged in the land of Gilead (east of the Jordan). He had 30 sons. He provided them recreation with thirty donkeys, and gave them rule over thirty "towns" when they grew up. The towns were called *Havvoth Jair*, meaning the "tent-villages of Jair." Nearly 300 years previously, the land of Gilead had been conquered by another Jair, a son of Manasseh (and probably an ancestor of judge Jair). The towns were first named *Havvoth-Jair* at that time (Num. 32:41; Deut. 3:14).

11. *Overlapping judgeships* (Judg. 10:6-16). Again the Israelites did evil in the eyes of the LORD. They worshiped the gods in all the nations around them. For doing this the LORD "sold them" into the hands of the Philistines from the west, and the Ammonites from the east (east of the Jordan). The Ammonites even crossed the Jordan to fight Judah, Benjamin, and Ephraim.

When Israel prayed for help, this time the LORD said, "Go and cry out to the gods you have chosen. Let them save you." God's longsuffering has a limit!

When the Israelites confessed their sin and got rid of their foreign gods, the LORD's heart could bear Israel's misery no longer, and He raised up another deliverer — *Jephthah*. Jephthah delivered Israel from Ammon near the same period when *Samson* was resisting the Philistines. Also it appears that *Eli* was serving as priest near that same period.

SAMSON, JEPHTHAH, & ELI the priest —
All three served near the same time period.

---

12. *Jephthah saves Israel from Ammon* (Judg. 10:17-32).
Outline of the Jephthah story:
    1. A difficult childhood (11:1-3)
    2. Jephthah accepts leadership (11:4-11)
    3. Futile negotiations with the king of Ammon (11:12-28)
    4. Vow of Jephthah (11:29-31)
    5. Victory over Ammonites (11:32-33)
    6. Jephthah's daughter offered (11:34-40)
    7. Conflict with jealous Ephraimites (12:1-7)

JEPHTHAH — HERO OF FAITH (Heb. 11:32).
MAKER OF A PAINFUL VOW.

JEPHTHAH'S FAITH AND GOOD ACTS:

1. Overcame the circumstances of his birth and childhood (11:1-3)
2. A mighty warrior (11:1)
3. Often spoke honoring the LORD (11:9,11,21,27,35)
4. Appealed to reason before fighting (11:12, 14-27)
5. The Spirit of the LORD came upon him (11:29)
6. Prayed to the LORD (11:30)
7. Had courage to confront enemies (11:32)
8. Kept his vow (11:35, 39; Eccl. 5:4-5)
9. Instilled faith in his daughter (11:36)

JEPHTHAH'S UNDESIRABLE QUALITIES AND ACTS

1. He became rough like his associates (11:3).
2. He held a grudge (11:7).
3. He wanted the highest office (11:9).
4. He thought he could influence God by sacrifices (11:31).
5. He vowed foolishly (11:31).
6. He treated some people rough (12:1-6).

The stories of Abimelech (ch. 9) and Jephthah both tell of boys rejected by their families when the boys were young. Both stories are tragic. Abimelech grew up vicious. Jephthah grew up with an outlaw gang (11:1-3), and developed enough roughness to make his own life sad and others around him uncomfortable. But Jephthah became a man of faith (Heb. 11:32-33) and had leadership ability. He had a daughter of apparently marriageable age, but his wife (or concubine) is never mentioned.

The location of *Mizpah*, where the Israelites chose Jephthah as their battle leader (10:17; 11:11), is uncertain; but it was probably in the land of Gilead north of the Jabbok River, and probably was the same place where Jacob bade farewell to Laban (Gen. 31:49).

Jephthah contacted the king of Ammon, and told him that when the Israelites had passed by Ammon, Edom, and Moab back in the days of Moses, they had not attacked or disturbed these peoples (11:18; Deut. 2:9, 18, 19; Num. 21:4). The only lands near Ammon that Israel took then were the lands occupied by Sihon, king of the Amorites. The Ammonites had not claimed those areas then, and Israel had lived in them for 300 years by the time of Jephthah. It was unreasonable that Ammon should claim these lands. But the king of Ammon paid no attention to the message from Jephthah. In the war that followed, Jephthah devastated twenty Ammonite towns, and Israel subdued Ammon.

13. *Jephthah's unwise vow* (Judg. 11:30-40). Jephthah had vowed that if the LORD gave him victory, he would offer as a burnt offering whatever came out the door of his house when he returned. Domesticated animals often stayed in (or under) houses in that land. But it was Jephthah's own daughter that came out of the house to greet her victorious father! Jephthah felt obligated to carry out this vow; and after two months of mourning "he did to her as he had vowed" (11:39).

Was it obligatory that Jephthah do this? Fulfilling vows was considered a sacred duty in the Old Testament (Eccl. 5:4-6; Deut. 23:21-23; Num. 30:1-2. Compare Matt. 5:33-37). However, the law of Moses had a provision that if a person thoughtlessly or carelessly made an oath to do anything, and then did not do it, though he was guilty, he could yet have the priest make atonement for him for his sin by offering a sin offering (Lev. 5:5-10). Perhaps Jephthah did not know this provision in the law.

Some Bible interpreters have said that Jephthah did not actually kill his daughter, but "sacrificed" her by devoting her to the service of the LORD at the door of the tabernacle for the rest of her life. (See G.L. Archer, *A Survey of O.T. Intro.*[1994], p.306.) The statement, "She knew no man," (13:39) has been used to support this view. But it seems almost certain that this statement is added to set forth in a stronger light the rashness of Jephthah and the heroism of his daughter. The fact that Jephthah was a hero of faith (Heb. 11:32) and "the Spirit of the LORD" came upon him did not prevent his doing some wrong things, even as King Saul later did (1 Sam. 11:6).

14. *Jephthah's conflict with the Ephraimites* (Judg. 12:1-6). The men of the tribe of Ephraim seem to have been envious for battle honors *after* the battles were over (Ps. 78:9; Isa. 11:13). Perhaps they liked the praise Deborah gave them (5:14). They had previously confronted Gideon about this (8:1). Gideon answered them very politely. Now they confronted Jephthah with the accusation that he had not called them to join the battle, and the threat that they would burn his house over his head. They said, "You Gileadites are just renegades from Ephraim and Manasseh." Jephthah did not have the gentility of Gideon. A war followed in which 42,000 Ephraimites were killed!

The Ephraimites who sought to escape back across the Jordan into Ephraim were asked to say the word *Shibboleth* as a password to prove they truly were Gileadites, not Ephraimites in disguise. Ephraimites could not say it correctly, and uttered "*Sibboleth*." This shows that differences of dialect had already developed among the tribes. The word *shibboleth* has passed into English to refer to expressions used by particular religious denominations to identify those whom they will accept as the "true believers." The Hebrew word *shibboleth* originally meant either a "flowing water stream" (as in Psalm 69:2), or an "ear of grain" (as in Zechariah 4:12).

"SHIBBOLETH." "Say it right, or you die!"

---

15. *Ibzan, Elon, Abdon* – Judges we scarcely know (Judg. 12:8-15). These three judges served after Jephthah, but probably served during the time of Samson and Eli. They served in the territories of Zebulun and Ephraim while Samson was mostly in Dan and Judah.

a. *Ibzan* (12:8-10). He had a large family, with thirty sons and thirty daughters. He had wealth sufficient to bring in young women as brides for his sons. He was from Bethlehem, probably not the famous Bethlehem in Judah, but another Bethlehem in the tribe of Zebulun (Josh. 19:10,15). He led Israel seven years (1096–1090 B.C.).

b. *Elon* (12:11-12) led Israel ten years (1089–1080 B.C.). He was buried in *Aijalon*, a site not yet identified in the land of Zebulun.

c. *Abdon* (12:13-15) followed Elon for eight years (1079–1071). Like judges Jair and Ibzan, Abdon had a very large family, with forty sons, and thirty grandsons. Like Jair, he provided them donkeys for recreation. He was from Pirathon, which was probably located about six miles southwest of Shechem, "in Ephraim, in the hill country of the Amalekites." The reference to Amalekites yet remaining in Ephraim is alarming (Judg. 7:12; 10:12; 1 Sam. 14:48).

16. *Chronology of the period of Samson.* The Philistines oppressed the Israelites for forty years (13:1). Samson led Israel during the first twenty years of this oppression (15:20; 16:31. 1090–1070 B.C.). The story of his birth appears to be retrospective, that is, it occurred during the time of the judges we previously read about, but is not related to us until the stories of earlier judges were finished.

The priest Eli served Israel for forty years as high priest at Shiloh (1 Sam. 4:18). It seems that he received the priesthood about twenty years before Samson began his career as deliverer of Israel. Eli's death occurred soon after Samson's death, so that the last twenty years of Eli's priesthood were also the twenty years of Samson's career.

The book of Judges ends chronologically with the death of Samson; and the story of the judges continues in the first book of Samuel. The stories in Judges 17–21 and the book of Ruth interrupt the narrative and may cause us not to see the close connection between the careers of Samson and Eli. When we open the book of 1 Samuel, we find Eli firmly established in his office and already of great age (1 Sam.1:9).

When Samson died, it was quite natural that the Philistines seized the occasion of his death to make a great attack on Israel, which led to the capture of the ark and the deaths of Eli and his sons.

Eli's death left Samuel the prophet as the judge of Israel. Samuel was attacked by the Philistines, but subdued them (1 Sam. 7:13). The twenty years of Samuel's ministry were the last half of the forty years of Philistine oppression.

OUTLINE OF THE SAMSON STORY
 1. Prediction of birth (Judg. 13:1-23). Birth (13:24)
 2. Failed marriage to woman of Timnah (14:1-19)
 3. Fights with Philistines (15:1-20)
 4. Sin and triumph at Gaza (16:1-3)
 5. Deception by Delilah (16:4-21)
 6. Death of Samson (16:23-31)

---

17. *Birth of Samson* (Judg. 13). In the time of Israel's anguish, the angel of the Lord came to a woman of the tribe of Dan. Her husband was named Manoah. The angel announced to her that she would bear a son. "He will begin the deliverance of Israel from the hands of the Philistines" (13:5). He would be a Nazirite, one of those men called to an unusual and special ministry. (Regarding Nazirites, see Numbers 6:2-21; Amos 2:11-12.) His deeds, his unshaven appearance, and style of life would draw great attention.

The territory of the tribe of Dan was immediately north of the area occupied by the Philistines on Israel's southwst coast. The Philistines frequently made raids into Dan, and attempted to encroach upon the territory of Dan. The villages of Zorah and Eshtaol, Samson's towns, were only about ten miles up into the hill country from the Philistine center of Ashdod (Judg. 18:2). The location of Samson's hometown made it almost inevitable that he would have contact with Philistines and probably conflict.

The angel of the LORD who announced Samson's birth was God Himself. The angel said that his name was "beyond understanding" (Hebrew, *Wonderful*), a title similar to that of the Messiah in Isaiah 9:6. When the angel burned the sacrifice of Manoah and his wife, Manoah said, "We are doomed to die!" "We have seen *God!*" (13:22). (See special study on pp. 364-366.)

The wife seems to have had more trust than Manoah during this announcement. She answered Manoah, "If the LORD had meant to kill us, he would not have accepted a burnt offering . . . from our hands" (13:23).

She named her son *Samson* (Heb. *Shimshon*), a name perhaps taken from the Hebrew word *shemesh*, meaning *sun*, and known for its strength (Judg. 5:31; Ps. 19:4-5).

Even in youth the Spirit of the LORD began to stir Samson while he was in Mahaneh Dan between Zorah and Eshtaol. (*Mahaneh Dan* means the Camp of Dan, probably a fortified place kept on alert for Philistine attacks. Judges 13:25; 18:12). Even in his youth Samson probably expressed outrage over the Philistines' aggression.

SAMSON — A weak strong man.
But also he was **SAMSON** — A hero of faith (Heb. 11:32).

---

18. *Failed marriage to woman of Timnah* (Judg. 14). Samson became enamored to a Philistine woman in the village of Timnah, which was only five miles from Samson's town of Zorah. A marriage was arranged (reluctantly) by Samson's

father. (Samson was self-controlled enough not to take the woman without marriage.) These events came to pass as a result of the LORD's direction in Samson's life to bring about a confrontation with the Philistines, who were then ruling over Israel. (The LORD does direct events in the lives of His servants, and in the world.)

Samson's immense strength was shown when he tore apart a young lion that came roaring toward him (14:5-6). This led to the making of a famous riddle that was uttered at Samson's seven-day wedding feast (14:14). Samson stormed out of the wedding feast when his bride-to-be discovered and revealed the secret meaning of the riddle to the thirty male "companions" of Samson. These "companions" threatened to burn the woman and her family to death if she did not obtain the secret of the riddle. (They later did burn the woman and her father [14:15; 15:6]. We see no gentleness or good will in these Philistines.)

To pay off his bet that the companions could not guess the riddle, Samson went down to the Philistine city of Ashkelon (fifteen miles southwest from Timnah) and "struck down" thirty Philistines and stripped them of their belongings and clothes to give to the wedding guests who "guessed" his riddle. The Spirit of the LORD gave him power to do this. Samson's "wife" was given to the friend who had attended him at his wedding (14:20).

Such tribulations would cause many people to abandon the LORD. But Samson had faith, and continued to cry to God.

19. *Samson's fights with the Philistines* (Judg. 15). Samson's anger flared when he returned to his "wife" and found that she had been given to the other man. He captured 300 foxes (probably jackals, carrion-eating wild dogs). We imagine a scene of snarling, snapping, and wild struggling! With torches tied to the foxes' tails, Samson ignited the wheat fields of the Philistines and burnt them "together with the vineyards and olive groves" (15:5). Such fires draw attention!

In the fight that followed, Samson "slaughtered many" of the Philistines (15:8). His Israelite kinsmen from Judah turned Samson over to the Philistines bound (15:13). Samson was gracious and careful not to attack the Judeans, even though they were delivering him to probable death (in their minds). Samson killed a thousand Philistines with a fresh jawbone of a donkey (15:15).

Then Samson said, "With a donkey's jawbone I have made donkeys of them." This could also be translated, "With an ass's jawbone, a heap, two heaps" (BDB Lexicon). There is play on words here, since *Hamor* in Hebrew means both an "ass" and a "heap." Samson used the jawbone of an *ass* for his weapon; and bodies were strewn about in *heaps*.

After the fray, Samson called the place *Ramath Lehi*, meaning *The Height of the Jawbone*. In great thirst he cried out to God. God split open the hollow place (resembling a mortar) at Lehi (meaning *Jawbone*), and water came out. Samson called the spring *En Hakkore*, meaning *The Spring of the One Who Cried* (15:19). Samson's faith shows throughout this conflict. God's power showed even more.

20. *Samson's sin and triumph at Gaza* (Judg. 16:1-3). At the Philistine city of Gaza, Samson saw a prostitute and "went in to her." The men of Gaza heard he was there and surrounded the place. They lay in wait all night at the city gate to keep him in the city. At midnight Samson arose, tore out the massive gates and the two gateposts, and carried them on his shoulders from Gaza (near sea level) *thirty* miles to the top of the mountain that faces Hebron (perhaps *Jebel Jalis*; 3300 ft.). Such an exploit should have inspired awe. God's continued use of Samson, even after his sin, shows the amazing greatness of God's grace toward people.

21. *Downfall and death of Samson* (Judg. 16:4-31). Samson's downfall came through Delilah, a woman in the Valley of Sorek (located a few miles west of Samson's town, Zorah). Possibly she was a Philistine, though the Bible does not say that. The huge bribes offered her by the rulers of the Philistines (the "lords" of the five chief cities) suggest that her loyalties were not wholly devoted to Philistia. She spoke of the Philistines in the third person (16:9,12,14). Probably she was a prostitute of no particular race.

Samson appears self-confident, even cocky, with her. He "kids" happily with her, offering false suggestions as to how he could be bound, even after she demonstrates that she is seeking to destroy him. Samson's third declaration to her about how he might become weak came perilously close to the truth. It involved his long hair. "If you weave the seven braids of my head into the fabric on the loom, and tighten it with the pin, I'll become as weak as any other man" (16:13).

O Samson, Samson,
> *Don't trust the godless woman !* (Prov. 2:16)
> *Don't trust your own heart !*
"He who trusts in himself is a fool" (Prov. 28:26).
"The heart is deceitful above all things and beyond cure" (Jer. 17:9).

After much nagging, Samson finally confessed that he was a Nazirite, and that if he broke the Nazirite vow by having his hair cut, he would become weak. We are amazed that he could sleep on her lap while a man shaved off the braids of his hair. Samson was awakened and seized. His eyes were gouged out, he was bound with bronze fetters, and he was set to grinding grain in the prison. But the hair on his head began to grow back again.

Samson died in the temple of Dagon (at Ashdod? 1 Sam. 5:1-2). Thousands of Philistines were present, celebrating the downfall of the man who "laid waste our land and multiplied our slain" (16:24). Samson asked the servant who held his hand to place him by the pillars that supported the temple roof. Samson prayed for vengeance for the blinding of his eyes; and his prayer was answered, probably because it was also God's vengeance on the heartless oppressors (Deut. 32:35; Isa. 35:4). With prayer and a final powerful push, Samson brought down the pillars, and the roof collapsed with its load of three thousnad men and women. "Thus he killed many more when he died than while he lived."

Samson had brothers and family, who brought his body

back and buried it in the tomb of his father. "He had led Israel twenty years" (16:31).

Questions on Section C
The Later Judges — Gideon to Samson (Judg. 6–16)

1. What people enslaved Israel after the peace under Deborah? (Judg. 6:1)
2. Where did the Israelites make shelters from the Midianites? (6:2-3)
3. How numerous were the Midianites? (6:5)
4. Why had the LORD oppressed Israel? (6:10)
5. Where was Gideon threshing wheat? Why there? (6:11)
6. What was Gideon sent to do for Israel? (6:14)
7. What did the angel do with Gideon's offering? (6:21)
8. What did Gideon do with his father's altar to Baal? (6:25,27)
9. What does the name *Jerub-Baal* mean? Why was Gideon called by that name? (6:30-32)
10. How did Gideon use a fleece to test whether God was really with him? (6:36-40)
11. How many men came to Gideon? How many fearful ones went home? (7:3)
12. How were the men who were to go with Gideon selected? (7:4-6). How many men were selected?
13. What dream did Gideon overhear a Midianite tell of? (7:13-14)
14. How many groups did Gideon divide his men into? (7:16)
15. What three things did Gideon give each man? (7:16)
16. What did Gideon's men shout? (7:20)
17. What caused the deaths of many Midianites? (7:22)
18. Name the two leaders of Midian. (7:24-25). Who killed them?
19. What did the Ephraimites complain of? (8:1)
20. Name the two Midianite kings. (8:5)
21. What two cities would not assist Gideon as he pursued the Midianite kings? (8:5,8)
22. What was done to the cities that refused to help Gideon? (8:16-17)
23. What had the Midianite kings done that caused Gideon to slay them? (8:18-19)
24. Name Gideon's firstborn son. (8:20)
25. What did Israel request Gideon to become? (8:22)
26. Who should have been Israel's true king? (8:23)

27. What did Gideon make of the earrings from the spoil? (8:21-27)
28. What did the Israelites do with the ephod?(8:27)
29. How many sons did Gideon have? (8:30)
30. Who was Gideon's son by the concubine at Shechem? (8:31)
31. What god did the Israelites serve after the death of Gideon? (8:33)
32. How did Abimelech win favor at Shechem? (9:1-3)
33. What relatives did Abimelech slay? (9:5)
34. Who escaped the massacre by Abimelech? (9:5)
35. What fable did the brother who escaped tell? (9:8-15)
36. Who was symbolized by the thornbush? (9:16)
37. Who led the revolt against Abimelech in Shechem? (9:26-28,39)
38. Who was Zebul? Whose side was he on? (9:30-31)
39. Who won in the fight between Abimelech and the men of Shechem? (9:40)
40. How did Abimelech kill those in the tower of Shechem? (9:48-49)
41. Where did Abimelech die? (9:50)
42. What two things caused Abimelech to die? (9:53-54)
43. Of what tribe was judge Tola? (10:1)
44. Which judge had thirty sons that rode on donkeys? (10:3-4)
45. What mocking command did God give when the Israelites cried to Him in distress? (10:14)
46. What did Israel need to make war against Ammon? (10:18)
47. Why had Jephthah been driven out from his family? (11:1-2)
48. What followers had Jephthah collected? (11:3)
49. What bargain did Jephthah make with the Gileadites? (11:9)
50. How did Jephthah first make contact with the king of Ammon? (11:12)
51. How long had Israel occupied Heshbon? (11:26)
52. What vow did Jephthah make? (11:30-31)
53. Who first met Jephthah when he returned home? (11:34)
54. How long did the daughter weep over her virginity? (11:38)
55. Why were the men of Ephraim angry with Jephthah? (12:1)
56. Who won the fight, Ephraim or the Gileadites? (12:4)
57. What was the password? How did the Ephraimites say it? (12:5-6)
58. What chapters in the book of Judges tell of Samson?
59. Name the father of Samson. (13:2)
60. Where did Samson's parents live? (13:2)
61. Who foretold Samson's birth? (13:3)
62. What prohibitions were imposed on Samson and on his mother before his birth? (13:4-5, 14)

63. Why did the messenger come back and repeat the prophecy about Samson's birth? (13:8-9)
64. Where did Samson find a woman he wanted? (14:1-2)
65. How did it happen that Samson became involved with the Philistine woman? (14:4)
66. What did Samson kill with his bare hands? (14:5-6)
67. Where had a swarm of bees settled? (14:8)
68. What was Samson's riddle and his bet? (14:12-14)
69. How was the solution to his riddle discovered? (14:15-16)
70. How did Samson pay off his bet? (14:19)
71. What caused Samson to burn the Philistines' fields?(15:1-2,6)
72. What did Samson use to spread the flames? (15:4-5)
73. Where did Samson stay after slaughtering the Philistines? (15:8)
74. Who handed over Samson to the Philistines? (15:11-13)
75. What did Samson use to slay Philistines? How many did he kill with it? (15:15)
76. Where did Samson obtain water after the slaughter? (15:18-19)
77. Where did Samson go in to a prostitute? (16:1)
78. What did Samson carry on his shoulders when he left this town? (16:3). Where did he carry it?
79. Where did Delilah live? (16:4)
80. What three lies did Samson tell Delilah about the source of his strength? (16:7,11,13)
81. Where was Samson when his hair was being shaved? (16:19)
82. How did the Philistines abuse Samson? (16:21)
83. To what Philistine god was a great sacrifice made? (16:23)
84. Why was Samson brought to the Philistine temple? (16:25)
85. Where did Samson ask to stand in the temple? (16:26)
86. How many Philistines were on the temple roof? (16:27)
87. How did Samson die? (16:30)
88. How long did Samson judge Israel? (16:31)

Section D
Conditions in the Time of the Judges (Judges 17–21)

1. *Events told in Judges 17–21 occurred early in the period of judges.* These events occurred long before (probably 200

years before) the life of Samson. This is indicated by (1) the fact that Moses' grandson Jonathan was still active (18:30); (2) Hosea's reference to the sin at Gibeah as Israel's *first* sin in the land (Hosea 10:9); (3) the fact that there was time enough before King David's seventh year (1003 B.C.) for the tribe of Benjamin to replenish its population from 600 men (Judg. 20:47) to many thousands (1 Chr. 12:29); (4) the fact that Aaron's grandson Phinehas' was still the priest (Judg. 20:28; Num. 25:7).

The events told in Judges 17–21 are disgusting and repulsive. These incidents illustrate conditions in Israel during the period of judges. Conditions were ungodly and unsafe. These events illustrate the way many people will live if they do not have a good king to control them. The verse that most vividly explains the conditions in those days is the last verse in the book (21:25): "In those days Israel had no king; everyone did as he saw fit." Nations will destroy themselves if their people are not controlled either by an internal governor (like the Holy Spirit and conscience), or by an external force, like a good king.

The preservation of the history in Judges 17–21 — of which Israel must have been ashamed — must be regarded as evidence of divine oversight, direction, and selection of the words and information in the Holy Scripture. No public relations committee would have selected the material in these chapters!

2. *The idolatry of Micah* (Judg. 17). An Ephraimite man stole 1100 pieces of silver (about 28 lb., or 13 kg.) from his mother. He became fearful when the mother pronounced a curse on the thief. He confessed and returned the money. His mother then consecrated the money to purchase for him some objects of worship — a carved image and a cast idol. Micah then made one of his sons his priest. (Micah was a superstitious, idolatrous, spoiled thief. God's children need not fear curses, hexes, and such (Prov. 26:2).

Later an unemployed Levite from Bethlehem in Judah came by Micah's house, and was hired to be Micah's priest. The Levite became "like one of his sons." Micah was sure that his having a *Levite* as his priest would guarantee him prosperity. We are shocked to read that this Levite (named Jonathan) was a son of Gershom, the son of *Moses*! (18:30). This is so appalling that the editors of the common Jewish Bible (the Hebrew Masoretic text) attempted to conceal the fact that Moses' grandson was a priest in an idol shrine. They inserted a *nun* (= *N*) into, but slightly above, the name *Moses,* so that "Moses" would be read as "Manasseh." (מְנַשֶּׁה, see KJV and NIV margin.) But no one named Manasseh was priest or prince at the time of this story.

3. *The Danites settle in Laish* (Judg. 18). The statement that "In those days Israel had no king" occurs four times in the final chapters of Judges (17:6; 18:1; 19:1; 21:25). It sounds like an apology for the wicked acts that are related. It shows that the Israelites sensed their need for a righteous king, and would soon be asking for a king (1 Sam. 8:5). Even the rule of an evil king would be better than the chaos in the time of judges.

The tribe of Dan lived along the Mediterranean coast, just north of the area occupied by the Philistines. The Philistines continually raided the areas around them to expand their territory (1 Sam. 13:5,17; Judg. 1:34-35). The Danites suffered anguish from this pressure, but did not have faith enough to seek God and fight the Philistines. The story in Judges 18 tells of the search by the Danites for safer land, and how they seized their new turf with great cruelty. They seemed to relish a fight (18:20-26).

On their way to find a safe new homeland, the Danites

The Dan-snake* coiled and struck!

The smitten city of Laish perished (Judg. 18:27).

*In his prophecy about his sons, Jacob said, "Dan will be a *serpent* by the roadside" (Gen. 49:17).

---

came by the house of Micah (17:1-5). They were amazed to meet there Jonathan the Levite, whom some of them had known before (18:3). Jonathan was very willing to prophesy that they would have a successful journey (18:6), and later to leave his employer, Micah, and to go with the tribe of Dan to be their priest (18:19-20). He was a "hired hand" (a hireling), and not a good shepherd (John 10:12).

The desire of the Danites for gods (18:14) and a priest who might bring them good fortune tells a lot about the religious conditions in Israel, and in most humans.

The place found by the Danites was named *Laish*, but they renamed it *Dan* (18:29). It is about 25 miles north of the Sea of Galilee, in the lush Jordan valley. Dan was over 120 miles north from the Danites' villages of Zorah and Eshtaol (Samson's towns; Judges 18:2; 13:25). The major source of the Jordan River waters spring forth at Dan, cold and pure, amidst dense woods. Dan was isolated from other cities (like Sidon in Phoenicia) that might have protected it from attackers by the the heights of Upper Galilee west of Dan, and by Mt. Hermon ten miles east.

Ater Dan was captured and renamed, the expression "from Dan to Beersheba" became a popular saying to refer to the entire country. Dan was in the far north end of the land, and Beersheba was in the far south (west of the Dead Sea).

The reference to the "captivity of the land" (18:30) does not prove that the book of Judges was written after the fall of the northern kingdom (Israel) to Assyria in 732 or 722 B.C. The reference to Shiloh (18:31) shows that the "captivity" refers to an earlier "captivity." Shiloh fell about 1050 B.C., three centuries before the fall of the northern tribes of Israel.

Archaeological research at Dan shows it was wealthy in the early Late Bronze Age (14th–13th centuries B.C.), but poorer in the last Bronze Age level (*New Ency. Arch. Exc. in Holy Land*, Vol. 1 [1993], p. 326).

4. *A Levite and his concubine* (Judg. 19). (A *concubine* was not a paramour or mistress, but a woman lawfully united in marriage to a man, but having a relationship [like slavery] inferior to that of a regular wife. Polygamy was common in ancient Israel.)

A Levite living in the tribe of Ephraim went south to the town of Bethlehem to bring back a concubine who had fled from him. The concubine had been "unfaithful to him," literally, "played the harlot against him" (19:2, NKJV). After getting away from her excessively hospitable father, the Levite, his concubine, and his servants journeyed north to the town of Gibeah, where they were housed by a nonlocal resident. That night the poor concubine was raped to death by the townsmen. The Levite took her dead body to his home, cut her into twelve pieces, and sent them to the tribes of Israel, with a call for justice and punishment upon the town of Gibeah and the Benjamites.

Geographically the story is easy to trace. The events took place on the "water-parting road" north and south through the mountainous central part of Israel. The tribe of *Ephraim* lay ten to forty miles north of Jerusalem. Jerusalem was then called *Jebus*, and its people Jebusites (19:10; 1:21). *Bethlehem* (19:1) was six miles south of Jerusalem. Gibeah (meaning "hill") was three miles north of Jerusalem on the east side of the road (19:13-14; 1 Sam.10:26). *Ramah* (hometown of Samuel the prophet [1 Sam. 7:17]) was six miles north of Jerusalem.

The overpowering hospitality of the concubine's father is tarnished by the fact that at some of their meals only the "*two* of them (the Levite and the concubine's father) sat down to eat and drink together" (19:6). The concubine was either left out, or did not desire to join them.

As his party travelled homeward the Levite chose not to stay in Jebus (Jerusalem), just six miles north of Bethlehem, because Jebus was inhabited by non-Israelites. They travelled on three miles north to the Israelite town of Gibeah, though the evening was becoming darkness. In Gibeah no one would take them into their homes. There were no inns in that period. Still, extending hospitality to strangers was a general custom. Abraham entertained three (very special!) strangers (Gen. 18:1-4). Hospitality to strangers is a godly service (Job 31:32; Matt. 25:35,38; Rom. 12:13; 1 Tim. 5:10; Ex. 22:21).

The attack by the men of Gibeah on the house where the Levite and his concubine were finally taken in reminds us of the acts of the men of Sodom (19:22; Gen. 19:5). "Bring out the man . . . so we can have sex with him" (Hebrew, "know him") (19:22). Homosexuality is strongly condemned in Scripture (Lev. 18:22; 20:13; 1 Cor. 6:9). Their acts brought destruction upon themselves. The Benjamites had no respect either for God's ministers (Levites) or for women. The people of Benjamin were characterized in Genesis 49:27: "Benjamin is a *ravenous wolf.*"

The offer of the Levite to sacrifice his concubine to the town rapists to save himself (19:24) shows that the Levite had no true devotion to her. Perhaps that was why she ran away. After the horrendous night, he came to the door where she lay dead, and said to her, "Get up; let's go." See Hosea 9:9; 10:9-10.

The Levite cut her body into twelve parts, probably one for each tribe (19:29), and sent the pieces throughout all the territory of Israel. Word of this spread, and caught everyone's attention. A century or two later King Saul cut up his oxen into pieces and sent them throughout all the territory of Israel as a call to war against Ammon (1 Sam. 12:7). Saul also got attention!

What were the Levite's motives in sending out the pieces of the concubine's body? Vengeance? Or was he attempting to make the people think about the guilt of the Benjamites rather than about HIS sins? He was correct in saying that their guilt was great: "Such a thing has never been seen or done" before (19:30).

5. *Israelites fight the Benjamites* (Judg. 20). Chapter 20 is a continuation of the story in chapter 19. After the Levite had alerted the Israelites about the rape and murder of his concubine, the entire Israelite nation got into a three-day war against the tribe of Benjamin at Gibeah. The Benjamites were outnumbered 400,000 to 26,000, but nonetheless inflicted over 40,000 casualties on the Israelites before they were defeated by an ambush attack. When the war was over only 600 Benjamite men survived.

The Israelites gathered at *Mizpah* to take counsel for war against Benjamin (20:1). Mizpah was possibly located at Tell en-Nasbeh nine miles north of Jerusalem, or perhaps at Nebi

Samwil on the high ridge six miles northwest of Jerusalem. Both locations are only 6–8 miles from Gibeah. The Israelites had sworn that none of them would give their daughters as brides to the wicked Benjamites (21:5).

The Benjamites knew of Israel's mass meeting against them (20:3), but did not seem in the slightest intimidated by it, and boycotted the gathering. "Pride goes before destruction" (Prov.16:18).

Like many wars, this one seems unjustified. The results of the war seem much worse than the crime that the war was designed to punish. The war seems to have been started by the Levite to divert attention from his suspicious reputation.

The Levite did not tell the "whole truth and nothing but the truth" about what happened at Gibeah the night when his concubine died. Compare Judges 20:4-5 with 19:22-25. Thousands died so he could look like an innocent bystander.

When the Israelites asked the Benjamites to turn over the rapists who had abused the concubine to death, they refused (20:13). They were willing to fight and die rather than to admit that any of them had done anything wrong. Confessing their sin was an act that the Benjamites could not bring themselves to do.

The Benjamites, though outnumbered, had some advantages in the battle. They were fighting for their lives on their home turf. The town of Gibeah was on a high hill, which provided an advantage to the defenders. The Benjamites had a special "force" of six hundred left-handed slingstone sharpshooters (20:16). (Slingstones in Bible times were about the size of baseballs!) Also the Benjamites were famous as warriors (Judg. 20:44; 1 Chr. 8:40; 12:2; 2 Chr. 14:8).

"The Israelites went up to *Bethel* (ten miles north of Jerusalem) and inquired of God" (20:18). The ark and tabernacle were then at Shiloh. Sometimes the ark was brought out to battlefields (1 Sam. 14:18). That seems to have been done on this occasion. The ark and Phinehas (Aaron's grandson, the priest) were brought to Bethel, close to the battle site of Gibeah (20:27-28).

God directed Israel in this battle. (See 20:18,23,28). God

surely knew that Israel would suffer many casualties (Isa. 46:10). Why then should He send them to death in battle? We believe that God is JUST, even as He is kind, and that both sides in this battle needed a stern lesson.

The Israelites lost their enthusiasm for this war when 22,000 of them perished the first day, and 18,000 the next day (20:21,24). They came "before the LORD" weeping and praying, "Shall we go up again to battle with Benjamin *our brother?*" (20:23,28). They had NOT talked that way before the battle.

Israelites offered "burnt offerings and fellowship (peace) offerings to the LORD" (20:26; 21:4). Their acts show that these sacrifices were familiar ordinances in Israel far back into its history (shortly after the time of Moses) and not the doctrines of some Priestly writer who lived near the time of the Babylonian captivity 800 years later, as some critics allege (N. Gottwald, *The Hebrew Bible* [1987], pp. 186, 188, 207).

The Benjamites were defeated on the third day when the Israelites prepared an attack from ambush, somewhat similar to the attack upon 'Ai (20:29; Josh. 8:12). The Benjamites lost 25,000 valiant fighters, and only six hundred men escaped (20:46-47). These few fled to the village of Rimmon (located about twelve miles northeast of Gibeah).

After pursuing the fleeing Benjamites, "the men of Israel went back to Benjamin and put all the towns to the sword . . . All the towns they came across they set on fire" (20:48). The author recalls his excavation experiences at Khirbet Raddana (just north of modern Ramallah), which is about eight miles north of Gibeah. There in rubble remaining from the Iron I Age (1200–1000 B.C.) a thick layer of fallen stones and ashes was clearly traceable. This layer may have been a result of the war described in Judges 20. (See Robert Cooley, in *Near East Archaeological Society Bulletin* # 5,1975, p. 13).

6. *Wives for the Benjamites* (Judg. 21). The final chapter of Judges tells that the Israelites grieved over the near annihilation of the tribe of Benjamin in the war at Gibeah (chap. 20). Apparently the women and children of Benjamin also perished in this war and in the slaughter throughout the tribe of

Benjamin that followed the victory (20:48).

Only 600 Benjamite men survived. They fled to Rimmon in the territory of Ephraim north of Benjamin. (Israelites have always taken casualties in war with great grief [Num. 31:49; 2 Sam. 2:30-31], and still do.)

Judges 21 tells of Israel's manipulations to provide wives for the 600 Benjamites, while making it appear that they had NOT willingly given their daughters to the Benjamites. They had sworn an oath "by the LORD not to give them any of our daughters in marriage" (21:7).

This led to the senseless slaughter of the men and women in the town of Jabesh Gilead (east of the Jordan River) — except for 400 virgin women who were taken from there as brides to the Benjamites (21:8-12).

If the Jewish historian Josephus is correct, virgins could be identified because they wore long-sleeved tunics reaching to their ankles, in order not to be exposed (*Antiquities*, VII, viii,1; [VIII, 174]. See 2 Sam. 13:18.)

The Israelites then set up an organized project of kidnapping 200 young women at Shiloh to be brides for the remaining Benjamites (21:20-21).

All of this was done to keep up a façade of piety and fidelity to one's oaths while actually breaking the oath. Surely God expected them to keep their word when they made oaths (Lev. 5:4-6; Ps. 15:4). But even the law in Leviticus that said that oaths had to be kept permitted sacrifices to be made for a broken oath uttered "thoughtlessly" (Heb., "to speak rashly, thoughtlessly." BDB Lexicon). To kill the people of a whole city to cover the fact that they had made a rash oath appears to be committing a great evil to prevent having to confess to a lesser evil.

Jabesh Gilead, the town where 400 virgins were taken and the rest of the people slain, lay about eight miles east of the Jordan River and fifty miles north of the tribe of Benjamin. To assemble and equip 12,000 troops to go that far was a huge effort and expense (21:10). All this was done to "save face."

The Israelites' scheme of having the remaining two hundred Benjamite men go to Shiloh during the annual feast (probably the Passover) to snatch dancing maidens for brides is amazing. When the girls' fathers protested the kidnapping of their daughters (without even payment of a dowry), the fathers' objections were brushed aside with the request, "Do us a kindness by helping *them* . . . you are innocent, since you did not *give* your daughters to them" (meaning "to us Benjamites").

Perhaps this chapter illustrates sin in its most basic nature — a mixture of lawlessness and self-justification (pride).

Questions on Section D
Conditions in the Time of the Judges (Judg. 17–21)

1. Are the events told in Judges 17–21 early in the period of judges, or late in the period? Give a reason for answer.
2. In which tribe did Micah live? (Judg. 17:1)
3. How much money was stolen? Who took it? (17:2)
4. What was done with the money? (17:3-5)
5. Where had the young Levite who visited Micah come from? (17:7)
6. What was the Levite's name? Who was his famous ancestor? (18:30)
7. What did the Levite become for Micah? (17:12)
8. What did the tribe of Dan desire? Why? (18:1)
9. Where did the Danites stop overnight as they were out looking for land? (18:2-3)
10. What place did the Danites find that they wanted to take? (18:7)
11. Whom did the Danites take with them to their new home? (18:18-19)
12. How did the priest who was taken feel about being taken? (18:20)
13. What did the Danites name their new city? (18:29)
14. What did the Levite in Ephraim take unto himself? (19:1)
15. Why did he go to Bethlehem? (19:2-3)
16. In what city did he try to find lodging when he returned from Bethlehem? (19:12-13)
17. Who died as the result of abuse in this city? (19:27)
18. What was done with the body? (19:29)
19. Who assembled for war? Against what tribe and what city? (20:1,14)
20. What unusual fighting force was among the Benjamites? (20:16).

21. How many days were required to defeat the Benjamites? (20:24-28)
22. How many Benjamites survived the war? (20:47)
23. What grieved the Israelites about the tribe of Benjamin? (21:1-3)
24. From what city were wives stolen for the Benjamites? (21:10-11)
25. At what city were the Benjamites to snatch additional women for wives? (21:19-21)
26. What final descriptive verse explains conditions in the days of the judges? (21:25)

Section E
Ruth

> ### *Truths from the book of Ruth*
>
> 1. Not everyone is bad, even in an evil age like the period of judges.
> 2. God cares about ordinary people and families, like Naomi and her family (not just about whole nations).
> 3. Sweet servant saints like Naomi attract loyal loved ones like Ruth.

The book of Ruth has been called the most beautiful short story ever written. Its charm attracts even the skeptics. Jews have read the book of Ruth during the Feast of Weeks (the feast also called Pentecost).

   a. *Authorship and date of Ruth.* Jewish tradition affirmed that Samuel the prophet was the author (Talmud, *Baba Bathra* 14b). Samuel lived at the right period to have written the book, and Samuel anointed David (who is named in Ruth 4:17) to be the future king (1 Sam. 16:13; Ruth 4:22). We believe Samuel probably was the author.

   The date of the book would be late in Samuel's life, possibly about 1055 B.C. Samuel died before David became king (1010 B.C.), but the book of Ruth does not refer to David as already being the king (Ruth 4:22; 1 Sam. 25:1).

b. *Purposes of the book of Ruth.* The book does not list the purposes for writing it. But the book illustrates MANY valuable truths. It shows that God accepts people from all nations. It shows that God's saints suffer hardships, but always triumph, if they continue in faith. It illustrates the functions of the Hebrew kinsman-redeemer (the GO'EL), who was a type (or symbol) of Christ, our Redeemer. The book gives a genealogical list leading up to King David, and ultimately to Christ. The book pictures true family love, and practical godliness. The book is captivating, just as a love story. "The book has something for everyone."

    c. *Outline of Ruth*:

        (1) Sad sojourn of Naomi in Moab (1:1-5)
        (2) Return to Bethlehem by Naomi with Ruth (1:6-22)
        (3) Ruth the gleaner in Boaz' field (ch. 2)
        (4) Meeting of Ruth and Boaz at the threshing floor (ch. 3)
        (5) Boaz makes arrangements to marry Ruth (4:1-12)
        (6) Birth of son (4:13-17)
        (7) The genealogy of David (4:18-22)

1. *Sad sojourn of Naomi in Moab* (Ruth 1:1-5). The book of Ruth begins (in Hebrew), "And it came to pass in the days when the Judges administered justice that there was a famine in the land." (Rotherham trans.)

Famines sometimes were the result of God's judgment upon a land (Deut. 28:23-24), but they occurred often as natural events in our world under the curse (Gen. 26:1).

The town of Bethlehem in Judah lay six miles south of Jerusalem. *Bethlehem* means "house of bread"; but there was a famine in the house of bread. Ephratha was a name for the district around Bethlehem (Gen. 35:19; 1 Sam. 17:12; Micah 5:2).

The name *Naomi* means *pleasant* or *lovely* (1:20). *Elimelech* means "My God is king." The names of Naomi's sons — *Mahlon* and *Kilion* — seem to mean "sickly" and "consumed." Their names probably had no association with their premature deaths.

The family of Elimelech went to sojourn in Moab during

the famine. They did not plan to stay there as permanent residents. *Moab* was the high, productive tableland east of the Dead Sea, south of the Arnon River. Food was available in Moab.

Naomi's husband and two sons both died in Moab. She was left with the two Moabite women who had married her sons.

Naomi's grief at the loss of her family did not destroy her faith in the LORD (1:8-9), but it left her rather embittered (1:13, 20). We do not know *why* God allowed these events to occur. But Naomi found that God is full of kindness in the outcome (Ruth 2:20).

2. *Return to Bethlehem by Naomi* (Ruth 1:6-22). Naomi heard that God had come to the aid of his people (lit., *visited* them) by providing food at Bethlehem. She set out to go back, and the daughters-in-law were coming with her.

Naomi had earned such great respect and love from her daughters-in-law that they were willing to go with her to her homeland, though the land of Judah was foreign to them. But Naomi was more concerned over their welfare than her own loneliness. She thought that they would more likely find new husbands in their own land than in a land foreign to them. She desired that they would find "rest" with a husband (1:9; 3:1), and she certainly had no more sons for them to marry.

Throughout the story in Ruth the custom of *Levirate* marriage is referred to, a custom that permitted a childless widow to be married to the brother (or closest relative) of her deceased husband. See Deuteronomy 25:5-10.

Naomi requested that the LORD (*not* a Moabite deity) show "kindness" to Ruth and Orpah (1:8). "Kindness" is from the Hebrew *ḥesed*, a word full of tender meaning and variously translated as "mercy" (KJV), "steadfast love" (NRSV), or "lovingkindness" (NASB).

Naomi spoke as if she blamed God for her painful experiences (1:13). Compare Job 19:7-11.

Orpah decided to return to her people and her "gods" (1:15). The word "*gods*" is *'elohim*, which may be either singular or plural in meaning. It therefore does not necessarily imply that Orpah worshiped many gods.

Ruth's response to Naomi (1:16-17) is a model speech to express total devotion to a loved one. Ruth gave up her ancestors' gods and her own people to go with Naomi. Ruth called upon Yahweh, the God of Israel. She swore her determination with a strong oath expression like that used by others (1 Sam. 3:17), that she would die rather than be apart from Naomi.

The arrival of Naomi back in Bethlehem with Ruth set the city into an uproar of murmuring. (The Hebrew verb הום has those meanings, but sounds like the English *hum*.) The question, "Is *this* Naomi?" suggests that she had aged in appearance.

Naomi told the women to call her *Mara'* (meaning *bitter*, a name similar to *Marah* in Exodus 15:23), and not to call her *Naomi*. She referred to God as the Almighty (Shaddai), a less intimate title for God often used in the book of Job.

Naomi and Ruth returned in the barley harvest season. This was in April/May. The wheat harvest began a few weeks later (1:22).

3. *Ruth the gleaner in Boaz' fields* (Ruth 2). The hero — Boaz — now enters the story. He was a "relative" (3:2) of Naomi's deceased husband. He was a "man of standing" (or "man of strength," or "man of wealth").

Ruth was not lazy. She volunteered to go forth and seek work picking up (gleaning) leftover grain, a hot and hard toil. The law of Moses directed landowners to leave some grain in their fields for the poor to glean (Lev. 19:9-10; 23:22; Deut. 24:19-21). (This was part of Israel's social "welfare" system.)

Ruth did not know Boaz. But it was hardly an accident that she found employment in his fields.

When Boaz came to his field, he greeted his employees, "The LORD be with you." Boaz' good will to his harvesters, and their gracious response to him are unusual and delightful. Boaz knew his employees, and noticed a new worker — Ruth.

Boaz conversed with Ruth, and invited her to continue working with his servant girls already there. Ruth responded with great humility and courtesy (2:10,13).

Boaz had already heard of Ruth's return with Naomi. He praised her with eloquent words: "You have come to take refuge under the *wings* of the LORD, the God of Israel." The Hebrew word for *wing* can also mean *corner* (as in Ruth 3:9). Ruth had come under God's "wings" (like a baby bird), but she ended under the "corner" (or "wing") of Boaz.

At mealtime Boaz himself offered her food. Meals were simple — bread, with wine vinegar to dip it in, and roasted grain. (Similar food is still eaten.) Boaz showed increasing interest in Ruth. He instructed the harvesters to leave extra grain for her.

When Ruth returned to Naomi, she had an ephah of barley, over half a bushel, enough to feed a person for several weeks, much more than a gleaner would usually get.

Naomi asked, "Where did you glean today?" In her reply Ruth did not say Boaz' name till the last word in her sentence, as if to arouse suspense in Naomi. When Ruth said *Boaz'* name, Naomi seemed electrified. "That man is our close relative; he is one of our kinsman-redeemers" (3:20). Did Ruth know what that might mean? Kinsmen-redeemers helped childless widows of their deceased relatives! (This is the first mention of the *go'el* in the book. Compare 3:9,12; 4:1, 6, 8,14.)

The Hebrew word for "kinsman-redeemer" is **GO'EL** (pronounced Go-ALE). The services to be performed by a *go'el* are stated in the Law of Moses:

a. To avenge a murdered relative (Num. 35:19).

b. To marry the childless widow of his deceased brother (or relative), that she might bear a child to carry on the name of her deceased husband (Deut. 25:5-10). This is called *Levirate* marriage (meaning "brother-in-law marriage").

c. To buy back family land that had been sold (Lev. 25:25; Jer. 32:6).

d. To redeem relatives sold as slaves (Lev. 25:47-49).

> # Jesus is our KINSMAN-REDEEMER,
> ## our GO'EL (גֹּאֵל) from heaven.

Ruth continued her work of gleaning in Boaz' fields till the barley and wheat harvests were finished (3:22). This would extend about seven weeks, till June.

4. *Meeting of Ruth and Boaz* (Ruth 3). How does a woman motivate a man to stop giving all his attention to his work and to marry her? She arranges a meeting with him that will get his attention.

Ruth chapter 3 tells of Ruth's meeting with Boaz at night at his threshing floor. Boaz was glad for her "kindness" (3:10).

A *threshing floor* is simply a circle of hard-packed soil or bedrock — about 50 to 100 feet across — where sheaves of wheat were unloaded. There oxen would drag a sled over them to break the grain loose from the husks. The wheat would then be winnowed by tossing it into the air so the breeze would blow chaff away from the heavier grains. A delightful article picturing the harvesting and winnowing of wheat at Bethlehem is in *National Geographic*, Dec. 1929, pp. 699-735. A photo of a landowner winnowing his threshing floor has the caption: "Winnowing is the task for the Master of the Harvest." His grain was his living. He guarded it personally.

Naomi wanted to find a "home" for Ruth (3:1), literally, a "rest." (Compare 1:9). Ruth's future was probably in danger if she did not marry.

"Perfume yourself" (3:3) is literally "anoint yourself" (with oils). A fragrance is not necessarily referred to.

Ruth came to Boaz' threshing floor at night and lay down at his feet. He awoke startled, asking "Who are you?" She reminded him that he was a redeemer-kinsman. (She did not say "MY redeemer-kinsman," or even "THE redeemer-kinsman.")

Boaz blessed her for her "kindness" (Hebrew, *ḥesed*; see notes on 2:20). She had sought him out, though he was older than she. "All my fellow townsmen know that you are a woman of *noble character*." (Literally: "All the gate of my people know that you are a *woman of strength*" [valor].) The same words are applied to the woman of *noble character* in

Proverbs 31:10. Boaz himself was called a "man of *standing*" (same Hebrew word) in 2:1. Boaz and Ruth were alike — people of *strength*.

There was no immorality involved in this meeting.

Boaz was eager to accept Ruth, but there was another relative more closely related to her dead husband than he was. He could not marry her unless the other kinsman gave consent. Boaz promised with an oath ("as surely as the LORD lives") that "I will do it." He investigated the matter the next morning.

Before daylight the next morning Boaz sent Ruth home with a large gift of grain — six measures of barley (the volume of the measures is not told). He said, "Don't let it be known that a woman (literally "*the* woman") came to the threshing floor."

Naomi greeted Ruth with the same question (in Hebrew) that Boaz asked her: "*Who are you*, my daughter?" ("Are you the widow of Mahlon? Or the bride-to-be of Boaz?")

5. *Boaz makes arrangements to marry Ruth* (Ruth 4:1-12).

TWO GREAT GIFTS FROM GOD

(1) A **WIFE** — Proverbs 19:14: A prudent wife is from the LORD.

(2) A **CHILD** — Psalm 127:3: Children are a heritage from the LORD.

Boaz received both of these gifts.

Ruth 4:1: "Now Boaz went up to the gate [of Bethlehem] and sat down there, and behold, the kinsman-redeemer that Boaz had spoken of was passing by! And he [Boaz] said, 'Turn aside, *Peloni Almoni* [Johnny No-name]'; and he did turn aside and sat down" (Author's paraphrase).

The Hebrew text indicates that the other kinsman-redeemer passed by soon after Boaz sat down at the gate. Boaz knew his name; but the Bible withholds the name, calling him (in Hebrew) *Peloni Almoni*. This title means "a certain person." (See its uses in 2 Kings 6:8 and 1 Samuel 21:2

[v. 3 in Hebrew]. F.B. Huey calls him "Mr. So-and-so" [*Expositor's Bible Com.*, Vol.3, p. 541].)

The gate of a town was the community gathering place. Stone seats were placed in some gates. Merchandise was bought and sold around the gate (Neh. 13:20, 22). Judges sometimes held court sessions by the gate (Job 29:7,16-17; Deut. 22:15; 2 Sam. 15:2). God's prophets sometimes reproved people at the gate (Amos 5:10). Boaz went to the right place to meet his relative, and to transact legal business.

Boaz said to him, "Naomi is selling the piece of land that belonged to our brother (relative) Elimelech." The Hebrew can be translated "has sold." The exact legal and financial status of the property is not related; but Naomi was clearly in need, and the property needed to be "redeemed" soon by a relative.

The other relative was willing to acquire the land, but declined to take it when Boaz informed him that if he took the property, he also acquired Ruth, the dead man's widow (4:5), to raise up children by her.

The custom used to show that property had been redeemed was to remove a sandal, and give it to the "redeemer." (See Ruth 4:7 and Deuteronomy 25:7-10.) The procedure as described in Deuteronomy also directed the woman to spit in the face of the redeemer who refused to take her. But in this case all the family involved were hoping that the other relative would not take Ruth. Therefore when he declined, no act of contempt was done to him. This custom of removing the sandal is said to have been practiced "in earlier times in Israel" (4:7). We do not know the exact date Ruth lived, but it was possibly about 1300 B.C.(?), a century after the writing of Deuteronomy. Samuel, the prophet and probable author of the book of Ruth, ministered about 1070–1050 B.C. By Samuel's time the custom of removing the sandal when property was redeemed seems to have ceased.

The elders who witnessed Boaz' transaction seemed eager to declare they were "Witnesses!" They wished him well, desiring that Ruth would become like Leah, Jacob's wife who bore him six sons, and like Rachel, who bore two sons. "May your family be like that of Perez, whom Tamar bore to Judah."

6. *Birth of a son* (Ruth 4:13-17). After Boaz took Ruth, "the LORD enabled her to conceive, and she gave birth to a son" (4:13). Ruth had borne no children during several years of marriage in Moab; so the conception of the child appeared as obviously a divine gift.

The local women involved themselves in the festivities of the new son's birth. They praised the LORD that Naomi would have yet another kinsman-redeemer, her son. The women gave the son his name, *Obed* (meaning *one who serves*, or a *worshiper*). They praised Ruth, saying she was better to Naomi than seven sons.

Naomi took much care of the child in her lap. She became a "nurse," (literally, one who supports).

7. *The genealogy of David* (Ruth 4:18-22). The book of Ruth closes with an important genealogy. Compare Matthew 1:3-6, and 1 Chronicles 2:3-15.

(1) *Perez*, son of Judah and his daughter-in-law, Tamar.

(2) *Hezron*, a prominent man (1 Chr. 2:21, 25).

(3) *Ram.*

(4) Amminadab, father-in-law of Aaron (Ex. 6:23).

(5) *Nahshon*, a very prominent leader (Num. 1:7; 2:3; 7:12).

(6) *Salmon* (or *Salma*), husband of Rahab (Matt. 1:4).

(7) *Boaz*, husband of Ruth.

(8) *Obed*. (The Bible tells nothing of Obed, except his name.)

(9) *Jesse*, father of King David.

(10) *David*, apparently in youth, not yet referred to as *King* David.

These men all were fleshly ancestors of Jesus our Lord. Ruth, the Moabitess, became an ancestor of the Messiah, Jesus.

Questions on Section E
Ruth

1. During what period did the story of Ruth occur? (Ruth 1:1)
2. What was Naomi's husband's name? Her sons' names? (1:2)

3. Where did they live? (1:1)
4. Where did they all go to live for a while? Why? (1:1-2)
5. Name the two Moabite women that Naomi's sons married.(1:4)
6. Who died in the land where they had gone? (1:3,5)
7. What did Naomi urge her widowed daughters-in-law to do?(1:8)
8. Which daughter-in-law clung to Naomi? (1:14)
9. Whose God did Ruth accept as her God? (1:16; 2:12)
10. What do the names *Naomi* and *Mara'* mean? (1:20)
11. Why did Naomi ask that she be called *Mara'*? (1:20)
12. At what agricultural season did Naomi return? (1:22)
13. Who was Naomi's husband's relative? (2:1)
14. What work did Ruth do? (2:2)
15. What kindnesses did Boaz show to Ruth? (2:8-9, 14-16)
16. How much grain did Ruth gather the first day? (2:17)
17. How did Naomi react when she heard that Ruth had gathered grain in the field of *Boaz*? (2:20, 22)
18. What did Naomi want to find for Ruth? (3:1) (Compare the translation of this verse with the King James version of it.)
19. Where did Naomi send Ruth? Why? (3:2-4)
20. Where did Boaz lie down to sleep? (3:7)
21. What did Ruth mean by saying, "Spread the corner of your garment over me"? (3:9)
22. What does the Hebrew word *go'el* mean? (3:9)
23. What did Boaz promise to do for Ruth? (3:13)
24. What hindered Boaz from marrying Ruth at once? (3:12)
25. What did Boaz give Ruth to carry home? (3:15)
26. At what place did Boaz meet the other kinsman-redeemer? Who else was present at the meeting? (4:1-2)
27. Did the near kinsman agree to redeem the land of Elimelech? (4:3-4)
28. Why did he not redeem it? (4:5-6)
29. What action showed that the land had been legally redeemed? (4:7-8)
30. What was the significance of the words, "May the LORD make the woman . . . like Rachel and Leah"? (4:11)
31. What was the name of the son of Ruth and Boaz? (4:17) Who gave him the name?
32. What woman took the child and cared for him? (4:16)
33. What relation was Ruth to King David? (4:17)
34. What significance does the genealogy in Ruth 4:18-22 have in the fulfillment of God's promise to Abraham? (Gen. 22:18; Matt. 1:1-6)

Section F
Eli and Samuel (1 Samuel 1–7)

Introduction to 1 & 2 Samuel

1. *Purpose of the books* — The books of 1 & 2 Samuel show the fulfillment of God's preparations and prophecies concerning *kings* for Israel. God had promised to Abraham and Sarah and Jacob that *"kings* will come from you" (Gen. 17:6, 16; 35:11). In the book of Deuteronomy God gave instructions about the *kings* that Israel might have (Deut. 17:14-17). God promised that He Himself would choose their king for them (Deut. 17:15). The book of Judges several times states that wicked events occurred when "Israel had no king." A good king is necessary.

A negative purpose of the books could be to show the failure of human kings. A *divine* king is needed (Isa. 31:1-2).

Hannah (Samuel's mother) said, The LORD . . . will give strength to his *king* and exalt the horn of his *anointed"* (1 Sam. 2:10).

2. *Contents of 1 & 2 Samuel*

---

1 Samuel tells of the prophet **Samuel** (chs.1-7), and also of King **Saul** (chs. 8-31).
2 Samuel tells of the reign of King **David**.

The books of Samuel seem to have been written as one book. But they contain so much information that one scroll large enough for it all was too big to carry easily. It was divided into two books when the O.T. was translated into Greek (about 285 B.C.). Hebrew Bibles printed after A.D. 1517 divided it into two books.

The Greek and Latin and Catholic Bibles call 1 & 2 Samuel *1 & 2 Kings* (or *Kingdoms*), and 1 & 2 Kings are called *3 & 4 Kings* (or *Kingdoms*).

3. *Endings of historical books:* (Memorize these.)
   a. 1 Samuel ends with the *death of King Saul.*
   b. 2 Samuel ends near the *death of King David.*
   c. 1 Kings ends near the *death of King Ahab.*
   d. 2 Kings ends with Israel in *captivity in Babylon.*
   e. 1 Chronicles ends with the *death of King David.*
   f. 2 Chronicles ends with the *release from captivity in Babylon.*

4. *Authorship.* The author of the books of Samuel is uncertain. The Jewish *Talmud* says that Samuel wrote the books that bear his name. But then it asks, Is it not written, *Now Samuel was dead* (1 Sam. 25:1)? Answer: The book was completed by Gad the seer (1 Chr. 29:29) and Nathan the prophet. This may be true.

Ahimaaz, the son of Zadok the priest, has been suggested as author of the book or parts of it (2 Sam. 15:36; 17:17-20; 18:19). The stories about Ahimaaz are told with vivid details, as if written by an eyewitness. But he was not an eyewitness of all events recorded.

The statement in 1 Samuel 27:6 that the town of Ziklag has "belonged to the kings of *Judah* ever since" the time of David indicates that the final author of the books of Samuel lived after Judah became a separate kingdom from the other tribes. This occurred after the death of King Solomon (931 B.C.).

5. *Prophetic character of the book of Samuel.* In the Hebrew Bible the book(s) of Samuel are included in the *Former Prophets,* which is the first part of the second section of the Hebrew Bible (called the *Prophets,* or *Nevi'im*). The Former Prophets include Joshua, Judges, 1 & 2 Samuel, and 1 & 2 Kings. The books tell much about prophets like Samuel, Gad, and Nathan. The author(s) appear to have been prophets. The books present their history from a religious and moral viewpoint, not from political or social perspectives. The books continue the prophetic perspective of the book of Deuteronomy, which stresses the truth that God blesses those who serve Him. The books in a true prophetic spirit expose the failings of the leading personalities, as well as their triumphs.

6. *Chronology of the period near Samuel's life:*
   a. Samuel born — about 1100 B.C.
   b. Ark captured — about 1070 B.C.
   c. Samuel's ministry — 1070-1050 B.C.
   d. Reign of King Saul — 1050-1010 B.C.
   e. Reign of King David — 1010-970 B.C. (Note that David was reigning in 1000 B.C.)

7. *Outline of the books of Samuel:* (Memorize main parts.)
   I. Samuel's career (1 Sam. 1-7)
      A. Birth and boyhood (1:1-2:10)
      B. Rejection of Eli and call of Samuel (2:11-3:21)
      C. The ark among the Philistines (4:1-7:1)
      D. Victory over Philistines (7:2-17)
   II. Reign of King Saul (1 Sam. 8-31)
      A. Rise of Saul (chs. 8-14)
      B. Decline of Saul and rise of David (chs. 15-31)
   III. Reign of David (2 Samuel)
      A. David's lamentation over Saul (ch. 1)
      B. Reign at Hebron over Judah (chs. 2-4)
      C. Reign in Jerusalem over all tribes (chs. 5-6)
      D. God's covenant with David (ch. 7)
      E. David's conquests (chs. 8-10)
      F. David's sin and repentance (chs. 11-12)
      G. Crimes of Amnon and Absalom (chs. 13-14)
      H. Absalom's rebellion (chs. 15-18)
      I. David restored to power (chs. 19-20)
      J. Famine; revenge of Gibeonites (21:1-14)
      K. Later wars with Philistines (21:15-22)
      L. David's song and last words (22:1-23:7)
      M. David's mighty men (23:8-29)
      N. David's census and its punishment (ch. 24)

8. *Memorize:* 1 Sam. 15:22; 16:7; 2 Sam. 7:12-13; 24:24.

Questions over Introduction to 1 & 2 Samuel

1. What is the *purpose* of the books of Samuel?
2. Who are the two principal persons in 1 Samuel? Which chapters apply to each person?

3. What does 2 Samuel tell of?
4. What are 1 & 2 Samuel called in the Greek and Latin Bibles? What are 1 & 2 Kings called?
5. What events are at the *ends* of 1 & 2 Samuel? 1 & 2 Kings? 1 & 2 Chronicles?
6. Who were the authors of the books of Samuel according to the Jewish *Talmud*?
7. In what part of the Hebrew Bible are the books of Samuel placed?
8. What was the date of Samuel's ministry? King Saul's reign?
9. What are the three main parts of the outline of 1 & 2 Samuel?

1. *Birth of Samuel* (1 Sam. 1:1-20). The hometown of Elkanah, father of Samuel, was *Ramathaim* (1:1). This was probably the same place as *Ramah*, the home of Samuel (1 Sam. 1:19; 7:17). *Ramah* means "height." *Ramathaim* is the dual form of *Ramah*, meaning "the two heights." It was in the tribe of Ephraim, about six miles (10 km.) northwest of Jerusalem, at the place called *Arimathea* in the N.T. (Matt. 27:57).

Elkanah is called a *Zuphite* (1 Sam. 1:1 — NIV, NRSV), meaning one from the land of *Zuph* (1 Sam. 9:5), the area around Ramah. The reading "Zuphite" requires a slight change from the Hebrew *Ramathaim Zophim* (KJV, NASB), which may mean Ramathaim of the Zuphites.

Elkanah was an Ephraimite by residence, but by ancestry he was a Levite of the Kohathite family (Josh. 21:5; 1 Chr. 6:2, 16, 22, 26-28, 37-38). Elkanah was not in the priestly branch of that family (Levi, Kohath, Amram, Aaron, etc.), but in the line of Kohath, Izhar, Korah, etc. Therefore, Samuel his son was a Levite, but not a priest.

1 Samuel 1:2-8 — The family life of Elkanah's home was damaged by rivalry between his two wives, Hannah ("Grace") and Peninnah ("Coral"). Peninnah had borne children, but Hannah had not. Barrenness was considered a great curse in O.T. times. (See Gen. 16:1-2; 1 Sam. 2:5; Prov. 30:16.)

Polygamy was often practiced in O.T. times, but it was not God's desire for mankind. God made one wife for one man,

Adam. And why just one? "Because he was seeking a godly offspring" (Mal. 2:15).

Israelite men were commanded to go to the central sanctuary (then at Shiloh) three times a year to offer sacrifice (Ex. 23:14). The holy day referred to in 1:3-4 was probably the Feast of Tabernacles (in early October). The people assembled for several days for this (Lev. 22:34-36).

Peninnah was quite persistent in taunting Hannah for her barrenness (1:6-7), even at the tabernacle. She "kept provoking" her, hoping to "irritate" Hannah (lit., "cause her to thunder"), to cause her to scream out some unseemly outburst that would damage Elkanah's love for her. Hannah afterwards prayed, "He will thunder against them from heaven" (2:10).

The reference to the "LORD Almighty" in 1:3 is the first use of this phrase in the Old Testament. Literally it reads "LORD (Yahweh) of *hosts*" (heaven's armies). Compare 1:11; 4:4.

1 Samuel 1:9-18 — At the tabernacle Eli was the priest, with his two evil sons named Hophni and Phinehas (1:3,9; 2:12). Eli was descended from Aaron, the first high priest, but through Aaron's son Ithamar, rather than through Eleazar, Aaron's son who was ancestor of the first several generations of priests. At some time during the period of judges the priesthood had shifted over to the family of Ithamar.

The tabernacle at Shiloh is called the LORD's *temple* (1:9; 3:3; Ps. 5:9; 30:1). Probably it had been made more temple-like after it had been permanently set at Shiloh.

At the tabernacle Hannah prayed in bitterness of soul, and made a vow that if the LORD would give her a son, she would give him to the LORD all his life, and the son would be an unshaven Nazirite (1:11; Num. 6:2,5). Hannah had a close and open relationship with God. Eli at first thought that Hannah was drunken; but after he learned that she was praying, he answered her more graciously, "May the God of Israel grant you what you have asked of him" (1:17).

409

PRIESTLY DESCENDANTS OF AARON

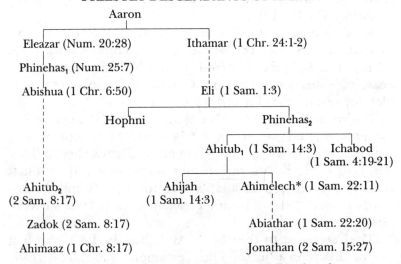

Aaron

Eleazar (Num. 20:28)   Ithamar (1 Chr. 24:1-2)

Phinehas₁ (Num. 25:7)

Abishua (1 Chr. 6:50)   Eli (1 Sam. 1:3)

Hophni   Phinehas₂

Ahitub₁ (1 Sam. 14:3)   Ichabod (1 Sam. 4:19-21)

Ahitub₂ (2 Sam. 8:17)   Ahijah (1 Sam. 14:3)   Ahimelech* (1 Sam. 22:11)

Zadok (2 Sam. 8:17)   Abiathar (1 Sam. 22:20)

Ahimaaz (1 Chr. 8:17)   Jonathan (2 Sam. 15:27)

*Christ referred to Ahimelech as "Abiathar." We therefore suppose that Ahimelech was also known by the name Abiathar, which was his son's name.

1 Samuel 1:19-20 — After Hannah returned home, the LORD "remembered" her, as He "remembered" Rachel (Gen. 30:22). She bore a son, and named him *Samuel*, which means *Name of God*. By a small play on the sound of the name, Hannah interpreted it to mean *"Asked of God."*

2. *Dedication of Samuel* (1 Sam. 1:21-28). Hannah kept the little son at home during the next "annual sacrifice" (lit., "sacrifice of the days"). With gracious words Elkanah reminded her of God's involvement with her promise. Elkanah supported Hannah in her vow to give Samuel. She remained at home and nursed (lit., suckled) her son until he was weaned.

The family took the young child (probably about three years old) to Shiloh, along with a three-year-old bull for sacrifice (Heb. MT, "three bulls"). The bull was sacrificed. (Leviticus 27:1-3 states that when people were dedicated to the LORD, a price was to be paid. The LORD does not become our debtor when we give to Him the people who are His. The privilege is ours.)

When she presented the lad to Eli, Hannah said, "And

also I myself asked for him for the L ORD all the days he will be [living]; he was asked for *for the* L ORD" (1:28; author's translation).

"And he worshiped the L ORD there." Who worshiped? Eli? Elkanah? Samuel? Samuel was very young, but probably he was fully capable of worship. Hannah had surely "coached" him for this day of his dedication. (The singular "he" in NIV 1:28 is a correct translation, instead of "they.")

3. *Prayer of Hannah* (1 Sam. 2:1-11). Hannah was not sad or distressed when she left Samuel at the temple with Eli. She was exultant and joyful. She prayed a prayer of triumph that has a military tone. Hannah had been profoundly hurt by the taunts of Peninnah. Now the L ORD had vindicated her. Her "horn" was "lifted high." ("Horn" is a symbol of strength and power.)

The "prayer" of Hannah is often called the *Song* of Hannah, because it has a poetic style (lyric) often used for songs. Her song resembles the Song of Moses (Ex. 15), the Song of Deborah (Judg. 5), the Song of David (2 Sam. 22), the "song" of Mary (the *Magnificat*) in Luke 1:46-55, and Zechariah's song (Luke 1:67-79).

The **Prayer of Hannah** (1 Sam. 2:1-10)

Theme — The L ORD humbles the mighty
but exalts the lowly.

Both Hannah and Mary became pregnant by miraculous help. In Mary's song she repeats several of the thoughts in Hannah's prayer. Both began by *rejoicing* in the L ORD (1 Sam. 2:1; Luke 1:47). Both said that the L ORD humbles the proud, but lifts up the humble (1 Sam. 2:3; Luke 1:51-52). Perhaps Mary had memorized Hannah's prayer and quoted from it.

Hannah mentions several contrasting classes of people whose status the L ORD often changes: (a) proud–humble; (b) the strong (warriors)–the weak; (c) full–hungry; (d) barren–child-bearing; (e) dead–living; (f) poor–rich.

411

Peninnah had tried to provoke Hannah to *thunder* out words that would harm her. Hannah declared, The LORD "will *thunder* against them from heaven" (1 Sam.1:6; 2:10. See Ronald Youngblood in *Expositor's Bible Commentary*, Vol. 3 [1992], pp. 571, 582.)

Hannah closed her prayer by saying, "He will give strength to his *king* and exalt the horn of his *anointed*." The word *anointed* is *Messiah*. This is the first use of this word in the Bible. David in his song also used the words *king* and *anointed* as parallel terms to refer to God's chosen king (1 Sam. 2:10; 2 Sam. 22:51). The title *Christ* (from the Greek) means the same thing as the Hebrew word *Messiah*. Jesus *Christ* was *anointed* with the Holy Spirit.

4. *Eli's wicked sons* (1 Sam. 2:12-26). There was a vivid contrast between the faithful servant boy Samuel and Eli's sons, Hophni and Phinehas (1:3; 2:1). They were wicked and grasping. They seized for themselves choice parts of the sacrifices brought to the LORD (2:16-17). They slept with the women who served at the entrance of the tabernacle (2:22). Exodus 38:3 refers to these women. They were not ceremonial prostitutes, but godly women, like Anna (Luke 2:36-37). Eli had failed to restrain his sons when they were young (3:13), and now in maturity they would not listen to his words (2:23-24). The LORD hardened their hearts, as He had hardened Pharaoh's heart (Ex. 10:27), that He might put them to death. Hophni and Phinehas had not learned from the examples of Nadab and Abihu (Lev. 10:1-2).

"Samuel was ministering before the LORD — a boy wearing a linen ephod" (2:18). This was a colorful garment worn by the priests. (See Ex. 28:6-7; 39:2-7.) The ephod was like a double apron, with front and back. Samuel served as a priest-in-training, though he was not from the priestly family of Aaron.

The loving service of Hannah in bringing to Samuel each year a little robe made with her own hands evokes precious memories to many sons who have had godly mothers (2:19). The LORD was gracious to Hannah, and she bore three sons and two daughters besides Samuel (2:21). "The barren has borne seven" (2:5). (*Seven* signifies completeness.)

5. *Prophecy against the House of Eli* (1 Sam. 2:27-36). A *man of God* came unto Eli and rebuked him. Eli had not lived according to the standards required of priests, such as his forefathers (2:28). "Why do *you* (plural, referring to Eli and his sons) scorn (lit., *kick*, as in Deut. 32:15) my sacrifice and offering?" "Why do you (sing.) honor your sons more than me by fattening yourselves on the choice parts of every (*all*) offering?" (2:29, 13-15; 3:13). (Did this cause Eli to be "heavy"? [4:18])

The consequences of Eli's failures were foretold. "I will cut short your strength (lit, *your arm*) and the strength of your father's house . . . there will never be an old man (in your family) . . .and all your descendants (lit., *all the multitude of your house*) will die in the prime of life" (lit., as *men*). Hophni and Phinehas would both die on the same day. (See 1 Sam. 2:34; 4:11.) God would raise up for himself a faithful priest to replace Eli's family. Eli's family would be reduced to begging for a tiny piece of silver.

This was fulfilled in the time of David, when only Abiathar (a descendant of Eli) escaped a massacre of the priests (1 Sam. 22:20), and he was later deposed from the priesthood (1 Kgs. 2:26-27).

Three titles for prophets –

(1) **"Man of God"** — This title emphasizes his character (1 Sam. 2:27; 9:9-10).

(2) **"Seer"** — Emphasizes his ability to "see" truths that most humans could not see (1 Sam. 9:9).

(3) **"Prophet"** — Emphasizes his speaking out the messages the LORD gave him (1 Sam. 3:20).

The "faithful priest" who would replace Eli would at first be Samuel, who did priestly acts (7:9; 9:12-13). Later, the family of Zadok received the priesthood (1 Kgs. 2:35). Ultimately, the faithful priest would be the Lord Jesus, a priest of the order of Melchizedek.

6. *The LORD calls Samuel* (1 Sam. 3:1–4:1). The LORD called
the boy Samuel one night (3:4,6,8). He told him that the guilt
of Eli's house would never be atoned for (covered) by sacrifice. On the next morning Eli insisted that Samuel tell him
what the LORD said, and Samuel did. Samuel learned early to
bear the prophet's cross, and speak painful messages. Samuel
grew up and was recognized by all Israel as a prophet of the
LORD.

In those days the word of God (prophetic revelation) was
rare (precious and costly). God had not yet revealed His
word even to the boy Samuel (3:1, 7).

Eli's eyes had become weak (3:2). Moses' eyes remained
clear until his death (Deut. 34:7). Blindness is NOT always a
punishment of God (John 9:1-3), but sometimes it was (Deut.
28:28).

The right answer to God's call:

"Speak, LORD, for your servant is listening" (1 Sam. 3:9).

When the LORD called Samuel the third time, "The LORD
came and *stood* there" (3:10). Samuel, like Abraham and
Jacob, saw God in some form.

When Samuel grew up, and God revealed Himself to
Samuel through His word (3:21), God let none of his words
"fall to the ground," that is, fail to happen exactly as God
foretold. God revealed TRUTH to Samuel, and God did not
forget what He had said.

Samuel was . . .

    (1) A **PRIEST**/**LEVITE** (1 Sam. 10:8; 1 Chr. 6:28).
    (2) The LAST **JUDGE** (1 Sam. 7:15-17).
    (3) The FIRST **PROPHET** in the continuous series
        from Samuel to Malachi (1 Sam. 3:20).

The priesthood was instituted by God to teach Israel (1 Chr.
15:3; Mal. 2:7). The priesthood failed in the time of Eli. God raised
up a new class of servants to teach His truth — His **prophets**.

The apostle Peter said, "All the prophets from *Samuel* on, . . . have foretold these days [the life of Christ and the start of Christ's church in Jerusalem on the feast of Pentecost]" (Acts 3:24). Samuel spoke Messianic prophecies, but we have none preserved.

7. *Israel defeated and the ark captured* (1 Sam. 4:1-11). The Philistines attacked Israel. In a battle at Aphek (in the coastal plains near Joppa) Israel was defeated. The sons of Eli brought out the ark of the LORD's covenant to the battlefield. But Israel was defeated with a slaughter of 30,000 men. Eli's two sons were killed in the battle. The ark was captured by the Philistines.

The Philistines immigrated from the Mediterranean islands around Crete into Israel in large numbers after 1200 B.C. They settled into the southern coastal area, around Gaza and Ashdod. They soon sought to expand their territory into the land occupied by Israelites. They camped at Aphek, eight miles northeast of Joppa (Tel Aviv). Aphek was a well-watered, strongly fortified place. The Israelites camped at Ebenezer two miles away. Ebenezer is thought to be modern Izbet Sarteh, a primitive outpost that was lived in only two centuries, 1200–1000 B.C. (See *Biblical Archaeology Review*, Sept.–Oct. 1978, pp. 18-21, 26-27.) Its destruction was probably the work of the Philistines.

After an initial defeat by the Philistines, the Israelites brought out the ark of the covenant from the tabernacle at Shiloh, (twenty-five miles away), and carried it into battle. Hophni and Phinehas, Eli's sons, were there with the ark (4:4).

The Philistines were frightened by the presence of the ark. "Woe to us! . . . these mighty gods . . . are the gods who struck the Egyptians with all kinds of plagues in the desert." (Their historical knowledge was inaccurate!)

Israel's defeat in the battle at Aphek fulfilled part of the prophecy of God to Samuel about Eli's family (2:34).

8. *The death of Eli* (1 Sam. 4:12-22). When the news came back to Shiloh about Israel's defeat and the capture of the ark, Eli fell backward off his chair at the gate and died (4:18).

He was less affected by the deaths of his sons than by the news about the ark. He had led (lit., *judged*) Israel forty years. His story is tragic.

Eli's daughter-in-law, Phinehas' wife — went into labor and delivered a son. She died after the birth, but named the son *Ichabod,* meaning "Where is the glory?" or "No glory." The name described the family of Eli and the whole nation of Israel at that time. More than that, the *glory* cloud that shone above the atonement cover (mercy seat) and indicated God's presence at the ark was gone from Israel, and in Philistine hands.

The town of Shiloh, where the ark had been, was itself destroyed about 1050 B.C., soon after the Israelites were defeated at Ebenezer. (See Jer. 7:12; 26:6; *Biblical Archaeology Review*, Jan.–Feb. 1986, pp. 22-41.)

9. *The LORD afflicts the Philistine cities* (1 Sam. 5). The Philistines had defeated Israel and taken the ark. But the Philistines had not defeated the LORD, the God of Israel. In the Philistine city of Ashdod, where the ark was placed, the idol of their god Dagon (probably a grain god) fell over and broke. The people were smitten with "tumors," probably plague boils, swellings of lymph nodes in bubonic plague. (These were not hemorrhoids, or emerods. See article "Diseases," in *Zondervan Pictorial Bible Dictionary,* 1966, p. 219.) The ark was moved to the city of Gath and then to Ekron. The tumors erupted wherever the ark was.

Ashdod was nearly due west of Jerusalem, on the Mediterranean coast. Ekron was at the place now called Tell Miqne, six miles north of Gath, in the Sorek Valley (*Biblical Archaeology Review,* Jan.–Feb. 1990, pp. 26-36).

10. *Return of the ark* (1 Sam. 6:1-7:1). By this time the Philistines recognized that they certainly had to return the ark to Israelite territory to save themselves more suffering. The ark was in the Philistine territory seven months (6:1).

On a cart pulled by cows the ark was taken up the Sorek River valley to Beth Shemesh. Some Israelites at Beth Shemesh looked into the ark, and many of them died. (NIV reads "seventy" died. The Hebrew and Greek texts both read "fifty thousand and seventy" men. This seems to be a huge number, nearly the entire population of the tribe of Dan.)

The ark was then transported on up into the hills to Kiriath Jearim (Forest City), ten miles west of Jerusalem, on the border between Judah and Benjamin. The ark remained at Kiriath Jearim most of the time for the next seventy years (about 1070–1000 B.C.), until King David brought it up to Jerusalem to place it in a new tent (2 Chr. 13, 15).

The Philistines sent an offering with the ark on the cart — five golden tumors and five gold rats — as if they wanted to be certain that the God of Israel knew exactly what the offerings were to bring them relief from.

The story of the ark being pulled by two cows who had never been "broken" to pull wagons, and who had new calves will amuse anyone who has been around cattle. These cattle would normally have gone berserk. But a divine power overruled their natural and maternal instincts, and they went placidly up the road, lowing as they went.

11. *Samuel delivers Israel from the Philistines* (1 Sam. 7:2-17). Samuel the prophet met with the Israelites and told them to get rid of their foreign idols. At a large assembly at Mizpah, Samuel and the Israelites worshiped the LORD and confessed their sins. The Philistines attacked the assembled people. Samuel prayed and offered sacrifice and the LORD sent a storm and threw the Philistines into a panic. Samuel pursued the Philistines. He set up a stone monument to this victory and called it EBENEZER — meaning *Stone of HELP* (1 Sam. 7:12).

EBENEZER means *Stone of Help*

At every point in our lives we should be able to say, "The LORD has helped me to this time and at this place."

Samuel did more to save Israel from the Philistines by his prayers and sacrifices than Samson did with his muscles. There is power in blood sacrifices (7:9; Rev. 12:11). Samuel recaptured all the towns the Philistines had taken from the Israelites (7:14).

Samuel met with the Israelites at *Mizpah* (7:5). This was probably located on the high ridge called *Nebi Samwil* seven miles northwest of Jerusalem, or at the mound named Tell en-Nasbeh nine miles north of Jerusalem.

Samuel travelled from Bethel to Gilgal to Mizpah, judging the people during his circuit (7:16). Gilgal is probably the famous place near Jericho where Israel encamped in the time of Joshua (Josh. 4:19). Khirbet el-Mefjir two miles northeast of Jericho is proposed as the location of Gilgal.

After Samuel's circuits to judge the people, he came back to his hometown of Ramah, six miles north of Jerusalem (7:17).

Questions on Section F
Eli and Samuel (1 Sam. 1–7)

1. Who was Samuel's father? (1 Sam. 1:1, 19-20)
2. Name the two wives of Elkanah. (1:2)
3. Where did they worship each year? (1:3)
4. Who was the priest? Name the priest's sons. (1:3)
5. From which son of Aaron was the priest descended?
6. What grieved Hannah? (1:5-6)
7. What request and vow did Hannah make to the LORD? (1:11)
8. Why did the priest think Hannah was drunk? (1:13-14)
9. Who was Hannah's son? (1:5-6)
10. Where did Hannah take her son? When? (1:24)
11. How did Hannah feel when she gave her child to the LORD? (2:1)
12. What song in the New Testament resembles Hannah's song?
13. What work did Samuel do at the house of God? (2:11)
14. What sort of men were Eli's sons? (2:12)
15. What did Hannah bring to Samuel each year? (2:19)
16. What other children did Hannah have? (2:21)
17. Why could Eli's sons not listen to their father? (2:25)
18. What did the man of God foretell about Eli's house? (2:31, 34)
19. How often did the LORD speak His word in those days? (3:1)
20. When did the LORD call to Samuel? (3:2-4)

21. How many times did the Lord call to Samuel? (3:8, 10)
22. What message did the Lord tell Samuel? (3:12-14)
23. What offices did Samuel hold?
24. Where did Israel encamp against the Philistines? (4:1) Where did the Philistines encamp?
25. What did the Israelites propose to do after their first defeat? (4:3)
26. How did the Philistines react to the presence of the ark? (4:7-8)
27. Tell three results of the second battle at Ebenezer. (4:10-11)
28. How old was Eli at his death? (4:15)
29. What was Eli's physical condition? (4:15, 18)
30. How did Eli react to the news of the battle? (4:18)
31. What happened to Phinehas' wife? (4:19-20)
32. Who was called *Ichabod*? What does the name mean? (4:21-22)
33. Where was the ark taken first? (5:1)
34. Who was Dagon? (5:2)
35. What happened to Dagon? (5:3-4)
36. What happened to the people of Ashdod? (5:6)
37. Where was the ark sent from Ashdod? (5:8)
38. Where was the third place the ark was sent? (5:10)
39. Where did the Philistines decide to send the ark? Why? (5:11-12)
40. How long was the ark in the land of the Philistines? (6:1)
41. What was sent back to Israel with the ark? (6:3-4)
42. By what means was the ark sent back?(6:7-9)
43. How did this show that the Lord had smitten the Philistines?
44. Where in Israel did the ark return to? (6:12)
45. During what season of the year did the ark return? (6:13)
46. Why did the Lord strike down the men of Beth Shemesh? How many men died? (6:19)
47. Where was the ark sent from Beth Shemesh? (6:21)
48. How long was the ark at Kiriath Jearim? (7:2)
49. What did Samuel command the Israelites to do? (7:3)
50. Where did Samuel gather all Israel? (7:5)
51. Who attacked as Israel was assembled? (7:7)
52. What did Samuel do to call on God to help the Israelites when they were attacked? (7:9)
53. How did God stop the Philistines' attack? (7:10)
54. What does the name *Ebenezer* mean? To what was the name given? Why? (7:12)

55. How much deliverance did Samuel give to Israel from the Philistines? (7:13-14)
56. What three cities formed Samuel's judicial circuit? (7:16)
57. What was Samuel's hometown? (7:17)

Period VIII — Period of the United Kingdom

The reigns of Saul, David & Solomon (1 Sam. 8–1 Kgs. 11; 1 Chr. 10–2 Chr. 9)

Section A
The Rise of Saul (1 Samuel 8–12)

KINGS OF THE UNITED KINGDOM OF ISRAEL

1. *SAUL* (1050–1010 B.C.) — Period of *weakness.*
2. *DAVID* (1010–970) — Period of *power.*
3. *SOLOMON* (970–931) — Period of *decay.*

---

1. *Israel asks for a king* (1 Sam. 8). National life in Israel made a major change during the old age of Samuel. Israel got a KING!

WHY ISRAEL ASKED FOR A KING

(1) The evil lives of Samuel's sons (1 Sam. 8:3,5)
(2) The desire to be like other nations (8:5, 20)
(3) A desire for an always-available leader in their battles (8:20)
(4) An attack upon them by Nahash, king of Ammon (12:12)

God had foreknown that Israel would have kings. He foretold to Abraham and Jacob, "Kings will come from you" (Gen. 17:6, 16; 35:11). The "scepter" would not depart from Judah (Gen. 49:10). Deuteronomy 17:14-17 states that God Himself would choose their king.

Samuel appointed his two sons as judges for Israel at Beersheba. This was not the LORD's appointment, nor the people's. Beersheba was over fifty miles from the area Samuel primarily served in. This shows that Samuel's authority was far-reaching, extending from Dan to Beersheba (3:20).

421

Samuel's sons were evil men who "turned aside after dishonest gain and accepted bribes, and perverted justice" (8:3). Samuel himself was a completely honest man (1 Sam. 12:3-4), but probably in his burdensome service as prophet and judge he had neglected his sons in their childhood. Israel was to select as judges men who feared God and hated "dishonest gain" (Ex. 18:21). Samuel's sons did not qualify in these ways.

Samuel was displeased with the people's request for a king, but he wisely prayed to the LORD before responding. The LORD said, "It is not *you* they have rejected; but they have rejected *me* as their king."

The Israelites had not examined their motives for asking for a king. They were placing more faith in human rulers than in God. Nonetheless, God granted them their request. He directed that a warning be spoken about the consequences of having a king.

Samuel told the people all the burdens and exactions that a king would lay upon them (8:10-18). "You yourselves will become his *slaves*" (8:17). But his warnings were not heeded.

Parts of the books of Samuel speak favorably of the kingship, and parts seem hostile to kingship. This has led some critics to say that the books had two or more authors, one favoring the monarchy and another opposed (Robert Pfeiffer, *Intro. to Old Testament* [New York: Harper, 1948], p. 341). More probably the books of Samuel give us a balanced view of the monarchy by a single author. The kingship was neither all good nor all bad.

2. *Samuel anoints Saul to be king* (1 Sam. 9:1–10:16). Saul, son of a prominent man named *Kish* from the tribe of Benjamin, was sent out to search for his father's lost donkeys (lit., *she-donkeys*). Kish was a "man of *standing*," like Boaz (Ruth 2:1), or Jeroboam I (1 Kgs. 11:28), or the woman in Proverbs 31:10.

In his search for donkeys Saul met the prophet Samuel, who honored Saul publicly, and then privately anointed Saul to be the leader over Israel. Samuel foretold to Saul that three groups of men would meet him as he journeyed homeward. These predictions by Samuel would prove to Saul beyond question that Samuel's words to him were God's words. God directed the journeys of Saul and others so they would meet at certain times and places.

> Saul went looking for lost donkeys,
> but found a kingdom!

Saul was a very complex personality. He was physically impressive, and yet timid (10:22-23). He was both self-sacrificing and self-seeking (13:15; 14:36), forgiving and yet jealous (11:13; 18:8-9). He honored God and yet disobeyed God.

Special Study
KING SAUL — GOOD OR BAD ?

"Saul and Jonathan — in life they were loved and gracious" (2 Sam. 1:23).

David praised King Saul and Jonathan after their deaths. We should do the same. Saul had his faults and failings, but mainly he was a noble king.

A. KING SAUL'S GOOD POINTS

1. *Courageous.* Saul never withdrew from a battle to protect his people, even when great odds were against him (1 Sam. 13:2-7; 14:2; 31:3).
2. *Forgiving* (at least during the first part of his reign) (1 Sam. 11:12-13).
3. *Worshipful* (part of the time). He called upon the LORD (1 Sam. 17:37; 14:37,41; 15:24-31).
4. *Good to his people.* ". . . Saul, who clothed you in scarlet and finery, who adorned your garments with ornaments of gold" (2 Sam. 1:24). Saul was a king with modest and simple tastes, unlike King Solomon, who lived in luxury at the expense of his people. The people got to enjoy their earnings. Judging from the archaeological evidence, King Saul's palace at Gibeah was rustic and quite plain.

B. KING SAUL'S BAD POINTS

1. *Impatient*, particularly with God (1 Sam. 13:8-9; 14:17-20, 36-37). We must learn to *wait* upon the LORD (Ps. 37:7).
2. *Jealous* (1 Sam. 18:7-8).
3. *Disobedient* (1 Sam. 15:19-23; 1 Chr. 10:13). He who has not learned to be obedient will not be able to cause others to obey him.

Saul's basic problem was that in his heart he wanted what **HE** wanted, not necessarily what God wanted. Pleasing God was not the major motivation in his life.

Saul was "impressive" (1 Sam. 9:2), literally, *good*, like David (1 Sam. 16:12) and Moses (Ex. 2:2).

Saul and his servant came to the town where Samuel was. "This town" was probably Ramah, Samuel's home (1 Sam. 9:6; 1:1,19; 7:17).

It was customary to give a prophet a gift when he gave information (9:7; 1 Kgs. 14:3). Some prophets were greedy for gain (Jer. 6:17). But Samuel was not a prophet for profit (1 Sam. 12:3).

> **Three titles for prophets like Samuel: (1 Sam. 9:9–10)**
> **"Man of God," "Seer," "Prophet." (See 1 Sam. 2:27.)**

The LORD *spoke* to Samuel (1 Sam. 9:15,17). The manner by which the LORD spoke is not stated; but the LORD's message was very specific and clear. Some critics brush aside the possibility that any God has ever really spoken to people (Robert Pfeiffer, *O.T. Intro.*, p. 50). But the consistent teaching of all the Bible is that "God has spoken" (Heb. 1:1).

When Samuel first told Saul he would become king, Samuel worded the news in somewhat concealed language: "To whom is all the desire of Israel turned, if not to you?" (1 Sam. 9:20). Saul seemed to understand what Samuel meant.

Saul and other leaders — Moses, Gideon, Jeremiah — have

felt unworthy of the divine honor and call, and protested that they were not adequate (1 Sam. 9:21; Ex. 3:11; Judg. 6:15; Jer. 1:6).

Samuel brought Saul into the large hall where thirty honored, invited guests were to eat (1 Sam. 9:22-24). Samuel had reserved a choice leg (or thigh) portion of meat for Saul, even before he met him. The piece was one usually reserved for the priests (Lev. 7:33).

Samuel anointed Saul when they were alone. Samuel poured a flask of oil on the head of Saul, and said, "Has not the LORD anointed you leader of his inheritance?" (10:1). (The LORD's "inheritance" is His people. Ps. 78:71)

Samuel foretold to Saul that, as he returned home, he would meet three groups of men doing very specific things (such as one man carrying three wriggly kid goats) (10:2-5). Saul himself would be overcome by the Spirit in the prophets he would meet, and would prophesy with them (10:6). The prophets would be playing "lyres, tambourines, flutes, and harps." These events would demonstrate to Saul that *God* was working out all the events that were happening to him, and therefore he should always trust and obey God.

First Samuel 10:5 mentions "Gibeah of God" (lit., *hill* of God). This probably was a name for the town of *Geba* six miles north-northeast of Jerusalem, where the Philistines had an outpost of troops (10:5; 13:3). It is not the same place as Gibeah of Benjamin (10:26; 13:2), which was Saul's home, three miles north of Jerusalem.

The existence of a "procession of prophets" (10:5) shows that after the time of Samuel the prophets in Israel became more numerous and more organized. The guild of prophets became known as the "*sons* (or company) *of the prophets*" (2 Kgs. 2:3,5; 6:1).

When Saul joined in prophesying with the prophets who met him, his former acquaintances all asked, "Is Saul also among the prophets?" (1 Sam. 10:11). They were clearly amazed by this. One resident went so far as to question the spiritual integrity of all the prophets, including Saul, saying, "Who is their father?" Saul encountered some suspicion and skepticism (10:27). The question "Is Saul among the prophets?" became a scornful popular saying to express suspicion or surprise about anything that might be the work of God. (Compare 19:24.) But prospects looked excellent for Saul.

Saul told his uncle Ner (1 Sam. 14:50) that he had met the prophet Samuel; but he did *not* tell him that Samuel had anointed him as leader over Israel (10:14-16). Ner probably was not prepared to accept his nephew as God's leader over Israel.

THE STORY OF KING SAUL

1. **Rise to power** (1 Sam. 9–12)
2. **Fall into disobedience** (1 Sam. 13–15)
3. **Descent to doom** (1 Sam. 16–31)

---

3. *Saul publicly made king* (1 Sam. 10:17-27). Samuel gathered the Israelites at Mizpah (See notes on 1 Samuel 7:5-6). He rebuked them sternly: "You have now rejected your God, who saves you" (10:19). Nonetheless, the procedure of selecting the king was carried out by drawing lots (Josh. 14:2; Prov. 16:33). Saul's name was selected.

Saul was found, though he had "hidden himself among the baggage" (10:22). The Hebrew word for "baggage" (KJV, "stuff") often has a military association (as in 1 Samuel 25:13). Perhaps Saul was hiding at the wagon containing Israel's weapons. (Is this a hint that Saul would become a great warrior?) The fact that he was *hiding* makes Saul appear very human and humble, almost to the point of insecurity.

When Saul was presented before the people, they shouted with joy, "Long live the king!"

Samuel "explained to the people the regulations of the kingship" (lit., the *decision*, or judgment, of the kingship). Probably he told them the story of how God had selected Saul. Samuel wrote these things down on a scroll (Heb. MT, "in *the* book," perhaps referring to their sacred Scriptures). He deposited the record "before the LORD," as Moses had placed his writings by the ark (Deut. 31:26).

Saul returned home to Gibeah, "accompanied by valiant men whose hearts God had touched" (10:26). (We should desire to join that company of men.) But certain troublemakers ("sons of Belial") said, "How can this fellow save us?" (10:27), and gave him no gifts or respect. (Compare 10:11-12; Proverbs 24:21.)

4. *Saul rescues the city of Jabesh Gilead* (1 Sam. 11:1-11). An opportunity soon came for Saul to demonstrate his divine appointment, authority and his ability. Nahash, leader of the Ammonites (who lived east of the tribe of Gad, east of the Jordan) went up and besieged the town of Jabesh Gilead. (Nahash is not called *king* in this passage; but compare 2 Samuel 10:2; 1 Chronicles 19:1.) Jabesh Gilead lay three miles east of the Jordan, ten miles southeast of Beth Shan. Its remains lie by a brook still called the Wadi *Yabis*, or Jabesh.

The Ammonites had shown an aggressive and unreasonable spirit back in the time of the judges, in the time of Jephthah (Judg. 10:7,17; 11:13). The Ammonites under Nahash again sought to humiliate all Israel. They would not even allow the people of Jabesh Gilead to surrender unless they consented to allow Nahash to gouge out the right eye of everyone. (Sin makes people cruel and vicious.)

A Dead Sea scroll of the book of Samuel (4QSam^a) adds that Nahash had already attacked and overcome the whole area east of Jordan, and had gouged out the right eyes of all the people there. Josephus gives a similar report (*Ant.* VI, v,1 [68-70]).

The elders of Jabesh Gilead managed to obtain seven days of reprieve from the Ammonites, and sent messengers into Israel calling for help. The messengers came to Gibeah, apparently unaware that Saul had been appointed as king or lived there.

When Saul heard of the plight of Jabesh, the Spirit of God came upon him in power. Saul was empowered by the Spirit in the way that Samson and the judges had been empowered. Saul gathered a huge army quickly (3-4 days?), by sending out pieces of oxen cut apart. (Compare Judges 19:29–20:1.) The men of Israel were numbered separately from the men of Judah (1 Sam. 10:8). This appears to be an early indication of the complete division that would occur later between Judah and Israel.

Saul gathered the forces at Bezek (located west of Jabesh Gilead, and west of Jordan, about ten miles). Word was sent into Jabesh that they would have deliverance "tomorrow." The men of Jabesh pretended to the Ammonites that they would surrender "tomorrow" (1 Sam. 11:10).

Saul attacked the Ammonites in the "last watch of the night" (lit., the *morning watch*, the third watch of the night, just before morning). This was the same "watch" as the time when the LORD thwarted the Egyptians at the Red Sea (Ex. 14:28).

Saul's victory at Jabesh Gilead was total. "No two Ammonites were left together." By this victory Saul became well-known.

5. *Saul's kingship reaffirmed* (1 Sam. 11:12–12:25). It appears that Samuel and many other non-combatants had come along to be near Saul's battle at Jabesh, perhaps to provide support for their fighting men (11:7,12).

After the victory Saul graciously refused to allow any vengeance to be inflicted upon those who had scorned him when he was first made king (11:12-13; 10:11-12, 27). He said, "No one shall be put to death today, for this day the LORD has rescued Israel." This may have been Saul's finest moment. Years later David spoke similiar words concerning Shimei (2 Sam. 19:22).

Samuel summoned the people to Gilgal to "reaffirm (or renew) the kingship." The *Gilgal* referred to was probably not the Gilgal near Jericho, but another place (now called Jiljiliah) seven miles north of Bethel, more in the center of the land.

Saul had been selected and installed as king first at Mizpah (1 Sam. 10:17,23). His kingship was confirmed in the presence of the LORD at a mass meeting and celebration at Gilgal (11:15). This meeting closed with a stern speech by Samuel to the people (12:1-25).

Outline of Samuel's farewell speech to the people

(1) Samuel's challenge about his uprightness (1 Sam.12:1-5)
(2) Samuel's review of Israel's unfaithfulness (12:6-15)
(3) Samuel's demonstration of God's power (12:16-19)
(4) Samuel's warning and promises to the people (12:20-25)

Samuel sounds quite defensive in upholding his own upright conduct (12:3-5). The lives of Samuel's evil sons were not mentioned out loud, but they could hardly have been forgotten (8:1-5).

Samuel reviewed Israel's record of forgetting the LORD ever since the time of Moses (1 Sam.12:6-11). Moses himself had confronted Israel with similar accusations (Deut. 9:24).

Jerub-Baal (12:11) was Gideon (Judg. 6:32). "Barak" in 12:11 is *Bedan* in Hebrew; the Greek reads "Barak." Perhaps his name was spelled both ways. Instead of "Samuel" in 12:11, some Greek manuscripts read "Samson." This would seem to be a more discreet name for Samuel to mention, though Samuel was not reticent in asserting his own authority.

To impress upon the people what an evil act they had done in asking for a king (and also, it would seem, to confirm his own authority), Samuel prayed the LORD to send thunder and rain (1 Sam. 12:17). It was then wheat harvest time (early June), when rain is almost never seen. (The author saw a brief sprinkle of rain in Hebron once on June 6.) Rain in harvest is a disaster (Prov. 26:1). The wheat is quickly struck down to the ground and imbedded in sticky red mud. The people acknowledged their sins, but they had gone too far to back out of their request for a king.

In his closing words Samuel warned them about idols (12:21), and about "doing evil." "Both you and your king will be swept away." Samuel promised to *pray* for them regularly, and to *teach* them the way that was good and right. (Compare Acts 6:4.)

A good leader's responsibility: "Far be it from me that I should sin against the LORD by failing to *pray* for you" (1 Sam. 12:23).

The main part of Samuel's life and judgeship ends at the close of chapter 12, although his life extended on to 1 Samuel 25:1, after the anointing of David. He was Israel's greatest judge.

The Greatness of Samuel

1. He alone saved Israel from military defeat by Philistines.
2. He almost alone kept Israel with the LORD.
3. He preserved the civil laws of the nation.
4. He kept the tribes united as one nation, in spite of the tendency of Judah to "go it alone" from Israel (1 Sam.11:8).
5. He anointed the first two kings of Israel.

Questions on Section A
The Rise of Saul (1 Sam. 8–12)

1 Samuel 8
1. Whom did Samuel make judges over Israel? Give their names. (8:1-2)
2. What special request did the people of Israel make to Samuel? Why did they ask for this? (8:4-6,19)
3. How did Samuel react to their request? (8:6)
4. Whom did God say that the people had rejected? (8:7)
5. Did God tell Samuel to grant the people's request? (8:9,22)
6. What warning was to be given to the people? (8:10-17)
7. Did the people change their request after the warning? (8:19)

1 Samuel 9
1. Who was Kish? (9:1)
2. How tall was Saul? (9:2; 10:23)
3. On what mission was Saul sent by his father? (9:3)
4. Why did Saul want to return home after being unsuccessful on his search? (9:5)
5. What is a *seer*? Who was the seer? (9:9,11,15)
6. Why did Saul and his servant desire to go to the seer? (9:8)
7. Who told Saul where he could find the seer? (9:11-12)
8. What information had the Lord revealed to the seer? (9:15-16)

9. From what enemy was the new leader to deliver Israel? (9:16)
10. Where did Saul sit while eating with the seer? What was given to Saul to eat? (9:19, 23-24)
11. Where did Saul and the seer talk, after coming down from the high place? (9:25)
12. Why did Samuel ask Saul to stay with him? (9:27)

1 Samuel 10
1. What was done to Saul when he was anointed? (10:1)
2. What three groups of men was Saul to meet after leaving Samuel? (10:2-3,6)
3. Where was Saul to wait until Samuel came?(10:8)
4. What proverbial saying arose after Saul prophesied? (10:12)
5. What did Saul tell his uncle Ner? What did he *not* tell him? (10:14-16)
6. Where did Samuel gather the people together? (10:17)
7. From what tribe was Saul? (10:20)
8. How was the new king selected and made known to the people? (10:20-21)
9. Who said that Saul was hidden among the baggage? (10:22)
10. How did the people react to the new king? (10:24)
11. Was everyone pleased with the new king? (10:27)

1 Samuel 11
1. Who was Nahash? (11:1; 12:12)
2. What city did Nahash attack? What was his condition for the people to surrender? (11:2)
3. Where did the city send messengers seeking help? (11:4)
4. What came upon Saul when he heard of the city's plight? (11:6)
5. What did Saul do to recruit an army? (11:7)
6. How did Saul divide up his troops when he attacked? (11:11)
7. What words of kindness did Saul utter after the battle? (11:13)
8. Where did Samuel call the people together? (11:14)
9. For what purpose did Samuel call the people together? (11:14)

1 Samuel 12
1. To whom did Samuel speak? (12:1)
2. Was Samuel then young or old? (12:2)
3. Why did Samuel challenge the people to accuse him of wrongdoing? (12:3; 8:5)
4. According to Samuel, had Israel always remembered their God? (12:9-11)
5. Which judges does Samuel mention? Who is *Bedan*? (12:11)
6. What would happen to Israel and its king if they feared the LORD and served Him? What would happen if they did not? (12:14-15)

431

7. What miraculous occurrence did Samuel cause to happen? (12:16-18)
8. What did Samuel say he would continue to do for Israel? (12:23)
9. What would be their punishment if Israel continued doing wickedly? (12:25)

Section B
Decline of Saul and Rise of David
(1 Samuel 13–2 Samuel 1)

1. *Philistine attack upon Israel* (1 Sam. 13:1-7). "Saul was thirty years old when he became king" (1 Sam. 13:1). This NIV translation of the verse is conjectural. Our present Hebrew text lacks the number telling how old Saul was when he became king. (NRSV translates it correctly by omitting the number. The Greek Bible omits 1 Samuel 13:1.) The last clause of 13:1 and part of 13:2 may be translated, "And he [Saul] ruled two years over Israel, and [then] Saul chose for himself three thousand [men] from Israel."

During the early part of Saul's reign his kingdom was so weak that the Philistines could come up from their cities in the coastal plains into the central hill country of Israel and make raids on towns like Geba and Michmash (seven miles northeast of Jerusalem). These raids caused a lot of Israelites to hide in caves or leave their homes as refugees (13:6-7).

At this critical time Jonathan, King Saul's son, became Israel's deliverer. He attacked the Philistine outpost at Geba. His act provoked the Philistines to heavier attacks.

The "Gilgal" of 13:7 where Saul remained may not be the famous Gilgal near Jericho in the Jordan valley, but a place about twenty miles north of Jerusalem. (See Barry Beitzel, *Moody Atlas of Bible Lands*, pp. 57, 134.)

2. *King Saul offers a foolish sacrifice* (1 Sam. 13:8-15). Saul waited for seven days at Gilgal with his quaking little army of two thousand, waiting for the prophet Samuel to arrive. Nearly three years before Samuel had told Saul, "Go down ahead of me to Gilgal. *I* [emphasized] will surely come down to you to sacrifice burnt offerings and fellowship (peace) offerings. Seven days you shall *WAIT* until I come to you and tell you what you are to do" (1 Sam. 10:8).

Saul waited the seven days. He saw many of his troops beginning to desert and scatter. Only about six hundred men were yet with him. Saul therefore offered the burnt offering himself. He had not yet had time to offer the fellowship offering, when LO! Samuel arrived. Saul must have heard that Samuel was near, for he went out to greet Samuel. Saul told Samuel how he had "felt compelled" (or "forced myself") to offer the sacrifice.

Samuel said, "You have acted foolishly . . . Now your kingdom will not endure," meaning that his descendants would not rule after him.

Saul's sin was not primarily in offering the sacrifice, though that work was reserved for priests only (Num. 3:10). Kings like David and Solomon sometimes offered sacrifices in unusual situations and were not punished (2 Sam. 24:25; 1 Kgs. 3:15). Samuel stated twice what Saul's sin was: "You have not kept the LORD's command" (1 Sam. 13:13, 14). Samuel's command for Saul to WAIT until he came was *God's* command. Saul could not be available for Samuel to instruct him what to do if he did not wait for Samuel.

Samuel had previously demonstrated his awesome power over the Philistines and the potency of burnt offerings he offered (1 Sam. 7:9-10). Saul had every reason to trust Samuel, and no reliable alternatives. But Saul had a rash impatience. If events did not occur just when he expected, he would take matters into his own hands and do something. He showed this spirit on several other occasions (1 Sam. 14:18-19, 36-39; 15:9,22; 28:5-7).

Samuel may indeed have arrived a few hours after the seven days had passed, and perhaps even on the next day. (See Exodus 22:29 for a grammatical comparison.) But Saul trusted more in the sacrifice itself than in the prophetic authority of Samuel or the protection of God. It is very difficult for some people to "*Wait* for the LORD" (Ps. 27:14; 37:7).

Saul had no dependable resources available to him to save Israel from the Philistines. Samuel would have told him some sure method. Because of Saul's disobedience Samuel left Gilgal without instructing Saul, and Saul went off to face the enemy ignorant of God's guidance. Only the courage and faith of his son Jonathan saved Israel in the fight that followed.

3. *Israel without weapons* (1 Sam. 13:16-22). The Philistines kept a monopoly on iron technology and blacksmithing, so that the Israelites had almost no weapons. (See J.D. Muhly, "Iron Technology," in *Biblical Archaeology Review,* Nov.–Dec.1982, pp. 40-54.) The Philistines charged the Israelites exorbitant rates to sharpen implements. They charged two-thirds of a shekel (Hebrew, *pîm*) to sharpen a plowshare. (A *shekel* was a unit of weight, about .4 oz.) A plowshare was a small cone of iron placed over the end of a wood post used to make furrows.)

While Israel was in this weakened state, the Philistines had occupied Michmash (eight miles northeast of Jerusalem), and from there were sending out raiding parties north and west and east toward the desert. The psychological effect was terrifying.

4. *Jonathan defeats the Philistines* (1 Sam. 14:1-48). Two men — King Saul's son Jonathan and his armor bearer — climbed down a deep valley, and up its other side to the village of *Michmash.* After an initial fight in which the two men slew twenty men in a small field, the entire Philistine army panicked, and Israel won a great victory that day (14:15).

This exciting story occurred about eight miles northeast of Jerusalem. Just south of Michmash is a deep valley (a wadi) now called the Wadi Suweinit. It extends eastward into the Wadi Qelt, which goes into the Jordan near Jericho. Just south of the ravine by Michmash is the village of Geba, less than two miles from Michmash. King Saul and the Israelites were camped at Geba. Jonathan and his armor bearer slipped away without telling anyone. At the bottom of the valley steep rock crags rim the brook. The crag on the north is named Bozez, and the one on the south is called Seneh. They are about fifty feet high. The valley forms a strong natural military defense line.

Jonathan's victory was a victory of faith. He said, "Perhaps the LORD will act in our behalf. Nothing can hinder the LORD from saving, whether by many or by few" (1 Sam. 14:6).

On Feb. 13, 1918, the British army captured the village of Michmash from the Turks. After reading the Bible account of Jonathan's victory, the brigade major sent out only a company of soldiers in the night across the deep valley and up to Michmash. Just before dawn they found themselves on a flat piece of ground, perhaps the same field mentioned in 1 Samuel 14:14. The Turks, who were sleeping, awoke, and thought they were surrounded by the armies of Lord Allenby and fled in disorder. Thus after three thousand years of time the tactics of Jonathan were repeated with success. (From Vivian Gilbert, *The Romance of the Last Crusade* [New York: Appleton-Century, 1923], pp. 180-186.)

The glory of Jonathan's victory was nearly ruined by the conduct of his father. Saul joined in the pursuit of the fleeing Philistines, and was so impatient to overtake them that he would not allow his men even to eat. Jonathan unknowingly broke the oath Saul had made his men swear to keep. Saul was ready to kill Jonathan. But Saul's men rescued Jonathan, and he was not put to death (13:45).

Saul in the following years fought against Israel's enemies on all sides. He delivered Israel from the hands of those who had plundered them (1 Sam. 14:47-48). Saul was courageous, and willing to lay down his life for his countrymen.

King Saul's Three Philistine Wars brought him no glory.

1. First war (at *Michmash*) — Jonathan was hero.
2. Second war (at *Valley of Elah*) — David was hero (David killed Goliath).
3. Third war (at *Mt. Gilboa*) — Saul killed himself.

---

5. *Saul's family* (1 Sam. 14:49-51)
   a. Father — Kish (of the tribe of Benjamin)
   b. Wife — Ahinoam
   c. Sons — Jonathan, Ishvi (Ish-Bosheth), Malki-Shua
   d. Daughters — Merab (pronounced May-RAHV)
                  Michal (Me-KHALL) (became David's wife)

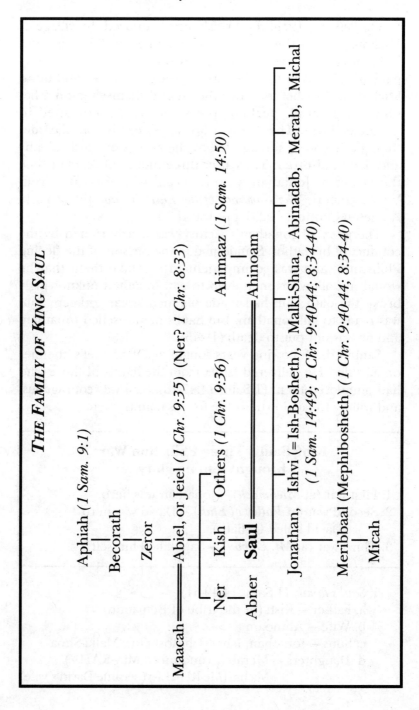

THE FAMILY OF KING SAUL

Aphiah (*1 Sam. 9:1*)

Becorath

Zeror

Maacah══Abiel, or Jeiel (*1 Chr. 9:35*) (Ner? *1 Chr. 8:33*)

Others (*1 Chr. 9:36*)

Ahimaaz (*1 Sam. 14:50*)

Ner

Kish

Abner

Saul══Ahinoam

Jonathan, Ishvi (= Ish-Bosheth), Malki-Shua, Abinadab, Merab, Michal
(*1 Sam. 14:49; 1 Chr. 9:40-44; 8:34-40*)

Meribbaal (Mephibosheth) (*1 Chr. 9:40-44; 8:34-40*)

Micah

e. Uncle — Ner

f. Cousin — Abner (son of Ner)

6. *Saul sent against the Amalekites* (1 Sam. 15:1-9). The LORD sent King Saul against the Amalekites, to attack them and destroy them and their possessions utterly. Saul carried out most of this mission (15:7-8). But he did spare their king, Agag, and spared the best of their livestock (15:9).

The Amalekites were descendants of Esau (Gen. 36:12). They were nomadic predators in the deserts. They had attacked the Israelites as they were travelling from Egypt to Mt. Sinai (Ex. 17:8-14). At that time God had sentenced them to be totally exterminated. God in His grace and patience had allowed four hundred years to pass before He finally took vengeance. King Saul himself had already had battles with the Amalekites (1 Sam. 14:48), who had plundered them. The Amalekites had demonstrated that they were NEVER going to change their cruel ways.

7. *Saul rejected as king* (1 Sam. 15:10-34). The LORD sent Samuel to confront Saul. Saul was very defensive about his actions (15:20-21). Samuel rebuked Saul in strong language:

Does the LORD delight in burnt offerings and sacrifices as much as in obeying the voice of the LORD?

To obey is better than to sacrifice! (1 Sam. 15:22).

Samuel pronounced God's judgment upon Saul:

"Because you have rejected the word of the LORD, **he has rejected you as king**" (1 Sam. 15:23).

Saul seized hold of Samuel's robe as Samuel began to depart, and the robe tore. Samuel used this as an object lesson: "The LORD has *torn* the kingdom of Israel from you today" (15:28). Saul was remorseful, but God "who is the Glory of Israel does not lie or change his mind" (1 Sam. 15:29).

Samuel himself executed Agag, king of the Amalekites. The New King James Version preserves the wording of the Hebrew text:

"Samuel hacked Agag in pieces before the LORD in Gilgal" (15:33).

King Saul's Acts of Disobedience and Their Punishments

1. *Offering sacrifice* himself (1 Sam. 13:8-14). His kingdom would not endure, that is, his family (or dynasty) would not rule after him.
2. *Not destroying the Amalekites* completely (1 Sam. 15:9, 23). God rejected Saul as king.
3. *Seeking the witch* (1 Chr. 10:13). Saul died.

---

8. *Samuel anoints David* (1 Sam. 16:1-13). The LORD sent Samuel to *Bethlehem* (six miles south of Jerusalem), to the house of *Jesse* (grandson of Ruth and Boaz), to anoint one of his sons to be Israel's next king in place of Saul. (Bethlehem is known as the "City of David," as is Jerusalem also [Luke 2:11].)

Samuel's arrival in Bethlehem caused anxieties (16:4). A man who could denounce one king (Saul) and kill another (Agag) was not a person to be trifled with.

Jesse had eight sons (1 Sam. 17:12; 1 Chr. 2:13-15). Jesse's three older sons were impressive in physical appearance. But none of them were chosen to become king.

"Man looks at the outward appearance, but the LORD looks at the heart" (1 Sam. 16:7).

David was brought back to his home from his work of tending sheep. David was ruddy, with a fine appearance and handsome. Samuel anointed him (poured a horn of oil upon his head) in the presence of his brothers. (Their reaction is not told, but they later showed some resentment toward their

little brother David [17:28].) From that day the Spirit of the
LORD came upon David in power.

> Psalm 89:20-21 — I have found **David** my servant; with my
> sacred oil I have *anointed* him. My hand will sustain him;
> surely my arm will strengthen him.

9. *David plays the harp to comfort Saul* (1 Sam. 16:14-23).
King Saul suffered much when the Spirit of the LORD
departed from him, and an "evil spirit" from the LORD tormented him (16:14).

How could the one great and good God send an "*evil*
spirit"? The adjective *evil* in the Scriptures often refers to
physical evils rather than to moral evils. A plague is evil
(1 Sam. 6:9); a storm is evil (Jonah 1:8); poisonous herbs are
evil (2 Kgs. 4:14); boils are evil (Job 2:7). Saul's depression of
mind (or whatever it might be called) certainly was an *evil*.
God does not tempt people to do moral evils (James 1:13),
but God does send physical evils of all types upon those who
disobey His commands.

God specifically warned in the law of Moses that if the
people disobeyed His commandments, He would send upon
them "confusion of mind" (Deut. 28:28). God specifically
mentioned that their king could be punished (Deut. 28:36).
King Saul received the punishment that God had forewarned
would come.

David was summoned to come to King Saul and play the
harp for him. David was probably about thirteen to sixteen at
this time. From David's town of Bethlehem to Saul's capital
at Gibeah is about ten miles, with Jerusalem in between
them. David's playing helped Saul much. Saul liked (lit.,
loved) David very much and David became an armor-bearer
for Saul (16:21). It is surely one of the greatest ironies of all
history that David should play the harp to comfort the
rejected king whom he was to replace. David never showed
rivalry or disrespect for Saul.

10. *David and Goliath* (1 Sam. 17). In Saul's second war with the Philistines, David came out to the battlefield to bring food to his older brothers in Saul's army. While he was there, David killed the Philistine giant Goliath with a slingstone. David probably was about eighteen to twenty when this occurred.

The battle with Goliath and the Philistines took place in the valley of *Elah*. This valley starts just west of Bethlehem and extends west to the Mediterranean. The battle site between Socoh and Azekah was less than twenty miles west of Bethlehem, so David did not have far to travel to get to it. The Philistines were camped on the south side of the valley, and the Israelites on the north.

David's battle with Goliath made David an instant celebrity. The obscure shepherd boy became known to the whole nation at once. This was God's way of bringing David to the throne. It brought David into contact with the royal family. David's battle with Goliath speeded up the process of King Saul's downfall. The battle delivered Israel from the Philistines for a time. The battle had great significance.

Goliath's weapons were frightening. The iron point on his spear weighed six hundred shekels, about fifteen pounds (like a sharpened shot put!). His body was protected with scale armor, and his legs with greaves (shin guards) of bronze (17:5-7).

David's brother Eliab, a soldier in Saul's army, scorned David's interest in the battle with Goliath. David replied, "Can't I even speak?" (King James Version: "*Is there* not a cause?" Both translations are permissible. They depend upon the meaning given to the Hebrew word *davar*, which can mean word, or thing, or matter, or affair, or even "cause." We prefer the older translation. David was not being flippant or casual when he mentioned fighting Goliath. It was a life-threatening decision for him. Henry P. Smith in the *International Critical Commentary* on Samuel translates the clause, "Is it not a matter of importance?")

David talked openly to King Saul about God, and openly to Goliath about God (17:36, 45).

The fact that King Saul offered to David his armor to wear

suggests that David must have been a husky youth. Saul was a very large man. He would not have asked David to wear his armor if David had been so small that the armor would be hanging beyond his hands (17:38-39).

David told Goliath that he would cut off his head "that the whole world will know that there is a God in Israel" (17:46). This battle was not just "the underdog" whipping the big dog. It was a battle about God vs. the enemies of God. David's devotion to God was very strong, even when he was a youth.

Slingstones used in warfare in Bible times were about the size of baseballs. David killed Goliath with one stone, while he was running toward Goliath and Goliath toward him.

After David had killed Goliath and beheaded him, Saul asked his army commander, Abner, "Whose son is that young man?" (17:55). That seems a strange statement in view of the fact that David played the harp for Saul and Saul loved him. But several months or years had intervened since then, and David had matured. Besides that, Saul had seen David when he was in a bad frame of mind, and not concentrating on remembering names.

The Philistines did not honor Goliath's promise to be slaves of the Israelites if one of them could kill Goliath! (17:9)

11. *David's relationships with Saul's family* (1 Sam. 18).

    a. Relationship with Jonathan — Love (18:1-4).

    b. With Saul — Jealousy and enmity from Saul (18:5-16).

    c. With Merab (Saul's daughter) — Cancelled marriage (18:17-19).

    d. With Michal (Saul's daughter) — Love, marriage (18:20-29).

The friendship of Jonathan and David was one of the greatest friendships in history. It reveals the possibility and preciousness of human friendship. To David, Jonathan's love was wonderful, "more wonderful than that of women" (2 Sam. 1:26). "A man of many companions may come to ruin, but there is a friend who sticks closer than a brother" (Prov. 18:24). The friendship of Jonathan continued all through the lives of both David and Jonathan. Jonathan gladly yielded his right of succession to his father's throne to David.

The song of the women about Saul and David created jealousy in Saul: "Saul has slain his thousands, and David his tens of thousands" (18:7). It is very probable that the women were NOT trying to contrast Saul with David. According to the patterns in Hebrew poetic parallelism (the relationship between successive lines), a numerical term in one line was sometimes made parallel to a number ten times as large in the next line, when both numbers referred to the same large but indefinite quantity. Thus in Psalm 91:7 — "A thousand may fall at your side, ten thousand at your right hand, but it will not come near you." Compare Micah 6:7; Psalm 144:13.

Saul did not take the song of the women as equal praise for himself and David. Nor did he seem willing to give David the honor that he truly deserved. Shortly thereafter, Saul attempted to spear David to the wall as David played for him (18:11). Saul did not often miss when he threw his spear at someone (2 Sam. 1:22).

Saul's scheme to get David killed by the Philistines while he was trying to obtain a hundred foreskins of Philistines as a purchase price for Saul's daughter Michal as wife seems ugly and cowardly and irrational (18:24-27). Perhaps we should pity Saul rather than condemn him.

"Michal loved David." This is one of very few statements in the Bible that a particular women loved her husband. Sadly, a beautiful love story ended with a breakup (2 Sam. 6:20-23).

David had continual success as a military leader in Saul's army (18:5, 30). David won the loyalty of a number of men (18:27), who stayed with David when he had to flee from Saul.

12. *Saul's continued enmity toward David* (1 Sam. 19). Jonathan interceded for David to his father Saul, who was seeking to kill David (19:1-7).

Saul sent men to David's house to watch it and to kill him in the morning (19:11). During the night Michal let David out of the house through a window. Psalm 59 was written by

David near this time. The title of the psalm says, "Of David . . . When Saul had sent men to watch David's house in order to kill him." (Read the psalm to learn David's feelings at that time.)

David's wife Michal saved David's life by stuffing his bed with an idol (*teraphim*, the same as the idols Rachel took [Gen. 31:19]). Michal said that David was ill in bed (19:11-17). (This does not mean that it is sometimes right to lie or to have idols in the house.)

David had to flee from Gibeah (Saul's capital, three miles north of Jerusalem) to Samuel at Ramah (just two miles north of Gibeah). ("Naioth" in 19:19, 23 seems to refer to a region or compound near Ramah.)

When Saul sent men to Ramah to capture David, they were seized by the divine Spirit of God and prophesied (19:18-20). Saul himself was overwhelmed by the same divine power (19:23-24). This marvelous event should have convinced David that he need never fear Saul nor anyone else, and convinced Saul that he could never harm David. Neither Saul nor David seemed to learn these lessons.

When Saul stripped off his clothes and prophesied, some people asked, "Is Saul also among the prophets?" (19:24). This same saying was expressed when Saul first became king (1 Sam. 10:12). The question expressed skepticism of Saul's credentials. By the time Saul prophesied at Naioth in Ramah, he was discredited both as a prophet and king.

1. *Gibeah* (1 Sam. 19:1-17)
   a. Jonathan intercedes for David. (19:1-7)
   b. Saul tries to spear David. (19:8-10)
   c. Michal helps David escape. (19:11-17)
2. *Ramah* (1 Sam. 19:18-24; Ps. 59)
   a. David visits Samuel. (19:18-19)
   b. Saul and his men prophesy. (19:20-24)
3. *Gibeah* (1 Sam. 20)
   a. David is absent from feast of new moon. (20:1-34)
   b. Jonathan warns David by arrows. (20:35-42)
4. *Nob* (1 Sam. 21:1-9) (Nob was located about 2.5 miles north of Jerusalem near the Mt. of Olives.)
   a. Ahimelech gives David food and weapons. (21:1-6, 8-9)

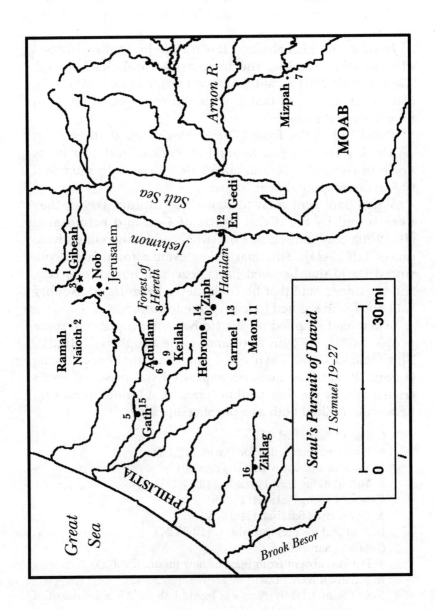

Saul's Pursuit of David
1 Samuel 19–27

30 mi

0

b. Doeg the Edomite witnesses Ahimelech's acts. (21:7)
5. *Gath* (1 Sam. 21:10-15; Ps. 34, 56)
   a. David pretends madness.
6. *Adullam* (1 Sam. 22:1-2; Ps. 142)
   a. David gathers 400 followers.
7. *Mizpah of Moab* (1 Sam. 22:3-5)
   a. David leaves his parents there for safety.
8. *Forest of Hereth* (1 Sam. 22:5-23; Ps. 52)
   a. Saul kills the priests at Nob. (22:5-19)
   b. Abiathar comes to David. (22:20-23)
9. *Keilah* (1 Sam. 23:1-12)
   a. David saves Keilah from the Philistines. (23:1-6)
   b. Saul pursues David. (23:7-12)
10. *Ziph* (1 Sam. 23:13-23)
    a. David escapes to the wilderness. (23:13-14)
    b. Jonathan's last visit with David. (23:15-18)
    c. Ziphites reveal David's hiding place to Saul. (23:19-23)
11. *Maon* (1 Sam. 23:24-28)
    a. David narrowly escapes Saul.
12. *En Gedi* (1 Sam. 23:29-24:22)
    a. David spares Saul.
13. *Carmel* (1 Sam. 25)
    a. Samuel dies. (25:1)
    b. Nabal refuses to give food to David's men. (25:2-13)
    c. Abigail's intercession. (25:14-35)
    d. Death of Nabal. (25:39-44)
    e. David marries Abigail. (25:39-44)
14. *Ziph* (1 Sam. 26)
    a. Ziphites reveal David's hiding place again. (26:1-3)
    b. David spares Saul. (26:4-25)
15. *Gath* (1 Sam. 27:1-4)
    a. David dwells with Achish.
16. *Ziklag* (1 Sam. 27:5-12)
    a. David receives Ziklag from Achish. (27:5-7)
    b. David raids southern tribes. (27:8-12)

20. *Jonathan shields David from his father* (1 Sam. 20). This chapter tells the start of David's experiences as an outlaw, one sought by the ruler "dead or alive." The friendship of Jonathan shines at its brightest at this time.

Jonathan went up to Ramah to see David. David said to

Jonathan a truth that we all could rightly say:

> "There is only a step between me and death" (1 Sam. 20:3).

Jonathan and David devised a communication signal, so Jonathan could let David know if it was safe for him to come in to the New Moon festival meal. Jonathan asked David to swear that he would never "cut off your kindness" to his family, even when all the rest of David's enemies were cut off (20:15). This request surprises us, but Jonathan knew David better than we do. David showed later that he could seek angry revenge (1 Sam. 25:12-13, 24). David never in his life sought to harm Saul, or even spoke harshly to him.

When David's place at the table was empty for a second day, Saul asked Jonathan about him. Saul was furious with Jonathan when he learned David was not coming. He called Jonathan a bad name, and hurled his spear at Jonathan. Jonathan was compelled to accept the fact that his father would never relent of his enmity to David. By shooting arrows Jonathan signalled to David to stay hidden. Afterwards Jonathan and David had a tearful affectionate farewell. They would see one another alive only one more time (1 Sam. 23:16-18).

21. *David with the priest at Nob* (1 Sam. 21:1-9). David fled from Gibeah to *Nob*, a place just north of Jerusalem near the Mt. of Olives. There he asked the priest Ahimelech (a descendant of Eli) for food and weapons. He received the only bread available, the Presence Bread used in the tabernacle, and the sword of Goliath. Doeg, an Edomite servant of King Saul, was detained at Nob, and saw David receive the food.

The priests were stationed at Nob, probably because the tabernacle site at Shiloh had been destroyed (1 Sam. 4:10).

Ahimelech's giving the sword of Goliath to David was clear evidence that the priest recognized that David would be the next king.

David lied to Ahimelech about why he was leaving the area in such a hurry that he had not even made basic preparations for travel (21:2-5). David's lie cost eighty-five priests their lives (22:18-22).

Whenever David trusted the LORD and asked for His guidance and protection, David was delivered and others were unharmed. Whenever David tried to save himself by depending upon himself or upon lies or human alliances, he always got into worse troubles and others suffered also.

22. *David's humiliation at Gath* (1 Sam. 21:10-15). David fled from Nob to the Philistine city of Gath to escape from pursuit by Saul. Gath is downstream from the place where David killed Goliath (1 Sam. 17:52). The first visit to Gath was triumph; this visit to Gath was utter humiliation. David was recognized and remembered by the Philistines. He had to act like a madman to save his life. David's intense feelings of pain at Gath are revealed in Psalm 56.

23. *David at Adullam and Mizpah* (1 Sam. 22:1-5). From Gath David journeyed to a large cave at *Adullam* (about twelve miles southwest from Bethlehem). About four hundred men joined him there, men in trouble with the law or discontented or in debt. Oppressive governments create social refugees.

David took his family from Bethlehem to the land of Moab east of the Dead Sea (22:3-4). David's great-grandmother was Ruth the Moabitess. At a later time David took cruel vengeance on the Moabites (2 Sam. 8:2). The Bible does not tell why he did that, but a Jewish tradition says that the Moabites murdered David's family.

After leaving Moab David stayed in the "stronghold" (22:4-5; 24:22). In Hebrew "stronghold" is *metsudah,* from which comes the name *Masada*, later applied to the huge cliff of rock west of the Dead Sea, where king Herod built a strong fortress. This would be a very secure hideout. David perhaps stayed there for a short period (1 Chr. 12:8, 16). The prophet Gad told David not to stay in the *stronghold*, but to go into the land of Judah. Gad is mentioned frequently later (2 Sam. 24:11; 2 Chr. 29:25).

24. *Saul and Doeg kill the priests* (1 Sam. 22:6-22). At Saul's capital Saul was bemoaning the fact that his servants would

not reveal what they knew about David (22:6-8). Doeg, the Edomite who saw David receive the Presence Bread, reported this event to Saul. Ahimelech the priest and all his family were brought to Gibeah and accused of disloyalty. Ahimelech was totally innocent and ignorant of David's intentions. But on the word of Doeg Saul ordered the priests to be slain. Doeg himself massacred eighty-five priests. (Was he trying to get even with the priests for detaining him? We cannot resist calling him Dirty Doeg.) The slaughter was continued at the town of Nob where the priests lived. Saul's madness had no limit.

Only one priest — Abiathar — escaped. He fled to David, and stayed with David all the hard years when David was an outlaw to Saul (23:6; 1 Kgs. 2:26). David was very sad that his lies had cost the priests their lives.

David wrote Psalm 52 concerning Doeg. He calls him "a mighty man," one who "loves evil" and loves "falsehood rather than speaking truth," and "a deceitful tongue."

25. *David at Keilah, Ziph, and Maon* (1 Sam. 23). David asked the LORD if he should go up to the town of Keilah and fight the Philistines who were looting the grain at the threshing floors at Keilah (pronounced Kee-EYE´-lah, or Keh-ee-LAH´ in Hebrew). Whenever David sought the guidance of the LORD, he was always triumphant. David risked his own life and that of his men to help people who were being afflicted. Keilah was located about eight miles northwest of Hebron (23:1-6).

King Saul learned that David was at Keilah, and he called up all his forces to go there to capture David and his men, now numbering about six hundred (23:13). David learned of this, and asked the LORD if the men of Keilah would turn him over to Saul. David left Keilah and fled to the Desert of Ziph (about six miles southeast of Hebron).

Jonathan visited David for the last time at Ziph (23:15-18).

David's experiences at Keilah show that the philosophy of Determinism is false. (Determinism is the belief that every event, act, or decision is the inevitable result of something that has happened previously and is beyond the control of human will.) If David had remained at Keilah, he would have been captured. But he had the ability to recognize the danger, and the ability to leave town, and delivered himself.

Some people at Ziph informed Saul that David was among them. Saul pursued David at Ziph, and on to Maon nearby. Saul almost took David at Maon. "Saul was going along one side of the mountain, and David and his men on the other side, hurrying to get away from Saul. As Saul and his forces were closing in on David and his men to capture them, a messenger came to Saul, saying, 'Come quickly! The Philistines are raiding the land.'" God timed the Philistine attack just right, so Saul could not catch David (23:26-27).The place where David escaped Saul was called *Sela Hammahlekoth*, meaning "rock of escapes," or "rock of parting."

26. *David spares Saul at En Gedi* (1 Sam. 24). En Gedi is located on the west shore of the Dead Sea, near its center. A deep wadi with sides over five hundred feet high cuts through the cliffs along the seashore. A spring at the head of the valley supplies water that cascades over a falls more than fifty feet and flows down the valley. This creates a strip of luxurious green in the valley bottom, while the hot tan desert of Judah lies on either side. Many caves can be seen in the cliffsides of the valley. Wild goats (Nubian ibexes) roamed the area long ago, and have been restocked in modern times. The beauty of En Gedi is mentioned in the Song of Solomon (1:14).

King Saul came to this place with three thousand men to pursue David (24:2). David spared Saul when he entered the very cave where David and his men were hiding "in the innermost recesses of the cave." Saul went in to relieve himself (lit., "cover his feet") and went to sleep. David silently cut off a corner of Saul's robe. When Saul left the cave, David called to him and showed him the corner of his robe he had cut off. David pleaded with Saul to recognize his innocence and good will. David compared himself to a dead dog and a flea (24:14). Saul was remorseful. He acknowledged that David would surely be the next king (24:20). He asked David not to cut off all his descendants or wipe out his family. (There was no need for Saul to make such a request to David. David had demonstrated many times that he would not retaliate against Saul.) But David gave his oath to Saul, and Saul returned to his home. David did not yet trust Saul and went up to the "stronghold" (Masada nearby?) (24:22).

Be like David, and do not take vengeance (1 Sam. 24:12).

Do not take revenge, my friends, but leave room for God's wrath, for it is written: "It is mine to avenge; I will repay," says the Lord (Rom. 12:19).

---

27. *David, Nabal, and Abigail* (1 Sam. 25). Samuel the great prophet died at this time (25:1; 28:3). He did not live to see David become king.

David came back to the area of Maon, where he had narrowly escaped from Saul (23:25). David and his men stayed near the ranch of a wealthy man named *Nabal.* His name means *fool* in Hebrew. *Abigail,* Nabal's wife, said, "He is just like his name — his name is Fool" (25:25). He was surly and mean ("churlish") in his dealings. David's men protected Nabal from thieves and prowlers, and stole nothing from Nabal (25:7, 15-16). When David asked for food from Nabal, he scornfully rejected the request. David was ready to wipe out Nabal's family.

Abigail took action, and brought a large supply of food for David's men. She spoke to David with gracious words that melted David's heart (25:24-31).

"A gentle answer turns away wrath, but a harsh word stirs up anger" (Prov. 15:1).

Abigail appealed to David not to shed blood needlessly:

Abigail said, "My master [David] will not have on his conscience the staggering burden of needless bloodshed or of having avenged himself" (1 Sam. 25:31).

David spared Nabal. But soon afterward, Nabal held a banquet, like that of the king. Nabal became very drunk. When he was sober the next morning and Abigail told him how near he had been to being wiped out by David, "his heart failed him, and he became like a stone" (25:37).

After Nabal's death David took Abigail as a wife. She responded to his proposal with very diplomatic words: "Here is your maidservant, ready to serve you and wash the feet of my master's servants" (25:41).

DAVID's WIVES (1 Sam. 25:42-44; 1 Chr. 3:1-19) –

(1) Michal, (2) Ahinoam, (3) Abigail, (4) Maacah, (5) Haggith, (6) Abital, (7) Eglah, (8) Bathsheba, (9) Wives and concubines in Jerusalem (2 Sam. 5:13-14).

---

28. *David again spares Saul, at Ziph* (1 Sam. 26). Some people of the village of Ziph had once before revealed to Saul where David was (25:19). They repeated their act (26:1). Saul came after David again with "three thousand chosen men" (26:1; 24:2). Saul camped with his army around him (26:5). Abner, his cousin and commander of his army, was with him.

David and his valiant nephew Abishai quietly approached Saul in the night, for "the LORD had put them into a deep sleep" (26:12). Abishai wanted to thrust Saul through with just "one thrust." (That act would doubtless have brought death upon David and Abishai.) David took Saul's spear and water jug, and left. (The spear that Saul had used to try to spear David and even Jonathan was no longer in his possession!) From a safe distance David called out to Abner and Saul. He taunted Abner for failing to guard Saul (26:14-16). He pleaded with Saul: "Do not let my blood fall to the ground far from the presence of the LORD" (26:20). Saul again was remorseful — for a little while — and returned home.

> **David spared Saul two times:**
>   (1) At *En Gedi*, in a cave (1 Sam. 24).
>   (2) At *Ziph*, camped out at night (1 Sam. 26).

29. *David goes over to the king of the Philistines* (1 Sam. 27). It was a major and strenuous move for David to transfer six hundred men and their families from the Ziph area to Gath of the Philistines (27:2-3). The journey was at least twenty-five miles.

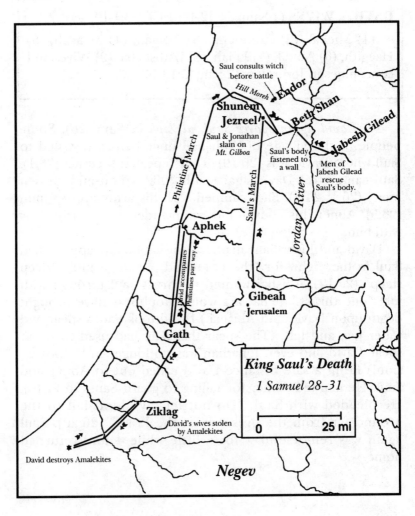

Saul consults witch before battle

Hill Moreh Endor

Shunem

Jezreel

Beth Shan

Jabesh Gilead

Philistine March

Saul & Jonathan slain on *Mt. Gilboa*

Saul's body fastened to a wall

Men of Jabesh Gilead rescue Saul's body.

Saul's March

Jordan River

Aphek

David accompanies Philistines part way

Gibeah

Jerusalem

Gath

King Saul's Death
1 Samuel 28–31

0   25 mi

Ziklag

David's wives stolen by Amalekites

David destroys Amalekites

Negev

David's going over to King Achish at the Philistine city of Gath was unnecessary and evil. The Bible does not say that David asked God's guidance in making this move, as he had asked on previous occasions (23:2, 4). God had protected David so many times that David should not even have considered this means to save himself from Saul. David had to pretend he had a loyalty to the Philistine king that he really did not have. He had to lie about his actions (27:8-12). He had to kill a lot of people to conceal his own deeds (27:11). His going to the Philistines almost got him into war against his own people (1 Sam. 29). He missed a chance to resist further Philistine occupation of Israel (28:1). David's act almost certainly delayed his acceptance as king over ALL Israel for seven years.

David killed the people in a number of the non-Israelite settlements near Philistia (27:8-9), but always reported his actions so that it sounded like he was fighting his own Israelite people.

David asked the Philistine king for a city of his own, and the king gave him *Ziklag*, located about fifteen miles northwest of Beersheba. David felt uneasy about being too close to the Philistines (27:5-6). God's people should not be too cozy with evil men.

30. *Saul and the witch at Endor* (1 Sam. 28). The Philistines resumed their aggression against the land of Israel, even though David was living among them (28:1, 4). The Philistines assembled their camp at Shunem, up in the east end of the great valley of Esdraelon, in the heart of Israel. A victory there would cut Israel into two parts (north and south) and permit the Philistines to control a passage clear to the Jordan River.

King Achish told David, "I will make you my bodyguard for life," literally, "Keeper of my head I will appoint you all the days" (28:2).

King Saul gathered all the Israelites and set up camp at Mt. Gilboa. The Israelite camp there would block further Philistine advance toward the Jordan.

King Saul had expelled all the mediums and spiritists

(witches) from the land of Israel (28:3). As he faced the military crisis he sought divine help (28:5, 15), but found none. In desperation Saul said, "Find me a woman who is medium." "There is one in Endor," they said (28:7). Endor is a village on the north side of the Hill of Moreh, less than five miles from Shunem, and ten miles north from Mt. Gilboa.

Witchcraft and communicating with the dead was forbidden in Israel (Ex. 22:18; Lev. 19:31; 20:6).

The medium at Endor appears to have been very suspicious of Saul. His large size may have given her a clue as to who Saul was (28:9, 12).

Saul asked her to bring up the spirit of Samuel the prophet. The woman was probably a deceiver of most of her clients. She seems to have been astounded at her own success in bringing up a spirit out of the ground. Apparently Saul did not see the spirit, but the woman's description of it was like that of Samuel as Saul remembered him.

Samuel said, "Why have you disturbed me?" (28:15). "Tomorrow you and your sons will be with me" — dead. "The LORD will also hand over the army of Israel to the Philistines" (28:19).

Saul fell over at full length. He had eaten nothing all that day and night. The woman asked to give him food. He refused, but finally relented. She prepared a fattened calf and unleavened bread (28:24). It was a meal fit for a king, and there was in it a demonstration of honor to her king. It was Saul's last meal upon earth. (We read and weep.)

First Chronicles 10:13-14 says, "Saul died because he was unfaithful to the LORD . . . and even consulted a medium for guidance, and did not inquire of the LORD."

31. *Achish sends David back to Ziklag* (1 Sam. 29). David had so thoroughly convinced the Philistine King Achish of his loyalty that Achish was quite willing to have David and his men go with him to fight against Saul. The Philistine commanders were angry with Achish about this, and did not trust David. They remembered the song, "David has slain his tens of thousands." Achish sent David back to Ziklag with many apologies. David pretended that he was offended by being sent

back to his town. But he departed, probably praising the LORD inwardly.

It surely was God's providence that the Philistine lords refused to allow David to join them in the battle against Saul and Jonathan. We feel that in the battle he would surely have turned upon the Philistines. Also it was providential that David be sent back to Ziklag just then, because the Amalekites had raided Ziklag and stolen David's two wives Ahinoam and Abigail.

32. *David destroys the Amalekites* (1 Sam. 30). Perhaps the Amalekies raided Ziklag in reprisal for David's raid upon them (30:1; 27:8). But they raided other places nearby in the same excursion and took spoil from all the places (30:16).

The discovery that their town had been raided and their wives stolen distressed David and his men so greatly that they wept until they had no strength left to weep (30:4). But David found strength in the LORD his God (30:6).

God directed David to pursue the Amalekites, and promised David victory (30:8).

David and his men crossed the Besor Ravine (better, Wadi Besor) in their pursuit of the Amalekites. They had been marching three days and some were exhausted. These were left at the Besor to stay with their supplies (30:24).

The LORD provided a guide to the Amalekite camp, a nearly-starved Egyptian, who had been abandoned by the Amalekites when he was ill (30:11-13).

There were many more Amalekites than men in David's army. The battle against the Amalekites was nearly a day long (30:17), but his victory was total (30:18-20).

David was magnanimous toward the weary warriors at the Wadi Besor. He established a rule that those who stayed with the supplies would receive the same portion of the spoils as those who fought in the battle (30:24-25).

Back in Ziklag David sent portions of the spoils he took from the Amalekites to all the various places in Judah where David had roamed, including a place not yet identified but named Bethel (30:26-30). David realized that he was soon to become king, and sought by this means to win favor from some of the people.

33. *Saul and his sons die at Mt. Gilboa* (1 Sam. 31; 1 Chr. 10). Mt. Gilboa is a mostly barren stony ridge, about 1696 feet high at its summit. It lies at the southeast corner of the Plain of Esdraelon. There King Saul and his three sons Jonathan, Abinadab, and Malki-Shua died fighting against the Philistines. "In death they were not parted" (2 Sam. 1:23). This says much about the character of Saul and his sons.

Saul was wounded by the archers, and took his own life by falling upon his sword. Saul was always courageous. He took his own life only when all else was lost. There was no value in letting the "uncircumcised" run their weapons through Saul and exercise themselves by abusing him (31:4).

Saul's death led to a general flight of Israelites from the area, and the Philistines entered the abandoned towns and occupied them.

Saul's body was found and beheaded. (Was this retaliation for what was done to Goliath?) Saul's headless body was fastened to the wall in the town of Beth Shan (seven miles east of Mt. Gilboa). Saul's head was hung in the temple of Dagon in Philistia (1 Chr. 10:10).

The men of the town of Jabesh Gilead east of the Jordan came at night twenty miles to Beth Shan and rescued Saul's heavy headless body. In their town the body was cremated, and his bones were buried under a tamarisk tree at Jabesh. The people of Jabesh had much gratitude to Saul, because at the start of his reign he had saved their city from the cruel Ammonites (1 Sam. 11:1-11).

34. *David learns of Saul's death* (2 Sam. 1). There is no reason to divide 1 Samuel from 2 Samuel. The books tell a continuous story. The length and weight of a single scroll large enough to contain the contents of both books has made the division into two books helpful.

David at Ziklag learned of the death of Saul from an Amalekite who had been on Mt. Gilboa when Saul died. He had in his possession the crown of Saul and his arm band. The story he told of Saul's death is very similar to what others said (as in 1 Sam. 31:4-6). The Amalekite lied by saying that he killed Saul when Saul asked him to do it. He thought this would win approval from David.

If King Saul had killed all of the Amalekites (1 Sam. 15:3), this one would not have been there to do his vile deed.

David wrote a touching lamentation over Saul and Jonathan. He called it "The BOW" (or Song of the Bow). (See 1:22; 1 Samuel 18:4; 20:20.) The song was to be placed in the Book of Jashar (1:18), which seems to have been a book of Hebrew hero stories written in poetry (Josh. 10:13).

David spoke of the anguish of their deaths. "O mountains of Gilboa, may you have neither dew nor rain . . . for there the shield of the mighty was defiled." He spoke of their bravery (1:22). David spoke of the generosity of King Saul: "O daughters of Israel, weep for Saul, who clothed you in scarlet and finery" (1:24).

"HOW THE MIGHTY HAVE FALLEN!" (1:25,27). This is the appropriate epitaph for Saul and Jonathan. Probably we should emphasize the word "mighty" more than we emphasize "fallen."

Questions on Section B
Decline of Saul and Rise of David (1 Sam.13–2 Sam.1)

1 Samuel 13
True or False? (Correct all false statements.)
1. Saul chose an army of men when he had reigned two years. (13:1-2)
2. Two thousand men were with Saul in Gibeah. (13:2)
3. Jonathan attacked the Philistine outpost at Geba. (13:3)
4. The people were summoned to join Saul in Gibeah. (13:4)
5. The Philistines encamped in Michmash after Saul left. (13:5)
6. The people of Israel stood up bravely against the Philistines. (13:6-7)
7. Saul waited seven days in Gilgal for Samuel. (13:8)
8. Saul had the priest to offer the burnt offering and the fellowship offerings. (13:9)
9. Saul went out to meet Samuel and to greet him. (13:10)
10. Samuel said that Saul had done foolishly, and now his kingdom would not endure. (13:13)
11. Saul had 600 men with him in Gilgal. (13:15)
12. Saul and Jonathan came and stayed in Geba. (13:16)

13. Philistine raiding parties came out of Michmash in five detachments. (13:17)
14. Israel had many iron workers to make weapons. (13:19)
15. The Philistines sharpened the Israelites' tools. (13:21)

1 Samuel 14

1. Who was Jonathan? (14:1)
2. Where did Jonathan and his armor-bearer go? (13:23–14:1)
3. What priest was with Saul? (14:3)
4. Where were the rocky cliffs between which Jonathan and his armor-bearer passed? (14:4-5)
5. What did Jonathan call the Philistines? (14:6)
6. What gave Jonathan courage to attack the Philistines? (14:6)
7. What did Jonathan say would be the signal for them to attack the Philistines? (14:8-10)
8. How did Jonathan get up to the Philistines? (14:13)
9. How many Philistines did they kill? (14:14)
10. What caused a great trembling? (14:15)
11. Who from a distance saw the Philistines melting away? (14:16)
12. Where was the ark of God? What did Saul want the ark to be used for? (14:18-19)
13. What did the fearful Israelites who had been in hiding do when they saw the Israelites were winning? (14:21-22)
14. What oath did Saul bind upon the people? (14:24)
15. Who violated the oath? How? (14:27)
16. Why did the people pounce on the spoil and eat meat with the blood? (14:31-33)
17. Why could Saul not get an answer when he sought guidance about pursuing the Philistines? (14:37-38)
18. What did Saul threaten to do to Jonathan? (14:44)
19. Who rescued Jonathan? (14:45)
20. Name five foreign enemies that Saul fought. (14:47-48)
21. Who were Merab, Michal, Abner, Ner, and Kish? (14:49-51)

1 Samuel 15

1. What people was Saul told to destroy? Why? (15:2-3)
2. Where were Saul's people numbered for war? (15:4)
3. What people were told to depart from the battle area? (15:6)
4. How fully did Saul destroy the enemy? (15:8-9)
5. Who was the king of the condemned people? (15:8)
6. Where did Saul set up a monument? (15:12)

7. Where did Samuel rebuke Saul for his sin? (15:12)
8. Whom did Saul blame for his sin? (15:15)
9. What is better than sacrifice? How did this truth apply to King Saul? (15:22)
10. What was Saul's penalty for his disobedience? (15:23)
11. What was torn by Saul? (15:27)
12. What name did Samuel use to describe God? (15:29)
13. What happened to Agag? (15:33)
14. To what places did Samuel and Saul go after the execution of King Agag? (15:34)

1 Samuel 16

1. What was Samuel to do with his horn? (16:1)
2. To what place was Samuel sent? To what man? Why?
3. How did the elders of this city react to Samuel's visit?(16:4)
4. How many sons did Jesse have? (1 Sam. 17:12)
5. Give the names of Jesse's three oldest sons. (16:6,8,9)
6. How did Jesse's oldest son impress Samuel? (16:6)
7. How does God look upon people differently than men do? (16:7)
8. Describe David's physical appearance. (16:12)
9. What came upon David after he was anointed? (16:13)
10. What tormented King Saul? (16:14)
11. How did Saul's servants seek to cheer him? Who was called to perform? (16:16)
12. How did Saul respond to David and to his playing? (16:2-3)

1 Samuel 17

1. What book and chapter contains the story of David and Goliath?
2. What people gathered for war against Israel? (17:1)
3. In what valley did they encamp? (17:2-3)
4. Who was the champion of the Philistines, and where did he come from? (17:4)
5. What was the champion's height? (17:4)
6. What did Goliath offer if an Israelite defeated him? (17:9)
7. Which of Jesse's sons were in Saul's army? (17:13)
8. For how many days did the Philistine challenge Israel? (17:16)
9. Why did David go to the battle area? (17:17-18)
10. What rewards were promised to the one who defeated Goliath? (17:25)
11. What were David's words concerning Goliath? (17:32)
12. How did Eliab feel when he heard what David said to the men? (17:28)
13. Why did Saul tell David that he could not go against Goliath? (17:33)

14. What animals had David killed while herding his sheep? (17:34)
15. Why wouldn't David wear Saul's armor? (17:39)
16. What were Goliath's first words to David? How did David reply? (17:43)
17. Whose sword did David use to behead Goliath? (17:51)
18. How far did Israel pursue the Philistines? (17:52)
19. What did David do with Goliath's head and his armor? (17:54)
20. What did Saul ask Abner concerning David? (17:55)

1 Samuel 18

1. Who became David's friend? How close was the friendship? (18:1)
2. What would Saul not allow David to do any more? (18:2)
3. What items did David's friend give to him? (18:3)
4. How did the people feel about David's promotion? (18:5)
5. What was the song of the women? (18:7)
6. How did Saul react to the song? (18:8)
7. Where did the evil spirit upon Saul come from? (18:10)
8. How did Saul attempt to harm David? (18:10-11)
9. Into what position did Saul place David? (18:13)
10. Who was Saul's older daughter? (18:17)
11. Why did Saul give his daughter Michal to David? (18:19-20)
12. How did Michal feel toward David? (18:20)
13. How many Philistines did David kill to provide a dowry to obtain Michal? Was this the number requested? (18:25, 27)

1 Samuel 19. Why did these things happen?

1. That David was staying in hiding? (19:1-2)
2. That Saul swore concerning David, "As the LORD lives, David will not be put to death?" (19:5-6)
3. That Saul drove his spear into the wall? (19:9-10)
4. That David escaped at night? (19:11-12)
5. That Michal let David down through a window in a basket?
6. That an idol was put in David's bed? (19:13)
7. That Michal lied to her father? (19:14)
8. That David came to Samuel at Ramah? (19:18)
9. That Saul's messengers failed in their mission? (19:19)
10. That Saul stripped off his clothes and prophesied? (19:23)

1 Samuel 20

1. Whom did David go to see after leaving Ramah? (20:1)
2. How far from death did David feel he was? (20:3)

3. What promise did Jonathan cause David to swear to him that he would do? (20:14-15)
4. What festival would Saul expect David to attend? (20:5)
5. To what event at Bethlehem did David say he had gone? (20:6)
6. Name the stone David was to wait behind. (20:19)
7. How many arrows did Jonathan shoot? (20:20)
8. What did Saul notice about David's place at the table? (20:25)
9. On what day did Saul ask about David? (20:27)
10. What did Saul hurl at Jonathan? (20:33)
11. Who went to find arrows? (20:35)
12. Who kissed one another? (20:41)

1 Samuel 21 — True or false? (Correct all false statements.)
1. David went to Ahimelech, to Nob the priest.
2. The priest came to meet David trembling because of the soldiers with David.
3. David lied to Ahimelech.
4. David said that he had some men with him, but he had told them to meet him at another place.
5. David asked for five loaves of bread.
6. David said that his men were (ceremonially) holy.
7. Doeg was an Ammonite.
8. Doeg was Saul's head shepherd.
9. David said that the king's business was urgent.
10. The sword of Goliath was wrapped in an ephod.
11. Nahash was king of Gath.
12. The song of the women of Gath refreshed David's heart.
13. David was very much afraid of Achish, the king of Gath.
14. David acted like a madman before the king.

1 Samuel 22 — What events are associated with the following?
1. Adullam.
2. About four hundred men.
3. Mizpah of Moab.
4. Gad.
5. The forest of Hereth.
6. Ahitub.
7. Doeg the Edomite.
8. Eighty-five men.
9. Abiathar.
10. Ahimelech.

Old Testament History

1 Samuel 23 — Multiple choice

1. The Philistines were looting the threshing-floors at (1) Keilah; (2) Ziph; (3) Maon.
2. Abiathar, son of Ahimelech, came to David with (1) a sword; (2) an ephod; (3) the ark.
3. From Keilah David went next to (1) the Desert of Ziph; (2) Maon; (3) En Gedi.
4. David then had about (1) 200; (2) 400; (3) 600 men.
5. Jonathan visited David in (1) the Desert of Ziph; (2) Keilah; (3) Gibeah. (23:14)
6. Saul wanted the Ziphites to (1) capture David and bring him to him; (2) locate David's hiding places; (3) take news to David.
7. Saul pursued David in (1) the Desert of Maon; (2) En Gedi; (3) the land of the Philistines. (23:24)
8. Saul (1) never got near David; (2) was on the other side of the mountain from David; (3) found David in the strongholds.
9. Saul returned from pursuing David because (1) he could not catch him; (2) he had a change of heart; (3) a Philistine raid was reported to him.

1 Samuel 24 — True or false?

1. Saul sought David on the crags of the wild goats.
2. David said when he discovered Saul in the cave, "This is the day the LORD spoke of . . . 'I will give your enemy into your hands.'"
3. David cut off a corner of Saul's robe.
4. David's conscience troubled him after he had cut the robe.
5. David stood right up and spoke to Saul man to man.
6. David said that Saul had been listening to the words of men who said that David was bent on hurting Saul.
7. David said that he would not hurt Saul because he loved his son Jonathan. (24:10)
8. David called upon the LORD to judge between him and Saul.
9. David called Saul a dead dog and a flea.
10. Saul wept. David's good overcame Saul's evil.
11. Saul actually asked the LORD to reward David well.
12. Saul would not admit that David would ever be king.
13. Saul asked the same thing that Jonathan did, that David would not cut off his descendants.
14. Saul went home and David went with him.

1 Samuel 25

1. Where was Samuel buried? (25:1)

462

2. Where did Nabal live? How wealthy was he? (25:2)
3. Who was Nabal's wife? (25:3)
4. What did David request from Nabal? How did Nabal respond? (25:8)
5. What did David determine to do to Nabal? (25:22)
6. Who prevented David's violence? How? (25:23)
7. What does the name *Nabal* mean? (25:25)
8. How did Nabal die? (25:37)
9. What happened to Abigail after Nabal's death? (25:40)

1 Samuel 26

1. How many men came with Saul to pursue David? (26:2)
2. Where did the events of chapter 26 take place? (26:2)
3. Who went with David as he came to Saul at night? (26:6)
4. What did David's companion desire to do to Saul? (26:8)
5. What did David take from Saul? (26:11)
6. Whom did David taunt? (26:14)
7. To what two creatures did David compare himself? (26:20)
8. How did Saul react when he realized that David had spared him? (26:21)

1 Samuel 27 — True or False? (Correct all false statements.)

1. David said that even if he went to the land of the Philistines, Saul would pursue him there.
2. David had six hundred men with him when he went to Gath.
3. Nahash was the king of Gath.
4. David had two wives with him in Gath.
5. Saul never found out where David was staying.
6. David stayed in the country of the Philistines for sixteen months.
7. The city of Gath was given to David.
8. David smote the Amalekites and the Geshurites.
9. David brought back the kings of these nations alive.
10. David lied to Achish about the people he fought against.
11. Achish was suspicious of David.

1 Samuel 28

1. Between what two peoples did fighting arise again? (28:1)
2. To what position did Achish appoint David?(28:2)
3. What people had Saul put out of the land? (28:3)
4. What sort of person did Saul seek to inquire of? Why? (28:7)
5. Where did the woman medium live? (28:7)
6. Whom did Saul seek to call back from the dead? (28:11)
7. How did the woman react when she saw Samuel? (28:12)

8. What was Samuel's message to Saul? (28:19)
9. Describe Saul's physical condition after he heard Samuel. (28:20)
10. What did the woman feed Saul? (28:24)

1 Samuel 29
1. Where did the Philistines gather, and where did Israel camp? (29:1)
2. Who objected to David's presence among the Philistines? (29:4)
3. Did David go with the Philistines to battle? (29:11)

1 Samuel 30
1. What did David find upon returning to Ziklag? (30:1-2)
2. What two people special to David had been taken captive? (30:5)
3. What reaction of the people greatly distressed David? (30:6)
4. Who told David to pursue the attackers? (30:8)
5. What ravine (wadi) did they cross? How many were left there? Why? (30:9)
6. Who was found in a field? (30:11)
7. What were the attackers doing when David overtook them? (30:16)
8. How complete was the rescue? (30:18-19)
9. What spoil was given to those who stayed by the baggage? (30:24)
10. Where did David send spoil from this battle? (30:26-31)

1 Samuel 31
1. Where was Israel defeated in battle? (31:1)
2. What three princes were killed in this battle? (31:2)
3. How did Saul die? (32:4)
4. What was done with Saul's body by the Philistines? (31:9)
5. Who rescued Saul's body? Why did they do this good deed? (31:11-13)

2 Samuel 1
1. How long after the death of Saul was it before David heard the news? (1:1-2)
2. Who reported the news of Saul's death to David? (1:2, 8)
3. What did the Amalekite tell David about Saul's death? Was it a true report? (1:6-10)
4. What possessions of Saul were brought to David? (1:10)
5. What happened to the Amalekite? (1:15)
6. What was the name of David's song of lamentation? (1:18)
7. In what book was this song written down? (1:18)
8. How precious had been the love of Jonathan for David? (1:26)

Section C
Introduction to Kings and Chronicles
(We introduce these books at this point because the reign of King David is recorded in 1 Chronicles, as well as in 2 Samuel.)

A. Kings (These are really one book divided into two books.)
1. The book of 1 Kings begins with David's old age (near his death), and ends after the death of King Ahab.
2. Second Kings begins with Ahab's son Ahaziah, and ends with the people of Judah in captivity in Babylon. Second Kings brings us down almost to the end of Old Testament history.
3. There is a major historical break between chapters 11 and 12 of 1 Kings. This is the division between the United Kingdom period and the Divided Kingdom period.
4. *Outline of 1 & 2 Kings.* (Memorize this.)
   I. Reign of King Solomon (1 Kgs. 1-11)
   II. Simultaneous reigns of kings of Judah and Israel (1 Kgs. 12 to 2 Kgs. 17).
   III. Kings of Judah to the captivity in Babylon (2 Kgs. 18-25)
5. The prophet *Jeremiah* (or his scribe, Baruch) was probably the final *author* and compiler of the books of Kings. The last chapter of Jeremiah's book is nearly identical to the last chapter of Kings. Jeremiah's book supplements the information in Kings. It appears probable that the author of Kings included in the books information from the official records in Judah and Israel. (See 1 Kings 11:41; 14:19,29.) Also (and more importantly) he copied sections of the writings of various prophets before him, who wrote of events in their own times. (See 1 Kings 9:21; 12:19; 2 Kings 16:6; 17:14.)
6. The books of Kings give an emphasis to the work of the **prophets**. The deeds of Elijah and Elisha occupy a large part of the books. They tell of schools of prophets called "sons of the prophets" (2 Kgs. 2:15; 6:1; etc.). These prophets knew the secrets of royal hearts and councils. They did not fear to condemn the sins of kings.

Differences between the books of Samuel–Kings and Chronicles	
Books of *Samuel & Kings*	Books of *Chronicles*
1. Tell of events in **all 12 tribes.**	1. Tell of **Judah only.**
2. **Prophetic** (in content and authorship). Emphasize the work of prophets, like Elijah.	2. **Priestly** (in content and authorship). Emphasize work of priests and temple.
3. **Pessimistic.** (Tell the unpleasant events, like David and Bathsheba. End with the Jews in captivity in Babylon.)	3. **Optimistic.** (Omit the unpleasant events. End with the Jews being released from captivity in Babylon.)
4. Mostly **pre-exilic** (before captivity in Babylon)	4. **Post-exilic** (after captivity in Babylon) in date and view-point
5. **Long time span** (500 yrs.)	5. **Longer time span** (3500 yrs. – from Adam to end of O.T. history)

B. Chronicles

1. Well over half of the information in Chronicles is parallel to (and perhaps taken from) the books of Samuel–Kings and Genesis. However, there are important differences between Chronicles and the other books. See the chart above.

    The books of Chronicles provided for the Jews who returned from Babylon a link with their past "roots."

2. The priestly emphasis in Chronicles is apparent by the many *genealogies* in Chronicles. (The genealogies were important, because the Messiah was to come from the families of Abraham and Judah and David.)

3. *Chronicles begins with Adam* and carries the history down to the decree of King Cyrus (536 B.C.), who permitted the Jews to return from captivity in Babylon. The genealogies in the book carry the history down even further, naming

several generations of the royal family after Babylonian captivity. (See 1 Chronicles 3:17-24.)

4. *Outline of Chronicles.* (Memorize.)

I. Genealogies from Adam to the return from Babylon (1 Chr. 1–9)

II. History of King David (1 Chr. 10–29)

III. History of King Solomon (2 Chr. 1–9)

IV. History of the kings of Judah (2 Chr. 10–36)

5. *Ezra,* the scribe and priest who came back from Babylonian captivity, was probably the author and compiler of Chronicles. The last paragraph in 2 Chronicles is repeated and continued at the start of Ezra's book. Ezra possibly used old temple records as sources of the genealogies in Chronicles.

6. Verses in Chronicles worthy of memorizing: 1 Chr. 29:14; 2 Chr. 7:14; 15:2; 31:21. (2 Chr. 7:14 especially)

Questions on Section C
Introduction to Kings and Chronicles

1. With what events does 1 Kings begin and end?
2. With what events does 2 Kings begin and end?
3. Where in 1 Kings is the major historical break? What two periods does it come between?
4. What book and chapters tell of King Solomon's reign?
5. Who was probably the final author or compiler of the books of Kings?
6. What sources of information did the final compiler of the books of Kings probably take much information from?
7. What two great prophets have much told about them in 1 & 2 Kings?
8. Which books tell of events in *all* 12 tribes — Kings or Chronicles?
9. Which books are *prophetic*? Which are *priestly*?
10. Which books give a *pessimistic* view of the history? *Optimistic?*
11. How long is the time span in the books of Kings? How long in Chronicles?
12. How much of the material in Chronicles is in other books?
13. What are the starting and ending events in Chronicles?
14. What information is in Part I of Chronicles (chs. 1–9)?
15. Whose history is in Part II (chs. 10–29) of Chronicles?
16. Who was probably author/compiler of 1 & 2 Chronicles?
17. Write 2 Chronicles 7:14 from memory.

Section D
David's Reign in Triumph
(2 Samuel 2–12; 1 Chronicles 11–20)

After the death of Saul, David soon became king.

TWO PARTS OF DAVID'S REIGN

1. REIGN in **TRIUMPH**; 2 Samuel 2–12.
2. REIGN in **TRAGEDIES**; 2 Samuel 13–1 Kings 2.
   (David's taking Bathsheba changed his reign from triumph to tragedies.)

---

1. David anointed king over Judah (2 Sam. 2:1-7). The battle at Mt. Gilboa left Israel in a defenseless state. Israel's army was defeated. Its king and his sons were dead. The only possible claimant to the throne — David — had been a loyal (?) associate of the Philistines. The entire coastal plain was now in the control of the Philistines, and also the Valley of Esdraelon, and the valleys east of it to the Jordan. Israel was two-thirds surrounded. The Philistines occupied many Israelite cities (1 Sam. 31:7).

In that dark time God raised up two men — Abner (commander of Saul's army) and David. They gradually drove out the Philistines from much of the territory they had taken.

David inquired of the LORD about what he should do (2:1). Perhaps he inquired through the priest Abiathar. The LORD directed David to go up to the city of Hebron in Judah.

Hebron was twenty miles south of Jerusalem, and it was the major city in Judah. David was from the tribe of Judah. David had sent to Hebron some of the spoils of battle taken from the Amalekites (1 Sam. 30:26,32). David, his two wives, and the men who were with him (hundreds of them!) moved to Hebron and settled there (1 Chr. 12:1-22).

At Hebron the men of Judah anointed David as king over the house (tribe) of Judah, and men from other tribes joined with him. It was needful that David's private anointing (1 Sam. 16) be publicly reconfirmed and shown to the public.

> **David's two capital cities** (2 Sam. 5:5)
> 1. **HEBRON** (7½ yrs.)
> 2. **JERUSALEM** (33 yrs.)

David did some "campaigning" to entice other tribes to recognize him as king. He sent sincere blessing and thanks to the people of Jabesh Gilead for their kindness in burying Saul. "The LORD bless you." (Compare Ruth 2:4; 1 Sam. 15:13.) David closed his communiqué by saying, "Now . . . Saul your master is dead, and the house of Judah has anointed me *king* over them" (2 Sam. 2:7).

2. *War between the houses of David and Saul* (2 Sam. 2:8–3:1).

Abner, Saul's commander, had escaped from death at Mt. Gilboa. Many Israelites fled after the battle there (1 Sam. 31:7). Abner took Saul's son *Ish-Bosheth* with him over east of the Jordan River to Mahanaim. There Abner made him king (2:9) over the tribes east of the Jordan, and over some of the tribes in "all Israel" (2:9).

Though Ish-Bosheth had the title "king," Abner had all the power (3:11; 4:1). Ish-Bosheth was a puppet in Abner's control.

Ish-Bosheth was probably the same person as Saul's son named *Ishvi* (1 Sam. 14:49). *Ish-Bosheth* means "man of shame." He was first called *Esh-Baal*, meaning "man of Ba'al" (1 Chr. 8:33; 9:39). But some Israelites would not say the name *Ba'al* (the name of the Canaanite god), and substituted the word *Bosheth* (meaning *shame*) for it. (In the same way, Jerub-Baal was called *Jerub-Besheth* [2 Sam. 11:21]; and Merib-Baal was called *Mephibosheth* [1 Chr. 8:34; 2 Sam. 9:6].)

Ish-Bosheth was forty years old when he was made king, and he reigned two years. We think that he was not made king until about five years after Saul's death, because David became king over all Israel shortly after Ish-Bosheth's death, and David reigned at Hebron over Judah for seven and a half years. It appears that during David's first five years of reign Abner was gradually pushing the Philistines back out of Israelite territory. Then Abner installed Ish-Bosheth as king, and Ish-Bosheth had the title of "king" only during David's last two years at Hebron.

The first conflict between the house of David and the men of Ish-Bosheth (led by Abner) occurred at the pool of Gibeon. Gibeon was a village six miles northwest of Jerusalem. Gibeon was the place that made a peace treaty with Joshua (Josh. 9). Gibeon is referred to in Jeremiah 41:12 as the place with the "great pool" (lit., "great waters").

Archaeologist James B. Pritchard discovered at Gibeon the "great pool" just inside the ancient city wall. It was a huge pit in bedrock, thirty-seven feet in diameter and thirty-five feet deep, with a smaller (6' diameter) hole going on down forty feet to water. (See Pritchard's book *Gibeon Where the Sun Stood Still.*)

It was a long hike (about eighty miles) for Abner and his men to come from Mahanaim east of Jordan to Gibeon. Gibeon was selected probably because to Abner it was a friendly and familiar place in Benjamin, the tribe of Saul. As David's men (under Joab) faced Abner's men across the pool at Gibeon, Abner said, "Let's have some of the young men get up and fight" (2:14). Literally, "Let the young men now arise and *play* before us." It was deadly *play*, for twenty-four young men were stabbed to death. In the battle that followed the initial fight, Abner and the men of Israel were defeated. Joab and David's men pursued Abner and his men eastward toward the Jordan. Joab's brother Asahel was fleet-footed as a wild gazelle, and overtook Abner. Abner was extremely strong and thrust the butt of his spear into Asahel's stomach, and the spear came out through his back (2:23). This event later caused Joab to kill Abner (3:27).

Joab continued his pursuit of Abner until reinforcements came to help Abner (2:25). Abner returned to Mahanaim east of Jordan and Joab went back to Hebron. Abner had lost three hundred and sixty men, and Joab had lost nineteen (2:30-31).

Thus began a long war (two years) between the house of David and the house of Saul. David grew stronger and stronger, but the whole house of Saul grew weaker and weaker (3:1).

FAMILY OF KING DAVID (I)

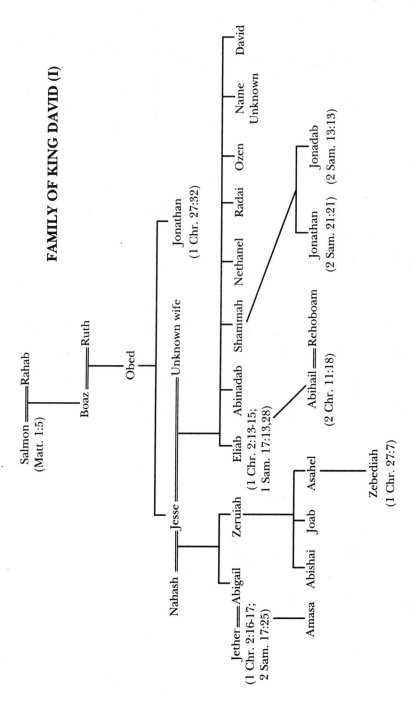

FAMILY OF KING DAVID (II)

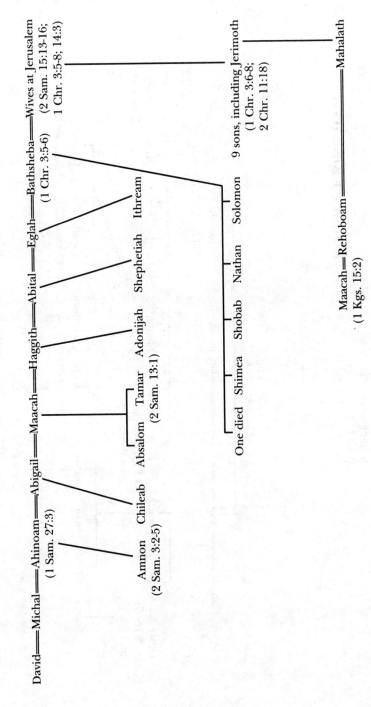

3. *Sons of David* (2 Sam. 3:2-5; 5:13-14; 1 Chr. 3:1-9).

David had six sons born to him at Hebron, and thirteen more born in Jerusalem. Besides these, there were sons born of his concubines and a daughter, *Tamar* (2 Sam. 13:1).

---

4. *Abner goes over to David* (2 Sam. 3:6-39). Ish-Bosheth accused Abner of taking his father's concubine Rizpah. Abner became angry and abandoned Ish-Bosheth. He went to David at Hebron to turn the other tribes over to David's rule. Joab was angry that David had welcomed Abner. Joab killed Abner. David was saddened over the murder of Abner, and buried him at Hebron with honor.

All of these events worked out to bring David to the throne over all Israel. In God's eternal plan, David was to become Israel's greatest king, and both a type and an ancestor of the Messiah. See Psalm 89:3-4, 20-37.

David's three harsh (rough-neck) nephews:

(1) *JOAB*; (2) *ABISHAI*; (3) *ASAHEL*. (2 Sam. 3:39)

These three were sons of David's half-sister Zeruiah (1 Chr. 2:16). Joab especially was a man of bloodshed (1 Kgs. 2:5).

Whether Ish-Bosheth's accusation against Abner was true or not, Abner became angry and abandoned Ish-Bosheth (3:7-8). For the rest of the story about Rizpah, see 2 Samuel 21:8-11.

Perhaps Abner had seen the handwriting on the wall, and perceived that David would soon become king (3:17-18). The accusation that Ish-Bosheth laid upon him gave him the excuse to go over to David's side.

David's insistence that his former wife Michal be returned to him before he would talk to Abner did not work out pleasantly for anyone. ("Do not arouse or awaken love until it so desires" [Song 3:5].) Michal's husband, Paltiel, had grown very fond of her. Ish-Bosheth was humiliated to have to force her to return to David. The relationship of David and Michal ended sadly (6:16, 20-23).

Joab was quite angry that David welcomed Abner. If Abner was accepted in David's administration, Joab would probably have lost his position as commander to Abner. Also Joab wanted vengeance on Abner for killing his brother Asahel. Joab treacherously killed Abner (3:26-27). David's curse upon the house of Joab (3:28-29) foreshadowed the fate of Joab (1 Kgs. 2:28-34).

Abner died like the "*lawless* die" (3:33). Literally this reads, "like the death of a *fool*" (Heb., *nabal*). Fools die for needless and trivial reasons. Abner had noble qualities and leadership.

5. *Ish-Bosheth murdered* (1 Sam. 4). Saul's son (Ish-Bosheth) was "alarmed" (terrified) when he heard of Abner's death. Soon after Abner's death Ish-Bosheth was assassinated by two of his "leaders of raiding bands" (princes of pillage). They brought the head of Ish-Bosheth to David at Hebron, expecting reward. David rebuked them sternly, and executed them, cutting off their hands and feet and hanging them.

The two killers of Ish-Bosheth were from Beeroth (meaning "wells") in the tribe of Benjamin. The exact location of Beeroth is uncertain, perhaps near Nebi Samwil five miles northwest of Jerusalem. Beeroth had been occupied by non-Israelites (like the Gibeonites), but they had fled as Abner pushed the Philistines out of Israelite territory, and went to Gittaim on the north edge of the plain of Philistia. Benjamites then occupied Beeroth.

Jonathan, David's friend, had a son named *Mephibosheth*, who was crippled by a childhood injury (4:4). This explains why he could not claim the throne of Israel, and also leads into the touching story of David's kindnesses to him later (9:1-13).

The assassins of Ish-Bosheth "stabbed" (lit., *struck*) and killed him and cut off his head (4:6,7).

The killers assumed (wrongly!) that David considered Saul as his enemy (4:9). David denounced them as worse killers than the Amalekite who took Saul's crown (4:9-10). They were killed, and their hands and feet were cut off, and their bodies hanged. The head of Ish-Bosheth was buried with honor. The contrast between the treatment of the bodies could not be more striking.

The story of Ish-Bosheth's death shows that God's king — David — had no malice toward those who might be his rivals. He was not involved in plots, assassinations and conspiracies. David hated evil deeds, even when they might appear to be advantageous to him. The story shows again that "All who draw the sword will die by the sword" (Matt. 26:52). A king's throne is upheld by his kindness.

6. *David anointed king over all Israel* (2 Sam. 5:1-5; 1 Chr. 11:1-3; 12:23-40). All the tribes of Israel, and the elders of Israel came to Hebron to David. David "cut a covenant" with them, and they anointed him king over Israel. A great feast lasting three days was held. David was recognized as the "shepherd" of Israel. (See Psalm 78:70-72.) The title "Shepherd" was a title of honor used by ancient kings.

7. *David conquers Jerusalem* (2 Sam. 5:6-12; 1 Chr. 11:4-9). David and his men marched to Jerusalem to attack the Jebusites, who lived there. Jerusalem was protected by deep valleys on its east and west, and by strong fortifications. The defenders thought that even the lame and blind could defend a city so secure. Jerusalem was indeed so secure that it had remained in Canaanite hands all through the period of judges (Judg. 19:11-12). David's men, led by David's nephew Joab, entered the city through a water tunnel. The tunnel had been dug from the spring *Gihon* on the east side of the city, back westward till it came under the city. A vertical shaft (now called Warren's shaft) led upward over thirty feet from the tunnel into the city. (See Terrence Kleven, "Water Spout," in *Biblical Archaeology Review,* July–Aug. 1994, pp. 34-35.)

David called Jerusalem the *City of David.* He built up the area around it, from the supporting terraces (Heb., *Millo'*) and inward. *Millo'* seems to refer to stone terraces along the steep eastern and western sides of Jerusalem that supported houses and walls. These terraces frequently needed repairing.

It was important for David to relocate his capital from Hebron. Hebron was much too deeply in the center of Judah to be acceptable to the other tribes, or to avoid the appearance of partiality to Judah. Jerusalem was in the territory of the tribe of Benjamin, though the tribe of Judah was "next door south," with the tribe's boundary going around the south edge of Jerusalem through the valley of Hinnom.

Jerusalem was a place that was defended by strong walls. Jerusalem had religious associations, from Melchizedek's residence there, and probably Abraham's sacrifice of Isaac at Moriah.

Jerusalem in David's time was a small (7–10 acres) city built on a tongue-shaped ridge between the Kidron Valley on its east side and the Tyropoeon Valley on its west. The north part of the City of David was called *Ophel.* The City of David lay outside of the modern walls of Jerusalem, south of Mt. Moriah, where Solomon built his temple and where the Dome of the Rock now stands.

Hiram, king of Tyre in Phoenicia, built a palace in Jerusalem for David (2 Sam. 5:11-12; 1 Chr. 14:1-2). Hiram was always a friend (lit., *lover*) of David (1 Kgs. 5:1).

8. *David's wives and children* (2 Sam. 5:13-16). Compare the lists in 1 Chronicles 3:5-8 and 14:4-7.

Jerusalem — Hills, Valleys, Springs
A. The hills of Jerusalem — "As the mountains surround Jerusalem, so the LORD surrounds his people both now and forevermore" (Ps. 125:2).
  1. *Zion* – The City of David
    a. This was the southeast hill. The north part was called *Ophel.*
    b. It was a long narrow hill, shaped like a gigantic human footprint, about 1250 feet long and 400 feet wide. Its walled-in area was about 8–10 acres.
    c. David called this hill *Zion* (Ps. 48:12; 76:1-2).
  2. *Mt. Moriah* (2435 feet high)
    a. This was the hill north of Mt. Zion and Ophel. Moriah was not in the city during most of David's reign.

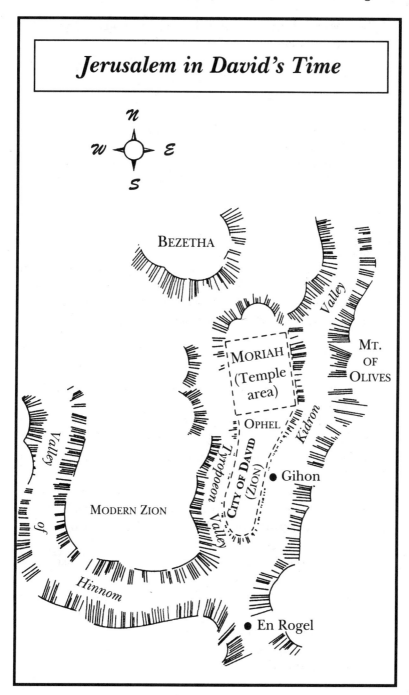

Jerusalem in David's Time

BEZETHA

MORIAH (Temple area)

MT. OF OLIVES

OPHEL

Kidron

Tyropoeon Valley

CITY OF DAVID (ZION)

● Gihon

MODERN ZION

Valley of

Hinnom

● En Rogel

      b. It was the location of Solomon's temple and also the later temples (2 Chr. 3:1).

      c. A depression between Ophel and Mt. Moriah was filled in by David and later kings.

   3. *Mt. of Olives* (2625 feet). (2 Sam. 15:30)

      a. This lies east of Jerusalem.

      b. David fled over the Mt. of Olives from his son Absalom.

   4. *Zion* (modern)

      a. This is the southwest hill, larger in area and higher than the City of David.

      b. This was not part of David's city. It has been wrongly called *Zion* since Crusader times.

   5. *Bezetha*

      a. A hill northwest of Moriah. It was partly included in the walls in New Testament times, but it is not mentioned in the Bible, nor was it part of David's city.

      b. The north part of this hill is now called "Gordon's Calvary."

B. The valleys of Jerusalem

   1. *Hinnom*

      a. This valley lies around the west and south of Jerusalem.

      b. It is also called *Gehenna* (2 Kgs. 23:10; Jer. 7:31).

   2. *Kidron*, or Jehoshaphat (Joel 3:2; 2 Sam. 15:23)

      a. This is the valley east of Jerusalem, between the Mt. of Olives on its east, and Moriah and Zion on its west.

      b. The Kidron joins the Hinnom at the southeast corner of Jerusalem. The name *Kidron* is retained on southeast of the junction of the valleys. The Kidron extends on to the Dead Sea.

      c. Water flows in the Kidron during the rainy season.

   3. *Tyropoeon*, or Central, valley

      a. This valley separated Mt. Ophel and the hill of modern Zion.

      b. This valley is not mentioned in Scripture. It is filled with with dirt and debris in modern times, except at the south end.

C. The springs of Jerusalem
   1. *Gihon* (1 Kgs. 1:33, 39, 45; 2 Chr. 32:30)
      a. This was located at the edge of the Kidron valley, on the east side of the City of David. It is now called the Virgin's Fountain.
      b. Tunnels from this spring were dug westward into the city in ancient times by the Jebusites and by King Hezekiah.
   2. *En Rogel* (Josh. 15:1; 2 Sam. 17:17)
      a. This spring (which is now a well, called Job's well) is located in the Kidron valley, south of the junction of the Kidron and Hinnom valleys.

Questions on Jerusalem

1. What was the name of the Jerusalem City of David?
2. What was the high north part of the City of David called?
3. Where was Mt. Moriah from the City of David?
4. Where is modern Zion from the City of David?
5. Where is the Kidron valley?
6. Where is the Tyropoeon valley?
7. What and where is the Gihon?
8. What and where was En Rogel?

9. *David defeats the Philistines twice* (2 Sam. 5:17-22; 1 Chr. 14:8-17). The Philistines decided to test Israel's new king quickly by an attack upon Jerusalem. They approached the city through the valley of Rephaim (meaning "Giants"). This fertile, relatively flat valley begins southwest of Jerusalem about five miles. It flows westward into the Sorek valley. David asked the LORD for guidance. David defeated the Philistines there, and called the place *Baal Perazim* ("Baal of Breaking Through").

In a second attack by the Philistines in the same valley, David circled behind them, and the LORD caused the Philistines to hear sounds of marching. This time David chased the Philistines back as far as Gezer (twenty miles west-southwest) and Gibeon (eight miles northwest).

In his battles with the Philistines in the Valley of Rephaim David longed for water from his father's well at Bethlehem. Three of his brave men risked their lives to sneak through the Philistine lines and get the water and bring it back to David. David poured out the water on the ground as an offering to the LORD (2 Sam. 23:13-17; 1 Chr. 11:15-19).

This act might seem ungrateful or wasteful. Our evaluation of the act will be determined by how aware we are of the reality of God's presence and power with us.

10. *The ark brought to Jerusalem* (2 Sam. 6; 1 Chr. 13, 15, 16). The ark of the covenant had been kept at the residence of Abinadab at Kiriath Jearim, ten miles west of Jerusalem, for nearly seventy years (1070–1003 B.C.) (1 Sam. 7:1). King Saul had taken it out into the battle one time (1 Sam. 14:18), but it had been returned to Kiriath Jearim. David prepared a new tent for the ark to be placed into (1 Chr. 15:1). The new tent was probably very well made.

David's bringing the ark up to Jerusalem established Jerusalem forever as the religious center of Israel.

David failed in his first attempt to bring up the ark, because they attempted to transport it on a cart, instead of having the Levites carry it (1 Chr. 15:13; Num. 3:6-10). The ark remained at the house of Obed-Edom the Gittite (Gathite) for three months. Then David went with the Levites and successfully brought the ark to Jerusalem.

Uzzah, son of Abinadab, the keeper of the ark, died when he touched the ark at the time they first attempted to bring it up to Jerusalem (6:3-7). David was angry about this for a while. Numbers 3:38 plainly said, "Anyone else (except priests and Levites) who approached the sanctuary (tabernacle) was to be put to death." God is often very strict about our doing exactly what he told us to do.

When David brought the ark up to Jerusalem, David selected a medley of Psalms to be sung. He delivered the songs to the musician Asaph (1 Chr. 16:7-36). The selected psalms were

(1) Psalm 105:1-15 (1 Chr. 16:8-22)

(2) Psalm 96:1-13 (1 Chr. 16:23-33)

(3) Psalm 106:1, 47-48 (1 Chr. 16:34-36).

David even quoted part of the benediction that is at the end of Book Four of the psalms (106:48). David's use of these psalms indicates that some of the psalms had already been written and collected into groups by the time of David's early reign.

David held a great celebration when the ark was brought to Jerusalem (2 Sam. 6:14-15). The event was greatly marred for David when his wife Michal (Saul's daughter) spoke sarcastically and scornfully to him for dancing so exuberantly as the ark was brought up. She *despised* him in her heart (2 Chr. 15:29). She said, "How the king of Israel has distinguished himself today, disrobing in the sight of the slave girls of his servants as any vulgar fellow would!" (6:20).

These words led to a hot exchange that permanently put a barrier between David and Michal. Both had risked their lives to have one another. But a few bitter words broke up their relationship (6:23).

After the ark was brought to Jerusalem, David appointed priests to minister there with the ark regularly (1 Chr.16:37). He appointed gatekeepers (16:37). The altar of burnt-offering was at Gibeon (6 miles northwest of Jerusalem). David appointed priests to minister there at the altar and musicians to give thanks to the LORD (16:41-42).

11. *God promises David an eternal kingdom* (2 Sam. 7:1-17; 1 Chr. 17:1-15; Acts 7:46). David desired to build for God a "house" (a temple) of cedar wood. God said that *He* would build a "house" for David, and David's offspring and kingdom would endure forever.

---

2 Samuel 7:12-13 — ONE OF THE GREATEST PROPHECIES IN THE BIBLE !

The LORD said to David, "When your days are over and you rest with your fathers, I will raise up your offspring to succeed you, . . . and I will establish his kingdom. He is the one who will build a *house* for my Name, and I will establish the throne of his kingdom *forever*."

This chapter (2 Sam. 7) was the source and foundation of the hope for the Messiah. This hope was elaborated by the prophets and in the Psalms, as God revealed more and more of His plan. (See Psalm 89:3-4, 29, 35-37; Jeremiah 23:5-6.)

Abigail, the gracious lady, foretold to David, "The LORD will certainly make for my lord an *enduring house*" (1 Sam. 25:28).

The fulfillment of the LORD's promise to David was spoken to Mary by the angel: "You will be with child and give birth to a son, and you are to give him the name Jesus. He will be great and will be called the Son of the Most High. The Lord God will give him the throne of his father *David*, and he will reign over the house of Jacob forever; his kingdom will never end" (Luke 1:31-33).

The New Testament begins, "A record of the genealogy of Jesus Christ the son of *David*, the son of *Abraham*" (Matt. 1:1). God gave to Abraham and to David the two greatest Messianic promises in the Scriptures — the promise that all nations would be *blessed* by Abraham's offspring, and the promise that an *eternal kingdom* would come from David's offspring. If Jesus were not a descendant of Abraham and David, He could not be the one to fulfill these promises. The New Testament begins by documenting the human descent of Jesus from these two men.

Chapter seven of 2 Samuel probably follows chapter eight chronologically. Compare 7:1 and chapter 8. But the promises of God to David in chapter seven are far more important than the record of David's military victories in chapter eight. The victories were temporary historical events; the promises are eternal realities.

WHY GOD DID NOT ALLOW DAVID TO BUILD A TEMPLE

1. God had never asked for a temple (2 Sam. 7:7).

2. God does not dwell in tents or temples (Acts 7:46, 48-49).

3. God wanted to make a "house" for David, rather than for David to make a "house" for God (2 Sam. 7:11, 27).

4. David was a man of war and had shed blood (1 Chr. 22:8; 28:3).

The word *house* has two different meanings in 2 Samuel 7:7,11.

God said to David, "I have not dwelt in a *house* from the day I brought the Israelites up out of Egypt to this day" (2 Sam. 7:6). God did not dwell in the tabernacle, but in His people (Ex. 25:8).

The prophet *Nathan* is mentioned for the first time in 2 Samuel 7:2, but Nathan is very prominent later (12:1).

The LORD's promises to David were a "covenant" (Ps. 89:28), although the word *covenant* is not found in 2 Samuel 7.

12. *David's prayer of submission* (2 Sam. 7:18-29; 1 Chr. 17:16-27). David's prayer to God after God refused to let him build a temple is very touching. Nine times in the prayer David calls himself "your servant. David was willing for God's will to be done, rather than his own will.

David's prayer of submission to God (2 Sam. 7:18-29)

(1) Acknowledgment of what is best (7:18-21).
(2) Praise to the the LORD (7:22-24).
(3) Submission to the LORD (7:25-29).

David's prayer is addressed to "Sovereign LORD," literally *Adonai Yahweh* (the lord, the eternal one).

David said to God, "You **know** your servant" (7:20).

13. *David's military victories* (2 Sam. 8; 1 Chr. 18). The Philistines attacked David early in his reign, and he had to fight two defensive battles (2 Sam. 5:17-25). After that David went on the offensive against the Philistines and took their "mother city" of Gath. "Metheg Ammah" probably means the "Bridle of the Mother City."

David defeated the Philistines on the west (2 Sam. 8:1).

David defeated the Moabites on the east (8:2).

David defeated the Arameans (Syrians) on the north (8:3-12).

David defeated the Edomites on the south (8:14).

David was cruel to the Moabites, even though he was descended from Ruth the Moabitess. David had left his family in Moab while he was a fugitive from King Saul (1 Sam. 22:3-4). A Jewish tradition says the Moabites murdered his family.

David defeated the Arameans in Zobah and the Arameans of Damascus. *Zobah* was an Aramean state in the northern part of the Lebanon Valley. David won a large military victory there, and took much gold and bronze as spoil (8:7-8). David conquered their land all the way to the Euphrates River (8:3). This fulfilled the promise in Genesis 15:18.

David increased his territory from 6,000 square miles to 60,000 square miles.

The accounts of David's victories are followed by a list of some of David's officials (8:15-18). David's nephew Joab was commander over David's army most of the time. Zadok and Ahimelech, son of Abiathar, were David's priests. Benaiah was over David's private army of mercenaries called the Kerethites. The Kerethites were non-Israelites (associated with the Philistines) who were loyal to David.

14. *David's kindness to Mephibosheth* (2 Sam. 9:1-13; 4:4; 16:1-4; 19:24-30). David desired to show "kindness" (Heb., *hesed*) to the family of Saul for the sake of his beloved friend Jonathan.

David learned of the crippled son of Jonathan named *Mephibosheth*, who lived in Lo Debar over east of the Jordan, perhaps southeast of the Sea of Galilee. *Lo Debar* probably means "No Thing," as if it were a very small place. Saul's servant named *Ziba* was caring for the land belonging to Saul's family, and probably coveting it. Ziba had fifteen sons and twenty servants!

David invited Mephibosheth to come to his palace at Jerusalem to live. David would provide food for him, and directed that he should receive the income from the land. Later events show that Mephibosheth was very grateful to

David for his kindness and did not covet the family land. Mephibosheth had a young son, Mica.

We, like Mephibosheth, are invited to come and live in the king's (Jesus') house. There we also place OUR club feet under the king's table. We sometimes have "club feet" of bad manners, thoughtlessness, pride, poor grammar and speech, laziness, rudeness, lust, selfishness, ignorance, and dishonesty.

The TRIUMPHS of DAVID (2 Sam. 3–10)

a. Gracious reception of Abner (2 Sam. 3).

b. Good will toward Ish-Bosheth. Execution of his killers (2 Sam. 4).

c. Becoming king over ALL Israel (2 Sam. 5).

d. Jerusalem captured and made the capital (2 Sam. 5).

e. Two victories over attacking Philistines (2 Sam. 5).

f. Ark transported to Jerusalem (2 Sam. 6).

g. Temple servants appointed and organized (1 Chr. 15–16). Priests and Levites organized (1 Chr. 23–24).

h. Obtained God's promise to establish his throne forever (2 Sam. 7).

i. Victories over surrounding nations (2 Sam. 8).

j. Kindness to Mephibosheth (2 Sam. 9).

k. Courtesy toward Ammonites (2 Sam. 10).

l. Victory over Ammonites (2 Sam. 10).

---

15. *David defeats the Ammonites and Arameans* (2 Sam. 10; 1 Chr. 19). David attempted to show kindness to the Ammonites at the death of their king, but his messengers of sympathy were treated with suspicion and humiliating abuse (10:1-4). The Ammonites lived east of Israel, east of the Jordan, by the desert.

The two-cent insult by the Ammonites, who cut off half the clothes of David's messengers, was hardly worth going to war over and getting thousands of people killed. David was sometimes quick to attack people for insults. He once set out to wipe out the family of Nabal, who talked abusively to him

(1 Sam. 25). God was not pleased with David's being a man of war (1 Chr. 28:3). Always be kind, even to your enemies (Rom. 12:17-21; Matt. 5:43-45).

The Ammonites hired the Arameans to help defend themselves against the Israelites. Joab and his brother Abishai defeated them at Medeba (east of Dead Sea north end). In a second battle at a place named Helam (2 Sam. 10:17) David's men defeated the Arameans.

DAVID'S THREE BATTLES AGAINST THE AMMONITES AND THE SYRIANS
(All of these occurred east of the Jordan River.)

1. At *MEDEBA* (1 Chr. 19:6-15). Incomplete victory. The Syrians fled. The Ammonites retreated into their city (Rabbah).
2. At *HELAM* (2 Sam. 10:15-19; 8:3-8; 1 Chr. 19:16-19). The Syrians were thoroughly defeated. (Helam was perhaps located at modern Alma, 22 miles northeast of Ramoth-Gilead, near the border of Syria.)
3. At *RABBAH*, capital of Ammon (2 Sam.12:26-29; 1 Chr. 20:1-3). Total victory for David. While Joab was besieging Rabbah, David was back in Jerusalem, and saw Bathsheba. David later captured Rabbah, and tortured its people (2 Sam. 20:1-3).

---

16. *David and Bathsheba* (2 Sam. 11). David in Jerusalem fell into the sin of adultery while his army was fighting to capture the city of Rabbah (11:1-4). In an attempt to conceal his sin, David arranged to have the woman's husband killed (11:14-15). These events changed David's reign from a rule in *triumph* to a rule in *tragedies.*

Rabbah was the capital city of Ammon. It was forty-five miles east of Jerusalem, and twenty-five east of the Jordan River. *Rabbah* means "great" (large). The place is now named *Amman,* the capital of Jordan. It has a high citadel in its center, and a lower "water supply" (literally, "the city of waters") in its lower part (12:27). David attacked Rabbah after the insult by the new king of Ammon (10:1-4), and after two battles against Ammon the previous year.

Wars were fought in the spring seasons. Winters are cold and rainy and muddy.

David's sin illustrates the words of James 1:14: "Each one is tempted when, by his own evil desire, he is dragged away and enticed." The story also shows our need for modest conduct.

From the top of the City of David (Zion) in Jerusalem, one can look down upon the rooftops of houses east of the Valley of Kidron. The text does not say *Bathsheba* was bathing on the top of her house roof, but from *his* roof David saw her.

David had been on his bed in the afternoon, and rose in the evening. "Loafing in the afternoon makes you sexy in the evening."

Bathsheba (Bathshua in 1 Chr. 3:5) was the daughter of *Eliam* (spelled *Amiel* by reversing the first and last syllables in 1 Chronicles). One of David's Thirty mighty men was named Eliam (2 Sam. 23:34). He was a son of Ahithophel the Gilonite, the counselor of David who quickly transferred his loyalty to David's rebellious son Absalom (2 Sam. 15:12). We think this is the same Eliam as the father of Bathsheba. If so, Ahithophel would be Bathsheba's grandfather. Ahithophel was probably hostile to David for what he had done to his granddaughter Bathsheba. David was probably older than Bathsheba and much younger than Ahithophel.

Bathsheba was the wife of *Uriah* the Hittite. Uriah was one of David's thirty mighty men (2 Sam. 23:24, 29). David had numerous foreign warriors, including some Hittites (1 Sam. 26:16). Uriah's loyalty to David was genuine, deep, and sacrificial. He would not indulge his natural longings while his king's men were on the field of battle.

David attempted to deceive Uriah into thinking that the child conceived in Bathsheba was his child (11:8-11). David even tried to weaken Uriah's resolve by making him drunk. Uriah carried his own death orders, and delivered them to Joab, David's commander.

When Joab sent word back to David that Uriah was dead, Joab had to conceal the real intent of his report to David from the messenger who delivered it. Joab made Uriah's death sound like an unanticipated casualty in war (11:18-21).

David pretended a callous attitude when he heard Uriah was dead (11:25). But if Psalm 32 tells of this time in his life, David's spirit was groaning with guilt day and night (Ps. 32:3-4).

"Cursed is the man who kills his neighbor secretly."
Then all the people shall say, "Amen" (Deut. 27:24).

---

17. *Nathan rebukes David* (2 Sam. 12:1-25). For almost nine months David had shut in his feelings of guilt. Near the birth of Bathsheba's son the LORD sent the prophet Nathan to David to convict him of sin. Nathan told to David a story of a rich man who took a poor man's one little ewe (female) lamb.

Stealing a lamb was not a huge crime. But David was angered by the rich man's callous disregard of another's feelings. David said (literally), "That man is a son of death!"

Then came the blow to David: "YOU are the man." David knew his sin was known. His heart was touched. He confessed his sin. (Compare Psalm 32:5.) Unlike King Saul, who tried to defend his wrongdoing (1 Sam. 15:20-21), David repented of his deeds.

Nathan gave a clue to David that the story might apply to him when he said, "The lamb was like a *daughter* to the poor man." "Daughter" in Hebrew is *bath*, as in *Bath*-sheba.

David said, "I have sinned against the LORD" (12:13). Compare Psalm 51:4: "Against you, you only, have I sinned." Sin hurts God most of all; but David had also sinned against Uriah, Bathsheba, himself, his unborn child, his family and all Israel. Sin's effects hurt those all around the sinner.

David's sin was forgiven (2 Sam. 12:13). However, he was punished for his deeds.

> ## Psalm 51 — David's psalm of repentance after he had gone in to Bathsheba*
>
> "Have mercy on me, O God, according to your unfailing love."
> "Create in me a pure heart, O God."
> "Do not cast me from your presence."
>
> ---
>
> *Psalm 32 may also have been written near that time.

> ## PUNISHMENTS FOR DAVID'S SIN
>
> 1. His son would die (2 Sam. 12:14, 18).
> 2. The sword would never depart from his house (12:10; 13:28).
>   (There would always be killing and bloodshed in his family.)
> 3. There would be open immoralities in his family (12:11-12).
>   (See 2 Samuel 16:21-22.)

David's sin had "made the enemies of the LORD show utter contempt" (12:14). KJV: "thou hast given great occasion to the enemies of the LORD to blaspheme."

(Second Samuel 12:14 is a difficult verse to translate. Some scholars consider the word "enemies" to be a euphemistic insertion into the text to shield David's reputation. See P.K. McCarter in *Anchor Bible* on 2 Samuel, p. 296. But the pi'el stem of the verb "show contempt" [or scorn] indicates the causation of a state or condition. See Bruce Waltke, *Biblical Hebrew Syntax* [1990], p. 400. Therefore it appears correct to translate the verse to state that David's deeds had caused sinners to scorn God.)

The son of David and Bathsheba became ill. David prayed and fasted; but the child died on the seventh day. David then went to worship and ate food. His behavior surprised his servants. David expressed a hope and faith in immortality: "While the child was still alive, I fasted and wept . . . But now that he is dead, why should I fast? . . . *I will go to him*, but he will not return to me" (12:22-23). Compare Isaiah 57:1-2; 2 Corinthians 5:8; Job 19:25-26.

The later birth of Solomon to David and Bathsheba gives

a vivid display of God's grace. The name *Solomon* means
peaceable. But the LORD called him *Jedidiah*, which means
Beloved by the LORD. Neither the past acts of David, nor the
failures of Solomon that would occur in the future dimin-
ished the love the LORD felt for Solomon (2 Sam. 12:24-25).

18. *Capture of Rabbah* (2 Sam.12:26-31; 1 Chr. 20:2-3). Joab
(David's commander) captured the lower portion of the city
of Rabbah (2 Sam. 11:1), called the "water supply" (lit. "the
city of the waters"). Joab called for David to come and complete the capture of the city. Probably he did this to win favor
with David. (Concerning the City of David, see *Biblical
Archaeology Review*, March–April 1988, pp. 14-27.)

David came and captured the city. He placed the crown of
their king upon his own head, though it weighed a talent of
gold (about seventy-five pounds). Then he tortured the
defeated Ammonites with hard labor.

We think this happened before the birth of Bathsheba's
son that died, while David was in a state of spiritual and emotional turmoil. David showed his inner turmoil by harsh treatment of others. The "meanwhile" at the start of 12:26 (NIV)
is not actually in the Hebrew text, and does not indicate that
David captured Rabbah *after* Solomon's birth.

DAVID, A MAN AFTER GOD'S OWN HEART

How could David be a man after God's own heart when
he was a killer and an adulterer? Several Scriptures affirm
that David was indeed called "a man after God's own
heart." (See Acts 13:22; 1 Samuel 13:14; Psalm 89:20.)

1. David really LOVED GOD (Ps. 116:1; 18:1; 63:1).
2. David loved the PEOPLE of God (Ps. 119:63; 42:4).
3. David loved the WORD of God (Ps. 119:97).
4. David loved the HOUSE of God (Ps. 84:1-2).
5. David loved his fellow men (1 Kgs. 5:1; 2 Sam. 10:1).
6. David sinned deeply, but he repented deeply (Ps. 51).

Questions on Section D
David's Reign in Triumph (2 Sam. 2–12)

1. Whom did David inquire of before going up to one of the towns of Judah? (2 Sam. 2:1)
2. What was the name of David's wife from Jezreel? (2:2)
3. Who was the wife of Nabal who became David's wife? (2:2)
4. To what city in Judah did David go first to be anointed king? (2:3)
5. To the men of what city did David send thanks for their burying the body of King Saul? (2:4)
6. How long did David reign at the city where he was first anointed king? (2:11)
7. Whom did Abner (commander of Saul's army) make king over Israel? (2:8)
8. At what town was Ish-Bosheth anointed king? (2:8)
9. How long did Ish-Bosheth reign? (2:10)
10. At what town did the first fight take place between David's men and Abner's men? (2:12)
11. Who chased Abner, but was killed by him? (2:18)
12. Was the war between the house of Saul and the house of David a long war or a short war? (3:1)
13. What did Ish-Bosheth accuse Abner of? (3:7)
14. What was Ish-Bosheth's reaction when Abner announced he was going to transfer the kingdom to David? (3:11)
15. What did David demand before he would negotiate with Ish-Bosheth? (3:14)
16. What did Abner offer to do for David? (3:21)
17. Who became infuriated when he learned of David's conversation with Abner? (3:24)
18. Who killed Abner? Why? (3:22)
19. Who killed Ish-Bosheth? (4:5-6)
20. Where did the killers bring Ish-Bosheth's head? (4:8)
21. What did David command his young men to do to the killers? (4:11-12)
22. Were there many Israelites or few who came to make David king over all Israel? (1 Chr. 12:23, 37)
23. What two reasons did the tribes of Israel give for wanting to have part in the anointing of David as king over all Israel? (5:1-3)
24. How old was David at the beginning of his reign? (5:4)
25. For how long was David king? (5:4)
26. What people lived in Jerusalem before David took it? (5:6)
27. Who — supposedly — could defend Jerusalem? (5:6)

28. Through what was entry made into Jerusalem? (5:8)
29. Which of David's men smote Jerusalem first? (1 Chr. 11:6)
30. Which is another name for Jerusalem given to it at this time? (5:9)
31. What king made an alliance with David by sending him logs and workmen to build David a palace in Jerusalem? (5:11)
32. Where did the Philistines gather twice to fight David? (5:18,22)
33. What was the outcome of the two battles with the Philistines? (5:20, 25)
34. In what town was the ark when David first decided to bring it to Jerusalem? (6:1; 1 Chr. 13:5-6)
35. At whose house had it been kept? (6:3; 1 Sam. 7:1)
36. Name the two sons who accompanied the ark on its first journey. (6:3)
37. Who died because he touched the ark? (6:7)
38. To whose house was the ark then taken? (6:11)
39. How long was the ark left at the house of Obed-Edom before it was transferred to Jerusalem? (6:11)
40. Whom did David call to bring up the ark to Jerusalem in his second attempt? (1 Chr. 15:2,4,13)
41. Who scorned David because of his dancing when the ark was finally brought up to Jerusalem? (2 Sam. 6:16,20)
42. Why did David think he ought to build a temple for the ark of God? (7:2)
43. To whom did David speak concerning building the temple? (7:2)
44. Why was David forbidden to build a temple? (1 Chr. 22:8; 2 Sam. 7:6-7)
45. What promises did God give to David concerning his offspring (seed)? (7:12-13)
46. Who would build a house for whom? (1 Chr. 17:10; 2 Sam. 7:27)
47. List five nations or peoples that David defeated after he became king over Israel. (2 Sam. 8:1-14)
48. Name the king of Hamath. (8:9-10)
49. Who was over David's army? (8:16)
50. Who were David's two priests? (8:17)
51. What groups of people were David's bodyguards? (8:18) Who was their leader?
52. Who were the three men appointed by David over the ministry of music? (1 Chr. 15:19; 25:1).
53. How many divisions (or courses) did David divide the priests into? (1 Chr. 24:1, 18-19; compare 24:10 and Luke 1:5.)
54. Who was Ziba? (2 Sam. 9:2)
55. Who was the son of Jonathan that David befriended? (9:3,6)

56. What did David do for Mephibosheth? (9:3,7)
57. Who was Hanun? How did he anger David? (10:1,4)
58. Where was the first battle against the Ammonites?(1 Chr.19:7)
59. Where was the second battle against the Ammonites? (2 Sam. 10:17)
60. What people did the Ammonites hire to help them fight David? (10:6)
61. Who was a military leader besides Joab? (10:10)
62. At what place was David's army fighting when David (at home) saw Bathsheba from the roof of the palace? (11:1)
63. Who was Bathsheba's husband? (11:6-7)
64. What was Bathsheba's husband doing at that time? (11:6-7)
65. How did David try to conceal his sin? (11:8,11,13)
66. What letter did Uriah faithfully deliver? (11:14-15)
67. How did the LORD feel about David's deeds? (11:27)
68. What prophet was sent to David to convict him? (12:1)
69. Fill in the words from 2 Sam.12:1-4: "There were _____ men in a certain town, one _____ and the other _____. The _____ man had a very large number of _____ and cattle, but the _____ man had nothing except one little _____ _____ he had bought. He raised it, and it grew up with him and his children. It shared his _____, drank from his _____ and even _____ in his arms. It was like a _____ to him. Now a _____ came to the _____ man, but the _____ man refrained from taking one his own _____ or cattle . . . Instead he took the _____ _____ that belonged to the _____ man and prepared it for the one who had come to him."
70. What was David's judgment upon the man who had taken the little ewe lamb? (12:5-6)
71. What were the prophet's four convicting words to David? (12:7)
72. Did David confess his sin? (12:13)
73. Which psalm (possibly 2) expresses David's repentance?
74. What was David's immediate punishment for his sin? (12:14)
75. What did David do while the child was ill? (12:16-17)
76. What did he do when the child died? (12:20-21)
77. What was the name of a second son born to David by Bathsheba? (12:24)
78. What name did the LORD give to the son through Nathan the prophet? (12:24). What does this name mean?
79. How did David treat the Ammonites after he defeated them? (2 Sam. 12:30-31; 1 Chr. 20:3)

Section E
David's Reign in Tragedies
(2 Samuel 13:1 — 1 Kings 2:11)

1. *Absalom, Amnon, and Tamar* (2 Sam. 13). The fulfillment of the punishments David had been forewarned he would suffer soon occurred (2 Sam. 12:10-11). David's son Amnon assaulted his half-sister Tamar. Then Tamar's brother Absalom killed Amnon. Absalom then fled to his grandfather's house in the distant land of Geshur.

It is incorrect to say that God caused any of these evil events. But God did not prevent them from happening, as He had at previous times protected David from evil schemes by people. ("Deliver us from evil" is a meaningful, important prayer!)

Amnon was the firstborn son of David (1 Chr. 3:1). The story of Amnon and Tamar in chapter 13 is only the opening part of a longer section (chs. 13–18) about Absalom's campaign to take over his father David's kingdom. Absalom's name is mentioned first in the Hebrew text of 13:1.

Absalom's sister Tamar was beautiful (13:1). People of great physical beauty were numerous in David's family: David himself (1 Sam. 16:12; 17:42); Absalom (14:25); Bathsheba (11:2); Absalom's daughter Tamar (14:27); Adonijah (1 Kgs. 1:6).

"Amnon became frustrated" on account of his sister Tamar. "There was a steadfast frame of mind [an obsession!] in Amnon to the point of making himself ill because of Tamar his sister, because she was a virgin; but in the eyes of Amnon it seemed hard (or astonishing) to do anything to her." (Author's translation. Compare BDB, p. 428.)

Amnon's downcast disposition was noticed by Jonadab, a son of David's brother Shimeah (13:3). He was "very shrewd" and very unprincipled. Possibly he was seeking political advancement by sharp observations of people and by confidential counsel. By following Jonadab's advice, Amnon arranged to be alone with Tamar, and quickly assaulted her (13:9-14).

Amnon had asked for Tamar to prepare and serve him some "special bread," (13:6), perhaps "heart-bread" or "heart-shaped pancakes" (BDB, 525). Was he hinting of *amor*?

Tamar protested to Amnon, "You will be like one of the wicked *fools* in Israel" (13:13). "Fools" is from *nebalim*, plural of *nabal*. (See 1 Samuel 25:25 and Proverbs 6:32.)

Amnon had said that he "loved" Tamar (13:4). But sex relations outside of God's permitted zone are dangerous and unsatisfying. Having forced himself upon her, then he felt a hatred toward her, even more than the "love" he felt. He said, "Get up, and get out." (Probably Amnon also hated himself, but was not admitting that.)

Tamar's experience soon became public knowledge. Her brother Absalom pretended unconcern, but inwardly he seethed with deadly silent hatred. David was "furious" (literally, "burning exceedingly"); but David's own sin with Bathsheba left him feeling unable to take stern action against Amnon.

Two years later Absalom's men killed Amnon at a sheepshearing festival at Baal Hazor (seventeen miles north of Jerusalem). A false rumor came back to David in Jerusalem that all his sons had been killed (13:30). David's nephew Jonadab (the one who had counselled Amnon to do evil!) reassured David that only Amnon was dead. (Jonadab took pains to know all about all scandalous events.)

Absalom feared to return to Jerusalem, and fled to the district of Geshur, a small Aramean (Syrian) state on the east side of the Sea of Galilee. Absalom's grandfather Talmai was the king of Geshur (2 Sam. 3:3; 1 Chr. 3:2). (Regarding Geshur, see *Biblical Archaeology Review*, July–Aug. 1992, pp. 30-44.)

Absalom stayed in Geshur three years. By that time David longed for Absalom. Literally, "David ceased to go toward Absalom" (to threaten him either verbally or physically) (13:39).

2. *Absalom returns to Jerusalem* (2 Sam. 14). Joab took action to cause David to let Absalom come back to Jerusalem from Geshur. He called for a wise woman from Tekoa to

come and speak to David. The woman told David a contrived story about one of her two sons killing his brother. Her eloquent speech led David to swear to protect the remaining brother from death. That oath led David to make an even greater concession — to allow Absalom to be brought back. But the return of Absalom was coldly received. David would not see Absalom in Jerusalem for two years.

Absalom meanwhile was flaunting his personal beauty and long hair. Each year he would publicly shear off five pounds (200 shekels) of hair.

Absalom finally set fire to Joab's grain field to gain attention to his personal frustrations. He was brought before the king. The meeting was outwardly affectionate, but probably strained (14:33).

Joab is called the "son of Zeruiah" (14:1). Zeruiah was David's half-sister (1 Chr. 2:13-16), and Joab was David's nephew.

Tekoa is a village six miles south-southeast of Bethlehem (twelve from Jerusalem) on the edge of the desert of Judah. Amos the prophet later came from Tekoa (Amos 1:1).

Joab "put words into the mouth" of the woman from Tekoa and sent her to David. The woman was eloquent and diplomatic (14:20). She told David a story about how one of her two sons had killed the other, and now the whole clan was planning to kill the other son. Joab and Abishai had followed this same custom and killed Abner for similar reasons (2 Sam. 3:30).

David agreed to protect the son; but the woman sought more than a non-specific promise like "I will issue an order on your behalf" (14:8). She finally provoked David into making an oath: "Not one hair of your son's head will fall to the ground."

The woman then made an association between David's protection of her son and his non-acceptance of Absalom in exile. The cases were not fully alike. Absalom was not David's only surviving son. No one was seeking to kill Absalom at that time. The story was clearly contrived, and David perceived Joab's manipulation (14:19). But the woman's speech did cause David to have Absalom brought back to Jerusalem.

**WHY WE SHOULD BE FORGIVING,
AND RECEIVE PEOPLE BACK**
(as stated by the wise woman from Tekoa)

1. We are all going to die, and be like water spilled on the ground. We'll be sorry then if we have been unkind.
2. We should be like God, who devises ways to restore a banished person back to fellowship (2 Sam. 14:14). (God sent Jesus to restore us to fellowship.)

Absalom's vanity about his beauty and long hair shows he was a man of very superficial understanding. Three sons and a beautiful daughter were born to Absalom (14:27). But 2 Samuel 18:18 says Absalom had no sons. All the three sons must have died within a few years.

Absalom's act of setting fire to Joab's field shows he was totally concerned with himself, and not considerate of others.

3. *Absalom's conspiracy* (2 Sam. 15:1-12). Absalom soon began to show an ambition for royal recognition. He was the third son of David (1 Chr. 3:1-2; 2 Sam. 3:2-3), and his older brother Amnon was dead. He provided (lit., *made*) for himself a chariot and fifty runners to go ahead of the chariot. (His brother Adonijah later did the same [1 Kgs. 1:5].)

Absalom stole the hearts (or loyalty) of the men of Israel from David, by personal attention to their complaints, by promises he could never fulfill, and by profuse kissing.

David's reign was at a low ebb at that time because of the scandal of Bathsheba, the wars with Ammon, and his family strife. David did not appoint judges till his later years (1 Chr. 23:1-4), a situation that Absalom exploited (2 Sam. 15:3). Psalm three was written at the time David fled from his son Absalom. The psalm says, "How *many* rise up against me! *Many* are saying of me, 'God will not deliver him'" (Ps. 3:1-2).

Absalom deceived David concerning his planned trip to Hebron. He pretended to be going to fulfill a vow, but was actually fomenting his revolt. He invited people to accompany him, so it would appear that he had many more supporters than he did. At Hebron Absalom offered sacrifices (an act that had brought King Saul's dynasty to an end), and was proclaimed king. He was anointed king, either at Hebron, or after he came back to Jerusalem triumphant (2 Sam. 19:11).

Absalom sent for Ahithophel the Gilonite, David's counselor, to join him. Ahithophel was probably the grandfather of Bathsheba. (See notes on 2 Sam. 11:3.) He was a counselor with great shrewdness, and his defection to Absalom was a fearsome threat to David. Giloh probably was located about twenty miles south-southwest of Hebron, near Debir. (See Joshua 15:51; and *Macmillan Bible Atlas,* map 130.)

Absalom's conspiracy was strong, and Absalom's following kept on increasing (15:12).

4. *David flees* (2 Sam. 15:13-37). When David heard of Absalom's revolt, he decided to flee immediately from Jerusalem. He correctly judged Absalom's cruelty, and feared he would "put the city to the sword."

David's officials remained loyal to him (15:15). He left ten of his many concubines to care for the palace. (These women come into the story later [16:21-22].) David's foreign troops (bodyguard) willingly stayed with David, and went "before the king." They provided security and military power for David. Joab and Abishai went with David (18:2). The people departing to go with David numbered in the thousands (18:1).

A newly-arrived visitor — Ittai the Gittite (a Philistine friend from Gath) — would not leave David (15:21), and became one of his battle commanders (18:2).

When leaving the city, David had to pass over the brook *Kidron* along the east side of Jerusalem, and then go up over the Mt. of Olives. East of the mount is the *desert* of Judah (15:23,30).

David would not allow the ark of God to be carried with him (15:25,29). He was submissive to God's punishments (15:26). David sent the priest Zadok back to Jerusalem to observe and send word to him (15:28). "Aren't you a seer?" David asked him (1 Sam. 9:9). The two sons of the priests — Ahimaaz, son of Zadok, and Jonathan, son of Abiathar — were to be couriers of any news.

The news of Ahithophel's defection to Absalom (15:12) alarmed David greatly. "O LORD, turn Ahithophel's counsel into foolishness" (15:31).

David's "friend" (confidant) Hushai the Arkite, met David on the summit of Olives. David sent him back to Jerusalem, to pretend to join Absalom, and to give bad advice to Absalom, advice that might defeat Ahithophel's shrewd but deadly counsel.

AHITHOPHEL – a prototype of JUDAS	
1. Betrayed David, the LORD's anointed one (2 Sam. 15:12, 31).	1. Betrayed Jesus, the LORD's anointed one (John 6:70-71; 13:2).
2. Probably was a trusted friend, who ate with David. (1 Chr. 27:33; Ps. 41:9 may refer to Ahithophel.)	2. Ate with Jesus (John 13:18, 26). "Friend" (Matt. 26:30).
3. Caused David to cross the brook *Kidron* and the Mt. of Olives (2 Sam. 15:23, 30).	3. Caused Jesus to stay beyond the Mt. of Olives (Luke 21:37), and to cross the *Kidron* into Gethsemane (Luke 22:39; John 18:1).
4. Suicide by strangulation (2 Sam. 17:23).	4. Suicide by hanging (Matt. 27:3-5; Acts 1:18-19).

5. *David and Ziba* (2 Sam. 16:1-4; compare 9:2-11.). While David was fleeing from Absalom, Ziba caught up with David a short distance east of the summit of the Mt. of Olives. Ziba had donkeys and food for David's group. ("String" of donkeys is better translated "couple" [as NRSV] or "pair.")

Ziba told David that Mephibosheth had stayed in Jerusalem "because he thinks (lit., "said"), 'Today the house of Israel will give me back my grandfather's (Saul's) kingdom.'"

That was a lie and a slander on Mephibosheth, as subsequent events showed (2 Sam. 19:24-30).

Ziba wanted the fields that David had granted to Mephibosheth (9:7; 19:29). Ziba pretended to have no motives except a humble desire for David's favor (16:4).

> ### Ziba *COVETED* the land.
> ### Jesus said, Beware of covetousness (Luke 12:15).

6. *Shimei curses David* (2 Sam. 16:5-14). In David's flight from Absalom he approached the village of Bahurim (located northeast of Jerusalem only about 1½ miles). There a Benjamite of the clan of Saul came out and cursed David, and threw rocks and showered dust. He called David a "man of blood." (The Hebrew plural for "blood" indicates blood that is *shed*.) Shimei said that the LORD had caused Absalom to take over David's kingdom.

Shimei's abusive words were very wrong. David had been lenient toward Saul and Abner and Absalom. Shimei also seems very reckless with his life, for David was protected by mighty men on his right and left.

David's warrior Abishai was able and eager to take off Shimei's head (16:9), and called him a "dead dog." (Abishai had once been eager to spear Saul. See 1 Samuel 26:8.) David refused to allow him to harm Shimei, leaving any vengeance to the LORD. David in later years did give Solomon instructions to do to Shimei what he had forbidden Abishai to do to him (1 Kgs. 2:8-9,46).

7. *The advice of Ahithophel and Hushai* (2 Sam.16:15-17:23).

A Jewish proverb says, "Beware of the advice of Ahithophel." But in the days of David and Absalom his advice was regarded like that of one who inquired of God (16:23).

Hushai arrived back in Jerusalem at the time Absalom entered the city (15:37). Absalom was justifiably suspicious of him. But Hushai spoke so convincingly of his loyalty to Absalom that he was accepted. (See 2 Samuel 15:34; Proverbs 18:21).

Ahithophel's first advice to Absalom was that Absalom should publicly "lie" with his father's ten concubines (16:21-22; 15:16). This was ungodly advice. (See Leviticus 18:8; Deuteronomy 22:30.) The effect of doing this was to destroy any possibility of future reconciliation between David and Absalom, and to force the people to accept that being FOR Absalom required being AGAINST David. The defiled concubines were later isolated by David (2 Sam. 20:3).

"Blessed is the man who does not walk in the *counsel of the wicked*" (like Ahithophel) (Ps. 1:1).

Ahithophel's second advice was that Absalom should let him set out that very night with 12,000 men to pursue David quickly and kill him, so that the people with him would be brought back under Absalom's control. That was good advice for Absalom, but bad for David.

Hushai (David's "friend") gave conflicting advice. He urged Absalom to remember that David was a man of war. David would be watching for any attacks, and be well hidden. Some of Absalom's people would probably get killed, and the report of this would demoralize Absalom's people. It would be better to mobilize all Israel against David, and then go after him like an overpowering wave.

This was good advice for David, but bad for Absalom. The result of following Hushai's advice would be to give David enough time to escape across the Jordan River into territory safe for him, and a long way from home for Absalom. Hushai made bad advice sound good. Absalom chose to follow it, because the LORD had determined to bring disaster (lit., "evil") on Absalom (17:14). This was the answer to David's prayer (2 Sam. 15:31).

Absalom did not at first state whose advice he was following. Hushai relayed word to David to cross the Jordan immediately before Absalom might attack. The message was sent to David by Jonathan and Ahimaaz (15:27-28), who were staying at En Rogel. This is a well southeast of Jerusalem (now called Job's well), near where the Kidron and Hinnom valleys merge.

Jonathan and Ahimaaz were seen and reported to Absalom. They fled for their lives. They were hidden in a well at Bahurim (16:5), under a covering of straw (17:18-19). (The story of their close brush with death is so filled with vivid specific details that some have suggested that Ahimaaz wrote this part of the book of Samuel or the whole book. Compare 18:28-29.)

The run by the priests' sons from Bahurim to David's camp near the Jordan would have taken about eight hours. But by daybreak the next morning every one of David's men was across the Jordan.

Ahithophel was proud, as well as ungodly. Seeing that Absalom had not taken his advice, he returned to his town of Giloh and hanged (lit., "strangled") himself (17:23).

8. *The doom of Absalom* (2 Sam. 17:24-19:8). David went to Mahanaim east of the Jordan (2 Sam. 17:24). (There Abner had made Ish-Bosheth king [2:8].)

Absalom followed David with a great army. (See 18:7, which tells that 20,000 were killed.) Absalom set *Amasa* over his army. He was a cousin of Joab. (Joab's mother and Amasa's mother were sisters.) Joab later killed Amasa (2 Sam. 19:13; 20:4-10).

At Mahanaim David was aided by three prominent men of the area (17:27-29):

(1) *Shobi*, son (or grandson) of Nahash (probably the same Nahash as in 2 Samuel 10:1).

(2) *Makir* of Lo Debar, former guardian of Mephibosheth (2 Sam. 9:4).

(3) *Barzillai*. See 17:27; 19:31-32; 1 Kings 2:7.

David had no chance to prepare for battle during his hasty flight from Jerusalem. At Mahanaim he placed his troops into three divisions, under Joab, Abishai, and Ittai the Gittite (2 Sam. 15:19-21).

David commanded the three leaders, "Be gentle with the young man Absalom for my sake" (18:5, 12).

> **A great and humble leader like David deserves all
> honor** (2 Sam. 18:3; Heb. 13:7).

The battle took place in the "forest of Ephraim" (18:6).
The land of the tribe of Ephraim was *west* of the Jordan River
from this battle. Perhaps the forest received its name from
the presence of Ephraimites there in the days of judge
Jephthah. (See Judges 12:4-6; 7:24.) "The forest claimed more
lives that day than the sword." Abner and the "army of
Israel" were defeated (18:7).

Absalom himself was yanked off his mule when his head
was caught in a tree limb as he rode through the thick
branches of a large oak. His long hair is not mentioned, but
perhaps it contributed to his being snagged (2 Sam. 14:11).

Joab spoke very brusquely to a soldier who had seen
Absalom hanging and did not kill him (18:11). Joab would
not listen to the man's rebuke of him for his eagerness to kill
Absalom and disobey David. Joab said, "I'm not going to wait
like this for you."

Joab killed the defenseless Absalom in the tree. A large
pile of rocks over a pit marked his humiliating burial place.
(Compare Joshua 7:26; 8:29.) All the Israelites fled to their
homes (2 Sam. 18:17; 19:8).

Absalom died having no son (14:27); but he had set up in
the King's Valley in Jerusalem (Gen. 14:17) a monument to
himself called the *Yad 'Abshalom* (Hand, or Monument, of
Absalom). There is still in Jerusalem in the Kidron valley just
east of the temple an impressive monument called Absalom's
monument. It is fifty-two feet tall, and has a cone-shaped top.
It is thought to have been made in Roman times (about the
time of Jesus), so it cannot be Absalom's original monument,
but may be near where it was.

Ahimaaz (son of the priest Zadok) asked Joab permission
to run and tell David of their victory. Joab, for reasons not
stated, did not want him to go. Joab asked the Cushite (an
Ethiopian, or Nubian) to go and report what he had seen.
Ahimaaz had not actually seen Absalom dead (18:29, 32).

After the Cushite left, Ahimaaz still insisted on running to bear the news, and by taking an easier route "by way of the plain," he outran the Cushite to David at Mahanaim. (He probably ran up through the valley of the brook Jabbok. See *Macmillan Bible Atlas*, map 110.)

David was more concerned about Absalom than about the battle. The Cushite diplomatically cushioned the news of Absalom's death: "May the enemies of my lord the king . . . be like that young man" (18:32).

David's grief was total. As he went into seclusion he was saying, "O my son Absalom! My son, my son Absalom! If only I had died instead of you."

David's grief affected the whole army. The people stole away into the city, not knowing what to say or do (19:2-4).

Joab rebuked David for allowing his emotions to overrule good judgment. "You love those who hate you, and hate those who love you" (19:6). Joab was probably correct. The people needed a leader. David had abandoned his throne when Absalom proclaimed himself king. Who was the ruler now that Absalom was dead? David needed to present himself before his people as ruler, or he would quickly lose power to someone else. "Now go out and encourage your men" (19:7). David did so, and all the people came before him in glad submission.

Joab's rebuke of David, plus all his previous cruel acts, soon cost him his position as commander (2 Sam. 19:6).

9. *David returns to Jerusalem as king* (2 Sam.19:9-43). The Israelites felt keenly their need for the king to be on the job (19:9-10). David himself took action, and asked the elders of Judah (his own tribe), "Why should you be the last [to offer] to bring the king back to his palace?" (19:11). David's offer was accepted at once, and the people rallied around him.

David offered to make Amasa the commander of his army in place of Joab (19:13). Amasa had been commander of Absalom's army. David's offer would help to restore the loyalty of those who had been with Absalom. Amasa was David's nephew (2 Sam. 17:25).

Shimei met David at the Jordan River bank, hoping to

save his life by asking David's forgiveness. Shimei had cursed David and thrown dust at him when David fled from Jerusalem. See 2 Samuel 16:5-13; 19:16-23. David spared Shimei, but later told Solomon to take his life (1 Kgs. 2:8-9).

Mephibosheth (Jonathan's crippled son) also came to meet David at the Jordan (2 Sam. 19:24-30; 16:5-13). Mephibosheth had been very grieved over David's forced departure from Jerusalem. As a result of Ziba's accusation that Mephibosheth was seeking David's throne, David had been uncertain about Mephibosheth's loyalty. Mephibosheth showed he was fully loyal, and did not desire even the wealth from his family's fields.

The old gentleman Barzillai the Gileadite also came to the Jordan to bid David farewell (19:34-39; 17:27-29). His presence was significant, because it showed that David was respected as king by honorable people in all areas of Israel. Barzillai had shown kindness to David when he first fled from Absalom. David could now repay the kindness to Barzillai, and was quite willing to take Barzillai's son Kimham with him to Jerusalem. Kindness produces rewards of the same kind.

The tribe of Judah and the other tribes of Israel had a shouting match over which tribes should escort David back to Jerusalem as king (19:40-43). Their angry and jealous words gave an advance indication of the split that would come between Judah and Israel, when they would become separate kingdoms (1 Kgs. 12:16-20).

Get rid of all bitterness, rage and anger (Eph. 4:31).

---

10. *The rebellion of Sheba against David* (2 Sam. 20). Among those present at the dispute between the tribe of Judah and the other tribes was a Benjamite named *Sheba*. Sheba is called a " troublemaker" (literally, "a man of Belial"). He felt that David was too partial to his own tribe of Judah. Sheba went ahead of David back to Jerusalem, and arrived there shortly before David did. He sounded the trumpet and said, "We

have no share in David . . . Every man to his tent, O Israel."
Sheba had not yet organized an armed rebellion, but he did
cause most of the people to boycott David's return to the
throne, and to follow him as leader. The incipient rebellion
was extensive: "All the men of Israel deserted David" (20:2).
Only the tribe of Judah remained loyal.

In Jerusalem David removed his ten concubines that
Absalom had lain with, and placed them in a house under
guard, where they lived as widows (20:3; 16:20-22). Absalom's
actions had greatly dishonored David (Lev.18:8; 20:11).

David sent forth Amasa, his new army commander, to capture the rebel Sheba. Amasa took too much time at the job.
David sent Abishai to pursue Sheba, and his brother Joab
(David's previous commander) went also. Amasa met them
on their way. Joab treacherously killed him (20:4-13). Joab's
cruelty was remembered in later years, and brought upon
him a sentence of death (1 Kgs. 2:5-6).

> Joab killed **ABNER** (2 Sam. 3:27), and **ABSALOM**
> (2 Sam. 18:14), and **AMASA** (2 Sam. 20:10). Joab got
> straight A's!

Joab pushed himself forward and took over leadership of
David's army. Joab pursued Sheba far into northern Israel, to
the village of Abel Beth Maacah, which is on a mound west of
the Jordan River, across from Dan. The people of Abel had a
reputation for great wisdom. There a wise woman negotiated
with Joab as he was besieging the town. She persuaded her
people to seize Sheba, behead him, and throw his head over
the city wall to Joab (20:14-22).

> **All who draw the sword will die by the sword** (Matt. 26:52).

The man in charge of David's forced laborers was named
Adoniram (Heb., *Adoram*) (20:24). The task master at the
start of the reign of King Rehoboam had the same name

(1 Kgs. 12:18). We suppose the same man is referred to in both passages. It seems menacing and fateful that David had a director of forced labor. (See Deuteronomy 20:11 on "forced labor.")

David's priests were Zadok and Abiathar (20:25). Abiathar later turned away from Solomon, and was deposed (1 Kgs. 1:7).

11. *The Gibeonites avenged* (2 Sam. 21:1-14). Three years of famine occurred in the days ("reign") of David. David did the right thing: he sought the face of the LORD. The LORD told him that it was because King Saul had put the Gibeonites to death. Israel had sworn to the Gibeonites that they would spare them (Josh. 9:19). The people of Israel were collectively responsible to do what they had sworn to do. We have no other information about Saul's slaughter of them (except perhaps 2 Samuel 4:2-3). Only a few Gibeonites survived, so few that they had "no place anywhere in Israel" (21:5).

David conferred with the Gibeonites, who asked that seven of the descendants of Saul be executed "before the LORD" (21:6, 9) in Gibeah of Saul — his very hometown and capital. David agreed to this, and turned over to them two sons of Saul's concubine Rizpah (2 Sam. 3:7), and five sons of Saul's daughter Merab (1 Sam. 14:49; 18:17-19). ("Merab" is the preferred reading, instead of "Michal," which is the name written in most Hebrew and Septuagint manuscripts.) The bodies were hanged and publicly exposed to view.

Rizpah guarded the bodies of her sons from animals and birds for many weeks or months, from the barley harvest (April) until the "rain poured down from the heavens on the bodies," (probably in October). This is a heart-wrenching display of motherly devotion. What a stench! What self-sacrifice!

David followed this up by reburying the bones of Saul and Jonathan, from Jabesh Gilead (east of the Jordan) to the family burial place in Benjamin (21:12-14). This appears to us to be a diversion of public attention from a very wrong act by David.

David's act of turning Saul's descendants over to the Gibeonites to be killed was wrong. David asked the LORD for

information about the cause of the famine, but there is no
record that he asked for directions as to what to do about it.
God's law to Moses had clearly said, "Fathers shall not be put
to death for their children, nor children put to death for
their fathers; each is to die for his own sin" (Deut. 24:16;
compare 2 Kgs. 14:6; Ezek. 18:19-20).

It is very unsafe to ask victims of a crime to decide the
punishment of one who has harmed them. They may seek
excessive vengeance, and not justice. The decision of a just
and impartial judge is better.

The law of Moses included provisions for sacrifices to be
made for breaking oaths or false swearing. See Leviticus 5:4-
6. Swearing falsely and breaking of oaths are indeed serious
offenses (Jer. 5:2; 7:9; Zech. 5:4; Matt. 5:33-34). But the sacrifice of the LORD has great power to make atonement for
(cover) sin. The purpose of the sacrifices that the LORD commanded was to *save* the lives of people, so that humans would
not be sacrificed.

12. *Battles with Philistine giants* (2 Sam. 21:15-22; 1 Chr.
20:4-8). David and his men fought four hazardous battles
with Philistine giants. David was nearly killed (21:16-17). The
four are called "the children of *Rapha*," the ancestor of a race
of giants. One of the giants was named *Lahmi*. He was a
brother of Goliath! (The reading in 1 Chronicles 20:4 seems
more correct than that in 2 Samuel 21:19. Goliath could
hardly have been killed *twice*.) One giant had six fingers on
each hand, and six toes on his feet (21:20). (See Richard D.
Barnett, "Polydactylism," in *Biblical Archaeology Review*,
May–June 1990, pp. 46-51.)

13. *David's song of praise for deliverance* (2 Sam. 22). The
song in this chapter is the same as that in Psalm 18. This song
was sung when David defeated the house of Saul and his
other enemies. Probably it would fit correctly after 2 Samuel
18, if it were in chronological position. The song can be outlined as follows:

    a. Opening praise (22:2-4)
    b. David's distress (22:5-6)
    c. David's prayer (22:7)

d. God's response to David's prayer (22:8-20)
"He rescued me because he delighted in me" (22:20).
e. David's righteousness (22:21-28)
f. David's testimony to God's help (22:29-49)
g. Closing thanks (22:50-51)

> "I call to the LORD, who is worthy of praise, and I am saved from my enemies" (2 Sam. 22:4).

14. *David's last words* (2 Sam. 23:1-7). This song tells of God's dealings with David. The words are beautiful and touch our hearts. David said, "The Spirit of the LORD spoke through me; his word was on my tongue" (23:2). David was conscious of the inspiration of God upon him.

The song can be outlined as follows:

INTRODUCTION — God had spoken through David's songs (23:1-3a; Luke 24:44).
I. Blessings from an ideal king (23:3b-4).
II. Failure of David to be an ideal king (23:5a).
III. God's blessings upon David in spite of his failure (23:5).
IV. Dangers from the ungodly (23:6-7).

The words in 2 Samuel 23:5 may be interpreted gramatically in two different ways. The interpretation given in the older versions (LXX, Vulgate, Syriac, King James, and ASV) gives the thought that David knew that his "house" had *not* risen to the level that God's righteous king should reach. Most modern versions prefer to take the clauses as questions: "Is not my house right with God?" The Hebrew allows for either rendering, but that of the ancient versions gives a higher idea of David's spiritual discernment (*Ellicott's Commentary* on Samuel).

15. *David's mighty men* (2 Sam. 23:8-39; 1 Chr. 11:10-41). David had thirty "mighty men" in his army (23:8, 23). They were powerful fighters and leaders. The list of their names includes *Abishai* (23:18; 20:6), *Benaiah* (apparently the same

Benaiah mentioned in 2 Sam. 20:23; 23:20), *Asahel* (23:24; 2:18-19), and *Uriah* the Hittite, husband of Bathsheba (23:39). Replacements in the elite Thirty increased their total to thirty-seven (23:39).

Besides the Thirty, three champion warriors achieved the highest battle honors: (1) Josheb-Basshebeth (or Jashobeam), who killed eight hundred men in one encounter (1 Chr. 27:2); (2) Eleazar (23:9-10), and Shammah (23:13-12). In our sinful world, warriors are often needed to preserve liberty for all the rest of us.

16. *The census and the plague that followed it* (2 Sam. 24; 1 Chr. 21). The LORD was justly angry with Israel (24:1). The LORD incited David to take a census of Israel. But Satan also incited David to do this (1 Chr. 21:1). We cannot say this is a contradiction, unless we are certain we have NEVER done anything because of mixed motives. The desire for self-glorification for doing good works is not uncommon!

Whenever Israel took a census they were to collect ransom money from each person. If they did not do this, a plague could follow (Ex. 30:12). We have no statement that David collected the ransom money. Israel certainly suffered a plague.

David's statement that he was ordering the census "so that I may know how many there are" hints that David was taking pride in the size of his military manpower more than in God's power (2 Sam. 24:2; 1 Chr. 21:2).

David's commander, Joab, took the census. He did not want the job and did the task poorly (1 Chr. 21:3-6; 27:23-24). The census totals in 2 Samuel and in Chronicles differ (2 Sam. 24:9; 1 Chr. 21:5). The books of Samuel give eight hundred thousand men from Israel and five hundred thousand from Judah.

David was presented with three choices as punishment — three years of famine, or three months of being swept away before enemies, or three days of plague. (The reading "three days" in 1 Chronicles 21:12 and the LXX of 2 Samuel 24:13 is preferred over the reading "seven days" in the Hebrew of 2 Samuel 24:13.). David chose the plague. He had experienced famine recently! He had nearly been killed in recent battles (2 Sam. 21:16).

The plague killed seventy thousand people in Israel. The angel that inflicted the plague stood between heaven and earth, with a drawn sword extended over Jerusalem (1 Chr. 21:16). The angel stood at the threshing floor of Araunah the Jebusite on Mount Moriah. The plague stopped at Jerusalem (2 Sam. 24:25).

David was told to build an altar on the threshing floor of Araunah (1 Chr. 21:18). David purchased the threshing floor for fifty shekels of silver, but for the entire site he paid six hundred shekels of gold (1 Chr. 21:25).

David would not accept the land as a gift from Araunah (24:23).

The king replied to Araunah, "No, I insist on paying you for it. I will not sacrifice to the LORD my God burnt offerings that cost me nothing" (2 Sam. 24:24).

David built an altar to the LORD there, and sacrificed burnt offerings and fellowship offerings. He called on the LORD, and the LORD answered him with fire from heaven on the altar of burnt offering (1 Chr. 21:26). This was similar to what happened when Aaron offered his first sacrifices (Lev. 9:24).

The place on Mt. Moriah where David offered sacrifices on the threshing floor of Araunah became the location of Solomon's temple and all the later temples in Jerusalem (1 Chr. 22:1).

THE TRAGEDIES OF DAVID

1. Son Amnon assaulted Tamar, his sister (2 Sam. 13).
2. Son Absalom killed Amnon (2 Sam. 13).
3. Son Absalom conspired to take David's kingdom (2 Sam. 15).
4. Shimei cursed David (2 Sam. 16).
5. Absalom was killed in war (2 Sam. 18).
6. Sheba starts a rebellion (2 Sam. 20).

> 7. Three years of famine occur (2 Sam. 21).
> 8. Plague kills 70,000 people (2 Sam. 24).
> 9. Son Adonijah conspired to become king (1 Kgs. 1).

17. *David's last acts as king* (1 Chr. 22–29). These chapters in 1 Chronicles follow the events of 2 Samuel 24. The chapters tell how David organized the nation and its religious observances. The books of Chronicles stress these events because of the *priestly* emphasis in those books.

a. *David prepares for construction of the temple* (1 Chr. 22). David loved the house of God (Psalm 84). He procured dressed stone blocks and iron and bronze and cedar logs, a hundred thousand talents of gold (twenty-five billion dollars worth!), and other materials. David ordered all the leaders of Israel to help Solomon (1 Chr. 22:17).

b. *Levites were numbered and divided into groups* (1 Chr. 23). After making Solomon king by public proclamation, David divided up the Levites for work in the temple. The sons of Moses were counted as part of the tribe of Levi (23:14). The age for Levites to begin their tabernacle work was lowered from thirty years down to twenty (23:27; Num. 4:3). David wanted everything to be done in a fitting and orderly way (1 Cor. 14:40).

c. *The priests were divided into groups* (1 Chr. 24). The many priests were divided into twenty-four divisions for rotation of work duties (24:1-19). David wanted everyone to have a share in the work. The most famous of the divisions ("courses") of the priests was that of Abijah (24:10; Neh. 12:4). Zechariah, the father of John the baptizer, was from the division of Abijah (Luke 1:5).

d. *Musicians were organized* (1 Chr. 25; 2 Chr. 35:15). Twenty-four groups of musicians were organized (25:7-31). The three principal leaders of the music were . . .

(1) *Asaph* (25:1-2; Titles of Psalms 50, 73–83).

(2) *Jeduthun* (25:3; Titles of Psalms 39, 62, 77).

(3) *Heman* (25:4; Title of Psalm 88). Heman had fourteen sons and three daughters, a choir in his own family.

The music was authorized by God (25:2; 2 Chr. 29:25).

e. *Temple gatekeepers were appointed* (1 Chr. 26). Gatekeepers were appointed before any gateways were built! David had great confidence in the future. The sons of Obed-Edom were included in the gatekeepers (25:4, 15; 2 Sam. 6:11-12). Treasurers and business officials were appointed (26:20).

f. *Army commanders and other officers appointed* (1 Chr. 27). Twelve army commanders were commanded over the divisions. Some names have been mentioned in previous stories — Jashobeam (2 Sam. 23:8), Benaiah (27:9; 2 Sam. 23:20), Asahel (27:7; 2 Sam. 2:18). Officers were appointed over the twelve tribes of Israel (27:16).

g. *A mass assembly to promote Solomon and the temple was held* (1 Chr. 28–29). David told why he did not get to build the temple (28:3; 22:8). Solomon was publicly proclaimed king (28:5). David publicly gave to Solomon the plans of the temple (28:11-12). (God had given to David the plans for the temple [28:19].) David gave an exhortation to Solomon that was similar to the one the LORD gave to Joshua (28:20; Josh. 1:5-6). After this a very large offering was given for the temple. David gave his personal treasures of gold and silver to the temple, and the people gave over five thousand talents of gold (29:7).

The people rejoiced . . . for they had given freely and wholeheartedly to the LORD (29:9).

David prayed a majestic prayer of praise (29:10-13).

He said . . .

> **"Everything comes from you, and we have given you only what comes from your hand"** (1 Chr. 29:14).

18. *Abishag brought to David* (1 Kgs. 1:1-4). David could hardly keep warm in his very old age. His servants suggested getting a beautiful virgin to be with him. Their suggestion was foolish and probably obscene. The reference here to Abishag is necessary to understand the later story of Adonijah (1 Kgs. 2:13-25).

19. *Adonijah attempts to become king* (1 Kgs. 1:5-53). David's

son Adonijah had grown up with NO discipline, not even any spoken correction (1:6). Adonijah recruited the support of a few key men and had himself proclaimed king at the water source of En Rogel. Both Solomon and Adonijah were proclaimed king at water sources — Adonijah at En Rogel and Solomon at the Gihon spring (1:23). There would always be an audience at these places. By declaring himself king Adonijah was openly defying what his father had publicly declared — that Solomon was to be his successor.

The prophet Nathan and Bathsheba informed David of Adonijah's plot. Nathan was a very effective communicator. He arranged for himself and Bathsheba to give David a one-two punch with the news. Previously Nathan had used the story of the ewe lamb (2 Sam. 12) to touch David's conscience. Be a communicator like Nathan!

Though he was old, David arranged quickly for Solomon to be proclaimed king at the Gihon. The anointing of Solomon at Gihon was received with favor and loud rejoicing. "The ground shook" (lit., *the earth broke open*). Adonijah's people a half mile away at En Rogel heard the sound. When they discovered what the sound indicated, they deserted Adonijah like people leaving a sinking ship (1:49).

It is not surprising that Joab forsook David to join Adonijah (1:7). It is surprising that Abiathar the priest joined Adonijah. Perhaps he was jealous over the obvious promotion of the priest Zadok over him. (See 1 Kings 2:26-27.) The departure of Abiathar led to the final fulfillment of God's promise of the fall of the house of Eli (1 Sam. 3:12-14).

20. *Final charges to Solomon* (1 Kgs. 2:1-12). "Be strong" (2:2). Keep "the law of Moses" (2:3).

Concerning Joab, David told Solomon, "Do not let his gray head go down to the grave (lit., *Sheol*) in peace." In other words, "Kill him."

Solomon did this. See 1 Kings 2:28-34.

Concerning Shimei, David gave Solomon similar advice: "Do not consider him innocent . . . Bring his gray head down to the grave (Sheol) in blood." (See 1 Kings 2:8-9; 2 Samuel 16:5-13; 19:18-23.)

David died and was buried in the City of David. The tomb of David has not conclusively been located as yet.

"So Solomon sat on the throne of his father David" (1 Kgs. 2:12). The throne of David is also called "the throne of the LORD" (1 Chr. 29: 23). In our days the greater offspring of David sits upon the throne of the LORD at the right hand of God, waiting until He has put all His enemies under His feet (1 Cor. 15:25; Mark 16:19; Rev. 3:21).

Questions on Section E
David's Reign in Tragedies (2 Sam. 13:1 — 1 Kgs. 2:11)

1. What was the name of Absalom's sister? (2 Sam.13:1)
2. Which son of David became frustrated because of lust for her? (13:2)
3. What friend helped him devise a plot against her? (13:3)
4. What plot was devised to entrap the woman? (13:5)
5. What was the feeling of Amnon toward Tamar after his sin? (13:15)
6. How much time passed before Absalom took vengeance on his half-brother? (13:23)
7. What was the occasion when vengeance was taken? (13:23)
8. To whom did Absalom escape after he killed Amnon? (13:37)
9. What relationship was this man to Absalom? (3:3)
10. How long did Absalom remain away from his father? (13:38)
11. Who realized that David's heart longed for Absalom? (14:1)
12. To what town did he send for a wise woman who would come and convince David he should send for Absalom? (14:2)
13. For how long after his return to Jerusalem was Absalom not allowed to see David? (14:28)
14. What did Absalom do to force Joab to arrange for him an appointment to see the king's face? (14:30-32)
15. How many men did Absalom provide to run ahead of him and his chariot as he travelled about? (15:1). What does this act indicate that Absalom was thinking about doing?
16. By what method(s) did Absalom steal the hearts of the men of Israel? (15:2-6)
17. What did Absalom do to deceive the king in order to get his permission to leave Jerusalem? (15:7-8)
18. How many men from Jerusalem went with Absalom on his mission to proclaim himself as king throughout all the tribes of Israel? (15:11)

19. What counselor of David went over to Absalom? (15:12)
20. What did David do when he heard that Absalom was making himself king over Israel? (15:14)
21. What foreigner (a Gittite, or Gathite) would not forsake David? (15:19-22)
22. Did David grant permission for the priests to bring the ark out of Jerusalem? (15:25)
23. What did David pray when he learned that his counselor had gone over to Absalom? (15:31).
24. What was David's friend Hushai sent back to Jerusalem to do? (15:32-34)
25. Name the sons of the priests Zadok and Abiathar. What were they appointed to do for David? (15:36)
26. What report did Ziba bring to David as David was fleeing? (16:1-3; 9:2-3). Was it the truth? (19:24-28)
27. Who was Shimei? What did he do to David? (16:5, 13)
28. Why did David spare Shimei when Abishai wanted to kill him? (16:9-12)
29. What advice was given to Absalom about David's concubines? Who gave this counsel? (16:20-21)
30. What advice did each of Absalom's two counselors give to him about attacking David? (17:1-3, 11-13)
31. Whose advice was followed? (17:14)
32. Who saw the sons of the priests and told Absalom? (17:17-18)
33. How did the sons of the priests escape death? (17:18-19)
34. Why did David and his people go across Jordan? (17:21-22)
35. How did Ahithophel die? (17:23)
36. Whom did Absalom appoint over his army? (17:25)
37. Name the three men who brought bedding and food to David and his people. (17:27)
38. Into how many divisions did David divide his army? Who was appointed leader of each division? (18:1-2)
39. What command concerning Absalom did David speak before all the troops? (18:5)
40. Where was the battle with Absalom fought? (18:6)
41. What killed more people than the sword? (18:8)
42. How did Absalom die? Who killed him? (18:9-14)
43. Who wanted to run and take the news to David? (18:19,23)
44. Who was sent to tell David of Absalom's death? (18:21)
45. How did David react to the news of Absalom's death? (18:33)
46. Who scolded David for his grief over Absalom? (19:5-6)

47. Why was it necessary for David to go forth and speak to his men after Absalom's death? (19:7-8)
48. Which tribe was summoned to bring David back to Jerusalem? (19:11, 14)
49. Did David spare Shimei when he met him? (19:16-17,23; compare 1 Kgs. 2:8-9,46.)
50. How had Mephibosheth felt during David's absence? (2 Sam. 19:24)
51. To whom were given the fields that had belonged to King Saul? (19:29)
52. What aged man would not return with David to Jerusalem? (19:32-34)
53. Who was Kimham (Chimham)? (19:37)
54. What argument arose between Judah and the other tribes of Israel? (19:41-43)
55. Who was Sheba? What did he do? (20:1-2)
56. What did David do with his defiled concubines? (20:3)
57. Who was sent to gather an army to pursue Sheba? (20:4)
58. Who was later sent to pursue Sheba? (20:6-7)
59. Who killed Amasa? Where? (20:8-10)
60. Where did Sheba die? How? (20:15, 22)
61. Why were there three years of famine in the land? (21:1)
62. Why did the Gibeonites seek revenge on Saul's descendants? (21:4-6)
63. How many of Saul's descendants were slain? (21:6)
64. Who was Rizpah? (21:8)
65. How long did Rizpah guard the bodies of her sons? (21:9-10)
66. Where were the bones of Saul and Jonathan buried? (21:14)
67. Who saved David's life during a battle with a giant? (21:16-17)
68. What relative of Goliath was slain? (1 Chr. 20:5). Who killed him?
69. How many fingers were on each hand of the giant from Gath? (2 Sam. 21:20)
70. What did David say in his song that the LORD was to him? (22:1-3; Ps. 18:2)
71. Who spoke through David, according to his last song? (23:1-2)
72. How many "mighty men" did David have? (23:8-9, 23-24).
73. Who was chief of the "Three"? (23:18)
74. Who incited David to number Israel? (2 Sam. 24:1; 1 Chr. 21:1)
75. Who protested the numbering? (24:3)
76. About how many men were numbered? (24:9; 1 Chr. 21:5)
77. What three punishments did God offer David a choice of? (24:13)
78. How many people died as a result of David's numbering? (24:15)
79. Where did the angel stop killing? (24:16)
80. Where was the angel seen? (24:16; 1 Chr. 21:16)
81. Where was David commanded to build an altar? (24:18; 1 Chr. 22:1)

Old Testament History

82. What was built in later years on the place where David built the altar? (1 Chr. 22:1)
83. What did Araunah offer to give David? (2 Sam. 24:22)
84. What happened to the burnt-offering on David's altar? (1 Chr. 21:29)
85. Where was the altar of burnt-offering in David's time? (21:29)
86. What people were gathered together to work on preparations for the temple? (22:2)
87. What materials did David collect for the temple? (22:3-4, 14)
88. What charge did David give to Solomon? (22:6)
89. Whom did David appoint to be the next king? (23:1)
90. What services did David organize the Levites to do? (23:4-5, 28-32; 26:1, 20,29)
91. At what age did David cause the Levites to enter into their service? (23:24,27)
92. How did this differ from the age given in the law? (Num. 4:1-3)
93. How many divisions (courses, or groups) were the priests divided into? (1 Chr. 24:1,18; compare 24:10 & Luke 1:5).
94. Name the three men whose sons were leaders in the temple music. (25:1)
95. Name the young virgin brought to David in his old age. (1 Kgs. 1:3)
96. Which son of David put himself forward in David's old age and said, "I will be king"? (1:5)
97. Which two leaders gave their support to this would-be king? (1:7)
98. Who told Bathsheba of the plot? (1:11)
99. Who first told David of the plot? (1:15)
100. Who came afterwards and told David of the plot? (1:22)
101. Who were summoned to anoint Solomon and proclaim that he was king? (1:32-34). Where was the announcement made?
102. How did the people react to Solomon's being made king? (1:40)
103. How did the would-be king and his followers react to the news that Solomon had been proclaimed king? (1:49-50)
104. Did Solomon kill the man who had tried to become king? (1:52-53; 2:25)
105. What dying charge did David give to Solomon? (2:1-3)
106. What instructions did David give to Solomon concerning Joab? (2:5-6) Concerning Barzillai? (2:7) Concerning Shimei? (2:8-9)
107. Where was David buried? (2:10)

518

Section F
The Reign of Solomon (1 Kings 2:12–11:43; 2 Chronicles 1–9)

King Solomon is famous for his . . .
1. Wisdom   2. Wealth
3. Wives   4. Temple

---

1. *Reign of Solomon – From glory to decay.* Solomon had been publicly placed upon the throne before his father David died (1 Kgs. 1:35). He reigned over Israel forty years, 970–931 B.C. (1 Kgs. 11:42). The LORD gave to Solomon wisdom greater than any man before or since (1 Kgs. 3:12). Solomon inherited from his father great riches (1 Chr. 29:3-4), and a large powerful kingdom. David had either conquered all the surrounding nations or had friendly relations with them. David had led the people in spiritual acts and worship, and had gathered materials for building a great temple. Thus Solomon was free to lead the nation in great spiritual growth.

But Solomon failed to serve the LORD. He made alliances with foreign nations by marrying the daughters of rulers (1 Kgs. 11:1-2). Solomon built places near Jerusalem for the worship of the gods of his wives (1 Kgs. 11:7-8). As a result, the LORD raised up adversaries against Solomon during the latter part of his reign (1 Kgs. 11:14) and his kingdom began to shrink.

Spiritual decay was followed by political decay. Solomon's reign closed with the prophecy that his son would rule only one of the twelve tribes (1 Kgs. 11:11-13).

The LORD appeared to King Solomon twice!
(1 Kgs. 3:5; 9:2)
But Solomon's heart turned away from the LORD!
(1 Kgs. 11:9)
"Be faithful, even to the point of death" (Rev. 2:10).

---

2. *Events early in Solomon's reign* (1 Kgs. 2:13–4:34).

a. *Punishments upon Adonijah, Abiathar, Joab, and Shimei* (1 Kgs. 2:13-46). Solomon's half-brother Adonijah had attempted to take over the throne of David late in David's reign, before Solomon could get established (1 Kgs. 1:5). He failed then, but he still had the audacity to ask Solomon's mother (Bathsheba) to intercede with Solomon to give him the virgin Abishag in marriage. (See 1 Kings 1:2-4.) It is surprising that Bathsheba was indulgent enough to make this request for Adonijah. There was a custom in those times that when a king died, his harem passed to his successor. (Note 2 Samuel 12:8; 16:21-22.) Thus Solomon considered this request as an attempt by Adonijah to "get his foot in the door" so he could later enter into kingship. Solomon ordered that Adonijah be executed (2:13-25).

Solomon banished the priest *Abiathar* to his own home village of Anathoth (a suburb of Jerusalem on its north side). Abiathar had joined in Adonijah's attempt to become king. But Solomon did not kill him because he had accompanied David in his hardships during the years David was fleeing from King Saul.

The removal of Abiathar from the priesthood was the final fulfillment of God's prophecy that the house of Eli would be removed from the priesthood (1 Kgs. 2:26-27; 1 Sam. 2:30-36).

Solomon ordered Benaiah (2 Sam. 23:20; 1 Kgs. 2:35) to execute *Joab*, David's army commander, as David had requested (1 Kgs. 2:5-6, 28-35). Joab is remembered mainly for his excessive eagerness in shedding blood.

"Six things the LORD hates" . . . *(Prov. 6:16-17)*
"HANDS THAT SHED INNOCENT BLOOD"

Solomon also ordered Benaiah to execute *Shimei*, the Benjamite who had thrown rocks and dust at David when he was fleeing from Absalom (2 Sam. 16:5-13; 1 Kgs. 2:36-46). Shimei seems to have felt he could talk his way out of any punishment (2 Sam. 19:18-20) and did not obey Solomon's rules for his probation. It is always wise to fear the LORD and the king! (Prov. 24:21)

These executions and punishments by Solomon did not cause any public uprising. Rather, "the kingdom was now firmly established in Solomon's hands" (1 Kgs. 2:46). Solomon's triumphs over his enemies were a foreshadowing (type) of the triumphs of the coming "son of David" (the Messiah) over all His enemies. (*Expositor's Bible Commentary*, Vol. 4, p. 42; 1 Cor. 15:25; Ps. 72:8-11.)

King Solomon — A Type of Jesus Christ	
1. **Son of David.** 1 Kgs. 2:12	1. Matt.1:1,6; Luke 1:32; Jer. 23:5
2. **Beloved of the LORD.** 2 Sam. 12:24-25	2. Matt. 3:17; Col. 1:13
3. **Anointed.** 1 Kgs. 1:39	3. Acts 10:38; Heb. 12:9
4. **King.** 1 Chr. 29:23; 1 Kgs. 2:12	4. Luke 1:32-33; Rev. 19:16
5. **Peaceable.** 1 Chr. 22:9	5. Isa. 9:6-7; John 14:27; Eph. 2:14
6. **Wise.** 1 Kgs. 3:12; 4:29-31	6. Matt. 12:42; Luke 11:31
7. **Built temple.** 1 Kgs. 7:51	7. **Built church.** Matt. 16:18
8. **Glorious.** Matt. 6:29	8. Matt. 16:27; Mark 8:38; Luke 9:29; Rev. 1:13-16
9. **Prosperous.** 1 Kgs. 10:7, 14-23; 1 Chr. 29:23	9. Isa. 53:10; 42:4; Matt. 12:20-21

b. *Solomon's administration and his wisdom* (1 Kgs. 3:1-4:34; 2 Chr. 1:1-17).

(1) Solomon's first act of foreign policy must have been to many Israelites a very startling one. "Solomon made an alliance with Pharaoh king of Egypt and married his

daughter" (1 Kgs. 3:1). This Pharaoh was probably *Siamun*, the next-to-last king of the Egyptian twenty-first dynasty. He ruled 978–959 B.C. from the northeastern Delta city of Tanis.

The law of Moses said, "You must not do as they do in *Egypt*, where you used to live" (Lev. 18:3). Solomon's bringing Pharaoh's daughter to Jerusalem seems to have caused some unease, even within Solomon himself. He kept her in the City of David only until he completed a palace for her (1 Kgs. 7:7; 2 Chr. 8:11). She was almost certainly a worshiper of some of the 2,000 gods of Egypt. Solomon had opened a door to spiritual compromise.

(2) The people of Israel were still sacrificing to the LORD at the high places, because the temple had not yet been built (1 Kgs. 3:2). (A "high place" was a worship center with an altar for sacrifices, sometimes built on a hilltop, though not always.) One special high place was at *Gibeon*, a village six miles northwest of Jerusalem (modern *El Jib*). "The tabernacle of the LORD, which Moses had made in the desert, and the altar of burnt offering were at that time on the high place at Gibeon" (1 Chr. 21:29; 2 Chr. 1:5).

Solomon went to the high place at Gibeon, and there offered a *thousand* burnt offerings on the altar (1 Kgs. 3:4). (God later said through the prophet Isaiah, "The multitude of your sacrifices — what are they to me?" [1:11]) But Solomon still *loved* the LORD at that time, and walked according to the ways of David, except for offering sacrifices and burning incense on the high places (1 Kgs. 3:3), a statement that hints that God was not pleased with the scattered high places, even though He tolerated them at that time. The high places hindered use of a central sanctuary, which God had directed Israel to have (Deut. 12:1-14). They were frequently places for Canaanite worship practices.

(3) At Gibeon God appeared to Solomon in a dream, and offered to give him whatever he requested. (Behold the goodness of God!) Solomon requested *wisdom* to govern the people. His request pleased God, who promised to give him greater wisdom than anyone had had before or would have

afterwards. God also promised him riches and honor, and possibly long life (1 Kgs. 3:5-15).

"The LORD gives **wisdom**" (Prov. 2:6).

"If any of you lacks **wisdom**, he should ask God" (James 1:5).

Probably the request for wisdom expressed by Solomon does not have as high a meaning as is sometimes ascribed to it. Solomon did not ask for that profound spiritual wisdom, which would teach him to know God and know his own heart. In this he was always far inferior to David. His prayer was for practical sagacity, sharp intelligence, and quick discernment to see the right from the wrong amid the mazes of duplicity which beset a judge, especially among some Oriental peoples. This gift he received. Solomon's wisdom is described in 1 Kings 4:29-34.

(4) The case of the *disputed baby* (1 Kgs. 3:16-28). Solomon soon had opportunity to use his gift of wisdom. He settled a dispute between two prostitutes over who was the real mother of a baby, by threatening to cut the baby in half! The reaction of the baby's real mother shows that kings in those days did such things, and the mother took him seriously. Solomon was wise enough to discern that probably one of these women was stupid enough to reveal that she was not the true mother by agreeing to what he had threatened. She walked into a very visible trap.

(5) *Solomon's officials* (1 Kgs. 4:1-19). The list of Solomon's government leaders shows that the land of Israel had become quite a bureaucracy since the time of the judges, when there was no king in Israel. Solomon's chief officials are listed in 1 Kings 4:1-6, and his regional district governors are named in 4:7-19. The fact that two of the governors were Solomon's sons-in-law suggests that this list was made about midway during Solomon's reign.

Zadok the priest was probably quite old during Solomon's reign. Abiathar was priest only by family connection, not by participation in priestly work, because he was banished. The "recorder" (4:3) was "the one who reminds." As such, he was the appointment coordinator, the one who kept the book of activities, and sent notices of activities and appointments.

The "district governors" controlled approximately the areas of the twelve tribes, but not precisely. They furnished provisions for Solomon and those who dined at his table (1 Kgs. 4:27-28). No governor was appointed for Judah, perhaps because it was so near Jerusalem that it could be governed by officials at the capital. Probably Judah received special privileges that created jealousy in other areas. (Solomon was a Judean.)

The bureaucracy of Solomon probably became part of the "heavy yoke" the Israelites later complained about (1 Kgs. 12:4).

(6) The *wisdom of Solomon* (1 Kgs. 4:20-34). Solomon's wisdom excelled that of all other men, including three famous men who are named but otherwise unknown (1 Chr. 2:6; Ps. 88, 89 titles). Much of Solomon's wisdom is given in the book of Proverbs. Many proverbs were Solomon's own writings; but some he collected from other writers (Prov. 22:17; 24:23). His wisdom was not speculative, but practical and religious. He dealt with honesty and kindness, avoiding adultery and alcohol, and with the necessity of work. "The fear of the LORD is the beginning of knowledge, but fools despise *wisdom* and discipline" (Prov. 1:7).

---

*Solomon spoke **3000 proverbs**, and his **songs** numbered a thousand and five (1 Kgs. 4:32).*

Writings by King Solomon:
1. *Proverbs*
2. *The Song of Songs* (also called *Canticles*)
3. *Ecclesiastes* (Called QOHELETH in Hebrew)
4. *Psalms 72 & 127*

The Song of Songs tells of the glowing love of a village maiden for her "beloved." Solomon sought passionately to have her, but apparently in vain. The song ends with the declaration "Love is as strong as death . . . Many waters cannot quench love" (Song 8:6,7).

Ecclesiastes tells of Solomon's search for what was truly good for man in this life (Eccl. 1:13, 17). He discovered that most of the things people value are "Utterly meaningless!" ("Vanity of vanities"). To fear God and keep His commandments is the whole fulfillment of a man (Eccl. 12:13).

---

3. *Solomon's preparations for building his temple* (1 Kgs. 5).

a. *Assistance was obtained from Hiram* (5:1-14; 2 Chr. 2:1-6). Solomon sent envoys to Hiram, king of the city of Tyre in Phoenicia (modern Lebanon), requesting that his men cut cedar logs from the mountains in Lebanon and send them to Solomon for use in constructing the temple. Hiram had always been on friendly terms with David (2 Sam. 5:11-12) and quickly accepted the request from Solomon. The cedar logs from Lebanon were greatly prized in ancient times for use in temples in Egypt, and in Mesopotamia. (See ANET pp. 27,243,268.) The logs were to be floated in rafts on the sea from Lebanon to the port of Joppa in Israel, and from there transported by wagons the forty miles up to Jerusalem (2 Chr. 2:16). Solomon paid Hiram and his men with wheat, barley, wine and oil for food. (Phoenicia was mountainous and deficient in agricultural products.)

Hiram also provided Solomon with a master craftsman named *Huram-Abi* (Huram, My Father) to work on the temple in metal casting, fabric installation, and engraving (2 Chr. 2:7,13-14).

b. *Building stones were quarried* (1 Kgs. 5:15-18; 6:7). Many large and "costly" stones were quarried in Israel and in Lebanon for the temple. 80,000 stonecutters were occupied with this! The stones were so precisely shaped at the quarry, that no sound of hammers or chisels were heard at the temple itself. (A large quarry known as "Solomon's quarries" lies below and south of the present north wall of Jerusalem.

Its modern name does not prove that Solomon actually quarried from it.)

4. *The building of Solomon's temple* (1 Kgs. 6; 2 Chr. 3). The information about the temple comprises over half of all the Bible story of Solomon.

Solomon's Temple – Good? Or Bad?

1. In all the ways that the temple was designed by *GOD*, the temple, like the tabernacle before it, was GOOD (1 Chr. 28:19,12).
2. In all the ways that the temple was designed and decorated by MAN, the temple was imperfect and potentially EVIL.
3. **EVIL** possibilities in the temple:
   a. It could show off human skill and art, and cause pride.
   b. It could become a place of false security (Jer. 7:4,11). "We have the temple of God! No enemy can defeat us!"
   c. It became a "den of thieves" (Matt. 21:11).
   d. It could make men think God was confined to a box, or to the inside of four walls (Acts 7:49; Isa. 66:1; Jer. 23:24).
4. **GOOD** possibilities in the temple:
   a. It was a house of prayer for all peoples (Isa. 56:7; Matt. 21:13).
   b. The Messiah would come suddenly to the temple (Mal. 3:1).
   c. Like the tabernacle, it was a picture of things in heaven (Heb. 9:23; 8:5).
   d. It was a type of the New Testament church, which is the true temple of the Lord (Eph. 2:21; 1 Pet. 2:5).
   e. All people were welcome there and could obtain help from God (1 Kgs. 8:30,41).

---

a. The exact date of the start of construction on the temple is stated. It was 480 years after Israel's exodus from Egypt. (The Greek LXX reads "440 years," but other versions do not agree with that reading.) It began in the fourth year of Solomon (966 B.C.), the second month (*Ziv*, April), the second day of the month (1 Kgs. 6:1; 2 Chr. 3:2). (This sounds like an eyewitness record.)

b. The temple was built on the top of *Mt. Moriah*, which

had formerly been the threshing-floor of Araunah (Ornan) the Jebusite. The whole temple area was enclosed by stone outer walls that formed a court about 600 feet square. The sanctuary itself was comparatively small because it was intended only for the ministries of the priests. The congregation assembled in the courts (1 Kgs. 7:9-12). In its main sections, the temple was similar to the model of the tabernacle. The chief differences between them were that the temple dimensions were double those of the tabernacle; and the temple included side rooms all around it, and a portico (porch) at its front, which the tabernacle did not have.

c. There were three principal rooms of the temple:

(1) The "inner sanctuary," twenty cubits cubed (1 Kgs. 6:20). This was the Most Holy Place (the Holy of Holies), called in Hebrew the *debir*, or "oracle" (KJV), because God communicated from there (Ex. 25:22). This room contained the same ark of the covenant that was in the tabernacle (2 Chr. 5:7-10), but also contained two large wooden statues of cherubim, with their wings stretching from wall to wall (1 Kgs. 6:19-28).

The temple also had "upper parts," possibly rooms above the inner sanctuary (1 Chr. 28:11; 2 Chr. 3:9), which would make the roof over it level with that of the "main hall."

(2) The "main hall," 20 by 40 cubits and 30 cubits high. This room is also called the "House" (1 Kgs. 6:17, KJV), and corresponded to the Holy Place in the tabernacle (Ex. 26:33). The main hall contained *one* altar of incense (like the tabernacle), but *ten* golden tables of the bread of the Presence (showbread; 1 Kgs. 7:48; 2 Chr. 4:8, 19), and *ten* lampstands similar to the one in the tabernacle. The main hall had "narrow clerestory windows," probably high up in the walls, above the side rooms that wrapped around the two central rooms (1 Kgs. 6:4).

Between the inner sanctuary and the main hall was a "curtain" (or veil), like that in the tabernacle (2 Chr. 3:14). But the temple also had there a wall, with a doorway, and two olive-wood doors, carved with figures and overlaid with gold (1 Kgs. 6:31-35).

(3) The "portico" (or porch) in front of the main hall was 10 by 20 cubits, and 30 high (1 Kgs. 6:3; 1 Chr. 28:11), Two large (18 cubits tall) bronze pillars (columns) stood before the portico, seemingly not attached to the building (1 Kgs. 7:15; Jer. 52:21).

Ruins of several temples with basic layouts similar to Solomon's temple have been found in Syria and Israel. (See G.E. Wright, *Biblical Archaeology* [1966], p. 138. Also *Biblical Archaeology Review*, July–Aug. 1987, pp. 38-49.) Perhaps these other temples were built in imitation of Solomon's glorious temple.

God said of Solomon's temple, "I have consecrated this temple, which you have built, by putting my Name there forever. My eyes and my heart will always be there" (1 Kgs. 9:3).

GOD HAS NOW CONSECRATED HIS TEMPLE MADE OF LIVING STONES !

---

5. *Solomon's palace and government buildings* (1 Kgs. 7:1-12). Solomon spent seven years building the temple, but thirteen to build his own palace. (He was persistent!) Probably fewer laborers worked on his palace than on the temple.

Within Solomon's palace was an administrative structure called the Palace of the Forest of Lebanon, because many cedar logs held up its roof. Besides that, Solomon made a separate judicial hall, the Hall of Justice, and paneled it totally with cedar.

6. *The temple's furnishings* (1 Kgs. 7:13-51; 2 Chr. 4).

a. Two bronze pillars, standing before the portico (7:15-22). They were 18 cubits (27 feet) high, plus the height of their capitals on top. (The "thirty-five cubits" of 2 Chr. 3:15 is probably a copyist's error. See *Expositor's Bible Commentary*, Vol. 4, p. 73.)

Jeremiah 52:21: "Each of the pillars was eighteen cubits high and twelve cubits in circumference; each was four fingers thick, and hollow."

The pillars were named *Jakin* (meaning "He will establish" it), and *Boaz* (probably meaning "In Him is strength"). These names suggest God's initiative in establishing the temple, and His strength in upholding His people, Israel.

b. The "Sea" (1 Kgs. 7:23-26; 2 Chr. 4:2-5,10). This was a huge, circular, bronze tank for water, 10 cubits (15 feet) in diameter, where the priests washed (2 Chr. 4:6). It had two rows of ornamental "gourds" around its rim, cast in one piece with the Sea. Twelve bronze bulls were cast as supports for the Sea. These were afterwards removed in the time of King Ahaz (2 Kgs. 16:17). The Sea had a function similar to that of the laver in the tabernacle (Ex. 30:19-21). (We also are now cleansed by the "washing with water through the word" [Eph. 5:26].)

c. The bronze *altar* (2 Chr. 4:1; 1 Kgs. 9:64; 16:14). This huge altar (30' x 30' x 15' high) was the place for offering sacrifices in the temple. As large as it was, it was not large enough to care for sacrifices numbering 120,000 sheep and goats (2 Chr. 7:5,7)! The cost of these many sacrifices should make us thankful for the blood of Jesus Christ, which is worth much more (Heb. 9:14).

d. Ten moveable *stands* of bronze, each bearing a *basin* for water (1 Kgs. 7:43, 27-33; 2 Chr. 4:6) (NKJV: "ten carts and ten lavers"). These "stands" were carts with wheels beneath. Each bore a large basin for water (40 baths, or 230 gallons). Bronze panels on the sides of the stands were decorated with figures of cherubim, lions, and bulls (showing that the second commandment did not exclude all sculpture in Israel). These basins were used to rinse the burnt offerings (2 Chr. 4:6).

A similar cart bearing a laver was discovered at a tomb in Cyprus, dated about 1150 B.C. (Werner Keller, *The Bible As History in Pictures* [1964], p. 190.)

e. Furnishings inside the temple included the golden altar of incense, the ten golden tables for the bread of the Presence (showbread), and the ten gold lampstands (1 Kgs. 7:48-51; 2 Chr. 4:7-8).

7. *Dedication of Solomon's temple* (1 Kgs. 8; 2 Chr. 5:2-7:10).

a. From a human point of view the "dedication" of Solomon's temple was the grandest spectacle since the giving of the law at Mt. Sinai. Certainly, God is not greatly impressed by human pageantry.

1 Kings 8:63 and 2 Chronicles 7:5 report that the king and the people "dedicated" the temple of the LORD when they offered many animal sacrifices to Him. Except for these references, the term *dedication* (Hebrew, **Hanukkah**) is applied only to the altar where *sacrifices* were made (2 Chr. 7:9). The same is true of Moses' tabernacle (Num. 7:10-11). The term *dedication* is applied to the second temple (Zerubbabel's; Ezra 6:16-17) and to the walls of Jerusalem (Neh.12:27). This suggests that a temple of stone cannot usually be dedicated to God. The only things that really can be dedicated are our hearts and the blood sacrifice.

The dedication of Solomon's temple was perhaps Solomon's finest hour. He showed a genuine recognition of God (8:23, 56). Solomon knew that the temple was not big enough to contain God (8:27). He wanted the temple to be an instrument which would cause all the earth to know the LORD is God (8:60). (The temple did affect the queen of Sheba [9:4].) He wanted the people to live by God's decrees (8:61).

References to the *time* of the dedication indicate that the dedication was held about eleven months after the temple construction was finished. The temple was completed in the eighth month (Oct.–Nov., 1 Kgs. 6:38). The dedication was held in the seventh month (Sept.–Oct., 1 Kgs. 8:2), at the time of the festival of Tabernacles (Succoth, or Booths). During that festival the Israelites were to dwell outside their houses for a week. It was an opportune time for the dedication gathering, which lasted fourteen days (1 Kgs. 8:65).

Events at the Dedication of Solomon's Temple

1. Mass assembly (1 Kgs. 8:2)
2. Ark brought into the temple (8:3)
3. MANY sacrifices (8:5)
4. Praise (2 Chr. 5:12-13)
5. Glory cloud covers temple (1 Kgs. 8:10)
6. Solomon's short speech and long prayer (8:12-53)
7. Many more sacrifices (8:63). Fire upon the altar (2 Chr. 7:1-3)
8. Feast (1 Kgs. 8:65)

Solomon's Temple

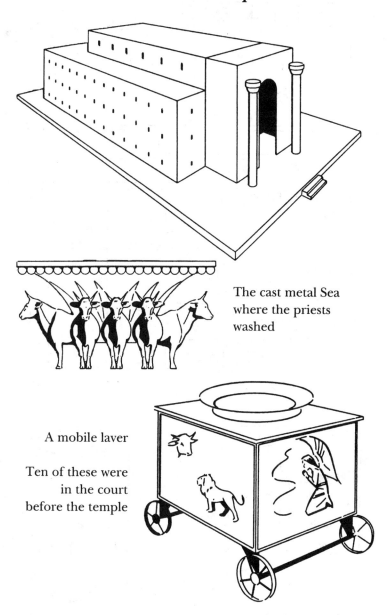

The cast metal Sea where the priests washed

A mobile laver

Ten of these were in the court before the temple

531

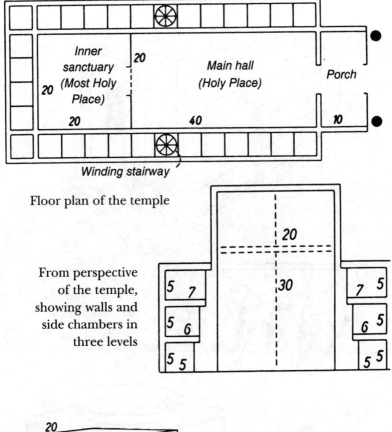

Floor plan of the temple

From perspective
of the temple,
showing walls and
side chambers in
three levels

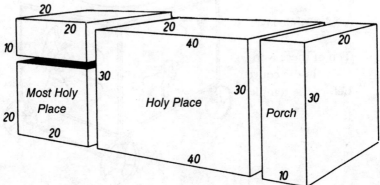

Principal compartment of the temple — side chambers not shown

The main hall or Holy Place

Area above the Most Holy Place (not described)

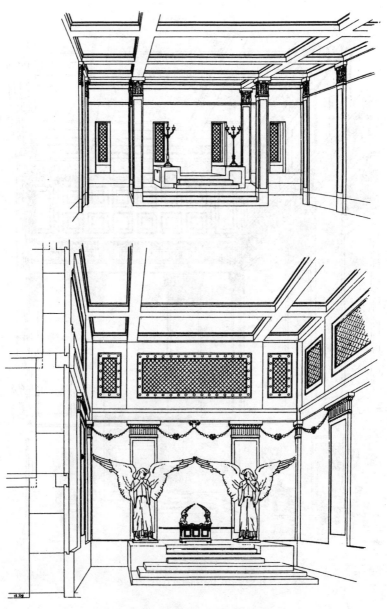

The inner sanctuary or Most Holy Place

Bringing the ark into the temple was an exciting moment (8:3-4). The ark was the visible symbol of God's presence with His people and of the LORD's covenant with them. It was the place for making atonement (covering) for their sins.

The ark with the poles used to carry it in the desert was placed in the Holy of Holies ("Oracle"). The ark was placed with its long axis north and south, so that it would be beneath the wings of the two large wooden cherubim in the room (8:6-7).

The ark then contained nothing except the two tablets of the Ten Commandments (8:9). What had happened to the jar of manna and Aaron's staff we do not know.

The cloud of glory filled the temple after the ark was brought in (8:10-11). A similar cloud had filled the tabernacle of Moses (Ex. 40:34). The cloud showed the presence of God in the temple, and Solomon perceived God's presence (Ex. 19:9). In a real, though outwardly less spectacular, way, the glory of the LORD now rests upon His people (Isa. 60:1; 2 Cor. 3:18).

Solomon's *prayer* at the temple dedication (1 Kgs. 8:22-53):

(1) Petition for God to fulfill His promise to David (8:22-26)

(2) Appeal for God to answer his prayer (8:27-30)

(3) Appeal for forgiveness in seven particular troubles (8:31-53)

The sacrifice of 22,000 cattle and 120,000 sheep (8:63) at the Dedication seems almost too many to imagine. That many cattle would be worth at least five million dollars. But the blood of Christ our Savior is worth far more. "It is impossible for the blood of bulls and goats to take away sins" (Heb. 10:4).

8. *The LORD's second appearance to Solomon* (1 Kgs. 9:1-9; 2 Chr. 7:11-22). The LORD appeared to him at night (2 Chr. 7:12).

God's response to Solomon's prayer at the dedication was conditional: "Yes — IF you do what I command you." If he did not obey, the temple would be rejected, and Israel would be cut off from their land. (Compare Jer. 7:4.) In the years after Solomon's reign Israel was often unfaithful. As a result their temple was destroyed, and the people were taken to foreign nations as captives (1 Kgs. 25:9-11).

> 2 Chr. 7:14 — If my people, who are called by my name, will **humble** themselves and **pray** and seek my face and turn from their wicked ways, then will I hear from heaven and will forgive their sin and will heal their land.

9. *Solomon's military activities, and others* (1 Kgs. 9:10-28; 2 Chr. 8:1-18).

a. Only one military campaign is recorded in Solomon's reign. He captured Hamath in Zobah, nearly three hundred miles north of Jerusalem, by the Orontes River (2 Chr. 8:3). Solomon's reign was mostly a reign in peace (1 Chr. 22:9).

b. Solomon gave to Hiram, king of Tyre, twenty cities in northern Galilee, near the border of Phoenicia (where Tyre was). They were payment for services rendered by Hiram in the construction of the temple. Hiram was not pleased with them, and called them the Land of *Cabul*. BDB Lexicon (p. 459) defines *Cabul* as meaning "as good as nothing." (Nothingsville!). The friendship of Hiram to Solomon was not impaired by this small unpleasant incident.

c. *Solomon's building projects* (1 Kgs. 9:15-24). 1 Kings 9:15 mentions the "forced labor Solomon conscripted." Mostly the forced labor gangs were made up of aliens living in the land (1 Kgs. 9:20-23). Solomon did not force all Israelites into compulsory service. The Israelites who later complained about their "heavy yoke" probably exaggerated their burdens (1 Kgs. 12:4).

Solomon rebuilt and fortified three large strategic cities — Hazor, Megiddo, and Gezer (1 Kgs. 9:15). Excavations at these three sites have exposed evidences that confirm several Biblical statements. All three of these cities have similar six-chambered gates, casemate walls, and water shafts and tunnels. (See *Biblical Archaeologist*, May 1967, p. 40, for drawings of the gates of these cities.)

Hazor was a huge (250-acre) mound about seven miles north of the Sea of Galilee. It controlled the roadway through the valley north of Galilee.

Megiddo is at the south side of the great plain of Jezreel (or Esdraelon). Megiddo controls the south entrance to that plain through the Valley of Iron, which goes through the Mt. Carmel range. Ruins found at Megiddo were formerly interpreted as being the "Stables of Solomon." Now they are thought to have been storage buildings made in the time of King Ahab (about 870 B.C., one hundred years after Solomon's time). (See Anson Rainey, "Megiddo Stables and Horse Sense," in *Eternity* magazine, Sept. 1975.) But many remains from the time of Solomon have been found at Megiddo, including a six-chambered gate and a double (casemate) wall.

Gezer (pronounced GEZZ-er) is a large (27-acre) mound, located about twenty miles south-southwest of Jerusalem, on the northernmost hill of the Shephelah foothills. From Gezer one has an excellent view across the coastal plains. Whoever controlled Gezer could monitor and intercept traffic going along the plain.

Solomon received the burned-up city of Gezer
as a wedding gift from the Egyptian Pharaoh when Solomon
married his daughter (1 Kgs. 9:16). An unusual gift!

At Gezer (in Field II) a burn layer 5–7 cm. thick in places was found. Dug into this burn layer were three courses of a large wall. The pottery fragments around these loci (places) were made in the mid-tenth century B.C. [the time of Solomon] at the latest. Probably these are debris from the destruction of Gezer by the Pharaoh who went up and captured Gezer and burnt it with fire (1 Kgs. 9:16). (See *Gezer I*, by Wm. G. Dever, H. Darrell Lance, & G. Ernest Wright [Jerusalem: Hebrew Union College, 1970], p. 61.)

"Supporting terraces" (Heb. *Millo'*) were built in Jerusalem (1 Kgs. 9:15, 24). The City of David was a tongue-shaped ridge with steep slopes along its east and west sides. To build upon these slopes, stone terraces had to be constructed and frequently repaired after rains or raids (2 Chr. 32:5).

d. Solomon sent ships to *Ophir* to get gold (1 Kgs. 9:26-28; 10:11; 2 Chr. 8:17-18). They sailed from his seaport at Ezion Geber on the north end of the Red Sea Gulf of Aqaba. The location of *Ophir* is uncertain (India? Southwest Arabia? East Africa?), but its existence has been confirmed by discovery of a potsherd bearing the inscription "Gold from Ophir for Beth-Horon." (Werner Keller, *Bible as History in Pictures* [New York: Morrow, 1964], p. 177.)

10. *The Queen of Sheba and Solomon* (1 Kgs. 10:1-13; 2 Chr. 9:1-12). The queen of Sheba said to King Solomon, "The report I heard in my own country about your achievements and your wisdom is true. But I did not believe these things until I came and saw with my own eyes. Indeed, **not even half was told me**; in wisdom and wealth you have far exceeded the report I heard" (1 Kgs. 10:6-7).

The queen travelled 1,500 miles from her homeland in the southwest corner of Arabia (modern Yemen) to Jerusalem to question King Solomon. His wisdom in answering her questions and the magnificence of his palace overwhelmed her. She gave to Solomon expensive gifts of gold (seventeen tons of it!) and spices and exotic wood. Solomon "gave the queen all she desired and asked for." All of this dramatized Solomon's wisdom and splendor.

Matthew 12:42 — Jesus said, "The Queen of the South will rise at the judgment with this generation and condemn it; for she came from the ends of the earth to listen to Solomon's wisdom, and now one greater than Solomon [Jesus Himself] is here."

Legends by Jews and Ethiopians and Hollywood that

Solomon fathered a son by the Queen are not verified by other evidences. The Scripture does not even hint of immoral relationships by them. Her praise to Yahweh would seem to lift their relationship above fleshly levels (1 Kgs. 10:9).

11. *Solomon's splendor* (1 Kgs. 10:14-29; 2 Chr. 9:13-28;1:14-17). In one year Solomon received 666 talents of gold (25 tons, six billion dollars worth), and that was not all he took in (1 Kgs. 10:14)!

Solomon imported exotic luxury items, like ivory, apes, and baboons. ("Peacocks" is now considered an incorrect translation.) See 1 Chronicles 9:21. (Werner Keller, *Bible as History in Pictures,* p. 177.)

Solomon made two groups of shields of gold, and placed them in his Palace of the Forest of Lebanon (1 Kgs. 10:16-17). These gold shields were later seized by Shishak, king of Egypt, in the days of Solomon's son Rehoboam (1 Kgs. 14:25-26).

Haggai 2:8 — **"The silver is mine and the gold is mine,"** declares the LORD Almighty.
God controls who gets to use His gold.

Solomon had "trading ships" (literally, "ships of Tarshish") (1 Kgs. 10:22). These ships were probably ships designed to carry ore and would therefore be sturdy enough to bring royal gifts from distant lands.

Solomon became the middleman in an import-export business of horses and chariots (1 Kgs. 10:28-29). He imported horses from Egypt and Kue (or *Keveh,* probably Cilicia in Asia Minor). He exported chariots and horses to kings of the Hittites and the Arameans (the Syrians in Damascus and nearby).

Matthew 6:28-29 — See how the lilies of the field grow . . . .
Yet I tell you that not even *Solomon* in all his splendor was dressed like one of these.

Solomon personally accumulated 1400 chariots and 12,000 horses. In doing this Solomon violated the commandment of God in Deuteronomy 17:16-17, where God forbade Israel's kings to acquire great numbers of *horses*, and many *wives* (1 Kgs. 11:3), and large amounts of *silver* and *gold*. Solomon's disobedience in these matters contributed to the decay and division of his kingdom.

12. *Solomon's wives* (1 Kgs. 11:1-13). "He had seven hundred wives of royal birth and three hundred concubines, and his wives led him astray." This is astounding. We are told that he held fast to them "in love." His attachment to them was sensual and emotional, as well as political. Many marriages were contracted in order to make political alliances with rulers in other lands. But In Ecclesiastes 2:8 Solomon wrote, "I acquired . . . a harem as well — the delights of the heart of man." He enjoyed it — too much.

God specifically forbade the Israelites to intermarry with Canaanites (Deut. 7:1-7; Josh. 23:12-13), and Ammonites and Moabites (Neh. 13:1; Deut. 23:3).

As Joshua had warned (Josh. 23:12-13), intermarriage with women devoted to other religions would lead the Israelites — including King Solomon — to depart from the LORD. Solomon built high places for the worship of the gods of his many wives. He built some of these on the mountain east of the City of David (Jerusalem), on the Mt. of Offense, the south end of the Mt. of Olives, where the village of Silwan now is.

Detestable gods followed by Solomon: (1 Kgs. 11:5-7)

(1) *ASHTORETH* — Canaanite goddess of Sidonians
(2) *MOLECH* — god of the Ammonites, to whom they burnt their children in fire (2 Kgs. 23:10)
(3) *CHEMOSH* — cruel god of Moabites

Because of Solomon's departing from the LORD, God determined to take away from his son the rule over all of the tribes except one. For the sake of God's promise to David that his offspring would rule forever, God did not take all the kingdom from Solomon and his evil offspring (1 Kgs. 11:11-13).

13. *Solomon's adversaries* (1 Kgs. 11:14-25). God raised up three enemies to Solomon in the last years of his reign, to bring about the downfall of his reign.

a. *Hadad* the Edomite (1 Kgs. 11:14-22). David and Joab smote most of the Edomites early in David's reign (1 Sam. 8:14; 1 Chr. 18:12). Hadad escaped this slaughter and fled to Egypt. From there he came back to Edom to resist Solomon.

b. *Rezon* the Aramean (Syrian) (1 Kgs. 11:23-25). Rezon came to Damascus in the time of Solomon and ruled there, and was continuously hostile to Israel.

c. *Jeroboam*, a very capable Israelite of the tribe of Ephraim. He became Solomon's most significant adversary. The prophet *Ahijah* met Jeroboam and gave to him ten pieces of a new robe that he had torn into twelve pieces. This symbolized that Jeroboam would rule ten of the twelve tribes. Solomon sought to kill Jeroboam. (That was an act of defiance against God Himself and his prophet.) Jeroboam fled to Egypt. From there he was brought back to Israel in the time of Solomon's son Rehoboam. Jeroboam did become king over ten tribes, mostly in the northern part of the land. (See 1 Kings 13.)

Solomon's son Rehoboam ruled over only one tribe — Judah (although Judah combined with Benjamin). Rehoboam's mother was Maacah, an Ammonite, one of those peoples that Israel was not to intermarry with.

What can be said as an epitaph to Solomon's life? Perhaps Solomon's own words in Ecclesiastes say it best: "Meaningless, meaningless" ("Vanity of vanities. All is vanity.") (Eccl. 1:2).

Solomon should have followed his own words: "Fear God and keep his commandments, for this is the whole duty of man" (Eccl. 12:13).

Questions on Section F
The Reign of Solomon (1 Kgs. 2–11)

1. Whom did Adonijah request as his wife? (1 Kgs. 2:17)
2. Who made the request for him? (2:13)
3. What punishment was inflicted upon Adonijah? (2:25)
4. Who carried out the punishment? (2:25)
5. What was the punishment given Abiathar because of his support of Adonijah? (2:26,27)
6. What punishment was given to Joab? (2:34)
7. Who was put in charge of Solomon's army at this time? (2:35)
8. Who became priest in Abiathar's place? (2:35)
9. What prophecy was fulfilled by the replacement of Abiathar? (1 Sam. 2:27-36)
10. Under what condition did Solomon promise to allow Shimei to live? (2:36-37)
11. To what place did Shimei go in disobedience to this restriction? (2:40)
12. Solomon married the daughter of what king? (3:1)
13. At what town did the Lord first appear to Solomon? (3:5)
14. What request did Solomon make of the Lord? (3:9)
15. What two other things did the Lord promise to give Solomon because of the request he had made? (3:13)
16. What was the condition of God's blessing upon Solomon? (3:14)
17. What event is recorded in the Scripture which led the people to respect highly Solomon's wisdom? (3:16-28)
18. What are the four things for which Solomon is famous?
19. Who was Solomon's priest? (4:2)
20. Who was in charge of forced labor? (4:6)
21. How many overseers were in charge of all Israel? (4:7)
22. Which three books of the O.T. did Solomon write most of?
23. Of how many proverbs was Solomon originator? (4:32)
24. How many songs?
25. Who was the king of Tyre who befriended Solomon? (5:1)
26. How many years had elapsed between the exodus from Egypt and the start of building the temple? (6:1)
27. How long was the temple? (6:2)
28. How wide was the temple? (6:2)
29. How high was the temple? (6:2)
30. What were the three principal compartments of the temple? (6:3,16-17,19)
31. Of what basic material was the temple constructed? (6:7)

32. How many years did it take to construct the temple? (6:38)
33. How many years did it take to construct the royal palace? (7:1)
34. For which of his wives did Solomon build a special house? (7:8)
35. What was the name of the craftsman in bronze brought from Tyre by Solomon? (7:13)
36. Of what tribe was his mother? (7:14)
37. What were the names of the pillars set up at the porch of the temple? (7:21)
38. How many bronze basins (lavers) were provided for the temple? (7:38)
39. Of what were the altar and the table for the bread of the Presence made? (7:48)
40. How many lampstands were in the temple? (7:49)
41. What was in the ark when it was transferred from Zion to the temple? (8:9)
42. Why were the priests unable to keep ministering in the house of the Lord? (8:10,11)
43. For what different situations (name seven) did Solomon ask God's favor in his dedicatory prayer? (8:30-53)
44. Did God promise to give Solomon what he prayed for? (9:2-5)
45. What name did the king of Tyre give the twenty cities presented to him by Solomon? (9:13)
46. What did Solomon construct in the City of David? (9:24)
47. How many times each year did Solomon offer burnt-offerings and fellowship-offerings at the altar? (9:25)
48. Where did Solomon build ships? (9:26)
49. From where came a queen to test Solomon with hard questions? (10:1)
50. What were her words after her inspection? (10:6-7)
51. How great were Solomon's wealth and wisdom in comparison with that of others of his day? (10:23)
52. How many wives did Solomon have? (11:3)
53. How many concubines did Solomon have? (11:3)
54. What *sins* of Solomon caused Jehovah's displeasure with him? (11:2,4)
55. Who was the goddess of the Sidonians? (11:5)
56. Who was the god of Moab? (11:7)
57. Who was the god of the Ammonites? (11:7)
58. Why did God not immediately take the kingdom from Solomon? (11:12)
59. Who were the three opponents with whom the Lord confronted Solomon? (11:14,23,26)
60. What did the prophet Ahijah give to one of Solomon's adversaries? What did this act foretell? (11:29-31)

61. Of what tribe was the son of Nebat to whom Ahijah promised ten tribes? (11:26)
62. To whom did the son of Nebat escape when Solomon attempted to kill him? (11:40)
63. For how long did Solomon rule Israel? (11:42)
64. What son of Solomon became king upon the death of his father? (11:43)

Period IX — Period of the Divided Kingdom
(1 Kgs. 12–2 Kgs. 25; 2 Chr. 10–36)

Section A
Neighboring Peoples of Israel and Judah

1. Amalekites	4. Assyrians	8. Moabites
2. Ammonites	5. Babylonians	9. Philistines
3. Arameans	6. Edomites	10. Phoenicians
(Syrians)	7. Hittites	

1. Amalekites

a. Ancestry — Descendants of *Esau* (Gen. 36:12,16). (The reference to Amalek in Genesis 14:7 seems to be proleptic, that is, the name *Amalek* is applied to territory later occupied by the Amalekites when Moses wrote of events that occurred there long before the Amalekites lived there.)

b. Location — Nomadic.
  (1) The Amalekites wandered in the Sinai peninsula, west of Edom toward Egypt (Ex. 17:8; 1 Sam. 27:8).
  (2) They also lived in the Negev, the southern desert part of Canaan (Num. 13:29).
  (3) Sometimes they invaded Palestine itself (Judg. 6:3, 33; 12:15).

c. Character — Warlike (Num. 14:45; Deut. 25:17-18).

d. History —
  (1) They made an unprovoked attack upon Israel at Rephidim, near Mt. Sinai (Ex. 17:8-13).
  (2) God determined that they would be utterly destroyed (Ex. 17:14; Num. 24:20; Deut. 25:17-19).
  (3) The Amalekites and Canaanites repulsed the Israelites when they attempted to enter Canaan from the south, after the spies' report (Num. 14:45).

(4) King Saul was told to destroy them (1 Sam. 15).

(5) The Amalekites destroyed David's city, Ziklag, and took its inhabitants captive (1 Sam. 27:6).

(6) A remnant of Amelekites remained until the time of King Hezekiah (1 Chr. 4:43).

   e. No certain archaeological discoveries have yet been made relating to the Amalekites.

Questions on the Amalekites:

1. Where did the Amalekites live?
2. What was their character?
3. When did Israel have its first contact with Amalekites?
4. What did God determine to do with the Amalekites?
5. Who was sent to destroy them?

2. Ammonites

   a. Descendants of Ben-Ammi, a son of Lot and his daughter (Gen. 19:38). A semi-nomadic people. Cruel.

   b. Located east of the tribes of Gad and Reuben (the former kingdom of Sihon) and north of Moab, from the Arnon River on the south to the brook Jabbok on the north.

   c. Historical notes:

(1) The Israelites were commanded to leave the Ammonites unharassed and unprovoked, as they journeyed toward the Promised Land (Deut. 2:19).

(2) The western borders of Ammon were fortified (Num. 21:24) by watchtowers. (See "The Material Civilization of the Ammonites" by George M. Landis, in *Biblical Archaeologist,* Sept. 1961, p. 68.)

(3) The Ammonites fought against Israel during the period of the judges (Judg. 11:13). Jephthah defeated them.

(4) The Ammonites attempted a conquest of Israel at the beginning of King Saul's reign, but were soundly defeated (1 Sam. 11).

(5) King David conquered their capital city, Rabbah (2 Sam. 12), and kept the Ammonites in submission

during the united kingdom. (Rabbah was also called Rabbath-Ammon, and was later called Philadelphia It is now known as Amman, the capital of the country of Jordan. King Solomon married Ammonite women and followed their god, Molech (1 Kgs. 11:1,5). Other Scriptures referring to the Ammonites include Jeremiah 40:14; 41:5-7; Amos 1:14; Nehemiah 2:10,19; Ezekiel 25:1-7.

(6) The Assyrian records of King Shalmaneser III tell of a contingent of troops from Ammon at the battle of Karkar in 853 B.C. in the coalition of troops that included those of King Ahab. (See James Pritchard, ed., *Ancient Near East*, Vol. 1 [Princeton, 1973], p.190.)

(7) The Ammonites paid tribute to the Assyrian kings Tiglath-pileser III and Esarhaddon (*Ancient Near East*, Vol.1, pp. 193, 201).

(8) The Ammonite ruler Tobiah opposed Nehemiah (Neh. 2:19).

The Tobiad family continued until the second century B.C.

(9) Judas Maccabeus fought the Ammonites (1 Macc. 5:6).

d. The Ammonites worshiped Molech (also spelled Moloch, Milcam, Milcom) with human sacrifices. ("Children passed through fire." Deut. 18:10; 2 Chr. 33:6; 2 Kgs. 21:6.)

Questions over the Ammonites:
1. From whom were the Ammonites descended?
2. Where was the land of Ammon?
3. What was the capital city of Ammon?
4. How did Ammon and Israel get along?
5. What was the name of the god of Ammon? How was it worshiped?

3. Arameans (Syrians)
a. Descendants of Shem (Gen. 10:22,23; 1 Chr. 1:17).
b. *Aram* is the correct name (the Hebrew name), but it is

very often translated *Syria*. (See 2 Samuel 8:5; 1 Kings 20:20; Amos 1:5).

c. Aram was located north and east of Israel, and covered a large area from the Mediterranean east beyond the upper Euphrates River. The Taurus Mountains were its northern boundary. Its southern border was against northern Israel, and included the Golan Heights east of the Sea of Galilee.

d. Aram consisted of several semi-independent states, with Damascus as the strongest city, and often the center of power.

    (1) *Aram-Naharaim* (meaning "Syria of the Two Rivers"). This was part of Mesopotamia around Haran, the home of Laban (Gen. 11:31; 24:10; 31:47).

    (2) *Aram-Damascus* (1 Kgs. 11:23,24). Damascus was a constant enemy of the northern kingdom of Israel. Damascus was captured by Assyria in 732 B.C. (2 Kgs. 16:9).

    (3) *Aram-Zobah* (2 Sam. 8:7), north of Damascus. Hadadezer was its most powerful ruler. He also ruled Maacah, Geshur, and Tob.

    (4) *Aram-Maacah*, east of Jordan, near Mt. Hermon (1 Chr. 19:6).

    (5) *Geshur*, east of Jordan, in the territory of the tribe of Manasseh. Absalom's mother was from this area (2 Sam. 3:3; 13:7). (See *Biblical Archaeology Review*, July–Aug. 1992, pp. 30-44.)

    (6) *Tob*, east of Jordan (2 Sam. 10:6).

e. Religiously, the Arameans were idolaters, worshiping gods like Rimmon (2 Kgs. 5:18) and Hadad.

f. King David conquered the Aramean states (2 Sam. 8:5-6), and Solomon extended his kingdom into these areas (2 Chr. 8:3).

g. "Rezon, son of Eliada," was raised up to chasten Solomon (1 Kgs. 11:23). He recaptured Damascus, and paved the way for the rise of the Aramean kingdom.

h. Kings of Aram at Damascus (from about 940–732 B.C.):

    (1) *Hezion*, probably the same person as *Rezon* in

1 Kings 15:18. (See 1 Kgs. 11:23.) (See M.F. Unger, *Archaeology & the Old Test.*, p. 239.)

(2) *Tab-Rimmon* (1 Kgs. 15:18). (Unger, ibid.)

(3) *Ben-Hadad I* (approx. 890–843 B.C.) King Ben-Hadad was hired by King Asa to attack Israel (2 Chr. 16:2) about 875 B.C. He seems to have been the same king as the Ben-Hadad who fought against King Ahab about 856 B.C. (1 Kgs. 20:1). (Unger, *op.cit.*, pp. 239-241).

(4) *Hazael*, a cruel oppressor of Israel (2 Kgs. 8:15). 843–801 B.C.

(5) *Ben-Hadad II* (2 Kgs. 13:24-25). Date uncertrain.

(6) *Rezin* (2 Kgs. 15–37). Approx. 750–732 B.C. (Unger, *op.cit.*, pp. 254-255.)

All six of these Aramean kings are known from archaeological records, as well as from the Bible.

i. Historical notes on the Arameans:

(1) After the division of the kingdom (931 B.C.), the Arameans of Damascus gained strength and became the foremost Syrian kingdom and Israel's chief enemy.

(2) Asa, king of Judah, sent gifts to King Ben-Hadad I of Aram, and thus formed an alliance with him. Ben-Hadad in turn invaded northern Israel (under King Baasha) (1 Kgs. 15:20-22).

(3) Ben-Hadad was kept at a distance during the reign of Omri in Israel (about 885 B.C.). Omri strengthened his position by alliances with foreign neighbors.

(4) During the reign of King Ahab (874–853 B.C.) the northern kingdom (Israel) became stronger (1 Kgs. 16:34; 22:39; 2 Kgs. 8:18,26). Ben-Hadad (with a coalition of thirty-two other kings) was soundly defeated about 856 at the battle of Samaria (1 Kgs. 20:1), and again in 855 at the battle of Aphek (east of the Sea of Galilee) (1 Kgs. 20:26-43). During this time the rising power of Assyria also checked Syrian advancement.

King Ahab of Israel was killed by the Arameans,

led by Ben-Hadad, in the battle at Ramoth-Gilead (1 Kgs. 22:1-40).

(5) Hazael became king at Damascus about 840 B.C. Because King Jehu of Israel would not join Hazael in resisting the king of Assyria, Hazael began to fight constantly against Israel (2 Kgs. 10:32-33). King Jehu paid tribute to the Assyrian king, Shalmaneser III, to keep peace with him. (This is pictured on the famous black obelisk of Shalmaneser displayed in the British Museum.)

(6) During the reign of King Jehoahaz in Israel (814–798 B.C.) Hazael reduced Israel's territory to a very small area (2 Kgs. 13:1-9, 22, 25). As Hazael advanced further south, he was kept out of Jerusalem only by the payment of a large amount of tribute obtained by sending sacred objects from the temple to Hazael (2 Kgs. 12:17, 18).

(7) The Arameans were weakened substantially by the Assyrians around 800 B.C. King Jehoash of Israel reclaimed much of the territory taken by Hazael. During the time of Israel's King Jeroboam II, Israel captured Damascus, and the northern boundaries were restored as they had been in the days of Solomon (2 Kgs. 14:28).

(8) When King Jeroboam II died in 753, Rezin, the last king of the Arameans, regained independence. In 732 B.C., in the days of King Ahaz of Judah, Tiglath-Pileser III, king of Assyria, captured Damascus, executed Rezin, and ended Aramean power permanently.

Questions over the Arameans:

1. What is another name for the *Arameans*?
2. Where was Aram?
3. Name four Aramean centers of power.
4. Name the six Aramean kings at Damascus.
5. When did the Arameans become Israel's chief enemy?
6. When did Damascus fall? To what king?

4. The Assyrians

"Woe to the *Assyrian*, the rod of my anger, in whose hand is the club of my wrath!" (Isa. 10:5).

a. Originally Assyria was a small tract of land between the upper Tigris River and the Zab River, its tributary. But Assyria grew to become a huge empire during the eighth and seventh centuries before Christ. The territory of Assyria lay in modern Iraq.

b. In the Hebrew Bible the name for Assyria is *Asshur.* The same name is used to denote both people and the country where they dwelt. See Ezra 4:2; Ezekiel 27:23.

c. The Assyrians were Semites (descendants of Noah's son Shem, Genesis 10:22). They were related to the Hebrews, Syrians, and others. Their language was a dialect of the Babylonian, and related to Hebrew.

d. *Nineveh* on the upper Tigris River was the capital of Assyria. Ruins of several palaces of Assyrian kings have been found at Nineveh and places near Nineveh.

e. Assyria is chiefly famous for its cruelty. The land of Assyria was not productive, being mostly desert. Irrigation from the rivers soon left salt in the land. Minerals and timber had to be imported. (They had oil, but it was not then used.)

To support its national economy the Assyrians conquered the nations all around them, and forced them to pay heavy tribute (2 Kgs. 17:4). The Assyrians enforced this by destroying cities, skinning prisoners alive, impaling them on posts, and deporting captives. They gloried in their cruelty, and pictured it in relief carvings on their palace walls. (See *Biblical Archaeology Review*, Jan.–Feb. 1991, pp. 52-61.) The prophet Nahum asked, "Who has not felt your endless cruelty?" (Nahum 3:19)

It was the policy of the Assyrians to deport peoples conquered in one land into another. See 2 Kings 17:23-24; 18:32. This practice was used to destroy the ability and will of the people to resist Assyria.

f. Several Bible prophets preached concerning Assyria and Nineveh. (Jonah preached *in* Nineveh.) See Isaiah 7:20;

Jeremiah 50:17; Hosea 11:5; Zephaniah 2:13; and
Zechariah 10:12. Nahum prophesied the eternal destruction of Nineveh (3:8-15).

g. Historical notes: (See S.J. Schwantes, *A Short History of
the Ancient Near East* [Grand Rapids: Baker, 1965],
pp. 110-133.)

(1) After several periods of strength and weakness, the
Assyrians reached the Mediterranean Sea about
1100 B.C. under *Tiglath-pileser I* (1115-1077 B.C.).

(2) The Aramean kingdom of Zobah became strong
about 1000 B.C., and this slowed the westward
advance of Assyria. When King David defeated
Zobah (2 Sam. 8:3), it became possible for the
Assyrians to resume expansionist policies.

(3) During the tenth century B.C. Assyria began its rise
to greatest power, and it became the dominating
power in the ancient world from the ninth to the
seventh centuries.

h. The kings of Assyria during its greatest strength:

(1) *Assurnasirpal II* (883-859 B.C.). Unspeakably cruel.
He conquered all the way to the Mediterranean Sea.

(2) *Shalmaneser III* (858-824). At the battle of Qarqar
(853 B.C.) he clashed in an indecisive battle with an
alliance of the king of Syria, *Ahab* of Israel, and
other kings. Ahab joined other kings to resist the
encroachments of mighty Assyria.

King Jehu of Israel paid tribute to Shalmaneser.
This is illustrated on the famous black obelisk of
Shalmaneser (in the British Museum).

(3) *Shamsi-Adad V* (823-811).

(4) *Adad-nirari II* (810-783). He subdued and collected
tribute from Tyre, Sidon, Israel, Edom, Philistia and
Damascus. Jehoahaz of Israel paid him tribute. He
defeated Ben-Hadad II of Damascus. He is possibly the
"deliverer" for Israel mentioned in 2 Kings 13:5. By
defeating Syria he saved Israel from attacks from Syria.

(5) *Shalmaneser IV* (782-773). Weak king. Possibly Jonah
the prophet preached in Nineveh during his reign.

(6) *Assur-dan III* (772-755). Weak king.

(7) *Asshur-nirari V* (754-745). Weak king.

(8) *Tiglath-pileser III* (744-727). Also called *Pul* (2 Kgs. 15:19). The most terrible Assyrian of all. He took Gaza (734 B.C.). He took Damascus and slew its king, Rezin (732). He took tribute from both Judah and Israel (2 Kgs. 15:19, 29). His monuments mention the Hebrew kings Azariah (Uzziah), Hoshea, Pekah, Menahem, Omri, and Ahab. He took the northern and eastern tribes of Israel (2 Kgs. 15:29). He conquered Babylon in his last year.

(9) *Shalmaneser V* (726-722). He took tribute from Hoshea (king of Israel) (2 Kgs. 17:3-5). He besieged Samaria for three years, and was probably the one who actually took the city (2 Kgs. 17:5; 18:9).

(10) *Sargon II* (721-705). He claims he captured Samaria, and deported 27,000 Israelites (2 Kgs. 17:6). He crushed Carchemish, the last stronghold of Hittite power, in 717. He took Ashdod in Philistia in 711 (Isa. 20:1).

(11) *Sennacherib* (704-681). He recaptured the western part of Assyria's empire — Ammon, Moab, Edom, and forty-six cities of Judah (including Lachish). He threatened to take Jerusalem in King Hezekiah's time; but the LORD's angel slew 185,000 of his troops in one night (2 Kgs. 18:13-19:36). He destroyed Babylon in 689.

(12) *Esarhaddon* (680-669). He restored Babylon, and took King Manasseh of Judah as a captive there (2 Chr. 33:11; Ezra 4:2). He defeated Tirhakah, king of Egypt, and occupied Memphis and lower Egypt (2 Kgs. 19:9).

(13) *Asshurbanipal* (668-631). Called *Osnappar* in Ezra 4:10. (See NRSV and Hebrew.) He was the last great king of Assyria. He took Thebes in Upper Egypt in 663 B.C. He was a lover of learning, and collected a library of about 100,000 cuneiform tablets, which have been discovered by archaeologists.

i. Nineveh was captured and destroyed by 612 B.C. by a confederation of Medes and Babylonians (under King Nabopolassar). The last Assyrian military force was destroyed at Carchemish in 605 B.C. (Jer. 46:2). The power of Assyria was broken forever, as the prophet Nahum had foretold (2:11; 3:11-19).

Questions on the Assyrians:

1. Where was the land of Assyria?
2. What was the capital city of Assyria?
3. What was the character of the Assyrian kings?
4. To what Assyrian king did Jehu pay tribute?
5. Who was the probable king of Assyria when Jonah the prophet preached in Nineveh?
6. Who was the greatest Assyrian king of all?
7. What Assyrian king threatened Jerusalem in the time of King Hezekiah?
8. When did Assyria fall? To what nations?

5. The Babylonians

a. The city of *Babylon (Babel)* was founded by Nimrod not long after the flood of Noah (Gen. 10:8-10). It was an important city throughout its history. Many battles were fought for control of it, and the city was destroyed and rebuilt a number of times.

b. The Euphrates River ran through Babylon. It was located in the area where the Tigris and Euphrates come close together. It was in a fertile area, and was within easy reach of the Persian Gulf.

c. Under King *Hammurabi* (1728-1686 B.C.) Babylon ruled a great empire, extending from the Persian Gulf to the middle Euphrates and the upper Tigris River area. After the time of Hammurabi Babylon was controlled by other peoples for nearly a thousand years — by Hittites, Kassites, Elamites, and Assyrians.

d. During this time several Babylonian rulers tried to assert independence without much success. *Merodach-baladan* (2 Kgs. 20:12-13) tried to revolt from Assyria, and did make Babylon independent twice briefly (722-710,

703–702 B.C.). He visited King Hezekiah of Judah, probably around 712 B.C. Sargon II of Assyria crushed this rebellion, and his son Sennacherib devastated Babylon in 689 B.C.

e. Sennacherib's son, Esarhaddon, rebuilt Babylon, and took Judah's King Manasseh to Babylon as a captive (2 Chr. 33:11).

f. In 626 B.C. *Nabopolassar* founded an independent dynasty at Babylon, and started the great Neo-Babylonian (or Chaldean) empire. Nabopolassar, in alliance with the Medes and other peoples, defeated and destroyed Nineveh in 612. He defeated other Assyrian units at Haran in 610. At Carchemish (on the upper Euphrates River) in 605 he and his son *Nebuchadnezzar* defeated an alliance of Assyrian army units allied with Egyptians under Pharaoh-Necho. This battle of Carchemish ended forever the existence of Assyria.

g. *Nebuchadnezzar* (605–562 B.C.) was the greatest king of the Neo-Babylonian empire. He was a great conqueror and a great builder. He captured all the territory that had once been held by the king of Egypt, from the brook (wadi) of Egypt to the River Euphrates (2 Kgs. 24:7). Nebuchadnezzar invaded Judah in 605 B.C. and took hostages (including Daniel). He invaded again in 597, when he took the prophet Ezekiel, King Jehoiachin, and 10,000 captives (2 Kgs. 24:1). He invaded again in 586 B.C., when he destroyed Jerusalem (2 Kgs. 25:1). He besieged Tyre for thirteen years (598–585 B.C.).

Nebuchadnezzar built structures in Babylon until it became the most glorious city on earth. Massive double walls with bronze gates extended eleven miles around the city. Its famous tower (ziggurat) was enlarged and repaired. The Hanging Gardens of Babylon became one of the Seven Wonders of the ancient world. See Daniel 4:30.

h. After Nebuchadnezzar's time the Neo-Babylonian empire declined rapidly. His son *Evil-Merodach* (Amel-Marduk) (2 Kgs. 25:27) reigned 562–560 and was assassinated by a son-in-law of Nebuchadnezzar, *Neriglissar* (called Nergal-Sharezer in Jeremiah 39:13), who reigned 560–556. Neriglissar's son *Labashi-Marduk* succeeded him in 556, but was deposed by a popular uprising. One of Nebuchadnezzar's generals, *Nabonidus*, who was probably a son-in-law of Nebuchadnezzar, was made king and ruled 556–539 B.C. Nabonidus appointed his son *Belshazzar* as co-regent in 553. Belshazzar did most of the actual ruling in Babylon while Nabonidus stayed at an Arabian desert resort named Teima.

The fall of Babylon in 539 B.C. is told in Daniel chapter 5, and in the writings of the Persian king Cyrus, and the Greek historians Herodotus and Xenophon. Cyrus took the city with little or no resistance, and Belshazzar was killed.

  i. Babylon declined in importance after its fall. It still existed in New Testament times (1 Pet. 5:13) — if the name *Babylon* in that passage is taken literally. In the sixth to ninth centuries after Christ the Jewish rabbis had a notable center of learning there. Today Babylon is in total desolation, and the ancient prophecy in Isaiah 13:17-22 about Babylon has been fulfilled. Saddam Hussein, dictator of Iraq, has attempted to rebuild part of Babylon, but with limited success.

Questions on the Babylonians
1. Who founded the city of Babylon?
2. On what river was Babylon built?
3. What great ruler ruled Babylon in the 17th century B.C.?
4. What Babylonian king visited King Hezekiah of Judah?
5. Who was the first king of the Neo-Babylonian empire?
6. Who was the greatest king of the Neo-Babylonian empire?
7. What contacts did Nebuchadnezzar have with Judah and Jerusalem?
8. Who were the last two kings of Babylon? What was their blood relationship? Who was the actual ruler in the land of Babylon?

6. Edomites (Idumeans)
  a. The Edomites were descendants of Esau, brother of

Jacob (Gen. 25:30; 36:1,8,9, 43). The name *Edom* means *red* (Gen. 25:24, 30).

b. The Edomites lived in Mt. *Seir*, the mountainous area south of the Dead Sea, just east of the Arabah valley (Gen. 32:3; 36:8). The south border of Edom reached as far as Elath on the north tip of the Gulf of Aqaba. On the north Edom extended to the brook Zered, which divided Edom from the land of Moab north of it (Deut. 2:12-13).

c. The original inhabitants of Mt. Seir were called the *Horites* (Deut. 2:12), probably the same people known as *Hurrians*. The name *Seir* was taken from Seir, the forefather of the Horites (Gen. 36:20-22; 14:6).

d. The ancient capital of Edom was Bozrah (Isa. 63:1; 34:5-6). But *Sela*, better known by its Greek name *Petra*, appears to have been Edom's principal stronghold in the days of Israel's divided kingdom (2 Kgs. 14:7). Petra was located about halfway between the Dead Sea and the Gulf of Aqaba.

e. Soon after the death of Isaac, Esau left Canaan and took possession of Mt. Seir (Gen. 35:28; 36:6,7,8). The Edomites drove out the Horites, and settled in their place.

f. The Edomites became idolaters.

g. The Edomites had a perpetual enmity against Israel (Amos 1:11). Edom refused to let the Israelites pass through their land during the time of Moses (Num. 20:14-21).

h. King Saul fought the Edomites (1 Sam. 14:47).

i. King David subdued the Edomites and thus became heir to the natural resources in Edom, such as copper and iron (2 Sam. 8:13-14).

j. King Solomon had contact with Edom. His seaports at Ezion-Geber and Elath were in Edomite territory (2 Chr. 8:17,18). Hadad the Edomite was an adversary against Solomon (1 Kgs. 11:14-23).

k. King Jehoshaphat defeated Edom (2 Chr. 20:22).

l. Edom revolted in the time of King Jehoram of Judah

(2 Chr. 21:8-10). Their hostility at this time may have been the occasion of the prophecy of *Obadiah* against them. The entire prophecy of the book of Obadiah is directed against Edom (2 Chr. 21:16-17; Obad. 1-16).

m. King Amaziah smote Edom and hurled many of them over the rock cliffs (2 Chr. 25:11-12).

n. Edom smote Judah in the time of King Ahaz (2 Chr. 28:17). (Perhaps this was the occasion of the prophecy of Obadiah, which is a book that is difficult to date.)

o. The perpetual anger of Edom against Judah all the time down to the time of Judah's fall to Babylon called forth condemnations by the prophets of God (Amos 1:11-12; Jer. 49:7-22; Ezek. 25:12-14; Ps. 137:7).

p. After the Babylonian captivity an Arab tribe called the *Nabateans* drove the Edomites out of the Mt. Seir area. The Edomites moved into the southern part of Palestine (the Negev) as far north as Hebron, and this area where they relocated became known as *Idumea*, which is the Greek form of the name *Edom*. See Mark 3:8. King Herod the Great was an Idumean.

The Nabateans developed a prosperous society in the area of Petra, and carved many spectacular structures into the stone cliffs at Petra. Many of the most prominent buildings now visible there are the work of the Nabateans.

Questions on the Edomites

1. Of whom were the Edomites descendants?
2. Where did the Edomites live?
3. What was the name of the original inhabitants of this area?
4. What was the capital of Edom?
5. How did the Edomites get along with the Israelites?
6. What Old Testament book of prophecy is entirely devoted to a condemnation of Edom?
7. Name the Arab tribe which drove the Edomites out of their territory.
8. What land is called *Idumea*?

7. The Hittites

a. The Hittites were descendants of Noah's son Ham through his son Canaan (Gen. 10:15). In archaeological inscriptions they are called the Hatti or Khatti or Heta.

b. The main center of the Hittite empire was in Asia Minor. Its capital was named Hattusas (now called Boghaz-koy). The Hittites also had several cities in Syria (such as Carchemish, Hamath, and Zinjirli) that were centers of their power.

c. Some Hittites lived as far south as Canaan in the time of Abraham (Gen. 15:20; 23:3-20). Esau married Hittite women (Gen. 26:34). They were so numerous in Canaan by the time of Joshua that he speaks of all Palestine and Syria as "all the Hittite country" (Josh. 1:4). King David (1000 B.C.) had some Hittite soldiers in his army (1 Sam. 26:6; 2 Sam. 11:3).

d. Up until the early twentieth century the Hittites were almost unknown outside of the Bible. Archaeological excavations have abundantly confirmed the Biblical notations about the Hittites. Their hieroglyphic writing has been deciphered and read on hundreds of tablets.

e. There were two main periods of Hittite power:

(1) The Old Kingdom, 1850–1550 B.C.

(2) The New Kingdom, 1450–1200 B.C.

The Hittites took Aleppo in 1570 and sacked Babylon in 1550. In the fifteenth century the Egyptians under such kings as Thutmose III, swept north into Hittite territory, and greatly weakened their kingdom. Joshua and the Israelites defeated the Palestinian Hittites.

The Hittites regained supremacy through the use of horse-drawn war chariots (1 Kgs. 10:29; 2 Kgs. 7:6). Their greatest monarch was *Suppiluliumas* (1385–1345 B.C.). He subdued the Hurrian kingdom of Mittani and extended his border to Lebanon. He brought order to the entire area. He was contemporary with the forty years of Israel's peace under Othniel (Judg. 3:11).

The Egyptian kings Seti I and Rameses II fought the Hittites and took Canaan and much of Syria from them.

f. The Sea People from the Mediterranean islands around Crete invaded the eastern Mediterranean area (including Egypt, Canaan, Ugarit, and Asia Minor) about 1200 B.C. (or a little later). (The Philistines were one tribe of the Sea People.) The Sea People destroyed the Hittite empire.

g. The Hittites still held a few centers of strength after the fall of their main empire. These included cities in Syria, such as Hamath and Carchemish (on the great bend of the upper Euphrates). Carchemish fell to the Assyrians in 717 B.C.

h. The Hittites had law codes which tolerated many sexual relationships outside of marriage without punishment. Also they tolerated sexual union with various animals. (See *Ancient Near Eastern Texts* [Princeton, 1955], pp. 196-197.) The Bible describes the Hittites as very immoral (Ezek. 16:3, 45).

Questions on the Hittites

1. Where was the main center of the Hittite empire?
2. Where else did they have centers of power?
3. Were Hittites numerous in Canaan (Palestine)?
4. Give the dates for the two main periods of Hittite power.
5. Who was the greatest of the Hittite kings?
6. What battle equipment helped the Hittites get supremacy?
7. What people finally destroyed the Hittites?

8. The Moabites

a. The Moabites were descendants of Lot and his daughter (Gen. 19:36-38).

b. The land of Moab was located east of the Dead Sea, between the Arnon River on the north and the Zered on the south. In their early history they controlled territory north of the Arnon.

c. Sihon, king of the Amorites, took much of Moab "as far as the Arnon" (Num. 21:26) before the Israelites arrived around 1406 B.C.

d. The Israelites were forbidden by God to harass or provoke the Moabites as they passed by Moab (Deut. 2:9).

e. Because of his fear of the Israelites who were camped in the "Plains of Moab" (just east of the Jordan River, across from Jericho), Balak, king of Moab, sent for the prophet Balaam to come and curse Israel (Num. 22:1–25:5). Balaam finally advised Balak to involve the Israelites in the Moabites' immoral worship of Baal at Peor (Num. 31:16; 25:1; Rev. 2:14).

f. During the period of judges Moab oppressed Israel for eighteen years, but was defeated by Ehud (Judg. 3:12-30).

g. Ruth, a Moabitess, became an ancestor of Christ (Ruth 1:4). The book of Ruth indicates that a friendly relationship existed between Moab and Israel during part of the period of judges.

h. King Saul fought against the Moabites (1 Sam. 14:47).

i. King David defeated the Moabites and brought them into subjection (2 Sam. 8:2).

j. During the reign of King Jehoshaphat (872–848 B.C.), Moab confederated with Ammonites, Edomites, and others against Judah. But the LORD delivered Judah (2 Chr. 20:1-25; 2 Kgs. 3:6-27).

k. Moab was subservient to Israel for nearly two hundred years. But in the days of the prophet Isaiah (about 700 B.C.) Moab seems to have regained some of her previous power and prosperity. (See Isaiah 15, 16; Jeremiah 48:47.)

l. The national deity of Moab was named *Chemosh* (Num. 21:29; Judg. 11:24; 1 Kgs. 11:7).

m. The Moabite Stone was discovered in A.D. 1868. It is a black stone 3' 10" tall, and gives the story of how King Mesha of Moab revolted from Israel in the days after King Ahab. The story on the stone gives Moab's version of the story told in 2 Kings 3:4-5. King Mesha gave praise to his god Chemosh for the success of his revolt. The stone contains the names of at least twenty-one Bible people and places, including the name of

YAHWEH, God of Israel. (See an excellent article on the Moabite Stone in *Biblical Archaeology Review*, May–June 1986, pp. 50-61.)

Questions on the Moabites
1. From whom were the Moabites descended?
2. Where was the land of Moab?
3. What was the name of the national deity (god) of Moab?
4. Were the Moabites friendly toward the Israelites?

9. The Philistines (Israel's archenemy)
a. The area of Philistia was located on the Mediterranean shore, from Joppa southward to the south of Gaza.
b. The Philistines were a non-Semitic people. A large number of them seem to have immigrated into Israel from the Greek islands around Crete in the Aegean Sea after about 1200 B.C. They were one of the tribes of the Sea People who invaded the eastern Mediterranean area. A few Philistines had immigrated into Canaan asfar back as the time of Abraham and Isaac (2000 B.C.) (Gen. 21:32; 26:1). (See Bryant G. Wood, "The Philistines Enter Canaan," in *BAR*, Nov–Dec. 1991, pp. 44-52.)
c. In Canaan the Philistines had a strong political system, with five dominating city-states, independent but cooperative in their expansionist military efforts. The cities were Gaza, Gath, Ashdod, Ashkelon, and Ekron (Josh. 13:3).
d. The Philistines knew the secret of smelting and hardening iron and thus were at a great military advantage. They forced the Israelites to come to their Philistine blacksmiths to sharpen their few iron tools — at exorbitant prices (1 Sam. 13:19-22). (See James D. Muhly article in *BAR*, Nov.–Dec. 1982, pp. 40-54.)
e. God used the Philistines to *test* Israel (Judg. 3:3-4). The presence of these cruel idolaters forced the Israelites to choose whether they truly trusted God or would compromise His word to "get along" with their neighbors.

f. Shamgar killed six hundred Philistines (Judg. 3:31), and Samson hindered the Philistine oppression greatly (Judg. 13:16).

g. About 1070 B.C. the Philistines destroyed the town of Shiloh where the tabernacle and the ark of the covenant had been. They removed the ark to their own territory (1 Sam. 4:4, 11; Jer. 7:12). (See Israel Finklestein, "Shiloh" in *BAR*, Jan.–Feb.1986, pp. 22-41, esp. p. 41.)

h. By the time of King Saul the Philistines held many cities within the territory of Israel (like Michmash; 1 Sam. 13:16-17). At the time of Saul's death the Philistines occupied all the Mediterranean coast to Mt. Carmel, and the valley of Esdraelon as far east as Beth Shan (near the Jordan), thus almost encircling Israel (1 Sam. 31:10).

i. King David won victories over the Philistines (1 Sam. 5:17-25; 2 Sam. 8:1). They never after that exerted powerful control in Israel.

j. The Philistines still remained an enemy during the divided kingdom occasionally (Joel 3:4-8; Amos 1:6-8; 2 Chr. 17:11; 21:16, 17).

Questions over the Philistines
1. Where was Philistia located in Israel?
2. Where did the Philistines come from?
3. What were the five chief cities of the Philistines?
4. What technology gave the Philistines a military advantage?
5. When was the major Philistine immigration into Israel?
6. Who permanently broke the Philistine control over Israel?

10. The Phoenicians
a. Phoenicia was a narrow strip of land along the eastern Mediterranean coast, north of Mt. Carmel and the bay of Akko. Phoenicia was the territory now in the country of Lebanon. The habitable coastal plains are hemmed in by the Lebanon mountains, rising scarcely ten miles east of the coast.

b. There was not a *nation* of Phoenicia. The political power was exercised by the cities, particularly by *Tyre* and *Sidon*

(Joel 3:4). *Gebal* (later called Byblos) was also strong (1 Kgs. 5:18; Ezek. 27:9). The village of *Zarephath* (Sarepta) in Phoenicia is famous as the place where Elijah fed the widow and raised her son (1 Kgs. 17).

c. The original Sidonians were descendants of Noah's son Ham (Gen. 10:15). But they came to speak a Semitic language similar to Hebrew, perhaps because of invasions by Semitic conquerors like Sargon of Akkad and the Assyrians.

d. The Phoenicians were famous for their seafaring activities (Ezek. 27:4-9). They developed trade routes to many points on the Mediterranean coast, and eventually up to Britain. They were noted as the most accurate sailors of the ancient world and were the first to use the North Star as a navigational guide.

The Phoenicians also were noted for their colonization of places outside their land. These colonies provided them seaports throughout the Mediterranean. Examples: Carthage in north Africa, and the island of Malta.

e. The Phoenician (Canaanite) *religion* was very immoral and cruel. Ezekiel the prophet railed against Tyre and Sidon (Ezek. 27, 28). Several Canaanite gods and rituals are mentioned in the Old Testament — Ba'al, Ashtoreth, Anath, El, and Dagon. Archaeological discoveries at Ras Shamra have revealed much about the Canaanite religion, exposing its cruelty and obscenity. (See Charles Pfeiffer, *Ras Shamra and the Bible* [Baker, 1962], pp. 29-39.)

f. A number of Phoenician kings were named *Hiram*, or Ahiram (1 Kgs. 5:1).

g. Friendship existed between Phoenicia and Israel during the reign of David and Solomon (2 Sam. 5:11; 1 Kgs. 5:1).

h. King Ahab married Jezebel, the daughter of the king of Sidon, and the idolatrous practices of Canaanite religion were introduced into Israel (1 Kgs. 16:31-33).

i. Several Assyrian kings besieged Tyre without taking it. Nebuchadnezzar of Babylon besieged Tyre for thirteen years (598–585), taking the mainland portion of the city, but not the island portion one-half mile out in the Mediterranean (Ezek. 29:18). Alexander the Great built a causeway of earth out to the island city of Tyre, making it part of a peninsula, and captured the city in 332 B.C. after a seven-month siege.

Questions over the Phoenicians

1. Where was Phoenicia?
2. What were the two chief cities of Phoenicia?
3. What was the principal business activity of the Phoenicians?
4. What was the nature of the religion of the Phoenicians?
5. What name did several Phoenician kings have?

Section B
From the Division of the Kingdom to the Fall of the House of Ahab (1 Kings 12–2 Kings 11; 2 Chronicles 10–23)

1. *Facts about the Divided Kingdom.* Very soon after the death of Solomon, the prophecy of Ahijah (1 Kgs. 11:29-31) was fulfilled. Solomon's kingdom, now ruled by his son Rehoboam, split in two, and the two parts formed separate kingdoms named JUDAH and ISRAEL (the name of the united kingdom).

Israel, the northern kingdom, was larger, about 9500 square miles, compared to Judah's area of 3500 square miles. The land of Israel was more productive than Judah.

On the other hand Judah, the southern kingdom, retained the capital city of Jerusalem, the center of organized government, and the material assets of the nation, such as the accumlated treasures of David and Solomon. Also Judah retained the authorized worship center of the temple in Jerusalem. In addition, Judah experienced a relative stability in its government, with all its kings being descendants of David, while Israel suffered the social upheavals of eight assassinations or violent deaths of kings. The elements of greatness were mostly on the side of the southern kingdom, Judah.

Period 9 — The DIVIDED KINGDOM (930–586 B.C.)

A. Israel split into two kingdoms:
   (1) ISRAEL — 10 northern & eastern tribes
   (2) JUDAH — 2 southern tribes

B. Both kingdoms went into captivity.
   (1) Israel to captivity in ASSYRIA
   (2) Judah to captivity in BABYLON

From the very first, the blot of rebellion clung to the breakaway kingdom of Israel. Jeroboam, the first king of the northern kingdom, had been selected by God to punish the sins of Solomon, and he had been promised an enduring dynasty (1 Kgs. 11:38); but he did not serve the LORD at all.

Jeroboam's very first act cut every religious bond to the LORD (Yahweh) and His worship, and Jeroboam's course was followed by every one of his successors. We frequently read such statements as "He walked in all the ways of Jeroboam son of Nebat and in his sin, which he caused Israel to commit" (1 Kgs. 16:26).

On the other hand, the kingdom of Judah was preserved from the utter spiritual falling away of Israel, for the sake of God's covenant with David (1 Kgs. 11:34), who had observed God's commands and statutes. The immediate consequence of Jeroboam's religious revolt was to drive all the priests and Levites in his kingdom to Jerusalem (2 Chr. 11:13-14). The result was that the kingdom of Israel lacked those qualities of love and goodness that were imparted to the people through the law of Moses. This produced a disposition of rebellion and violence in the people, which was an underlying cause of the frequent assassinations and upheavals in Israel.

Certainly Judah and the house of David was deeply corrupted, mainly by its alliance with the wicked house of Ahab of Israel. But Judah boasted the names of very *good* kings, like

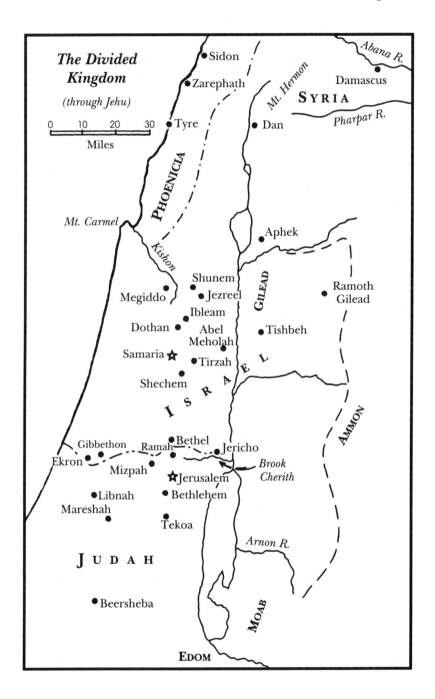

The Divided Kingdom

(through Jehu)

0   10   20   30
Miles

Sidon

Abana R.

Zarephath

Mt. Hermon

Damascus

SYRIA

Tyre

Dan

Pharpar R.

PHOENICIA

Mt. Carmel

Kishon

Aphek

Shunem

GILEAD

Megiddo

Jezreel

Ramoth Gilead

Ibleam

Dothan

Abel Meholah

Tishbeh

Samaria ☆

Tirzah

Shechem

I S R A E L

AMMON

Gibbethon

Bethel

Ramah

Jericho

Ekron

Brook Cherith

Mizpah

☆ Jerusalem

Libnah

Bethlehem

Mareshah

Tekoa

Arnon R.

J U D A H

MOAB

Beersheba

EDOM

Asa, Jehoshaphat, Uzziah, Jotham, Hezekiah, and Josiah. Israel's kings, on the other hand, were every one branded as doers of evil by the prophets sent from God.

The two kingdoms were distinguished by their final fates. The sentence of captivity was executed upon Israel about 130 years sooner than on Judah. The ten tribes never made a unified return to their homeland, but a large remnant of the tribe of Judah returned to its land and became a small but strong nation. Judah was not free from the faults of its fathers, but the zeal of the remnant that returned prepared the way for the establishment of the true spiritual kingdom under Jesus, the last great son of David.

1. Names of the two kingdoms	**ISRAEL**	**JUDAH**
2. Number of tribes in each kingdom	Ten	Two (Judah merged with Benjamin)
3. Area included	Northern & eastern	Southern
4. First kings	Jeroboam	Rehoboam
5 Total number of kings	19	19 plus 1 usurper
6. Number of dynasties	Nine	One (the house of David)
7. Character of the kings	All bad, some worse	Some bad, some good
8. Capitals of the kingdoms	Samaria. (Earlier at Shechem and Tirzah (2 Kgs. 12:25; 14:17)	Jerusalem
9. Fate of the kingdoms, and date	Conquered and deported to Assyria, 722 B.C.	Conquered and deported to Babylon, 586 B.C.

(Memorize the contents of the chart above.)

WHY STUDY THE DIVIDED KINGDOM ?

1. Bible sections about the divided kingdom are part of God's word; and **all** Scripture is *profitable* (2 Tim. 3:16-17).
2. There are many references to the divided kingdom *in*

the *New Testament* — references to Elijah, Elisha, Naaman, Jezebel, the kings of Judah, and others.

3. The divided kingdom is the historical *setting for many of the prophets* — Hosea, Amos, Isaiah, Jonah, Jeremiah, etc.

4. Many *archaeological discoveries* relate to kings and events in the divided kingdom period.

5. The divided kingdom period *shows God's training*, discipline, and blessings upon Israel. We learn much about GOD!

6. The divided kingdom period *shows the fulfillments of* many earlier *prophecies*, such as those spoken by Jacob (Gen. 49), by Moses (Deut. 28, 33), and to Solomon (1 Kgs. 9).

7. It furnishes many valuable *illustrations of human character* and behavior. It is a course in psychology.

8. The divided kingdom *covers a long period of Bible history* — 350 years. Our historical knowledge has a huge gap if we do not know about it.

9. The people and history of the divided kingdom are truly *interesting*.

2. *The Kings of Israel and Judah* (As the various kings are studied, students should refer to the following chart and memorize the names of the kings and the principal events associated with each. Roman numerals along the margin indicate dynasties. The names of the kings are positioned on the chart so as to show which kings in Israel and Judah were reigning at the same time.)

ISRAEL	JUDAH
1. *Jeroboam*	1. *Rehoboam* (evil)
a. Made golden calves	a. Split the kingdom
b. His altar denounced by the	b. Invaded by Shishak
young prophet	2. *Abijam* (evil)
	a. Victory over Jeroboam
2. *Nadab*	3. *Asa* (good)
a. Assassinated by Baasha	a. Beat a million Ethiopians
3. *Baasha*	b. Religious reforms
a. Destroyed the family of	c. Backslid a mile (hired Ben-
Jeroboam	Hadad)

I (left margin, dynasty marker for items 1–2 Israel)
II (left margin, dynasty marker for item 3 Israel)

Baasha (continued)
  b. Fortified Ramah against Asa
  c. Denounced by the prophet
    Jehu
4. **Elah**
  a. Assassinated by Zimri
5. **Zimri**
  a. Destroyed the family of
    Baasha
  b. Seven-day rule
6. **Omri**
  a. Mighty
  b. Made Samaria the capital
7. **Ahab**
  a. Jezebel and Baal worship
  b. Contest with Elijah
  c. Two victories over Ben-
    Hadad
  d. Naboth slain
  e. Battle of Ramoth-Gilead
8. **Ahaziah** (son of Ahab)
  a. Accident and sickness
  b. Elijah predicts his death
9. **Jehoram** (son of Ahab)
  a. Mesha of Moab revolted.
  b. Ministry of Elisha
  c. Siege & famine at Samaria
  d. Wounded at Ramoth-Gilead
  e. Slain by Jehu
10. **Jehu**
  a. Killed the house of Ahab and
    Ahaziah of Judah
  b. Destroyed Ba'al worship

11. **Jehoahaz**
  a. Lost most of his kingdom to
    Syria
12. **Jehoash**
  a. Smote Syria three times
  b. Conquered Amaziah and
    Judah
13. **Jeroboam II** (the mightiest)
  a. Restored territory to Israel
  b. Took Damascus and Hamath

4. **Jehoshaphat** (good)
  a. Appointed righteous judges
  b. Alliance with Ahab
  c. Victory over Moab and
    Ammon
  d. Shipwreck
  e. Went with Jehoram to fight
    Moab

5. **Jehoram** (one of the worst!)
  a. Married Athaliah
  b. Killed his six brothers
  c. Edom and Libnah revolted
  d. Letter from Elijah
  e. Hideous death
6. **Ahaziah** (evil)
  a. Visited uncle Jehoram of Isr.
  b. Slain by Jehu
X. **Athaliah** (evil usurper)
  a. Killed all but one of the house
    of David
  b. Slain in a plot by Jehoiada
7. **Joash** (good and bad)
  a. The boy king
  b. Repaired the temple
  c. Forgot the kindness shown to
    him
8. **Amaziah** (good and bad)
  a. Conquered Edom and took its
    gods
  b. Defeated by Jehoash
  c. Assassinated

Period IX: Divided Kingdom

Jeroboam II (continued)
  c. Amos announced the end of the kingdom (Amos 7:11)

V 14. **Zechariah**
  a. Slain by Shallum after 6 months

VI 15. **Shallum**
  a. Slain by Menahem after 1 month

VII 16. **Menahem**
  a. Cruel in war
  b. Invaded by Pul of Assyria
17. **Pekahiah**
  a. Slain by Pekah

VIII 18. **Pekah**
  a. Joined Rezin in attacking Ahaz
  b. Invaded by Tiglath-pileser
  c. Slain by Hoshea

IX 19. **Hoshea**
  a. Tribute to Shalmaneser
  b. Conspiracy with Egypt
  c. Siege of Samaria and fall of Israel

END OF ISRAEL !

9. **Uzziah** (or Azariah) (good)
  a. Mighty
  b. Became a leper

10. **Jotham** (good)
  a. Mighty
  b. Threatened by Rezin & Pekah
11. **Ahaz** (one of the worst)
  a. Introduced idolatry
  b. Attacked by Rezin & Pekah
  c. Hired Tiglath-pileser to attack Israel
  d. Made an altar like one in Damascus
  e. Damaged the temple wilfully
12. **Hezekiah** (one of the best)
  a. Temple reopened and cleansed
  b. Great Passover
  c. Sennacherib's invasion
  d. Life extended 15 years
  e. Visitors from Babylon
13. **Manasseh** (the worst of all)
  a. Idolatry unlimited
  b. Cruelty unlimited
  c. Announcement of fall of Judah
  d. Captive in Babylon
  e. Repentance and reformation
14. **Amon** (evil)
  a. Continued evils of father
  b. Assassinated
15. **Josiah** (the best!)
  a. Temple repaired
  b. Book of law found
  c. Idolatry purged and true religion enforced

571

Josiah (continued)
  d. Altar at Bethel defiled
  e. Slain by Pharaoh-Necho
16. *Jehoahaz* (or Shallum) (evil)
  a. Three months' reign
  b. Deposed and taken to Egypt
17. *Jehoiakim* (evil)
  a. Enthroned by Pharaoh
  b. Servitude to Babylon
  c. Cut up Jeremiah's scroll
  d. First deportation to Babylon
18. *Jehoiachin* (evil) (also called Jeconiah and Coniah)
  a. Three months' reign
  b. Captured and taken to Babylon
  c. Second deportation to Babylon
19. *Zedekiah* (evil)
  a. Rebelled against Babylon
  b. Siege and destruction of Jerusalem
  c. Third deportation to Babylon

END OF JUDAH !

3. *Chronology of the Divided Kingdom*

Dates of the Kings:

ISRAEL	JUDAH
1. Jeroboam — 931–910 B.C.	1. Rehoboam — 931–913 B.C.
	2. Abijam — 913–911
	3. Asa — 911–870
2. Nadab — 910–909	
3. Baasha — 909–886	
4. Elah — 886–885	
5. Zimri — 885	
6. Omri — 885–874	
7. Ahab — 874–853	4. Jehoshaphat — 873–848
8. Ahaziah — 853–852	
9. Jehoram — 852–841	5. Jehoram — 848–841
	6. Ahaziah — 841

Jehu killed Jehoram of Israel and Ahaziah of Judah (841 B.C.).

10. Jehu — 841–814	X. Athaliah — 841–835

7. Joash — 835-796

11. Jehoahaz — 814-798
12. Jehoash — 798-782   8. Amaziah — 796-767
13. Jeroboam II — 793-753   9. Uzziah — 790-739
14. Zechariah — 753-752
15. Shallum — 752
16. Menahem — 752-742   10. Jotham — 751-736
17. Pekahiah — 742-740
18. Pekah — 752-732   11. Ahaz — 742-728
19. Hoshea — 732-722   12. Hezekiah — 728-695
End of Israel — 722 B.C.

13. Manasseh — 695-642
14. Amon — 642-640
15. Josiah — 640-609
16. Jehoahaz — 609
17. Jehoiakim — 609-597
18. Jehoiachin — 597
19. Zedekiah — 597-586

a. The history of the divided kingdom contains dozens of chronological statements, such as: "In the eighteenth year of the reign of Jeroboam son of Nebat, Abijah became king of Judah, and he reigned in Jerusalem three years" (1 Kgs. 15:1-2). With these many notations it would seem that the chronology of this period would be the most clearly indicated and most easily reckoned of all the periods.

b. However, upon serious study these chronological notes have given great difficulty. The difficulties are of two main types:

(1) The total numbers of years obtained by adding up the numbers of years each king is said to have reigned do not seem to agree with the synchronisms stated for the other kingdom. (Judah's kings are synchronized with years in the reigns of Israel's kings and vice versa.) For example, the total number of years stated for Israel's first four kings equals fifty (Jeroboam 22, Nadab 2, Baasha 24, Elah 2). This total is synchronized with King Asa's 27th year (1 Kgs. 16:10, 15). However, King Rehoboam's 17 years, plus 3 for Abijah and 27 for Asa total 47, not 50.

(2) The dates apparently indicated in the Hebrew

573

Scriptures do not seem to agree with the carefully recorded year-by-year dates preserved in the records of the Assyrians and Babylonians (called the "Eponym Lists" or "King lists").

c. These difficulties have appeared impossible to be solved until recent years. With increased knowledge of Assyrian and Babylonian records and more careful study of the Bible, we now know that the Biblical numbers are generally reliable. (I feel they will be found to be totally reliable.) Our understanding of the Bible has been at fault, not the Bible itself.

Some helpful books on chronology have been produced in recent years by Edwin R. Thiele. These include *The Mysterious Numbers of the Hebrew Kings*, rev. ed., Grand Rapids: Eerdmans, 1965. A shorter book by the same author is *A Chronology of the Hebrew Kings*, Grand Rapids: Zondervan, 1977. See also the article by Leslie McFall in the journal *Themelios*, Oct.–Nov. 1991 (Vol. 17, No. 1), pp. 6-11. The dates proposed by Thiele have gained a wide acceptance, and we have mostly followed them, except for his date of King Hezekiah. Thiele dates Hezekiah 715–686 B.C. This creates a conflict with the statement that King Hezekiah began to reign in the third year of Hoshea, the last king of the northern kingdom of Israel (2 Kgs. 18:1). Hoshea reigned nine years (2 Kgs. 17:1,9), up until the fall of Israel in 722 B.C. Therefore we should date the start of Hezekiah's reign (or possibly a joint reign with his father) at 728 B.C., six years before the fall of Israel.

If there was a co-regency of Hezekiah with his father until 715 B.C., that date would be the start of Hezekiah's sole reign and would place the invasion by the Assyrian king Sennacherib (which occurred in 701 B.C.) in the "fourteenth year" of Hezekiah as sole ruler. This harmonizes with the statement in 2 Kings 18:13.

The researches by Thiele and others have shown that our difficulties in understanding the chronology of the Hebrew kings have been caused by several factors:

(1) One factor is that several kings in both Judah and Israel had *overlapping reigns* by father and son, or with a rival.

King Jotham ruled jointly with his father (2 Kgs. 15:5-6). Several other kings also appear to have had joint reigns. The total number of years they reigned would therefore not equal the total of number of years of both added together.

The existence of joint reigns raises problems. If the start of the reign of one country's king is synchronized with a specific year of a king ruling in another country, does the historian date the start of the new ruler's reign from the start of the joint reign of the neighboring king, or from the start of his sole reign after his father died? This is sometimes difficult to determine.

(2) Different countries have reckoned the first years of their rulers in different ways. If a king died in the middle of a calendar year, that year was sometimes counted as the dead king's last year, and the remainder of the year until the next New Year's day was counted as the new king's first year. (This is called a *non-accession* year system of dating.) Other countries counted the remainder of the calendar year when the new king first ruled as his "accession year" and did not include it in the total number of years he ruled. It is obvious that the non-accession year system would make the total number of years ruled by several kings appear to be more than the actual number of calendar years that passed. It appears that the kingdom of Israel followed a non-accession year system of dating at least in the first part of its history, while Judah used an accession-year system.

(3) Countries sometimes shifted from the accession-year method of counting lengths of reigns to a non-accession year method. The kingdom of Judah appears to have adopted the dating system used by Israel when the two countries formed an alliance in the time of Judah's King Jehoram. Then in the time of Judah's King Amaziah, Judah returned to its former method of computing reigns. This complicates the chronology.

(4) A small but real problem was the time of starting the new years. Some countries started their years in the spring and some in the autumn. Because of this, two kings who began to reign on the same day could a few months later

find one king spoken of as being in his official "second year" while the other was still in his "accession year," not even in his official first year.

d. The "twenty years" of the reign of King Pekah is also a difficult feature of the chronology (2 Kgs. 15:27). King Menahem, a predecessor of King Pekah, paid tribute to Tiglath-pileser III of Assyria. This is told both in the Bible and Tiglath-pileser's inscriptions. Tiglath-pileser is dated 745–727. If we count back from the fall of Israel in 722, and add the nine years of King Hoshea to twenty of Pekah, we are brought back to 752 B.C., a date *before* the time of Tiglath-Pileser. If this were true, Menahem could not have paid tribute to Tiglath-pileser.

The solution seems to be (as Thiele suggests) that Pekah set up a rival dynasty east of the Jordan in Gilead at the time when King Menahem ascended to the throne in Samaria. (See 2 Kings 15:25.) Thus Menahem's reign of ten years was at the same time as the first ten years of Pekah. When Pekah finally came into power over all Israel, it was natural that he would maintain that he had always been the only true king of Israel, even from 752. This is a possible, though not a proven explanation.

4. *King Rehoboam of Judah.*

REHOBOAM of Judah — 931–913 B.C. (*Evil*)
(1 Kgs. 12:1-24; 14:21-31; 2 Chr. 10,11,12)
   a. He split the kingdom.
   b. He was invaded by Shishak (king of Egypt).

Rehoboam was the son of Solomon by *Naamah*, an Ammonite princess. Ammonite idolatry probably influenced Rehoboam (1 Kgs. 11:5).

The name of the *mother* of nearly every king of Judah is given in the opening verses telling of their reigns. (This is done in the books of Kings. Chronicles does not name the mothers of the kings after good King Hezekiah.) Only the names of the mothers of King Asa, and of two very evil kings

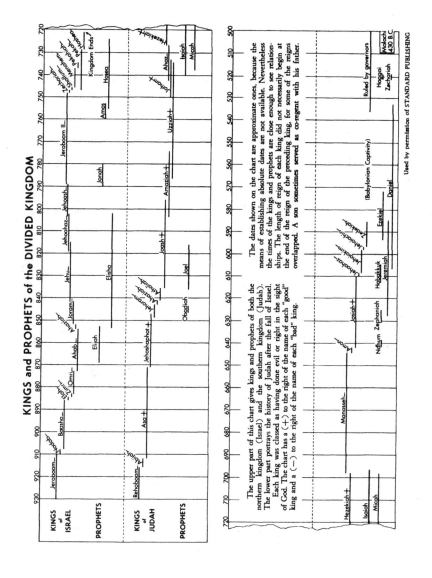

KINGS and PROPHETS of the DIVIDED KINGDOM

The upper part of this chart gives kings and prophets of both the northern kingdom (Israel) and the southern kingdom (Judah). The lower part portrays the history of Judah after the fall of Israel.

Each king was classed as having done evil or right in the sight of God. The chart has a (+) to the right of the name of each "good" king and a (—) to the right of the name of each "bad" king.

The dates shown on the chart are approximate ones, because the means of establishing absolute dates are not available. Nevertheless the times of the kings and prophets are close enough to see relationships. The length of reign of each king did not necessarily begin at the end of the reign of the preceding king, for some of the reigns overlapped. A son sometimes served as co-regent with his father.

Used by permission of STANDARD PUBLISHING

— Jehoram and Ahaz — and of the usurper Athaliah [Jezebel!] are not named. The mothers of the kings of *Israel* are not named. Stating the mothers' names shows the importance of motherhood.

As Rehoboam was forty-one when he became king, he must have been born about the time his father was installed as king by his grandfather David. The luxury in which he was brought up gave him a light and headstrong character, into which his father's precepts in the book of Proverbs did not enter.

Rehoboam was scarcely seated on the throne before the old jealousy between Judah and the other tribes flared up (2 Sam. 19:42-43; Isa. 11:13). To soothe the old animosity, Rehoboam traveled up to Shechem (40 miles north of Jerusalem) to meet with the dissidents assembled there. The Israelites of the northern tribes had sent for JEROBOAM to come back out of Egypt and be their spokesman and potential leader (2 Kgs. 12:2-3; 2 Chr. 10:3). The Israelites asked for relief from the "heavy yoke" that Solomon had laid upon them. Rehoboam requested time to make his decision. He rejected the counsel of his elders that he give the people a favorable and gracious answer. (Respect for older people and their wisdom usually was the rule among the Hebrews and related peoples. See Leviticus 19:32; Job 32:6-7.) But Rehoboam followed the advice of young men who had grown up with him, and let them place harsh words in his mouth: "My little finger is thicker than my father's waist." By this he implied, "Think how much my waist will weigh when I sit upon you!" "My father scourged you with whips; I will scourge you with *scorpions*" (1 Kgs. 12:11). The "scorpions" were terrifying, though non-specific threats.

Rehoboam did not heed the advice of his father:
"A gentle answer turns away wrath, but a harsh word stirs up anger" (Prov. 15:1).

All of this occurred to fulfill the word of the LORD which He had spoken to Jeroboam through Ahijah, the prophet from Shiloh (1 Kgs. 11:29-38). God's word never fails to come to pass.

The result of Rehoboam's speech was the opposite of what he sought. Instead of meekly submitting to him, the people rebelled and ten of the tribes formed a separate kingdom. Rehoboam had to flee from Shechem to save his life, and his "enforcer" Adoniram was stoned to death. (The spelling of his name alternates between *Adoram* and *Adoniram*. See 2 Samuel 20:24; 1 Kings 4:6; 5:14; 12:18.)

Back in Jerusalem Rehoboam began to muster troops to crush the revolt by war. But God spoke to Rehoboam and to the people through Shemaiah, "the man of God," forbidding them to fight against their "brothers, the Israelites." ("Man of God" is a common title for God's prophets. See 1 Kings 13:1; 20:28. Concerning Shemaiah, see 2 Chronicles 11:2,15; 12:5-7.) God's plans will not be overthrown by human conceit and schemes.

"Only the tribe of Judah remained loyal to the house of David" (1 Kgs. 12:20). Judah absorbed the territory of Benjamin, where Jerusalem was (1 Kgs. 12:21). Although the tribe of Simeon was completely enclosed within the territory of Judah, it appears that the loyalties and practices of the Simeonites caused them to be regarded as a part of the northern kingdom of Israel.

2 Chronicles 15:9 says that large numbers of people from Ephraim, Manasseh and *Simeon* came to Jerusalem in the time of King Asa, for people "had come to him from *Israel.*" Beersheba in Simeon had a center of false worship to which Amos forbade the people of the northern kingdom to go (Amos 5:5).

Rehoboam built up about fifteen fortified towns for defense in Judah, mostly in the south to protect his southern frontier from Philistines, Egyptians, and Edomites (2 Chr. 11:5-12; 21:10). (See C. Rasmussen, *Zondervan NIV Atlas of the Bible*, pp. 124-125.) Events soon showed that Rehoboam was in real danger from the Egyptians. He did not fortify his northern border, perhaps because he felt he could defeat Israel in any conflict.

Priests and Levites fled from the northern tribes ruled by Jeroboam, who had set up an entirely different religious system from that commanded in the law of Moses. Priests came from Israel into Jerusalem, and these strengthened the kingdom of Judah and supported Rehoboam (2 Chr. 11:13-17).

Godliness strengthens a nation. "Blessed is the nation whose God is the LORD" (Ps. 33:12).

Rehoboam followed his father Solomon as a role model by having many wives. Rehoboam had eighteen wives and sixty concubines (2 Chr. 11:21; 1 Kgs. 11:3).

Rehoboam appointed his son *Abijah* to become king (2 Chr. 11:22; his name is spelled *Abijam* in 1 Kings 15:1,8). In spite of Rehoboam's faults, he "acted wisely" in administering his country (2 Chr. 11:23).

When Rehoboam's position as king was established, he abandoned the law of the LORD. As a result of this the LORD permitted King Shishak of Egypt to invade Judah in Rehoboam's fifth year (2 Chr. 12:1-11; 1 Kgs. 14:25-28). Shishak captured many fortified cities of Judah, and came as far as Jerusalem (2 Chr. 12:4). Shishak took everything, including the gold shields that Solomon had made (2 Chr. 12:9; 1 Kgs. 10:16-17).

Shishak's invasion caused the leaders of Israel and King Rehoboam to humble themselves, and say, "The LORD is just." The LORD then spared Jerusalem from total destruction by Shishak (2 Chr. 12:12).

Rehoboam attempted to preserve the appearance of glory by making bronze shields to replace the golden ones. The brazen shields of Rehoboam became a symbol of Rehoboam's lost glory, and probably of all religious institutions that forsake the LORD and lose His protection. (See Harry Rimmer, *Dead Men Tell Tales* [Chicago, 1946], pp. 247-266.)

In the Egyptian writings Shishak is called *Sheshonq I* (about

945–924 B.C.) The conquests of Shishak up into Canaan are memorialized on a huge relief carving (nearly thirty feet high) on the south wall of the Temple of Karnak at Thebes (Luxor) in Upper Egypt. The carving shows about 154 names in ovals (cartouches) bearing the names of conquered places. Each oval is carved below a figure of a captive with arms tied behind his back at the elbows. The conquered places listed include Gath, Gibeon, Bethhoron, Megiddo, and other Biblical towns. From these names it is possible to reconstruct partially the route of Shishak's campaign. (See Carl Rasmussen, *Zondervan NIV Atlas of the Bible.* Grand Rapids, 1989, pp. 124-125. Also "Shishak's Military Campaign in Israel Confirmed," by Kenneth A. Kitchen, in *Biblical Archaeology Review*, May–June 1989, pp. 30-33.) Shishak's name is preserved on a fragment of a stele found at Megiddo, verifying his presence at that location (Kitchen, *op.cit.*, p. 33).

There was continual warfare between Rehoboam and King Jeroboam of the northern kingdom (1 Kgs. 14:30). Rehoboam was honored in death by burial with his fathers in the city of David (1 Kgs. 14:30-31).

5. *King Jeroboam of Israel.*

JEROBOAM I of Israel — 931–910 B.C.
(1 Kgs. 12:20, 25-33; 13:1–14:19)
    a. He made golden calves.
    b. His altar was denounced by the young prophet.

---

a. *Jeroboam's capital and shrines* (1 Kgs. 12:25-33). After the ten northern tribes made Jeroboam king over them, he fortified *Shechem* as his first capital. He also built up *Penuel* east of Jordan as his eastern administrative center (1 Kgs. 12:25). Penuel was by the Jabbok River, where Jacob wrestled the angel (Gen. 32:30; Judg. 8:8,17). Shechem is in the valley between Mt. Ebal and Mt. Gerizim, and is not easily defended. Perhaps for that reason, Jeroboam relocated his "house" to *Tirzah* (1 Kgs. 14:17-18), which is seven miles northeast of Shechem, in a beautiful location at the headwaters of the brook Faria. King Zimri later burned the palace at Tirzah (1 Kgs. 16:15-18).

Jeroboam's first act as ruler was to make a complete break with the beliefs and practices of his forefathers, which were preserved at Jerusalem in the kingdom of Judah. Jeroboam introduced new gods for the people — golden calves — but he presented them as the gods "who brought you up out of Egypt." (Jeroboam used the same words as the idolaters at Mt. Sinai who made the golden calf there. See Exodus 32:8.) Jeroboam set these up at the north and south ends of his kingdom, at Dan and Bethel. No one could leave his kingdom without passing by imposing worship centers. No one would need to go to Jerusalem to worship!

Perhaps the Israelites under Jeroboam rationalized that the golden calves made by Jeroboam were only animal figures on whose backs stood the invisible God (*Expositor's Bible Commentary*, Vol. 4, p. 118). But God's prophets declared plainly that God regarded the calves as idols. (See 2 Kings 14:9; 17:16.)

Archaeological excavations at Dan have discovered part of a statuette of an Egyptian king wearing the white crown of Osiris. This may be associated with Jeroboam's stay in Egypt (1 Kgs. 11:40). Also two large jars bearing snake decorations, and an incense stand were found. (Avraham Biran, *Biblical Dan*, Jerusalem, 1994, pp. 177-183.) Also at Dan a large platform 8 meters wide and 19 meters long, made of 2 courses of large cut stones was found. Perhaps it was the platform on which the golden calf once stood, though no trace of the calf was found. The platform had been burned, perhaps in the attack on Dan by the Syrian king Ben-Hadad (1 Kgs. 15:20). (Article "Dan" in *New Encyclopedia of Archæological Excavations in the Holy Land*, Vol. 1, 1993, p. 327.)

Jeroboam changed not only the place for Israel's worship, but also its festivals and priesthood. Instead of the feast of Tabernacles commanded in the law of Moses to be kept in the seventh month, he instituted a festival in the *eighth* month. (Josephus says that Jeroboam decided to invent his own religious festivals as the Feast of Tabernacles was approaching, to protect his kingdom, and perhaps his own life. *Antiquities* VIII, 225 [viii,4].) Instead of using only Levites as priests, Jeroboam appointed all sorts of people as priests. This was a violation punishable by death according to the law of Moses (Num. 3:5-10).

Jeroboam's disregard of God brought about his doom.
(See 1 Kings 13:34; 14:7-11.)

---

b. *The Man of God from Judah* (1 Kgs. 13). A "man of God" came from Judah to Bethel, and denounced the altar of Jeroboam, predicting it would be split apart. Jeroboam ordered his officers to seize him, but Jeroboam's hand instantly became shriveled and unusable. The prophet showed the true spirit of God by praying for the hand of the king who had tried to seize him. Nineteen times in the chapter the prophet is called the "man of God."

The man of God foretold the future coming of a king named *Josiah*, who would sacrifice priests on the altar of Jeroboam, and burn bones there, making it unclean (1 Kgs. 13:2; Num. 19:11). This prophecy was fulfilled, almost exactly three hundred years later (about 630 B.C.). See 2 Kings 23:15-18.

The man of God was deceived by an old prophet in Bethel, one who had not reproved Jeroboam's altar. He lied, saying that an angel had told him to bring back the man of God to his house to eat. (We must be alert not to be deceived.)

Neither men nor angels have authority to change the word of God (1 Kgs. 13:18; Gal. 1:8).

A lion killed the man of God as he was returning to Jerusalem (ten miles south from Bethel). It might seem unfair that the man of God should die violently while the old prophet who deceived him lived on. But the old prophet died a thousand deaths; the man of God died only once. The old prophet sought to appear noble by associations with the man of God, rather than by personal achievement. Even in death his main desire was to be buried beside the bones of the man of God (1 Kgs. 13:31).

Jeroboam did not change his evil ways even after the man of God had demonstrated clearly that God's power was working through him (1 Kgs. 13:33). This illustrates the power of sin to blind the eyes of our hearts to clear evidences of God's reign in the world (2 Cor. 4:3).

c. *Ahijah's prophecy against Jeroboam* (1 Kgs. 14:1-20). Jeroboam's son *Abijah* became ill. In consternation Jeroboam sent his wife to the prophet *Ahijah* at Shiloh, to obtain a prophecy concerning what would happen to the boy. Ahijah had previously foretold to Jeroboam that he would become king over ten tribes (1 Kgs. 11:31). Jeroboam's desperate scheme shows a curious mixture of faith in Ahijah's ability to prophesy truth, while at the same time a feeling that he could deceive Ahijah as to who his wife was. Ahijah must have known the family well enough to recognize Jeroboam's wife by sight; but he had become blind. (Note Jeroboam's desire to "save face" and shield himself from any rebuke by the prophet.)

By the time in his reign when Jeroboam sent his wife to Ahijah, Jeroboam had relocated his capital to Tirzah, northeast of Shechem eight miles (1 Kgs. 14:17). Shiloh, where Ahijah lived, was then in ruins, and the tabernacle was no longer there (Jer. 7:12).

The "boy" (Heb., *child*) of Jeroboam was the only one in his home in whom the LORD found anything good (1 Kgs. 14:13). Ahijah foretold that the child would die when his mother returned and set foot in the city. That their only good son should die to escape the doom of his family will seem strange to some. "The righteous perish, and no one ponders it in his heart; . . . that the righteous are taken away to be spared from evil" (Isa. 57:1-2).

Ahijah foretold that God would cut off from the family of

Jeroboam every last male in Israel (14:10). (The Hebrew expression for "male" is "he that urinates on a wall.") To compare the future burning of Jeroboam's house to the burning of *dung* was supremely demeaning; but the prophecy was fulfilled very completely (1 Kgs. 15:29). "The LORD struck him down and he died" (2 Chr. 13:20).

The death of Abijah must have affected Jeroboam deeply, but there is no record of changes in his ways of living.

    d. *Jeroboam's relationships with Rehoboam* (1 Kgs. 15:30; 14:21-32; 2 Chr. 10,11,12). "There was continual warfare between Rehoboam and Jeroboam." Abijam won a great victory over Jeroboam, so that Jeroboam did not regain power during the time of Abijah (2 Chr. 13:20). Concerning *Rehoboam, King of Judah*, see notes on 1 Kings 12:1-24. Though Rehoboam's reign started reasonably well, it degenerated until it was little better than that of Jeroboam. In Judah they set up high places, sacred stones (*masseboth*) and Asherah poles on every high hill and under every spreading tree. There were even male shrine prostitutes in the land (1 Kgs. 14:23; 15:12). Such practices ultimately brought about the doom of Judah. See notes on 1 Kings 12:1-24 concerning *Shishak*.

    6. *King Abijah/Abijam of Judah.*

ABIJAH (Abijam) of Judah — 913–911 B.C. (*Evil*)
(1 Kgs. 15:1-8; 2 Chr. 13:1–14:1)
    a. Victory over Jeroboam

Abijah's name is spelled *Abijam* in the Hebrew of 1 Kings. Chronicles spells it *Abijah*. (The Greek and Latin Bibles support the different spellings in Kings and Chronicles.) The difference in spelling is minor, and perhaps indicates that both ways of spelling his name were used in his lifetime.

The reign of Abijah was brief, bad, and braggy. Why Abijah's reign lasted only three years is not stated. He "committed (lit., *walked in*) all the sins his father had done" (1 Kgs. 15:3; 2 Chr. 12:14). Abijah would probably have had an even shorter reign, except for the LORD's promise to David (1 Kgs. 15:3-5).

Second Chronicles 13:3-19 records a decisive victory by Abijah over King Jeroboam of the northern kingdom. Though Jeroboam had twice as many men (2 Chr.13:3), "God routed Jeroboam and all Israel." God's control over the outcome of wars is often stated in Scripture (Josh. 23:10).

The location of this battle by Mt. Zemaraim is not certain, but it was near Bethel, just a few miles north of Judah's territory (Josh. 18:22). After the battle Abijah occupied Bethel and nearby villages. (The border between Judah and Israel frequently floated northward or southward. See 1 Kings 15:17.)

During the battle Abijah boasted on the mountaintop to the armies of Israel about how very "orthodox" the kingdom of Judah was in its religious observances (2 Chr. 13:8-12). Abijah felt security in being a descendant of David, to whom God had given the kingship forever by a "covenant of salt." This may refer to salt as a symbol of preservation, rather than to a particular ritual involving use of salt. (See Numbers 18:19.) As his boasting proceeded, Jeroboam was setting men in position to ambush Abijah. Abijah's boasting in external religious ordinances sounds very hollow. The divine judgment was that "He committed all the sins his father had done." We cannot gain security by keeping rituals or by our connection with godly ancestors, unless we, like them, have a heart that is right with the LORD (Jer. 7:4-10).

7. *King Asa of Judah.*

ASA of Judah — 911–870 B.C. (*Good*)
(1 Kgs. 15:9-24; 2 Chr. 14,15,16)
    a. Beat a million Cushites (Ethiopians).
    b. Made religious reforms.
    c. Backslid a mile (hired Ben-Hadad).

The story of King Asa in Chronicles is longer than his record in Kings. Chronicles records four events in his reign:
    (a) Asa's early period of reform and prosperity (2 Chr. 13:1-8).

(b) Asa's victory over a million Cushites (2 Chr. 14:9-15).

(c) A thorough religious reform (2 Chr. 15:1-19).

(d) Asa's backsliding, in hiring King Ben-Hadad (2 Chr. 16:1-14).

a. *Early prosperity of King Asa* (2 Chr. 14:2-8). After twenty years of rule by evil kings, Judah acquired a king who did what was right — King Asa. He reigned a long time in Jerusalem — forty-one years.

Asa began with religious reforms: "He removed the foreign altars and the high places (*bamoth*), smashed the sacred stones (*masseboth*), and cut down the Asherah poles" (2 Chr. 14:3; compare 2 Kgs. 14:23!). These three types of religious objects were used in Canaanite worship (Ex. 23:24; 1 Kgs. 16:32-33). Asa's reforms resulted in a ten-year period of peace from the LORD.

King Asa said, "The land is still ours, because we have sought the LORD our God; we sought him and he has given us rest on every side" (2 Chr. 14:6-7). Asa built up a very strong army (2 Chr. 14:8).

b. *Asa's victory over a million Cushites* (2 Chr. 14:9-15). King Asa was attacked by a huge army from Africa, led by Zerah the Cushite. *Cush* was the land south of Egypt, also called Ethiopia, and Nubia, and now the Sudan. (See 1 Chronicles 1:8.) The Cushites had been mercenaries in the Egyptian army that raided Judah in the time of King Rehoboam (926 B.C. 2 Chr. 12:3).

The raid by Zerah the Cushite occurred after King Asa's tenth year, about 900 B.C. Asa went out with troops to Mareshah to resist Zerah. Mareshah is about twenty-five miles southwest of Jerusalem, near Lachish, in the Shephelah foothills. Mareshah had been fortified by King Rehoboam in anticipation of such an attack as this (2 Chr. 11:5-8).

Asa had a large army of over 580,000 troops from Judah and Benjamin. But Zerah confronted him with "a thousand thousand" (a million, or some huge number), and three hundred chariots. He had "great numbers of chariots and horsemen" (2 Chr. 14:9; 16:8).

Zerah is not referred to in any known writings other than the Bible. Zerah is not called "king." The king of Egypt at that time was named Osorkon I (924–889 B.C.). Osorkon was a son of King Shishak who invaded Rehoboam. Zerah was probably an Ethiopian mercenary soldier leading an army of Egyptians, Libyans and others (2 Chr. 16:8). Probably they were seeking to steal wealth from Judah as Shishak had. The mention of *camels* in 2 Chronicles 4:15 hints that the army of Zerah included Arab Bedouin fighters.

When King Asa went out to resist Zerah, he called openly upon the Lord for help (2 Chr. 14:11). The Lord struck the Ethiopians before Asa and Judah, and the Lord's victory was total. Asa's army pushed the Cushites southward as far as Gerar (over thirty miles from Mareshah) on the Wadi Besor. Asa destroyed all the villages around Gerar, and carried off a large amount of plunder. This shows that the southern portion of Judah was not at that time friendly to Judah or fully under Judean control. The area was still under Philistine influence. (See 2 Chronicles 21:16.)

KEYS TO VICTORY BY KING ASA (and by us):
1. *Pray* as if everything depended on God.
2. *Work* and fight as if everything depended on us.

---

c. *Asa's thorough religious reforms* (2 Chr. 15:1-19; 1 Kgs. 15:9-15). After King Asa's victory over Zerah, a prophet named Azariah (son of Oded) met Asa, and encouraged him to be strong in the Lord's work. This prophet Azariah is mentioned only in 2 Chronicles 15:1.

Azariah said to Asa and all Judah, "**The Lord is with you when you are with him**." (If we are separated from the Lord, who has left whom?)

Azariah referred to "a long time [when] Israel was without the true God, without a priest to teach" (2 Chr. 14:3; Lev. 10:11). This time was probably the long, godless period of the judges, and perhaps also refers to part of the reigns of Kings Solomon, Rehoboam, and Abijam.

Asa responded to the words of Azariah by removing all the idols from the whole land of Judah and Benjamin, and even up into Ephraim (2 Chr. 15:10-15).

King Asa even deposed his grandmother Maacah from her honored position as queen mother, because she had made a wooden pole, the symbol of the Canaanite goddess Asherah (2 Chr. 15:16-17; 1 Kgs. 15:13). Maacah had been the favorite wife of King Rehoboam (2 Chr.11:21), and the mother of King Abijah, Asa's father (1 Kgs. 15:10). She must have been staunch, outspoken and influential in her idolatry. (Asa's own mother is not named in Scripture.)

King Asa deposed his grandmother for her idolatry.

Jesus said, "Anyone who loves his father or mother more than me is not worthy of me; anyone who loves his son or daughter more than me is not worthy of me" (Matt. 10:37).

King Asa's reforms brought nearly twenty-five years of peace (2 Chr. 15:19; 14:1). God creates peace (Isa. 57:19-21).

   d. *Asa's backsliding, by hiring Ben-Hadad* (2 Chr. 16:1-14; 1 Kgs. 15:16-24). In King Asa's later years Baasha, king of the northern kingdom of Israel, began to encroach upon Asa's kingdom of Judah. Baasha began to push southward into Judah. Perhaps at this time Baasha recaptured Bethel (2 Chr. 13:15). Soon he reached Ramah, which is only six miles north of Jerusalem, and began to dig in and fortify it. He was concerned about his people leaving and entering the territory of Judah. (Compare 1 Kgs. 12:27.)

Asa's reaction to this threat was very disappointing. He hired King Ben-Hadad of Aram (Syria) to attack the northern end of Baasha's kingdom. Asa hired Ben-Hadad with treasures from the LORD's temple! Ben-Hadad was very willing to attack Israel and take some of its land. He took several fortified cities in northern Israel (2 Chr. 16:4; Josh. 19:35). In the years that followed, Asa's son Jehoshaphat had to fight alongside the king of Israel *against* Ben-Hadad!

Baasha did cease attacking Judah, and returned to his capital at Tirzah (1 Kgs. 15:21; 14:17). Asa reoccupied Ramah and fortified the nearby towns of Geba and Mizpah (2 Chr. 16:6). He dug a great pit to protect himself from Baasha (Jer. 41:9).

Why did Asa hire Ben-Hadad to protect himself? In the face of a small invasion by Baasha, Asa showed none of the great faith he once had shown when attacked by a million invaders under Zerah the Cushite! Perhaps Asa's own strength and success as king had gradually eroded away his dependence upon God. His example illustrates the warning "If you think you are standing firm, be careful that you don't fall" (1 Cor. 10:12).

God sent the prophet (seer) Hanani to rebuke Asa: "From now on you will be at war" (2 Chr. 16:9). Asa was enraged at Hanani for this reproof. Asa imprisoned Hanani and oppressed some of the people. He showed the evil that had grown silently in his heart.

In his later years Asa suffered a disease in his feet, "very severe." (Literally, this may mean that the inflammation and swelling had gone "upward" from his feet.) But Asa did not seek help from the LORD, but sought the physicians. (The Egyptians were known for their physicians.) When Asa died, they buried him in the City of David (in Jerusalem; 1 Kgs. 2:10). They covered his body with spices and perfume. But the odor of a corrupted faith can hardly be concealed by perfume.

In spite of his failures in old age, the divine evaluation of King Asa was that "he did what was good and right in the eyes of the LORD" (2 Chr. 14:2). God's grace covers many sins.

8. *King Nadab of Israel.*

NADAB of Israel — 910–909 B.C. (1 Kgs. 15:25-32)
 a. Walked in father's footsteps
 b. Assassinated by Baasha
"Nadab, the Nothing." "Nadab, the Father-Follower."

Jeroboam's son *Nadab* ruled only two years. He was assassinated by Baasha of the tribe of Issachar. Nadab walked in the ways of his father (Jeroboam), who had caused Israel to sin. Baasha killed Nadab while Israel was besieging the Philistine town of Gibbethon (15:27; 16:15). Gibbethon was located three and half miles west of Gezer, or twenty-two miles west of Jerusalem, on the east edge of the Plain of Philistia. Baasha killed Jeroboam's whole family. He did not leave Jeroboam anyone that breathed. This slaughter fulfilled God's threatened punishment, which was spoken by Ahijah, the prophet at Shiloh (1 Kgs. 14:10).

9. *King Baasha of Israel.*

BAASHA of Israel — 909–886 B.C. (1 Kgs. 15:27-16:7)
   a. Destroyed the family of Jeroboam
   b. Fortified Ramah against Asa
   c. Denounced by the prophet Jehu
"Baasha, the Basher." "Baasha, the Barrier-Builder."

Baasha (pronounced BAY´-ah-shah in English, and Bah-SHAH´ in Hebrew) founded the second dynasty of kings over the Northern Kingdom of Israel. The dynasty lasted only twenty-six years, and had only two kings. The kings were warlike, aggressive, and wicked. King Baasha killed the whole family of the former king.

Baasha continued all the sins that the previous dynasty of Jeroboam had practiced (1 Kgs. 15:34; 16:7). He did not fear the judgment of God. He did not learn from the fate of his predecessor that he might suffer the same fate, if he did the same evils.

God pronounced doom upon Baasha and his family through a prophet named Jehu, son of Hanani (1 Kgs. 16:1,7, 12; 2 Chr. 19:2; 20:34). "I will make your house like that of Jeroboam." "Dogs will eat those belonging to Baasha . . . and the birds of the air will feed on those who die . . ." (1 Kgs. 16:4).

There was war between King Asa of Judah and Baasha of Israel throughout their reigns (1 Kgs. 15:16). Baasha attempted to encroach upon the land of Judah and occupy territory south of Bethel to Ramah. (See notes above on 1 Kings 15:17-22, in the section on King Asa of Judah.)

10. *King Elah of Israel.*

ELAH of Israel — 885–886 B.C. (1 Kgs. 16:8-14)
   a. Assassinated by Zimri
"Elah, the Alcoholic."

Baasha, king of Israel, was succeeded by his son *Elah*, who reigned only two years, and was assassinated by *Zimri*, one of his officials who had command of half of his chariots. Zimri killed off Baasha's whole family, as the prophet Jehu had foretold.

At the time of his death, King Elah was in Tirzah getting drunk (lit., "drinking *himself* drunk") at the house of Arza, who was "the man in charge of the palace (lit., *house*) at Tirzah."

"It is not for kings . . . to drink wine, nor for rulers to crave beer, lest they drink and forget what the law decrees" (Prov. 31:4-5).

---

11. *King Zimri of Israel.*

ZIMRI of Israel — 885 B.C. (1 Kgs. 16:9-12, 15-20)
   a. Destroyed the family of Baasha
"Zimri, the Zapper." "Zimri, the Royal Roast."

King Zimri (ZIM´-rye in English; Zim-REE´ in Hebrew) reigned only seven days in the capital of Tirzah. In those few days he killed off the entire family of the former dynasty of Baasha.

The army of Israel was camped at the town of Gibbethon on the edge of Philistia (15:27). According to Josephus, Zimri took advantage of the absence of the army from Tirzah to kill Elah (*Antiquities*, VIII, xii, 4 [VIII, 308]. *Omri*, the commander, left Gibbethon and laid siege to Tirzah to do away with Zimri. Zimri burned down the palace at Tirzah over himself.

Though his reign was very brief, Zimri still "walked in the way of Jeroboam, and in his sin" (1 Kgs. 16:19). The worship of the golden calves was very ingrained.

As brief as his reign was, Zimri gained a reputation as a killer and assassin. Queen Jezebel later called Jehu, who killed her and her son, a "Zimri" (2 Kgs. 9:31).

12. *King Omri of Israel.*

OMRI of Israel — 885-874 B.C. (1 Kgs. 16:17, 21-28)
  a. Mighty
  b. Made Samaria the capital

The third dynasty of Israel was one of its two *high* points in military strength. This third dynasty was its *low* point in its idolatry and social oppression. Four kings ruled: OMRI, AHAB, AHAZIAH, and then his brother JEHORAM, for a period of forty-four years.

Little is told of Omri in Scripture. He defeated a rival named Tibni for title to the throne (16:21-22). He was mighty (16:27). He bought a large hill site and made it into the new capital, *Samaria.* Omri is chiefly famous as the father of King Ahab, who followed him. Omri did evil in the eyes of the LORD more than all those before him. Micah 6:16 says of the country of Judah, "You have observed the statutes of *Omri* and the practices of Ahab's house." Omri was a bad influence.

Omri is known from several archaeological inscriptions, which add to the historical background of his reign. Jehu, "son of Omri," paid tribute to the Assyrian king Shalmaneser III about 840 B.C. (*Ancient Near East*, Vol. 1, p. 191). The Assyrians called King Jehu (841-814) the "son of *Omri*," though Jehu was founder of the next dynasty. Either the name of *Omri* was so famous that it came to be used to refer to the country of Israel in all periods, or perhaps Jehu actually was the son of Omri and half-brother to Ahab. Omri is mentioned in the Moabite inscription of King Mesha (about 849 B.C.), which says that Omri afflicted the land of Moab many years (*Ancient Near East*, Vol. 1, p. 209).

Omri's choice of the hill of *Samaria* as Israel's next capital was a good one. Samaria lies eight miles WNW of Shechem. The hill is isolated, without any "saddle" (ridge) of land connecting it to other heights. It is high, and its sides are steep enough to make it hard to attack. The top was fortified with a double (casemate) wall nearly thirty feet across, and enclosing about twelve acres. The king of Assyria spent three years besieging Samaria before it fell (2 Kgs. 17:5-6).

13. *King Ahab of Israel.*

AHAB of Israel — 874–853 B.C. (1 Kgs. 16:29–22:40)
  a. Jezebel and Baal worship
  b. Contest with Elijah
  c. Two victories over Ben-Hadad
  d. Naboth's vineyard
  e. Killed in battle at Ramoth Gilead

---

a. *Ahab, Israel's worst king* (1 Kgs. 16:29-34). Ahab was the most famous king of the northern kingdom, Israel, probably because of his infamous wife Jezebel. He "did more evil in the eyes of the LORD than any of those before him" (16:30). Not only did Ahab continue the golden calf worship of Jeroboam, but he introduced the worship of *Baal* as Israel's state religion. Baal worship was brought into Israel by Ahab's wife Jezebel, the daughter of *Eth-baal*, king of Sidon, a city in Phoenicia. Ahab also made an *Asherah*, a wooden pole set up as a cult symbol of the Canaanite goddess Asherah, one of several godesses of sex and fertility.

During the reign of Ahab a man named Hiel rebuilt the city of Jericho which Joshua had destroyed over five hundred years before. Hiel suffered the punishments foretold by Joshua, the deaths of his oldest and youngest sons (1 Kgs. 16:34; Josh. 6:26). God does not forget His warnings nor His promises.

Ahab was a great builder in Israel, and a great warrior in battles. Ahab added on to the cult center at Dan that Jeroboam built. He rebuilt the city of Megiddo on a new city plan and made it into a chariot city. Storage buildings were built at Hazor. The impressive palace ruins at Samaria are the work of Ahab, at least in part. (See *The New Encyclopedia of Archaeological Excavations in the Holy Land*, Vols. 1, 3 (1993), Articles on "Dan" and "Megiddo," pp. 329, 1020–1021.)

The inscriptions of the Assyrian king Shalmaneser III (the "Monolith Inscriptions") tell that Ahab the Israelite and Hadadezer of Damascus were the principal leaders of a coalition of twelve kings that fought against Shalmaneser at Karkar (on the Orontes River north of Israel). Ahab alone contributed 10,000 foot soldiers in that battle (853 B.C.). (*Ancient Near East*, Vol. 1, p. 190.)

b. *Elijah resists King Ahab* (1 Kgs. 17:1). At this time of outward prosperity and inward decay, the LORD sent to Israel a great but unusual prophet, *ELIJAH*. He was the most dramatic prophet of the Old Testament. He came from the village of Tishbeh, in the cultural backwoods east of the Jordan. He wore a garment of hair with a leather belt around his waist (2 Kgs. 1:8). He was a man charged with divine feelings. "He prayed earnestly that it would not rain, and it did not rain on the land for three and half years" (James 5:17). Elijah truly wanted to see Ahab defeated, and the LORD exalted. Elijah appeared at Samaria with the news: "There will be neither dew nor rain in the next few years except at my word." Dew is common in Israel because of the sea breezes and the cool air from Mt. Hermon.

c. *Elijah protected at the brook Kerith and at Zarephath* (1 Kgs. 17:2-24). Elijah hid from Ahab at the Wadi Kerith east(?) of the Jordan. The identification of the brook Kerith is uncertain. The text says only that it was "before" Jordan (17:5). "Before" usually means "east of" when referring to places, but not always (Josh. 18:16; 13:25). We think the deep canyon of the Wadi Qelt (Kelt) west of Jericho was very probably the "Kerith Ravine." (See J.W. McGarvey, *Lands of the Bible* [Nashville: Gospel Advocate, 1957], p. 234.) There Elijah was

Life of Elijah

1. *Tishbeh* (in Gilead). Home of Elijah (1 Kgs. 17:1).

2. *Samaria*. Predicts drought (1 Kgs. 17:1).

3. *Cherith* (Kerith). Fed by ravens (1 Kgs. 17:2-7).

4. *Zarephath*. At widow's house (1 Kgs. 17:8-24).

5. Somewhere in *Israel*. Meets Obadiah and Ahab (1 Kgs. 18:1-18).

6. *Mt. Carmel*. Fire upon altar (1 Kgs. 18:19-45).

7. *Jezreel*. Flees from Jezebel (1 Kgs. 18:45; 19:1-2).

8. *Beersheba*. Fed by angel (1 Kgs. 19:3-7).

9. *Mt. Horeb*. Still small voice (1 Kgs. 19:8-18).

10. *Abel Meholah*. Elisha called (1 Kgs. 19:19-21).

11. *Jezreel*. Ahab denounced in Naboth's vineyard (1 Kgs. 21:17-29).

12. Somewhere in *Israel*. Meets King Ahaziah's messengers going to Ekron (2 Kgs. 1:1-16).

13. *East of Jordan*. Elijah taken to heaven (2 Kgs. 2:1-12).

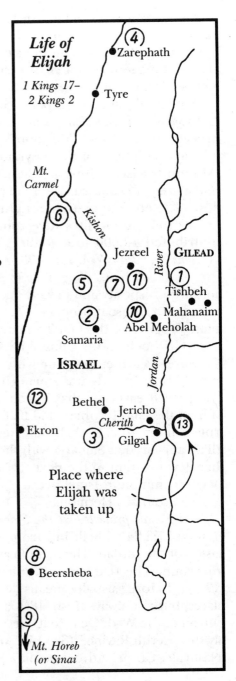

Life of Elijah

1 Kings 17– 2 Kings 2

Zarephath ④

Tyre

Mt. Carmel

⑥

Kishon

Jezreel   GILEAD

⑤ ⑦ ⑪   Tishbeh ①

② ⑩ Mahanaim

Abel Meholah

Samaria

ISRAEL

Jordan

⑫ Bethel

Jericho

Cherith

Ekron ③ Gilgal

⑬

Place where Elijah was taken up

⑧
Beersheba

⑨

Mt. Horeb (or Sinai

fed by ravens which brought him meat and bread each day. (Even the unclean birds helped Elijah defeat Ahab!)

When the brook Kerith dried up, Elijah was sent up into Phoenicia, to the village of Zarephath (Sarepta) on the Great Sea coast south of Sidon (1 Kgs. 17:8). At Zarephath Elijah stayed with a widow and her son. Jesus said, "There were many widows in Israel in Elijah's time . . . yet Elijah was not sent to any of them, but to a widow in Zarephath in the region of Sidon" (Luke 4:25-26). The LORD provided them food until the drought was over. Elijah raised her son back to life when he became ill and died.

Elijah gave the woman a severe test of faith, asking her to *first* make a small cake of bread for him out of her meager supply of flour (1 Kgs. 17:13). There was always enough flour (meal) and oil for another day.

> **"Seek *first* his kingdom and his righteousness, and all these things will be given to you as well"** (Matt. 6:33).

When Elijah resurrected the widow's son, he cried to the LORD, "O LORD, my God, let this boy's *life* return to him!" . . . and the boy's *life* returned to him (1 Kgs. 17:21-22). The word for *life* here is *nephesh*. It is often translated "soul" and probably should be here also. Compare Genesis 35:18; 2 Peter 1:13-14; Psalm 16:10. It is true that individually we *are* souls; but it is also true that we *have* souls.

d. *The contest at Mt. Carmel* (1 Kgs. 18). Elijah was sent back to Israel to confront King Ahab again. Elijah met Obadiah, the God-fearing servant of Ahab (18:3-4). Obadiah had saved a hundred of the LORD's prophets when Jezebel was killing the prophets. Obadiah was fearful Elijah would disappear again when he reported to Ahab that he had seen him (18:12).

When Elijah met Ahab, Ahab said, "Is that you, you *troubler* of Israel?" Evil men usually consider anyone who rebukes them a troubler, when it is they who have caused the trouble upon the land.

Elijah called upon Ahab to hold a dramatic test. Go to Mount Carmel. Let the priests of Baal pray to Baal to send fire upon the sacrifice on his altar. Elijah would pray for the LORD to send fire on His altar.

Mt. Carmel is the large "hump" on the coast of Israel. It is a ridge about fourteen miles long, six hundred feet high near the coast, and rising to a summit of 1,742 feet. On its high point is the traditional location of Elijah's sacrifice. It is named *Muhraqa*, meaning "the place of burning." There at the side of Mt. Carmel, the small brook Kishon is scarcely a quarter of a mile away (18:40). A large flat area (now an olive orchard) is there on the slope of the mountain, large enough for four hundred and fifty prophets of Baal, plus four hundred prophets of Asherah, and many spectators.

Elijah mocked the prophets of Baal as they called upon their non-existent god to do something (18:27-29). "The One enthroned in heaven laughs; the Lord scoffs at them" (Ps. 2:4).

The LORD's triumph was total (18:38). Only a burned-out hole remained where the altar and sacrifice had been.

The prophets of Baal were slaughtered by the brook Kishon. The Baal prophets had killed little children and God's prophets (Jer. 32:35; Deut. 12:31). We must not feel they were unjustly slain.

Elijah said to Ahab, "There is the sound of a heavy rain" (18:41). No rain was yet falling, but Elijah's faith in God's revelation was total. "He [Elijah] prayed, and the heavens gave rain, and the earth produced its crops" (James 5:18).

Elijah climbed to the top of Carmel and sent his servant up seven times to look toward the sea. Each time the servant reported, "There is nothing there." The seven ascents up Mt. Carmel showed Elijah's total faith, and also focused attention strongly on what was about to happen. The seventh time the servant said, "A cloud as small as a man's hand is rising from the sea" (18:44). Soon "the sky grew black with clouds . . . a heavy rain came." Ahab in his chariot raced off Mt. Carmel down the twisty road and eastward twenty miles to the town of Jezreel. (Jezreel was Ahab's winter palace. In summer it is uncomfortably hot.)

The power (lit., "hand") of the LORD was upon Elijah, and "he ran ahead of Ahab all the way to Jezreel."

Elijah was soon to learn that miracles — even undeniable ones — do not always lead people to repent. The heart must be touched first before the mind and the will respond.

ELIJAH — A type of JOHN the baptizer
(Mal. 4:5; Matt. 11:14; 17:10-13; John 1:21)

1. **Both were rustic** (2 Kgs. 1:8; Matt. 1:21).

2. **Both preached judgment** (1 Kgs. 17:1; Matt. 3:7-10).

3. **Both denounced a king** (1 Kgs. 21:19; Matt. 14:4).

4. **Both were brought down by a woman.**

5. **Both became discouraged** (1 Kgs. 19:4, 10; Matt. 11:2-3).

6. **Both were followed by a greater prophet** — Elijah by Elisha, and John by Jesus (1 Kgs. 19:9; Matt. 3:11-12).

---

e. *Elijah flees to Mt. Horeb* (1 Kgs. 19:1-18). When Jezebel heard from Ahab everything which Elijah had done on Mt. Carmel, she was not intimidated, not even impressed. She threatened that by the next day Elijah would be dead like the Baal prophets.

Elijah was afraid and ran for his life. He ran to Beersheba, at least one hundred and twenty miles southward, in the kingdom of Judah. Probably he neither ate nor slept during the trip. At Beersheba (which is in the north part of the Negev desert), he went a day's journey out into the desert, and lay down under a broom tree and wished to die. (The broom tree is a desert bush with sparse slender leaves. It grows only to twelve feet high. The shade it provides is scant, but welcome. It burns well and makes good charcoal.)

An angel fed Elijah twice with baked bread and water.

"The *angel* of the LORD encamps around those who fear him, and he delivers them" (Ps. 34:7).

Elijah journeyed on for forty days to Mt. Horeb, also called Mt. Sinai. This was a journey of two hundred and fifty miles, through rugged and barren country. At Horeb he went into a cave and spent the night. We assume that Mt. Horeb is the same mountain (Jebel Musa) now called Mt. Sinai (Deut. 4:15; Ex. 19:20). A cave (grotto) and chapel on top of the mountain is pointed out as the grotto of Elijah, though without proof.

**The LORD's question to Elijah (and to us) —
"What are you doing here?"** (1 Kgs. 19:9, 13).

Elijah felt that he was the only person left alive who was trying to serve the LORD (1 Kgs. 19:10). But there were seven thousand in Israel who had not bowed their knees to Baal (19:18). We must not fall into the temptation of feeling we are all alone and helpless.

The LORD wanted Elijah to go out of the cave, "for the LORD is about to pass by" (19:11). At Sinai Moses had desired to see God, but Elijah was too depressed to wish to do anything except hide. Elijah saw and felt a powerful wind, and then an earthquake, and then a fire. God's presence is sometimes shown by these violent events (Nahum 1:3-6). But God spoke to Elijah in a "gentle whisper" (a "still, small voice") (19:12).

Elijah was sent back to Israel with the command to anoint three people:

---

1. Anoint **HAZAEL** king over Aram (Syria) (1 Kgs. 19:15).
2. Anoint **JEHU** king over Israel (19:16).
3. Anoint **ELISHA** as the prophet to succeed you.

(These men would be God's agents to punish evildoers.)

When Elijah returned to Israel, he came to Abel Meholah, near the center of the Jordan valley west of the river. There he cast his cloak (mantle) around Elisha, as a symbol of his call. Elisha was a busy working man. But he gave his oxen and implements to the people for food, and set out to follow Elijah. In many respects Elisha became a greater prophet than Elijah.

    f. *Two victories by Ahab over Ben-Hadad* (1 Kgs. 20).

King Ahab's Three Wars with Ben-Hadad (king of Aram)

1. At *Samaria* (1 Kgs. 20:1-21) — Result: Victory for Ahab.
2. At *Aphek* (1 Kgs. 20:22-43) — Results: Victory for Ahab; Ben-Hadad spared.
3. At *Ramoth Gilead* (1 Kgs. 22:1-38) — Results: King Jehoshaphat was almost killed. King Ahab was killed.

    The power of the land of Aram (Syria) increased greatly after the deaths of David and Solomon, who had subjugated Aram. (See Period IX, Section A, 3.) During the early part of the Divided Kingdom period, Aram was Israel's strongest and most determined enemy. King Ahab of Israel had three significant wars with Ben-Hadad, king of Aram.

    In these three battles it seems that the LORD was showing special favor to Ahab, as if He was saying, "See what I am able to do for you, and want to do for you. Why do you not serve me?"

    Some striking and impressive statements were made in these battles. Ahab said to Ben-Hadad as he threatened to annihilate Samaria, "One who puts on his armor should not boast like one who takes it off" (1 Kgs. 20:11).

    The Syrians were puzzled as to why they were defeated in their first battle at Samaria. Their officials with great wisdom (?) advised the king, "Their (the Israelites') gods are gods of the *hills*. That is why they were too strong for us. But if we fight them on the *plains*, surely we will be stronger than they" (1 Kgs. 20:23). [Samaria is in a very hilly area.] The LORD, who fills heaven and earth (Jer. 23:24) took this as a personal insult, and the Syrians were defeated at *Aphek* the following year.

    Aphek (1 Kgs. 20:26) was located about four miles east of the Sea of Galilee, on the mostly level plateau of the Golan

Heights. Its modern name is *Fiq*. It is east of the ruins of Hippos (Susita).

After his great victory at Aphek, Ahab learned that King Ben-Hadad was still living. Ahab said, "He is my *brother*" (20:32). This is a surprising statement, seeing that Ben-Hadad had tried to destroy Ahab in two recent wars. The reason for Ahab's favor to Ben-Hadad was probably his fear of the rising power of the nation of Assyria, which lay east of Aram. Ahab had previously (853 B.C.) been allied with the Arameans in a battle against the Assyrian king Shalmaneser III. Ahab needed a strong and friendly buffer state between Israel and Assyria, and Aram was that buffer state.

The LORD had determined that King Ben-Hadad should die (1 Kgs. 20:42; Amos 1:3-4). For sparing Ben-Hadad, Ahab was himself sentenced to death: "It is your life for his life" (20:42). After hearing this judgment, Ahab went back to his palace in Samaria sullen and angry (20:43).

g. *Naboth's vineyard* (1 Kgs. 21). Near the palace of Ahab in Jezreel was a vineyard belonging to Naboth the Jezreelite.

Jezreel is located in the southeastern part of the Plain of Esdraelon, just north of Mt. Gilboa. Ahab desired the vineyard, but Naboth would not part with his family heritage. With the cruel help of Jezebel, Ahab killed Naboth and took possession of the vineyard. Naboth's sons were killed, as well as Naboth (2 Kgs. 9:26). In Israel not even a king could seize a man's land without cause, but in Phoenicia (where Jezebel came from) the king or queen was accustomed to taking whatever they wanted by any means they chose to employ.

Elijah the prophet appeared at Jezreel and denounced Ahab. "This is what the LORD says: In the place where dogs licked up Naboth's blood, dogs will lick up your blood — yes yours!" "I will make your house like that of Jeroboam son of Nebat and (like) that of Baasha." "Concerning Jezebel the LORD says: 'Dogs will devour Jezebel by the wall [or rampart] of Jezreel' " (21:19-23).

When Ahab heard these words, he tore his clothes, put on sackcloth and fasted. He lay in sackcloth and went around meekly (quietly), as if he feared that any noise might arouse

God to strike him. God's gracious response was that because Ahab had humbled himself "I will not bring this disaster in his day, but I will bring it on his house in the days of his son" [Jehoram]. See 2 Kings 9:24-26. This illustrates how God punishes the children for the sins of the fathers, but shows love to those who love him and keep his commandments (Ex. 20:5-6).

The fearsome prophecies concerning Ahab and Jezebel were fulfilled completely. See 1 Kings 22:37-38 and 2 Kings 9:30-37.

    h. *Alliance of Ahab and Jehoshaphat* (1 Kgs. 22:1-4; 2 Chr. 18:1-3). King Jehoshaphat of Judah began to reign in the fourth year of Ahab. Jehoshaphat went down to see the king of Israel, and while there he agreed to join forces with Ahab to recapture the city of Ramoth in Gilead. Ramoth Gilead (*the heights of Gilead*) lay about thirty miles east of the Jordan River, up near the Yarmuk River, on the frontier of Israel by Aram (Syria). Wars were frequently fought there with Syria for possession of this town (2 Kgs. 8:28; 9:14; 2 Chr. 22:5).

The early kings of Judah — Rehoboam, Abijam, and Asa — had continual wars with the northern kingdom of Israel (1 Chr. 12:15; 1 Kgs. 15:16). King Jehoshaphat himself was a very good and godly king. But *Jehoshaphat made alliance* with the northern kingdom (1 Kgs. 22:44). Jehoshaphat joined forces with both Ahab and his son Jehoram in battles (2 Kgs. 3:7; 2 Chr. 18:1-3). He joined King Ahaziah (also Ahab's son) in building a fleet of ships (2 Chr. 20:35). The alliance of Judah and Israel continued down until the time of King Joash. Jehu the prophet rebuked Jehoshaphat for these alliances: "Should you help the wicked and love those who hate the LORD?" (2 Chr. 19:2).

King Jehoshaphat's son ***JEHORAM*** *married* ***ATHALIAH,*** the daughter of Ahab and Jezebel (2 Kgs. 8:18, 26-27; 2 Chr. 21:6). This marriage led to the destruction of Jehoram, and his son Ahaziah, and almost the entire royal family of Jehoshaphat.

Jehoshaphat's alliances with the family of Ahab led to the SHIPWRECK of his fleet and his family (1 Kgs. 22:48; 2 Chr. 22:10). When Jehoshaphat's daughter-in-law, Athaliah, took over the queenship after her son was killed, she killed all the royal family of the house of Judah, except for one little son (Joash).

i. *Prophecy of Micaiah against Ahab* (1 Kgs. 22:5-28; 2 Chr. 18:4-27). Before Jehoshaphat and Ahab went out to battle to recapture Ramoth Gilead, Jehoshaphat asked that they inquire of a prophet of the LORD. Ahab's four hundred false prophets all urged them to go, and promised victory. One brave — but hated — prophet foretold that in the battle Israel would be scattered like sheep without a shepherd. The LORD said, "These people have no master" (1 Kgs. 21:17). With these words Micaiah clearly predicted the death of Ahab. The false prophets were quite upset, and one Zedekiah slapped Micaiah. Ahab sent Micaiah back to prison, to be fed on bread and water "until I return safely." Micaiah declared, "If you ever return safely, the LORD has not spoken through me" (1 Kgs. 21:28).

Lying spirits enticed Ahab to go out to battle, so he would be killed (1 Kgs. 21:21-22). Those who will not receive the love of the truth may receive *powerful delusions*, so that they will believe a lie and be condemned (2 Thess. 2:10-11).

---

j. *King Ahab killed at Ramoth Gilead* (1 Kgs. 21:29-40; 2 Chr. 18:28-34). In the battle at Ramoth Gilead King Jehoshaphat was nearly killed (21:32-33). Ahab was killed by an arrow shot into the air at random. Micaiah's prophecy came true. Ahab's blood in the chariot was washed out, and the dogs licked up his blood, as the word of the LORD through Elijah had foretold (1 Kgs. 21:19).

"Do not be deceived. God cannot be mocked. A man reaps what he sows" (Gal. 6:6). King Ahab certainly did.

First Kings 2:39 mentions Ahab's house of *ivory*. In the excavations at Samaria about five hundred pieces of ivory were found, of which two hundred were carved, and apparently had been inlaid into woodwork or furniture. Also a four inch ivory lion was found in the palace of Ahab and Jezebel. (See Richard D. Barnett, "Ancient Ivories," in *Qedem* # 14 [1982], p. 49. Also Harry Rimmer, *Dead Men Tell Tales*, p. 227.)

14. *King Jehoshaphat of Judah.*

JEHOSHAPHAT of Judah — 873-848 B.C. (*Good*)
(1 Kgs. 22:41-50; 2 Chr. 20:31-21:1)
    a. Appointed righteous judges
    b. Alliance with Ahab
    c. Victory over Moab and Ammon
    d. Shipwreck
    e. Went with Jehoram to fight Moab

King Jehoshaphat of Judah was one of the few good kings of Judah. "He did what was right in the eyes of the LORD" (1 Kgs. 22:43). At least twice he sent out religious teachers to teach the law of the LORD to the people (2 Chr. 17:7-9; 19:4). He appointed honest, God-fearing judges in the land (2 Chr. 19:6-10). (Jehoshaphat's name meant "*Jehovah is judge*." His name matched his actions.)

Jehoshaphat's one failure was his making the alliance with Ahab and his family. Because Jehoshaphat did this, his son Jehoram was united in marriage to Athaliah, daughter of Ahab and Jezebel. When she took control, she killed all the royal family except one son. (More about Jehoshaphat is told below.)

15. *King Ahaziah of Israel.*

AHAZIAH of Israel — 853-852 B.C.
(1 Kgs. 22:51-53; 2 Kgs. 1:1-18)
    a. Accident and injury
    b. Elijah predicts his death

King Ahab's son Ahaziah never learned anything from all the discipline his father had suffered in his conflict with the LORD. Ahaziah continued to worship the idols of Jeroboam, and also he served and worshiped Baal and provoked the LORD to anger, just as his father had done.

The nation of Moab rebelled against Israel's control after the death of Ahab (2 Kgs. 1:1). King David had subdued Moab (2 Sam. 8:2). Moab remained under Israelite control until the death of Ahab. The rebellion of Moab was led by King Mesha, and reached its full bloom in the time of Israel's King Jehoram (2 Kgs. 3:4-5).

Ahab's son Ahaziah had a fall and injury (2 Kgs. 1:2). He sent messengers to the town of Ekron to the temple of Baal-Zebub to learn if he would recover from his injury. This act shows a complete rejection of the LORD Yahweh. *Ba'al* means *lord*, or master. *Zebub* means habitation, residence, or dwelling; but as a collective word it means *flies* (Eccl. 10:1). *Ba'al Zebub* therefore meant *lord of flies* (as in LXX). The name is a distortion of *Ba'al Zebul*, meaning "lordly Ba'al." In the New Testament it appears as *Beelzebub* (Matt. 12:24).

The messengers from King Ahaziah met Elijah the prophet, who predicted the death of Ahaziah. Elijah knew what the king's mission was and the route and time of the messengers' journey. This miraculous knowledge should have impressed Ahaziah so much that he would stop his stubborn idolatry, but it did not. Three groups of fifty men, each with a captain, attempted to compel Elijah to come with them, and twice the groups were consumed by fire. (Courtesy and humility saved the third captain!) The King James Version of Luke 9:54 refers to this event: "Lord, wilt thou that we command fire to come down from heaven, and consume them, even as Elias [Elijah] did?"

King Ahaziah died. He had no son, and was succeeded by his brother named *Jehoram*, another son of Ahab and Jezebel (2 Kgs. 1:17).

16. *Elijah taken up to heaven* (2 Kgs. 2:1-18). In our minds we walk with Elijah and Elisha down the lonely road from Gilgal (probably the Gilgal eight miles north of Bethel), to

Bethel, to Jericho and on to the Jordan. We share Elisha's pain at the coming departure of his master Elijah, but also his exhilaration in awareness that God's power was sweeping over. Other prophets too were allowed to know of it (2:3,5). A deep flowing river did not slow the progress of holy prophets going to meet God (2:8).

Elisha asked for a "double portion" of Elijah's spirit (2:10), not meaning that he hoped to be twice as great as Elijah, but that he might have a greater prophetic spirit than most of the prophets at that time (Gen. 48:22; Deut. 21:17).

Elijah was taken up to heaven not in the chariot of fire, but by the whirlwind. The chariot served to separate Elijah from Elisha.

The chariot of fire and the tornadic wind that took Elijah away make us ask, "Will it be like that when all the dead arise?" (1 Thess. 5:17) Yes, though there will be differences (Matt. 16:27; 25:31). Christ shall come in great glory.

Elijah truly had been "the chariots and horsemen of Israel" (2:12). Neither kings nor nations had power against Elijah.

**Only Enoch and Elijah have been taken
from earth without dying.**

The "company of the prophets" (literally, "sons of the prophets") that met Elisha coming back from the Jordan carrying Elijah's cloak wanted to go and search for Elijah. We should not, as they did, conceive of God as limited to the radius of our vision.

17. *Elisha, the miracle worker* (2 Kgs. 2:19-25). Elisha did over fifteen miracles that are described in some detail. Several of these resembled the miracles of Christ. (Prepare a list of his miracles, from 2 Kings 2 through 13.) His first three miracles were (1) parting the Jordan (2:14); (2) healing the waters of Jericho (2:19-22), and (3) calling down a curse upon the youths who mocked him and sending two bears after them (2:23-25).

The spring at Jericho is now called Elisha's Fountain (and also called the Sultan's Spring) and still flows with abundant wholesome water and irrigates several hundred acres.

The trip from Jericho to Bethel is twenty-five miles uphill. Mockers greeted Elisha there. Sadly, disrespect for worthy men is common in youths, unless they have been taught respect by godly fathers. The "youths" who were cursed are called "little" youths (in the Hebrew). (Also see NRSV.) The Hebrew word for "youth" (*na'ar*) (2:23) is applied to men like Rehoboam (age 41; 2 Chr. 13:7) and Joseph (age 17; Gen. 37:2), but also to younger lads (Gen. 21:12).

18. *King Jehoshaphat's greatness* (2 Chr. 17, 19, 20). The books of Kings tell little about King Jehoshaphat of Judah (1 Kgs. 22:41-45). (See previous notes [IX, 13, h].) The books of Chronicles tell much about Jehoshaphat.

a. *Great strength and godliness* (2 Chr. 17). Jehoshaphat was strong because the LORD was with him (17:3). His heart was devoted to the ways of the LORD (17:6). He sent out officials to teach the people from the book of the law of the LORD (17:9). He built forts and store cities in Judah (17:12). His commanders were powerful leaders of thousands. One commander named Amasiah willingly offered himself unto the LORD, and with him two hundred thousand mighty men of valor (2 Chr. 17:16). Even warriors may be dedicated servants of God.

b. *God-fearing judges were appointed* (2 Chr. 19). Jehoshaphat told the judges, "Consider carefully what you do, because you are not judging for man, but for the LORD" (19:6).

c. *Victory over Moab and Ammon* (2 Chr. 20). Jehoshaphat was invaded by armies of Moabites, Ammonites, and Edomites (from Mt. Seir). Jehoshaphat prayed a long prayer for deliverance (20:5-12). He said that the LORD had not allowed Israel to invade these nations when they came out of Egypt, but Israel had passed around them (20:10). A prophet named Jahaziel said, "You will not have to fight this battle . . . stand firm and see the deliverance (lit., *salvation*) the LORD will give you" (20:17). (These words are like those Moses spoke to Israel beside the Red Sea [Ex. 14:13].) Jehoshaphat appointed men to sing to the LORD and praise Him as they went out to face the enemies (20:21). The invading Moabites and Ammonites attacked the Edomites with them; and then they helped to destroy one another (20:23). Jehoshaphat's men spent three days collecting plunder, and on the fourth day they assembled in the Valley of Beracah (meaning *Blessing*) to praise the LORD. This is a green valley between Bethlehem and Hebron.

19. *Moab revolts* (2 Kgs. 3). *Joram* (also spelled *Jehoram*), son of Ahab, became king over Israel after the death of his brother Ahaziah (1:17). Jehoram was not quite as evil as his father, but he did continue to cling to the sins of Jeroboam. The king of Moab revolted from the control of Israel in his time (1:1; 3:4). (See notes on 1:1.)

JEHORAM* of Israel — 852–841 B.C.
(2 Kgs. 1:17; 3:1-3; chs. 3-9)
    a. King Mesha of Moab revolted
    b. Ministry of Elisha
    c. Siege and famine at Samaria
    d. Wounded at Ramoth Gilead
    e. Killed by Jehu
*Judah also had a king named *Jehoram*. He was a brother-in-law of this Jehoram.

The revolt of Moab was led by its king named *Mesha*. He is famous because his own record of this revolt has been found on a black stone slab nearly four feet tall at Dibon east of the Dead Sea. The stone is called the Moabite Stone. Mesha gives credit to the Moabite god *Chemosh* for his victory (?) over Israel. He tells how he retook city after city from the Israelites. He does NOT tell what the Bible tells, how he was nearly defeated in an attack by Kings Jehoram of Israel and Jehoshaphat of Judah, and how he had to sacrifice his first-born son on the wall of his city to deter the invasion of his land (2 Kgs. 3:26-27).

The Moabite Stone contains the names of twenty-one Bible people and places, including the name of Yahweh, God of Israel, and King Omri. The Bible is a historical book, and trustworthy.

On their way to fight the Moabites, the Israelites traveled around the south end of the Dead Sea, and ran out of water in that very desolate area (3:9). The prophet Elisha was present with the army and instructed them that they should dig ditches, which would fill with water (3:16-20). Elisha was not very willing to prophesy for Jehoram of Israel, but he would speak to help Jehoshaphat (3:14).

Moab was nearly defeated (3:24-25). In a desperate move to save himself, the king of Moab sacrificed his firstborn son on the city wall (3:27). This barbaric custom of sacrificing a son to save a city was practiced by Canaanites on numerous occasions. Canaanite inscriptions have been found which tell of it. (See *Biblical Archaeology Review*, Nov.–Dec. 1986, pp. 50-61, for an interesting article about the Moabite Stone, and a translation of it, and quotations of Canaanite texts about sacrificing a son.)

20. *Miracles by Elisha* (2 Kgs. 4). 2 Kings chapter four tells of four miracles by Elisha, miracles that have heart-touching features in them. Elisha was much more of a pastor who lived among his people than was Elijah, who was often out of sight for long periods and then appeared for dramatic confrontations.

a. *The widow's oil increased* (2 Kgs. 4:1-7). The destitute woman had nothing in her house except a small jar of oil. But she had faith to borrow many jars when Elisha told her to. From the little jar she poured oil and filled all the borrowed vessels. She received just as much oil as she had faith to go and borrow vessels to put the oil in. "According to your faith it will be done to you" (Matt. 9:29). Often we limit how greatly God might bless us by our own small faith, as shown by the small goals we seek after.

> "I'm empty, LORD, But full thou art.
> So on my part, I only bring My jar or thing.
> I know that thou Wilt fill it now,

As full as faith will thee allow.
Please fill my jar, My EVERY jar."

b. *The Shunammite's son restored to life* (2 Kgs. 4:8-37; 8:1-2). Elisha was appreciative of the hospitality of a "well-to-do" woman (lit., a *great* woman). She lived at Shunem, a village on the south side of the Hill of Moreh in the Valley of Esdraelon. Elisha passed through her village and stayed at her home when he made his pastoral circuits. He granted her the gift of a SON (4:17), and then later brought the son back to life, after he had died from what sounds like a heat stroke (4:18). The story is full of tender emotion and suspense. The story seems like a foreshadowing of Christ, who resurrected the son of a widow at Nain (Luke 7:11-15).

c. *"Death in the pot!"* (2 Kgs. 4:38-41). Elisha made harmless a pot of stew containing shredded gourds that the "company (lit., *sons*) of the prophets" were eating during a famine. They cried out, "O man of God, there is death in the pot!" Those who seek to serve God will often be poor by the world's standards. But there is divine power in God and in His Prophet (Acts 3:20, 22). "There was *nothing harmful* in the pot," literally, "not an evil thing."

d. *Feeding of a hundred* (2 Kgs. 4:42-44). The miracle of feeding a hundred men with twenty "loaves" (each loaf just an individual serving) has several remarkable resemblances to the story of Jesus feeding the five thousand (John 6:1-13).

(1) There were few pieces of bread (2 Kgs. 4:42; John 6:9).
(2) The men were counted (2 Kgs. 4:43; John 6:10).
(3) Skepticism was expressed (2 Kgs. 4:43; John 6:9).
(4) Bread was left over (2 Kgs. 4:44; John 6:13).

21. *Naaman the leper* (2 Kgs. 5). The LORD gave victories to some non-Israelite kingdoms and people (like Naaman), even though the LORD's main attention in the Mosaic dispensation was upon Israel (2 Kgs. 5:1). God planned to bless *all nations* (Gen. 22:18).

Human greatness cannot prevent even the mightiest of men from suffering the effects of man's fall. Naaman had leprosy!

The young girl who served Naaman's wife had been taken captive from Israel. Yet she had good will toward her Syrian mistress and master (2 Kgs. 5:2-3). She is a model of obedience in children.

Naaman felt humiliated to be asked to do a simple act of obedience (2 Kgs. 5:11-12). But *obedience* was more important for him than was sacrfice, as it had been for King Saul (2 Kgs. 5:5, 10-11).

The Hebrew verb meaning "to dip" (*ṭabal*) in 2 Kings 5:14 is translated "baptize" (dip) in the Greek Old Testament (LXX).

The sin of covetousness is an easy one for God's ministers (like Gehazi) to fall into (2 Kgs. 5:20). But we never get to enjoy our dishonest gain (2 Kgs. 5:26-27). Gehazi was struck with the leprosy that Naaman had had!

22. *An axhead floats!* (2 Kgs. 6:1-7). The miracle of the floating axhead may seem trivial and perhaps more amusing than significant. But to the destitute prophet who borrowed the axe, the miracle probably meant the difference between his having food for the next few days or not. God is our helper in the small events that make up most of life, as well as in the historic happenings.

The floating axhead demonstrated again the divine commission of Elisha.

The Jordan River was about twelve feet deep and muddy in the vicinity where the axhead was floated. Elisha could not have fished out the axhead by poking around for it. The miracle was great.

23. *Elisha turns back the Arameans* (2 Kgs. 6:8-23). The Arameans (Syrians) had unending hostility toward Israel. They planned raid after raid, but Elisha told the king of Israel (Jehoram) their plans, and the Israelites prepared to meet the attacks. The Arameans were certain they had a spy among them. When they learned that Elisha was revealing their plans, they decided to capture him. (How could they do that, if he knew all their plans?)

The Arameans came to Dothan and surrounded the city. Dothan is twelve miles north of the capital city of Samaria. At

Dothan the servant of Elisha was very afraid when he saw the armies. Elisha revealed to him that the hills around Dothan were full of (angelic) horses and chariots of fire all around Elisha (6:17).

"The **angel** of the LORD encamps around those who fear him, and he delivers them" (Ps. 34:7; Matt. 18:10; Heb. 1:14).

Elisha struck the Syrians with blindness and marched them twelve miles to Samaria before breakfast! At Samaria Elisha told King Jehoram to feed them, not to kill them. So he prepared a great *feast* for them and sent them back home.

Elisha **overcame evil with good** (Rom. 12:20-21). This unexpected and astounding action caused the Syrians to quit raiding into Israel for a while (2 Kgs. 6:23).

24. *Siege and famine at Samaria* (2 Kgs. 6:24–7:20). A later siege by the Arameans at Samaria caused a great famine. The famine was so terrible that a donkey's head sold for eighty shekels of silver, about fifty dollars. (A donkey was unclean, and the head was the most inedible part of it [Lev. 11:3].)

Jehoram saw two women by the wall, one of whom cried out that they had eaten one of their sons (6:29). (The law of Moses had forewarned that if the people were unfaithful to the LORD, they would eat their own children [Lev. 26:29; Deut. 28:53, 57].) Jehoram tore his robes, which showed he was wearing sackcloth underneath.

Jehoram determined to execute Elisha, as if that would solve the famine problem (6:31). Elisha knew the executioner was coming to his house, and he said, "Don't you see how this *son of a murderer* [Jehoram, son of Ahab, who had murdered Naboth] is sending someone to cut off my head?" (6:32, author's translation).

Elisha predicted that the famine would be over by that time tomorrow, so that a seah (two gallons) of flour would sell for a shekel (about sixty cents). The captain was incredulous. Elisha told him he would see it happen, but he would not get to eat any of it. (We should be careful what we say before God! God sometimes turns our words into judgments upon ourselves.)

Things happened exactly as Elisha foretold. The Arameans abandoned their siege camp the next day, thinking they were under attack by the Hittite and Egyptian kings (7:6). When food was found in the abandoned Aramean camp, the people stampeded into the camp for food, and the officer was trampled to death.

Four lepers at the entrance of the city gate were the first to disover that the Aramean camp was abandoned. When they found the abundance of food, they said, "We're not doing right. This is a day of good news and we are keeping it to ourselves" (7:9). We also have good news that we should be sharing.

25. *The Shunammite woman's land restored* (2 Kgs. 8:1-6; compare 4:8-37). We may suffer distress and famine with the rest of the people in the world, but the LORD will sustain His people.

It was an amazing coincidence that after seven years the king was talking to Gehazi about the Shunammite woman at the very moment she came back to the king of Israel to beg for her house and land. (Probably it was NOT a coincidence.)

Second Kings 8:1-6 must have occurred before chapter five, because the king would hardly have talked to a confirmed leper.

26. *Hazael becomes king of Aram* (Syria) (2 Kgs. 8:7-15). Elijah had been sent to anoint *Hazael* as the next king of Aram (1 Kgs. 19:15), but Elisha carried out this assignment. Ben-Hadad had been king of Aram nearly fifty years, and was then ill. Ben-Hadad's representative Hazael came to Elisha with *many* gifts. In answer to the question about Ben-Hadad's recovery, Elisha said, "Say to him, You certainly could live, but the LORD has shown me that you will certainly die" (author's trans.). Elisha wept as he faced Hazael. Elisha said to him, "You will set fire to their (the Israelites') fortified places, kill their young men with the sword . . . and rip open their pregnant women" (8:12). Hazael acted greatly offended. Hazael became a very cruel persecutor of Israel, just as Elisha

foretold (2 Kgs. 10:32; 12:17; 13:3, 22; Amos 1:3-5). The very next day after his visit with Elisha, Hazael smothered the old king (Ben-Hadad) with a wet cloth.

27. *King Jehoram of Judah.*

JEHORAM* of Judah — 848–841 B.C.
(One of Judah's *worst* kings). (2 Kgs. 8:16-24; 2 Chr. 21)
    a. Married Athaliah (daughter of Ahab & Jezebel)
    b. Killed his six brothers
    c. Edom and Libnah revolted
    d. Letter from Elijah
    e. Hideous death

*The kingdom of Israel also had a king named Jehoram. He was a brother-in-law to Jehoram of Judah.

Jehoram, king of Judah, was very cruel, and killed all his six brothers (2 Chr. 21:4). "He walked in the ways of the kings of Israel . . . for he married a daughter of Ahab." The city of Libnah revolted from his authority, as did the country of Edom (2 Kgs. 8:20; 2 Chr. 20:22).

The prophet **OBADIAH** prophesied against the *Edomites,* probably in the time of Jehoram, king of Judah, about 845 B.C. (2 Kgs. 8:20-22). See Gleason L. Archer, *A Survey of Old Testament Introduction* (1994), pp. 332–338. Other scholars date Obadiah near the fall of Jerusalem to the Babylonians.

King Jehoram received a letter from the prophet Elijah, foretelling that he would die a painful and repulsive death (2 Chr. 21:12-15, 18-19). How could Elijah have sent the letter to Jehoram AFTER Elijah was taken up to heaven? Possibly the story of Elijah's being taken up is out of chronological order, or the sending of the letter occurred early in the reign of Jehoram.

Jehoram passed away "to no one's regret" (2 Chr. 21:20).
28. *King Ahaziah of Judah.*

AHAZIAH* of Judah — 841 B.C. (*Evil*)
(2 Kgs. 8:25-29; 9:21-29; 2 Chr. 22:1-9)
    a. Visited his uncle Jehoram in Israel
    b. Killed by Jehu
*The kingdom of Israel also had a king named Ahaziah. He was
a son of Ahab, and uncle of Ahaziah of Judah.

Ahaziah's mother was Athaliah, the daughter of Ahab and
Jezebel (2 Chr. 22:2). Ahaziah went down to Jezreel (winter
capital of the kings of Israel) to visit his wounded uncle (his
mother's brother) Jehoram. Jehoram had been wounded in
battle at Ramoth Gilead, the town on the border with Aram,
where many battles were fought. While Ahaziah was with his
uncle Jehoram, a revolt occurred, and *Jehu* took over the
kingship of Israel and killed both Jehoram (king of Israel)
and Ahaziah (king of Judah).

God brought about the downfall of Ahaziah and Jehoram
to complete the destruction of the house of Ahab (2 Chr.
22:7-8). (Ahaziah was Ahab's grandson.)

The details of the death of Ahaziah in the books of Kings
and Chronicles are hard to harmonize. Chronicles says
Ahaziah was found hiding in Samaria and brought to Jehu (at
Jezreel?) and killed. The books of Kings tell that Jehu pursued Ahaziah and wounded him, but he escaped to Megiddo
and died there (2 Kgs. 9:27). We believe both accounts are
true and can be harmonized, but we do not know all the
details of the events. Perhaps Ahaziah escaped from Jehu
after they brought him back from Samaria, and then Jehu
pursued him. (Compare Josephus, *Antiquities*, IX, vi, 3
[IX,120-121].)

29. *Jehu anointed king of Israel* (2 Kgs. 9:1-13). Elisha sent a
man from the "sons of the prophets" to Ramoth Gilead to
anoint Jehu to be the next king over Israel. The distance
From Jezreel to Ramoth Gilead is about fifty miles. The army

officers with Jehu mocked the prophet, calling him a "mad-man" (2 Kgs. 9:11), but they were enthusiastic to accept his words when they discovered that he had anointed Jehu king.

30. *Jehu kills Joram, and Ahaziah, and Jezebel* (2 Kgs. 9:14-37; 2 Chr. 22:7-9). (See notes in section 28 above.) Before Jehu arrived at Jezreel from Ramoth Gilead his identity was known by the furious speed of his chariot.

"The driving is like that of *JEHU* son of Nimshi — he drives like a madman" (2 Kgs. 9:20).

Queen Jezebel faced her meeting with Jehu with defiance and strength to her end. (Would that people of God were as strong for God as Jezebel was strong in dedication to her evil causes!) She painted her eyes, arranged her hair, and looked out of the upstairs window. She called Jehu a "Zimri" and "murderer of your master" (Jehoram). (Zimri killed the house of Baasha [1 Kgs. 16:10-11].) Jezebel was thrown out the window. Jehu ran over her, and then went to eat and drink. When Jehu sent men to bury her, they found the dogs had eaten her body, except for skull, feet, and hands. The prophecy of Elijah had come to pass (1 Kgs. 21:23; 2 Kgs. 9:10).

31. *Ahab's family killed* (2 Kgs. 10:1-17). Jehu wrote letters to Samaria and other places where Ahab's family members were. Seventy "sons" of Ahab were beheaded at Samaria and their heads were brought to Jezreel. Jehu pretended he was shocked, though he had ordered the massacre. He killed some relatives of King Ahaziah of Judah (who were related to Ahab's family). Jehu went to Samaria, and rode through its streets with a man named Jehonadab son of Recab, killing all who who were left there of Ahab's family.

God had told Jehu to "destroy the house of Ahab" (2 Kgs. 9:7). But Jehu did this with such gusto and apparent pleasure and excessive killing that he came under God's judgment. Hosea 1:4 gives God's words about Jehu: "I will soon punish the house of Jehu for the massacre at Jezreel." Proverbs 6:16-

17: "There are six things the LORD hates . . . hands that shed innocent blood."

JEHU of Israel — 841–814 B.C. (2 Kgs. 9:1–10:36)
   a. Killed the house of Ahab and Ahaziah of Judah
   b. Destroyed Baal worshipers

---

32. *Jehu kills worshipers of Baal* (2 Kgs. 10:18-36). With crafty deceit Jehu assembled all the worshipers of Baal in the Baal temple (at Samaria?). They were put to death, and the Baal temple was used for a latrine "to this day." (This phrase shows that this section of 2 Kings was written before the fall of Israel in 722 B.C. Compare 2 Kgs. 13:23; 16:6.)

The NIV says the "ministers" of Baal were the ones who were killed. The Hebrew simply says "his servants." NRSV translates it "his worshipers" (10:19), which is probably the better translation.

Though Jehu destroyed Baal worship in Israel, he continued the worship of the golden calves (10:29). He was not careful to keep the law of God. The result was that God allowed Hazael, king of Aram, to take nearly all of Jehu's territory east of the Jordan (10:32-33).

33. *Queen Athaliah and Joash* (2 Kgs. 11:1-21; 2 Chr. 22:10-23:21).

ATHALIAH in Judah — 841–835 B.C. (*Evil*)
(2 Kgs. 11:1-21; 2 Chr. 22:10-23:21)
   a. Killed all but one of the house of David
   b. Slain in a plot led by Jehoiada

When Athaliah, the widow of Judah's King Jehoram, saw that her son (Ahaziah) was dead, she proceeded to destroy the whole royal family in Judah. Satan is a murderer, and all who (like Athaliah) follow Satan are potentially killers (John 8:44; 1 John 3:12).

Athaliah thought she had wiped out all the house of David. But God had promised that the house of David would reign forever (2 Sam. 7:13). Though Athaliah killed almost all, one son of the royal family (named *Joash*) was saved, and he later became king. People cannot thwart God's determined plans.

The infant Joash was saved by his aunt, *Jehosheba* (spelled Jehoshabeath in 2 Chr. 22:11), his father's sister. She hid him for six years.

The priest *Jehoiada* organized a plot to install Joash upon the throne, though he was only seven years old then (2 Kgs. 11:21). Jehoiada gathered the Levites and priests from throughout Judah to come to Jerusalem (2 Chr. 23:2). Jehoiada divided them into three companies. They brought the boy king out, and put the crown upon him, and presented him "the Testimony." (NIV, "*copy*" of the covenant." "Copy" is not in the Hebrew.) The term *testimony* is most often applied to the stone tablets bearing the Ten Commandments (Ex. 31:18; 25:21), but it is sometimes applied to the entire law of Moses (Ps. 78:5; Isa. 8:20). Probably Joash held the official temple copy of the law of Moses (or the autograph itself!).

When Athaliah realized what was happening, she cried out, "Treason! Treason!" She thought it was treason to plot against her, but had not considered it treason when she killed all the royal family. She herself was killed, and also Mattan, the priest of Baal in Jerusalem (2 Kgs. 11:18).

Jehoiada proceeded to organize the government during the childhood years of Joash. Jehoiada organized the priests, the Levites, and doorkeepers (2 Chr. 23:18-19).

Questions on Section B
From the Division of the Kingdom to the Fall of the House of Ahab (1 Kgs. 12–2 Kgs. 11)

Facts About the Divided Kingdom
   1. What were the names of the two kingdoms in the divided kingdom?

2. Which kingdom was northern in location? Which was southern?
3. What was the approximate land area of each kingdom?
4. How many tribes were in each kingdom?
5. Who were the first kings in each kingdom?
6. What was the total number of kings in each kingdom?
7. What was the number of dynasties in each kingdom?
8. What was the character of the kings in each kingdom?
9. What were the capitals of the two kingdoms?
10. What nations defeated and destroyed each kingdom?
11. What was the date of the fall of each kingdom?
12. Why was the kingdom of Judah consistently stronger?

Jeroboam I (king of Israel)

1. How many tribes were in Jeroboam's kingdom? (1 Kgs. 11:31)
2. What cities were Jeroboam's capitals? (12:25)
3. What idol did Jeroboam make? Why? Where? (12:26-29)
4. Whom did Jeroboam appoint to be priests? (12:31)
5. What day did Jeroboam designate as a feast day? (12:32)
6. Who denounced Jeroboam's altar? (13:1-2)
7. What was the name of the king who was to be born and defile the altar? (1 Kgs. 13:2; 2 Kgs. 23:15-17)
8. How was Jeroboam's attempt to seize the man of God defeated? (1 Kgs. 13:4)
9. Would the man of God eat with the king? Why or why not? (13:7-10)
10. Who went to overtake the returning man of God? (13:11-14)
11. What lie did the old prophet tell? (13:8)
12. What disturbing message was revealed as the prophets ate? (13:20-22)
13. What happened to the man of God? (13:24)
14. Where was the man of God buried? (13:29-30)
15. What was the consequence of Jeroboam's sin upon his house? (13:33-34)
16. What was the name of Jeroboam's sick son? (14:1)
17. What was the son's character? (14:13)
18. Who was sent to Ahijah the prophet? (14:2)
19. What message about the son and about Jeroboam's family did Ahijah give? (14:7-12)

Rehoboam (king of Judah)

1. Where did Rehoboam go to be made king? (1 Kgs. 12:1)
2. What request did the people make to Rehoboam? (12:4)
3. Who was the spokesman for the people of Israel? (12:3)

4. What counsel did the old men give to Rehoboam? The younger men? (12:6-11)
5. Whose counsel did Rehoboam follow? (12:13)
6. Why did Rehoboam speak so foolishly? (12:15)
7. What was Israel's response to Rehoboam's speech? (12:16, 19)
8. What happened to Adoniram when Rehoboam sent him to the Israelites? (12:18)
9. Why did Rehoboam not fight Israel? (12:22-24)
10. Was Rehoboam a good king? (2 Chr. 12:14; 1 Kgs. 14:21)
11. Who was Rehoboam's mother? (1 Kgs. 14:21)
12. What defensive preparations did Rehoboam make in Judah? (2 Chr. 11:5-6)
13. What religious people came into Rehoboam's kingdom? From where? Why? (11:13-16)
14. What effect did these religious people have on Rehoboam's kingdom? (11:17)
15. How many wives and concubines did Rehoboam have? (11:21)
16. What evils were practiced in Judah in Rehoboam's time? (1 Kgs. 14:22-23)
17. Who was Shishak? (14:25)
18. What did Shishak take from Rehoboam? (1 Kgs. 14:26; 2 Chr. 12:9-10)
19. What did the king and the princes do when Shishak invaded? (2 Chr. 12:6)
20. What did God do when they humbled themselves? (12:6-8)
21. What substitute was made for golden shields? (1 Kgs. 14:27)
22. How did Rehoboam and Jeroboam get along? (14:30)

Abijah (king of Judah)
1. Was Abijah a good king? (1 Kgs. 15:3)
2. Why did God not destroy Judah in Abijah's time? (15:4)
3. How did Abijah and Jeroboam get along? (15:7)
4. Where did Abijah deliver a speech against Jeroboam? (2 Chr. 13:4-5)
5. What was the main point in Abijah's speech? (13:4-12)
6. How did Jeroboam try to defeat Abijah? (13:3)
7. What was the result of the battle between Abijah and Jeroboam? (13:15-16)

Asa (king of Judah)
1. Was King Asa good or bad? (1 Kgs. 15:11)
2. What did Asa put out of the land? (15:12)
3. For how long did Asa have peace? (2 Chr. 14:1)
4. Who attacked Asa? With how large a force? (14:9)
5. How did Asa get help for the battle? (14:11)
6. What prophet encouraged Asa? (15:1)
7. When is the LORD with you? (15:2)

8. What did Asa lead Judah to make a covenant to do? (15:12)
9. Who was Maacah? What was done with her? Why? (1 Kgs. 15:13)
10. What king of Israel captured and fortified a city in Asa's kingdom? (2 Chr. 16:1)
11. How did Asa stop the fortifying of Ramah? (16:2-4)
12. What was done with the stones of Ramah? (16:6)
13. What prophet rebuked Asa? (16:7)
14. What was to be Asa's punishment? (16:9)
15. What did Asa do when the prophet rebuked him? (16:10)
16. What afflicted Asa in his old age? (16:2)

Nadab (king of Israel)
1. What was Nadab's character? (1 Kgs. 15:26)
2. What city did Nadab besiege? (15:27)
3. Who assassinated Nadab? (15:27)

Baasha (king of Israel)
1. Was King Baasha good or bad? (1 Kgs. 15:34)
2. What did Baasha do to the house of Jeroboam? (15:29)
3. What prophet denounced Baasha? (16:1)
4. What did the prophet say was going to happen to the house of Baasha? (16:2-3)
5. What town did Baasha capture and fortify against King Asa? (15:17)

Elah (king of Israel)
1. Who conspired against Elah and killed him? (1 Kgs. 16:9)
2. What was Elah doing when he was assassinated? (16:9)

Zimri (king of Israel)
1. Whose family (house) did Zimri destroy? (1 Kgs. 16:11)
2. How long did Zimri reign? (16:15)
3. What city was under siege when Zimri became king? (16:15)
4. What did the people do when they heard that Zimri had killed the king? (16:15)
5. Who attacked the city where Zimri was? (16:17)
6. How did Zimri die? (16:18)
7. Did Zimri gain a good reputation? (1 Kgs. 16:19-20; 2 Kgs. 9:31)

Omri (king of Israel)
1. Who was temporarily a rival to Omri for king? (1 Kgs. 16:21)
2. What hill did Omri buy for a new capital? From whom? (16:24)
3. Was Omri strong or weak? (16:27)

4. Who was Omri's son, who became a much more famous king? (16:28)

Ahab (king of Israel) and **Elijah** the prophet

1. How did Ahab compare in character with Israel's other kings? (1 Kgs. 16:30)
2. Who was Ahab's wife? (16:31)
3. Who was the father of Ahab's wife? (16:32)
4. What religion was introduced into Israel by Ahab and his wife? (16:32)
5. Who rebuilt Jericho in Ahab's time? (16:34; Josh. 6:26)
6. Where was Elijah the prophet from? (17:1)
7. What was Elijah's proclamation to Ahab? (17:1; James 5:17)
8. By what brook was Elijah fed? (17:5)
9. Where was Elijah sent after the brook dried up? (17:9)
10. What two things did Elijah ask the widow for? (17:10-11)
11. How much food did the widow have? (17:12)
12. Where did Elijah and the widow obtain food? (17:16)
13. Whom did Elijah raise from the dead? (17:17-22)
14. What did Elijah pray about the boy's soul (life)? (17:21-22)
15. Does every person have a *soul* that is distinct from the body? (Compare Gen. 35:8; Matt. 10:28; 2 Pet. 1:13-14; Eccl. 12:7)
16. Who sent Elijah back to Ahab? (1 Kgs. 18:1)
17. Who was in charge of Ahab's household and property? What sort of man was he? (18:3)
18. How had a hundred prophets been saved alive? (18:4)
19. What mission did Ahab and his servant go out on? (18:5-6)
20. Why did Ahab's servant fear to tell Ahab that he had met Elijah? (18:8-12)
21. What did Ahab call Elijah when they met? (18:17)
22. How many prophets of Baal were there? How many prophets of Asherah (the grove)? (18:19)
23. Where did Elijah call upon Ahab to go to test who was God? (18:19, 21)
24. What test did Elijah propose to prove who was God? (18:23-24)
25. How long did the prophets of Baal pray? (18:26,29)
26. How many containers of water did Elijah have poured on his altar? (18:33-34)
27. What did the fire from heaven burn up? (18:38)
28. What was done with the prophets of Baal? Where? (18:40)
29. Where did Elijah send his servant to go and look? How many times? (18:43)
30. How big was the cloud? (18:44)
31. Where did Elijah and Ahab hurry to? Who arrived first? (18:45-46)
32. What did Jezebel threaten to do to Elijah? (19:2)

33. To what place did Elijah flee from Jezebel? (19:3)
34. Under what sort of tree did Elijah request to die? (19:4)
35. How did Elijah get food there? (19:5-6)
36. Where did Elijah go after eating the food? (19:8)
37. What question did God ask Elijah at Mt. Horeb? (19:9)
38. What three violent events occurred in Elijah's presence? (19:11-12)
39. What sort of voice did Elijah hear? (19:12)
40. What three people was Elijah sent to anoint? (19:15-17)
41. How many people in Israel had not bowed to Baal? (19:18)
42. What was Elisha doing when Elijah found him? (19:19)
43. How did Elijah demonstrate his call to Elisha? (19:19)
44. Name the king of Aram (Syria) who besieged Samaria. (20:1)
45. What two demands did the king of Aram make? (20:3-6)
46. Did King Ahab yield to these demands? (20:9)
47. What men were to give the Arameans into Ahab's hands? (20:13-14)
48. What was the king of Aram doing when Israel attacked? (20:16-17)
49. What was the outcome of the battle at Samaria? (20:20-21)
50. What explanation did the Arameans give for their defeat? (20:23)
51. Where was the Arameans' next battle with Ahab? (20:26)
52. What did the army of Israel look like? (20:27)
53. How did the second battle with Aram turn out? (20:29)
54. Who suggested that the king of Aram ask for mercy? (20:31)
55. What did King Ahab call the king of Aram? (20:32)
56. What did King Ben-Hadad promise to grant to Ahab? (20:34)
57. What happened to a prophet who would not strike his fellow-prophet? (20:35-36)
58. Where did the prophet wait after being struck? (20:38)
59. How had his prisoner escaped, according to the prophet? (20:39-40)
60. To whom was the story of the escaping prisoner applied? (20:41-42)
61. What penalty was pronounced on King Ahab for letting Ben-Hadad go free? (20:42)
62. Whose vineyard did Ahab desire? Where was it? (21:1)
63. Would the owner of the vineyard give it to Ahab? (21:3)
64. Who volunteered to obtain the vineyard? (21:7)
65. How was the vineyard owner slain? (21:8-10)
66. Who met Ahab in the vineyard? (21:17-18)
67. What penalty was pronounced upon Ahab? Upon his house? Upon Jezebel? (21:19-24)

68. What did God say when Ahab humbled himself? (21:29)
69. What royal visitor came to see Ahab? (22:2)
70. What city did Ahab propose that they attack? (22:3)
71. Who requested that they ask the counsel of the LORD before going to battle? (22:5)
72. How many prophets were gathered before the king? (22:6)
73. What one prophet of the LORD was brought? (22:7-9)
74. How did Ahab feel toward this prophet? Why? (22:8)
75. What prophet made horns of iron? What were these horns supposed to illustrate? (22:11)
76. What did Micaiah at first tell the kings to do? Was this message sincere? (22:15-16)
77. What vision of Israel's armies did Micaiah relate? (22:17)
78. What vision concerning the prophets did Micaiah relate? (22:19-23)
79. What did Zedekiah do to Micaiah? (22:25)
80. What disguise did Ahab put on for battle? (22:30)
81. What instructions had the king of Aram given his troops for the battle? (22:31)
82. How did King Jehoshaphat nearly lose his life? (22:32-33)
83. How was King Ahab killed? (22:34-35)
84. What prophecy was fulfilled when blood was washed from Ahab's chariot? (22:38; 21:19)
85. What material was used for decoration in Ahab's palace? (22:39; compare Amos 6:4; 3:15.)

Jehoshaphat (king of Judah)
1. Was Jehoshaphat a good king? (1 Kgs. 22:43)
2. Whom did Jehoshaphat send throughout the cities of Judah? For what purpose? (2 Chr. 17:7-9)
3. What foreign nations sent tribute to Jehoshaphat? (17:11)
4. Was Jehoshaphat strong or weak? (17:12)
5. What good thing did Jehoshaphat's commander Amasiah do? (17:16)
6. How did Jehoshaphat become associated with the house of Ahab? (21:6)
7. With what words did the prophet rebuke Jehoshaphat for helping Ahab? (19:2)
8. What did Jehoshaphat instruct the judges whom he appointed to do? (19:5,7,9)
9. What peoples invaded Jehoshaphat's kingdom? (20:1)
10. What did Jehoshaphat do to prepare for battle? (20:3-12)

Old Testament History

11. What prophet predicted deliverance for Jehoshaphat? (20:14-15)
12. Where did Jehoshaphat and his army go to face the enemies? (20:20)
13. What did Judah do as the battle began? (20:21-22)
14. How did the battle turn out? (20:23)
15. What was the place where the spoil was collected called? What does the name mean? (20:26)
16. Where did Jehoshaphat build ships? What were the ships designed to do? (20:35-36; 1 Kgs. 22:48)
17. What happened to the ships? (20:37)
18. What offer by King Ahaziah did Jehoshaphat refuse? (1 Kgs. 22:49)

Ahaziah (king of Israel)

1. How did Ahaziah compare with his father in character? (1 Kgs. 22:51-53)
2. What kingdom rebelled against Israel after Ahab's death? (2 Kgs. 1:1)
3. How was Ahaziah injured? (1:2)
4. Where did Ahaziah send for information about his sickness? (1:2)
5. What message did Elijah send to Ahaziah? (1:4)
6. Whom did Ahaziah send to Elijah? (1:9)
7. What happened to two captains and two groups of fifty men? (1:10-12)
8. What did Elijah tell King Ahaziah? (1:16)
9. Name the four places Elijah and Elisha passed by on the way to Elijah's being taken up. (2:1,2,4,6)
10. What did the sons of the prophets tell Elisha on the way? (2:3,5)
11. How did Elijah and Elisha cross Jordan? (2:8)
12. What last request did Elisha make of Elijah? (2:9)
13. What divided Elisha from Elijah? (2:11)
14. How was Elijah taken into heaven? (2:11)
15. Why did the company of the prophets want to search for Elijah? (2:16)
16. Where was the water bad? (2:15, 19)
17. How did Elisha heal the waters? (2:21)
18. Where did youths mock Elisha? (2:23)
19. What punishment came upon the youths? (2:24)

Jehoram (king of Israel) and *Elisha* the prophet

1. Who was Jehoram's father? (2 Kgs. 3:1)
2. What act of Jehoram shows he was a little better than his father? (3:2)
3. Who was king of Moab? (3:4)
4. Whom did Jehoram get to help in his battle against Moab? (3:6-7)
5. What dangers beset the armies as they marched? (3:9)
6. What prophet was with the armies? (3:11)

7. How did Elisha speak to Jehoram? (3:14)
8. What accompaniment did Elisha have as he prophesied? (3:15)
9. How was water obtained for the troops? (3:16-20)
10. What did the king of Moab think when he saw the water? (3:22)
11. What was done to the land of Moab? (3:25)
12. What desperate act saved Moab from total destruction? (3:27)
13. What complaint did a widow of one of the prophets bring to Elisha? (4:1)
14. How did the widow obtain money to pay her debts? (4:2-7)
15. Where did Elisha often stay and eat as he traveled? (4:8)
16. What did the woman and her husband make for Elisha? (4:10)
17. What did Elisha promise the woman? (4:16)
18. How did the woman's son die? (4:18-20)
19. Where did the woman go seeking Elisha? (4:24-25)
20. Who was Elisha's servant? (4:25)
21. Who rode back to the woman's house first? (4:31)
22. What did Elisha do in bringing the child back to life? (4:33-35)
23. What painful condition existed in the land in those days? (4:38)
24. What ingredient made the prophets' pottage deadly? (4:39-40)
25. How was the pottage made non-poisonous? (4:41)
26. From what place did a man come bringing food for the prophet? (4:42)
27. How much food was brought? How many men did it feed? (4:43)
28. Who was Naaman? (5:1)
29. What was Naaman's affliction? (5:1)
30. Who told about the prophet who could heal Naaman? (5:2-3)
31. Who sent Naaman to Israel? To what person in Israel was he sent? (5:5)
32. How did the king of Israel react to Naaman's arrival? (5:7)
33. What did Elisha tell Naaman to do to be healed? (5:10)
34. Name the two rivers of Damascus. (5:12)
35. How was Naaman persuaded to obey Elisha? (5:13)
36. What rewards did Elisha accept? (5:16)
37. What did Naaman ask to take back with him? Why? (5:17)
38. Who covetously overtook Naaman and asked for a gift? (5:20)
39. What excuse did he give for asking for the gift? (5:22)
40. How was Gehazi's act made known to Elisha? (5:26)
41. What was Gehazi's punishment? (5:27)
42. What complaint did the prophets have about their dwelling place? (6:1)
43. What happened to a borrowed axe? (6:5)
44. How did Elisha retrieve the axhead? (6:6-7)

45. What military secrets did Elisha reveal? (6:8-10)
46. Where did the king of Syria attempt to capture Elisha? (6:13)
47. How did Elisha's servant react when he saw the city surrounded? (6:15)
48. What did Elisha pray the Lord would show his servant? (6:17)
49. Where did Elisha lead the blinded Syrians? (6:19)
50. What did Elisha tell the king to do to the Syrians? (6:22)
51. What was the effect of the kindness to the Syrians? (6:22)
52. What was the effect of the siege upon Samaria? (6:25)
53. How much was a donkey's head sold for in Samaria? (6:25)
54. What very horrible act occurred during the famine? (6:26-29; compare Lev. 26:29; Deut. 28:53)
55. What was Jehoram wearing as an undershirt? (6:30)
56. What unreasonable decision did Jehoram make about Elisha? (6:31)
57. How was Jehoram the "son of a murderer"? (6:32; 1 Kgs. 21)
58. What dramatic change in the famine did Elisha promise? (2 Kgs. 7:1)
59. What did Elisha tell Jehoram's captain would happen to him? (7:2)
60. Who discovered that the Syrians had fled? (7:3)
61. Why had the Syrians fled? (7:6)
62. What did the king think about the Syrians' departure? (7:12)
63. How was Elisha's prophecy about the captain seeing abundant food, but not eating of it, fulfilled? (7:18-20)
64. Where had Elisha sent the Shunammite woman? For how long? Why? (8:1)
65. What remarkable coincidence occurred when the woman returned? (8:4-5)
66. What was returned to the woman? (8:6)
67. What foreign city did Elisha visit? (8:7)
68. Whom did Ben-Hadad send to Elisha to inquire about his sickness? (8:8)
69. What did Elisha say about Ben-Hadad's recovery? (8:10)
70. What did Elisha predict about Hazael's deeds? (8:11-12)
71. How did Ben-Hadad die? (8:15)

Jehoram (king of Judah)
1. Was Jehoram's life good or bad? (2 Kgs. 8:18)
2. Who was Jehoram's wife? (8:18,26)
3. What did Jehoram do to his brothers when he became king? (2 Chr. 21:4)
4. What country and what city revolted in Jehoram's time? (2 Kgs. 8:20,22)
5. What prophet wrote Jehoram a letter? (2 Chr. 21:12)
6. What did the letter predict concerning Jehoram? (21:14-15)
7. What peoples invaded Judah and Jerusalem in Jehoram's time and carried away all the goods? (21:16-17)

8. Which prophet (probably) wrote God's message against the Edomites for cruelty during Jehoram's reign?
9. How did Jehoram die? (21:18-19)
10. How did the people feel about Jehoram when he died? (21:20)

Ahaziah (king of Judah)

1. Why was Ahaziah made king when he was his father's youngest son? (2 Chr. 21:17; 22:1)
2. Who counseled Ahaziah to do wickedly? (22:3)
3. Whom did Ahaziah accompany to battle? To what place? (22:5)
4. Where did Ahaziah go to visit his sick uncle? (22:6)
5. Where did Jehoram of Israel and Ahaziah meet Jehu? (2 Kgs. 9:21)
6. Where did Ahaziah flee from Jehu? (9:27)
7. At what city did Ahaziah die? (9:27)
8. Where was Ahaziah buried? (9:28)

Jehu (king of Israel)

1. How many sons did Ahab have in Samaria? (2 Kgs. 10:1)
2. What challenge did Jehu make to those who cared for the sons of Ahab? (10:2-3)
3. How did Ahab's sons die? (10:7)
4. How thoroughly did Jehu destroy Ahab's house? (10:11, 17)
5. Whom did Jehu meet at Beth Eked of the Shepherds in Samaria? (10:12-13)
6. What happened to these men at the well of Beth Eked? (10:14)
7. Who accompanied Jehu on his mission of massacre in Samaria? (10:15-17)
8. What pretense did Jehu make to the worshipers of Baal? (10:18-19)
9. How were the worshipers of Baal made obvious and distinct? (10:22)
10. What was done to the worshipers of Baal? (10:25-28)
11. Did Jehu serve Jehovah with his heart? (10:31)
12. What portion of Israel was lost to Syria in Jehu's time? (10:32-33)

Athaliah (usurper in Judah)

1. Who had been Athaliah's husband? (2 Kgs. 8:16,18)
2. Who had been Athaliah's son? (8:26)
3. What did Athaliah do when her son was dead? (11:1)
4. How near did Athaliah come to destroying all the descendants of David? (11:1-2)
5. Who was saved? Whose son was he? (11:2)
6. Who hid the young prince? (2 Chr. 22:11)
7. How long was he hidden? (2 Kgs. 11:3)
8. What did Athaliah do to the temple? (2 Chr. 24:7)

9. Who was the leader of the plot against Athaliah? (23:1)
10. From where and at what place were Levites gathered to oppose Athaliah and appoint a new king? (23:2-3)
11. Into how many groups were the Levites gathered for the revolt? (23:4)
12. Who was to be protected from all intruders? (2 Kgs. 11:8)
13. What was given to the boy when he was made king? (11:12)
14. What did Athaliah hear that aroused her? (11:13)
15. What did Athaliah say when she saw the new king? (11:14)
16. Where was Athaliah slain? (11:15-16)
17. Who led the people in making a covenant between the king, the people and God? (11:17)
18. What was done to Baal worship in Jerusalem? (11:18)

Section C
From Joash to the End of Israel (2 Kings 12:1-18:12)

1. *King Joash of Judah.*

JOASH of Judah — 835-796 B.C. (*Good and bad*)
(2 Kgs. 12; 2 Chr. 24)
    a. The boy king (7 yrs. old)
    b. Repaired the temple
    c. Forgot the kindness shown to him

The prophet **JOEL** prophesied probably about 835 B.C., during the minor years of King Joash.

In the book of Joel no kings or princes are mentioned. But elders and priests are referred to (Joel 1:1, 13).

The background of Joel's prophecy is a terrible *locust plague*. The deliverance from this plague is used to lead into a presentation of future blessings.

The apostle Peter quoted the book of Joel on the day of Pentecost, when the church of the Lord Jesus Christ was established in Jerusalem:

"Afterward, *I will pour out my Spirit* on all people" (Joel 2:28; Acts 2:16-17).

King *Joash* (also spelled *Jehoash*) did what was right in the eyes of the LORD all the years (lit., *days*) of Jehoiada the priest (2 Chr. 24:2). With his limited social contacts in early childhood, Joash needed much counsel in personal relationships.

Joash decided to repair the temple of the LORD. The sons of Athaliah had broken up the temple of God (2 Chr. 24:4, 7). At the kings's command and at the action of Jehoiada, a chest was prepared with a hole bored in its side. This was placed beside the altar to collect money for repairing the temple.

When the priest Jehoiada died, he was buried like a king, with the kings in the City of David (2 Chr. 24:16).

After the death of Jehoiada, the officials of Judah came to King Joash and "paid homage" and also persuaded him to ease up on the strict religious standards Jehoiada had enforced. Soon the people were abandoning the temple of the LORD, and worshiping Asherah poles and idols. The Spirit of God came upon Zechariah, son of Jehoiada the priest, who had placed Joash on the throne. He rebuked Joash and the people for their idolatry. At the order of the king they stoned this prophet in the very courtyard of the LORD's temple! Thus Joash *did not remember the kindness* that Zechariah's father had shown to him, but killed his son, who said as he lay dying, "May the LORD see this and call you to account." Let us never forget the kindnesses of our parents, Sunday school teachers, preachers, etc., as Joash did.

(Note — The "Zechariah, son of Berekiah" that Jesus mentioned in Matthew 23:35 is the prophet Zechariah, whose book is next to the last in the Old Testament. He lived three hundred years after the Zechariah that Joash killed. Both prophets were martyred, but they certainly were not the same individual.)

A sellout never saves people. Joash was soon invaded by the army of Aram led by Hazael (2 Kgs. 12:17). The invaders killed all the leaders of the people! (2 Chr. 24:23). Joash himself was wounded, and then two of his officals murdered him.

Joash was buried in the City of David, but not in the tombs of the kings (2 Chr. 24:25). Jehoiada had the character of a king, though not the title of king. He was buried like a king. Joash had the title of king, but not the character of a king. He was not buried with the kings. Character is more important than a title.

2. *King Jehoahaz of Israel (son of Jehu).*

JEHOAHAZ of Israel — 814–798 B.C. (2 Kgs. 13:1-9)
    a. Lost most of his kingdom to Aram (Syria).

The dynasty of Jehu lasted eighty-nine years, by far the greatest length of any dynasty of Israel's kings. Under King Jeroboam II, Israel reached the greatest power and size it ever had, almost to the size it had in the days of Solomon. But after this dynasty collapsed, the whole country fell apart, and within thirty years it was conquered and taken into captivity.

The **JEHU** dynasty — the "J" Kings:
  JEHU, JEHOAHAZ, JEHOASH, JEROBOAM II, ZECHARIAH

Jehoahaz, son of Jehu, did evil in the eyes of the LORD, and the Lord for a long time kept them under the power of Hazael, king of Aram and King Ben-Hadad II, his son.

When Jehoahaz sought the LORD, the LORD provided a "deliverer" for Israel. This deliverer was probably the Assyrian king Adad-nirari III, who in 803 B.C. defeated Ben-Hadad II and thus took the pressure of Aram off of Israel.

Jehoahaz was brought so low that he had left to him only fifty horsemen and ten thousand foot soldiers (2 Kgs. 13:7). This is almost the only information that is reported in Scripture about Jehoahaz. (What will we be mostly remembered for?)

3. *King Jehoash (or Joash) of Israel.*

JEHOASH of Israel — 798–782 B.C.
(2 Kgs. 13:10-25; 14:8-16)
    a. Defeated Syria three times
    b. Conquered King Amaziah in Judah

Jehoash called himself the "**cedar of Lebanon**" and called Judah's King Amaziah the "thistle of Lebanon" (2 Kgs. 14:9).

Jehoash, king of Israel was mighty (13:12). He defeated Amaziah, king of Judah, when Amaziah had the audacity to challenge Jehoash (14:11-14). Jehoash broke down a long (six hundred feet) section of the wall of Jerusalem.

In the reign of Jehoash Elisha the prophet did his final miracles. He predicted three victories of Jehoash over the Arameans. Also, after Elisha died, a dead man's body was hastily placed in Elisha's tomb. The body came back to life. The power of the God of Elisha clearly continued on after Elisha was dead.

Elisha — then very old — told Jehoash to "Shoot" an arrow out the window. Elisha said, "The arrow of victory over Aram!" Then Elisha told him to strike the ground with the arrows. Jehoash struck the ground three times and stopped. Elisha said that each blow would bring one victory over Aram. "You should have struck the ground five or six times; then you would have defeated Aram and completely destroyed it." We might ask, "How could Jehoash have known he should strike the ground many times?" Perhaps Jehoash's stopping his striking so soon showed a basic lack of enthusiasm for it. In the Lord's work, we should get earnestly involved.

4. *King Amaziah of Judah.*

AMAZIAH of Judah — 796-767 B.C. (*Good and bad*)
(2 Kgs. 14:1-22; 2 Chr. 25)
   a. Conquered Edom and took its gods
   b. Defeated by Jehoash (king of Israel)
Amaziah is called the "thistle of Lebanon" (2 Kgs. 14:9).

Amaziah collected a large army from Judah and hired mercenary soldiers from Israel (2 Chr. 25:5-6). He sent the troops from Israel home at the command of a man of God (a prophet) (2 Chr. 25:7). The Israelite troops went on a rampage of killing when they were sent home (2 Chr. 25:13). Amaziah defeated the Edomites with a great slaughter (2 Chr. 25:11-12). Amaziah challenged the king of Israel to fight him (2 Chr. 25:17). Amaziah was defeated (2 Chr. 15:22). Amaziah was assassinated at Lachish (2 Chr. 25:27).

There are curious resemblances between Amaziah and his father, Joash:
(1) Both were zealous for God in the early years of their reigns.
(2) Both forsook God.
(3) Both disregarded the rebukes of prophets.
(4) Both were conspired against and were slain.

Amaziah was very foolish in saving and bringing back to Judah the gods of the Edomites, when he had just defeated the Edomites (2 Chr. 25:14-15). A prophet asked him, "Why do you consult this people's gods, which could not save their own people from your hand?"

5. *King Jeroboam II of Israel.* King Jeroboam II was Israel's most powerful king ever. He reigned a long time, forty-one years. During his rule the country became prosperous, and conquered the nations north and east of Israel, so that Israel was almost as large as it had been in the time of Kings David and Solomon. But beneath this favorable exterior, there was much social oppression of the poor (Amos 5:11), and much immorality and violence. (See Hosea 4:1-2.) After the time of Jeroboam II, the country of Israel just collapsed. Six kings ruled in a space of only thirty years. Then the country was taken captive to Assyria.

JEROBOAM II of Israel — 793-753 B.C. (2 Kgs. 14:23-29)
  a. Restored territory to Israel
  b. Conquered Damascus and Hamath
  c. Amos announced the end of the kingdom of Israel.

There was an overlap (co-regency) of about twelve years in the reigns of Jeroboam II and his father Jehoash. See 2 Kings 13:10; 14:1-2, 23; 15:1. Jehoash ruled about 798-782, and Jeroboam II about 793-753.

There were several great *prophets* who proclaimed their messages during the reign of Jeroboam II and shortly thereafter.

THREE GREAT PROPHETS IN ISRAEL IN THE TIME OF KING JEROBOAM II

1. *JONAH* – Sent to Nineveh, about 780 B.C. (2 Kgs. 14:25)

2. *AMOS* – Announced the captivity of Israel (Amos 5:27; 6:7; 7:18). (760 B.C.)

3. *HOSEA* – Revealed God's heartbreak over His "marriage" to Israel. (760–725 B.C.)

By the time of Jeroboam II, *Assyria* had become the most powerful nation in the Bible lands. It was only a matter of time until they captured Aram (Syria) and Israel. The Assyrians were notorious for their cruelty. (See notes on Period IX, A, 4.)

JONAH – Jonah was probably a popular preacher in Israel because he foretold the restoration of lands in Israel which had been conquered by their enemies (2 Kgs 14:25).

God sent Jonah to Nineveh, the capital of the cruel Assyrians. Jonah did *not* want God to be merciful to the Assyrians and fled in the opposite direction from where Nineveh was. God brought Jonah back, riding inside a great fish, to do his duty. Jonah learned that God is gracious to all nations.

Jonah became a great type of Christ Jesus. See Matthew 12:39-41. "As Jonah was three days and three nights in the belly of the great fish, so will the Son of Man (Jesus) be three days and three nights in the heart of the earth." Christ compared His death, burial, and resurrection to Jonah's being swallowed up in the fish, and then being vomited out.

The prophet *Hosea* was commanded to go and marry an adulterous wife. Many tragedies and heartbreaks followed this marriage. God used the experiences of Hosea to dramatize His heartbreaking relationships with Israel as His bride. God had sought to "marry" Israel, when He made the covenant with them at Mt. Sinai to become His chosen people. But Israel sought all kinds of other "lovers" — idols, foreign alliances, and sins of every kind.

635

HOSEA	GOD
1. Married a harlot (Hosea 1:2)	1. Married a faithless people (Israel) at Mt. Sinai (Jer.31:22)
2. Wife was faithless (2:1-5)	2. Israel was faithless (Hos. 7:1-8)
3. Children of grief! (1:4-9) a. *Jezreel* — Bloodshed! b. *Lo-Ruhamah* — No mercy! c. *Lo-Ammi* – Not my people	3. Children of grief! a. Bloodshed in Israel (4:2) b. No more mercy (1:6; 2:1) c. Rejection of Israel
4. Strained relationship with wife (3:1-3)	4. Strained relationship with Israel (3:4-5; 4:17)
5. Steadfast love and hope (1:10–2:1)	5. Steadfast love and hope for Israel (11:8-9)

6. *King Uzziah (or Azariah) of Judah.*

UZZIAH of Judah — 790–739 B.C. (*Good*)
(2 Kgs. 14:21-22; 15:1-7; 2 Chr. 26)
   a. Mighty
   b. Became a leper

Uzziah was a very good king, and a very strong one. But his greatest fame may be his relationship with the prophet *Isaiah*: "In the year that King *Uzziah* died, I saw the Lord seated on a throne, high and exalted" (Isa. 6:1).

Uzziah defeated the Philistines and other nations (2 Chr. 26:6). He fortified Jerusalem and other cities. He loved agriculture and developed rural areas (2 Chr. 26:10). He made war engines to hurl arrows and large stones (2 Chr. 26:15). He was smitten with leprosy when he became proud and attempted to offer incense in the temple, which only priests were authorized to do. After he became a leper he ruled jointly with his son Jotham. (Concerning Jotham, see 2 Kings 15:32-38.)

7. *Israel's last kings* (2 Kgs. 15:8-31). Israel's last six kings ruled during a period of only thirty years. God had set His plumb line among His people Israel, and would spare them no longer (Amos 7:8).

ZECHARIAH of Israel — 753–752 B.C (2 Kgs. 15:8-12)
   a. Killed before the people by Shallum after six months
(Zechariah was the last king in the dynasty of Jehu.)

The fact that Shallum could kill Zechariah in front of the people and still succeed him as king shows that conditions were bad at that time.

SHALLUM of Israel — 752 B.C. (2 Kgs. 15:13-15)
   a. Killed by Menahem after one month

Shallum led a conspiracy to kill Zechariah, but himself fell victim to the cruel conspirator Menahem.

MENAHEM of Israel — 752–742 B.C. (2 Kgs. 15:16-22)
   a. Cruel in war (2 Kgs. 15:16)
   b. Invaded by King Pul of Assyria

Probably the reign of Menahem in Samaria was at the same time as the first ten years of Pekah (a later king), who ruled (?) in the land of Gilead (east of Jordan). (See notes on Period IX, B, 3, d.)

Menahem's cruelty was as bad as that of the Aramean king Hazael (2 Kgs. 15:16; 8:12). Can you believe that Menahem's name means *comfort?*

Menahem's kingdom was invaded by King *Pul* of Assyria, who is more commonly known by the name Tiglath-Pileser III. In the days of Jonah (about 780 B.C.) the Assyrians at Nineveh had repented, even if only to a limited degree. Forty years later the army commander Pul (or Pulu) took over the land, and the Assyrians went back to their old cruel ways of conquest and forced extortion of tribute money. Menahem had to collect fifty shekels of silver from every wealthy man to give to the king of Assyria.

PEKAHIAH of Israel — 741–740 B.C. (2 Kgs. 15:23-26)
   a. Slain by Pekah

Pekahiah was a son of Menahem. He was killed by one of his chief officers, *Pekah*. Pekah attacked him with fifty men from Gilead. This causes us to think that Pekah may have been ruling over part of Gilead (east of Jordan) at the same time as Menahem and Pekahiah were ruling at Samaria west of the Jordan.

PEKAH of Israel — 752–732 B.C. (2 Kgs. 15:27-31)
  a. Joined Rezin in attacking King Ahaz (of Judah)
  b. Invaded by Tiglath-Pileser
  c. Slain by Hoshea

Pekah is famous to us mainly because of the famous reference to him in Isaiah the prophet (7:1). Pekah, king of Israel, allied himself with the last king of Aram, *Rezin*, and marched up to Jerusalem to attack King *Ahaz*, and probably to compel him to join with them in resisting Assyria. (See 2 Kings 15:37.)

In that attack Pekah, son of Remaliah, killed a hundred and twenty thousand soldiers in Judah — because Judah had forsaken the LORD (2 Chr. 28:6). Little wonder that the heart of Judah's King Ahaz and his people were shaken as the trees of the forest are shaken by the wind (Isa. 7:2).

At that dangerous time Isaiah offered to King Ahaz any miraculous sign he might wish to ask for, if he would only believe that the LORD would help him (Isa. 7:11-12). Ahaz refused the offer from God, because he planned to send messengers to Tiglath-Pileser to seek help (2 Chr. 28:16, 19). He trusted the arm of flesh more than the power of God.

Isaiah told Ahaz that the LORD would give a sign whether Ahaz cooperated or not — the sign of a son born of a virgin, and named *Immanuel*, which means "God with us" (Isa. 7:14; Matt. 1:23).

In the time of Pekah, Tiglath-Pileser III invaded Israel and captured all the northern tribes and the lands east of the Jordan (2 Kgs. 15:29). This was the first phase in the defeat and deportation of Israel. The rest of the land would soon fall also.

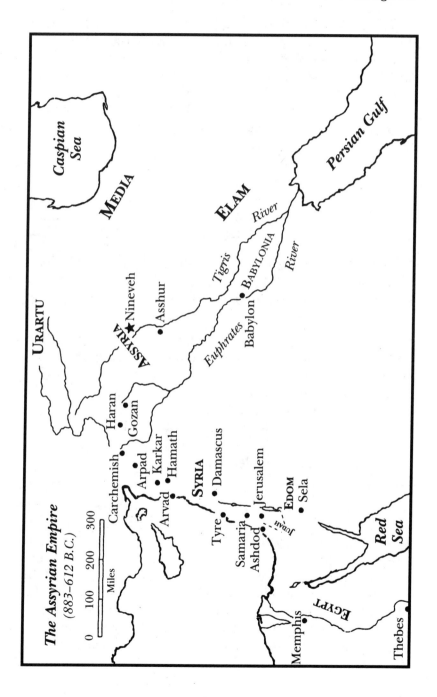

The Assyrian Empire
(883–612 B.C.)

Miles
0   100   200   300

Caspian Sea

MEDIA

ELAM

Persian Gulf

URARTU

Tigris River

Euphrates River

BABYLONIA

Nineveh
Asshur
ASSYRIA
Babylon

Haran
Gozan
Carchemish
Arpad
Karkar
Hamath
Arvad
SYRIA
Damascus
Jerusalem
EDOM
Sela
Tyre
Samaria
Ashdod
Judah

Red Sea

EGYPT

Memphis

Thebes

The story of Israel's last king — *Hoshea* — is related to us in 2 Kings 17:1-6. Hoshea assassinated Pekah (2 Kgs. 15:30).

8. *King Jotham of Judah.* Jotham was a good king and mighty. He "ordered his ways" before the LORD his God (2 Chr. 27:6, ASV). Jotham won a significant victory over the Ammonites (2 Chr. 27:5). Much of Jotham's reign was a joint reign with his father Uzziah, when he was a leper.

JOTHAM of Judah — 751-736 B.C. (*Good*)
(2 Kgs. 15:32-38; 2 Chr. 27)
    a. Mighty (2 Chr. 27:6)
    b. Threatened (but NOT invaded) by Rezin and Pekah.

---

9. *King Ahaz of Judah.* (See notes on Pekah, section 7, above.) King Ahaz was one of the *worst* kings ever in Judah. It amazes us to learn that he was so extremely evil when he had a good grandfather and father.

AHAZ of Judah — 743-728 B.C. (One of the *WORST*)
(2 Kgs. 16; 2 Chr. 28)
    a. Introduced idolatry
    b. Attacked by Rezin and Pekah
    c. Hired Tiglath-Pileser III to attack Israel
    d. Made an altar like one in Damascus
    e. Damaged the temple willfully

Ahaz practiced idolatry. He even sacrificed his son in the fire (2 Kgs. 16:3). Ahaz was attacked by Pekah, the king of Israel, allied with Rezin, the king of Aram from Damacus (2 Kgs. 16:5). This attack resulted in the deaths of one hundred and twenty thousand soldiers in Judah! (2 Chr. 28:6). In his distress Ahaz would not seek the LORD, nor accept the offer of a miraculous sign from God (Isa. 7:10-11). Instead, he hired Tiglath-Pileser III of Assyria to attack Damascus. Tiglath-Pileser was quite willing to do that. (He planned to do it anyway!)

> **In 732 B.C. Tiglath-Pileser III captured Damascus** and killed Rezin, the last king of the Aramean kingdom. This decisive event caused Assyria to become Israel's major threat. Israel fell to the Assyrians in 722, just ten years after Aram fell.

When Ahaz went up to Damascus to pay off Tiglath-Pileser, Ahaz saw an altar there and desired to make one like it to place in his temple in Jerusalem (2 Kgs. 16:10). He kept the old altar, for the remote chance that he might sometime wish to inquire of the LORD (2 Kgs. 16:15).

Ahaz found that the "help" he received from Tiglath-Pileser was much more trouble than help (2 Chr. 28:20).

Ahaz shut up the LORD's temple and set up altars at every street corner in Jerusalem (2 Chr. 28:24).

10. *Hoshea, the last king of Israel.* Hoshea's name is actually the same name in Hebrew as the famous prophet *Hosea*, but the names are usually spelled differently to prevent confusion. The form *Hoshea* is more like the Hebrew.

> **HOSHEA** of Israel — 732–722 B.C. (2 Kgs. 17:1-6; 15:30)
> a. Tribute to Shalmaneser (king of Assyria)
> b. Conspiracy with King So of Egypt
> c. Siege of Samaria and fall of Israel

The last king of Israel was not quite as evil as the kings before him. He even allowed King Hezekiah to send messengers from Judah up into Israel, to invite them to the great Passover feast held by Hezekiah (2 Chr. 30:1, 10-11). But it was too late to save Israel. If Hoshea had made common cause with Hezekiah, king of Judah, and with the LORD, he might have delayed the fall of Israel. But Hoshea chose the path of rebellion, after he had sworn to be the vassal of Shalmaneser.

In Hoshea's time the Assyrian king Shalmaneser V (son of Tiglath-Pileser) invaded Israel when he learned that Hoshea had sent envoys to King *So* of Egypt, and had not paid the tribute money to Assyria. (*So* was perhaps a short form of the name of the Egyptian king O*SO*rkon IV (730–715 B.C.). After a three-year siege of Samaria, Shalmaneser captured the city in the year 722 B.C. Shalmaneser died in December of that year, after the fall of Samaria.

Shalmaneser's successor as king of Assyria, Sargon II, wrote that he captured Samaria, and had captured 27,280 persons. Sargon was second-in-command under Shalmaneser, but his claims to have taken Samaria are not regarded as true.

The Israelites were taken from their land, and deported to Assyria. They were resettled in Gozan on the Habor River, and in the towns of the Medes farther east (in modern Iran).

11. *Israel exiled because of sin. Israel resettled with foreigners* (2 Kgs. 17:7-41). The final writer of the books of Kings (probably Jeremiah) wrote an extended explanation of why the northern kingdom of Israel was deported (17:7-23). It was because of their continual idolatry. People may not be willing to acknowledge it, but God controls the destiny of nations. "So the people of Israel were taken from their homeland into exile in Assyria, and they are still there" (lit., "to this day"). See notes on 2 Kings 10:27.

Foreigners were brought into Samaria from Babylon and other places conquered by the Assyrians (2 Kgs. 17:24). These foreigners were the ancestors of the *Samaritans*, who lived there in the time of Christ, and were so despised by the Jews. Further colonization of Samaria is ascribed to Esarhaddon, grandson of Sargon, and to the "great and honorable Ashurbanipal" (or Osnapper), the last great king of Assyria (668–633 B.C.) (Ezra 4:2,10). These imported people brought in their own idols with them and practiced the worship of them in Samaria. They burned their children in fire to their gods (2 Kgs. 17:31) as they did before.

The LORD did not allow Himself to be forgotten as the ruler in Israel, and He sent lions among the Samaritan settlers. To relieve that crisis the Samaritans did not cease to worship their own gods, but only brought back a priest to the land to conduct worship to the LORD, as well as to their own gods. They worshiped (lit., *feared*) the LORD, but they also served their own gods" (1 Kgs. 17:33).

12. *King Hezekiah of Judah, before the fall of Israel* (2 Kgs. 18:1-12; 2 Chr. 29, 30, 31). Hezekiah began to reign (probably jointly with his father Ahaz) in 728 B.C. He was one of Judah's best kings ever.

Hezekiah was king in Judah in 722 B.C., when the northern kingdom of Israel fell. This was Hezekiah's sixth year.

Hezekiah followed his "father" David, and not his immediate father, Ahaz (18:3). Hezekiah removed the pillars and poles that were symbols of idolatry. He even broke into pieces the bronze snake that Moses had made in the desert, because the Israelites were worshiping it (2 Kgs. 18:4), and he called it *Nehushtan*, meaning "just a piece of bronze" (Num. 21:8-9).

HEZEKIAH of Judah — 728-695 B.C. (One of the *BEST*)
(2 Kgs. 18:1-8, 13-37; chs. 19-20; 2 Chr. 29-32)
    a. Reopened and cleansed the temple
    b. Great Passover feast
    c. Sennacherib's invasion
    d. Life extended 15 years
    e. Visitors from Babylon

The books of Chronicles tells much about the reforms that King Hezekiah made in his early years, before the fall of Israel. His acts include (1) reopening and repairing the temple [Ahaz had closed it.] (2 Chr. 29:3-11); (2) purifying (cleansing) the temple (2 Chr. 29:12-19); (3) starting again the sacrifices and praise in the temple (2 Chr. 29:20-36); (4) celebrating a great Passover feast, to which the people of the northern kingdom were invited (2 Chr. 30:1-31); (5) collecting tithes from the people for the support of priests and

Levites (2 Chr. 31:6). Hezekiah himself contributed from his own possessions for the morning and evening burnt offerings (2 Chr. 31:3).

Hezekiah's men found a document written by King Solomon with some proverbs not included in his previous collection. Hezekiah's men copied these out, and included them with the proverbs already recorded (Prov. 25:1).

Militarily, Hezekiah showed an example of the power of trust in the LORD to his neighboring king, Hoshea. Hezekiah trusted in the LORD. He rebelled against the king of Assyria, and did not serve him (2 Kgs. 18:7). The Assyrians did NOT tolerate that type of insubordination. Hezekiah's courage wavered a little after the Assyrians conquered the northern kingdom, and he sent tribute to them on at least one occasion (2 Kgs. 18:14-15). But Hezekiah's courage grew again, and he was successful in resisting the Assyrians, for the LORD was with him (2 Kgs. 18:7).

"In everything that he (Hezekiah) undertook in the service of God's temple and in obedience to the law and the commands, he sought his God and worked wholeheartedly. And so he prospered" (2 Chr. 31:21).

There was a great eruption of activity by the *prophets* in the time of Hezekiah. *Isaiah* was the prophet in Jerusalem for nearly sixty years (740–681 B.C.). *Micah* was a country (rural) prophet about 739–710 B.C. The prophet Hosea's testimony in Israel continued down into the time of Hezekiah.

The Prophet MICAH

1. Rural prophet in Judah, at Moreshath-Gath, 739–710 B.C.

2. Message: Social justice is required (Micah 2:1-2, 8-9).
   The LORD will triumph (Micah 4:1-3; 5:2-4).

3. Micah prophesied that the Messiah-king would come from *Bethlehem* in the land of Judah (Micah 5:2; Matt. 2:5-6).

4. Micah 6:8 — "He has showed you, O man, what is good. And what does the LORD require of you? To act justly and to love mercy and to walk humbly with your God."

The greatest of the prophets was *Isaiah.* His name means "Salvation of the LORD." The name was very fitting for Isaiah. (See Isaiah ch. 12.) Isaiah was greatest in the comprehensiveness and length of his book. His prophecies cover topics from sin (ch. 12) to deliverance in the new heavens and earth (Isa. 66:22; Rev. 21:1). Isaiah prophesied deliverance from Aram (Syria) (ch. 8), from Asssyria (ch. 10), and from Babylon (chs. 13,14; 48:14, 20).

Isaiah was the greatest prophet in the vividness of his prophecies about the *Messiah* to come. He foretold the coming of the suffering servant of the LORD, upon whom "the LORD has laid the iniquity of us all" (Isa. 52:13–53:12). See also Isaiah 42:1-4; 32:1-3; 7:14; 9:6-7. Isaiah foretold the coming of "A voice of one calling" in the desert for the people to prepare the way for the LORD (Isa. 40:3). This was a prophecy of John the baptizer (John 1:23).

Outline of the Prophecies of Isaiah

1. **Prophecies of judgment** (chs. 1–35).
   In this section prophecies are made of the coming menace from Assyria (10:5-19). Judgments upon many nations (chs. 13–24).
2. **Historical interlude** (chs. 36–39).
   These chapters show the fulfillment of Isaiah's earlier prophecies about Assyria. This gave reason to trust his future prophecies. The chapters introduce the future menace from Babylon (ch. 39). These chapters are a bridge between what preceded and what follows them.
3. **Prophecies of comfort** (and peace) (chs. 40–66).
   These chapters foretell deliverance from Babylon and from all sin and distress.

Questions on Section C
From Joash to the End of Israel (2 Kgs. 12:1–18:12)

Joash (king of Judah)
1. How old was Joash when he began to reign? (12:1)
2. Was Joash good or evil? (12:2)
3. Who was the good counselor of Joash? (2 Chr. 24:2)
4. What project did Joash undertake? (24:4)
5. How did Joash first try to raise money? (24:5)
6. How did this first financial drive work out? (24:5-6)
7. How was money finally raised? (24:8,11; 2 Kgs. 12:9)
8. How did the temple repair project progress? (24:13)
9. Who came appealing to Joash after Jehoiada's death? (24:17)
10. What prophet denounced Joash for backsliding? (24:20)
11. What happened to this prophet? (24:21-22)
12. What enemy army invaded Judah in Joash's time? (24:32)
13. What city did Hazael take? (2 Kgs. 12:17)
14. Why did Hazael not take Jerusalem? (12:18)
15. Who slew Joash and why? (2 Chr. 24:25; 2 Kgs. 12:20)
16. Where was Joash buried? (24:25)

Jehoahaz (king of Israel)
1. What Syrian king had power over Israel continually during Jehoahaz' reign? (2 Kgs. 13:3)
2. How did Jehoahaz obtain some deliverance? (13:4-5)
3. How many troops, horsemen and chariots were left to Jehoahaz? (13:7)

Jehoash (king of Israel)
1. Was Jehoash a strong or weak king? (2 Kgs. 13:12)
2. Who visited Elisha in his final sickness? (13:14)
3. What did Elisha predict by the shooting of an arrow? (13:17)
4. What miracle was done by Elisha after his death? (13:20-21)
5. Why did God not permit Syria to wipe out Israel? (13:23)
6. Who succeeded Hazael as king of Syria? (13:25)
7. How many times did Jehoash smite Syria? (13:25)

Amaziah (king of Judah)
1. Was Amaziah a good king? (2 Kgs. 14:3)
2. What did Amaziah do to the murderers of his father (Joash)? (14:5)
3. With what nations did Amaziah war? (14:7,11)

4. What mercenary troops did Amaziah hire? (2 Chr. 25:6)
5. Did he keep and use the mercenary troops? (25:7)
6. What did the Israelite troops do when dismissed? (25:10,13)
7. What people did Amaziah slaughter? (25:11,14)
8. How many did Amaziah throw off a rock cliff? (25:12)
9. What terrible thing did Amaziah do in Edom? (25:14)
10. How did Amaziah receive a prophet sent to reprove him? (25:16)
11. What challenge did Amaziah issue to Jehoash of Israel? (2 Kgs. 14:8)
12. With what fable did Jehoash answer him? (14:9)
13. Who won — Amaziah or Jehoash? (14:13)
14. What did Jehoash do to Jerusalem? (14:13)
15. How did Amaziah die? Where? Why? (14:19; 2 Chr. 25:27)
16. Who succeeded Amaziah? (2 Kgs. 14:21)

Jeroboam II (king of Israel)
1. Was Jeroboam II strong or weak? (2 Kgs. 14:25)
2. What territory and cities did Jeroboam recover and capture? (14:25,28)
3. What three prophets prophesied in Israel in the time of Jeroboam II? (14:25; Amos 1:1; Hosea 1:1)
4. What prophet foretold Jeroboam's successes? (2 Kgs. 14:25)

Uzziah (Azariah) (king of Judah)
1. How long did Uzziah reign? (2 Kgs. 15:1-2; 2 Chr. 26:3)
2. Was Uzziah good or bad? (2 Chr. 26:4-5)
3. Was Uzziah strong or weak? (26:6)
4. What peoples did Uzziah conquer? (26:6-8)
5. What unusual weapons were devised in Uzziah's time? (26:15)
6. What presumptuous act did Uzziah attempt to do? (26:16; compare Num. 18:7)
7. Who opposed Uzziah's presumptuous act? (26:17)
8. What was Uzziah's punishment? (26:19-21)
9. What prophet wrote the acts of Uzziah? (26:22)
10. Who was co-regent with Uzziah? (2 Kgs. 15:5)
11. What prophet saw the Lord in the year that King Uzziah died? (Isa. 6:1)

Zechariah (king of Israel)
1. How long did Zechariah reign? (2 Kgs. 15:8)
2. Who slew Zechariah? Where did the assassination occur? (15:10)
3. Whose dynasty ended with the death of Zechariah? (15:12)

Shallum, Menahem, Pekahiah and Pekah (kings of Israel)

1. How long did Shallum reign? (2 Kgs. 15:13)
2. Who slew Shallum? (15:14)
3. What did Menahem do to the city of Tiphsah? (15:16)
4. What person seems to have begun to reign over Israel in Gilead at the same time that Menahem began to reign? (15:25)
5. What foreign king came upon Menahem? (15:19)
6. How much tribute did Menahem have to pay? (15:19)
7. Who succeeded Menahem? (15:23)
8. How long did Pekahiah reign? (15:23)
9. Who slew Pekahiah? (15:25)
10. What foreign king invaded Israel in the days of Pekah? (15:29)
11. What area in Israel did the Assyrian king conquer? (15:29)
12. Who slew Pekah? (15:30)

Jotham (king of Judah)

1. Was Jotham a good or bad king? (2 Kgs. 15:32-34)
2. Was Jotham a strong or weak king? (2 Chr. 27:6)
3. What kings began to invade Judah during the time of Jotham? (2 Kgs. 15:37; compare Isaiah 7:1)
4. How did the people live in Jotham's time? (2 Chr. 27:2)
5. What nations did Jotham fight against? (27:5)

Ahaz (king of Judah)

1. Was Ahaz good or bad? (2 Kgs. 16:2-4)
2. What idolatry did Ahaz practice? (2 Chr. 28:2-3)
3. What nations smote Ahaz and Judah? (28:5)
4. What reassurance did Isaiah extend to Ahaz? (Isa. 7:3-4; 10-11)
5. What prevented many Judeans from being permanently enslaved in Israel? (2 Chr. 28:8-11)
6. To whom did Ahaz send for help? (28:16)
7. What city did Tiglath-pileser conquer? (2 Kgs. 16:9)
8. Did Assyria really help Judah? (2 Chr. 28:21)
9. Why did Ahaz sacrifice to the gods of Damascus? (28:33)
10. What altar did Ahaz build? (2 Kgs. 16:10)
11. Where did Ahaz erect altars in Jerusalem? (2 Chr. 28:24)
12. What damage did Ahaz do to the temple? (2 Kgs. 16:17-18)

Hezekiah (king of Judah) *before Israel's fall*

1. Was Hezekiah good or bad? (2 Kgs. 18:3,5)
2. What did Hezekiah reopen and repair? (2 Chr. 29:3)

3. What did Hezekiah set the Levites in the temple to do? (29:25)
4. Where did the command to use instrumental music come from? (29:25)
5. Whom did Hezekiah invite to a great feast? What feast was it? (30:1)
6. How were Hezekiah's messengers treated in Israel? Did any Israelites respond favorably? (30:10-11)
7. What was done to permit those who were unclean to eat the Passover? (30:18-20)
8. How great was Hezekiah's passover feast? (30:26)
9. What did the returning Israelites do after the Passover? (31:1)
10. How did Hezekiah provide for the priests? (31:4-5)
11. Were the priests adequately cared for by Hezekiah's system? (31:10)
12. What literary work did the men of Hezekiah do? (Prov. 25:1)
13. What brass object did Hezekiah destroy? What did he call it? What does this name mean? (2 Kgs. 18:4; compare Num. 21:8)
14. What foreign nation did Hezekiah rebel against? (18:7)
15. What people did Hezekiah smite? (18:8)

Hoshea and the Fall of Israel

1. Who was the last king of Israel? (2 Kgs. 17:1)
2. What Assyrian king invaded Hoshea's kingdom? (17:3)
3. With what other foreign king did Hoshea make a conspiracy? (17:4)
4. How long did the king of Assyria besiege Samaria? (17:5)
5. What was done with the people of Israel when Samaria was captured? (17:6)
6. Name the places where the Israelites were taken. (17:6)
7. What had caused Israel to be deported? (17:7)
8. Had the Israelites lived better than the Canaanites that God had thrust out before them? (17:8)
9. Whom had God sent to warn Israel of the consequences of their ungodliness? (17:13)
10. How had Israel treated the prophets? (17:14)
11. What gods and idolatrous practices had Israel taken up? (17:16-17)
12. Had Judah kept the commandments of God? (17:19)
13. What king of Israel had made Israel sin? (17:22)
14. What people were imported into Samaria? By whom? (17:24)
15. How did God show his displeasure to these imported peoples in Samaria? (17:25)
16. How did the imported peoples react to God's punishment? (17:26-27)
17. Who was brought back to Bethel to teach the law of the LORD? (17:28)
18. Did the LORD become the exclusive God at Samaria? (17:29-32)

19. Did God's chastening make Israel understand? (17:34,41)
20. Who was king in Judah when Samaria and Israel fell? (18:9-10)

Section D
Judah after the Fall of Israel (1 Kings 18:13–25:26)

1. *The Assyrian menace* (Isa. 10:1-18; 20:1). When the northern kingdom of Israel was defeated and deported by the Assyrians, Judah was threatened. Judah was "next door" south from Samaria and Israel. The Assyrians had captured city after city and country after country all over Syria and areas nearby, and appeared invincible.

In Jerusalem Isaiah the prophet warned, "The Assyrian" is the rod of God's anger "in whose hand is the club of my wrath! I send him against a godless nation [Judah!], I dispatch him against a people who anger me [the Jews!], to seize loot and snatch plunder . . . But this is not what he [the Assyrian king] intends . . . his purpose is to destroy, to put an end to many nations" (10:5-7).

Isaiah had words of reassurance, as well as threats. "When the Lord has finished all his work against Mount Zion and Jerusalem, he will say, 'I will punish the king of Assyria for the willful pride of his heart and the haughty look in his eyes'" (10:12). "Assyria will fall by a sword that is not of man; a sword, not of mortals, will devour them" (Isa. 31:8).

There was in Judah a large political "party" that trusted in *Egypt* to save them from the Assyrians (and still later trusted the Egyptians to save them from the Babylonians). Isaiah pronounced "Woe to those who go down to *Egypt* for help, who rely on horses, who trust in the multitude of their chariots . . . but do not look to the Holy One of Israel, or seek help from the LORD" (Isa. 31:1; 30:1-2). The Egyptians proved to be of no help at all to the Jews. The Assyrian Rabshekeh ("field commander") was correct in his description of Egypt as a "splintered reed . . . which pierces a man's hand and wounds him if he leans on it" (2 Kgs. 18:21).

King Sargon II of Assyria in 720 B.C., after the fall of

Israel, swept down the Philistine coast, capturing Ekron and Gaza, and advanced to the very gates of Egypt, which for the first time was defeated and forced to pay tribute. Again in 712 Sargon's forces were sent into Philistia against Ashdod, led by the Tartan ("supreme commander"). See Isaiah 20:1! Ashdod was captured and organized into a new Assyrian province. (See W.W. Hallo and W.K. Simpson, *The Ancient Near East* [New York: Harcourt, Brace Jovanovich, 1972], pp. 138-142).

Sargon died on a military expedition far from his native land and was succeeded by his son *Sennacherib* (703–681 B.C.).

2. *Invasion of Judah by Sennacherib* (2 Kgs. 18:13–19:37; 2 Chr. 32:12-33). Sennacherib was a successful military commander, but arrogant and created hatred everywhere. He even alienated his own sons (2 Kgs. 19:37). Sennacherib's invasion of Judah and its surrounding countries is one of the best documented events in all ancient history. We have the Prism of Sennacherib, a fifteen-inch high hexagonal clay prism that gives Sennacherib's own boastful version of this campaign. (See *Ancient Near East*, Vol. 1 [Princeton Univ., 1973], pp. 199-201.) In addition to Sennacherib's record, many rooms filled with relief carvings of Sennacherib's battle at Lachish were found at Nineveh. (These can be seen at the British Museum.) Also, the actual excavations at Lachish show clear evidences of the siege of Lachish by the Assyrians. (See *Biblical Archaeology Review*, March–April 1984, pp. 48-65, 66-73.)

An important date — **701 B.C.** —
The invasion of Judah by King Sennacherib of Assyria.

Hezekiah temporarily wavered, and sent tribute money to Sennacherib (2 Kgs. 18:14-16). However, Hezekiah's courage grew again, probably from the preaching of Isaiah. Isaiah said that Assyria was like a great tree, but the LORD would lop off its branches with great power (Isa. 10:5,33).

When King Sennacherib sent his supreme commander and other top officers (the Tartan [Isa. 20:1], the Rabsaris, and the Rabshakeh) from Lachish to Jerusalem to demand that Hezekiah surrender and give hostages to them, Hezekiah told his people on the wall of Jerusalem not even to answer him (2 Kgs. 18:36,17). Jerusalem was a safe place with the deep valleys and high walls around it. Unless they undertook an all-out long siege, all the Assyrians could do at Jerusalem was bluster.

King Sennacherib boasted in his record that he shut up Hezekiah the Jew like a bird in a cage at Jerusalem. (See *Ancient Near East,* Vol. 1, p. 200.) When a bird is in a room with a large cat, the safest possible place for it to be is in its cage! If Sennacherib had actually captured Hezekiah, he would have gloated about it, as he gloated over other kings that he captured and tortured to death.

When the Assyrian Rabshekeh (field commander) left Jerusalem to return to Sennacherib, he found he had left the siege of Lachish, because he had heard a rumor that he was about to be attacked by King Tirhaka the Cushite (Ethiopian) (2 Kgs. 19:7,9). Sennacherib had moved his forces ten miles northeast, to Libnah. From Libnah, Sennacherib wrote a threatening letter to Hezekiah in Jerusalem (2 Kgs. 19:9, 4). Hezekiah read the letter in the temple, with the letter spread out "before the LORD" (19:14). The prophet Isaiah sent word to Hezekiah that Sennacherib "will not enter this city or shoot an arrow here" (19:32).

That night the angel of the LORD went out and put to death a hundred and eighty-five thousand men in the Assyrian camp. When the people got up the next morning — there were all the dead bodies! (19:35). Sennacherib and his surviving forces went back to Nineveh, where he was slain by two of his sons.

Sennacherib's defeat was commemorated by a poem by Lord Byron.

THE DESTRUCTION OF SENNACHERIB

The Assyrian came down like the wolf on the fold,
And his cohorts were gleaming in purple and gold;

And the sheen of their spears was like stars on the sea,
When the blue wave rolls nightly on deep Galilee.

Like the leaves of the forest when Summer is green,
That host with their banners at sunset were seen:
Like the leaves of the forest when Autumn hath blown,
That host on the morrow lay wither'd and strown.

For the Angel of Death spread his wings on the blast,
And breathed in the face of the foe as he pass'd;
And the eyes of the sleepers wax'd deadly and chill,
And their hearts but once heaved, and forever grew still!

And there lay the steed with his nostril all wide,
But through it there roll'd not the breath of his pride:
And the foam of his gasping lay white on the turf,
And cold as the spray of the rock-beating surf.

And there lay the rider distorted and pale,
With the dew on his brow and the rust on his mail;
And the tents were all silent, the banners alone,
The lances unlifted, the trumpet unblown.

And the widows of Ashur are loud in their wail,
And the idols are broke in the temple of Baal;
And the might of the Gentiles, unsmote by the sword,
Hath melted like snow in the glance of the Lord!

3. *Hezekiah's illness* (2 Kgs. 20:1-11; 2 Chr. 32:24-26; Isa. 38:1-22). King Hezekiah became ill to the point of death with an infected boil (Isa. 38:21). Also, Hezekiah's heart was proud (2 Chr. 32:25). Isaiah the prophet delivered to him God's message: "Put your house in order, because you are going to die." Hezekiah was very distressed, and prayed a prayer that his life be spared (Isa. 38:9-20).

The LORD promised to let Hezekiah live fifteen more years. Hezekiah died in 698 B.C. His deliverance from death would have been about 713 B.C. To reassure Hezekiah God gave him a miraculous sign. At Hezekiah's request, the shadow on the stairway (or sundial?) of Ahaz was to go backwards ten steps (or degrees). (King Ahaz refused to accept a sign from God [Isa. 7:11-12]. King Hezekiah does not seem to have benefited much by the sign he saw.)

During the fifteen years Hezekiah's life was extended, a

son — Manasseh — was born to him. Manasseh was twelve years old when he became king (2 Kgs. 21:1). Manasseh became by far the worst king Judah ever had. He filled Jerusalem with innocent blood (2 Kgs. 21:16). Because of his sins, Judah was sentenced to captivity (2 Kgs. 24:3-4; 21:13-14). It would have been better for the nation if Hezekiah had died when God directed, and Manasseh had never been born. There is a proper time to die (Eccl. 3:2), and God knows better than humans do when that time is.

4. *Messengers from Babylon to Hezekiah* (2 Kgs. 20:12-19; Isa. 39:1-8). It appears that soon after Hezekiah's recovery from illness, he received messengers from Merodach-Baladan (Marduk-apla-iddina II), the king at the city of Babylon. This "king" ruled at Babylon 721–710 B.C., in opposition to the kings of Assyria (principally Sargon II), seeking to form an independent kingdom. Sargon chased him from the throne in 710. It is probable that he was seeking some alliance or friendship with King Hezekiah, as he was anticipating the attack by Sargon. Merodach-Baladan had a second rule at Babylon, but it lasted only six months in 702 B.C., when he was chased out by the Assyrian king Sennacherib.

King Hezekiah of Judah showed to the messengers from Babylon all his treasures in Jerusalem. Isaiah the prophet rebuked Hezekiah for this and foretold that the time was coming when all those treasures would be taken and carried off to Babylon (2 Kgs. 20:17). Worse than that, Hezekiah's own "descendants" (lit., "sons") would be taken away and be eunuchs in the palace of the king of Babylon (20:18). (Could Daniel and his three friends have been some of these? [Dan. 1:3,6]). King Hezekiah does not seem to have been concerned about the warning by Isaiah (20:19).

5. *Hezekiah's construction projects* (2 Kgs. 20:20-21; 2 Chr. 32:5, 30-31). Hezekiah made a tunnel to bring water into the city of Jerusalem (2 Kgs. 20:20-21 and 2 Chr. 32:5, 30-31). This tunnel extended the Jebusite tunnel, which went westward from the spring Gihon into Jerusalem. Hezekiah's tunnel was dug under Jerusalem through bedrock 1,749 feet, and led to the Pool of Siloam (John 9:7). It follows a large

S-shaped path. (See *Biblical Archaeology Review*, March–April 1980, pp. 9-11.) Hezekiah dug this tunnel to keep the Assyrians from finding a water supply when they brought their army to Jerusalem (2 Kgs. 18:17).

Hezekiah also enlarged Jerusalem very much. He built a new wall westward from the temple court to a location near the modern Jaffa gate of Jerusalem, and then southward around the hill called modern Zion, and back east to the City of David. A segment of this wall of Hezekiah (eighteen feet wide and one hundred fifty feet long) has been found. This wall more than doubled the size of Jerusalem. Probably the new walled-in area was necessary because of a large population increase in Jerusalem produced by refugees from the northern kingdom when it fell to the Assyrians in 722 B.C. (See the *New Encyclopedia of Archaeological Excavations in the Holy Land*, Vol. 2, article "Jerusalem," pp. 706-707 for map and photo.)

6. *Wicked King Manasseh of Judah* (2 Kgs. 21:1-17; 2 Chr. 33:1-20). The worst king ever in the kingdom of Judah (Manasseh) followed one of its best kings (Hezekiah). (It is interesting to speculate about why this occurred.)

MANASSEH of Judah — 695–642 B.C. (The *WORST*!)
(2 Kgs. 21:1-18; 2 Chr. 33:1-20).
    a. Idolatry unlimited
    b. Cruelty unlimited
    c. Announcement of Judah's end
    d. Captive in Babylon
    e. Repentance and reformation

As a result of Manasseh's extreme wickedness, the LORD pronounced the sentence of doom upon Judah (2 Kgs. 24:4; 21:12-13). Also, the LORD allowed him to be taken to Babylon as a captive by the Assyrian king Esarhaddon. Esarhaddon's father, Sennacherib, had destroyed Babylon in 689 B.C. to punish it for its attempts to become independent of Assyria.

Esarhaddon rebuilt the city. He was the only Assyrian ruler who actually ruled at Babylon. Esarhaddon wrote that he forced twenty-two kings to transport bulding materials to Nineveh, and he specifically names Manasseh king of Judah (*Ancient Near East*, Vol. 1, p. 201).

In Babylon Manasseh repented, and prayed to God. The Lord brought him back to Jerusalem, where he rebuilt the outer wall of the city of David and made other developments at Jerusalem (2 Chr. 33:14-16).

The short document called the *Prayer of Manasses* is included in the fourteen books of the Apocrypha. Its words sound very appropriate for Manasseh's repentance. The Jews did not include the document in their Scriptures. The majority of scholars date it in the second century before Christ, but this is uncertain.

7. *King Amon of Judah.* He was evil. He did not learn any lesson from his father's captivity at Babylon or his father's repentance. Amon was assassinated.

AMON of Judah — 642–640 B.C. (*Evil*)
(2 Kgs. 21:19-26; 2 Chr. 33:21-25)
    a. Continued his father's evils
    b. Assassinated

---

8. *King Josiah, Judah's best king.* Josiah became king at age eight. He was Judah's best king ever. He repaired the temple (2 Kgs. 22:6).

JOSIAH of Judah — 640–609 B.C. (The *BEST* of all)
(2 Kgs. 22:1–23:30; 2 Chr. 34:1–35:27)
    a. Temple repaired
    b. Book of the law found
    c. Idolatry purged and true religion enforced
    d. Altar at Bethel defiled
    e. Slain at Megiddo by Pharaoh Neco

In the repair work on the temple, the book of the law was found. (It was concealed either by rubble or in a hidden place provided for it.) We are of the opinion that the book was the original writing by Moses, or the official temple copy of it. The book was brought to King Josiah by Hilkiah the priest, and it was read by Shaphan the scribe. Josiah tore his robes in distress. The book warned of fearsome punishments for forsaking the LORD, and Josiah knew that his father and grandfather had done that. Josiah was reassured by the prophetess Huldah that although the punishments that were described in the book of the law were surely coming upon Judah, they would not come in his lifetime. "Your eyes will not see all the disaster I am going to bring on this place" (2 Kgs. 22:20).

Prominent people associated with King Josiah:
1. HILKIAH — the high priest (2 Kgs. 22:4)
2. SHAPHAN — the scribe (2 Kgs. 22:9)
3. HULDAH — the prophetess (2 Kgs. 22:14)
4. JEREMIAH — the prophet (Jer. 1:2-3)

The contents of the book that was found in the temple are not clearly stated. It seems to have included warnings of punishment for forsaking the LORD. These possibly included Deuteronomy 27 and 28 and Leviticus 26.

There is a popular theory that the book that was found was just the book of Deuteronomy. Many writers say that the book had just been written a few years or months before by people who were influenced by the preaching of prophets and believed in the doctrine of "divine retribution," that is, if we do good we will be rewarded, and if we do evil we will be punished. These people (supposedly) also believed that the worship should be conducted ONLY by the Levites, and only in one place, the central sanctuary at Jerusalem. To promote these beliefs, the author(s) wrote this book in a way that made it sound as if Moses wrote it. The author(s) of this writing is called "D," for Deuteronomist. They planted it in the temple where it would be found when young Josiah's men began to repair the temple. When this book was found, it became the first Scripture ever accepted as "holy" by the Israelites.

If we accept this theory, we must conclude that all the many statements in the book of Deuteronomy about Moses writing it are false. We believe that the theory is false, and the Scriptures are truth. See the Introduction to Deuteronomy, Period V, F, 1, g.

Josiah led the people in a great covenant assembly to declare publicly they would keep the law of Moses, which they found written in the scroll (2 Kgs. 23:1-3). Josiah then forcibly destroyed the idols and altars all over the country. He closed down the many sanctuaries outside of Jerusalem, where people were worshiping the LORD and idols in their own ways. God forbade people to bring their sacrfices to places other than at the central place which He designated (Deut. 12:1-14). Archaeological evidence of the destruction of the out-of-Jerusalem worship centers has been found at places such as Beersheba and Arad. King Hezekiah had closed down some of the illegal worship places, but Josiah's reform was more thorough.

The Prophet ZEPHANIAH

Zephaniah is a rather obscure prophet who spoke during the days of King *Josiah*. He writes of a great danger coming upon the land of Judah (1:2-3). Perhaps this was the Scythian invasion from the north in 627 B.C. Zephaniah's prophecies seem to have been given before Josiah made the great reformation in 621 B.C. after the book of the law was found.

The theme of Zephaniah is **THE DAY OF THE LORD**. See 1:7, 14-18. It would be a time of judgment against many nations and against Jerusalem. He foretold the fall of Assyria and Nineveh (2:13-15). Perhaps Zephaniah's strong preaching helped Josiah, and caused many of the people to repent.

Zephaniah 3:9 — "Then I will purify the lips of the peoples, that all of them may call on the name of the LORD."

Josiah destroyed what was left of the altar at Bethel, where Jeroboam made the golden calf (2 Kgs. 23:15-18). Almost exactly three hundred years before (930 B.C.) a man of God from Judah had foretold that a king named *Josiah* would be born and come and burn the bones of priests upon Jeroboam's altar (1 Kgs. 13:1-3). Josiah came to Bethel and did this about 620 B.C.

During the reign of King Josiah the great prophet *Jeremiah* was very conspicuous. He began to prophesy in the thirteenth year of Josiah (627 B.C.) and his prophetic ministry continued on into the period of the captivity in Babylon (580 B.C.?). Jeremiah was the last great prophet in Judah in the period just before Judah fell to Babylon. He wrote a lamentation over the death of Josiah (2 Chr. 35:26).

Josiah was killed at the city of Megiddo in 609 B.C. by the Egyptian Pharaoh Neco (609–593 B.C.). Neco was alarmed by the rise of the power of the kingdom of Babylon. The Babylonians had already captured the city of Nineveh in 612 B.C. and ended the rule of the Assyrians. Egypt had been in subjection to the Assyrians at least as far back as 661 B.C., when the Assyrian king Ashurbanipal destroyed Thebes, the capital of upper Egypt.

The new Egyptian king Pharaoh Neco wanted to help the remnants of the Assyrian army at Carchemish to resist the Babylonians. Carchemish was on the "great bend" of the upper Euphrates River, west of Haran. To get to Carchemish Pharaoh Neco had to leave Egypt and go north across the territory of Judah. King Josiah knew how the Assyrians had savagely raided his country in the time of his great-grandfather Hezekiah. He did not want Pharaoh Neco to go through his land to help the Assyrians. Josiah tried to head off Neco at the pass at Megiddo. The Valley of Iron leading through the Carmel range to Megiddo is one of the few places where armies could pass through the Carmel range to go on north.

Josiah was the last good king of Judah. The country fell apart after he died, and lasted only twenty-two years. During that time Judah had four kings, who included three sons of Josiah and one grandson. Then Jerusalem was captured by the Babylonians, (586 B.C.), and the people of Judah were taken into captivity in Babylon for seventy years.

The Battle of CARCHEMISH — 605 B.C.

This battle ended the power of the Assyrian empire forever. It caused Babylon to be the next ruling empire for nearly a century, and led to the capture of JUDAH by BABYLON.

ASSYRIAN ARMY **REMNANTS**   **VS.**   *BABYLON.*
Allied with **Egyptians**   (Babylon won!)

---

9. *King Jehoahaz of Judah.* Jehoahaz also had the name *Shallum* (Jer. 22:11).

JEHOAHAZ of Judah — 609 B.C. (*Evil*)
(2 Kgs. 23:30-34; 2 Chr. 36:2-4; Jer. 22:11)
    a. Three months' reign
    b. Deposed and taken to Egypt

---

10. *King Jehoiakim of Judah.*

JEHOIAKIM of Judah — 609–597 B.C. (*Evil*)
(2 Kgs. 23:34-24:7; 2 Chr. 36:5-8; Jer. 35,36)
    a. Enthroned by Pharaoh
    b. Servitude to Babylon
    c. Cut up and burned Jeremiah's scroll
    d. First deportation to Babylon

Jehoiakim was a brother to Jehoahaz, whom Pharaoh Neco had removed from the throne. Pharaoh changed his name from Eliakim to Jehoiakim. Jehoiakim was so evil and vicious that the LORD sent against him several foreign nations — Babylonians, Arameans, Moabites and Ammonites (2 Kgs. 24:2).

Jehoiakim was a cruel opponent of the prophet Jeremiah and tried to capture and kill him (Jer. 36:26). Jehoiakim captured the prophet Uriah (or Urijah) in Egypt, and killed him (Jer. 26:20-24).

During the reign of Jehoiakim important international events occurred. The famous battle at Carchemish (referred to above [section 8]) was finally fought in 605 B.C. and won by the Babylonians. This battle ended over two centuries of rule by the Assyrians and allowed the Babylonians to rule the "world" for nearly a century. The great king of the Babylonians was *Nebuchadnezzar* (605–562 B.C.).

Following the battle of Carchemish, Nebuchadnezzar came to Jerusalem, and the LORD delivered Jehoiakim into his hand (Dan. 1:1-2). Nebuchadnezzar took some captives from Jerusalem to Babylon. These included the famous Daniel and his three friends — Shadrach, Meshach, and Abednego (Dan. 1:6). Jehoiakim swore allegiance to his new masters, the Babylonians, but then broke his oath and did not send the tribute to Babylon as he promised (2 Kgs. 24:1).

Jehoiakim would not listen to the scroll of all the messages the LORD gave to Jeremiah, but cut the scroll to pieces and burned them (Jer. 36:23). His efforts to destroy Jeremiah's book were not successful. After the first book was burned, the LORD told Jeremiah to get a new scroll and rewrite all the words that Jehoiakim king of Judah had burned in the fire, and Jeremiah added many similar words to them, including the story of how Jehoiakim burned the first edition (Jer. 36:28, 32).

In the reign of Jehoiakim the heart-touching story of the Recabites occurred (Jer. 35). These nomadic, Bedouin-type people had come into Jerusalem during the invasion by Nebuchadnezzar (35:11). When Jeremiah offered them wine to drink, they refused, because their forefather Jonadab son of Recab had commanded them not to drink wine, or to build houses or plant crops (35:8). They obeyed their forefather. The LORD said that the Recabites had obeyed their father, but Judah had not obeyed Him as their father. The Recabites would always continue, but Judah would perish. From this story we learn the lessons of obedience to parents, the dangers of strong drink, and, most important of all, obedience to God.

Jehoiakim died in disgrace when the king of Babylon came to Jerusalem to capture him. He died, and his dead body was thrown out and exposed to heat by day and frost by night (Jer. 36:30). He was buried with the burial of a donkey, dragged away and thrown outside the gates of Jerusalem (Jer. 22:19). His son Jehoiachin was placed on the throne, but only reigned three months.

JEREMIAH — The Weeping Prophet

a. Jeremiah was the great prophet in Judah in the time of Kings Josiah, Jehoiakim, and Zedekiah. He had a long ministry, from the thirteenth year of Josiah (627) until after the captivity began in 586 B.C.

b. God knew him even before he was born and set him apart to be a prophet (Jer. 1:5).

c. Jeremiah had to announce the seventy years of captivity in Babylon (Jer. 25:9-11; 29:10). Jeremiah urged the people to surrender to Babylon (38:17-18).

d. Jeremiah's scribe's name was Baruch (Jer. 36:4). He was a very efficient, but quite forthright man (Jer. 45:1-5).

e. Jeremiah was mocked, beaten, and imprisoned. One time he was lifted out of a muddy pit by a kind Ethiopian named Ebed-Melech (Jer. 38:7-12).

f. Jeremiah cried, "Oh, that my head were a spring of water and my eyes a fountain of tears! I would *weep* day and night for the slain of my people."

The prophet *HABAKKUK* prophesied about 605 B.C., at the time when the Babylonians had not yet taken Judah but had become known as fierce warriors. God told Habakkuk that He would use the Babylonians to punish the Judeans (Hab. 1:6). Habakkuk was pained at that news.

God told to Habakkuk the good news that "the righteous will live by his *faith*" (Hab. 2:4; Rom. 1:17).

---

11. *King Jehoiachin of Judah.* Jehoiachin was also called by

the names *Jeconiah* and *Coniah* (Jer. 24:1; 27:20; 37:1). Jehoiachin was an eighteen-year-old king who had wives and servants (2 Kgs. 24:15, 12).

JEHOIACHIN of Judah — 597 B.C. (*Evil*)
(2 Kgs. 24:8-16; 2 Chr. 36:9-10)
  a. Three months' reign
  b. Captured and taken to Babylon
  c. Second deportation to Babylon

Nebuchadnezzar had come to Jerusalem to take Jehoiakim, but he had died. Nebuchadnezzar instead took Jehoiachin captive and also took a great host of others. Nebuchadnezzar besieged the city, and Jehoiachin surrendered. They bound him with bronze shackles and brought him to Babylon (2 Chr. 36:6).

PROPHETS and Contemporary Kings

Prophet and date of his ministry	Area involved	Contemporary kings or events
1. Elijah (approx. 864–846 B.C.)	Northern kingdom	Ahab, Ahaziah, Jehoram
2. Elisha (approx. 846–796)	Northern kingdom	Jehoram to Jehoash
3. Obadiah (848–841?)	Edom	Jehoram of Judah (?)
4. Joel (830?)	Judah	Joash of Judah (?)
5. Jonah (780?)	Nineveh	Jeroboam II
6. Amos (760)	Northern kingdom	Jeroboam II
7. Hosea (755–725)	Northern kingdom	Jeroboam II
8. Isaiah (740–681)	Judah	Uzziah, Jotham, Ahaz, Hezekiah
9. Micah (736–710)	Judah	Jotham, Ahaz, Hezekiah
10. Jeremiah (627 till after 586)	Judah	Josiah until after fall of Judah
11. Zephaniah (627?)	Judah	Josiah. Scythian invasion?
12. Nahum (625?)	Nineveh	Before the fall of Nineveh (612 B.C.)
13. Habakkuk (605?)	Judah	Jehoiakim; Battle of Carchemish (605)

14. Ezekiel	Jews in Babylon and in Judah	Babylonian captivity
15. Daniel (605–536)	Babylon	Babylonian captivity
16. Haggai (520)	Judah	Post-exilic period
17. Zechariah (520–480)	Judah	Post-exilic period
18. Malachi (430?)	Judah	Post-exilic period

The Deportations of the Jews to Babylon

1. 605 B.C. — Fourth year of King Jehoiakim. Daniel and a few others were taken.
2. 597 B.C. — Reign of Jehoiachin. Those taken: King Jehoiachin, the prophet Ezekiel, Kish (great-grandfather of Mordecai), 10,000 Jews (2 Kgs. 24:14).
3. 586 B.C. — Eleventh year of King Zedekiah. Those taken: nearly all the remaining Jews, except a few of the poorest people, and the prophet Jeremiah (Jer. 40:1-6).
4. 582 B.C. — Minor deportation (Jer. 52:30)

Jehoiachin was regarded as the last king of Judah. He lived in Babylon as a prisoner at least thirty-seven years (2 Kgs. 25:27-30). He was finally released when King Nebuchadnezzar died. He was given food from the king's table. A clay tablet was found in Babylon which lists the names of prisoners to receive food allowances. The list includes the name of Jehoiachin. (See *Ancient Near Eastern Texts* [Princeton Univ., 1955], p. 308.)

12. *Zedekiah, the last king of Judah.*

ZEDEKIAH of Judah — 597–586 B.C. (*Evil*)
(2 Kgs. 24:18-25:7; 2 Chr. 36:11-14; Jer. 27:1,12; 32:1-5; ch. 37)
    a. Rebelled against Babylon
    b. Siege and destruction of Jerusalem
    c. Third deportation to Babylon
END OF JUDAH !

Zedekiah was a morally weak person. He felt many needs, and asked for prayer (Jer. 37:3). But when Jeremiah gave him God's word, he feared his advisers and princes more than he feared God, and would not follow Jeremiah's advice, even though he treated Jeremiah better than others did (Jer. 37:20-21).

In the ninth year of Zedekiah, King Nebuchadnezzar of Babylon came to Jerusalem to besiege it and destroy it. The siege lasted until Zedekiah's eleventh year, when there was a great famine in the city (2 Kgs. 25:3). King Zedekiah tried to escape from Jerusalem, but he was captured in the plains of Jericho (2 Kgs. 25:5). They brought him to the king of Babylon at Riblah (far north of Judah, up on the Orontes River). There they killed Zedekiah's sons before his eyes and then put out his eyes (2 Kgs. 25:7).

13. *Judah into captivity* (2 Kgs. 25:8-26; 2 Chr. 36:15-21; Jeremiah 39–44). The temple at Jerusalem was burned (2 Kgs. 25:9). Jerusalem's walls were torn down (2 Kgs. 25:10). Almost all of the people were taken away to Babylon. The valuable articles in the temple were carried away to Babylon (2 Kgs. 25:13-17). Many of the chief priests and officers were executed (2 Kgs. 25:18-21). Nebuchadnezzar appointed a governor named Gedaliah over the few Jews left in the land (2 Kgs. 25:23; Jer. 39:14). Gedaliah was assassinated (Jer. 40:7-41:15). The Jews who remained in the land were afraid and fled to Egypt, though Jeremiah told them to stay in the land of Judah (Jer. 41:16–43:13). In Egypt the Jews who fled there worshiped the goddess they called the Queen of Heaven in defiance of God's words through Jeremiah. Jeremiah warned them that they would perish by sword and famine until they were all destroyed.

Remains of a Jewish temple have been found on the island of Elephantine (Jeb) in the Nile River at Aswan in upper Egypt. The Jews there experienced the destruction of their temple but still did not serve the LORD as their only God. (See Keith N. Schoville, *Biblical Archaeology in Focus* [Grand Rapids: Baker, n.d.], pp. 268-270.)

Questions on Section D
Judah After the Fall of Israel
(2 Kgs. 18:13–25:26; 2 Chr. 32–36)

Hezekiah (after Israel's Fall)
1. What Assyrian king attacked Judah in Hezekiah's time? (2 Chr. 32:1-2)
2. What did Hezekiah do with the sources of water near Jerusalem? (32:3)
3. What did Hezekiah do to the walls of Jerusalem? Why? (32:5; 25:23)
4. What reassurance did Hezekiah give the men of Judah? (32:6-8)
5. How much success did the king of Assyria have in Judah? (2 Kgs. 18:13)
6. To what place did Hezekiah send a message of submission to the king of Assyria? (18:14)
7. What riches did Hezekiah send the king of Assyria? (18:15-16)
8. What messengers did the king of Assyria send to Hezekiah? Who was their spokesman? (18:17,19)
9. What two sources of help did the Assyrians urge the Judeans not to trust in? (18:21-22)
10. In what language did the Jewish leaders ask the Assyrians to speak? Why? (18:26-27)
11. What did the Assyrians demand Judah and Jerusalem to do? (18:31-32)
12. How did the Jews respond to the Assyrians' demands? (18:37;19:1-3)
13. What prophet reassured Hezekiah? (19:6)
14. What Egyptian (or Ethiopian) king caused the Assyrians to move? (19:8-9)
15. What was sent to Hezekiah from the Assyrian king? (19:14)
16. What did Hezekiah do with the item mentioned in question 15? (19:14)
17. Who sent word to Hezekiah that God would save Jerusalem? (19:20,34)
18. What caused many Assyrians to die? Where? How many? (19:8,35)
19. How did Sennacherib die? (19:36-37)
20. Who succeeded Sennacherib? (19:37)
21. What fearsome message came to Hezekiah while he was sick? (20:1)
22. What did Hezekiah do when he heard this news? (20:2-3)
23. How many years were added to Hezekiah's life? (20:5-6)
24. What medication was prescribed for Hezekiah? (20:7)
25. What miracle showed Hezekiah that he would be healed and go up to the house of the Lord? (20:8-11)
26. What Babylonian king came to visit Hezekiah? (Isa. 39:1-2)
27. What did Hezekiah show his visitors? (2 Kgs. 20:13)
28. What did Isaiah predict would happen because Hezekiah showed all his precious things to the Babylonians? (20:14-17)

29. Did Hezekiah seem to be alarmed over Isaiah's warnings? (20:19)

Manasseh

1. How old was Manasseh when he began to reign? (2 Kgs. 21:1)
2. What idolatry did Manasseh practice? (21:3,6)
3. Where did Manasseh build altars? (21:4-5)
4. Where did he set up idols? (21:7)
5. How wicked was Manasseh? (21:11)
6. What did God say he would do because of Manasseh's evils? (21:12-14)
7. What cruelty did Manasseh practice? (21:16)
8. Where was Manasseh taken captive? By whom? (2 Chr. 33:11)
9. What change took place in Manasseh while he was a captive? (33:12-13)
10. What building projects did Manasseh undertake after his captivity? (33:14-16)

Amon

1. What evils did Amon practice? (2 Chr. 33:22-23)
2. How did Amon die? (33:24)

Josiah

1. How old was Josiah when he began to reign? (2 Chr. 34:1)
2. When in his reign did he begin to seek God? (34:3)
3. What did Josiah destroy? (34:3-4)
4. What did Josiah do with bones of priests? Why? (34:5; Num. 19:11)
5. What project did Josiah undertake in his eighteenth year? (34:8,10)
6. Who was priest in Josiah's time? (34:14)
7. Who was the scribe in Josiah's time? (34:15)
8. What was found in the temple? (34:14)
9. Who read the law to the king? (34:18)
10. How did Josiah react when he heard the reading? (34:20)
11. Why did Josiah send some people to go inquire of the Lord? (34:21)
12. What position did Huldah have? (34:22)
13. Summarize the message of Huldah to Josiah. (34:24-28)
14. What people did Josiah gather at the house of Jehovah? (34:29-30)
15. What did Josiah do at this gathering at the house of Jehovah? (34:30)
16. What did the king make before the Lord? (34:31) What other people joined with him in making this? (34:32)
17. What did Josiah destroy in Jerusalem? (2 Kgs. 23:6,12-14)
18. What did Josiah destroy in Bethel? (23:15)
19. What sepulchre and monument in Bethel did he spare? Why? (23:16-18; 1 Kgs. 13:1-2)
20. What feast did Josiah keep? (2 Chr. 35:1)

21. How great was this feast compared to other such feasts? (35:18)
22. How did Josiah compare in character to the other kings? (2 Kgs. 23:25)
23. Why did Josiah's goodness not save Judah? (23:26-27)
24. What king of Egypt went to a battle? Where was he going? Through whose land did he pass? (2 Chr. 35:20; 2 Kgs. 23:29)
25. Who were the opposing sides in the battle of Carchemish? Why is this battle one of the decisive battles of history?
26. What warning did the king of Egypt send to Josiah? (2 Chr. 35:21)
27. What did Josiah do with his appearance before going to fight? (35:22)
28. How did Josiah die? Where? (35:22-23; 2 Kgs. 23:29)
29. What two prophets prophesied in Josiah's time? (Jer. 1:1; Zeph. 1:1)
30. What prophet lamented for Josiah? (2 Chr. 35:25)

Jehoahaz

1. Who made Jehoahaz king? (2 Kgs. 23:30)
2. How long did he reign? (23:31)
3. Who put Jehoahaz in bonds? (23:33)
4. Where was Jehoahaz taken and kept till his death? (23:34)
5. Who was made king in place of Jehoahaz? (23:34) What was his name changed to?
6. What was the relationship of the king that followed Jehoahaz to Jehoahaz? (23:34)

Jehoiakim

1. What taxation did Jehoiakim impose on the people? Why? (2 Kgs. 23:33,35)
2. What king took over Judah and other nearby lands from Egypt? (24:1,7)
3. Who was taken captive in the fourth (or third) year of Jehoiakim? (Dan. 1:1,6)
4. Whom did Jehoiakim rebel against? (2 Kgs. 24:1)
5. What peoples invaded Judah in Jehoiakim's time? (24:2)
6. What did Jehoiakim do with the roll of Jeremiah's prophecy? (Jer. 36:22-23)
7. Who was Jeremiah's scribe? (36:4)
8. Who came to Jerusalem to capture Jehoiakim? (2 Chr. 36:6)
9. How did Jehoiakim die? (Jer. 22:18-19)

Jehoiachin

1. By what two other names is Jehoiachin known? (Jer. 24:1; 22:24)
2. How long did Jehoiachin reign? (2 Kgs. 24:8)
3. Who captured Jerusalem in the days of Jehoiachin? (24:10)
4. How many people were deported? (24:14)
5. What prophet was deported to Babylon at this time?
6. What was done with the temple in Jehoiachin's time? (24:13)

7. What was done with Jehoiachin? (24:15)
8. Who was made king in the place of Jehoiachin? To what was his name changed? (24:17)
9. How long did Jehoiachin survive his captivity? (25:27)
10. What Babylonian king released Jehoiachin? (25:27-30)

Zedekiah

1. How old was Zedekiah when he began to reign and how long did he reign? (2 Kgs. 24:18)
2. What had Zedekiah sworn to do which he did not do? (2 Chr. 36:13)
3. What rebellion did Zedekiah make? (2 Kgs. 24:20-25:1)
4. Who came and besieged Jerusalem? (25:1-2)
5. How many years did the siege last? (25:1-2)
6. What foreign army came to resist Babylon during the siege of Jerusalem? (Jer. 37:5)
7. What did Jeremiah predict about Pharaoh's army and the fate of Judah? (37:7-10)
8. Why did Zedekiah try to flee Jerusalem? (2 Kgs. 25:3-4)
9. Where was Zedekiah captured? (25:5)
10. What was the last thing Zedekiah ever saw? (25:7)
11. Who was captain of the guard of the king of Babylon? (25:8)
12. What was done with the valuables of the temple? (25:13-15)
13. What was done to the temple? To Jerusalem? (25:9, 10)
14. What was done with the people of Jerusalem? (25:11)
15. What leaders of the Jews were executed? (25:18-21)
16. How long was the land of Judah desolate and kept its Sabbaths? (2 Chr. 36:21)
17. What privileges were granted to Jeremiah after Jerusalem fell? (Jer. 39:11-12)
18. What choices were given to Jeremiah by the Babylonians? Which choice did he make? (40:2-6)

Judah after its Fall

1. Whom did the king of Babylon make governor over the land? (Jer. 40:7)
2. What did the governor urge the Judeans to do? (40:9)
3. What agricultural produce did the people gather? (40:12)
4. Who hired an assassin to kill the governor? Who was the assassin? (40:14)
5. Whom did the assassins slay? (41:2-3)
6. Where were the bodies cast? (41:9)
7. Who fought the assassins? (41:11-12)
8. Where did the Jews think they should go? (41:17)

9. What did Jeremiah prophesy to the Jews about their proposed trip? (42:15-17,19)
10. Did the Jews accept Jeremiah's prophecy? (43:2,7)
11. What prophecy did Jeremiah make in Egypt? (43:10-11; 44:13-14)
12. What did the Jews in Egypt say to Jeremiah in response to his prophecy? (44:16-19)

Period X — Captivity in Babylon
(Daniel and Ezekiel; Psalm 137)

Section A
Introduction to the Period of Captivity

1. The seventy years of captivity of the Jews in Babylon may be calculated from the first deportation in 605 B.C. to the close of the captivity (536 B.C.), if both the starting and closing years are counted. (See the chart of the deportations to Babylon in Period IX, Section D, 11.) It has also been calculated from the actual fall of Jerusalem (586 B.C.) to the rebuilding of the temple (516 B.C.). See Zechariah 7:5.

2. The books of Ezekiel and Daniel are our principal sources of information about life during the period of captivity. These prophets guided and encouraged the captives. Psalm 137 also tells of the time of captivity.

3. King Jehoiachin of Judah was released from imprisonment in Babylon during the captivity (561 B.C.) (2 Kgs. 25:27-30).

4. The Jews lived nearly normal lives in Babylon. They were not enslaved or persecuted. They had liberty to marry, build homes, plant gardens (Jer. 29:5-6), to assemble (Ezek. 20:1), and to rise to positions of prominence, as Daniel did.

5. There were times of discouragement and painful memories (Ps. 137). Some additional captives were brought into Babylon (Jer. 52:30). Idolatry was enforced upon them at least once (Dan. 3). Some of the Jews were bitter against the LORD; some were indifferent; and some were disobedient (Ezek. 18:2, 25; 33:31). Nonetheless, many never forgot their homeland and were ready to return when opportunity came.

6. Tribal identity and genealogies were preserved by the scribes during the period (Ezra 2:59-62).

7. The Jews dispersed in foreign lands imparted to the people in whose lands they lived the knowledge of the one true God and the hope of the Messiah to come. When Jesus was born, Magi from the East were looking for the coming of the "king of the Jews" (Matt. 2:2).

8. The bitter experience of captivity in Babylon permanently cured the Jews of idolatry, at least those Jews who returned to Jerusalem after the captivity.

9. *Synagogues* probably first came into use during the captivity in Babylon. We have no historical records of exactly when or where synagogues were first organized. But the book of Ezekiel mentions groups of Jews gathering with the prophet Ezekiel (14:1; 20:1). With their temple destroyed, it was almost inevitable that small groups of Jews would gather for reading and teaching of the law, and that such groups would become organized into assemblies like the synagogues. By New Testament times synagogues were to be found in every village of the Jews, even after the temple was rebuilt.

10. *Rulers of Babylon*:

   (1) *Nebuchadnezzar* (605–562 B.C.)

   (2) *Evil-Merodach* (562–560 B.C. Son of Nebuchadnezzar. 2 Kgs. 25:27)

   (3) *Nergal-Sharezer* (560–556. Brother-in-law of Evil-Merodach. Jer. 39:13)

   (4) *Labashi-Marduk* (556. Son of Nergal-Sharezer. Killed by priests.)

   (5) *Nabonidus* (556–539. A military officer placed on the throne. His wife was *Nitocris*, probably the daughter of Nebuchadnezzar. He placed his son Belshazzar on the throne at Babylon from his third year of reign till his seventeenth year, so that they ruled jointly.)

   (6) *Belshazzar* (553–539. Dan. 5:1,30. Killed by the Persians.)

Belshazzar was probably a grandson of Nebuchadnezzar, through his mother. Note that Jeremiah predicted that all nations would serve Nebuchadnezzar, and *his son* and *his grandson* until the time came for his land to be overthrown (Jer. 27:7). Second Chronicles 36:17,20 says that the Jews were car-

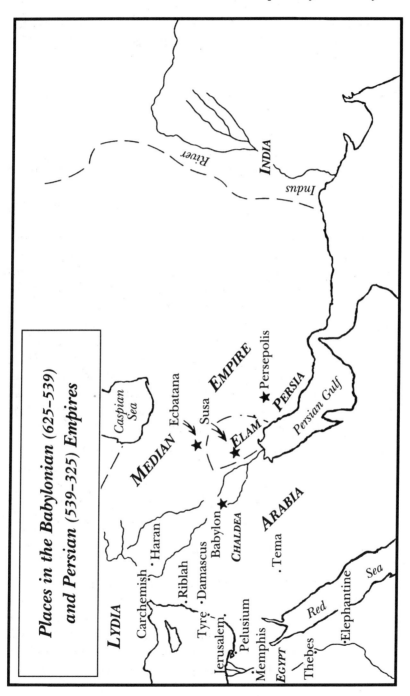

Places in the Babylonian (625–539) and Persian (539–325) Empires

ried to Babylon by Nebuchadnezzar and became servants to him and *his sons* until the kingdom of Persia came to power.

Section B
Daniel

The Hebrew Scriptures do not refer to Daniel as a "prophet" but as a godly government official. Jesus did speak of him as "the prophet Daniel" (Matt. 24:15). Daniel exercised the ministry of a prophet, but did not have the title or office of "prophet."

1. *Daniel and his fellows excel* (Dan. 1). Nebuchadnezzar, the king of Babylon, was the ultimate mighty tyrant. He was led to know God by a few godly young men, such as Daniel, Hananiah (renamed Shadrach), Mishael (Meshach), and Azariah (Abednego). They remained steadfastly true to their God even in Babylon. They determined not to eat the king's royal food and wine, even if that jeopardized their opportunities to enter respected careers and possibly their lives. God gave the young men knowledge and understanding so that King Nebuchadnezzar found them ten times better than all the magicians and wise men in his whole kingdom (1:20). Then they served in the king's government.

> Proverbs 2:6 — For the LORD gives wisdom, and from his mouth come knowledge and understanding.
> "Wisdom . . . will bring you honor" (Prov. 4:7-8, NKJV).

2. *Nebuchadnezzar's dream of a great statue* (Dan. 2). (Daniel 2:4 — 7:28 is written in the Aramaic language.)

Early in the reign of Nebuchadnezzar (his "second year," 603 B.C.) the "great God" whom Daniel served (2:45) showed to Nebuchadnezzar that He knew what kingdoms would rise and fall in the future, and that Daniel was His spokesman. God revealed to Daniel what the king had dreamed, so that Daniel could explain the meaning of the dream. It was an impressive dream, revealing by symbols what kingdoms would rise and fall during the following six hundred years:

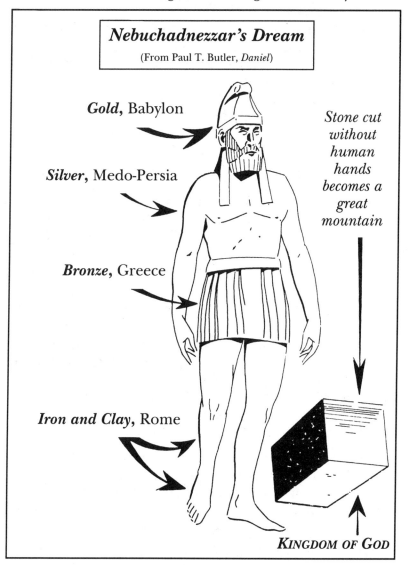

Nebuchadnezzar's Dream
(From Paul T. Butler, *Daniel*)

Gold, Babylon

Silver, Medo-Persia

Bronze, Greece

Iron and Clay, Rome

Stone cut without human hands becomes a great mountain

KINGDOM OF GOD

Nebuchadnezzar was deeply impressed by Daniel's revelation, and said, "Surely your God is the God of gods and the Lord of kings" (Dan. 2:47-49).

675

SYMBOLS IN NEBUCHADNEZZAR'S DREAM IMAGE
(Daniel 2)

1. **Gold** head — Symbolized **BABYLON**, the kingdom of Nebuchadnezzar (625–539 B.C.)
2. **Silver** arms and chest — Kingdom of Medes and **PERSIANS** (539–331 B.C.)
3. **Bronze** belly & thighs — **GREEK** kingdoms of Alexander the Great and his successors (331–63 B.C.)
4. **Iron** legs and feet — **ROMAN** empire (63 B.C.–A.D. 476). (The feet were partly of iron and partly of baked clay, showing that this kingdom was made of disunited peoples.)
5. The **ROCK** cut out of a mountain not by human hands — symbol of the **KINGDOM of GOD**, which is the church of Jesus Christ, established in the time of the Roman empire, on the great day of Pentecost (Acts 2).

---

3. *Trial of the blazing furnace* (Dan. 3). Nebuchadnezzar showed how quickly people can forget God. He showed folly and conceit by assuming that a man is able to create a god! On one occasion when Daniel was absent from Babylon, Nebuchadnezzar made a towering image of gold and compelled all his officials to bow to his image. Shadrach, Meshach, and Abednego would not fall down and worship it. They were thrown into the blazing furnace tied up. Then the king saw an amazing sight in the blazing furnace.

"Look! I see four men walking around in the fire, unbound and unharmed, and the fourth looks like a son of the gods" (Dan. 3:25).

When Shadrach, Meshach, and Abednego were delivered, the king praised their God. "Praise be to the God of Shadrach, Meshach and Abednego, who has sent his angel and rescued his servants! They trusted in him and defied the king's command and were willing to give up their lives rather

676

than serve or worship any god except their own God" (Dan. 3:28).

4. *Nebuchadnezzar's dream of a tree* (Dan. 4). King Nebuchadnezzar dreamed of a great tree that was cut down, and its stump in the ground was bound with iron and bronze shackles.

Daniel was again called to interpret this dream. He explained that the tree symbolized King Nebuchadnezzar himself, and the dream foretold that he would lose his mind and his throne, and would act and eat like an animal "until seven times (years?) pass by."

All this happened to the king just twelve months later. He was smitten by God. "He was driven away from people and ate grass like cattle. . . . his hair grew like the feathers of an eagle" (4:33).

When Nebuchadnezzar recovered, he praised the Most High God of Daniel: "Now I, Nebuchadnezzar, praise and exalt and glorify the King of heaven, because everything he does is right . . . And those who walk in pride he is able to humble" (4:37).

A hand-sized leather document was found among the Dead Sea Scrolls in Cave IV, which slightly resembles the story in Daniel chapter four. It supposedly quotes the Babylonian king Nabonidus (who reigned 556–539 B.C., after Nebuchadnezzar). He says that he was smitten with a malignant disease for a period of seven years and became unlike men. But a Jewish magician (like Daniel?) gave him directions that enabled him to be healed. (See J.T. Milik, *Ten Years of Discovery in the Wilderness of Judaea* [London: SCM Press, 1959], pp. 36-37.)

The connection between this document and Daniel chapter four is uncertain. We suppose that the Dead Sea document (which was written several centuries after Daniel) was a corrupted version of the story in Daniel four, in which the name of the later King Nabonidus was substituted for that of Nebuchadnezzar.

Nebuchadnezzar "ate grass like cattle" (Dan. 4:33). The illness of Nebuchadnezzar appears to be a rare form of mental illness in which the victims take the personality and behavior of animals. Some people have acted as wolves (werewolves) or chickens. R.K. Harrison tells of observing an actual case of *boanthropy* (humans taking the character of cattle). The victim was in a British mental institution in 1946. He wandered around the grounds, plucking up and eating handfuls of grass as he went along. His fingernails were coarse and thickened. (*Introduction to the Old Testament* [Grand Rapids: Eerdmans, 1969], p. 1116.)

Nebuchadnezzar triggered his illness when he said, "Is not this [city] the great Babylon [which] I have built as the royal residence, by my mighty power and for the glory of my majesty?" (Dan. 4:30).

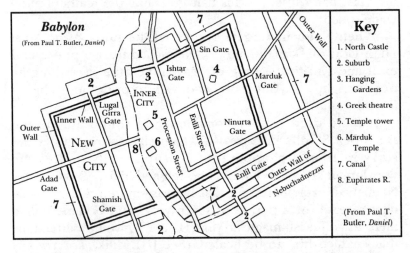

The city of Babylon in Nebuchadnezzar's time was a glorious city. It was eleven miles around its walls. The walls were eighty-five feet thick, made of baked mud bricks set in asphalt. The great Euphrates River flowed through the center of the city. A moat of water supplied by the Euphrates surrounded the walls. A broad street (the Processional Street) ran across the city. The walls along the street were decorated with glass-like tiles, which had figures of bulls, lions, or dragons upon them. The Processional Street ended at the high-arched Ishtar gate, nearly forty feet high. The Hanging

Gardens of Babylon were one of the Seven Wonders of the Ancient World. (See "Babylon" in *The Biblical World*, Chas. F. Pfeiffer, ed. [Grand Rapids: Baker, 1966].)

The prophets Isaiah and Jeremiah foretold that Babylon would become a total and permanent desolation (Isa. 13:19-22; Jer. 50:23, 39-40; 51:29-32). In our time Babylon remains in ruins, as the prophets foretold, in spite of attempts by modern rulers in Iraq to restore it.

5. *The Persians attack Babylon. End of Babylonian empire* (Dan. 5). Belshazzar made a great feast. At the feast they ate and drank and praised the gods of gold and silver. The fingers of a human hand appeared, writing upon the wall. The king watched and grew pale as it wrote. No one could interpret the writing. The queen (or queen mother) remembered Daniel. Daniel was then an old man perhaps eighty years old. He was called in and told that he would be made *third highest ruler* in the kingdom if he could interpret the writing. (Belshazzar was ruling jointly with his father, Nabonidus, so that the country already had two rulers.)

Daniel rebuked Belshazzar sternly (5:22-23). But Daniel gave the interpretation of the handwriting on the wall.

That very night Belshazzar, king of the Babylonians, was

THE HANDWRITING ON THE WALL
(applied to King Belshazzar)

מְנֵא מְנֵא *MENE, MENE* — *"Numbered, Numbered."* God has given your kingdom a certain *number* of days to exist, and the number ends tonight.

תְּקֵל *TEKEL* — *"Weighed"* (related to the word *shekel*). God has weighed you in His balances, and you are a lightweight (too small to remain on God's team).

וּפַרְסִין *U-PHARSIN* — "And *divisions.*" The *U* is "and." *Pharsin* is the word for "divisions" but is also the word for *Persians.* Your kingdom will be divided to the Medes and Persians (Dan. 5:25-28).

---

slain (Dan. 5:30). Darius the Mede took over the kingdom of Babylon. Darius was probably the commander known as Gubaru in the Babylonian records, and Gobryas in the Greek. (See John Whitcomb, *Darius the Mede* [Grand Rapids: Eerdmans, 1959], p. 24.) King Cyrus himself entered Babylon about two weeks later.

The events on the night Babylon fell are somewhat uncertain. The Greek historians tell us that Cyrus dug a canal or trench from the Euphrates River and let the river run into the canal, so that the river water level dropped, and his men were able to enter the city through the bed of the river. They raced to the palace, where those inside opened the gates to see what the uproar was about! The Persian soldiers dashed into the presence of the king, who arose with his dagger in his hand. He was overpowered and slain before most of the people of Babylon knew their city had been invaded. (See Herodotus, *Histories*, I, 191; also Xenophon, *Cyropaedia*, VII, v, 8-30.) This account seems to harmonize with Daniel 5:30.

In Cyrus' own account he says that his men marched to Babylon with their weapons packed away, and entered the city without any battle (*The Ancient Near East*, Vol. 1, James B. Pritchard, ed. [Princeton Univ. Press, 1958], p. 207). The *Babylonian Chronicles* also report that Cyrus' troops entered Babylon without battle (*Op. cit.*, p. 204).

The prophet Isaiah foretold that the LORD would subdue nations before Cyrus and "open doors before him so that gates will not be shut" (Isa. 45:1). Jeremiah the prophet foretold that there would be some fighting during the fall of Babylon (Jer. 51:3, 11-12). All of the accounts of the fall of Babylon agree that very little fighting occurred.

6. *Daniel in the lions' den* (Dan. 6). Daniel continued to serve as a government official even after the Persians took over Babylon. He lived to see the glorious time of the first return of his people from the Babylonian captivity (536 B.C.), though he did not die even then.

Because of jealousy in some of the Persian officials who resented Daniel's promotion (6:3), a plot was laid against Daniel. Daniel was thrown into a den of lions to be devoured

(6:7). Daniel was saved because God sent His angel and shut the mouths of the lions. (Daniel would then have been nearly ninety years old.)

The LAWS OF THE MEDES & PERSIANS

could not be repealed or changed, once the king had signed the law (Dan. 6:8, 12; Esth. 1:19).

Daniel showed to the Persians, as he had shown to the Babylonian king Nebuchadnezzar, that his GOD was the true and living God. After Daniel was delivered from the lions, the Persian king Darius wrote to all the people throughout the land . . .

"IN EVERY PART OF MY KINGDOM PEOPLE MUST FEAR AND REVERENCE THE GOD OF DANIEL" (6:26).

Officially Daniel was thrown into the lions' den because he had prayed to some other god than the king (6:7,13). Daniel prayed three times a day with his window open toward Jerusalem. King Solomon had prayed at the dedication of his temple, "If [your people] . . . in the land of their enemies who took them captive . . . pray to you . . . toward the city you have chosen [Jerusalem] and the temple, . . . hear their prayer and their plea" (1 Kgs. 8:48-49).

DANIEL PRAYED THREE TIMES EVERY DAY (Dan. 6:10).

Psalm 55:17 — Evening, morning and noon I cry out . . . and he hears my voice.

Do you pray to God three times each day? (1 Thess. 5:17)

---

7. *Daniel's dream of four beasts* (Dan. 7). In the first year of King Belshazzar (553 B.C.) Daniel had a dream which

foretold by symbols the rise of future kingdoms. The kingdoms are similar to those foretold by the dream image of Nebuchadnezzar in Daniel 2.

VISION OF FOUR BEASTS — Daniel 7

1. **Winged *LION*** — Symbol of kingdom of *Babylon* (8:4). (By the time of Belshazzar Babylon was nearly ready for its wings to be torn off.)
2. A ***BEAR*** raised up on one side — Empire of Medes and Persians. (8:5. The three ribs in the bear's mouth may symbolize the kingdoms of Egypt, Lydia, and Babylon, which were all conquered by the Persians.)
3. Four-winged ***LEOPARD*** — Greek kingdoms (8:6).
4. Terrible ten-horned BEAST — Roman empire (8:7-8).
5. Little ***HORN*** on the ten-horned beast — False forces which persecute God's saints (8:21), and try to change the laws of God (8:25).

The Four Symbolic Beasts (Daniel 7)
(From Paul T. Butler, *Daniel*)

In the vision Daniel saw "one like a son of man" come with the clouds of heaven to the Ancient of Days (God). He was given authority and sovereign power. The experiences of the "son of man" described in this vision are like those of Jesus. When Christ ascended in clouds to heaven (Acts 1:9), all authority was given to Him in heaven and earth and He sat down upon a throne at the right hand of God (Matt. 28:18; Mark 16:19; Rev. 3:21).

8. *Vision of a Ram and He-goat* (Dan. 8).

Daniel's Vision of a Ram and a He-goat (Dan. 8)

1. *RAM* — Kingdom of the Medes and Persians (8:20)
2. *He-GOAT* — The king of Greece (8:20)
3. *LARGE HORN* on the he-goat — Alexander the Great, who conquered the "world" for the Greeks (334–323 B.C.)
4. *FOUR HORNS* from stump of large horn — Four Divisions of the kingdom of Alexander the Great after he died.
5. *SMALL* (little) *HORN* — King Antiochus IV, called *Epiphanes* (meaning the Shining, or Radiant, One). (175–163 B.C. He persecuted the Jews and stopped their sacrifices in the temple [1 Maccabees 1:10, 44-50]. His cruelty led to the revolt by the Jews, led by the Hasmonean [Maccabean] family).

In the third year of King Belshazzar (551 B.C.) Daniel (probably living then in Babylon) saw an amazing vision that left him exhausted and ill for several days (8:27). Daniel saw himself in the citadel of the distant city of Susa, in the land of Persia. There he saw a two-horned ram, and after that a male goat. These animals aggressively charged about. The goat had a single prominent horn between his eyes. The goat came from the west. The goat attacked the ram and destroyed it. The goat's big horn broke off, but from the stump of the big horn grew four prominent horns. Then from one of these four horns grew a branch or prong, a small horn which developed in size. It became a persecuting power that took away the daily sacrifice from the sanctuary of God.

The Ram and the He-Goat (Dan. 8)

From Paul T. Butler, *Daniel*

Daniel saw this vision even before King Cyrus, who founded the Persian empire, came to power, and twelve years before Cyrus captured the city of Babylon.

9. *Vision of the Seventy "Sevens"* (Weeks) (Dan. 9). The famous prophecy of the *seventy sevens* (weeks) was given to Daniel after an intense prayer of confession (9:4-19). The prophecy came in the first year of Darius the Mede (539 B.C.), who in cooperation with Cyrus had captured Babylon (Dan. 5:30).

Daniel was an intense student of Scripture. He had learned from Jeremiah's book that the Jews' captivity was to last seventy years (Jer. 25:11). Sixty-six years had passed since Daniel himself was deported in 605 B.C., and he saw no indications that the Jews would be going back on schedule. The people were not being obedient to God even then. This was a call to prayer for Daniel.

The angel Gabriel was sent to Daniel to reveal to him God's timetable of future events (9:21-22). He revealed that Israel would indeed return and restore their land and that the Messiah (the Anointed One) would come (9:25). All of these events would occur in a period of "seventy sevens." ("Sevens" is an accurate translation, better than "weeks," the translation given in most older versions). Seventy times seven is four hundred and ninety. We assume that this refers to a period of four hundred and ninety *years*, because four hundred and ninety days is too short a time for all the events to occur within it.

The starting point of the "seventy sevens" is either the decree of King Cyrus (536 B.C.) or the later letter of authorization to Ezra (458 B.C.). Cyrus' decree authorized only the building of the temple (Ezra 1:3), but the prophecy in Daniel 9:25 spoke of restoring and rebuilding Jerusalem. The authorization to Ezra allowed him to do whatever he chose with any money he had left over after restoring the temple sacrifices (Ezra 7:18).

Starting then at the 458 B.C. date, and going down through sixty-nine of the seventy "sevens" (483 years), we come down to A.D. 25 (9:25). That was the exact year when Christ Jesus was baptized and began His ministry (Luke 3:23). (When our calendar was first adopted, the time of the birth of Christ was set four or five years too late, so that Christ was actually thirty years old in A.D. 25.)

During these 483 years Jerusalem was to be rebuilt "in times of trouble." Ezra and Nehemiah had lots of troubles.

In the midst of the seventieth "seven" (3½ yrs.), the Messiah was to be "cut off" and "have nothing" (9:26). Jesus' ministry was almost exactly three and a half years long. When He died, he had brought in "everlasting righteousness" (9:24; Rom. 1:17), and made an end to sacrifice and offering by the sacrifice of Himself (Dan. 9:27; Heb. 10:12). Following these events an "abomination that causes desolation" would come, that is, some hateful person who causes desolation. The city (Jerusalem) and the sanctuary would be destroyed. This refers to the Romans, who came and destroyed Jerusalem in A.D. 70 (Dan. 9:27; Matt. 24:15).

10. *Vision of the "man" to Daniel* (Dan. 10). On the bank of the Tigris (Hiddekel) River Daniel had a vision of a glorious "man" who closely resembled Christ Jesus as John saw him on the island of Patmos (Dan. 10:4-6; Rev. 1:12-16). He came to explain what would happen to Daniel's people in the future (10:14).

11. *Wars of the Kings of the South and North* (Dan. 11). The chapter foretells the wars between the two Greek kingdoms of Syria (the Seleucids) and Egypt (the Ptolemies) for the mastery of Judea (323–163 B.C.). The prophecies were fulfilled in precise detail. (See Paul T. Butler, *Daniel* [Joplin, MO: College Press, 1976].)

12. *The time of the end* (Dan. 12). At some point in the prophecy (12:1 perhaps), the revelations of the "man" to Daniel shifted to events far in the future. He spoke of the resurrection of the bodies of the dead (12:2,13). He spoke of everlasting glory for those who lead many to righteousness (12:3). He foretold that many would go here and there, and knowledge would increase (12:4). Daniel did not understand these things (12:8). He was told that the words were closed up and sealed until the time of the end.

The heavenly "man" speaks to every generation as he spoke to Daniel:

> "Many will be purified, made spotless and refined, but the wicked will continue to be wicked. None of the wicked will understand, but those who are wise will understand" (12:10).

13. *Subsequent history of Babylon.* Babylon remained the second city of the Persian empire and the residence of the kings during the greater part of each year. Alexander the Great ended his career in the city, which he had planned to renovate for his capital. The Seleucid kings of Syria transferred the capital to Antioch. They selected another site on the Tigris for the frontier city of Seleucia, to which most of the inhabitants moved. Jews in Babylon copied out their Babylonian *Talmud* in the third and fourth centuries. The houses of Babylon were finally deserted and the walls became quarries for building materials. The site of the city was swept over by the neglected river, while the mounds around it crumbled into the moat. As Jeremiah foretold, "Her towns will be desolate, a dry and desert land where no one lives" (51:43). Thus it remains to this day.

Section C
Ezekiel

Ezekiel — the prophet of individual responsibility

Ezekiel was taken to Babylon in 597 B.C., in the deportation with King Jehoiachin and ten thousand other Jews (Ezek. 1:2; 2 Kgs. 24:14-15).

Ezekiel was a priest (Ezek. 1:3). Priests and Levites began their services at age thirty (1 Chr. 23:3). Ezekiel was therefore probably older than Daniel, even though he was taken into captivity eight years after Daniel was taken, because Daniel was probably just a teenager when he was taken into captivity.

Ezekiel was called to be a "watchman" for his people, to warn them of the dangers brought on by their sins (Ezek. 3:17; 33:7).

Ezekiel had a very difficult ministry in Babylon. The people were still very rebellious toward God, even in captivity (Ezek. 2:6; 3:26; 12:3). They paid little heed to Ezekiel. God said to Ezekiel, "Indeed, to them you are nothing more than one who sings love songs with a beautiful voice and plays an instrument well, for they hear your words but do not put them into practice" (Ezek. 33:32). Ezekiel also suffered the anguish of his wife's death in Babylon, and he was forbidden to weep (Ezek. 24:18).

Ezekiel kept contact with the Jews in Jerusalem, even though he lived in Babylon (8:1-3). The people in Jerusalem continued their idolatry and evils, even though two groups of them had already been deported (8:6, 17). Ezekiel was in Babylon when he heard the fearsome news: "The city (Jerusalem) has fallen" (33:21).

Neither the Jews in Babylon nor in Jerusalem would repent. They blamed their troubles on their forefathers' sins. They said, "The fathers eat sour grapes, and the children's teeth are set on edge" (Ezek. 18:2).

God told the people through Ezekiel that they themselves were responsible for their sins and sufferings, not their forefathers.

> **"The soul who sins is the one who will die.** The son will not share the guilt of the father, nor will the father share the guilt of the son. The righteousness of the righteous man will be credited to him, and the wickedness of the wicked will be charged against him" (Ezek. 18:20).

Ezekiel preached the doctrine of **individual responsibility.** This truth is stated throughout God's word: Each of us will give an account of *himself* to God (Rom. 14:12).

In the midst of Ezekiel's stern and painful words, God spoke some glowing truths and promises:

a. "As surely as I live, declares the Sovereign LORD, I take no pleasure in the death of the wicked, but rather that they turn from their ways and live" (Ezek. 33:11).

b. "I will bless them . . . I will send down showers in season; there will be showers of blessing" (Ezek. 34:26).

c. "My servant David will be king over them, and they will all have one shepherd" (Ezek. 37:24). (This is a prophecy of Christ Jesus.)

d. "I will give you a new heart and put a new spirit in you; I will remove from you your heart of stone and give you a heart of flesh" (Ezek. 36:26).

Questions on Period X
Captivity in Babylon

1. Where were the Jews taken into captivity? (Jer. 25:11)
2. For how long?
3. Which Bible books are our main sources of information about this period? Which psalm tells of the period?
4. What dates mark the start and end of the period of captivity?
5. Did the Jews in exile have freedom or slavery?
6. What meeting places for reading and teaching the law probably came into existence during this period?
7. What effect did the captivity of the Jews have on their previous idolatry?
8. Who was the greatest king of Babylon? (Jer. 25:9)

9. Who were Shadrach, Meshech and Abednego? (Dan. 1:7; 2:49; 3:12)
10. What dream did Daniel interpret for Nebuchadnezzar? (Dan. 2)
11. What did the four parts of the dream image Nebuchadnezzar saw stand for (the gold head, silver chest and arms, bronze belly, and iron legs)? What did the rock cut out of a mountain stand for? (2:34,45)
12. Why were they thrown into a blazing furnace? (3:13-23)
13. What Judean king was released by Evil-Merodach? (Jer. 52:31; 2 Kgs. 25:37)
14. Which Babylonian king made a feast for a thousand of his nobles? (Dan. 5:1) Who was this king's father? Grandfather?
15. Explain the handwriting: *Mene, Mene, Tekel, Upharsin.* (5:25-28)
16. Why was Daniel made *third* ruler in the kingdom? (5:16,29)
17. Who was the king of Persia who conquered Babylon? (10:1)
18. Who was the Mede who governed Babylon? (5:31)
19. Which prophet foretold the coming of Cyrus by name?
20. What did each of the four beasts in Daniel 7 symbolize (the lion, the bear, the leopard, the ten-horned beast)?
21. In the vision in Daniel, chapter eight, what did the ram symbolize? (8:20)
22. What did the shaggy male goat symbolize? (8:5,21)
23. What did the big horn on the goat symbolize? (8:5,21)
24. Who did the *small horn* in Daniel 8:9,23-25 stand for?
25. What did Daniel foretell would happen at the time of the end? (12:4)

Period XI — Period of Return and Restoration
From the Decree of Cyrus to the close of the Old Testament Canon. (536–423 B.C.)

Section A
Introduction to Ezra, Nehemiah, and Esther

1. The three historical books — Ezra, Nehemiah, and Esther — and the three books of prophecy — Haggai, Zechariah, and Malachi — were written during the *period of return and restoration* after captivity in Babylon, after 536 B.C. During this period many of the Jews *returned* to their land from Babylon and *restored* their worship, their temple, their social structure, and Jerusalem.

2. These books deal with the time when the *Persian* empire ruled the world. The Persians and Medes captured Babylon in 539 B.C. Archaeologists call the period from King Cyrus to Alexander the Great the *Persian period*.

3. Kings of Persia (after the fall of Babylon):
   a. Cyrus II (the Great) . . . . .549–530 B.C.
   b. Cambyses II . . . . .530–522 B.C.
   c. Gomates (Pseudo-Smerdis) . . . . .522 B.C.
   d. Darius I (the Great, son of Hystaspes) . .522–486 B.C.
   e. Xerxes I (Ahasuerus) . . . . .486–465 B.C.
   f. Artaxerxes I (Longimanus) . . . . .465–424 B.C.
   g. Xerxes II . . . . .424–423 B.C.
   h. Darius II (Nothus) . . . . .423–404 B.C.
   i. Artaxerxes II (Mnemon) . . . . .404–359 B.C.
   j. Artaxerxes III (Ochos) . . . . .359–338 B.C.
   k. Arses . . . . .338–336 B.C.
   l. Darius III (Codomannus) . . . . .336–330 B.C.

(Alexander the Great overthrew Darius III at the battle of Arbela in 331 B.C., ending the Persian empire.)

4. *Chronology of Bible events* during the period of Return and Restoration:
   a. First return of the Jews to Jerusalem, 536 B.C.
   b. Foundation of the temple laid, 535 B.C. (Ezra 3:8, 10)
   c. Ministries of Haggai and Zechariah, 521 B.C. (Hag. 1:1; Zech. 1:1)
   d. Temple completed, 516 B.C. (Ezra 6:15)
   e. Queen Esther saves her people, 479 B.C. (Esth. 2:16)
   f. Ezra returns to Jerusalem, 458 B.C. (Ezra 7:1,7)
   g. Ezra breaks up mixed marriages, 458 B.C. (Ezra 9)
   h. Possible failed attempt by Ezra to rebuild walls of Jerusalem. (Ezra 4:7, 12-13; 9:9)
   i. Nehemiah's return and first governorship, 444–443 B.C. (Neh. 1:1; 13:6). Walls rebuilt, 444 B.C.
   j. Nehemiah returns to Persia, 433 B.C. (Neh. 13:6)
   k. Ministry of prophet *Malachi*, near 430 B.C.
   l. Nehemiah's second governorship, 428–423(?) B.C.
   m. Accession of Persian king Darius II, 423 B.C. (Neh. 12:22). This is the last event referred to in the Old Testament.
5. *Outline of the book of Ezra* (Memorize the headings.)
   I. Restoration under Zerubbabel (chs. 1–6).
   II. Reforms under Ezra (chs. 7–10).
6. *Facts about the book of Ezra*:
   a. Parts of the book of Ezra are written in the Aramaic language rather than Hebrew. Aramaic sections are Ezra 4:8–6:18 and 7:12-26.

   b. The Jewish *Talmud* says that Ezra wrote the book that bears his name (*Baba Bathra*, 14b). We agree.
   Nehemiah's book is told in first person and is clearly Nehemiah's own record. Some biblical critics have taught that only *one* author-editor produced both Ezra and Nehemiah, and also 1 and 2 Chronicles. It is highly probable that Ezra was the editor of Chronicles, as well as his own book. But it does not seem true that he wrote the book of Nehemiah also.
   c. There is a long time gap between Part I of Ezra and

Part II, about 78 years. The account in Ezra 7–10 is Ezra's own story; but the previous chapters contain older material probably recorded by others (Zerubbabel?), which Ezra later combined with his own record.

d. Ezra 4:6-23 is out of chronological order with the rest of the book. In Ezra 4:5 information is given about the opposition to the rebuilding of the temple in the time of King Darius II. Then in 4:6-23 a summary of the later oppositions to the rebuilding is given. In 4:24 the discussion returns to events in the time of Darius II.

e. It appears there was an abortive attempt in the time of Ezra to rebuild the walls of Jerusalem (Ezra 4:7, 12-13; 9:9). If Ezra actually failed in an attempt to do this, his failure may account for the lack of references to him in the early part of the book of Nehemiah.

7. *Outline of book of Nehemiah* (Memorize headings.)
  I. Restoration of the walls by Nehemiah (chs. 1–7)
  II. Reforms by Ezra and Nehemiah (chs. 8–13)

8. *Outline of the book of Esther* (Memorize headings.)
  I. Danger of the Jews (chs. 1–3)
  II. Deliverance of the Jews (chs. 4–10)

9. *Facts about the book of Esther:*

a. King *Xerxes* in the book of Esther is the king of Persia who is famous for his wars with Greece. Some Bible versions spell his name *Ahasuerus* (Hebrew, *Aḥašveroš*). The events in the book pertaining to Esther took place in Xerxes' seventh year (479 B.C.), after he returned from the defeat of his navy at Salamis (in southern Greece). According to the Greek historian Herodotus, Xerxes sought consolation with his harem after this disaster. This may have a connection with the events told in Esther 2:1-2.

b. The book of Esther is peculiar in that it does not mention God's name. However, it does refer to fasting (4:16; 9:31), and probably to prayer (literally, "their crying out," Esth. 9:31) and to providence (4:14). It is not God's wish that His name not be mentioned. "My name will be great among the nations" (Mal. 1:11). But in view of the very compromised moral situation of the Jews in Persia who had chosen not to return to their homeland, it is probably no less surprising that God's name is not mentioned in the book than it is that God continued to protect and bless them.

Esther 4:14 is a wonderful verse, worthy to be memorized: The verse closes by asking,
"Who knows but that you have come to royal position **for such a time as this?**"
(God had a special job for Esther — and for us!)

Questions on Section A
Introduction to Ezra, Nehemiah, and Esther

1. What three historical books and what three books of prophecy were written in the period after the return from Babylonian captivity?
2. What title have we given to this period of time?
3. What empire ruled the "world" after the Babylonian captivity? (Ezra 1:1)
4. Give the dates of (1) the first return of the Jews back to Jerusalem; (2) Ezra's return to Jerusalem; and (3) Nehemiah's first return and governorship.
5. Write from memory the headings of Parts I and II of the outlines of Ezra, Nehemiah, and Esther.
6. In what language was part of the book of Ezra written?
7. By what other name is King Xerxes known?
8. What name surprisingly is not found in the book of Esther? Does this mean Esther is not a religious book?
9. Memorize Esther 4:14. Write it or recite it from memory.

Section B
Return and Restoration under Zerubbabel (Ezra 1–6)

1. *Cyrus' proclamation and the first return* (Ezra 1). After King Cyrus of Persia captured Babylon, he made a proclamation that the Jews could return to their homeland and rebuild the temple of the LORD (Ezra 1:3).

Cyrus' decree in Ezra 1:1-4 is a repetition and continuation of his words given in 2 Chronicles 36:22-23.

The Jewish historian Josephus says that Cyrus had read the writings of Isaiah (c. 700 B.C.), which said that Cyrus was to become king of many nations and "send my people their own land and build my temple" (*Antiquities*, XI, i, 1; Isa. 44:28–45:4). Isaiah had prophesied this about 160 years before Cyrus came to power.

A nine-inch clay cylinder was found at Babylon which gives Cyrus' own record of his capture of Babylon. It quotes Cyrus as saying that he gathered all the former inhabitants of conquered nations that he found in his kingdom and returned them to their habitations. Cyrus gave credit to Marduk, the city god of Babylon. (See *Ancient Near East*, James Pritchard, ed. [Princeton Univ. Press, 1973], p. 208).

This is in harmony with Isaiah 45:4, which says that the LORD had called Cyrus even though Cyrus did *not* know Him.

Cyrus ordered that the people provide the Jews with silver and gold and goods for their temple (Ezra 1:4,6).

Those whose hearts God had moved (1:5) quickly prepared to go back to Jerusalem.

The returning Jews (numbering about 50,000) were led by *Sheshbazzar* (Ezra 1:8,11; 5:14,16). In Ezra 2:2; 3:2 and other passages the leader is named *Zerubbabel*. Both men are called "governor" (Ezra 5:14; Hag. 1:1). Both are said to have laid the foundation of the temple (Ezra 5:16; Zech. 4:9). Nehemiah 12:1 lists priests and Levites who "returned with Zerubbabel." We think that Sheshbazzar and Zerubbabel are two names referring to the same person. But most scholars consider them to be two individuals living at the same period. It is uncertain.

There was great joy
when the Jews returned from Babylon to Jerusalem.

Isaiah 48:20 — "Leave Babylon, flee from the Babylonians!
Announce this with shouts of *JOY*."

---

2. *A list of those who returned* (Ezra 2). The first group of those returning from Babylon was led home by Zerubbabel (the governor), and by Jeshua (the high priest) and others (2:2). They numbered about 50,000 (Ezra 2:64-65). These people included the ancestors of Jesus and Mary and Peter! They were God's chosen remnant (Ezra 9:8, 15; Isa. 10:21-22; Rom. 9:27). God would work out His program through them. They were those "whose heart God had moved" (Ezra 1:5).

Zerubbabel is called the son of Shealtiel in Ezra 3:2, 8; 5:2; Nehemiah 12:1; Haggai; and Matthew 1:12. However, 1 Chronicles 3:19 states that his father was Pedaiah. Possibly Pedaiah was his biological father by Levirate marriage, and Shealtiel was his legal father through marriage to Zerubbabel's mother.

The leaders are named (2:2). The other returnees are listed as groups descended from a prominent ancestor (vv. 3-20), or from the towns where their families had formerly lived (vv. 21-35). Many of these returnees settled back into their ancestral towns.

The "temple servants" (Hebrew *Nethinim*, the "given ones,") were the descendants of hereditary temple slaves (Ezra 2:8; 8:20), such as the Gibeonites (Josh. 9:27). They were some of the first to resettle back into their own towns (1 Chr. 9:2).

Jeshua (or Joshua), the high priest at the time of the first return (Hag. 1:1), is a prominent personality in the book of Ezra, and Haggai, and especially in Zechariah. He was one of the most impressive "types" of the Christ to come. (Christ is called the "Branch" in Zechariah 3:8.) Joshua was a "priest upon his throne"; so also is Christ (Zech. 6:12-13).

Those who could not find records of their family ancestry were not allowed full participation in the worship of the returned Jews (Ezra 2:62-63). This indicates the importance attached to genealogies.

The list of returnees in Ezra chapter two is repeated in Nehemiah chapter seven, with some variations in the statistics.

God keeps lists of His people. Is your name there?

---

3. *Altar built and temple foundation laid* (Ezra 3). The Israelites probably left Babylon in the spring and spent about five months travelling to Jerusalem. (See Ezra 7:8-9.) They settled into their towns (2:70). That probably required several weeks.

In the seventh month (Sept.–Oct.), under the leadership of their chief priest, Jeshua, they began to build the altar for sacrifice, and soon were offering daily burnt offerings, in spite of fear of their unfriendly neighbors.

They observed the Feast of Tabernacles, which started on the seventh month, fifteenth day, and lasted eight days (Lev. 23:33-36). During that feast they would "camp out."

In the following spring, in the 2nd month (April–May) under the leadership of the governor Zerubbabel, they laid the foundation for their new temple. That event was celebrated with music and very loud praise. But some who had seen the former temple wept "with a great voice."

Restoring and maintaining the worship of God was their top priority in going back to their land. So ought it always to be.

4. *Opposition to the rebuilding* (Ezra 4). The peoples living near the Jews requested to be allowed to help them rebuild their temple. Ezra 4:1 calls them the "enemies." Their unkind and slanderous conduct toward the Jews shows that the description was correct. The Jewish leaders (Zerubbabel, Jeshua, and others) refused their request, though they worded their refusal so it sounded as if King Cyrus' decree prevented them from accepting help from others.

These "enemies" appear to be mainly the Samaritans, descendants of foreigners brought into Samaria after the fall of the northern kingdom. These people had adopted a worship of Yahweh, but they continued to worship their old gods and practice abominations, like sacrificing their sons and daughters in fire (2 Kgs. 17:17). They feared the LORD, but served their own gods. It was prudent of the Jews to decline their offer of assistance.

When their request was refused, the enemies hired counselors (advisers, lawyers) to work against the Jews. These counselors slandered the Jews, saying that if their temple were built they would pay "no more taxes" (4:13), an accusation sure to get attention from government officials. This continued all through the reign of Cyrus (until 530), and on into the reign of Darius. Work on the temple was suspended until the second year of Darius (520 B.C.).

Ezra 4:6-23 relates further acts of opposition to the Jews during the reigns of later kings of Persia, Xerxes I and Artaxerxes I. Seemingly the Jews made an attempt to rebuild their city wall (4:12). All progress on this project was stopped by force.

Those who are enemies of God will be enemies of God's people (Ps. 68:1; Mark 13:13).

---

5. *Rebuilding of temple resumed. Letter of Tattenai to King Darius* (Ezra 5). In the second year (520 B.C.) of the Persian king Darius I, dramatic events happened in Judah. Darius had been occupied in crushing revolts during the first two years of his reign (according to his famous monument called the Behistun inscription). When Darius completed destroying the rebels, God had a matter for his attention!

In that second year of Darius, the word of the LORD came through (lit., *by the hand of*) the prophets *Haggai* and *Zechariah* unto Zerubbabel the governor and Jeshua the high priest.

Haggai spoke a stirring prophecy (Hag. 1:2-4):

This is what the LORD Almighty [Lord of *heaven's* armies] says: "These people say, 'The time has not yet come for the LORD's house to be built.'" Then the word of the LORD came through the prophet Haggai: "Is it a time for you yourselves to be living in your paneled houses, while this house [the temple] remains a ruin?"

The words of the prophet Zechariah were equally stirring:

"The hands of *Zerubbabel* have laid the foundation of this temple; his hands will also complete it . . . . Who despises the day of small things? Men will rejoice when they see the plumb line in the hand of Zerubbabel" (Zech. 4:9-10).

(People may scorn what they view as small, but God does not!)

These two prophets aroused the Jews to resume construction on the temple, even though they were under government orders to cease (5:1; 6:14). Tattenai, the governor of Trans-Euphrates (the area west of the Euphrates, including Judah), challenged them, saying, "Who authorized you to rebuild this temple?" But the eye of their God was watching over the elders of the Jews, and they were not stopped until a report could go to Darius, the king, and his written reply be received (5:5).

Tattenai sent the letter to Darius, asking that a search be made in royal archives of Babylon, to see if the former king Cyrus had indeed issued a decree to rebuild a temple in Jerusalem. If such a law had ever been issued, it could never be revoked, for that was the custom of the law of the Medes and Persians (Dan. 6:12).

The *temple* was important. "Then suddenly the Lord . . . will come to his *temple*" (Mal. 3:1). The Lord Jesus began His ministry by cleansing the temple.

6. *The decree of Darius about the temple* (Ezra 6:1-12). King Darius initiated a search in the archives for a copy of the decree by Cyrus authorizing the rebuilding of the temple in Jerusalem (Ezra 6:1). Though it could not be found in Babylon, a copy of Cyrus' memorandum was found at Ecbatana (Heb. *Achmetha*). Ecbatana was the capital of the province of Media near modern Tehran. (King Cyrus the Persian had conquered the Medes early in his reign.)

The memorandum as quoted in Ezra 6:2-5 appears to be a government version of the more personal document quoted in Ezra 1:2-4. The file version does not mention Yahweh by name. Cyrus had sent his proclamation throughout all his huge realm and put it in writing (Ezra 1:1). Perhaps that was the occasion when a copy was placed in Ecbatana.

After discovering the document King Darius issued an emphatic order that his officials NOT interfere with the building of the temple and that they should actually contribute to its costs (Ezra 6:6-12).

Darius desired that the elders of the Jews pray for the well-being (lit., *life*) of the king and his sons (6:10). His feelings about their cause were earnest and personal.

7. *Completion of the temple. Passover held* (Ezra 6:13-22). The temple was completed in the sixth year of King Darius (516 B.C.). Twenty years had passed since the temple was started. The dedication ceremony included many sacrifices (6:17), in particular twelve male goats as a sin offering for the tribes of Israel (though most of the returnees were from the tribes of Judah or Benjamin).

A Passover feast was held at the newly completed temple about a month after it was completed (6:19,15). The returned Israelites ate it, with certain others who had separated themselves from the unclean practices of Gentile neighbors. The feast was a genuine spiritual feast, held with sincere joy and thanks that the LORD had changed the attitude (lit., *heart*) of the king of Assyria. The "king of Assyria" mentioned here is clearly Darius, king of Persia. He ruled the large territory once ruled by the nation of Assyria. Assyria was still remembered.

The completion of the temple was a large step toward the fulfillment of God's promise in Haggai 2:7:

"I will shake all nations, and the desired of all nations will come, and *I will fill this house with glory.*"

Questions on Section B
The Return and Restoration under Zerubbabel (Ezra 1–6)

1. Give the headings and Scripture references of the two parts of the outline of the book of Ezra.
2. What king of Persia let the Jews return to Judah? (Ezra 1:1)
3. To whom did the Persian king give credit for his being king? (1:2)
   Did the king of Persia know the LORD? (Isa. 45:1,4)
4. What did the king declare that God had charged him to do? (1:2)
5. What was to be given to assist the Jews who returned? (1:4)
6. What vessels were brought forth for the Jews to take back with them? (1:7)
7. Who was the prince of Judah? (1:8)
8. How many vessels were given to the Jews? (1:11)
9. From what city did the Jews return? (1:11)
10. Whose name heads the list of returning Jews? (2:2)
11. Whose name is second in the list of returning Jews? (2:2; compare 3:2 and Zechariah 6:11.)
12. Why were some Jews who returned excluded from the priesthood? (Ezra 2:62)
13. How many returned with Zerubbabel? (2:64-65)
14. What was given by some of the Israelites for the house of God? (2:68-69)
15. What item of temple equipment was restored first? (3:2)
16. What feast was kept by the returned Jews? (3:4)
17. From where were cedar trees for the new temple brought? (3:7)
18. Who supervised the work of rebuilding the temple? (3:8)
19. How was the laying of the foundation celebrated? (3:10-11)
20. What mixed sounds were heard when the temple foundation was laid? (3:12-13)
21. What did the enemies of Judah ask for? (4:1-2)
22. What did the enemies do when their request was refused? (4:4-5)
23. How does Ezra 4:6-23 fit (or not fit) into the narrative in Ezra?
24. What Assyrian king had brought people into the city of Samaria? (4:10)
25. How did the enemies of the Jews stop the building of the temple in the days of King Artaxerxes? (4:7,11,23)
26. What two prophets stirred up the people to resume the building of the temple? (5:1)
27. Who questioned the Jews' right to rebuild the temple? (5:3)
28. What did the governor request Darius to search for in the royal archives? (5:6,17)

29. Where was the old decree of Cyrus found? (6:1-2)
30. What order concerning the rebuilding of the temple did King Darius give? (6:7-11)
31. During the reign of what king was the temple completed? (6:15)
32. How many years did it take to build the temple?
33. What feeling did the Israelites have at the dedication of the temple? (6:16)
34. How many goats were offered as sin offerings at the dedication? Why was this number offered? (6:17; compare 8:35.)
35. What feast was kept after the temple was completed? (6:19)
36. How did Zerubbabel's temple compare with Solomon's?

Section C
Esther

1. *Xerxes' banquet. Queen Vashti deposed.* (Esth. 1). During the interval between the first return of the Jews under Zerubbabel (536 B.C.) and the second return under Ezra (458 B.C.) incidents with far-reaching effects occurred in Susa (Shushan), the wintertime capital of the Persian kings.

In 486 B.C. Darius I was succeed by his son Xerxes I, whose defeat in Greece fills so notable a page in the history of Europe. In the Hebrew Bible his name is spelled *Aḥašveroš*, and in English *Ahasuerus* (KJV).

During Xerxes' third year before his campaign in Greece he made a great feast in Susa, lasting one hundred and eighty days. During this feast he demanded that his queen, Vashti, come before the assembled princes and display her beauty. When she refused, she was deposed at the suggestion of the king's wise men, who feared that other women would follow her example and disobey their husbands.

2. *Xerxes defeated in Greece. Esther added to his harem. Mordecai reports a plot* (Esth. 2). During the years that followed, Xerxes made a trip to Greece with a great navy. He was stopped at Thermopylae, defeated at the naval battle of Salamis and nearly annihilated at Plataea (479 B.C.). He returned to Persia, and in his seventh year he sought consolation with his harem according to Herodotus (ix. 108).

Many fair virgins were brought to him, among them one

Hadassah (*Myrtle*), a Hebrew maiden better known by the name Esther (Akkad. *Ishtar,* Latin *Venus*), who had been brought up by an older cousin named *Mordecai.* Esther won such favor both with the king and his servants that she was made queen in the place of Vashti (Esth. 2:1-18).

Greek historians tell that Xerxes had an infamous wife named Amestris as his queen at that time. On one occasion Amestris had fourteen noble Persian youths buried alive as a thank-offering to the god of the underworld (Herodotus vii. 113). Esther is not the same woman as Amestris. It is not surprising that the Greek historians do not mention Esther; they mention only those people connected with their own history. Xerxes was notably polygamous. It is not surprising that the Greeks mentioned two wives of Xerxes not mentioned in the Bible and that the Bible mentions Vashti and Esther, who are not mentioned by the Greeks.

In those times Mordecai at the king's gate overheard a plot on the king's life and reported it through Esther. The plotters were executed and a record made of Mordecai's deed (Esth. 2:21-23).

3. *Haman honored. Haman obtains a decree to destroy Jews* (Esth. 3). A prince of Xerxes named Haman was promoted to a high position. Haman was greatly disturbed by Mordecai, however, because Mordecai would not bow down to him. Haman obtained a decree from the king to destroy all Jews, including Mordecai. The day for this massacre was selected by casting lots (dice) called (in Assyrian) *pur* (Heb. pl. *purim*). This decree was circulated throughout the vast empire of Xerxes from India to Cush (Ethiopia), including Judah (Esth. 3).

If this decree had been carried out, all of God's promises to Abraham, to Moses, to David — all the promises of the Messiah — would have failed. But the word of the Lord shall stand forever (Isa. 40:8).

4. *Mordecai sends Esther to Xerxes. Esther's banquet. Haman plots to hang Mordecai* (Esth. 4–5). Mordecai, in great weeping over the decree, sent word to Esther in the palace, asking her to petition the king about the decree. In words of great elo-

quence he declared that she may have come to the kingdom "for such a time as this" (4:14). Esther bravely accepted this duty, knowing that if she approached the king without an invitation, she would be put to death unless the king extended his scepter toward her as a gesture of acceptance (4:11).

Esther's faith was rewarded. The king received her warmly and accepted an invitation to a banquet prepared by her that day. To this banquet Haman also was invited. At the banquet Esther requested their presence at a similar banquet the next day. Haughty Haman was exultant at the supposed honor to him, but upon seeing Mordecai as he went home he was again angered. At the suggestion of his wife, Zeresh, he prepared that day a high gallows, and that night went to the king to obtain permission to hang Mordecai upon them (Esth. 5).

5. *The chronicles read to Xerxes. Mordecai honored and Haman humiliated. Haman's plot exposed. Haman hanged* (Esth. 6–7). That night sleeplessness struck Xerxes and he requested that the chronicles of his kingdom be read to him. He heard of Mordecai's report of the assassins and learned that no reward had been given Mordecai. At that moment Haman came in to ask to execute Mordecai. The king asked Haman what should be done to one whom the king wished to honor. Supposing that it was he himself, Haman proposed that the honored one be royally paraded through the city on a horse led by a most noble prince. Haman was assigned the job of leading the horse as Mordecai was royally honored. Upon returning home in humiliation, his wife expressed her fear that Haman had started an irreversible fall before Mordecai the Jew. The unique power of the Jews was hated but recognized (6:13).

At that hour Haman was summoned to the second banquet. At this banquet Esther revealed to Xerxes that she was a Jewess and that Haman's plot would destroy her and her people. Xerxes stalked out in anger. Haman fell before Esther, pleading. Mistaking this for an attack upon her, Xerxes condemned Haman, and he was hung upon the gallows that had been prepared for Mordecai.

6. *The Jews defend themselves. The feast of Purim* (Esth. 8). While the laws of the Medes and Persians could not be altered or taken away, other laws could be added to them. Therefore Esther and Mordecai, who had been appointed to Haman's position, obtained from Xerxes a further decree permitting Jews to assemble to fight and defend themselves on the day that Haman had chosen for their extermination. This decree brought joy to the Jews and caused many Gentiles to become proselytes to the Jewish faith.

On the fearsome day scheduled for the slaughter of Jews and on the day after, the Jews throughout the empire gathered and defended themselves. They slew 800 enemies in Susa and 75,000 throughout the empire (Esth. 9:12,15).

To commemorate this deliverance Mordecai sent out letters to Jews everywhere to keep a holiday on the fourteenth and fifteenth days of the twelfth month, a feast called PURIM, after the name of the lots cast by Haman (Esth. 9).

7. *Xerxes' taxation. Mordecai's greatness.* After this Xerxes laid a tax on the lands and islands of his empire, perhaps to pay for the expenses of his disastrous Grecian wars.

Mordecai became very great in the kingdom of Xerxes. His name has been found on a clay tablet verifying before all people his place in the history of Persia and of Israel (G.L. Archer, *A Survey of O.T. Intro.* [1994], p. 466).

Questions on Section C
Esther

1. What were the limits of Xerxes' kingdom? (Esth. 1:1)
2. What is another spelling of Xerxes' name?
3. In what city was his palace? (1:2)
4. In what year of his reign did he make a great feast? (1:3)
5. How long did the feast last? (1:4-5)
6. Does 1:6-7 sound like an eyewitness report of the feast?
7. Who was Vashti? (1:9)
8. What did Vashti refuse to do? (1:11-12)
9. Why did the wise men urge that Vashti be deposed? (1:18,20)

10. What did the king afterwards seek for himself? (2:2)
11. Who was Mordecai? (2:5-6)
12. Who was Hadassah? (2:7)
13. What did Esther not tell the Persians? (2:10)
14. How was Esther received by the king? (2:17)
15. What plot did Mordecai overhear? (2:21)
16. Where was a record made of Mordecai's report? (2:23)
17. Who was Haman? (3:1)
18. What honor did Haman receive? (3:2)
19. What made Haman angry? (3:5)
20. What did Haman decide to do with the Jews? (3:6)
21. What is *pur*? (3:7)
22. What law did Haman get passed? (3:13)
23. How did Mordecai react to the decree? (4:1)
24. How did Esther find out about the plot against the Jews? (4:7-8)
25. What request did Mordecai send to Esther? (4:8)
26. What danger was there in Esther's entering the king's court? (4:11)
27. What confidence did Mordecai have about the future of the Jews? (4:14)
28. What preparation did Esther make for going in to see the king? (4:16)
29. What was the king's reaction to Esther's visit? (5:2)
30. What did Esther ask of the king? (5:4)
31. What did Esther ask for at the first banquet? (5:8)
32. How did Haman feel about being invited to the banquet? (5:9,12)
33. What made Haman angry after the banquet? (5:9)
34. Who was Zeresh? (5:10)
35. How did Haman's wife propose that Mordecai be slain? (5:14)
36. How did the king occupy his mind when he could not sleep? (6:1)
37. About whom did the reader read to the king? (6:2-3)
38. Who appeared at that moment and for what purpose? (6:4)
39. What question did the king ask Haman? (6:6)
40. What suggestion for honoring a man did Haman offer? (6:8-9)
41. How was Haman humiliated? (6:10-12)
42. What prophetic word was uttered by Haman's wife? (6:13)
43. How did Xerxes react to Esther's accusation of Haman? (7:6-7)
44. What was Haman's fate? (7:9-10)
45. Who took the office of Haman? (8:2)
46. What did Mordecai write to the Jews after Esther had obtained the king's consent? (8:11)

47. How was this decree spread abroad? (8:14)
48. Why did many Gentiles become Jews? (8:17)
49. What happened on the day the Jews were to be slain? (9:2)
50. How many enemies of the Jews were slain in Shushan? (9:6,15)
51. How many were slain throughout the kingdom? (9:16)
52. What happened to Haman's ten sons? (9:10,13-14)
53. How was the deliverance of the Jews commemorated? (9:21)
54. What is *Purim*? (9:26)
55. What did Xerxes lay upon the land? (10:1)
56. Who became great in the kingdom of Xerxes? (10:2-3)

Section D
Return of Ezra (Ezra 7–10)

1. *Ezra authorized to return* (Ezra 7). King Artaxerxes I (king of Persia 465–423 B.C.) authorized Ezra the scribe ("teacher") to go back to Jerusalem and promote the temple sacrifices and to teach the people (7:17-25). Artaxerxes granted Ezra everything he asked for (7:6), and more. The king provided Ezra with gold and silver (nearly twenty million dollars worth of silver), and gave him unrestricted use of it (7:18, 22). He gave a long letter of authorization to Ezra (7:11-26).

King Artaxerxes was called Longimanus, meaning "long-handed" because his right hand was longer than the left.

Ezra responded to the king's generosity with praise to God (7:27): "Praise be to the LORD, the God of our fathers, who has put it into the king's heart to bring honor to the house of the LORD."

Ezra was a "teacher [literally, *scribe*] well versed [or "ready"] in the law of Moses" (7:6). The scribes were men who copied the law of God, and became expert scholars and teachers of the law. Ezra's name is short for Azariah, and the Greek form of his name is *Esdras*.

Ezra was also a priest (Ezra 10:10). A list of fifteen of Ezra's forefathers is given in 7:1-5. The list goes back to Aaron, the first high priest of Israel.

Ezra was authorized to appoint magistrates and judges (7:25). Ezra, however, proved to be more of a priest and scholar than an administrator.

Ezra came up from Babylon to Jerusalem in the seventh year of King Artaxerxes I (458 B.C.) (7:6,8). Ezra's journey took four months (119 days), from April to August.

Three goals of Ezra (Ezra 7:10):

(1) To seek the law of the LORD
(2) To do the law
(3) To teach the decrees and laws

(These goals should be our goals also.)

---

2. *Ezra returns to Jerusalem* (Ezra 8). Because of the gracious hand of God, Ezra recruited a large group of Israelites to go with him to Jerusalem, the home of their forefathers (8:18). They had a long but safe journey (8:31-32). Their journey took four months. (See 7:8-9.)

Ezra chapter 8 begins with a list of the people who came back with Ezra. These and the Levites recruited later made a group of about 1800 people.

Ezra assembled the group at the canal (literally, *river*) that flows toward Ahava (a place not yet identified). No Levites were present in the group. The Levites did the menial work of the temple, and apparently found life more comfortable in their exile in Babylon than what their forefathers endured in Jerusalem. Twenty willing Levites were found to join Ezra's group, and also 220 temple servants (*Nethinim*) (8:19-20; 2:43).

By the Ahava Canal Ezra assembled his group to fast and pray for a safe journey. Ezra had told the king how their God would protect them. But when the time came time to depart they felt uneasy. Because of his boasting that God would care for them, Ezra was ashamed to ask the king to send soldiers to escort them on their long journey. Ezra had to live a life of faith, not just talk about it.

A very large amount of silver and gold was taken back to Jerusalem by Ezra's group — 650 talents of silver and 100 talents of gold (8:26). (One hundred talents of gold is four tons of it, worth thirty million dollars!). The treasures were weighed when their journey began, and weighed again when they arrived in Jerusalem. (God's people should avoid even any appearance of dishonesty.)

"Satraps" (mentioned in 8:36 and Esther 3:12 and often in Daniel) were rulers in the small provinces of the Persian empire.

3. *Ezra's distress over mixed marriages* (Ezra 9). Certain people and priests reported to Ezra that many Israelites (even some priests) had married women of other races than Jews. This news distressed Ezra visibly. He tore his tunic, pulled hair from his head, and kept throwing himself down with his hands spread out to the LORD (9:3-5; 10:1).

Marriages to women from most of the nations listed in Ezra 9:1 was strictly forbidden (Ex. 34:11; Deut. 7:1-3), though marriage with Egyptians was not totally forbidden (Deut. 23:7-8). Marriages to Ammonites and Moabites were particularly forbidden (Deut. 23:3-6).

Much of Ezra chapter 9 is Ezra's prayer of confession of the guilt of Israel in intermarrying with other races (9:6-15). Ezra recited God's mercies to them (8–9), but confessed their great guilt (9:13-15).

Ezra's confession – and ours!
"You have punished us less than our sins have deserved" (Ezra 9:13).

---

4. *Ezra breaks up mixed marriages* (Ezra 10). Ezra's prayer and confession to God drew a crowd of people. They confessed their guilt and promised to send away the foreign women they had married. Ezra gathered all the people together at a cold rainy time. Though a few people objected, the people did put away the foreign women they had married. The names of approximately a hundred men who did

this are listed. The proceedings took three months to complete.

Ezra compelled the people to assemble on the ninth month, the twentieth day of the month (Dec. 19, 458 B.C.). This is in the rainy season (Oct.–April), and the weather is cold in December and January (10:9,13). (The people's mood probably matched the weather.)

The actual divorce proceedings extended from the tenth month, the first day (Dec. 31), until the first day of the first month (March 17). There were doubtless many tears and some anger, but "they all gave their hands in pledge to put away their wives" (10:19).

The truth of this narrative is shown by the candor with which the opposition to the divorce proceedings is recorded (*Expositor's Bible Commentary*, Vol. 4, p. 672).

Was Ezra justified in breaking up marriages to foreigners? The actions of Ezra seem very strict and severe; but it does seem that Ezra was fully justified.

The book of the prophet Malachi, which was written near the time of Ezra, spoke of the evil of marriages to women outside their faith:

> **Malachi 2:11 — Judah has broken faith. A detestable thing has been committed in Israel . . .** *marrying* **the daughter of a foreign god.**

The approval by Shechaniah (Ezra 10:2-4) and by most of the people (Ezra 10:12-14) shows that Ezra's actions were generally recognized as right.

Nehemiah had to deal forcibly with the same problem of mixed marriages that Ezra dealt with (Neh. 9:2; 10:18-31; 13:23-39). If Ezra was wrong, Nehemiah was wrong also.

God's blessings upon Ezra lead us to think he did the right thing (Ezra 7:6; 8:21-23).

In the Christian age, God's people are still to marry only those who "belong to the Lord" (1 Cor. 7:39). We are not to be yoked together with unbelievers (2 Cor. 6:14). But if we are married, the marriages are to be preserved if at all possible, regardless of the race or the faith of the man or woman (1 Cor. 7:10-14; 1 Pet. 3:1; Col. 3:11).

Questions on Section D
Return of Ezra

1. During the reign of what king did Ezra return? (7:1,8)
2. What was the date of his return?
3. What was Ezra's office? (7:6; compare KJV.)
4. What three things had Ezra set his heart to do? (7:10)
5. What did the king give to Ezra that authorized his return? (7:11)
6. How much money was given to Ezra? (7:15-16)
7. How did Ezra react to the king's generosity and help? (7:27-28)
8. Approximately how many came back with Ezra? (8:1-14)
9. By what canal (or river) did the returnees gather as they started their journey home? (8:15)
10. Why was a fast proclaimed by the river? (8:21-22)
11. How was the safe delivery of the silver and gold checked? (8:26,33)
12. Did the returnees have a safe journey? (8:31-32)
13. What evil in Judah was reported to Ezra? (9:1-2)
14. How did Ezra react to this news? (9:3)
15. What did Ezra confess in prayer? (9:6-7,12)
16. Who gathered as Ezra prayed? (10:1)
17. How did the people show their guilt? (10:1)
18. What did Israel make a covenant with God to do? (10:3)
19. Where were the people to assemble to put away foreign wives? (10:7) What would happen to them if they did not come? (10:8)
20. What was the weather like when the people assembled? (10:9)
21. Did the people agree to put away the foreign wives? (10:12-13) Did all agree? (10:15)
22. How long did the divorce proceeding require? (10:9-17)
23. What groups of Israelites had married foreign women? (10:18,23,24,25)

Section E
Return of Nehemiah

1. *Nehemiah heard grievous news about Jerusalem* (Neh. 1:1-4). The walls of Jerusalem had been destroyed by Nebuchadnezzar in 586 B.C. The walls were still in ruins one hundred and forty years later when Nehemiah came back to Jerusalem, (444 B.C.). Some Jews had returned to Jerusalem from Babylon and Persia from 536 on. They had rebuilt their temple, but the city walls had not been rebuilt though over ninety years had passed by. The Scripture hints that an ineffective, futile attempt had been made to rebuild the walls (Ezra 4:12).

Nehemiah heard this sad news about Jerusalem from his brother Hanani (Neh. 1:2; 7:2), who had come back from Judah. Nehemiah was living in the city of *Susa* (*Shushan*) in Persia, where he served as a cupbearer to King Artaxerxes I (Neh. 1:1; Gen. 40:5). (A cupbearer would be responsible to protect the king from being poisoned.) Artaxerxes I was king 464–424 B.C. Susa was the administrative capital of Persia in its southern part, about 200 miles east of Babylon.

The distressing news about Jerusalem caused Nehemiah to fast and pray.

Nehemiah was a MAN OF PRAYER.
1. He prayed when he heard bad news (1:4)
2. When he feared the king's displeasure (1:2,4)
3. When he was ridiculed (4:1-5)
4. When he had done good for the people (5:19)
5. When enemies were trying to trap him (6:9,14)
6. When he had to confront evils by the people (13:14, 22, 29, 30)

---

2. *Prayer of Nehemiah* (Neh. 1:5-11). Nehemiah praised God (1:5) and petitioned Him to hear his prayer (1:6). Nehemiah confessed the sin of the Israelites (1:6-7) and asked

God to remember His promise to forgive them (1:8-9). *Remember* is a key word in the book of Nehemiah, occurring nine times (5:19; 13:31).

3. *King Artaxerxes sent Nehemiah to Jerusalem* (Neh. 2:1-10). God heard Nehemiah's prayer. In the month of Nisan (March–April), four months after Nehemiah heard the bad news about Jerusalem, the king himself asked Nehemiah why he looked so sad. The king readily granted Nehemiah's request to be allowed to go back to Jerusalem and rebuild it. Nehemiah requested a military escort, and a royal order for timber (2:8).

OPPOSITION TO NEHEMIAH

The opposition to Nehemiah developed through several stages:
(1) Mockery and ridicule (2:19)
(2) Public anger and ridicule (4:1)
(3) Plots and threats of violence (4:8, 11)
(4) Request for a conference (6:2, 7)
(5) Attempts to "frame" and "smear" him (6:10, 13)

Opposition to Nehemiah's coming to Jerusalem quickly arose (2:10, 19). His three chief opponents were:

a. *Sanballat*, the governor in Samaria. Sanballat is called a Horonite, that is, a person from Beth-Horon (Josh. 10:10-11).

A dynasty of kings that included three named *Sanballat* has become known from papyrus scrolls found in caves north of Jericho. These men were governors of Samaria and ruled from about 485 to 300 B.C., which would include the time of Nehemiah. (See Frank Cross, "Samaria Papyri," in *Biblical Archaeologist*, Dec. 1963, p. 120.) *Sanballat I* was ruler at the time of Nehemiah.

b. *Tobiah*, the governor in Ammon east of Jordan. A dynasty of kings named Tobiah is known. Remains of the palace of the Tobiads have been found near modern

Amman, Jordan (*Biblical Archaeologist*, Sept. 1957, pp. 63-76). Many people in Judah were supporters of Tobiah (6:17-19).

c. *Geshem*, the Arab (6:2, 6). Probably he was governor of the Persian province of Arabia. These were very powerful enemies to Nehemiah. They were determined that Jerusalem would not become independent and strong enough to dominate them. Jerusalem was an economic market for them (Neh. 13:16).

4. *Nehemiah inspects Jerusalem's ruins* (Neh. 2:11-20). Nehemiah with a few men secretly examined the ruins of Jerusalem at night. He went mostly along the south end of Jerusalem, where the Dung Gate and the Fountain Gate were (2:13, 14), near the Pool of Siloam (3:15). The ruins were so massive and tumbled that Nehemiah's horse could not go over them (2:14; 4:10).

After his inspection Nehemiah the next day met with the priests, nobles, and others, and urged them to rebuild. Their response was quick and positive.

"Let us start rebuilding!" (Neh. 2:18).
(Literally, "Let us rise up and build.")
(An inspiring leader gets people working.)

Nehemiah refused to let the enemies have any part in the rebuilding of the city walls (2:21).

5. *Builders of the walls* (Neh. 3). This chapter tells the names of many people who worked to rebuild the walls of Jerusalem and what sections of the walls they worked on. The chapter reads like the record of an eyewitness. Forty-one men are named, along with the names of several towns in Judah from which men came to work. Town names include Jericho (3:2), Tekoa (3:5,27), Gibeon (3:7); Janoah (3:13), and Keilah (3:17,18). (Tekoa was a village six miles south of Bethlehem. It was famous because it was the home town of the prophet Amos.)

This account is our most important source of information about the walls and gates of Jerusalem in the time of

Nehemiah. Ten gates are named. They proceed from the northern end of the city in a counterclockwise direction, clear around the walls.

The Ten Gates of Jerusalem (Nehemiah 3) —

Northern gates — Sheep Gate (3:1; John 5:2); Fish Gate (3:3);
 Jeshanah Gate (3:6)
Western gate — Valley Gate (3:13)
Southern gate — Dung Gate (3:13)
Eastern gates — Fountain (spring) Gate (3:15); Water Gate
 (3:26); Horse Gate (3:28); East Gate (Golden Gate?)
 (3:29); Inspection (Heb., *Miphkad*) Gate (3:31)

The walls of Jerusalem as Nehemiah rebuilt them enclosed approximately the same area as the walls in the time of King Solomon. They enclosed the City of David (Zion) and Mt. Moriah north of it, where the temple was. Jerusalem in the days of King Hezekiah had grown until it enclosed the southwest hill of the present walled city, called Zion (modern "Zion"). This area was not enclosed by Nehemiah's walls; but the city did grow to include this area in the Hellenistic period, in the fourth and third centuries B.C. (See *Israel Exploration Journal*, Vol. 4 [1954]; pp. 239-248.)

Eliashib, the high priest in the time of Nehemiah, was prominent among the workers on the wall (3:1-2, 20). He was a grandson of Jeshua, high priest at the time the first group of Jews returned to Jerusalem (Ezra 10:6).

Ezra the scribe is not mentioned among the workers, through he was almost certainly living nearby when the walls were being built. Probably Nehemiah kept Ezra out of sight until the walls were completed. Then Ezra was called to read the law publicly (8:1), and had a prominent part in the dedication of the walls (12:36).

6. *Construction during opposition* (Neh. 4). Nehemiah's success aroused violent opposition. His enemies had an "army" (4:1). They planned to come into the midst of the Jews and

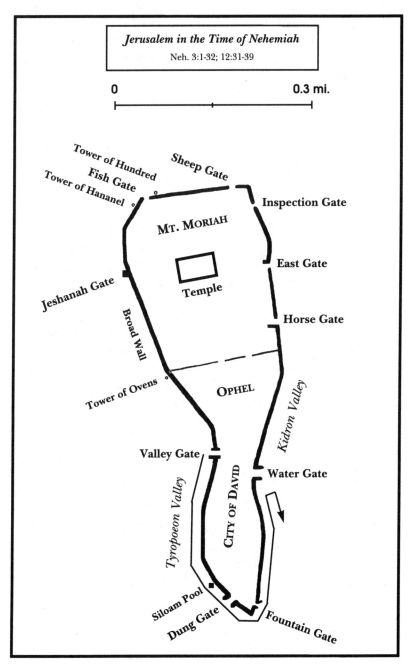

Jerusalem in the Time of Nehemiah
Neh. 3:1-32; 12:31-39

0   0.3 mi.

Tower of Hundred

Sheep Gate

Fish Gate

Tower of Hananel

Inspection Gate

MT. MORIAH

East Gate

Temple

Jeshanah Gate

Broad Wall

Horse Gate

Tower of Ovens

OPHEL

Kidron Valley

Valley Gate

Water Gate

Tyropoeon Valley

CITY OF DAVID

Siloam Pool

Dung Gate

Fountain Gate

Walls and gates of Jerusalem as described in Nehemiah 3.

kill them and cause the work to cease (4:11). The Jews who lived near their enemies told Nehemiah "ten times" (meaning "over and over, many times" [Gen. 31:41; Job 19:3]). "Wherever you turn, they will attack us" (4:12).

Nehemiah stationed half his men as guards, while the others worked. They toiled each day from the light of dawn till the stars came out (4:21).

"So we rebuilt the wall" (Neh. 4:6). Faith combined with prayer and labor always triumphs (4:9,21).

---

7. *Nehemiah delivers the poor from exploitation* (Neh. 5). Nehemiah forced the Jewish nobles to stop charging interest on loans to their poor people. The poor had mortgaged their lands to get money to pay the king's taxes (Neh. 9:36-37).

The Persian rulers collected huge amounts of gold and silver from their provinces, and little was ever returned. The removal of gold and silver from the provinces left the people without money and at the mercy (?) of loan sharks. According to the Greek historian Arrian, Alexander the Great found 50,000 talents of silver (twenty tons) in the city of Susa alone (where Nehemiah had come from), plus other valuables in possession of the king. (Arrian, *Campaigns of Alexander* [Middlesex, England: Penguin, 1981], p. 174; A.T. Olmstead, *History of the Persian Empire* [Univ. of Chicago, 1959], p. 298).

NEHEMIAH — A MODEL GOOD GOVERNOR

1. More concerned for his people than for himself (Neh. 1:4; 5:14-15; 7:2)
2. Self-sacrificing (5:14-18; 7:2; 13:6)
3. Decisive (2:5, 17; 5:6-7, 10; 6:3; 7:7; 13:7-8, 10-11)
4. God-fearing and prayerful (1:4,11; 2:4; 4:9; 5:19; 10:1; 13:14, 31)
5. Courageous (2:19-20; 4:13-14; 6:10-13)

Nehemiah demanded that the Jewish nobles stop their usury (charging interest), and immediately give back to the people their lands. Nehemiah dramatized his demand by shaking out the folds of his robe (5:11-13).

During his time as governor Nehemiah did not collect the food allowance legally due to him as governor (5:14, 18). He personally bore the expense of feeding one hundred and fifty people every day (7:17).

8. *The walls completed during opposition* (Neh. 6:1-7:3). Having failed to stop Nehemiah's progress on the walls by force, his enemies then invited him to a conference with them in the Plains of Ono (located near Lod, southeast of Joppa). Nehemiah would probably have been killed on the road if he had gone to this.

An attempt was then made to frighten Nehemiah into hiding when no danger actually threatened (6:10-13). If he had done this, his act would have broadcast everywhere. It was a tactic to "frame" and "smear" him. Nehemiah saw through this plot.

Several prayers by Nehemiah were uttered in this dangerous time (6:9,14).

"So **the wall was completed** on the twenty-fifth of Elul, (Aug.-Sept.) in fifty-two days" (Neh. 6:15).

The walls had lain in ruins for over ninety years even after the Jews first came back to Jerusalem. Under Nehemiah's leadership they were rebuilt in less than two months. Good leadership is a precious gift from God.

Nehemiah turned over the administration of Jerusalem to his brother, Hanani (7:2; 1:2). Nehemiah did not lust for authority and power.

9. *Nehemiah found the genealogical record* (Neh. 7:4-73). Nehemiah wanted to fill the newly fortified city of Jerusalem with enough people to supply the social and economic needs of the people. God put it into his heart to register all the families. Nehemiah found the genealogical record of those who

had come back from Babylon first. It was the same list as that given in Ezra 2.

Making a list of the residents enabled Nehemiah to do intelligent urban planning. He caused the people to select one out of every ten rural residents in Judah to move into Jerusalem (11:1-2).

The spellings and statistics in Ezra 2 and Nehemiah 7 have some differences. (See *Expositor's Bible Commentary*, Vol. 4, pp. 717-718.) We believe that the Scriptures are true and permanent. The differences in readings between Ezra 2 and Nehemiah 7 are probably only the result of careless copying work by ancient scribes.

10. *Ezra read the law* (Neh. 7:73b–8:12). Reading God's word brings joy (Ps. 119:14, 72). It also brings correction and cleansing (Ps. 119:9). Ezra the scribe was called to bring the book (scroll) of the Law of Moses and to read it to the people (8:1,5,18). They gathered in the square before the Water Gate.

Ezra began to read on the first day of the seventh month (mid-September). This was the day for the Feast of Trumpets (Lev. 23:23-25). On that day Ezra with the help of Levites read from the Book for at least five hours, from dawn till noon (8:3). When Scripture is read well, it is gripping and powerful.

The Levites gave explanations of what was read, "making it clear" (8:8). This expression has been interpreted by some to mean that they gave a translation and paraphrase of the Hebrew Scriptures that were read into the Aramaic language. Such translations into the Aramaic language are called *Targums*. None of the Targums that have been discovered are as old as the time of Nehemiah.

The people wept when they heard from the law the many things they had neglected or done wrong. Nehemiah and the Levites said to them:

> "Do not grieve, for **the joy of the LORD is your strength**" (Neh. 8:10).

11. *Feast of Tabernacles* (Neh. 8:13-18). On the second day of reading, the Israelites learned from the law that they were to keep the Feast of Booths (Tabernacles), during which they were to live in shelters made of tree branches for a week (8:13). During that feast the law was to be read every seventh year (Deut. 31:10-11). It took several days to prepare for this event, which began on the fifteenth day of the month. During the seven days of the Feast of Tabernacles Ezra read the book from the first day to the last (8:18). The final assembly after the seventh day would have come on the twenty-second day of the month. Two days later the Israelites returned to make confession of sins (9:1-2).

No such enthusiastic observance of the Feast of Tabernacles had been held since the time of Joshua (a thousand years before), although the feast had been kept occasionally (Ezra 3:4; 1 Kgs. 8:2, 65; 2 Chr. 5:3; 7:9).

Christians are not required to keep the feasts of the law, such as the Feast of Tabernacles (Gal. 4:9-10). But they should not neglect meeting together (Heb. 10:25). "All the believers were together" (Acts 2:44).

12. *Public confession of sins* (Neh. 9:1-37). The people were moved by their own consciences and devotion to come together and confess their sins. They assembled again on the twenty-fourth of the month, two days after the end of the Feast of Tabernacles. They read from the Book of the Law, and confessed, and worshiped the LORD (9:4). The Levites led in the praise.

> **"Stand up and praise the LORD your God,**
> who is from everlasting to everlasting" (Neh. 9:5).

In their *confession* the Levites mentioned several events in their history when God had blessed them, and yet they had continued to be unfaithful to Him:

 a. God's creating the world (9:5-6)
 b. His covenant with Abraham (9:7-8)
 c. The exodus (9:9-12)

d. The Law at Mt. Sinai (9:13-15)
e. Their rebellions in the desert (9:16-21)
f. The conquests of land (9:22-24)
g. Their rebellions in the promised land (9:26-35)

Our confession to God — "In all that has happened to us, you have been just; you have acted faithfully, while we did wrong" (Neh. 9:33).

The Sabbath was mentioned as a blessing from God: "You came down on Mount Sinai; . . . You *made known* to them your holy Sabbath" (9:13-14). The observance of the Sabbath was not commanded until the law was given at Mt. Sinai. But it was blessing for both man and beast. "The Sabbath was made for man" (Mark 2:27).

13. *The people's promised agreement* (Neh. 9:38–10:39). The Levites and the people made a binding agreement and put it in writing that they would follow the law of God given through Moses (9:38; 10:29). These public commitments were made immediately after the reading of the law during the Feast of Tabernacles (Neh. 8:14, 18). The power of the law on the people was great.

---

444 B.C. — *IT WAS AN EXCITING YEAR* for Nehemiah.

① Dec. 445 — Jan. 444 (month Kislev) — **NEWS THAT JERUSALEM WAS STILL IN RUINS** (Neh. 1:1)

② March 444 — **King Artaxerxes SENDS NEHEMIAH TO JERUSALEM** (2:6)

③ July 444 — **Start of REBUILDING the WALLS of Jerusalem**

④ Sept. 444 (month Elul) — **WALLS COMPLETED in 52 days** (6:15)

⑤ Oct. 444 — **LAW READ in Jerusalem during Feast of Tabernacles** (8:14; 9:1)

⑥ Oct. 444 — **The PEOPLE PUBLICLY PROMISE to FOLLOW GOD'S LAW** (10:29)

The first one to sign the agreement was Nehemiah the governor. Twenty-one names are listed, including leaders, Levites, and priests. The names of the great priests like Eliashib and Joiada and Johanan are not on the list! (12:10-11, 22; 13:7). Those who signed the document affixed their "seals" to it. These seals (bullae) were impressions of the names or emblems of the ones who signed, impressed into a clay lump attached to the document.

The commitments made by these men included such promises as not to contract marriages with the people of other nations, not to buy things or work on the Sabbath, to keep the Sabbatical year (10:31; Ex. 23:10-11), and other promises (10:30-39).

14. *New residents brought to Jerusalem* (Neh. 11). The leaders of the Jews and the people cast lots (similar to dice) to select people living outside of Jerusalem to come and live in Jerusalem (11:1). "A large population is a king's glory, but without subjects a prince is ruined" (Prov. 14:28). It was a sacrifice to give up the peace and roominess in a small town to serve in the city, even if it was "the holy city." Those who volunteered were commended. Residents were brought into Jerusalem from Judah and Benjamin and from the Levites scattered throughout the land. There were 3,044 new residents brought in.

Nehemiah 11 closes with a list of some towns of Judah and Benjamin that had been restored to functioning by the time of Nehemiah. People were living all the way from Beersheba to the Valley of Hinnon at the south edge of Jerusalem (11:25-36).

15. *Priests and Levites in the time of Nehemiah* (Neh. 12:1-26). Nehemiah 12:1-9 lists the priests and Levites at the time when Zerubbabel returned. Then a list of the high priests in consecutive order is given (12:10-11):

    a. *Je[ho]shua* (priest at the time of the return in 536 B.C.)
    b. *Joiakim* (12:12, 26)
    c. *Eliashib* (priest in the time of Nehemiah, 444 B.C.)
    d. *Joiada* (12:22; 13:28).

Joiada had a brother named *Johanan,* or *Jehohanan* (Neh.

12:23). He was probably the one whose room Ezra entered to weep (Ezra 10:6). He is not called *a* high priest.

e. *Jonathan* (12:11). His name is spelled *Johanan* in Nehemiah 12:22, and he was called *John* by Josephus. He was probably the same person as the "high priest *Johanan*" named in a papyrus document found at Elephantine island in Egypt, and dated 407 B.C. (*Ancient Near Eastern Texts*, Vol. I, p. 492).

f. *Jaddua* (12:22). Josephus says that Jaddua was high priest in the time of Alexander the Great (332 B.C.), and that Alexander met him and said that back in Macedonia he had dreamed of meeting the priest in the very robes he was wearing (Josephus, *Antiquities*, IX, vii, 2; IX, viii, 4-5). Josephus' story is doubtful, because Jaddua would have been over ninety years old by the time of Alexander.

Nehemiah 12:21-26 lists priests who were in office during the priesthoods of Joiakim and Eliashib. King "Darius the Persian" named in 12:22 is probably the Persian king called *Darius Nothus*, who ruled 423–404 B.C.

16. *Dedication of the walls of Jerusalem* (Neh. 12:27-43). The dedication of the walls was postponed until Jerusalem had enough people in it to be secure. An earlier dedication might have stirred up an attack upon Jerusalem. The dedication activities included music, both instrumental and choral (12:23, 31).

The main dedication event was the "March Around the Walls." Two choirs marched around the top of the walls, going in opposite directions. One group was led by Nehemiah the governor, and one by Ezra the scribe. The marchers started on the west side of the city near the Valley Gate. The group led by Ezra went south toward the Dung Gate, and turned northward, going along the east wall, and went up to the temple at the north of the city. It was a long walk and mostly uphill. The city was about a kilometer in length.

The group led by Nehemiah went north to the Sheep Gate and up into the house of God. The groups rejoined and sang out jubilantly under the direction of Jezrahiah (12:42). The sound could be heard far away.

After the dedication, storerooms were staffed to provide

places to store the tithes (tenths) of the produce of the land. The Levites were supported by the tithes of the people (Neh. 12:44-47; Num. 18:21, 26).

The prophet *Malachi* (who prophesied about 430 B.C., probably in between the two periods when Nehemiah was governor) preached about the tithes:

> **"Bring the whole TITHE into the storehouse,** that there may be food in my house. Test me in this," says the LORD Almighty, "and see if I will not throw open the floodgates of heaven and pour out so much blessing that you will not have room enough for it" (Mal. 3:10).

No godly people in the Bible ever gave less than a tithe. Many — like the widow and the early church after Pentecost — gave everything they had (Mark 12:42-44; Acts 5:32).

17. *Nehemiah's final reforms* (Neh. 13).

a. Foreigners were excluded (13:1-9). This reform occurred back at the time the law was read aloud (Neh. 8:13, 18). The Law of Moses excluded Moabites and Ammonites (Neh. 13:1; Deut. 23:3-5). It was simply inexcusable that the Jewish high priest should have prepared a large room in the temple for Tobiah the Ammonite. Nehemiah threw his stuff out.

Nehemiah had left Jerusalem after twelve years as governor (444–432 B.C.). We are not told how long he was back in Persia (five years perhaps?). When he returned to Jerusalem for his second term as governor, he was quite stern, and took harsh actions (13:8, 21, 25). The sins that Malachi preached against, Nehemiah took strong action against.

Similar sins opposed	by Malachi	by Nehemiah
1. Corruption of priests	1:6; 2:1-9	13:4,28
2. Marrying foreigners	2:11	13:23
3. Tithes neglected	3:8-10	13:10-12
4. Sabbath violated	4:4	13:15

b. Tithes were distributed to the Levites (13:10-13).

c. Sabbath violations were stopped by force (13:15-22).

d. Marriages to foreign women were broken up (13:23-29). "I beat some of the men and pulled out their hair" (13:25). Ezra had done the same thing about thirty years previously (Ezra 9, 10). People can depart from the LORD in one generation.

e. Priests and Levites were assigned to their duties (13:30).

Nehemiah's book closes with one of the many prayers in it: "Remember me with favor, O my God."

Nehemiah may have been the best leader Israel ever had.

An interesting statement about Nehemiah is found in II Maccabees 2:13: "In the records that concern Nehemiah; and how he, founding a library, gathered together books about the kings and prophets and the *books* of David, and letters of kings about sacred gifts."

This passage is not part of the Jews' Scripture, but it may be at least partly true. Nehemiah did have a great interest in promoting the Scriptures (Neh. 8:9). The *canon* of sacred Scriptures was completed by the time of Ezra and Nehemiah, and probably they were the ones who led in this important project. (The *canon* is the list of accepted books.)

Questions on Section E
Return of Nehemiah

1. Give the headings of the two parts of the outline of Nehemiah.
2. At what city did Nehemiah serve the king of Persia? (Neh. 1:1)
3. What was Nehemiah's position with the king? (1:11)
4. Under what king did Nehemiah serve? (2:1)
5. Who was Hanani? (1:2; 7:2)
6. What report about Jerusalem was given to Nehemiah? (1:3)
7. What did Nehemiah confess to God? (1:6-7)
8. For what did Nehemiah pray when he heard the bad news about Jerusalem? (1:11)
9. What did the king observe about Nehemiah? (2:2)

10. How prominent was prayer in Nehemiah's life? (2:4; 4:4; etc.)
11. What did Nehemiah ask of the king? (2:5)
12. Name Nehemiah's three adversaries. (2:10,19)
13. When did Nehemiah inspect Jerusalem? (2:12-13)
14. What did Nehemiah challenge the Jews to do? (2:17-18)
15. What was the first reaction of the enemies to the wall-building project? (2:19)
16. Does Nehemiah chapter 3 sound like an eyewitness account?
17. Name the seven gates of Jerusalem mentioned in Nehemiah 3.
18. What very unnoble behavior is reported about some nobles? (3:5)
19. How did Sanballat express his anger? (4:1)
20. What was stated about a fox and the wall? (4:3)
21. Why was the wall so quickly built to half its height? (4:6)
22. What violent plot did the enemies make? (4:8,11)
23. How was the plot prevented? (4:9,13)
24. What did half the workmen do as the work was being done? (4:16)
25. What did Nehemiah use as an alarm system? (4:20)
26. What were the working hours as they built the wall? (4:21)
27. What did the people cry to Nehemiah about? (5:1-2)
28. What had the people borrowed money to pay? (5:4)
29. What is *usury*? (5:7)
30. What demand did Nehemiah make of the nobles and rulers? (5:7-10)
31. How did Nehemiah dramatize his insistence that the nobles stop taking usury? (5:13)
32. How much salary had Nehemiah collected as governor? How much money for food allowance had he received? (5:14,18)
33. How many people did Nehemiah feed each day? (5:17)
34. What did Nehemiah's enemies request when they saw the walls completed? (6:1-2)
35. Where was Ono? (6:2)
36. What did one of the Jews urge Nehemiah to do? Why did he urge him to do this? (6:10-13)
37. How long did it take to build the wall? (6:15)
38. Why were many in Judah sympathetic to their enemies? (6:17-19)
39. Whom did Nehemiah appoint over Jerusalem? (7:2)
40. What precaution was taken about opening the gates? (7:3)
41. What was lacking in Jerusalem after the walls were built? (7:4)
42. What came into Nehemiah's heart to do after the walls were built? (7:5)
43. Who requested that the law be read? (8:1)

44. How long did Ezra read? (8:3)
45. Who instructed the people while the law was being read? (8:7)
46. In what manner was the law read? (8:8)
47. What was spoken during the reading besides the words of the law? (8:8)
48. How were the people told to feel when the law was read? (8:9)
49. What feast was observed after the law was read? (8:14-15; Lev. 23:42)
50. In what frame of mind did Israel assemble later that month? (9:1-2)
51. From what did the Israelites separate themselves? (9:2)
52. What history was narrated in the prayer of the Levites? (9:6-37)
53. When was the Sabbath day made known to man? (9:13-14)
54. How far did Israel's rebellion go in the time of Moses? (9:17)
55. How did Israel have clothing during the wilderness wanderings? (9:21)
56. What did the people promise God that they would make with Him? (9:38; 10:28-29)
57. Who was the first one to seal the covenant to obey God? (10:1)
58. What things did those who sealed the covenant promise to do? (10:29-32,35,37)
59. How was the population of Jerusalem increased? (11:1-2)
60. How many generations of priests does Nehemiah 12:10-11 trace?
61. Who were brought to Jerusalem for the dedication of the walls? (12:27)
62. Who led the two companies that marched around the walls of Jerusalem on opposite sides of town? (12:31,36)
63. How loud was the praise when the two groups converged? (12:40,43)
64. What nations were excluded from the house of God? Why? (13:1-2; Deut. 23:3-5)
65. Who was Eliashib? (13:4)
66. What prophet probably prophesied during Nehemiah's absence after his first governorship? (13:6)
67. For whom had Eliashib prepared a large room (or apartment)? (13:5)
68. What did Nehemiah do with Tobiah's stuff? (13:8)
69. How did Nehemiah provide the living for the priests? (13:10-12)
70. What was being done on the Sabbath days? (13:15-16)
71. How did Nehemiah stop the Sabbath activity? (13:15-22)
72. How did the children of mixed marriages speak? (13:23-24)
73. Whom had Eliashib's grandson married? (13:28)
74. What did Nehemiah do to Eliashib's grandson? (13:28)
75. Who collected the books of the Old Testament into one canon?
76. Where did the Samaritans build a temple?

Special Study — Between the Testaments

By Seth Wilson

History of the Interval

Although no Old Testament books record the history of this period, there were Jewish writings during the time. Some of these are the "Apocrypha," about 14 books or portions to be added to the Old Testament books, which have been "canonized" as a part of the Old Testament by the Roman Catholic Church. Of these, the first Book of Maccabees is the most valuable as history. Josephus, a Jewish historian who was born in the decade after Jesus' crucifixion, wrote two important works — *The Antiquities of the Jews* and *The Jewish Wars* — which give an account of the Jews from 170 B.C., through the destruction of Jerusalem by Titus in A.D. 70. The history of the empires of the world during this period between the Old and New Testaments is well covered by Greek and Roman historians. Moreover, this period is pictured with amazing accuracy prophetically in the Book of Daniel (Dan. 2:36-45; 7:3-8, 17; 8:3-22; 11:2-45). The history of the Jews in these times may be divided into six periods:

1. *The Persian Period* (538-332 B.C.). The return from Babylon took place under Persian rule (Ezra 1). Under the Persians, the Jews were usually governed by their own high priest, subject to the Syrian satrap or governor. Persian rule was usually mild and often very favorable toward the Jews (e.g., the stories of Zerubbabel, Ezra, Nehemiah, Esther, Daniel). The Samaritans and renegade Jews caused the most trouble in this period. The Samaritan temple on Mt. Gerizim was built about 423 B.C., a seat of degenerate Judaism that continues until today.

2. *The Greek or Macedonian Period* (332-323 B.C.). The Persian rule was broken by the world-sweeping conquests of Alexander the Great, out of Macedonia. Alexander showed consideration for the Jews and did not destroy or plunder Jerusalem. His short but brilliant career had far-reaching

results in the introduction of Greek language over Palestine and all the Mediterranean area.

3. *The Egyptian Period* (323-198 B.C.) On the death of Alexander, his empire was divided among four of his generals. Seleucus ruled Syria and Ptolemy ruled Egypt. Palestine, between them, was claimed by both of them. The Ptolemies early attached Palestine to Egypt. "They extended such privileges to Jewish settlers on the Nile, that Alexandria became the center of a large Jewish population and a celebrated seat of Jewish learning." It was, for the most part, a century of prosperity for the Jews. The most important event was the translation of the Old Testament into Greek at Alexandria. The Greek version is known as the Septuagint (meaning "seventy"), from the traditional number of translators.

4. *The Syrian Period* (198-167 B.C.). The Seleucidae (Greek kings of Syria) finally recovered Palestine from Egypt.

> The period of Syrian rule was the darkest yet most glorious in the whole four hundred years. The Seleucidae were dissolute tyrants. Antiochus Epiphanes (175-164 B.C.) was the most notorious of them all. Returning on one occasion from defeat in Egypt, he vented his vengeance on Jerusalem. He massacred forty thousand of its population, stripped the temple of its treasures and outraged the religious sense of the Jews by sacrificing a sow on the altar and sprinkling the interior of the temple with the liquor in which a portion of the unclean beast had been boiled. He sought by every means to stamp out the Hebrew religion and spirit and transform the nation into Greeks. He shut up the temple and, on pain of death, prohibited the Jewish religion. Multitudes heroically sacrificed their lives rather than their faith. — B.S. Dean.

5. *The Maccabean Period* (167-63 B.C.). A heroic revolt against such violence and sacrilege was led by a family of priest-patriots known as the Maccabees. An old priest, named Mattathias, and his five sons, in turn, led the Jews in a war for independence, which was finally gained after thirty years of struggle. Judas Maccabeus (166-161 B.C.) led in a remarkable series of victories and reopened, cleansed and rededicated

the temple in honor of which the Feast of Dedication continued to be kept (John 10:22). Judas fell in battle but his brothers (first Jonathan, then Simon) fought on, and taking
advantage of political deals with rivals for the Syrian throne,
obtained in turn the dual office of Governor and high priest
recognized by Syria. Simon lived his last days in peace and
made a league with Rome. He was succeeded by his son,
John Hyrcanus, who was subdued by the Syrian ruler for a
time, but found opportunity to throw off the yoke and went
on to conquer much additional territory. His change from
the Pharisee party to the Sadducees caused much bitter strife
at home. His son was ambitious and murderous, took the
title of king, ended the glory of a great family and started it
on its decline, a period of 60 years filled with intrigue and
barbarous civil war.

6. *The Roman Period* (63 B.C., through the New Testament
period). Pompey captured Jerusalem in 63 B.C. The plots
and murders of the different members of the Maccabean
family continued to curse the land. Antipater, of Idumea
(Edom), and his famous infamous son Herod, took part in
the rivalries and the deals with Rome until Herod finally conquered Judea, amidst shocking atrocities in 37 B.C. He
destroyed the rest of the Maccabean family, including his
wife, Mariamne. This Herod rebuilt the temple (larger than
Solomon's and much richer than Zerubbabel's), and slaughtered the babies of Bethlehem in an attempt to murder the
Messiah (Matthew 2). He gave to the kingdom the greatest
external splendor it ever knew, save in the reigns of David
and Solomon. Yet the moral and religious quality of his reign
was deplorable. Despite the outward splendor, Israel chafed
under the yoke of subjection to Rome and under the crimes
of Herod's regime.

> The tabernacle of David was, indeed, fallen, and the elect
> spirits of the nation, the "Israel within Israel," looked and
> longed for him who should raise it up again and build it as
> in the days of old (Amos 9:12). — B.S. Dean

There arose a party of *Herodians* who favored the rulers of
the Herod family and their collaboration with Rome. An

opposite party of *Zealots* worked "underground" to bring violent action against all such. The *Sadducees*, a small but influential party mostly of priests, became political opportunists, conniving at wrongs and losing faith in the Scriptures. The *Pharisees*, who began as faithful upholders of the law against all Gentile influences, became self-righteous and hypocritical formalists, seeking public acclaim and political influence. Even devout believers among the common folk became political-minded and materialistic and found it hard to accept the spiritual nature of the kingdom of Christ as the fulfillment of Israel's hopes.

Preparations for the Coming of Christ

Throughout this dark period God was working His own plan for Israel. Several developments in these centuries helped to bring about the "fullness of time" for the Messiah to come.

1. *The Dispersion of the Jews.* Many more were scattered abroad throughout the empire than lived in the homeland, yet everywhere they remained Jews. Thus they became world-wide missionaries of the knowledge of the true God and a message of hope in a hopeless world.

2. *The Synagogue*, which perhaps arose to meet the needs of the exiles in Babylon, became the center of worship for many of them who were too far separated from the temple and the place of instruction for all. The reading in the synagogue every Sabbath fixed the eyes of Israel more firmly on their Scriptures and the promised Messiah. Thus the synagogue everywhere became the great missionary institute, imparting to the world Israel's exalted Messianic hopes. Then after the gospel of Christ was given, synagogues became key places to begin its proclamation, and they furnished prepared persons for leadership and oversight in the new church.

3. *The Spread of the Greek language* prepared the world for the Word of God.

4. *The Septuagint Translation of the Old Testament*, spread throughout the world by the Jews and their synagogues, pre-

pared the world for the gift of God in His Son. The Septuagint thus is a distinct forward movement in the fulfillment of the Abrahamic promise (Gen. 12:3; 18:18).

5. *Rome made of the world one empire* and Roman roads made all parts of it accessible, while Roman stress on law and order maintained a comparatively high degree of peace and safety, which encouraged travel and communication.

6. "The Jews themselves, embittered by long-continued martyrdoms and suffering, utterly carnalized this Messianic expectation in an increasing ratio as the yoke of the oppressor grew heavier and the hope of deliverance grew fainter. And thus when their Messiah came, Israel recognized Him not, while the heart-hungry heathen humbly received Him (John 1:9-14). The eyes of Israel were blinded for a season, 'till the fullness of the Gentiles shall be gathered in' (Rom. 9:32;11:25)." (H.E. Dosker)

7. *The Silence of Prophecy for Four Hundred Years*, immediately preceded by the clear prediction of the coming of a great messenger like Elijah (Mal. 3:1; 4:5,6), put dramatic emphasis upon the message of John the Baptist. It strongly accented every inspired utterance that announced the coming of the Christ.

Bibliography on the Period Between the Testaments

Dana, H.E. *The New Testament World*, 3rd ed. Nashville: Broadman, 1937, pp. 7-106.

Free, Joseph P., Revised by Vos, Howard F. *Archaeology and Bible History*. Grand Rapids: Zondervan, 1992, pp. 215-229.

International Standard Bible Encyclopedia (1982). Art. "Intertestamental Period."

Payne, J. Barton. *An Outline of Hebrew History*. Grand Rapids: Baker, 1954, pp. 162-219.

Pfeiffer, Charles F. *Between the Testaments*. Grand Rapids: Baker, 1959.

The Hope of the Messiah

The prophets — like Isaiah, Jeremiah, and Daniel — spoke often about the *Messiah* who was to come.

The faith and hope that the Messiah would come and "redeem" Israel supported the Israelites during the four "silent centuries" between the Old and New Testaments (Luke 24:21).

1. A child is coming, who is *IMMANUEL* (God with us)! He will bring peace and righteousness (Isa. 7:14; 9:6).
2. *GOD* is coming! (Mal. 3:1; Micah 5:2; Isa. 7:14; 9:6).
3. A righteous BRANCH will grow up from King David's offspring, and He will be called The LORD OUR RIGHTEOUSNESS (Jer. 33:15-16).
4. A ruler will be born at BETHLEHEM in Judah (Micah 5:2).
5. ELIJAH will come before the LORD (Mal. 4:5-6).
6. An announcer in the desert will prepare the way for the LORD (Isa. 40:3-5).
7. The Lord's Servant will preach good news to the poor (Isa. 61:1-2).
8. The king will come to Jerusalem riding on a donkey (Zech. 9:9). The Redeemer will come to Zion (Isa. 59:20).
9. The LORD's servant will bear our iniquities (Isa. 53:5-6).
10. The body of the LORD's holy one will not decay (Ps. 16:10).
11. The Holy Spirit will come upon all people (Joel 2:28).
12. The LORD's servant will be a light to the *Gentiles* (Isa. 49:6).
13. Israel will come back and seek the LORD their God and David their king (Hosea 3:4-5).

Index

Page numbers of maps, charts, and other illustrations are in *italics*.